D1257934

POLYBIUS
IV

LCL 159

POLYBIUS

THE HISTORIES

BOOKS 9–15

TRANSLATED BY

W. R. PATON

REVISED BY

FRANK W. WALBANK
AND
CHRISTIAN HABICHT

HARVARD UNIVERSITY PRESS
CAMBRIDGE, MASSACHUSETTS
LONDON, ENGLAND
2011

First published 1925

Revised 2011

LOEB CLASSICAL LIBRARY® is a registered trademark
of the President and Fellows of Harvard College

Library of Congress Control Number 2009937799
CIP data available from the Library of Congress

ISBN 978-0-674-99659-5

Composed in ZephGreek and ZephText by
Technologies 'N Typography, Merrimac, Massachusetts.
Printed on acid-free paper and bound by
The Maple-Vail Book Manufacturing Group

CONTENTS

THE HISTORIES OF POLYBIUS

ΠΟΛΥΒΙΟΥ

FRAGMENTA LIBRI IX

I. EX PROOEMIO

1. Αἱ μὲν οὖν ἐπιφανέσταται πράξεις τῶν ὑπὸ τῆς προειρημένης ὀλυμπιάδος περιληφθεισῶν καὶ τοῦ τετραετοῦς διαστήματος, ὅ φαμεν δεῖν ὀλυμπιάδα νομίζειν, εἰσὶν αὗται· περὶ ὧν ἡμεῖς ἐν δυσὶ βυβλίοις

2 πειρασόμεθα ποιεῖσθαι τὴν ἐξήγησιν. οὐκ ἀγνοῶ δὲ διότι συμβαίνει τὴν πραγματείαν ἡμῶν ἔχειν αὐστη- ρόν τι καὶ πρὸς ἓν γένος ἀκροατῶν οἰκειοῦσθαι καὶ

3 κρίνεσθαι διὰ τὸ μονοειδὲς τῆς συντάξεως. οἱ μὲν γὰρ ἄλλοι συγγραφεῖς σχεδὸν ἅπαντες, εἰ δὲ μή γ', οἱ πλείους, πᾶσι τοῖς τῆς ἱστορίας μέρεσι χρώμενοι πολλοὺς ἐφέλκονται πρὸς ἔντευξιν τῶν ὑπομνημάτων.

4 τὸν μὲν γὰρ φιλήκοον ὁ γενεαλογικὸς τρόπος ἐπι- σπᾶται, τὸν δὲ πολυπράγμονα καὶ περιττὸν ὁ περὶ τὰς ἀποικίας καὶ κτίσεις καὶ συγγενείας, καθά που καὶ παρ' Ἐφόρῳ λέγεται, τὸν δὲ πολιτικὸν ὁ περὶ τὰς

5 πράξεις τῶν ἐθνῶν καὶ πόλεων καὶ δυναστῶν. ἐφ' ὃν ἡμεῖς ψιλῶς κατηντηκότες καὶ περὶ τοῦτον πεποιη- μένοι τὴν ὅλην τάξιν, πρὸς ἓν μέν τι γένος, ὡς

FRAGMENTS OF BOOK IX

I. FROM THE PREFACE

1. These are the principal events included in the above-mentioned Olympiad, that is in the space of four years which we term an Olympiad, and I shall attempt to narrate them in two books. I am not unaware that my work owing to the uniformity of its composition has a certain severity, and will suit the taste and gain the approval of only one class of reader. For nearly all other writers, or at least most of them, by dealing with every branch of history, attract many kinds of people to the perusal of their works. The genealogical side appeals to those who are fond of a story, and the account of colonies, the foundation of cities, and their ties of kindred, such as Ephorus, also remarks somewhere or other, attracts the curious and lovers of recondite lore, while the statesman is interested in the doings of nations, cities, and monarchs. As I have confined my attention strictly to these last matters and as my whole work

προεῖπον, οἰκείως ἡρμόσμεθα, τῷ δὲ πλείονι μέρει τῶν
ἀκροατῶν ἀψυχαγώγητον παρεσκευάκαμεν τὴν ἀνά-
6 γνωσιν. τίνος δὲ χάριν τἆλλα μέρη τῆς ἱστορίας
ἀποδοκιμάσαντες αὐτὰ τὰ κατὰ τὰς πράξεις προειλά-
μεθα γράφειν, ἐν ἑτέροις ἡμῖν εἴρηται διὰ πλειόνων,
κεφαλαιωδῶς γε μὴν οὐδὲν ἐπέχει καὶ νῦν ἐμφάσεως
χάριν ὑπομνῆσαι τοὺς ἀκούοντας.

2. Πολλῶν γὰρ καὶ πολλαχῶς ἐξηριθμημένων τά τε
περὶ τὰς γενεαλογίας καὶ μύθους καὶ περὶ τὰς ἀποι-
2 κίας, ἔτι δὲ συγγενείας καὶ κτίσεις, λοιπὸν ἢ τὰ
ἀλλότρια δεῖ λέγειν ὡς ἴδια τὸν νῦν περὶ τούτων
πραγματευόμενον, ὃ πάντων ἐστὶν αἴσχιστον, ἢ τοῦτο
μὴ βουλόμενον προδήλως ματαιοπονεῖν, ὑπὲρ τοιούτων ὁμολογοῦντα συντάττεσθαι καὶ φροντίζειν, ἃ
διὰ τῶν προγενεστέρων ἱκανῶς δεδήλωται καὶ παρα-
3 δέδοται τοῖς ἐπιγινομένοις. ταῦτα μὲν οὖν παρελείφθη
4 τούτων ἕνεκα καὶ πλειόνων ἑτέρων· ὁ δὲ πραγματικὸς
τρόπος ἐνεκρίθη πρῶτον μὲν διὰ τὸ καινοποιεῖσθαι
συνεχῶς καὶ καινῆς ἐξηγήσεως δεῖσθαι τῷ μὴ συμ-
βατὸν εἶναι τοῖς ἀρχαίοις τὸ τὰς ἐπιγινομένας πρά-
5 ξεις ἡμῖν ἐξαγγεῖλαι, δεύτερον δὲ καὶ διὰ τὸ πάντων
ὠφελιμώτατον αὐτὸν καὶ πρὸ τοῦ μέν, μάλιστα δὲ νῦν
ὑπάρχειν, τῷ τὰς ἐμπειρίας καὶ τέχνας ἐπὶ τοσοῦτον
προκοπὴν εἰληφέναι καθ᾽ ἡμᾶς ὥστε πᾶν τὸ παρα-
πῖπτον ἐκ τῶν καιρῶν ὡς ἂν εἰ μεθοδικῶς δύνασθαι
6 χειρίζειν τοὺς φιλομαθοῦντας. διόπερ ἡμεῖς οὐχ οὕτως
τῆς τέρψεως στοχαζόμενοι τῶν ἀναγνωσομένων ὡς

treats of nothing else, it is, as I say, adapted only to one sort of reader, and its perusal will have no attractions for the larger number. I have stated elsewhere[1] at some length my reason for choosing to exclude other branches of history and chronicle actions alone, but there is no harm in briefly reminding my readers of it here in order to impress it on them.

2. Since genealogies, myths, the planting of colonies, the foundations of cities and their ties of kinship have been recounted by many writers and in many different styles, an author who undertakes at the present day to deal with these matters must either represent the work of others as being his own, a most disgraceful proceeding, or if he refuses to do this, must manifestly toil to no purpose, being constrained to avow that the matters on which he writes and to which he devotes his attention have been adequately narrated and handed down to posterity by previous authors. So omitting these things for the above and various other reasons, I decided on writing a history of actual events; firstly, because there is always something fresh in them which demands novel treatment—since it was not in the power of the ancients to narrate events subsequent to their own time—and secondly, owing to the great practical utility of such a history, both formerly and especially at the present day, when the progress of the arts and sciences has been so rapid, that those who study history are, we may almost say, provided with a method for dealing with any contingency that may arise. My aim, therefore, being not so much to entertain readers as to benefit those who pay

---

[1] Not in the preserved parts.

τῆς ὠφελείας τῶν προσεχόντων, τἄλλα παρέντες ἐπὶ
7 τοῦτο τὸ μέρος κατηνέχθημεν. περὶ μὲν οὖν τούτων οἱ
συνεφιστάνοντες ἐπιμελῶς ἡμῶν τοῖς ὑπομνήμασι βε-
βαιότατα μαρτυρήσουσι τοῖς νῦν λεγομένοις.

II. RES ITALIAE

3. Ἀννίβας δὲ κύκλῳ περιλαμβάνων τὸν χάρακα
τοῦ Ἀππίου τὸ μὲν πρῶτον ἠκροβολίζετο καὶ κατεπεί-
2 ραζε, βουλόμενος ἐκκαλεῖσθαι πρὸς μάχην· οὐδενὸς
δὲ συνυπακούοντος τέλος ἐγίνετο πολιορκίᾳ παραπλήσιον τὸ συμβαῖνον, τῶν μὲν ἱππέων ἐπιφερομένων
ταῖς ἴλαις καὶ μετὰ κραυγῆς εἰσακοντιζόντων εἰς τὴν
παρεμβολήν, τῶν δὲ πεζῶν κατὰ σπείρας προσ-
3 πιπτόντων καὶ διασπᾶν τὸ χαράκωμα πειρωμένων. οὐ
μὴν ἀλλ᾽ οὐδ᾽ ὡς ἐδύνατο κινῆσαι τοὺς Ῥωμαίους ἐκ
τῆς ὑποκειμένης προθέσεως, ἀλλὰ τοῖς μὲν εὐζώνοις
ἀπετρίβοντο τοὺς προσπίπτοντας πρὸς τὸν χάρακα,
τοῖς δὲ βαρέσι τῶν ὅπλων ἀσφαλιζόμενοι τὴν ἐπιφορὰν τῶν βελῶν ἔμενον ἐν τάξει κατὰ τὰς σημαίας.
4 Ἀννίβας δὲ δυσαρεστούμενος τοῖς ὅλοις διὰ τὸ μήτε
παραπεσεῖν εἰς τὴν πόλιν δύνασθαι ⟨μήτ᾽ ἐκκαλεῖ-
σθαι⟩ τοὺς Ῥωμαίους, ἐβουλεύετο περὶ τῶν ἐνεστώ-
5 των τί χρὴ ποιεῖν. ἐμοὶ δ᾽ οὐ μόνοις ἂν δοκεῖ Καρχηδονίοις τὰ τότε συμβαίνοντα παρέχειν ἀπορίαν, ἀλλὰ
6 καὶ τῶν ἄλλων ἀνθρώπων τοῖς πυθομένοις. τίς γὰρ
οὐκ ἂν ἀπιστήσαι πῶς Ῥωμαῖοι, πολλαῖς μὲν ἥττη-

careful attention,[2] I disregarded other matters and was led to write this kind of history. The best testimony to the truth of what I say will be that of those who study this work with due application.

II. AFFAIRS OF ITALY

Siege of Capua

3. Hannibal surrounding the camp of Appius Claudius[3] at first harassed him by skirmishing with the object of provoking him to come out and give battle. But as none paid any attention, his attack finally became very much like an attempt to storm the camp, the cavalry advancing in squadrons, and with loud cries hurling their javelins into the camp, while the infantry attacked in maniples and attempted to tear down the palisade. But even thus he was unable to move the Romans from their purpose; they used their light-armed forces to repel the assault on the palisade, and kept their heavy-armed troops in their ranks under their standards protecting themselves from the shower of missiles. Hannibal was dissatisfied in general at being unable either to penetrate into the town or to provoke the Romans to battle, and began to consider what it was best to do under the circumstances. It seems to me indeed that the state of matters was such as might puzzle not only the Carthaginians, but anyone who heard of it. For who could believe that the Romans, who had been beaten in so many

211
B.C.

---

[2] This comes close to Thucydides' famous statement in 1.22.4.

[3] The consul of 212, now (211) proconsul, besieging Capua while Hannibal tries to lift the siege (5.2).

μένοι μάχαις ὑπὸ Καρχηδονίων, οὐ τολμῶντες δὲ
κατὰ πρόσωπον ἔτι συγκαθίστασθαι τοῖς ὑπεναντίοις, ὅμως οὔτ᾿ εἴκειν οἷοί τ᾿ ἦσαν οὔτ᾿ ἐκχωρεῖν τῶν
7 ὑπαίθρων· καὶ τὸν μὲν πρὸ τοῦ χρόνου ἀντιπαρῆγον
μόνον ἀεὶ ταῖς ὑπωρείαις, τότε δὲ καθίσαντες εἰς τὰ
πεδία καὶ τὸν ἐπιφανέστατον τόπον τῆς Ἰταλίας ἐπο-
λιόρκουν τὴν ἰσχυροτάτην πόλιν, κύκλῳ προσμαχο-
μένων αὐτοῖς τῶν πολεμίων, πρὸς οὓς οὐδ᾿ ἐπινοή-
8 σαντες οἷοί τ᾿ ἦσαν ἀντοφθαλμεῖν· Καρχηδόνιοί τ᾿,
ἀδιαλείπτως νικῶντες ταῖς μάχαις, οὐχ ἧττον ἐνίοις
9 καιροῖς ἐδυσχρηστοῦντο τῶν ἡττωμένων. δοκεῖ δέ μοι
<παρ>αίτιον τοῦτο γεγονέναι τῆς ἑκατέρων προαιρέ-
σεως, τὸ παρ᾿ ἀμφοῖν συντεθεωρῆσθαι διότι τὸ παρ᾿
Ἀννίβου σύνταγμα τῶν ἱππέων αἴτιον ἦν καὶ τοῦ
νικᾶν τοὺς Καρχηδονίους καὶ τοῦ λείπεσθαι τοὺς
10 Ῥωμαίους. διόπερ αἵ τε τῶν ἡττωμένων στρατοπέδων
ἀντιπαραγωγαὶ μετὰ τὰς μάχας εὐθέως κατὰ λόγον
ἐγίνοντο· διὰ γὰρ τόπων τοιούτων ἀντιπαρῆγον ἐν οἷς
οὐδὲν ἔμελλε βλάψειν αὐτοὺς τὸ τῶν ὑπεναντίων ἱππι-
11 κόν. τά τε περὶ τὴν Καπύην τότε συμβαίνοντ᾿ εἰκότως
ἑκατέροις ἀπήντα.

4. Τὸ μὲν γὰρ τῶν Ῥωμαίων στρατόπεδον ἐξιέναι
μὲν πρὸς μάχην οὐκ ἐθάρρει τῷ δεδιέναι τοὺς τῶν
2 πολεμίων ἱππεῖς, ἔμενε δ᾿ ἐν τῇ παρεμβολῇ τετολμη-
κότως, σαφῶς εἰδὸς ἀβλαβῆ τὴν ἵππον αὐτοῖς ἐσο-
3 μένην, ὑφ᾿ ἧς ἐν ταῖς μάχαις ἡττᾶτο. οἵ τε Καρχηδόνιοι πάλιν εὐλόγως οὔτε στρατοπεδεύσαντες μετὰ
τῆς ἵππου μένειν ἐδύναντο πλείω χρόνον διὰ τὸ τὰ μὲν

battles by the Carthaginians, and did not yet even dare to face the enemy in the field, nevertheless refused to retire or to abandon the open country? While up to now they had contented themselves with following the enemy's movements upon the hills, they had now established themselves in the plain in the finest district of Italy, and were besieging the strongest city of all, with that very enemy surrounding and attacking them whom they could not even bear the thought of confronting; while the Carthaginians who had won an unbroken series of victories were at times in equal difficulties with the losers. In my opinion the reason of this conduct on the part of both, was that both had perceived that it was to Hannibal's force of cavalry that the Carthaginians owed their victories and the Romans their defeats. Consequently both the former tactics of the beaten armies after the battles in moving along parallel to their adversaries were justified, since they were marching through country where the enemy's cavalry could not hurt them, and the present conduct of both before Capua was only what was to be expected.

4. As a fact the Roman army had not the courage to go out and give battle since they were afraid of the enemy's cavalry, but they remained in their camp with complete confidence since they well knew that the cavalry to which they had owed their defeat in the battles could do them no harm there. The Carthaginians again obviously could not remain there longer encamped together with their cavalry,

ἐν τῇ παρακειμένῃ χώρᾳ χορτάσματα πάντα κατ-
εφθαρκέναι τοὺς Ῥωμαίους αὐτοῦ τούτου χάριν, τοῖς
δὲ νώτοις οὐκ ἐφικτὸν εἶναι τοσαύτῃ μὲν ἵππῳ, τοσ-
ούτοις δ᾽ ὑποζυγίοις καταννύσαι χόρτον ἢ κριθὰς κομί-
4 ζοντας ἐκ μακροῦ διαστήματος· οὔτε μὴν ἄνευ τῶν
ἱππέων παραστρατοπεδεύσαντες ἐθάρρουν πολιορκεῖν
χάρακα καὶ τάφρον προβεβλημένους τοὺς ὑπεναντίους, πρὸς οὓς καὶ τὸν ἐξ ἴσου κίνδυνον αὐτοῖς
5 ἀμφίδοξον εἶναι συνέβαινε χωρὶς τῶν ἱππέων. ἔτι
δὲ πρὸς τούτοις ἠγωνίων καὶ τοὺς ἐπικαθισταμένους
ὑπάτους μὴ παραγενηθέντες ἐπιστρατοπεδεύσαιεν καὶ
πολλὴν ἀπορίαν σφίσι παραστήσαιεν, ἀφελόμενοι
6 τὴν τῶν χορηγιῶν ἐπάρκειαν. ἐξ ὧν συλλογιζόμενος
Ἀννίβας ἀδύνατον ὑπάρχον τὸ διὰ τῆς ἐκ χειρὸς βίας
λῦσαι τὴν πολιορκίαν, ἐπ᾽ ἄλλης ἐγένετο γνώμης.
7 ὑπέλαβε γάρ, εἰ λαθραίαν ποιησάμενος τὴν πορείαν
αἰφνιδίως ἐπιφανείη τοῖς κατὰ τὴν Ῥώμην τόποις,
ἴσως μὲν ἂν καὶ περὶ τὴν πόλιν ἀνύσασθαί τι τῶν
χρησίμων, ἐκπλήξας τῷ παραδόξῳ τοὺς ἐνοικοῦντας·
8 εἰ δὲ μὴ τοῦτο, τούς γε περὶ τὸν Ἄππιον ἀναγκάσειν ἢ
λύειν τὴν πολιορκίαν, σπεύδοντας τῇ πατρίδι βοηθεῖν, ἢ διαιροῦντας τὴν δύναμιν εὐκαταγωνίστους
ὑπάρξειν καὶ τοὺς βοηθοῦντας καὶ τοὺς ἀπολειπομένους αὐτῶν.

5. Ἃ διανοηθεὶς ἐξέπεμψε γραμματοφόρον εἰς τὴν
Καπύην, πείσας τινὰ τῶν Λιβύων αὐτομολῆσαι πρὸς
τοὺς Ῥωμαίους, κἀκεῖθεν εἰς τὴν πόλιν, προνοηθεὶς
2 τῆς τῶν γραμμάτων ἀσφαλείας· πάνυ γὰρ ἠγωνία μὴ

since the Romans had with this very object destroyed all the forage in the neighborhood, and it was impossible to get carried up on beasts of burden from such a long distance enough hay and barley for so many horses and mules; nor again if they remained in their position without their cavalry were they bold enough to assault an enemy having the advantage of protection by a trench and palisade, an engagement with whom on equal terms would be attended with doubtful success now they were deprived of their cavalry. Besides this they were in dread of the new consuls[4] appearing and establishing themselves in their rear, and thus placing them in great difficulties by cutting off their supplies. For these reasons Hannibal thought it would be impossible to raise the siege by force of arms and changed his plan. For he thought that if by a secret march he could appear suddenly before Rome, he might possibly by the surprise and dismay he would cause among the inhabitants manage to gain some advantage against that city itself; or if not would at least compel Appius either to raise the siege and hasten to the help of his native town, or to break up his army, so that both the force that went to relieve Rome and that which was left behind would be easy to overcome.

5. With this project in his mind he sent a letter bearer to Capua, inducing one of the Libyans to desert to the Roman camp and thence to the city, taking every precaution for the security of the letter. For he was in great dread lest the

4 Fulvius and Sulpicius, named in 6.6.

θεωρήσαντες αὐτὸν ἀπαλλαττόμενον οἱ Καπυανοί,
κἄπειτα διατραπέντες ὡς ἀπηλπισμένοι, παραδῶσι
3 τοῖς Ῥωμαίοις ἑαυτούς. διὸ γράψας ὑπὲρ τῆς ἐπιβολῆς τῆς κατὰ τὴν ἀναζυγὴν ἀπέστειλε τὸν Λίβυν, ἵνα
συνέντες τὴν πρόθεσιν αὐτοῦ καὶ τὸν χωρισμὸν εὐ-
4 θαρσῶς ὑπομένοιεν τὴν πολιορκίαν. τοῖς δ' ἐν Ῥώμῃ
προσπεπτωκότων τῶν περὶ τὴν Καπύην, διότι παρ-
εστρατοπεδευκὼς Ἀννίβας πολιορκεῖ τὰς δυνάμεις
αὐτῶν, ὀρθοὶ ταῖς διανοίαις καὶ περίφοβοι πάντες
ἦσαν, ὡς καὶ πρὸς τὰ ὅλα διατεινούσης τῆς ἐνεστη-
5 κυίας κρίσεως· διὸ καὶ ταῖς ἐξαποστολαῖς καὶ ταῖς
παρασκευαῖς πρὸς τοῦτο τὸ μέρος ὅλοι καὶ πάντες
6 ἐνενεύκεισαν. οἱ δὲ Καπυανοὶ κομισάμενοι τὰ παρὰ
τοῦ Λίβυος γράμματα καὶ γνόντες τὴν ἐπίνοιαν τῶν
Καρχηδονίων, ἔμενον ἐπὶ τῶν ὑποκειμένων, κρίνοντες
7 ἔτι ταύτην ἐξελέγξαι τὴν ἐλπίδα. Ἀννίβας δὲ μετὰ
πέμπτην ἡμέραν τῆς παρουσίας, δειπνοποιησάμενος
καὶ καταλιπὼν τὰ πυρὰ καιόμενα, τοιαύτην ἐποίησε
τὴν ἀναζυγὴν ὥστε μηδένα συνεῖναι τῶν πολεμίων τὸ
8 συμβαῖνον. χρησάμενος δὲ ταῖς πορείαις διὰ τῆς
Σαυνίτιδος ἐνεργοῖς καὶ συνεχέσι καὶ τοὺς περὶ τὴν
ὁδὸν τόπους αἰεὶ ταῖς προπορείαις ἐξερευνώμενος καὶ
9 προκαταλαμβάνων, ἔτι τῶν ἐν τῇ Ῥώμῃ ταῖς διανοίαις περὶ τὴν Καπύην καὶ τὰς ἐκεῖ πράξεις ὄντων ἔλαθε
διαβὰς τὸν Ἀνίωνα ποταμὸν καὶ συνεγγίσας, ὥστε μὴ
πλεῖον τετταράκοντα σταδίων ἀποσχὼν τῆς Ῥώμης
ποιήσασθαι τὴν παρεμβολήν.

6. Οὗ γενομένου καὶ προσπεσόντος εἰς τὴν Ῥώμην,

Capuans on witnessing his departure should think he despaired of saving them and in their consternation surrender to the Romans. He therefore wrote explaining his purpose in leaving, and sent off the Libyan, so that when they heard of his purpose and learned why he had left they might continue to sustain the siege courageously. Now when the news from Capua first reached Rome that Hannibal had encamped parallel to their lines and was besieging them, it caused universal excitement and dismay, as they felt that the impending decision would influence the whole war. Consequently the whole attention of everyone was at present directed to the preparation and dispatch of succor to that quarter. The Capuans on receiving the letter from the Libyan, and on understanding the Carthaginian plan, continued to maintain their resistance, being resolved to try the chance of this expedient. Hannibal on the fifth day from his arrival, after giving his men their supper, left his fires burning and retreated in such a manner that none of the enemy had any notion of what was happening. By a series of rapid marches through Samnium, and by sending his outposts on each day to reconnoiter and occupy the district near the road, he succeeded, while the minds of the Romans were still occupied with Capua and what was happening there, in crossing the Anio unperceived and getting so near to Rome that he established his camp at a distance of not more than forty stades[5] from the walls.

6. When the news reached Rome it caused universal

[5] About five miles.

εἰς ὁλοσχερῆ συνέβη ταραχὴν καὶ φόβον ἐμπεσεῖν
2 τοὺς κατὰ τὴν πόλιν, ἅτε τοῦ πράγματος αἰφνιδίου
μὲν ὄντος καὶ τελέως ἀνελπίστου διὰ τὸ μηδέποτε τὸν
Ἀννίβαν ἐπὶ τοσοῦτον ἀπηρκέναι τῆς πόλεως, ὑπο-
τρεχούσης δέ τινος ἅμα καὶ τοιαύτης ἐννοίας ὡς οὐχ
οἷόν τε τοὺς ἐναντίους ἐπὶ τοσοῦτον ἐγγίσαι καὶ κατα-
θαρρῆσαι μὴ οὐ τῶν περὶ Καπύην στρατοπέδων ἀπο-
3 λωλότων. διόπερ οἱ μὲν ἄνδρες τὰ τείχη προκατελάμβανον καὶ τοὺς πρὸ τῆς πόλεως εὐκαίρους τόπους, αἱ
δὲ γυναῖκες περιπορευόμεναι τοὺς ναοὺς ἱκέτευον τοὺς
θεούς, πλύνουσαι ταῖς κόμαις τὰ τῶν ἱερῶν ἐδάφη·
4 τοῦτο γὰρ αὐταῖς ἔθος ἐστὶ ποιεῖν, ὅταν τις ὁλοσχε-
5 ρὴς τὴν πατρίδα καταλαμβάνῃ κίνδυνος. ἄρτι δὲ τῶν
περὶ τὸν Ἀννίβαν κατεστρατοπεδευκότων καὶ διανοουμένων τῇ μετὰ ταῦθ᾽ ἡμέρᾳ καταπειράζειν αὐτῆς τῆς
πόλεως, γίνεται παράδοξόν τι καὶ τυχικὸν σύμπτωμα
6 πρὸς σωτηρίαν τοῖς Ῥωμαίοις. οἱ γὰρ περὶ τὸν Γνάιον
καὶ Πόπλιον τοῦ μὲν ἑνὸς στρατοπέδου πρότερον
πεποιημένοι τὴν καταγραφὴν ἐνόρκους εἶχον τοὺς
στρατιώτας εἰς ἐκείνην τὴν ἡμέραν ἥξειν ἐν τοῖς
ὅπλοις εἰς τὴν Ῥώμην, τοῦ δ᾽ ἑτέρου τότε τὰς κατα-
7 γραφὰς ἐποιοῦντο καὶ δοκιμασίας. ἐξ οὗ συνέβη
πλῆθος ἀνδρῶν αὐτομάτως ἀθροισθῆναι πρὸς τὸν
δέοντα καιρὸν εἰς τὴν Ῥώμην. οὓς ἐξαγαγόντες εὐθαρσῶς οἱ στρατηγοὶ καὶ παρεμβαλόντες πρὸ τῆς πόλεως
8 ἐπέσχον τὴν ὁρμὴν τῶν περὶ τὸν Ἀννίβαν. οἱ γὰρ
Καρχηδόνιοι τὸ μὲν πρῶτον ὥρμησαν, οὐχ ὅλως ἀπ-
ελπίζοντες αἱρήσειν κατὰ κράτος αὐτὴν τὴν Ῥώμην·

panic and consternation among the inhabitants, the thing being so sudden and so entirely unexpected, as Hannibal had never before been so close to the city. Besides this, a suspicion prevailed that the enemy would never have approached so near and displayed such audacity if the legions before Capua had not been destroyed. The men, therefore, occupied the walls and the most advantageous positions outside the town, while the women made the round of the temples and implored the help of the gods, sweeping the pavements of the holy places with their hair—for such is their custom when their country is in extreme peril. But just after Hannibal had established his camp, and while he was contemplating an attempt on the city itself for the following day, an unexpected stroke of luck intervened to save Rome. Gnaeus Fulvius and Publius Sulpicius had completed the enrolment of one legion, and had engaged the soldiers on their oath to present themselves in arms at Rome exactly on this day, and they were now engaged in enrolling and testing the men for a second legion; and the consequence was that a large number of men were spontaneously collected in Rome just when they were required. The consuls led them out confidently, and drawing them up in front of the city put a check on Hannibal's ardor. For the Carthaginians had at first eagerly advanced not without hope of taking Rome itself by assault, but when they saw

συνθεασάμενοι δὲ τοὺς ὑπεναντίους παρατεταγμένους
καὶ ταχέως διά τινος αἰχμαλώτου πυθόμενοι τὸ γεγονός, τῆς μὲν ἐπὶ τὴν πόλιν ἐπιβολῆς ἀπέστησαν, τὴν
δὲ χώραν ἐδῄουν ἐπιπορευόμενοι καὶ τὰς οἰκίας ἐν-
9 επίμπρασαν. τὰς μὲν οὖν ἀρχὰς ἀναρίθμητον περι-
ελασάμενοι λείας πλῆθος ἤθροισαν εἰς τὴν παρεμβολήν, ὡς ἂν εἰς ἄγραν ἥκοντες τοιαύτην εἰς ἣν οὐδεὶς
οὐδέποτε πολέμιον ἥξειν ἤλπιζε·

7. μετὰ δὲ ταῦτα τῶν ὑπάτων τολμησάντων ἐν δέκα
σταδίοις ἀντιστρατοπεδεῦσαι σφίσι παραβόλως, Ἀννίβας ἅμα μὲν λείας πλῆθος ἠθροικώς, ἅμα δὲ τῆς
2 κατὰ τὴν πόλιν ἐλπίδος ἀποπεπτωκώς, τὸ δὲ μέγιστον, συλλογιζόμενος τὰς ἡμέρας, ἐν αἷς ἤλπιζε κατὰ
τὴν ἐξ ἀρχῆς ἐπίνοιαν πυθομένους τοὺς περὶ τὸν
Ἄππιον τὸν περὶ τὴν πόλιν κίνδυνον ἤτοι λύσαντας
τὴν πολιορκίαν ὁλοσχερῶς παραβοηθήσειν τοῖς ἐπὶ
τῇ Ῥώμῃ πράγμασιν ἢ μέρος τι καταλιπόντας τῷ
3 πλείονι βοηθήσειν κατὰ σπουδήν· ὧν ὁπότερον ἂν
συμβῇ, δεόντως ἕξειν ὑπειληφὼς ἐκίνει τὴν δύναμιν
4 ἐκ τῆς παρεμβολῆς ὑπὸ τὴν ἑωθινήν. οἱ δὲ περὶ τὸν
Πόπλιον διασπάσαντες τὰς ἐπὶ τοῦ προειρημένου
ποταμοῦ γεφύρας καὶ συναναγκάσαντες αὐτὸν διὰ
τοῦ ῥεύματος περαιοῦν τὴν δύναμιν, προσέκειντο τοῖς
Καρχηδονίοις περὶ τὴν διάβασιν καὶ πολλὴν παρ-
5 εἶχον δυσχρηστίαν. ὁλοσχερὲς μὲν οὖν οὐδὲν ἐδύναντο πρᾶξαι διὰ τὸ πλῆθος τῶν ἱππέων καὶ τὴν πρὸς
πάντα τόπον εὐχρηστίαν τῶν Νομάδων· τῆς δὲ λείας
ἱκανόν τι μέρος ἀφελόμενοι καὶ περὶ τριακοσίους

16

the enemy drawn up in battle order, and when very soon afterward they learned the truth from a prisoner, they abandoned the project of attacking the city and took to overrunning and plundering the country and burning the houses. At first they drove into their camp a vast collection of captured animals, as they were in a country which no one ever expected would be entered by an enemy;

7. but afterward, when the consuls had the extreme boldness to encamp opposite them at a distance of ten stades, Hannibal retired. He had now collected a large quantity of booty, but he had given up his hope of taking Rome, and most important of all he reckoned that the time now had elapsed in which he expected, according to his original calculation, that Appius on learning of the danger that threatened Rome would either raise the siege and come with his whole force to save the city, or, leaving a part of it behind, would hasten to the rescue with the greater portion. In either event he considered that his purpose would have been attained, and he therefore moved his army out of the camp at daybreak. Publius,[6] who had destroyed the bridges on the Anio and compelled Hannibal to take his army across by fording the stream, attacked the Carthaginians as they were crossing and caused them no little distress. He could strike no decisive blow owing to the numbers of the enemy's cavalry and the ease with which the Numidians rode over any kind of ground; but after recovering a considerable part of the booty and killing

6 The consul P. Sulpicius.

17

καταβαλόντες τῶν πολεμίων τότε μὲν ἀνεχώρησαν
6 πρὸς τὴν παρεμβολήν, μετὰ δὲ ταῦτα νομίσαντες τοὺς
Καρχηδονίους διὰ φόβον σπουδῇ ποιεῖσθαι τὴν ὑπο-
7 χώρησιν, εἵποντο κατόπιν ταῖς παρωρείαις. Ἀννίβας
δὲ τὸ μὲν πρῶτον ἠπείγετο, σπεύδων ἐπὶ τὸ προκεί-
μενον· μετὰ δὲ πέμπτην ἡμέραν προσαγγελθέντος
αὐτῷ μένειν ἐπὶ τῆς πολιορκίας τοὺς περὶ τὸν Ἄππιον,
οὕτως ὑποστὰς καὶ προσδεξάμενος τοὺς ἑπομένους
8 ἐπιτίθεται νυκτὸς ἔτι τῇ στρατοπεδείᾳ, καὶ πολλοὺς
μὲν αὐτῶν ἀπέκτεινε, τοὺς δὲ λοιποὺς ἐκ τῆς παρεμ-
9 βολῆς ἐξέβαλε. τῆς δ᾽ ἡμέρας ἐπιγενομένης συνθεω-
10 ρήσας τοὺς Ῥωμαίους πρός τινα λόφον ἐρυμνὸν ἀπο-
κεχωρηκότας, τοῦ μὲν ἔτι προσκαρτερεῖν τούτοις
ἀπέγνω, ποιησάμενος δὲ τὴν πορείαν διὰ τῆς Δαυνίας
καὶ τῆς Βρεττίας ἐπέστη τοῖς κατὰ τὸ Ῥήγιον τόποις
ἀνυπόπτως, ὥστε παρ᾽ ὀλίγον μὲν καὶ τῆς πόλεως
κυριεῦσαι, πάντας δὲ τοὺς ἐπὶ τὴν χώραν ἐκπεπορευ-
μένους ἀποτεμέσθαι καὶ πλείστων γενέσθαι Ῥηγίνων
κύριος ἐν ἐκείνῃ τῇ παρουσίᾳ.

8. Δοκεῖ δέ μοι δικαίως ἄν τις ἐπισημήνασθαι κατὰ
τοῦτον τὸν καιρὸν τάς τε Καρχηδονίων καὶ Ῥωμαίων
2 ἀρετὰς καὶ φιλοτιμίας ἐν τῷ πολεμεῖν. καθάπερ γὰρ
Ἐπαμινώνδαν τὸν Θηβαῖον θαυμάζουσι πάντες, διότι
παραγενόμενος εἰς Τεγέαν μετὰ τῶν συμμάχων καὶ
θεωρήσας τοὺς Λακεδαιμονίους αὐτούς τε πανδημεὶ
παραγεγονότας εἰς Μαντίνειαν καὶ τοὺς συμμάχους
3 εἰς ταύτην ἠθροικότας τὴν πόλιν, ὡς παραταξομένους
τοῖς Θηβαίοις, δειπνοποιήσασθαι τοῖς αὑτοῦ καθ᾽

18

about three hundred of the enemy he retired to his camp, and afterward thinking that it was out of fear that the Carthaginians were retreating so precipitately, he followed them, keeping to the hills Hannibal at first marched with great speed, being anxious to attain his object, but when in five days he received the news that Appius was continuing the siege he halted until the part of his army which was following him came up and then attacked the enemy's army by night, killing a considerable number and driving the rest out of their camp. When, however, day dawned and he saw that the Romans had retired to a strong position on a hill, he gave up any thought of further molesting them, and marching through Daunia and Bruttium descended on Rhegium[7] so suddenly that he came very near taking the town itself, and did cut off from it all the inhabitants who had gone out to the country, making a number of Rhegians prisoners by this sudden appearance.

8. We are fully justified, I think, on this occasion in noting with admiration the high courage and determined spirit which both Romans and Carthaginians displayed in the war. To take a somewhat similar instance, Epameinondas of Thebes[8] is universally admired for his conduct in the following circumstances. On reaching Tegea with the allies, and discovering that the Lacedaemonians had arrived at Mantinea in full strength and had collected their allies there with the object of giving battle to the Thebans, he or-

362
B.C.

---

[7] Reggio di Calabria.

[8] The story (8–12) is told more fully in X. *HG* 7.5.8–16.

ὥραν παραγγείλας ἐξῆγε τὴν δύναμιν ἄρτι τῆς νυκτὸς
ἐπιγινομένης, ὡς τῆς παρατάξεως χάριν σπεύδων εὐ-
4   καίρους τινὰς προκαταλαβέσθαι τόπους, τοιαύτην δὲ
τοῖς πολλοῖς δόξαν ἐνεργασάμενος προῆγε, ποιού-
5   μενος τὴν πορείαν ἐπ᾽ αὐτὴν τὴν Λακεδαίμονα, προσ-
μίξας δὲ περὶ τρίτην ὥραν τῇ πόλει παραδόξως καὶ
καταλαβὼν τὴν Σπάρτην ἔρημον τῶν βοηθησόντων,
μέχρι μὲν ἀγορᾶς ἐβιάσατο καὶ κατέσχε τῆς πόλεως
6   τοὺς ἐπὶ τὸν ποταμὸν ἐστραμμένους τόπους. γενομένης δὲ περιπετείας, καί τινος αὐτομόλου τὴν νύκτα
διαπεσόντος εἰς τὴν Μαντίνειαν καὶ διασαφήσαντος
Ἀγησιλάῳ τῷ βασιλεῖ τὸ συμβαῖνον, καὶ τῶν βοηθούντων παραγενομένων εἰς τὸν τῆς καταλήψεως και-
7   ρόν, ταύτης μὲν τῆς ἐλπίδος ἀπεσφάλη, μετὰ δὲ ταῦτα
περὶ τὸν Εὐρώταν ἀριστοποιησάμενος καὶ προσανα-
λαβὼν τὴν δύναμιν ἐκ τῆς κακοπαθείας, ὥρμα πάλιν
8   ἐξ ὑποστροφῆς τὴν αὐτὴν ὁδόν, συλλογιζόμενος ὅτι
συμβήσεται τῶν Λακεδαιμονίων καὶ τῶν συμμάχων
παραβεβοηθηκότων εἰς τὴν Σπάρτην ἔρημον πάλιν
9   καταλείπεσθαι τὴν Μαντίνειαν· ὃ καὶ συνέβη γενέσθαι. διὸ παρακαλέσας τοὺς Θηβαίους καὶ χρησάμενος ἐνεργῷ τῇ νυκτοπορείᾳ παρῆν καὶ προσέμισγε τῇ
Μαντινείᾳ περὶ μέσον ἡμέρας, ἐρήμῳ τελέως ὑπαρ-
10   χούσῃ τῶν βοηθησόντων. οἱ δ᾽ Ἀθηναῖοι κατὰ τὸν
καιρὸν τοῦτον σπουδάζοντες μετασχεῖν τοῦ πρὸς τοὺς
Θηβαίους ἀγῶνος τοῖς Λακεδαιμονίοις κατὰ τὴν συμ-
11   μαχίαν παρῆσαν. ἤδη δὲ τῆς Θηβαίων πρωτοπορείας
συναπτούσης πρὸς τὸ τοῦ Ποσειδῶνος ἱερόν, ὃ κεῖται

dered his troops to take their supper at an early hour, and a little after nightfall led them out as if he was anxious to occupy in time some favorable ground for the battle. Having conveyed this impression to people in general he advanced and marched straight on Sparta, and reaching that city at about the third hour of the day took it by surprise, and finding no one there to defend it forced his way as far as the marketplace, occupying all that part of the town which faces the river. A mischance however occurred, a deserter having escaped in the night to Mantinea and informed King Agesilaus of the facts, so that upon the Spartans coming up to help just as the city was being occupied, Epameinondas was disappointed of his hope, but after breakfasting on the banks of the Eurotas, and refreshing his troops after their hard march, he marched back again by the same road, reckoning that since the Lacedaemonians and their allies had come to the help of Sparta, Mantinea would now be left without defenders, as indeed was the case. Exhorting the Thebans, therefore, to exert themselves, and marching rapidly all night, he reached Mantinea about midday, finding it with scarcely a soul to defend it. But just at this time the Athenians, who were anxious to take part in the battle against the Thebans, arrived to help the Lacedaemonians, as stipulated in their treaty[9] of alliance. So at the very time that the leading column of the Thebans had reached the temple of Poseidon, which is at

[9] *StV* 274 of 369.

πρὸ τῆς πόλεως ἐν ἑπτὰ σταδίοις, ὥσπερ ἐπίτηδες
συνεκύρησεν ἅμα καὶ τοὺς Ἀθηναίους ἐπιφαίνεσθαι
12 κατὰ τὸν τῆς Μαντινείας ὑπερκείμενον λόφον· εἰς οὓς
ἐμβλέψαντες οἱ καταλελειμμένοι τῶν Μαντινέων μόλις ἐθάρρησαν ἐπιβῆναι τοῦ τείχους καὶ κωλῦσαι τὴν
13 τῶν Θηβαίων ἔφοδον. διόπερ εἰκότως οἱ συγγραφεῖς
ἐπιμέμφονται τοῖς προειρημένοις ἔργοις, φάσκοντες
τῷ μὲν ἡγεμόνι πεπρᾶχθαι πᾶν ὅσον ἀγαθῷ στρατηγῷ, καὶ τῶν μὲν ὑπεναντίων κρείττω, τῆς δὲ τύχης
ἥττω γεγονέναι τὸν Ἐπαμινώνδαν.

9. Τὸ δὲ παραπλήσιον ἄν τις εἴποι καὶ περὶ τῶν
2 κατ' Ἀννίβαν. καὶ γὰρ τὸ προσβαλόντα τοῖς πολεμίοις πειραθῆναι διὰ τῶν ἐκ μέρους ἀγώνων λύειν τὴν
3 πολιορκίαν, καὶ τὸ ταύτης ἀποπεσόντα τῆς προσβολῆς ἐπ' αὐτὴν ὁρμῆσαι τὴν Ῥώμην, κἄπειτα μὴ
καθικόμενον τῆς προθέσεως διὰ τὰς ἐκ ταὐτομάτου
περιπετείας αὖθις ἐξ ὑποστροφῆς συμπέμψαι μὲν τοὺς
ἑπομένους, ἐφεδρεῦσαι δὲ τῷ κατὰ λόγον, εἰ συνέβη
γενέσθαι κίνημα περὶ τοὺς τὴν Καπύην πολιορκοῦν-
4 τας, τὸ δὲ τελευταῖον μὴ λήξαντα τῆς προθέσεως εἰς
τὴν τῶν ἐχθρῶν βλάβην ἀποσκῆψαι, μόνον οὐ δ'
5 ἀναστάτους ποιῆσαι Ῥηγίνους, τίς οὐκ ἂν ἐπισημήναιτο καὶ θαυμάσαι τὸν προειρημένον ἐπὶ τούτοις
6 ἡγεμόνα; καὶ μὴν Ῥωμαίους Λακεδαιμονίων ἀμείνους
7 ἄν τις ἐν τούτῳ τῷ καιρῷ κρίνειεν. Λακεδαιμόνιοι μὲν
γὰρ τῇ πρώτῃ προσαγγελίᾳ συνεκχυθέντες τὴν μὲν
Σπάρτην ἔσωσαν, τὴν δὲ Μαντίνειαν τὸ καθ' αὑτοὺς
8 μέρος ἀπέβαλον· Ῥωμαῖοι δὲ καὶ τὴν πατρίδα διεφύ-

seven stades' distance from the town, the Athenians happened as if by design to appear on the hill above Mantinea. When the few Mantineans who were left in the town saw the Athenians, they just managed to pluck up enough courage to man the wall and keep off the assault of the Thebans. Writers, therefore, very properly apportion the blame for the ill success of these operations, when they tell us that the commander did all that behooved a good general, and that Epameinondas here overcame his enemies but was worsted by Fortune.[10]

9. Very much the same may be said of Hannibal. Who can refuse admiration to this general, who considers how he first fell on the enemy and attempted to raise the siege by a series of combats, how failing in his attack he marched on Rome itself, and then when his design on the city was frustrated by the merest accident, how he both carried the pursuing enemy along with him and kept watch so that, in the likely event of the forces besieging Capua making some move, he might take advantage of it, and how finally, still holding to his purpose, he applied himself to the destruction of the enemy, and all but destroyed Rhegium? As for the Romans, we must pronounce that they behaved better on this occasion than the Lacedaemonians. For the latter, flocking off to the rescue when the news first reached them, saved Sparta indeed, but as far as it depended on them lost Mantinea, while the Romans not only

[10] As in the case of Epameinondas, so with Hannibal (chapter 9): the best planning of a commander is worsted by Tyche; see n. on 1.4.1.

λαξαν καὶ τὴν πολιορκίαν οὐκ ἔλυσαν, ἀλλ' ἔμειναν
ἀσαλεύτως καὶ βεβαίως ἐπὶ τῶν ὑποκειμένων καὶ τὸ
λοιπὸν ἤδη τεθαρρηκότως προσέκειντο τοῖς Καπυ-
9 ανοῖς. ταῦτα μὲν οὖν οὐχ οὕτως τοῦ Ῥωμαίων ἢ
Καρχηδονίων ἐγκωμίου χάριν εἴρηταί μοι—τούτους
μὲν γὰρ ἤδη πολλάκις ἐπεσημηνάμην—τὸ δὲ πλεῖον
τῶν ἡγουμένων παρ' ἀμφοτέροις καὶ τῶν μετὰ ταῦτα
μελλόντων χειρίζειν παρ' ἑκάστοις τὰς κοινὰς πρά-
10 ξεις, ἵνα τῶν μὲν ἀναμιμνησκόμενοι, τὰ δ' ὑπὸ τὴν
ὄψιν λαμβάνοντες ζηλωταὶ γίνωνται παράβολον ἔχειν
τι καὶ κινδυνῶδες, τοὐναντίον ἀσφαλῆ μὲν τὴν τόλμαν, θαυμασίαν δὲ τὴν ἐπίνοιαν, ἀείμνηστον δὲ καὶ
καλὴν ἔχει τὴν προαίρεσιν καὶ κατορθωθέντα καὶ
διαψευσθέντα παραπλησίως, ἐὰν μόνον σὺν νῷ γένηται τὰ πραττόμενα. . . .

Ἄτελλα , πόλις Ὀπικῶν Ἰταλίας μεταξὺ Καπύης
καὶ Νεαπόλεως. τὸ ἔθνικὸν Ἀτελλανός, ὡς Πολύβιος
ἐνάτῃ "Ἀτελλανοὶ παρέδοσαν αὐτούς."

11 [Τῶν γὰρ Ῥωμαίων πολιορκούντων Τάραντα] Βο-
μίλκας ὁ τῶν Καρχηδονίων ναύαρχος εἰς τὸ συμμα-
χήσειν μετὰ δυνάμεως πλείστης καὶ μηδὲν δυνηθεὶς
ἐπικουρῆσαι τοῖς ἔνδον διὰ τὸ τοὺς Ῥωμαίους ἀσφαλῶς θέσθαι τὰ περὶ τὴν στρατοπεδείαν, ἔλαθεν ἀνα-

---

11 P. encourages future statesmen to emulate Epameinondas
and Hannibal. The rest of the sentence is defective and open to
various interpretations; see WC 2.132–133, and J. Davidson, *JRS*
81 (1991), 11.

preserved their native town, but far from raising the siege remained firm and unshaken in their purpose, and henceforth pressed the Capuans with greater confidence. It is not for the purpose of extolling the Romans or the Carthaginians that I have offered these remarks—I have often had occasion to bestow praise on both peoples—but rather for the sake of the leaders of both these states, and of all, in each and every state, who shall be charged with the conduct of public affairs, so that by recalling or picturing to themselves these events they are moved to emulation,[11] and not shrink from undertaking designs, which may seem indeed to be fraught with risk and peril, but on the contrary are courageous without being hazardous, are admirable in their conception, and their excellence, whether the result be success or failure alike, will deserve to live in men's memories for ever, always provided that all that is done is the result of sound reasoning.

Atella, a city of the Opicans in Italy between Capua and Naples; the ethnic is Atellanus, as Polybius has it in Book 9: "the Atellani surrendered."

Tarentum

[When the Romans were besieging Tarentum][12] Bomilcar, the Carthaginian admiral, <sent> a very large fleet in support, and finding himself unable to render any assistance to those in the town, as the Roman camp was so securely defended, he used up his supplies before he was

---

[12] These are not the words of P. but of the Anonymous, from whom the passage is taken and who has misunderstood the situation. See Livy 26.20.7–11.

λώσας τὴν χορηγίαν. καὶ μετὰ παρακλήσεως πρότερον ἀφικέσθαι ἐκβιασθεὶς καὶ ὑποσχέσεων μεγάλων,
ὕστερον μεθ᾽ ἱκετηρίας τῶν ἔνδον ἀποπλεῦσαι ἀπ-
ηναγκάσθη.

III. RES SICILIAE

10. Οὐκ ἐκ τῶν ἔξω κοσμεῖται πόλις, ἀλλ᾽ ἐκ τῆς
τῶν οἰκούντων ἀρετῆς. . . .

2 Ἐκρίθη μὲν οὖν διὰ τοῦτο τοῖς Ῥωμαίοις τὰ προειρημένα μετακομίζειν εἰς τὴν ἑαυτῶν πατρίδα καὶ
3 μηδὲν ἀπολιπεῖν· πότερα δ᾽ ὀρθῶς τοῦτο καὶ συμφερόντων αὐτοῖς ἔπραξαν ἢ τἀναντία, πολὺς ἂν εἴη
λόγος, πλείων γε μὴν εἰς τὸ μὴ δεόντως σφίσι πεπρᾶχθαι μηδ᾽ ἀκμὴν νῦν πράττεσθαι τοῦτο τοὔργον.
4 εἰ μὲν γὰρ ἐκ τοιούτων ὁρμηθέντες προεβίβασαν τὴν
πατρίδα, δῆλον ὡς εἰκότως ταῦτα μετέφερον εἰς τὴν
5 οἰκείαν, δι᾽ ὧν ηὐξήθησαν. εἰ δ᾽ ἁπλουστάτοις χρώμενοι βίοις καὶ πορρωτάτω τῆς ἐν τούτοις περιττό-
τητος καὶ πολυτελείας ἀφεστῶτες ὅμως ἐπεκράτουν
τούτων αἰεὶ παρ᾽ οἷς ὑπῆρχε πλεῖστα καὶ κάλλιστα τὰ
τοιαῦτα, πῶς οὐ νομιστέον εἶναι τὸ γινόμενον ὑπ᾽

---

13 Following the fall of Syracuse to the Romans under Marcus
Claudius Marcellus in 211, the city was thoroughly plundered.
See *RE* Marcellus 2748–2749 (F. Münzer).

14 M. Pape, *Griechische Kunstwerke aus Kriegsbeute und ihre
öffentliche Aufstellung in Rom* (Diss. Hamburg 1975).

15 P. to the end of this chapter criticizes what happened after

well aware of it. He had been forced to come by urgent entreaties and large promises, and he was now compelled to sail off at the earnest request of the inhabitants.

III. AFFAIRS OF SICILY

The Spoils of Syracuse

10. A city is not adorned by external splendors,[13] but by the virtue of its inhabitants. . . .

The Romans, then, decided for this reason to transfer all these objects to their own city and leave nothing behind.[14] As to whether in doing so they acted rightly[15] and in their own interest or the reverse, there is much to be said on both sides, but the more weighty arguments are in favor of their conduct having been wrong then and still being wrong. For if they had originally relied on such things for the advancement of their country, they would evidently have been right in bringing to their home the kind of things which had contributed to their aggrandizement. But if, on the contrary, while leading the simplest of lives, very far removed from all such superfluous magnificence, they were constantly victorious over those who possessed the greatest number and finest examples of such works, must we not consider that they committed a mistake? To

the fall of Syracuse. Similar examples of Roman plundering happened in 189, when Pyrrhus' former residence Ambracia fell (C. Habicht, *Demetrias* 1 [Bonn 1976], 176), after the defeat of King Perseus in 168 (Livy 45.40.1–2) and after the destruction of Corinth in 146. See G. Waurick, "Kunstraub der Römer. Untersuchungen zu seinen Anfängen anhand der Inschriften," *JRGZM* 22 (1975 [1977]), 1–46.

6 αὐτῶν ἁμάρτημα; τὸ γὰρ ἀπολιπόντας τὰ τῶν νικών-
των ἔθη τὸν τῶν ἡττωμένων ζῆλον ἀναλαμβάνειν,
προσεπιδραττομένους ἅμα καὶ τὸν ἐξακολουθοῦντα
τοῖς τοιούτοις φθόνον, ὃ πάντων ἐστὶ φοβερώτατον
ταῖς ὑπεροχαῖς, ὁμολογούμενον ἂν εἴποι τις εἶναι τῶν
7 πραττόντων παράπτωμα. οὐ γὰρ οὕτως ὁ θεώμενος
οὐδέποτε μακαρίζει τοὺς τἀλλότρια κεκτημένους, ὡς
<ἐν τῷ> φθονεῖν ἅμα καί τις ἔλεος αὐτὸν ὑποτρέχει
τῶν ἐξ ἀρχῆς ἀποβαλόντων. ἐπὰν δὲ καὶ προβαίνῃ τὰ
8 τῆς εὐκαιρίας καὶ πάντα συνάγῃ πρὸς αὐτὸν τὰ τῶν
ἄλλων, καὶ ταῦτα συγκαλῇ τρόπον τινὰ τοὺς ἐστερη-
9 μένους ἐπὶ θέαν, διπλάσιον γίνεται τὸ κακόν. οὐ γὰρ
ἔτι τοὺς πέλας ἐλεεῖν συμβαίνει τοὺς θεωμένους, ἀλλὰ
σφᾶς αὐτούς, ἀναμιμνησκομένους τῶν οἰκείων συμ-
10 πτωμάτων. ἐξ ὧν οὐ μόνον φθόνος, ἀλλ᾽ οἷον ὀργή τις
ἐκκαίεται πρὸς τοὺς εὐτυχοῦντας· ἡ γὰρ τῶν ἰδίων
περιπετειῶν ἀνάμνησις ὡς ἂν εἰ προτροπή τις ἐστι
11 πρὸς τὸ κατὰ τῶν πραξάντων μῖσος. τὸ μὲν οὖν τὸν
χρυσὸν καὶ τὸν ἄργυρον ἀθροίζειν πρὸς αὑτοὺς ἴσως
ἔχει τινὰ λόγον· οὐ γὰρ οἷόν τε τῶν καθόλου πραγμάτων ἀντιποιήσασθαι μὴ οὐ τοῖς μὲν ἄλλοις ἀδυναμίαν
ἐνεργασαμένους, σφίσι δὲ τὴν τοιαύτην δύναμιν ἑτοι-
12 μάσαντας. τὰ δ᾽ ἐκτὸς ὑπάρχοντα τῆς προειρημένης
δυνάμεως ἦν ἐν τοῖς ἐξ ἀρχῆς τόποις ἅμα τῷ φθόνῳ
καταλιπόντας ἐνδοξοτέραν ποιεῖν τὴν σφετέραν πατρίδα, μὴ γραφαῖς καὶ τύποις, ἀλλὰ σεμνότητι καὶ
13 μεγαλοψυχίᾳ κοσμοῦντας αὐτήν. οὐ μὴν ἀλλὰ ταῦτα
μὲν εἰρήσθω μοι χάριν τῶν μεταλαμβανόντων ἀεὶ τὰς

abandon the habits of the victors and to imitate those of the conquered, not only appropriating the objects, but at the same time attracting that envy which is inseparable from their possession, which is the one thing most to be dreaded by superiors in power, is surely an incontestable error. For in no case is one who contemplates such works of art moved so much by admiration of the good fortune of those who have possessed themselves of the property of others, as by envy as well as pity for the original owners. And when material wealth increases, and the victor collects around him all the treasures of other peoples, and these treasures may be almost said to invite those who were robbed of them to come and inspect them, things are twice as bad. For now spectators no longer pity their neighbors, but themselves, as they recall to mind their own calamities. And hence not only envy, but a sort of passionate hatred for the favorites of fortune flares up, for the memories awakened of their own disaster move them to abhor the authors of it. There were indeed perhaps good reasons for appropriating all the gold and silver: for it was impossible for them to aim at a world empire without weakening the resources of other peoples and strengthening their own. But it was possible for them to leave everything which did not contribute to such strength, together with the envy attached to its possession, in its original place, and to add to the glory of their native city by adorning it not with paintings and reliefs but with dignity and magnanimity. At any rate these remarks will serve to teach all those who succeed to empire, that they should not strip

δυναστείας, ἵνα μὴ σκυλεύοντες τὰς πόλεις κόσμον
ὑπολαμβάνωσιν εἶναι ταῖς ἑαυτῶν πατρίσι τὰς ἀλλο-
τρίας συμφοράς· Ῥωμαῖοι δὲ μετακομίσαντες τὰ προειρημένα ταῖς μὲν ἰδιωτικαῖς κατασκευαῖς τοὺς αὑτῶν
ἐκόσμησαν βίους, ταῖς δὲ δημοσίαις τὰ κοινὰ τῆς
πόλεως.

IV. RES HISPANIAE

38. Σὺν γὰρ τοῖς ἐπιδεδεμένοις φορτίοις τὰ
κανθήλια λαβόντας ἐκ τῶν ὄπισθεν προθέσθαι πρὸ
αὑτῶν ἐκέλευσε τοὺς πεζούς. οὗ γενομένου συνέβη
παρὰ πάντας χάρακας ἀσφαλέστατον γενέσθαι τὸ
πρόβλημα. [Suda K 313 Adler]

11. Ὅτι οἱ τῶν Καρχηδονίων ἡγεμόνες, κρατήσαντες τῶν ὑπεναντίων, σφῶν αὐτῶν οὐκ ἠδύναντο
2 κρατεῖν, καὶ δόξαντες τὸν πρὸς Ῥωμαίους πόλεμον
ἀνῃρηκέναι πρὸς αὑτοὺς ἐστασίαζον, ἀεὶ παρατριβό-
μενοι διὰ τὴν ἔμφυτον Φοίνιξι πλεονεξίαν καὶ φιλαρ-
3 χίαν. ὧν ὑπάρχων Ἀσδρούβας ὁ Γέσκωνος εἰς τοῦτο
κακοπραγμοσύνης προήχθη διὰ τὴν ἐξουσίαν, ὡς
τὸν πιστότατον τῶν κατ᾽ Ἰβηρίαν φίλων Ἀνδοβάλην,
πάλαι μὲν ἀποβαλόντα τὴν ἀρχὴν διὰ Καρχηδονίους,
ἄρτι δὲ πάλιν ἀπειληφότα διὰ τὴν πρὸς ἐκείνους
4 εὔνοιαν, ἐπεβάλετο χρημάτων πλῆθος αἰτεῖν. τοῦ δὲ
παρακούσαντος διὰ τὸ θαρρεῖν ἐπὶ τῇ προγεγενημένῃ
πίστει πρὸς τοὺς Καρχηδονίους, ψευδῆ διαβολὴν ἐπ-
ενέγκας ἠνάγκασε τὸν Ἀνδοβάλην δοῦναι τὰς ἑαυτοῦ
θυγατέρας εἰς ὁμηρείαν.

cities under the idea that the misfortunes of others are an ornament to their own country. The Romans on the present occasion, after transferring all these objects to Rome, used such as came from private houses to embellish their own homes, and those that were state property for their public buildings.

IV. AFFAIRS OF SPAIN

38. He gave orders to the infantry to take the beasts of burden with their packs on from the rear and place them in their front, and when this was done the protection afforded was more effective than any stockade.

11. The Carthaginian commanders had mastered the enemy,[16] but were unable to master themselves, and while thinking they had put an end to the war against the Romans began quarrelling with each other, constant friction being caused by that covetousness and love of domination which is innate in Phoenicians. Hasdrubal, son of Gescon, was one of them, and his abuse of the authority he wielded went so far that he attempted to extract a large sum of money from Andobales,[17] the most faithful friend the Carthaginians had in Spain, who had formerly been deprived of his principality by them and had recently been restored to it because of his attachment to them. When he now refused to pay, relying on his loyalty in the past to Carthage, Hasdrubal brought a false accusation against him and compelled him to give his daughters as hostages.

211
B.C.

[16] Alludes to the defeat of the brothers Scipio in 211.
[17] See n. at 3.76.6.

V. RES ITALIAE

11a. Ὅτι οἱ Ῥωμαῖοι πρεσβευτὰς ἐξαπέστειλαν
πρὸς Πτολεμαῖον, βουλόμενοι σίτῳ χορηγηθῆναι διὰ
2 τὸ μεγάλην εἶναι παρ' αὐτοῖς σπάνιν, ὡς ἂν τοῦ μὲν
κατὰ τὴν Ἰταλίαν ὑπὸ τῶν στρατοπέδων ἅπαντος
ἐφθαρμένου μέχρι τῶν τῆς Ῥώμης πυλῶν, ἔξωθεν δὲ
μὴ γενομένης ἐπικουρίας, ἅτε κατὰ πάντα τὰ μέρη τῆς
οἰκουμένης πολέμων ἐνεστώτων καὶ στρατοπέδων
3 παρακαθημένων, πλὴν τῶν κατ' Αἴγυπτον τόπων. εἰς
γὰρ τοσοῦτον κατὰ τὴν Ῥώμην προεβεβήκει τὰ τῆς
ἐνδείας ὥστε τὸν Σικελικὸν μέδιμνον πεντεκαίδεκα
4 δραχμῶν ὑπάρχειν. ἀλλ' ὅμως τοιαύτης οὔσης τῆς
περιστάσεως οὐκ ἠμέλουν τῶν πολεμικῶν. . . .
12. Πολλὴν μὲν ἐπισκέψεως χρείαν ἔχει τὰ συμ-

---

18 It is uncertain whether this embassy is the same as the one
mentioned for 210 by Livy 27.4.10. Livy's statement is erroneous:
Ptolemy's queen was Arsinoe (not Cleopatra), and she never was
co-regent. The fact of an embassy, however, may be true. See W.
Huss, *Untersuchungen zur Aussenpolitik Ptolemaios' IV* (Munich
1976), 176.

19 The Sicilian *medimnus* was about 11.5 gallons (WC 2.138).

20 In the long digression on generalship (12–20), which is
partly nourished by P.'s experience as commander of the Achaean
cavalry in 169/8, P. discusses a number of rules a general ought to
observe (12–16) and then mentions cases in which neglect of one
or the other of these rules had bad consequences (17–20). Chapter 13 enumerates mandatory requirements, chapter 14 ways to
learn these, in particular through the study of astronomy and ge-

V. AFFAIRS OF ITALY

Roman Embassy to Ptolemy

11a. The Romans sent envoys[18] to Ptolemy wishing to procure a supply of corn, as they were suffering from a great scarcity of it, all the crops in Italy up to the gates of Rome having been destroyed by the armies, and no help from abroad having been forthcoming, since all over the world except in Egypt there were wars in progress and hostile forces in the field. The scarcity at Rome had reached such a pitch that the Sicilian medimnus[19] cost fifteen drachmae. But in spite of this distress the Romans did not neglect their military preparations. . . .

210
B.C.

On the Art of a Commander[20]

12. The accidents attendant on military projects re-

ometry. As any military action has to be timed, time reckoning is essential. The following examples of failure by generals are discussed in these chapters: 17.1–10: Aratus in one of his earlier strategies, perhaps in 241 (F. W. Walbank, *JHS* 56 [1936], 64–71), before the Arcadian town of Cynaetha; 18.1–4: Cleomenes of Sparta in May 223 at Megalopolis (see 2.55.5); 18.5–9: Philip V in 218 before Melitaea (see 5.97.5–6); 19.1–4: Nicias of Athens at Syracuse in the summer of 413 (Th. 7.50.3- 4). Cleomenes and Nicias failed because they lacked the knowledge of astronomy, Philip because he had his geometry wrong, Aratus because he was inexperienced in the use of signals. These samples led P. to stress again the need to know something of geometry (chapter 20), and Philip's abortive attempt at Melitaea makes him explain, as he had promised previously (5.98. 11), how to determine the length of ladders needed to scale the walls of a city (19.5–9).

βαίνοντα περὶ τὰς πολεμικὰς ἐπιβολάς· ἔστι δὲ δυνατὸν ἐν ἑκάστοις αὐτῶν εὐστοχεῖν, ἐὰν σὺν νῷ τις

2 πράττῃ τὸ προτεθέν. ὅτι μὲν οὖν ἐστι τῶν κατὰ πόλεμον ἔργων ἐλάττω τὰ προδήλως καὶ μετὰ βίας ἐπι-
τελούμενα τῶν μετὰ δόλου καὶ σὺν καιρῷ πραττομένων, εὐχερὲς τῷ βουλομένῳ καταμαθεῖν ἐκ τῶν ἤδη

3 γεγονότων· ὅτι γε μὴν αὐτῶν τῶν ἐν καιρῷ πάλιν
ἐνεργουμένων πλείω γίνεται τὰ διαμαρτανόμενα τῶν
κατορθουμένων, οὐδὲ τοῦτο γνῶναι χαλεπὸν ἐκ τῶν

4 συμβαινόντων. καὶ μὴν διότι παρὰ τὰς τῶν ἡγουμένων ἀγνοίας ἢ ῥᾳθυμίας ἐπιτελεῖται τὰ πλεῖστα τῶν

5 ἁμαρτημάτων, οὐδεὶς ⟨ἂν⟩ τοῦτ' ἀπορήσειε. τίς οὖν ὁ
τρόπος τῆς τοιαύτης διαθέσεως σκοπεῖν ἤδη πάρεστι.

6 Τὰ μὲν οὖν ἀποθέτως ἐν τοῖς πολεμικοῖς συμβαίνοντα πράξεις μὲν οὐδαμῶς ἁρμόζει λέγειν, περι-

7 πετείας δὲ καὶ συγκυρήσεις μᾶλλον· διὸ καὶ λόγον οὐκ
ἔχοντα μεθοδικὸν οὐδ' ἑστῶτα παραλειπέσθω· τὰ δὲ
κατὰ πρόθεσιν ἐνεργούμενα, ταῦτα δηλούσθω· περὶ

8 ὧν ὁ νῦν δὴ λόγος. πάσης δὴ πράξεως ἐχούσης
καιρὸν ὡρισμένον καὶ διάστημα καὶ τόπον, καὶ προσδεομένης τοῦ λαθεῖν καὶ συνθημάτων ὡρισμένων, ἔτι
δὲ καὶ δι' ὧν καὶ μεθ' ὧν καὶ τίνι τρόπῳ πραχθήσεται,

9 φανερὸν ὡς ὁ μὲν ἑκάστου τούτων εὐστοχήσας οὐχ
ἁμαρτήσεται τῆς ἐπιβολῆς, ὁ δ' ἑνὸς ὀλιγωρήσας

10 σφαλήσεται τῆς ὅλης προθέσεως. οὕτως ἡ φύσις πρὸς
τὰς ἀποτυχίας τῶν ἐπινοηθέντων ἱκανὸν ἓν καὶ τὸ
τυχὸν ἐποίησε τῶν κατὰ μέρος· πρὸς δὲ τὸ κατορθοῦν
μόλις ἱκανὰ πάντα.

quire much circumspection, but success is in every case possible if the steps we take to carry out our plan are soundly reasoned out. That in military operations what is achieved openly and by force is much less than what is done by stratagem and the use of opportunity, can easily be learned from the history of former wars. And it is no less easy to be convinced by facts that in those actions depending on the choice of opportunity failure is far more frequent than success. Nor can anyone doubt that most of the failures are due either to error or to negligence on the part of the commander. We must therefore inquire in what such faults consist.

It is by no means proper to describe as actions things in war which occur undesignedly, but such events should be rather styled accidents or coincidences. As therefore they fall under no systematic or fixed rules, I may neglect them, and deal only, as I will now proceed to do, with such things as are accomplished by design. Since every such action requires a fixed time for its commencement, and a fixed period, and an appointed place, and also requires secrecy, definite signals, proper persons through whom and with whom to act and the proper means, it is evident that the commander who is happy in his choice of each and all of these will not meet with failure, but the neglect of anyone of them will ruin the whole design; so true is it that nature makes a single trivial error sufficient to cause failure in a design, but correctness in every detail is barely enough for success.

13. διὸ χρὴ μηδενὸς ἀφροντιστεῖν ἐν ταῖς τοιαύταις
2 ἐπιβολαῖς τοὺς ἡγουμένους. ἔστι δ' ἀρχὴ μὲν τῶν
προειρημένων τὸ σιγᾶν, καὶ μήτε διὰ χαρὰν παραδόξου προφαινομένης ἐλπίδος μήτε διὰ φόβον μήτε
διὰ συνήθειαν μήτε διὰ φιλοστοργίαν μεταδιδόναι
3 μηδενὶ τῶν ἐκτός, αὐτοῖς δὲ κοινοῦσθαι τούτοις, ὧν
χωρὶς οὐχ οἷόν τε τὸ προτεθὲν ἐπὶ τέλος ἀγαγεῖν, καὶ
τούτοις μὴ πρότερον, ἀλλ' ὅταν ὁ τῆς ἑκάστου χρείας
4 καιρὸς ἐπαναγκάζῃ. χρὴ δὲ σιγᾶν μὴ μόνον τῇ γλώτ-
5 τῃ, πολὺ δὲ μᾶλλον τῇ ψυχῇ· πολλοὶ γὰρ ἤδη κρύψαν-
τες τοὺς λόγους ποτὲ μὲν δι' αὐτῆς τῆς ἐπιφάσεως,
ποτὲ δὲ καὶ διὰ τῶν πραττομένων φανερὰς ἐποίησαν
6 τὰς ἑαυτῶν ἐπινοίας. δεύτερον δ' ἐπεγνωκέναι τὰς
ἡμερησίους καὶ νυκτερινὰς πορείας καὶ τὰ διανύσματα τούτων, μὴ μόνον κατὰ γῆν, ἀλλὰ καὶ κατὰ
7 θάλατταν. τρίτον καὶ μέγιστον, τῶν ἐκ τοῦ περιέχοντος καιρῶν ἔχειν ἔννοιαν καὶ δύνασθαι τούτων
8 κατὰ τὸ κριθὲν εὐστοχεῖν. καὶ μὴν οὐδὲ τὸν τόπον τῆς
πράξεως ἐν μικρῷ θετέον, ἐπειδὴ πολλάκις παρὰ
τοῦτο τὰ μὲν ἀδύνατα δοκοῦντ' εἶναι δυνατά, τὰ δὲ
9 δυνατὰ πέφηνεν ἀδύνατα. τὸ δὲ τελευταῖον συνθημάτων καὶ παρασυνθημάτων, ἔτι δὲ τῆς ἐκλογῆς, δι' ὧν
καὶ μεθ' ὧν ἐνεργηθήσεται τὸ κριθέν, οὐκ ὀλιγω-
ρητέον.

14. Τῶν δὲ προειρημένων τὰ μὲν ἐκ τριβῆς, τὰ δ' ἐξ
ἱστορίας, τὰ δὲ κατ' ἐμπειρίαν μεθοδικὴν θεωρεῖται.
2 κάλλιστον μὲν οὖν τὸ γινώσκειν αὐτὸν καὶ τὰς ὁδοὺς
καὶ τὸν τόπον, ἐφ' ὃν δεῖ παραγενέσθαι, καὶ τὴν φύσιν

13. Therefore in such enterprises commanders must be careful about every detail. The first and foremost requisite is to keep silence, and never either from joy if some unexpected hope shall present itself, or from fear, or from familiarity with or affection for certain persons, to reveal one's design to anyone unconcerned in it, but to communicate it only to those without whom it cannot be put in execution, and even to these not earlier than when the need of their services renders it imperative. And we must keep not only our tongues tied but even more so our minds. For many who have kept their own counsel have revealed their projects either by the expression of their faces or by their actions. The second requisite is to be well versed in the question of night and day movements and voyages, knowing exactly how far they will bring us, not only by land but also by sea. The third and most important is to have an appreciation of the right time derived from observing the heavens and to make a successful use of this for furthering one's ends. Nor is the place fixed for the intended coup de main a matter of small importance; for often this shows seemingly impossible things to be possible and seemingly possible ones to be impossible. Finally, we must pay due attention to signals and counter signals, and to the choice of those by whose agency and in whose company our project is to be executed.

14. These things are learned either by routine or by inquiry or by experience systematically acquired. It is of course far best for a general to be himself acquainted with the roads, the spot he is bound for and the nature of the

τοῦ τόπου, πρὸς δὲ τούτοις, δι᾿ ὧν μέλλει καὶ μεθ᾿ ὧν
3 πράττειν. δεύτερον δ᾿ ἱστορεῖν ἐπιμελῶς καὶ ⟨μὴ⟩
πιστεύειν τοῖς τυχοῦσι· τὴν δὲ τῶν καθηγουμένων
πίστιν ἐπί τι τῶν τοιούτων ἐν τοῖς ἑπομένοις ἀεὶ δεῖ
4 κεῖσθαι. ταῦτα μὲν οὖν καὶ τὰ τούτοις παραπλήσια
δυνατὸν ἴσως καὶ δι᾿ αὐτῆς τῆς στρατιωτικῆς τριβῆς
περιγίνεσθαι τοῖς ἡγουμένοις, τὰ μὲν ἐξ αὐτουργίας,
5 τὰ δ᾿ ἐξ ἱστορίας· τὰ δ᾿ ἐκ τῆς ἐμπειρίας προσδεῖται
μαθήσεως καὶ θεωρημάτων, καὶ μάλιστα τῶν ἐξ
ἀστρολογίας καὶ γεωμετρίας, ὧν τὸ μὲν ἔργον οὐ
μέγα πρός γε ταύτην τὴν χρείαν, τὸ δὲ χρῆμα μέγα
καὶ μεγάλα συνεργεῖν δυνάμενον πρὸς τὰς προειρη-
6 μένας ἐπιβολάς. ἀναγκαιότατον δ᾿ αὐτοῦ τὸ περὶ τὰς
νυκτερινὰς θεωρίας καὶ τὰς ἡμερινάς. εἰ μὲν γὰρ ἴσας
εἶναι συνέβαινεν ἀεὶ ταύτας, οὐδ᾿ ἧστινος ἂν ἀσχο-
λίας τὸ πρᾶγμα προσεδεῖτο, κοινὴ δ᾿ ἂν ἦν ἁπάντων ἡ
7 γνῶσις· ἐπεὶ δ᾿ οὐ μόνον ἔχει τὰ προειρημένα πρὸς
ἄλληλα διαφοράν, ἀλλὰ καὶ πρὸς αὐτά, δῆλον ὡς
ἀνάγκη γινώσκειν τὰς αὐξήσεις καὶ μειώσεις ἑκατέ-
8 ρων. πῶς γὰρ ἄν τις εὐστοχήσειε πορείας καὶ δια-
νύσματος ἡμερησίου, πῶς δὲ νυκτερινοῦ, μὴ κατανοή-
9 σας τὰς τῶν προειρημένων διαφοράς; καὶ μὴν οὐδὲν
πρὸς τὸν δέοντα καιρὸν ἐξικέσθαι δυνατὸν ἄνευ τῆς
τούτων ἐμπειρίας, ἀλλὰ ποτὲ μὲν ὑστερεῖν, ποτὲ δὲ
10 προτερεῖν ἀνάγκη. μεῖζον δὲ τὸ προτερεῖν ἐν μόνοις
11 τούτοις ἁμάρτημα τοῦ καθυστερεῖν· ὁ μὲν γὰρ ὑπ-
ερᾶρας τὸν ὡρισμένον καιρὸν αὐτῆς ἀποτυγχάνει τῆς
ἐλπίδος—τὸ γὰρ γεγονὸς ἐξ ἀποστήματος ἐπιγνοὺς

ground, as well as with the people by whose agency and in concert with whom he is going to act. But the next best thing is to make careful inquiries and not to rely on chance informants. The pledges of good faith given by those who act as guides in such a case must be in the hands of those who follow their guidance. Skill, therefore, in these and similar matters can perhaps be acquired by a general just through military routine, partly by practice, and partly by inquiry; but what depends on systematically acquired experience requires a scientific education more especially in astronomy and geometry, which, while no very deep study of them is required for this purpose at least, are exceedingly important and capable of rendering the greatest services in projects such as we are speaking of. The most necessary part of astronomy is that dealing with the variations of day and night. If day and night were always of equal length, the matter would give us no trouble and the knowledge of it would be common property; since, however, days and nights differ not only from each other, but also from themselves it is evidently necessary to be acquainted with the increase and decrease of both. For how can one rightly calculate the distance traversed in a day's march or in a night's march without knowing the different lengths of day and night? Indeed it is impossible for anything to come off at the proper time without such knowledge; it is sure to be either too late or too soon. And in such matters alone it is a worse fault to be in advance than behind hand. For he who arrives later than the hour decided upon is disappointed merely in his hope—since he becomes aware of

αὖθις ἀπολύεται μετ᾽ ἀσφαλείας—ὁ δὲ προλαβὼν τὸν
12   καιρόν, ἐγγίσας καὶ γνωρισθεὶς οὐ μόνον ἀποτυγχάνει τῆς ἐπιβολῆς, ἀλλὰ καὶ κινδυνεύει τοῖς ὅλοις.

    15. κρατεῖ δ᾽ ἐπὶ πάντων μὲν τῶν ἀνθρωπείων
2   ἔργων ὁ καιρός, μάλιστα δὲ τῶν πολεμικῶν. διὸ προχείρως ἰστέον τῷ στρατηγῷ τροπὰς ἡλίου θερινὰς
⟨καὶ χειμερινάς⟩, ἔτι δ᾽ ἰσημερίας καὶ τὰς μεταξὺ
τούτων αὐξήσεις καὶ μειώσεις ἡμερῶν καὶ νυκτῶν·
3   οὕτως γὰρ ἂν μόνως δύναιτο συμμετρεῖσθαι πρὸς
λόγον τὰ διανύσματα καὶ κατὰ γῆν καὶ κατὰ θάλατ-
4   ταν. καὶ μὴν τοὺς κατὰ μέρος καιροὺς ἀναγκαῖον
εἰδέναι, καὶ τοὺς τῆς ἡμέρας καὶ τοὺς τῆς νυκτός, πρὸς
τὸ γινώσκειν πηνίκα ποιητέον καὶ τὰς ἐξεγέρσεις καὶ
5   τὰς ἀναζυγάς· οὐ γὰρ οἷόν τε τοῦ τέλους τυγχάνειν μὴ
6   οὐ τῆς ἀρχῆς εὐστοχήσαντα. τοὺς μὲν οὖν τῆς ἡμέρας
καιροὺς τῇ σκιᾷ θεωρεῖν οὐκ ἀδύνατον, ἔτι δὲ τῇ κατὰ
τὸν ἥλιον πορείᾳ καὶ τοῖς ἐπὶ τοῦ κόσμου γινομένοις
7   αὐτοῦ τούτου διαστήμασι· τοὺς δὲ τῆς νυκτὸς δυσχερές, ἐὰν μή τις ἐπὶ τοῦ φαινομένου τῇ τῶν δώδεκα
ζῳδίων οἰκονομίᾳ καὶ τάξει συμπεριφέρηται· πάνυ δὲ
καὶ τοῦτο ῥᾴδιον τοῖς τὰ φαινόμενα πεπολυπραγμονη-
8   κόσιν. ἐπεὶ γὰρ ἀνίσων οὐσῶν τῶν νυκτῶν ὅμως ἐν
πάσῃ τῇ νυκτὶ τῶν δώδεκα ζῳδίων ἐξ ἀναφέρεσθαι
συμβαίνει, φανερὸν ὡς ἀναγκαῖον ἐν τοῖς αὐτοῖς
μέρεσι πάσης νυκτὸς ἴσα μέρη τῶν δώδεκα ζῳδίων
9   ἀναφέρεσθαι. τοῦ δ᾽ ἡλίου γνωριζομένου καθ᾽ ἡμέραν,
ποίαν μοῖραν ἐπέχει, δῆλον ὡς δύναντος τούτου τὴν
10   κατὰ διάμετρον ἐπιτέλλειν ἀνάγκη. λοιπὸν ὅσον ἂν τὸ

the fact while still at a distance and can get away in security—but he who arrives too soon, approaching the enemy and being discovered by him, not only fails in his attempt, but runs the risk of total destruction.

15. It is choice of the right moment, indeed, which rules all human action and especially the affairs of war. So that a general must be familiar with the dates of the summer and winter solstices, and the equinoxes, and with the rate of increase and decrease of days and nights between these; for by no other means can he compute correctly the distances he will be able to traverse either by sea or land. He must also be acquainted with the subdivisions of day and night so as to know when to arouse the men and when to be on the march; for it is impossible to obtain a happy end unless the beginning is happily timed. Now for the time of day there is nothing to hinder our observing it either by the shadow or by the sun's course or by his position and height in the heavens, but it is difficult to tell the hour of the night, unless one is familiar with the system and order of the twelve signs of the Zodiac in the starry sky, knowledge of which it is quite easy to gain by studying the constellations. For since, though nights are of unequal length, yet during the course of every night six out of the twelve signs of the Zodiac must appear above the horizon, it follows of necessity that during the same portions of every night equal portions of the twelve signs must needs rise above the horizon. As the position each day of the sun in the Zodiac is known, it is evident that at his setting the part diametrically opposite must rise. So that the portion of the

μετὰ ταύτην μέρος ἀνατεταλκὸς φαίνηται τοῦ ζῳδι-
11 ακοῦ, τοσοῦτον εἰκὸς ἠνύσθαι τῆς νυκτὸς αἰεί. γνωρι-
ζομένων δὲ τῶν ζῳδίων καὶ κατὰ τὸ πλῆθος καὶ κατὰ
τὸ μέγεθος, τοιούτους γίνεσθαι μετὰ ταῦτα συμβαίνει
12 καὶ τοὺς κατὰ μέρος καιροὺς τῆς νυκτός. ἐν δὲ ταῖς
συννεφέσι νυξὶ τῇ σελήνῃ προσεκτέον, ἐπεὶ διὰ τὸ
μέγεθος ὡς ἐπίπαν αἰεὶ τὸ ταύτης ἐμφαίνεται φῶς,
13 καθ᾽ ὃν ἂν ᾖ τόπον τοῦ κόσμου. καὶ ποτὲ μὲν ἐκ τῶν
περὶ τὰς ἀνατολὰς καιρῶν καὶ τόπων στοχαστέον,
14 ποτὲ δὲ πάλιν ἐκ τῶν περὶ τὰς δύσεις, καθυπαρχούσης
καὶ περὶ τοῦτο τὸ μέρος ἐννοίας ἐπὶ τοσοῦτον ὥστε
συμπεριφέρεσθαι ταῖς καθ᾽ ἡμέραν διαφοραῖς τῶν
ἀνατολῶν. ἔστι δὲ τρόπος εὐθεώρητος καὶ περὶ ταύ-
15 την· ὅρος γὰρ εἷς μὴν ὡς τύπῳ, καὶ πρὸς αἴσθησιν
τοιοῦτοι πάντες.

16. ᾗ καὶ τὸν ποιητὴν ἄν τις ἐπαινέσειε, διότι
παρεισάγει τὸν Ὀδυσσέα, τὸν ἡγεμονικώτατον ἄνδρα,
τεκμαιρόμενον ἐκ τῶν ἄστρων οὐ μόνον τὰ κατὰ τοὺς
2 πλοῦς, ἀλλὰ καὶ τὰ περὶ τὰς ἐν τῇ γῇ πράξεις. ἱκανὰ
γὰρ καὶ τὰ παρὰ δόξαν γινόμενα ⟨μὴ δυνάμενα⟩
τυγχάνειν προνοίας ἀκριβοῦς εἰς τὸ πολλὴν ἀπορίαν
3 παρασκευάζειν καὶ πολλάκις, οἷον ὄμβρων καὶ ποταμῶν ἐπιφοραὶ καὶ πάγων ὑπερβολαὶ καὶ χιόνες, ἔτι δ᾽
ὁ καπνώδης καὶ συννεφὴς ἀὴρ καὶ τἆλλα τὰ παρα-
4 πλήσια τούτοις. εἰ δὲ καὶ περὶ ὧν δυνατόν ἐστι προϊδέσθαι, καὶ τούτων ὀλιγωρήσομεν, πῶς οὐκ εἰκότως
5 ἐν τοῖς πλείστοις ἀποτευξόμεθα δι᾽ αὐτούς; διόπερ οὐκ
ἀφροντιστητέον οὐδενὸς τῶν προειρημένων, ἵνα μὴ

night which is past is to be judged by the portion of the Zodiac which has risen after this; and the number and size of the signs of the Zodiac being known, the subsequent[21] subdivisions of the night correspond to them. On cloudy nights, however, we must observe the moon, because as a rule, owing to her size, her light is visible in whatever part of the heaven she may be situated. We can guess the hour at times from the time and place of her rising and at times again from those of her setting, if here too we have sufficient previous knowledge to be familiar with the daily difference in the hour of her rising. Here also there is an easy method of reckoning, for the period of her revolution is generally speaking one month, and all the months are similar as far as we can perceive.

16. Homer is therefore deserving of praise in representing Odysseus, the most capable of commanders, as observing the stars to direct not only his course at sea, but his operations on land. For those accidents which take us by surprise and cannot be accurately foreseen are quite sufficiently numerous to expose us to great and frequent difficulties, I mean sudden rains and floods, exceeding great frosts and snowfalls, a foggy and clouded state of the atmosphere and the like, and if we pay no attention even to such things as can be foreseen, we are sure to fail in most enterprises by our own fault. So that none of the abovementioned matters must be neglected, if we are not to

[21] On this obscure passage see WC 2.142.

τοιούτοις ἀλογήμασι περιπίπτωμεν οἵοις φασὶ περι-
πεσεῖν ἑτέρους τε πλείους καὶ τοὺς νῦν ὑφ' ἡμῶν
λέγεσθαι μέλλοντας ὑποδείγματος χάριν.

17. Ἄρατος ὁ τῶν Ἀχαιῶν στρατηγὸς ἐπιβαλό-
μενος πραξικοπεῖν τὴν τῶν Κυναιθέων πόλιν, συνετάξατο πρὸς τοὺς ἐκ τῆς πόλεως αὐτῷ συνεργοῦντας
ἡμέραν, ἐν ᾗ τὸν μὲν Ἄρατον ἔδει νυκτὸς παραγενη-
θέντα πρὸς τὸν ἀπὸ Κυναίθης ῥέοντα ποταμὸν ὡς ἐπὶ
τὴν ἕω μένειν ἐνσχολάσαντα μετὰ τῆς δυνάμεως,
2 τοὺς δ' ἔνδοθεν περὶ μέσον ἡμέρας, ὅτε λάβοιεν τὸν
καιρόν, ἕνα μὲν αὐτῶν μεθ' ἡσυχίας ἐν ἱματίῳ διὰ τῆς
πύλης ἐκπέμψαι, καὶ κελεῦσαι προελθόντα στῆναι
3 πρὸ τῆς πόλεως ἐπὶ τὸν συνταχθέντα τάφον, τοὺς δὲ
λοιποὺς προσενεγκεῖν τὰς χεῖρας τοῖς ἄρχουσι, κοι-
μωμένοις κατὰ μέσον ἡμέρας, τοῖς εἰθισμένοις τηρεῖν
4 τὴν πύλην. γενομένου δὲ τούτου σπουδῇ καταταχεῖν
τοὺς Ἀχαιοὺς ἐκ τῆς ἐνέδρας ἔδει πρὸς τὴν πύλην.
5 τούτων δὲ διατεταγμένων καὶ τοῦ καιροῦ συνάψαντος,
ὁ μὲν Ἄρατος ἧκε καὶ κρυφθεὶς κατὰ τὸν ποταμὸν
6 ἔμενε τηρῶν τὸ σύνθημα· περὶ δὲ πέμπτην ὥραν ἔχων
τις πρόβατα μαλακὰ τῶν εἰθισμένων περὶ πόλιν τρέ-
φειν, δεηθεὶς ἐκ τοῦ καιροῦ πυθέσθαι τι τοῦ ποιμένος
βιωτικόν, ἐξῆλθε διὰ τῆς πύλης ἐν ἱματίῳ καὶ στὰς
7 ἐπὶ τὸν αὐτὸν τάφον περιεβλέπετο τὸν ποιμένα. οἱ δὲ
περὶ τὸν Ἄρατον ἀποδεδόσθαι σφίσι τὸ σύνθημα
νομίσαντες σπουδῇ πρὸς τὴν πόλιν ἐφέροντο πάντες.
8 ταχὺ δὲ τῆς πύλης κλεισθείσης ὑπὸ τῶν ἐφεστώτων
διὰ τὸ μηδέπω μηδὲν ὑπὸ τῶν ἔνδον ἡτοιμάσθαι,

commit such blunders as many other generals are said to have committed besides those I am about to cite as examples.

17. Aratus, the Achaean strategus, having formed the project of getting Cynaetha betrayed to him, came to an agreement with those in the city who were working for him, fixing a day on which he himself was to march by night to the river that runs down from Cynaetha toward the east and remain there quietly with his forces. Those in the city about midday, whenever they had the opportunity, were to send out quietly through the gate one of their number dressed in a mantle with orders to advance as far as a certain tomb outside the city and take up his post on it. Meanwhile the rest of them were to attack the officers who used to keep the gate, while they were taking their midday sleep. Upon this the Achaeans were to issue from their ambush and make for the gate at full speed. Such being the arrangement, when the day came Aratus arrived and hid in the riverbed waiting for the signal. But at about the fifth hour of the day the owner of some of those delicate sheep whose habit it was to pasture them near the town, having some urgent private business with his shepherd, came out of the gate dressed in a mantle and went and stood on the identical tomb looking round for the shepherd. Aratus and his troops, thinking that the signal had been given them, made a rush for the town, but the gate was at once closed in their faces by its keepers, as their friends inside the town

συνέβη μὴ μόνον τῆς πράξεως ἀποτυχεῖν τοὺς περὶ
τὸν Ἄρατον, ἀλλὰ καὶ τοῖς ἐκ τῆς πόλεως συμπράτ-
τουσιν αἰτίους γενέσθαι τῶν μεγίστων συμπτωμάτων·
καταφανεῖς γὰρ γενόμενοι παραχρῆμα προβληθέντες
9 ἀπέθανον. τί οὖν εἴποι τις ἂν τῆς περιπετείας αἴτιον
γεγονέναι; τὸ ποιήσασθαι τὸν στρατηγὸν ἁπλοῦν τὸ
σύνθημα, νέον ἀκμὴν ὄντα καὶ τῆς τῶν διπλῶν συνθημάτων καὶ παρασυνθημάτων ἀκριβείας ἄπειρον.
10 οὕτως αἱ πολεμικαὶ πράξεις ἐν μικρῷ τὸ διαφέρον
ἔχουσι τῆς ἐφ' ἑκάτερα ῥοπῆς τῶν ἐκβαινόντων.

18. Καὶ μὴν Κλεομένης ὁ Σπαρτιάτης προθέμενος
διὰ πράξεως ἑλεῖν τὴν τῶν Μεγαλοπολιτῶν πόλιν,
συνετάξατο τοῖς τὸ τεῖχος φυλάττουσι τὸ κατὰ τὸν
Φωλεὸν καλούμενον νυκτὸς ἥξειν μετὰ τῆς δυνάμεως
κατὰ τρίτην φυλακήν· τοῦτον γὰρ ἐφύλαττον τὸν και-
2 ρὸν τὸ τεῖχος οἱ συμπράττοντες αὐτῷ. οὐκέτι δὲ προνοηθεὶς ὅτι περὶ τὴν τῆς Πλειάδος ἐπιτολὴν τελέως
ἤδη βραχείας εἶναι συμβαίνει τὰς νύκτας, ἐκίνησε
τὴν δύναμιν ἐκ τῆς Λακεδαίμονος περὶ δυσμὰς ἡλίου.
3 λοιπὸν οὐ δυνάμενος καταχεῖν, ἀλλὰ τῆς ἡμέρας
καταλαμβανούσης εἰκῇ καὶ ἀλόγως βιαζόμενος,
αἰσχρῶς ἐξέπεσε, πολλοὺς ἀποβαλὼν καὶ κινδυνεύ-
4 σας τοῖς ὅλοις· ὃς εἰ κατὰ τὸ συνταχθὲν ηὐστόχησε
τοῦ καιροῦ καὶ κρατούντων τῆς εἰσόδου τῶν συνεργούντων εἰσήγαγε τὴν δύναμιν, οὐκ ἂν διεψεύσθη τῆς
ἐπιβολῆς.

5 Πάλιν ὁμοίως Φίλιππος ὁ βασιλεύς, ὡς ἐπάνω
προεῖπον, πρᾶξιν ἔχων ἐκ τῆς τῶν Μελιταιῶν πόλεως

had as yet taken no measures, and the consequence was that not only did the coup that Aratus had planned fail, but they brought destruction on those of the citizens who were acting with him, for they were at once detected, dragged forward, and executed. If we ask what was the cause of the disaster, the answer must be that it was the use of a single signal by the commander, who was still young and ignorant of the accuracy secured by double signals and counter signals. On such small matters does success or failure depend in military operations.

18. Again Cleomenes of Sparta, having formed a plan for taking Megalopolis by treachery, agreed with those of the defenders who guarded the wall near what is called the Den to come there with his army at the third watch of the night, for it was at this hour that his partisans were on guard. But not reflecting that toward the rising of the Pleiades the nights are already quite short, he marched out of Lacedaemon about sunset. So that he was unable to arrive in time, but being overtaken by daylight was rash and imprudent enough to attempt to force his way into the town and was driven out with disgrace and considerable loss, very narrowly escaping complete disaster. Had he succeeded in arriving at the time agreed upon and led his troops in while his partisans were masters of the entrance, he would not have met with failure.

King Philip, to take another instance, having, as I stated above,[22] a proposal from Melitaea to betray the town to

22 See Book 5.97.

κατὰ δύο τρόπους ἥμαρτε· καὶ γὰρ τὰς κλίμακας
ἐλάττους ἔχων ἦλθε τῆς χρείας καὶ τοῦ καιροῦ δι-
6 έπεσε. συνταξάμενος γὰρ ἥξειν περὶ μέσας νύκτας
κατακεκοιμημένων ἤδη πάντων, πρὸ τοῦ δέοντος καιροῦ κινήσας ἐκ Λαρίσης καὶ προσπεσὼν πρὸς τὴν
τῶν Μελιταιῶν χώραν, οὔτ' ἐπιμένειν ἐδύνατο, δεδιὼς
μὴ προσαγγελθείη τοῖς ἔνδον, οὔτ' ἀνακάμψας ἔτι
7 λαθεῖν. διόπερ ἀναγκαζόμενος εἰς τοὔμπροσθεν προάγειν, ἧκε πρὸς τὴν πόλιν ἀκμὴν τῶν ἀνθρώπων
8 ἐγρηγορότων. ὅθεν οὔτε διὰ τῶν κλιμάκων ἠδύνατο
βιάζεσθαι διὰ τὴν ἀσυμμετρίαν οὔτε διὰ τῆς πύλης
εἰσελθεῖν τῷ μὴ δύνασθαι τοὺς ἔνδον αὐτῷ συνεργεῖν
9 διὰ τὸν καιρόν. τέλος διερεθίσας τοὺς ἐν τῇ πόλει καὶ
πολλοὺς τῶν ἰδίων ἀποβαλών, μετ' αἰσχύνης ἄπρα-
κτος ἐπανῆλθε, πᾶσι καὶ τοῖς ἄλλοις παρηγγελκὼς
ἀπιστεῖν αὐτῷ καὶ φυλάττεσθαι.

19. Καὶ μὴν Νικίας ὁ τῶν Ἀθηναίων στρατηγός,
δυνάμενος σῴζειν τὸ περὶ τὰς Συρακούσας στρά-
τευμα, καὶ λαβὼν τῆς νυκτὸς τὸν ἁρμόζοντα καιρὸν
εἰς τὸ λαθεῖν τοὺς πολεμίους, ἀποχωρήσας εἰς ἀσφα-
λές, κἄπειτα τῆς σελήνης ἐκλειπούσης δεισιδαιμονή-
σας, ὥς τι δεινὸν προσημαινούσης, ἐπέσχε τὴν ἀνα-
2 ζυγήν. καὶ παρὰ τοῦτο συνέβη κατὰ τὴν ἐπιοῦσαν
αὐτοῦ νύκτα ποιησαμένου τὴν ἀναζυγήν, προαισθο-
μένων τῶν πολεμίων, καὶ τὸ στρατόπεδον καὶ τοὺς
ἡγεμόνας ὑποχειρίους γενέσθαι τοῖς Συρακοσίοις.
3 καίτοι γε παρὰ τῶν ἐμπείρων ἱστορήσας μόνον περὶ
τούτων δυνατὸς ἦν οὐχ οἷον παραλιπεῖν διὰ τὰ τοι-

him, made two mistakes. Firstly he came there with ladders too short for the purpose, and secondly he did not arrive at the right time. He had arranged to arrive about midnight when everyone was asleep, but he started from Larisa before the proper hour, and on entering the territory of Melitaea, neither could remain there, as he feared that news of his arrival would reach the city, nor could he get back without being noticed. Being compelled, therefore, to advance he reached the city while people were still awake. So that he could neither take the place by escalade, owing to the defective size of his ladders, nor could he get in through the gate, as owing to the earliness of the hour his partisans within could not cooperate with him. Finally, after merely provoking the garrison and losing many of his own men he made a shameful retreat with his purpose unaccomplished, having thus given public notice to everyone else to mistrust him and be on their guard.

19. Nicias, again, the Athenian general, could have saved the army before Syracuse, and had fixed on the proper hour of the night to withdraw into a position of safety unobserved by the enemy; but on an eclipse of the moon taking place he was struck with superstitious terror as if it foreboded some calamity, and deferred his departure. The consequence of this was that when he abandoned his camp on the following night, the enemy had divined his intention, and both the army and the generals were made prisoners by the Syracusans. Yet had he only inquired from men acquainted with astronomy so far from throwing away his opportunity owing to such an occur-

αὗτα τοὺς ἰδίους καιρούς, ἀλλὰ καὶ συνεργοῖς χρῆσα-
4 σθαι διὰ τὴν τῶν ὑπεναντίων ἄγνοιαν· ἡ γὰρ τῶν
πέλας ἀπειρία μέγιστον ἐφόδιον γίνεται τοῖς ἐμπεί-
ροις πρὸς κατόρθωσιν.

5 Ἐκ μὲν οὖν ἀστρολογίας μέχρι τῶν προειρημένων
πολυπραγμονητέον. περὶ δὲ τῆς τῶν κλιμάκων συμμε-
6 τρίας τοιοῦτός τίς ἐστιν ὁ τρόπος τῆς θεωρίας. ἐὰν μὲν
γὰρ διά τινος τῶν συμπραττόντων δοθῇ τὸ τοῦ τείχους ὕψος, πρόδηλος ἡ τῶν κλιμάκων γίνεται συμ-
μετρία· οἵων γὰρ ἂν δέκα τινῶν εἶναι συμβαίνῃ τὸ τοῦ
τείχους ὕψος, τοιούτων δώδεκα δεήσει τὰς κλίμακας
7 δαψιλῶν ὑπάρχειν. τὴν δ’ ἀπόβασιν τῆς κλίμακος
πρὸς τὴν τῶν ἀναβαινόντων συμμετρίαν ἡμίσειαν
εἶναι δεήσει τῆς κλίμακος, ἵνα μήτε πλεῖον ἀφιστά-
μεναι διὰ τὸ πλῆθος τῶν ἐπιβαινόντων εὐσύντριπτοι
γίνωνται μήτε πάλιν ὀρθότεραι προσερειδόμεναι λίαν
8 ἀκροσφαλεῖς ὦσι τοῖς προσβαίνουσιν. ἐὰν δὲ μὴ
δυνατὸν ᾖ μετρῆσαι μηδ’ ἐγγίσαι τῷ τείχει, ληπτέον
ἐξ ἀποστάσεως παντὸς ὕψους τὸ μέγεθος τῶν πρὸς
9 ὀρθὰς ἐφεστώτων τοῖς ὑποκειμένοις ἐπιπέδοις. ὅ τε
τρόπος τῆς λήψεως καὶ δυνατὸς καὶ ῥάδιος τοῖς βου-
λομένοις πολυπραγμονεῖν ⟨τὰ⟩ παρὰ τῶν μαθημα-
τικῶν.

20. Διὸ πάλιν ἐν τούτοις φανερὸν ὅτι δεήσει τοὺς
βουλομένους εὐστοχεῖν ἐν ταῖς ἐπιβολαῖς καὶ πρά-
ξεσι γεγεωμετρηκέναι μὴ τελείως, ἀλλ’ ἐπὶ τοσοῦτον
ἐφ’ ὅσον ἀναλογίας ἔννοιαν ἔχειν καὶ τῆς περὶ τὰς
2 ὁμοιότητας θεωρίας. οὐ γὰρ περὶ ταῦτα μόνον, ἀλλὰ

rence, he could have utilized the ignorance of the enemy. For nothing contributes more to the success of well-informed men than the lack of instruction in their neighbors.

So far as the points I have mentioned are concerned it is to astronomy that we should address our inquiries, but the method of discovering the right length for ladders is as follows. If any of our partisans can give us the height of the wall the required length of the ladders is evident. For if the height of the wall be, let us say, ten of a given measure, the length of the ladders must be a good twelve. The distance from the wall at which the ladder is planted must, so as to achieve a proper relationship to those ascending, be half the length of the ladder, for if they are placed farther off they are apt to break when crowded and if set up nearer to the perpendicular are very insecure for the scalers. If however it is impossible to measure the wall or approach it, the height of any object which stands perpendicular on a plane surface can be taken from a distance, the method of determining it being practicable and easy for anyone who chooses to study mathematics.

20. So here again it is evident that those who aim at success in military plans and surprises of towns must have studied geometry, if not thoroughly at least enough to have a notion of proportion and the principles of equations; for this kind of knowledge indeed is necessary not only for

51

καὶ περὶ τὰς τῶν σχημάτων μεταλήψεις ἐν ταῖς στρατοπεδείαις ἀναγκαῖός ἐστιν ὁ τρόπος, χάριν τοῦ δύνασθαι ποτὲ μὲν πᾶν σχῆμα μεταλαμβάνοντας τηρεῖν
τὴν αὐτὴν συμμετρίαν τῶν ἐν ταῖς παρεμβολαῖς περι-
3 λαμβανομένων, ποτὲ δὲ πάλιν ἐπὶ τῶν αὐτῶν σχημάτων μένοντας αὔξειν ἢ μειοῦν τὸ περιλαμβανό-
μενον τῇ στρατοπεδείᾳ χωρίον, κατὰ λόγον ἀεὶ τῶν
προσγινομένων ἢ τῶν χωριζομένων ἐκ τῆς παρεμ-
4 βολῆς· ὑπὲρ ὧν ἡμῖν ἐν τοῖς περὶ τὰς τάξεις ὑπομνή-
5 μασιν ἀκριβέστερον δεδήλωται. οὐ γὰρ οἴομαι τοῦτό
γε μετρίως ἡμῖν ἐποίσειν οὐδένα διότι πολλά τινα
προσαρτῶμεν τῇ στρατηγίᾳ, κελεύοντες ἀστρολογεῖν
6 καὶ γεωμετρεῖν τοὺς ὀρεγομένους αὐτῆς. ἐγὼ δὲ τὰ μὲν
ἐκ περιττοῦ παρελκόμενα τοῖς ἐπιτηδεύμασι χάριν
τῆς ἐν ἑκάστοις ἐπιφάσεως καὶ στωμυλίας πολύ τι
μᾶλλον ἀποδοκιμάζων, παραπλησίως δὲ καὶ τὸ πορ-
ρωτέρω τοῦ πρὸς τὴν χρείαν ἀνήκοντος ἐπιτάττειν,
περὶ τἀναγκαῖα φιλοτιμότατός εἰμι καὶ σπουδάζων.
7 καὶ γὰρ ἄτοπον τοὺς μὲν ὀρχηστικῆς ἢ τοὺς αὐλητι-
κῆς ἐφιεμένους ἐπιδέχεσθαι τήν τε περὶ τοὺς ῥυθμοὺς
καὶ τὰ μουσικὰ προκατασκευήν, ἔτι δὲ τὰ περὶ τὴν
παλαίστραν, διὰ τὸ δοκεῖν προσδεῖσθαι τὸ τέλος ἑκα-
8 τέρου τῆς τῶν προειρημένων συνεργίας, τοὺς δὲ στρατηγίας ἀντιποιουμένους ἀσχάλλειν, εἰ δεήσει τῶν
9 ἐκτὸς ἐπιτηδευμάτων μέχρι τινὸς ἀναλαβεῖν. ὥστε
τοὺς περὶ τὰς βαναύσους τέχνας ἀσκοῦντας ἐμμε-
λεστέρους εἶναι καὶ φιλοτιμοτέρους τῶν περὶ τὰ κάλλιστα καὶ σεμνότατα προαιρουμένων διαφέρειν· ὧν

the above purpose but for making changes in the plan of camps, so as to enable us either in changing the whole plan of the camp to keep up the same proportion between the different parts enclosed in it, or at other times while adhering to the same plan, to increase or diminish the space included in the camp proportionately to the number of fresh arrivals or departures. About this matter I have entered into greater detail in my notes on tactics. I do not think anyone can fairly maintain that I attach too many qualifications to the art of generalship, by thus urging those who aim at mastering it to study astronomy and geometry. On the contrary I strongly disapprove of all such superfluous acquirements in a profession as serve but for ostentation and fine talk, but while also disinclined to insist on any studies beyond those that are of actual use, in the case of necessary knowledge I am most exacting and earnest. It is indeed strange that those who wish to learn the arts of dancing and flute playing should consent to study as a preliminary the theory of rhythm and music and even to acquire some gymnastic training, because it is thought that perfection in either cannot be attained without such aid, while those who aspire to the command of armies regard it as a grievance if we demand of them a certain slight acquaintance with other sciences. This would mean that those who practice illiberal arts show greater diligence and emulation than those whose aim is to excel in the most honorable and serious of all employments—a proposition

10   οὐδὲν ἂν ὁμολογήσειε νοῦν ἔχων οὐδείς. καὶ περὶ μὲν
τούτων ἐπὶ τοσοῦτον ἡμῖν εἰρήσθω. . . .

21. Ὅτι τοιαύτης διαθέσεως ὑπαρχούσης περί τε
τοὺς Ῥωμαίους καὶ Καρχηδονίους, καὶ παλιντρόπων
ἑκατέροις ἐκ τῶν ὑπὸ τῆς τύχης ἀπαντωμένων ἐναλ-
λὰξ προσπιπτόντων, κατὰ τὸν ποιητὴν ἅμα λύπην καὶ
χαρὰν ὑποτρέχειν εἰκὸς ἦν τὰς ἑκάστων ψυχάς. . . .

22. Ὅτι τῶν ἑκατέροις, Ῥωμαίοις φημὶ καὶ Καρχηδονίοις, προσπιπτόντων καὶ συμβαινόντων εἷς ἦν
2   ἀνὴρ αἴτιος καὶ μία ψυχή, λέγω δὲ τὴν Ἀννίβου. τά τε
γὰρ κατὰ τὴν Ἰταλίαν ὁμολογουμένως οὗτος ἦν ὁ
χειρίζων, τά τε κατὰ τὴν Ἰβηρίαν διὰ τοῦ πρεσβυ-
τέρου τῶν ἀδελφῶν Ἀσδρούβου, μετὰ δὲ ταῦτα διὰ
3   τοῦ [πρεσβύτου] Μάγωνος· οἱ γὰρ τοὺς τῶν Ῥωμαίων
στρατηγοὺς ἀμφοτέρους ἀποκτείναντες [ἅμα] κατὰ
4   τὴν Ἰβηρίαν ἦσαν οὗτοι. καὶ μὴν τὰ κατὰ τὴν Σικελίαν ἔπραττε τὰς μὲν ἀρχὰς διὰ τῶν περὶ τὸν Ἱππο-
5   κράτην, ὕστερον δὲ διὰ Μυττόνου τοῦ Λίβυος. ὁμοίως
δὲ καὶ κατὰ τὴν Ἑλλάδα καὶ τὴν Ἰλλυρίδα· καὶ τὸν
ἀπὸ τούτων τῶν τόπων φόβον ἀνατεινόμενος ἐξ-
έπληττε καὶ περιέσπα Ῥωμαίους διὰ τῆς πρὸς Φίλιπ-
6   πον κοινοπραγίας. οὕτως μέγα τι φύεται χρῆμα καὶ
θαυμάσιον ἀνὴρ καὶ ψυχὴ δεόντως ἁρμοσθεῖσα κατὰ

---

23 An account of recent gains and losses for both sides, as reported by Livy 26.37.1–9 (following P.).

to which no sensible man would give his assent. But these remarks must suffice on this subject. . . .

21. Such being the respective positions of the Romans and Carthaginians,[23] experiencing in turn the opposite extremes of fortune, it was natural that, as Homer says, pain and joy[24] at once should possess the minds of each. . . .

The Character of Hannibal

22. Of all that befell both nations, Romans and Carthaginians, the cause was one man and one mind—Hannibal. It was he indisputably who had the management of the Italian campaign, and he also directed that in Spain through the elder of his brothers, Hasdrubal, and afterward through Mago, these being the generals who killed the two Roman commanders in that country. Besides this he managed affairs in Sicily, first of all through Hippocrates and subsequently through Myttonus the African,[25] and he was likewise active in Greece and Illyria, threatening the Romans from these parts and keeping them alarmed and distracted by his understanding with Philip.[26] Such a great and wonderful product of nature is a man with a

---

[24] P. has replaced Homer's χάρμα καὶ ἄλγος (*Od.* 19.471) by λύπη καὶ χαρά, inverting the two notions.

[25] A Libyophoenician; *RE* Myttones 1428–1430 (V. Ehrenberg). An able commander who later defected and surrendered Agrigentum to the Romans (Livy 26.40.1–12). He received Roman citizenship and fought twenty years later for the Romans against Antiochus III. At Delphi he and his four sons were made *proxenoi* in 190/89 (*SIG* 585.86–88).

[26] P. refers to their alliance (7.9.1–17).

τὴν ἐξ ἀρχῆς σύστασιν πρὸς ὅ τι ἂν ὁρμήσῃ τῶν
ἀνθρωπίνων ἔργων.

7   Ἐπεὶ δ' ἡ τῶν πραγμάτων διάθεσις εἰς ἐπίστασιν
ἡμᾶς ἦχε περὶ τῆς Ἀννίβου φύσεως, ἀπαιτεῖν ὁ καιρὸς δοκεῖ μοι τὰς μάλιστα διαπορουμένας ἰδιότητας
8 ὑπὲρ αὐτοῦ δηλῶσαι. τινὲς μὲν γὰρ ὠμὸν αὐτὸν οἴονται γεγονέναι καθ' ὑπερβολήν, τινὲς δὲ φιλάργυρον.
τὸ δ' ἀληθὲς εἰπεῖν ὑπὲρ αὐτοῦ καὶ τῶν ἐν πράγμασιν
9 ἀναστρεφομένων οὐ ῥᾴδιον. ἔνιοι μὲν γὰρ ἐλέγχεσθαί
φασι τὰς φύσεις ὑπὸ τῶν περιστάσεων, καὶ τοὺς μὲν
ἐν ταῖς ἐξουσίαις καταφανεῖς γίνεσθαι, κἂν ὅλως τὸν
πρὸ τοῦ χρόνον ἀναστέλλωνται, τοὺς δὲ πάλιν ἐν ταῖς
10 ἀτυχίαις. ἐμοὶ δ' ἔμπαλιν οὐχ ὑγιὲς εἶναι δοκεῖ τὸ
λεγόμενον· οὐ γὰρ ὀλίγα μοι φαίνονται, τὰ δὲ πλεῖστα, ποτὲ μὲν διὰ τὰς τῶν φίλων παραθέσεις, ποτὲ δὲ
διὰ τὰς τῶν πραγμάτων ποικιλίας, ἄνθρωποι παρὰ
τὴν αὐτῶν προαίρεσιν ἀναγκάζεσθαι καὶ λέγειν καὶ
πράττειν.

23. γνοίη δ' ἄν τις ἐπὶ πολλῶν τῶν ἤδη γεγονότων
2 ἐπιστήσας. τίς γὰρ Ἀγαθοκλέα τὸν Σικελίας τύραννον οὐχ ἱστόρηκε διότι δόξας ὠμότατος εἶναι κατὰ τὰς
πρώτας ἐπιβολὰς καὶ τὴν κατασκευὴν τῆς δυναστείας, μετὰ ταῦτα νομίσας βεβαίως ἐνδεδέσθαι τὴν
Σικελιωτῶν ἀρχὴν πάντων ἡμερώτατος δοκεῖ γεγονέ-
3 ναι καὶ πρᾳότατος; ἔτι δὲ Κλεομένης ὁ Σπαρτιάτης οὐ
χρηστότατος μὲν βασιλεύς, πικρότατος δὲ τύραννος,
εὐτραπελώτατος δὲ πάλιν ἰδιώτης καὶ φιλανθρωπό-
4 τατος; καίτοι γ' οὐκ εἰκὸς ἦν περὶ τὰς αὐτὰς φύσεις

56

mind properly fitted by its original constitution to execute any project within human power.

But since the course of affairs has called our attention to the character of Hannibal, I think I am called upon at present to state my opinion regarding those peculiar traits in it which are the subject of most dispute. For some accuse him of excessive cruelty and others of avarice. Now it is no easy thing to state the truth about him or in general about men who are engaged in public affairs. For some say that men's real natures are revealed by circumstances, the truth being in the case of some brought to light by possession of power, even if they have hitherto managed to disguise it entirely, and in that of others by misfortune. But I cannot myself regard this view as sound. For it appears to me that not in a few cases only but in most cases men are compelled to act and speak contrary to their real principles by the complexity of facts and by the suggestions of their friends.

23. There are many previous instances a consideration of which will show that this is so. Take Agathocles the tyrant of Sicily. Do not all historians[27] tell us that after showing himself exceedingly cruel in his first enterprises and in the establishment of his power, afterward, when once he thought that he had securely attached the Sicilians to his rule, he became to all appearance the gentlest and mildest of men? Again, was not Cleomenes of Sparta at once a most excellent king and a most cruel tyrant, and then again in private intercourse most urbane and courteous? Now we can hardly suppose that dispositions so diametrically

---

[27] Timaeus (see 1.5.1) was not one of them, as he remained hostile to Agathocles throughout.

τὰς ἐναντιωτάτας διαθέσεις ὑπάρχειν· ἀλλ' ἀναγκαζό-
μενοι ταῖς τῶν πραγμάτων μεταβολαῖς συμμετατίθε-
σθαι τὴν ἐναντίαν τῇ φύσει πολλάκις ἐμφαίνουσι
διάθεσιν ἔνιοι τῶν δυναστῶν πρὸς τοὺς ἐκτός, ὥστε
μὴ οἷον ἐλέγχεσθαι τὰς φύσεις διὰ τούτων, τὸ δ'
5 ἐναντίον ἐπισκοτεῖσθαι μᾶλλον. τὸ δ' αὐτὸ καὶ διὰ τὰς
τῶν φίλων παραθέσεις εἴωθε συμβαίνειν οὐ μόνον
ἡγεμόσι καὶ δυνάσταις καὶ βασιλεῦσιν, ἀλλὰ καὶ
6 πόλεσιν. Ἀθηναίων γοῦν εὕροι τις ἂν ὀλίγα μὲν τὰ
πικρά, πολλὰ δὲ τὰ χρηστὰ καὶ σεμνὰ τῆς πολιτείας
Ἀριστείδου καὶ Περικλέους προεστώτων, Κλέωνος δὲ
7 καὶ Χάρητος τἀναντία· Λακεδαιμονίων <δ'> ἡγουμένων τῆς Ἑλλάδος ὅσα μὲν διὰ Κλεομβρότου τοῦ
βασιλέως πράττοιτο, πάντα συμμαχικὴν εἶχε τὴν
8 αἵρεσιν, ὅσα δὲ δι' Ἀγησιλάου, τοὐναντίον· ὥστε καὶ
τὰ τῶν πόλεων ἔθη ταῖς τῶν προεστώτων διαφοραῖς
9 συμμεταπίπτειν. Φίλιππος δ' ὁ βασιλεύς, ὅτε μὲν
Ταυρίων ἢ Δημήτριος αὐτῷ συμπράττοιεν, ἦν ἀσεβέστατος, ὅτε δὲ πάλιν Ἄρατος ἢ Χρυσόγονος, ἡμερώτατος.

24. Παραπλήσια δέ μοι δοκεῖ τούτοις καὶ τὰ κατ'
2 Ἀννίβαν γεγονέναι· καὶ γὰρ περιστάσεσι παραδόξοις

---

28 Recalled from exile in 480 on the eve of Xerxes' invasion of
Greece. After the foundation of the Delian League in 478/7, he
was commissioned to assess the tributes of the individual member
states; his performance earned him the epithet "the Just." Plu-
tarch wrote his *Life.* J. K. Davies, *Athenian Propertied Families
600–300 B.C.,* Oxford 1971, no. 1695

opposite existed in the same natures. The fact is rather that some princes are compelled to change with the change of circumstances and often exhibit to others a disposition which is quite the opposite of their real nature, so that so far from men's natures being revealed by such means they are rather obscured. And a like effect is usually produced by the suggestions of friends not only on generals, princes, and kings but on cities. At Athens at least we find that during the government of Aristides[28] and Pericles the state was the author of a few cruel actions, but of many kind and praiseworthy ones, while under Cleon[29] and Chares[30] it was quite the reverse; and again when the Lacedaemonians were supreme in Greece, all that King Cleombrotus[31] did was done in the spirit of friendly alliance, but it was the reverse with Agesilaus;[32] so that the character of cities also changes with that of those who govern them. And so with King Philip, when he had Taurion and Demetrius to act with him he was most wicked, but when he had Aratus and Chrysogonus he was most gentle.

24. It was very much the same, I think, with Hannibal. He had to deal with circumstances of such an exceptional

[29] The dominant politician after Pericles' death in 429 until his own in 422; well-known from Thucydides and Aristophanes.

[30] Athenian general against King Philip II and, in the service of Darius III, against Alexander the Great. Berve, *Alexanderreich* 2:403, no. 819.   [31] King of Sparta 380–371; he fell at Leuctra against the Thebans.

[32] King of Sparta 399–360, often disregarding the autonomy of other Greek states despite the pertinent clause in the King's peace of 387. See P. Cartledge, *Agesilaos and the Crisis of Sparta* (Baltimore 1987). See also X. *Ages.* and Plu. *Ages.*

THE HISTORIES OF POLYBIUS

καὶ ποικίλαις ἐχρήσατο καὶ φίλοις τοῖς ἔγγιστα
μεγάλας ἐσχηκόσι διαφοράς, ὥστε καὶ λίαν ἐκ τῶν
κατ᾽ Ἰταλίαν πράξεων δυσθεώρητον εἶναι τὴν τοῦ
3 προειρημένου φύσιν. τὰς μὲν οὖν τῶν περιστάσεων
ὑποβολὰς εὐχερὲς καὶ διὰ τῶν προειρημένων καὶ διὰ
τῶν μετὰ ταῦτα ῥηθησομένων καταμαθεῖν, τὰς δὲ τῶν
φίλων οὐκ ἄξιον παραλιπεῖν, ἄλλως τε καὶ διὰ μιᾶς
γνώμης ἱκανὴν τοῦ πράγματος ἔμφασιν ⟨ἐξὸν⟩ λα-
4 βεῖν. καθ᾽ ὃν γὰρ καιρὸν Ἀννίβας ἐξ Ἰβηρίας τὴν εἰς
Ἰταλίαν πορείαν ἐπενόει στέλλεσθαι μετὰ τῶν δυνάμεων, μεγίστης προφαινομένης δυσχρηστίας περὶ τὰς
τροφὰς καὶ τὴν ἑτοιμότητα τῶν ἐπιτηδείων τοῖς
στρατοπέδοις, ἅτε καὶ κατὰ τὸ μῆκος ἀνήνυτον ἔχειν
τι δοκούσης τῆς ὁδοῦ καὶ κατὰ τὸ πλῆθος καὶ τὴν
5 ἀγριότητα τῶν μεταξὺ κατοικούντων βαρβάρων, τότε
δοκεῖ καὶ πλεονάκις ἐν τῷ συνεδρίῳ περὶ τούτου τοῦ
μέρους ἐμπιπτούσης ἀπορίας εἰς τῶν φίλων Ἀννίβας
ὁ Μονομάχος ἐπικαλούμενος ἀποφήνασθαι γνώμην
διότι μία τις ὁδὸς αὐτῷ προφαίνεται, δι᾽ ἧς ἐστιν εἰς
6 Ἰταλίαν ἐλθεῖν ἐφικτόν. τοῦ δ᾽ Ἀννίβου λέγειν κελεύ-
σαντος, διδάξαι δεῖν ἔφη τὰς δυνάμεις ἀνθρωποφα-
7 γεῖν καὶ τούτῳ ποιῆσαι συνήθεις . . . . Ἀννίβας δὲ
πρὸς μὲν τὸ τόλμημα καὶ τὸ πρακτικὸν τῆς ἐπινοίας
οὐδὲν ἀντειπεῖν ἐδυνήθη, τοῦ δὲ πράγματος λαβεῖν
ἔννοιαν οὔθ᾽ αὑτὸν οὔτε τοὺς φίλους ἐδύνατο πεῖσαι.
8 τούτου δὲ τἀνδρὸς εἶναί φασιν ἔργα καὶ τὰ κατὰ τὴν
Ἰταλίαν εἰς Ἀννίβαν ἀναφερόμενα περὶ τῆς ὠμότητος, οὐχ ἧττον δὲ καὶ τῶν περιστάσεων.

60

and complex nature, and his nearest friends differed so widely in character, that from his actions when in Italy it is very difficult to discover the man's real nature. As for what was due to the promptings of circumstance, that can easily be learned from my preceding narrative and that which is to follow, but we must not ignore what he owed to the suggestions of his friends, especially as it is possible to get a very adequate notion of their nature from one single piece of advice. At the time when Hannibal contemplated marching on Italy from Spain with his army, it was foreseen that he would be very hard put to it to feed the troops and keep them constantly provided with supplies, the difficulties of the march seeming almost insuperable both owing to the distance and to the numbers and savage character of the barbarous inhabitants of the intervening countries. It seems that the difficulty was more than once discussed in the Council, and that one of Hannibal's friends, Hannibal surnamed Monomachus *(gladiator),* stated that he foresaw only one way by which it would be possible to reach Italy. When Hannibal asked him to explain himself, he said he must teach his troops to eat human flesh and accustom them to this . . . Hannibal had nothing to say against the boldness and usefulness of this suggestion, but he could persuade neither himself nor his friends actually to entertain it. They say that the acts of cruelty[33] in Italy of which Hannibal is accused were the work of this man, but in no less degree that of circumstances.

[33] Whether true for Hannibal, or to what degree, cannot be known.

25. Φιλάργυρός γε μὴν δοκεῖ γεγονέναι διαφερόντως καὶ φίλῳ κεχρῆσθαι φιλαργύρῳ Μάγωνι τῷ ⟨τὰ⟩
2 κατὰ τὴν Βρεττίαν χειρίζοντι. ταύτην δὲ τὴν ἱστορίαν ἐγὼ παρέλαβον μὲν καὶ παρ᾽ αὐτῶν Καρχηδονίων·
3 ἐγχώριοι γὰρ οὐ μόνον τὰς τῶν ἀνέμων στάσεις κατὰ τὴν παροιμίαν, ἀλλὰ καὶ τὰ τῶν ἐγχωρίων ἀνθρώπων
4 ἤθη κάλλιστα γινώσκουσιν· ἔτι δὲ Μασαννάσου . . . ἀκριβέστερον διήκουσα, φέροντος ἀπολογισμοὺς καθόλου μὲν περὶ πάντων Καρχηδονίων, μάλιστα δὲ περὶ τῆς Ἀννίβου καὶ Μάγωνος τοῦ Σαυνίτου προσ
5 αγορευομένου φιλαργυρίας. πρὸς γὰρ τοῖς ἄλλοις ἔφη γενναιότατα κεκοινωνηκότας ἑαυτοῖς πραγμάτων τοὺς προειρημένους ἀπὸ τῆς πρώτης ἡλικίας καὶ πολλὰς μὲν πόλεις κατ᾽ Ἰβηρίαν, πολλὰς δὲ κατὰ τὴν Ἰταλίαν εἰληφότας ἑκατέρους, τὰς μὲν κατὰ κράτος,
6 τὰς δ᾽ ἐκ παραδόσεως, οὐδέποτε μετεσχηκέναι τῆς αὐτῆς πράξεως ἀλλήλοις, ἀλλ᾽ ἀεὶ μᾶλλον ἑαυτοὺς ἢ τοὺς πολεμίους στρατηγεῖν χάριν τοῦ μὴ συμπαρεῖναι θάτερον θατέρῳ πόλεως καταλαμβανομένης, ἵνα μήτε διαφέρωνται πρὸς σφᾶς ἐκ τῶν τοιούτων μήτε μερίζωνται τὸ λυσιτελές, ἐφαμίλλου τῆς ὑπεροχῆς αὐτῶν ὑπαρχούσης.

26. Πλὴν ὅτι γε καὶ τὴν Ἀννίβου φύσιν οὐ μόνον ἡ τῶν φίλων παράθεσις, ἔτι δὲ μᾶλλον ἡ τῶν πραγμάτων περίστασις ἐβιάζετο καὶ μετετίθετο πολλάκις, ἔκ τε τῶν προειρημένων καὶ τῶν λέγεσθαι μελλόντων

25. He does indeed seem to have been exceedingly fond of money, and so was his friend Mago who commanded in Bruttium. I have been told about this matter both by Carthaginians[34] themselves—for the natives of a place do not only know best, as the saying is, the direction of the wind, but the character of their compatriots—and more in detail by Massinissa,[35] when he discoursed on the love of money displayed by Carthaginians in general and especially by Hannibal and by this Mago who was known as the Samnite. Among other things he told me that while these two men had from their earliest youth most generously shared all kinds of enterprises with each other and had each taken many cities both in Spain and Italy by force or by betrayal, on no single occasion had they both participated in the same enterprise, but had always maneuvered more carefully against each other than against the enemy, so that the one should not be present when the other took a city, to avoid any differences arising between them from such causes and any sharing in the profits as they were of equal rank.

26. But that it was not only the suggestions of friends that changed and did violence to Hannibal's real nature but also the force of circumstances clearly appears from my narrative, both that which precedes and that which is to

---

[34] It is not known where and when P. met them.

[35] Prince of the Massyli, fought with his Numidians on the Punic side in Spain until 206, then joined P. Scipio and contributed in 202 to Hannibal's defeat at Zama. After that, until his death in 149, the *nemesis* of Carthage. *RE* Massinissa 2154–2166 (W. Schur). P. met him in 150 along with Scipio Aemilianus.

2 ἐστὶ φανερόν. ἅμα γὰρ τῷ γενέσθαι τὴν Καπύην τοῖς
Ῥωμαίοις ὑποχείριον εὐθέως ἦσαν, ὅπερ εἰκός, αἱ
πόλεις μετέωροι, καὶ περίβλεπον ἀφορμὰς καὶ προ-
3 φάσεις τῆς πρὸς Ῥωμαίους μεταβολῆς· ὅτε δὴ καὶ
δοκεῖ μάλιστα δυσχρηστηθεὶς Ἀννίβας εἰς ἀπορίαν
4 ἐμπεσεῖν ὑπὲρ τῶν ἐνεστώτων. οὔτε γὰρ τηρεῖν τὰς
πόλεις πάσας πολὺ διεστώσας ἀλλήλων δυνατὸς ἦν,
καθίσας εἰς ἕνα τόπον, τῶν πολεμίων καὶ πλείοσι
στρατοπέδοις ἀντιπαραγόντων, οὔτε διαιρεῖν εἰς πολ-
5 λὰ μέρη τὴν αὑτοῦ δύναμιν οἷός τ᾽ ἦν. εὐχείρωτος γὰρ
ἔμελλε τοῖς ἐχθροῖς ὑπάρξειν καὶ διὰ τὸ λείπεσθαι τῷ
πλήθει καὶ διὰ τὸ μὴ δύνασθαι πᾶσιν αὐτὸς συμπαρ-
6 εῖναι. διόπερ ἠναγκάζετο τὰς μὲν προδήλως ἐγκατα-
λείπειν τῶν πόλεων, ἐξ ὧν δὲ τὰς φρουρὰς ἐξάγειν,
ἀγωνιῶν μὴ κατὰ τὰς μεταβολὰς τῶν πραγμάτων
7 συγκαταφθείρῃ τοὺς ἰδίους στρατιώτας. ἐνίας ⟨δὲ⟩
καὶ παρασπονδῆσαι᾽ ὑπέμεινε, μετανιστὰς εἰς ἄλλας
8 πόλεις καὶ ποιῶν ἀναρπάστους αὐτῶν τοὺς βίους. ἐξ
ὧν προσκόπτοντες οἱ μὲν ἀσέβειαν, οἱ δ᾽ ὠμότητα
9 κατεγίνωσκον. καὶ γὰρ ἁρπαγαὶ χρημάτων ἅμα τοῖς
προειρημένοις καὶ φόνοι καὶ βίαιοι προφάσεις ἐγίνοντο διά τε τῶν ἐξιόντων καὶ διὰ τῶν εἰσιόντων
στρατιωτῶν εἰς τὰς πόλεις, ἑκάστων ὑπειληφότων
ὅσον οὐκ ἤδη τοὺς ὑπολειπομένους μεταβαλεῖσθαι
10 πρὸς τοὺς ὑπεναντίους. ἐξ ὧν καὶ λίαν δυσχερὲς
ἀποφήνασθαι περὶ τῆς Ἀννίβου φύσεως, διά τε τὴν
τῶν φίλων παράθεσιν καὶ τὴν τῶν πραγμάτων περί-

follow. On Capua[36] falling into the hands of the Romans
all the other cities naturally began to waver in their allegiance, and were on the lookout for pretexts and occasions
for going over to Rome. Hannibal seems at this crisis to
have been in great difficulty and doubt as to how to deal
with the situation. For he was neither able to keep watch
over all the cities, far distant as they were from each other,
if he established himself at one spot, with several hostile
armies ready to intercept his movements, nor was he able
to subdivide his forces much, as he would then be easily
overcome by the enemy owing to numerical inferiority and
the impossibility of his being personally present everywhere. He was therefore obliged to abandon openly some
of the cities and to withdraw his garrisons from others,
from fear lest if they transferred their allegiance he should
lose his own soldiers as well. In some cases he even allowed
himself to violate the treaties he had made, transferring
the inhabitants to other towns and giving up their property
to plunder, thereby causing such offense that he was accused both of impiety and cruelty. For as a fact these measures were accompanied by robbery of money, murders,
and violence on no matter what pretext at the hands both
of the departing and the incoming troops, everybody acting on the supposition that the citizens who were left behind were just on the point of joining the enemy. All this
makes it very difficult to pronounce an opinion on the real
nature of Hannibal, as we have to allow for the influence of
his friends and the force of circumstances. But at any rate

---

[36] It fell to the Romans after Hannibal's march on Rome (5.1–
7).

11 στασιν. κρατεῖ γε μὴν ἡ φήμη παρὰ μὲν Καρχηδοίοις
    ὡς φιλαργύρου, παρὰ δὲ Ῥωμαίοις ὡς ὠμοῦ γενο-
    μένου [αὐτοῦ].

VI. RES SICILIAE

26a. Οἱ δὲ πλεῖστοι τῶν ἀνθρώπων ἐξ αὐτῆς τῆς
    περιμέτρου τεκμαίρονται τὰ μεγέθη τῶν προειρημέ-
2   νων. λοιπὸν ὅταν εἴπῃ τις τὴν μὲν τῶν Μεγαλοπολι-
    τῶν πόλιν πεντήκοντα σταδίων ἔχειν τὸν περίβολον,
    τὴν δὲ τῶν Λακεδαιμονίων ὀκτὼ καὶ τετταράκοντα, τῷ
    δὲ μεγέθει διπλῆν εἶναι τὴν Λακεδαίμονα τῆς Μεγά-
    λης πόλεως, ἄπιστον αὐτοῖς εἶναι δοκεῖ τὸ λεγόμενον.
3   ἂν δὲ καὶ συναυξῆσαί τις βουλόμενος τὴν ἀπορίαν
    εἴπῃ διότι δυνατόν ἐστι τετταράκοντα σταδίων πόλιν
    ἢ στρατοπεδείαν ἔχουσαν τὴν περιγραφὴν διπλασίαν
    γίνεσθαι τῆς ἑκατὸν σταδίων ἐχούσης τὴν περίμε-
    τρον, τελέως ἐκπληκτικὸν αὐτοῖς φαίνεται τὸ λεγό-
4   μενον. τοῦτο δ᾽ ἐστὶν αἴτιον ὅτι τῶν ἐν τοῖς παιδικοῖς
    μαθήμασι παραδιδομένων ἡμῖν διὰ τῆς γεωμετρίας οὐ
5   μνημονεύομεν. περὶ μὲν οὖν τούτων προήχθην εἰπεῖν
    διὰ τὸ μὴ μόνον τοὺς πολλοὺς ἀλλὰ καὶ τῶν πολιτευ-
    ομένων καὶ τῶν ἐν ταῖς ἡγεμονίαις ἀναστρεφομένων
    τινὰς ἐκπλήττεσθαι, θαυμάζοντας ποτὲ μὲν εἰ δυνατόν
    ἐστι μείζω τὴν τῶν Λακεδαιμονίων πόλιν εἶναι, καὶ
6   πολλῷ μείζω, τῆς τῶν Μεγαλοπολιτῶν, τὸν περίβολον
    ἔχουσαν ἐλάττω, ποτὲ δὲ τὸ πλῆθος τῶν ἀνδρῶν
    τεκμαίρεσθαι, στοχαζομένους ἐξ αὐτῆς τῆς περιμέ-

among the Carthaginians he was notorious for his love of money and among the Romans for his cruelty.

VI. SICILIAN AFFAIRS

Computation of the Size of Cities

26a.[37] Most people judge of the size of cities simply from their circumference. So that when one says that Megalopolis is fifty stades in circumference and Sparta forty-eight, but that Sparta is twice as large[38] as Megalopolis, the statement seems incredible to them. And when in order to puzzle them still more, one tells them that a city or camp with a circumference of forty stades may be twice as large as one the circumference of which is one hundred stades, this statement seems to them absolutely astounding. The reason of this is that we have forgotten the lessons in geometry we learned as children. I was led to make these remarks by the fact that not only ordinary men but even some statesmen and commanders of armies are thus astounded, and wonder how it is possible for Sparta to be larger and even much larger than Megalopolis, although its circumference is smaller; or at other times attempt to estimate the number of men in a camp by taking into con-

[37] In these eleven paragraphs P. returns once more to his statement that a general needs to have some knowledge of geometry (14.5 and 20).

[38] This is incorrect; it is in fact smaller, amounting only to about sixty percent of that of Megalopolis.

7 τρου τῶν στρατοπεδειῶν. παραπλήσιον δέ τι καὶ ἕτερον ἀδίκημα συμβαίνει περὶ τὰς τῶν πόλεων ἐπιφά-
σεις. οἱ γὰρ πολλοὶ τῶν ἀνθρώπων τὰς περικεκλασμέ-
νας καὶ βουνώδεις πλείους οἰκίας ὑπολαμβάνουσι

8 κατέχεσθαι τῶν ἐπιπέδων. τὸ δ᾽ οὐκ ἔστι τοιοῦτον διὰ
τὸ τὰ τειχία τῶν οἰκοδομιῶν μὴ τοῖς ἐγκλίμασι τῶν
ἐδάφων ἀλλὰ τοῖς ὑποκειμένοις ἐπιπέδοις οἰκοδομεῖ-
σθαι πρὸς ὀρθάς, ἐφ᾽ ὧν καὶ τοὺς λόφους αὐτοὺς

9 βεβηκέναι συμβαίνει. γνοίη δ᾽ ἄν τις ἐκ τοῦ φαινο-
10 μένου παιδικῶς ὅμως τὸ λεγόμενον. εἰ γὰρ νοῆσαι τις
εἰς ὕψος ἀνατεταμένας τὰς ἐν τοῖς κλίμασιν οἰκίας
οὕτως ὥστε πάσας ἰσοϋψεῖς ὑπάρχειν, φανερὸν ὡς
ἑνὸς ἐπιπέδου γενομένου τοῦ κατὰ τὰ τέγη τῶν οἰκιῶν,
ἴσον καὶ παράλληλον ἔσται τοῦτο τῷ τοῖς λόφοις
ὑποκειμένῳ καὶ τοῖς τῶν τειχῶν θεμελίοις ἐπιπέδῳ.

11 περὶ μὲν οὖν τῶν ἡγεῖσθαι καὶ πολιτεύεσθαι βουλομένων, ἀγνοούντων δὲ τὰ τοιαῦτα καὶ θαυμαζόντων,
ἐπὶ τοσοῦτον ἡμῖν εἰρήσθω.

Agrigentum

27. Ἡ δὲ τῶν Ἀκραγαντίνων πόλις οὐ μόνον κατὰ
τὰ προειρημένα διαφέρει τῶν πλείστων πόλεων, ἀλλὰ
καὶ κατὰ τὴν ὀχυρότητα, καὶ μάλιστα κατὰ τὸ κάλλος

2 καὶ τὴν κατασκευήν. ἔκτισται μὲν γὰρ ἀπὸ θαλάττης
ἐν ὀκτωκαίδεκα σταδίοις, ὥστε μηδενὸς ἀμοίρους

3 εἶναι τῶν ἐκ ταύτης χρησίμων· ὁ δὲ περίβολος αὐτῆς
καὶ φύσει καὶ κατασκευῇ διαφερόντως ἠσφάλισται.

sideration its circumference alone. Another very similar error[39] is made concerning the surface area of cities. Most people suppose that a broken and hilly surface area can contain more houses than a flat one. This is not so, as the walls of the houses are not built at right angles to the slope, but to the horizontal plane underlying these on which the hill itself rests. The truth of this can be made manifest to the intelligence of a child. For if one supposes the houses on a slope to be raised to such a height that their roofs are all level with each other, it is evident that the flat space thus formed by the roofs will be equal in area and parallel to the flat space in which the hill and the foundations of the houses rest. So much for those who aspire to political power and the command of armies but are ignorant of such things and surprised by them.

Agrigentum

27. The city of Agrigentum[40] is superior to most cities not only in the ways I have mentioned but in strength and especially in the beauty of its site and buildings. It stands at a distance of eighteen stades from the sea, so that it enjoys all the advantages of a seacoast town. It is encircled by natural and artificial defenses of unusual strength, the wall

---

39 It seems clear that $\dot{a}\delta i\kappa\eta\mu a$ here has to have that meaning.

40 See 1.17.5 and WC 2.157–161 with map. For the city's foundation see A. J. Graham, *Colony and Mother City in Ancient Greece* (Manchester 1964), 20–22.

4 κεῖται γὰρ τὸ τεῖχος ἐπὶ πέτρας ἀκροτόμου καὶ περιρ-
ρῶγος, ᾗ μὲν αὐτοφυοῦς, ᾗ δὲ χειροποιήτου, περι-
5 έχεται δὲ ποταμοῖς· ῥεῖ γὰρ αὐτῆς παρὰ μὲν τὴν
νότιον πλευρὰν ὁ συνώνυμος τῇ πόλει, παρὰ δὲ τὴν
ἐπὶ τὰς δύσεις καὶ τὸν λίβα τετραμμένην ὁ προσαγο-
6 ρευόμενος Ὕψας. ἡ δ' ἄκρα τῆς πόλεως ὑπέρκειται
κατ' αὐτὰς τὰς θερινὰς ἀνατολάς, κατὰ μὲν τὴν ἔξωθεν ἐπιφάνειαν ἀπροσίτῳ φάραγγι περιεχομένη, κατὰ
δὲ τὴν ἐντὸς μίαν ἔχουσα πρόσοδον ἐκ τῆς πόλεως.
7 ἐπὶ δὲ τῆς κορυφῆς Ἀθηνᾶς ἱερὸν ἔκτισται καὶ Διὸς
8 Ἀταβυρίου, καθάπερ καὶ παρὰ Ῥοδίοις· τοῦ γὰρ
Ἀκράγαντος ὑπὸ Ῥοδίων ἀπῳκισμένης, εἰκότως ὁ
θεὸς οὗτος τὴν αὐτὴν ἔχει προσηγορίαν ἣν καὶ παρὰ
9 τοῖς Ῥοδίοις. κεκόσμηται δὲ καὶ τἆλλα μεγαλοπρεπῶς
ἡ πόλις ναοῖς καὶ στοαῖς. καὶ ⟨μὴν⟩ ὁ τοῦ Διὸς τοῦ
Ὀλυμπίου νεὼς παντέλειαν μὲν οὐκ εἴληφε, κατὰ δὲ
τὴν ἐπιβολὴν καὶ τὸ μέγεθος οὐδ' ὁποίου τῶν κατὰ
τὴν Ἑλλάδα δοκεῖ λείπεσθαι.

10   Πολύβιος δὲ τὸν ποταμὸν καὶ τὴν πόλιν ἀπὸ τῆς
χώρας ὠνομάσθαι Ἀκράγης διὰ τὸ εὔγεων ⟨φησί⟩ (St.
Byz. A167 Billerbeck)

Agathyrna

11   Ἀγάθυρνα, πόλις Σικελίας, ὡς Πολύβιος ἐνάτῃ. Ὁ
12 δὲ Μάρκος δοὺς πίστεις ὑπὲρ ἀσφαλείας ἔπεισεν
ἐκχωρεῖν εἰς Ἰταλίαν, ἐφ' ᾧ λαμβάνοντας μέτρημα

being built on a ridge of rock either naturally steep and precipitous or artificially rendered so. It is also surrounded by rivers, that which has the same name as the town running along the southern side and the Hypsas along the west and southwest sides. The citadel overlooking the town is due northeast from it, being surrounded on its outer side by an impassable ravine and having on its inner side but one approach from the town. On its summit stand the temples of Athena and Zeus Atabyrius as in Rhodes; for since Agrigentum was founded by the Rhodians this god naturally bears the same title as in Rhodes. The other temples and porticoes which adorn the city are of great magnificence, the temple of Olympian Zeus being unfinished but second it seems to none in Greece in design and dimensions.

Polybius, however, says that the river and the city were named from the land Acrages.[41]

Transfer of the People of Agathyrna

Agathyrna, a city of Sicily. Polybius in Book 9. Marcus Valerius[42] persuaded the fugitives to retire to Italy, giving them pledges for the security of their persons, on condition that they should receive pay from the people of

---

[41] The Greek name was Akragas, in Polybius probably ἄκρα γῆς or γᾶς, as Schweighaeuser proposed.

[42] The consul of 210 (8.1.6). For his action see Livy 26.40.16–18.

παρὰ τῶν Ῥηγίνων πορθεῖν τὴν Βρεττιανήν, κυρίους
ὄντας ὧν ἂν ἐκ τῆς πολεμίας ὠφεληθῶσι.

4   40. Οἱ δὲ Ἀκαρνᾶνες πυνθανόμενοι τὴν τῶν Αἰτωλῶν ἔφοδον ἐπὶ σφᾶς, τὰ μὲν ἀπαλγοῦντες ταῖς ἐλπίσι, τὰ δὲ καὶ θυμομαχοῦντες ἐπί τινα παράστασιν
κατήντησαν (Suda A 2880 Adler)

5   Εἰ δέ τις λειπόμενος μὴ θάνοι, φύγοι δὲ τὸν κίνδυνον, τοῦτον μήτε πόλει δέχεσθαι μήτε πῦρ ἐναύειν.

6   περὶ τούτων ἀρὰς ἐποιήσαντο πᾶσι μέν, μάλιστα
δὲ τοῖς Ἠπειρώταις, εἰς τὸ μηδένα τῶν φευγόντων
δέξασθαι τῇ χώρᾳ (Suda E 1136 Adler)

VII. RES GRAECIAE

28. Ὅτι μὲν οὖν, ὦ ἄνδρες Λακεδαιμόνιοι, τὴν
Μακεδόνων δυναστείαν ἀρχὴν συνέβη γεγονέναι τοῖς
Ἕλλησι δουλείας, οὐδ᾽ ἄλλως εἰπεῖν οὐδένα πέ-
2   πεισμαι τολμῆσαι· σκοπεῖν δ᾽ οὕτως ἔξεστιν. ἦν τι
σύστημα τῶν ἐπὶ Θρᾴκης Ἑλλήνων, οὓς ἀπῴκισαν
Ἀθηναῖοι καὶ Χαλκιδεῖς, ὧν μέγιστον εἶχε πρόσχημα
3   καὶ δύναμιν ἡ τῶν Ὀλυνθίων πόλις. ταύτην ἐξανδρα-
ποδισάμενος Φίλιππος καὶ παράδειγμα ποιήσας οὐ
μόνον τῶν ἐπὶ Θρᾴκης πόλεων ἐγένετο κύριος, ἀλλὰ
καὶ Θετταλοὺς ὑφ᾽ αὑτὸν ἐποιήσατο διὰ τὸν φόβον.

---

43 For the reasons to insert 40.4 and 40.5–6 here, see WC 2.13.

44 The speaker, named in 31.7, is the Aetolian Chlaeneas from
Calydon, in 207 or 206 a member of the Amphictionic Council, F.
Lefèvre, *L'amphictionie pyléo-delphique: histoire et institutions*
(Paris 1998), 106.

Rhegium and plunder Bruttium, retaining whatever booty they carried off from the enemy's country.

40.4 The Acarnanians, on learning of the Aetolian invasion, partly from despondency and partly from fury came to a desperate resolution. . . .

40.5 If anyone survived and escaped from the battle no one might receive him in a city or give him fire.

40.6 They delivered a solemn curse on all and especially on the Epirots who should receive any fugitives in their country. . . .[43]

In 211 B.C. the Acarnanians were threatened with invasion by the Aetolians and resorted to the desperate resolution to which these fragments relate. See Livy, 26.25.

VII. AFFAIRS OF GREECE

Speeches of Chlaeneas the Aetolian and Lyciscus the Acarnanian at Sparta

28. "Men of Lacedaemon,[44] I am convinced indeed that no one would venture to deny that the slavery of Greece owes its origin to the kings of Macedon, but the matter may be looked at thus. There was once a group of Greek cities toward Thrace founded by the Athenians and Chalcidians, of which Olynthus[45] was the most eminent and powerful. Philip, by selling its inhabitants into slavery and making an example of it, not only obtained possession of the Thracian cities, but intimidated the Thessalians into

[211 B.C.]

---

[45] The principal city of the League of the Chalcidians, for which see M. Zahrnt, *Olynth und die Chalkidier* (Munich 1971). The city was destroyed by Philip II in 349.

THE HISTORIES OF POLYBIUS

4 μετ᾽ οὐ πολὺ δὲ μάχῃ νικήσας τοὺς Ἀθηναίους ἐχρήσατο μεγαλοψύχως τοῖς εὐτυχήμασιν, οὐχ ὅπως Ἀθηναίους εὖ ποιήσῃ, πολλοῦ γε δεῖν, ἀλλ᾽ ἵνα διὰ τῆς
πρὸς ἐκείνους εὐεργεσίας προκαλέσηται τοὺς ἄλλους
εἰς τὸ ποιεῖν ἐθελοντὴν αὐτῷ τὸ προσταττόμενον.
5 ἦν ἔτι τὸ τῆς ὑμετέρας πόλεως ἀξίωμα, δοκοῦν ἂν
6 σὺν καιρῷ προστήσεσθαι τῶν Ἑλλήνων. τοιγαροῦν
πᾶσαν ἱκανὴν ποιησάμενος πρόφασιν ἧκε μετὰ τῶν
7 δυνάμεων, καὶ κατέφθειρε μὲν τέμνων τὴν γῆν, κατέφθειρε δ᾽ αἴθων τὰς οἰκίας. τὸ δὲ τελευταῖον ἀποτεμόμενος καὶ τὰς πόλεις καὶ τὴν χώραν ὑμῶν προσ-
ένειμε τὴν μὲν Ἀργείοις, τὴν δὲ Τεγεάταις καὶ
Μεγαλοπολίταις, τὴν δὲ Μεσσηνίοις, ἅπαντας βουλόμενος καὶ παρὰ τὸ προσῆκον εὐεργετεῖν, ἐφ᾽ ᾧ
8 μόνον ὑμᾶς κακῶς ποιεῖν. διεδέξατο παρ᾽ αὐτοῦ τὴν
ἀρχὴν Ἀλέξανδρος. οὗτος πάλιν ὑπολαβὼν βραχύ τι
τῆς Ἑλλάδος ἔναυσμα καταλείπεσθαι περὶ τὴν Θηβαίων πόλιν, τίνα τρόπον αὐτὴν διέφθειρε, πάντας
ὑμᾶς οἴομαι κατανοεῖν.

29. Καὶ μὴν περὶ τῶν διαδεξαμένων τούτου τὰ
πράγματα πῶς κέχρηνται τοῖς Ἕλλησι, τί με δεῖ κατὰ
2 μέρος λέγειν; οὐδεὶς γάρ ἐστι τῶν ὄντων ⟨οὕτως⟩
ἀπράγμων ὃς οὐχὶ πέπυσται πῶς Ἀντίπατρος μὲν ἐν
τῇ περὶ Λαμίαν μάχῃ νικήσας τοὺς Ἕλληνας κάκιστα

46 The submission of Thessaly was completed in 344–342.

47 At Chaeronea in 338, Philip's victory over Athens and
Thebes.

74

submission.[46] When, shortly afterward, he had defeated[47] the Athenians in a battle he made a generous use of his success, not with the object of benefiting the Athenians, far from it, but in order that his kindness to them might induce others to obey his orders without resistance. The prestige of your city still survived then and it seemed as if in time you would be the leading power in Greece. Consequently, alleging as sufficient any pretext that offered itself, he came here[48] with his army and inflicted great damage, cutting the crops and trees and burning the homesteads, and finally partitioning your cities and your territory, he assigned[49] part of it to the Argives, part to the Tegeans and Megalopolitans, and part to the Messenians, wishing to confer ill-merited benefits on all of them if by doing so he could only damage you. He was succeeded by Alexander. That king again, because he thought there was left in Thebes a little spark of the Greece that once was, destroyed that city[50] in the manner that you all, I take it, know.

29. "And as for the successors of Alexander, need I tell you in detail how they treated the Greeks? For no one is so indifferent to facts as not to have heard how Antipater after his victory over the Greeks at Lamia[51] treated the un-

---

[48] Philip's invasion of Sparta: A. Momigliano, *Filippo il Macedone* (Florence 1934), 162–163; G. Cawkwell, *Philip of Macedon* (London 1978), 168–169.

[49] On this passage and the corresponding one in the speech of Lyciscus (33.11–12), see K. Harter-Uibopuu, *Das zwischenstaatliche Schiedsverfahren im Achäischen Koinon* (Cologne 1998), 83–86.

[50] In 335.   [51] In 322.

3   μὲν ἐχρήσατο τοῖς ταλαιπώροις Ἀθηναίοις, ὁμοίως δὲ
καὶ τοῖς ἄλλοις, εἰς τοῦτο δ' ὕβρεως ἦλθε καὶ παρανομίας ὡς φυγαδοθήρας καταστήσας ἐξέπεμψε πρὸς τὰς
πόλεις ἐπὶ τοὺς ἀντειρηκότας ἢ καθόλου λελυπηκότας

4   τι τὴν Μακεδόνων οἰκίαν. ὧν οἱ μὲν ἐκ τῶν ἱερῶν
ἀγόμενοι μετὰ βίας, οἱ δ' ἀπὸ τῶν βωμῶν ἀποσπώ-
μενοι, μετὰ τιμωρίας ἀπέθνησκον, οἱ δὲ διαφυγόντες
ἐκ πάσης ἐξενηλατοῦντο τῆς Ἑλλάδος· φύξιμον γὰρ
οὐδὲν ἦν πλὴν ἑνὸς αὐτοῖς τοῦ τῶν Αἰτωλῶν ἔθνους.

5   τά γε μὴν Κασσάνδρῳ καὶ Δημητρίῳ πεπραγμένα,
σὺν δὲ τούτοις Ἀντιγόνῳ τῷ Γονατᾷ, τίς οὐκ οἶδε; διὰ
γὰρ τὸ προσφάτως αὐτὰ γεγονέναι τελέως ἐναργῆ

6   συμβαίνει τὴν γνῶσιν αὐτῶν ὑπάρχειν. ὧν οἱ μὲν
φρουρὰς εἰσάγοντες εἰς τὰς πόλεις, οἱ δὲ τυράννους
ἐμφυτεύοντες οὐδεμίαν πόλιν ἄμοιρον ἐποίησαν τοῦ

7   τῆς δουλείας ὀνόματος. ἀφέμενος δὲ τούτων ἐπάνειμι
νῦν ἐπὶ τὸν τελευταῖον Ἀντίγονον, ἵνα μὴ τὴν ἐκ
τούτου πρᾶξιν ἀκάκως τινὲς ὑμῶν θεωροῦντες ὑπό-

8   χρεοι χάριτι νομίζωσιν εἶναι Μακεδόσιν. οὔτε γὰρ
Ἀχαιοὺς σῴζειν προαιρούμενος Ἀντίγονος ἐπανείλετο
τὸν πρὸς ὑμᾶς πόλεμον οὔτε τῇ Κλεομένους τυραννίδι
δυσαρεστούμενος, ἵνα Λακεδαιμονίους ἐλευθερώσῃ·

9   καὶ λίαν γὰρ ὅ γε τοιοῦτός ἐστι τρόπος εὐήθης, εἴ τις
10 ἄρα ταύτην ὑμῶν ἔχει τὴν διάληψιν· ἀλλ' ὁρῶν οὐκ ἐν
ἀσφαλεῖ τὴν ἑαυτοῦ δυναστείαν ἐσομένην, ἐὰν ὑμεῖς
τὴν Πελοποννησίων ἀρχὴν κατακτήσησθε, πρὸς δὲ
τοῦτο βλέπων εὖ πεφυχότα τὸν Κλεομένην καὶ τὴν

11 τύχην ὑμῖν λαμπρῶς συνεργοῦσαν, ἅμα φοβηθεὶς καὶ

happy Athenians as well as the other Greeks in the harshest manner, going so far in his wanton and lawless violence as to appoint and send round to the different cities exile hunters[52] to catch those who had opposed or in any way offended the royal house of Macedon. Some forcibly driven out of the temples and others dragged from the altars perished by torture, while those who escaped were expelled from the whole of Greece, having no single place of refuge except the territory of the Aetolian League. And who is ignorant of the actions of Cassander, Demetrius, and Antigonus Gonatas, all so recent that the memory of them is quite vivid? Some of them by introducing garrisons[53] to cities and others by planting tyrannies left no city with the right to call itself unenslaved. Leaving them aside, I will now pass to the last Antigonus, in case any of you, regarding his action without suspicion, consider themselves under a debt of gratitude to the Macedonians. It was not for the purpose of saving the Achaeans that Antigonus undertook the war against you, nor because he disapproved of the tyranny of Cleomenes and desired to set Sparta free. If anyone entertains such a notion he must be very simpleminded. But seeing that his own power would not be safe if you acquired the supremacy in the Peloponnese, that Cleomenes was just the man to effect this and that Fortune was working for you splendidly, he came here actuated

[52] Especially the infamous Archias of Thurii; among his victims were Demosthenes and Hyperides.

[53] The usual instrument of the kings of Macedon to ensure the loyalty of Greek cities within their realm.

φθονήσας παρῆν, οὐ Πελοποννησίοις βοηθήσων, ἀλλὰ τὰς ὑμετέρας ἐλπίδας ἀφελούμενος καὶ τὴν ὑμετέ-
12 ραν ὑπεροχὴν ταπεινώσων. διόπερ οὐκ ἐπὶ τοσοῦτον
ἀγαπᾶν ὀφείλετε Μακεδόνας, ⟨ὅτι⟩ κυριεύσαντες τῆς
πόλεως οὐ διήρπασαν, ἐφ' ὅσον ἐχθροὺς νομίζειν καὶ
μισεῖν, ὅτι δυναμένους ὑμᾶς ἡγεῖσθαι τῆς Ἑλλάδος
πλεονάκις ἤδη κεκωλύκασι.

30. Περί γε μὴν τῆς Φιλίππου παρανομίας τίς
2 χρεία πλείω λέγειν; τῆς μὲν γὰρ εἰς τὸ θεῖον ἀσεβείας
ἱκανὸν ὑπόδειγμ' αἱ περὶ τοὺς ἐν Θέρμῳ ναοὺς ὕβρεις,
τῆς δ' εἰς τοὺς ἀνθρώπους ὠμότητος ἡ περὶ τοὺς
3 Μεσσηνίους ἀθεσία καὶ παρασπόνδησις . . . Αἰτωλοὶ
γὰρ μόνοι μὲν τῶν Ἑλλήνων ἀντωφθάλμησαν πρὸς
Ἀντίπατρον ὑπὲρ τῆς τῶν ἀδίκως ἀκληρούντων ἀσφαλείας, μόνοι δὲ πρὸς τὴν Βρέννου καὶ τῶν ἅμα τούτῳ
βαρβάρων ἔφοδον ἀντέστησαν, μόνοι δὲ καλούμενοι
4 συνηγωνίζοντο, βουλόμενοι τὴν πάτριον ἡγεμονίαν
τῶν Ἑλλήνων ὑμῖν συγκατασκευάζειν.

5 Ταῦτα μὲν οὖν ἡμῖν ἐπὶ τοσοῦτον εἰρήσθω. περὶ δὲ
τοῦ νῦν ἐνεστῶτος διαβουλίου γράφειν μὲν καὶ χειρο-
τονεῖν ἀναγκαῖόν πώς ἐστιν ὡς περὶ πολέμου βουλευ-
ομένοις, τῇ μέντοι γ' ἀληθείᾳ μὴ νομίζειν τοῦτον εἶναι
6 πόλεμον. Ἀχαιοὺς μὲν γὰρ οὐχ οἷον διανοησομένους
βλάπτειν ὑμῶν τὴν χώραν, μεγάλην δὲ χάριν ἕξειν
αὐτοὺς ὑπολαμβάνω τοῖς θεοῖς, ἐὰν δύνωνται τὴν
ἰδίαν τηρεῖν, ἐπειδὰν αὐτοῖς ὁ πόλεμος ὑπ' Ἠλείων
καὶ Μεσσηνίων διὰ τὴν πρὸς ἡμᾶς συμμαχίαν, ἅμα

both by fear and envy, not to help the Peloponnesians but to cut short your hopes and humiliate your prestige. So instead of feeling affection[54] for the Macedonians because they did not plunder your city when masters of it, you should consider them your enemies and hate them for preventing you more than once when you had the power of attaining supremacy in Greece.

30. "And regarding Philip's offenses why need I speak more? As for his impiety to heaven it is sufficient to cite his outrages on the temples at Thermi,[55] and as for his cruelty to men I need but mention his perfidy and treachery to the Messenians.[56] . . . For the Aetolians alone among the Greeks dared to face Antipater and demand security for the unfortunate victims of his injustice, they alone withstood the attack of Brennus[57] and his barbarians, and they alone when called upon came to fight by your side and help you to recover your hereditary position of supremacy.

"I have spoken at sufficient length on this subject, but as regards the present deliberation one may say that while it is necessary to draw up your decree and to vote as if you were deciding on war, as a matter of fact you need not look on this as war. So far from the Achaeans being able to inflict any damage on your territory, I fancy they will be only too grateful to the gods if they can protect their own when encircled by foes, the Eleans and Messenians attacking them on one side owing to their alliance with us, and ourselves

[54] Antigonus was venerated as "Savior" and "Benefactor" in Sparta, S. le Bohec, *Antigone Dôsôn* (Nancy 1993), 458; *IG* V 1.1122 (from Geronthrae).   [55] 5.9.1–12.8.

[56] 7.11.10–12.10; 8.8.1– 5.

[57] In 279/8; see notes at 1.6.5 and 4.46.1 and below 35.4.

7 δὲ τούτοις ὑφ᾽ ἡμῶν περισταθῇ. Φίλιππον δὲ πάντως
πέπεισμαι λήξειν τῆς ὁρμῆς κατὰ μὲν γῆν ὑπ᾽ Αἰτωλῶν πολεμούμενον, κατὰ δὲ θάλατταν ὑπό τε Ῥω-
8 μαίων καὶ τοῦ βασιλέως Ἀττάλου. λίαν δ᾽ εὐμαρῶς
ἔστι συλλογίσασθαι τὸ μέλλον ἐκ τῶν ἤδη γεγονό-
9 των. εἰ γὰρ πρὸς μόνους Αἰτωλοὺς πολεμῶν μηδέποτε
δυνατὸς ἦν χειρώσασθαι τούτους, ἢ που συμβεβηκότων <τοσούτων> ἀξιόχρεως ἂν εἴη πρὸς τὸν ἐνεστῶτα πόλεμον;

31. Ταῦτα μὲν οὖν εἰρήσθω μοι κατὰ τὴν ἐξ ἀρχῆς
πρόθεσιν χάριν τοῦ γνῶναι πάντας ὑμᾶς διότι καὶ μὴ
προεισδεδεμένους, ἀλλ᾽ ἐξ ἀκεραίου βουλευομένους,
μᾶλλον Αἰτωλοῖς ἡμᾶς ἢ Μακεδόσιν ἐχρῆν συμ-
2 μαχεῖν. εἰ δὲ καὶ προκατέχεσθε καὶ προδιειλήφατε
3 περὶ τούτων, τίς ἔτι καταλείπεται λόγος; εἰ γὰρ συν-
έθεσθε τὴν νῦν ὑπάρχουσαν ὑμῖν πρὸς ἡμᾶς συμμαχίαν πρότερον τῶν ὑπ᾽ Ἀντιγόνου γεγονότων εἰς
ὑμᾶς εὐεργετημάτων, ἴσως ἦν εἰκὸς διαπορεῖν, εἰ δέον
ἐστί, τοῖς ἐπιγεγονόσιν εἴκοντας παριδεῖν τι τῶν πρό-
4 τερον ὑπαρχόντων. ἐπεὶ δὲ συντετελεσμένης ὑπ᾽ Ἀντιγόνου τῆς πολυθρυλήτου ταύτης ἐλευθερίας καὶ σωτηρίας, ἣν οὗτοι παρ᾽ ἕκαστον ὑμῖν ὀνειδίζουσι, μετὰ δὲ
ταῦτα βουλευόμενοι καὶ πολλάκις ἑαυτοῖς δόντες
λόγον, ποτέροις ὑμᾶς δεῖ κοινωνεῖν πραγμάτων, Αἰτωλοῖς ἢ Μακεδόσιν, εἴλεσθε μετέχειν Αἰτωλοῖς, οἷς
ἐδώκατε περὶ τούτων πίστεις καὶ <κατ>ελάβετε παρ᾽

58 A reference to the treaty of Rome with the Aetolians of 212

on the other. As for Philip, I feel sure that his aggressiveness will soon cease with the Aetolians fighting him on land and the Romans[58] and King Attalus at sea. It is indeed very easy to conjecture what will happen from the past. For if when he was at war with the Aetolians alone he was never able to subdue them, how with <such strong forces>[59] allied against him will he be able to support the present war?

31. "I have spoken so in order that, as was my purpose from the outset, you should all recognize that even if you did not stand in any way committed but were considering the question for the first time, you ought rather to ally yourselves with the Aetolians than the Macedonians. But if as is the fact you stand engaged and have made up your minds about the matter, what remains to be said? If indeed you had formed your present alliance with us previous to the favors[60] conferred on you by Antigonus, it might perhaps have been an open question for you whether you should not as a concession to subsequent circumstances neglect earlier obligations. But since it was after the establishment by Antigonus of this much vaunted liberty and security that they are constantly throwing in your teeth, since it was after frequently discussing among yourselves whether you should enter into alliance with the Aetolians or the Macedonians that you decided to join the Aetolians, with whom you have interchanged pledges, side by side

(StV 536), wherein the possibility that Elis, Sparta, Attalus I, and the Illyrians Pleuratus and Scerdilaidas might join the alliance was envisaged.

[59] The addition is Reiske's.

[60] The speaker ridicules what others considered benefactions bestowed by the king on Sparta.

ἡμῶν, καὶ συμπεπολεμήκατε τὸν πρῴην συστάντα
πόλεμον ἡμῖν πρὸς Μακεδόνας, τίς ἔτι δύναται περὶ
5 τούτων εἰκότως ἐπαπορεῖν; τὰ μὲν γὰρ πρὸς Ἀντίγονον καὶ Φίλιππον ὑμῖν ὑπάρχοντα φιλάνθρωπα
6 παρεγράφη τότε. λοιπὸν ἢ δι' Αἰτωλῶν ἀδίκημά τι δεῖ
μετὰ ταῦτα γεγονὸς εἰς ὑμᾶς δεικνύειν ἢ διὰ Μακεδόνων εὐεργεσίαν ἢ μηδετέρου τούτων ἐπιγεγονότος,
πῶς, οἷς πρότερον ἐξ ἀκεραίου βουλευόμενοι δικαίως
οὐ προσέσχετε, τούτων νῦν ἐντραπέντες ἀνασκευάζειν
μέλλετε συνθήκας, ὅρκους, τὰς μεγίστας πίστεις παρ'
ἀνθρώποις;
7   Ὁ μὲν οὖν Χλαινέας τοιαῦτα διαλεχθεὶς καὶ δόξας
δυσαντιρρήτως εἰρηκέναι κατέπαυσε τὸν λόγον.

32. μετὰ δὲ ταῦτα Λυκίσκος ὁ τῶν Ἀκαρνάνων
πρεσβευτὴς εἰσελθὼν τὸ μὲν πρῶτον ἐπέσχε, θεωρῶν
τοὺς πολλοὺς ἐν αὑτοῖς διαλαλοῦντας ὑπὲρ τῶν προ-
2 ειρημένων, ἐπεὶ δέ ποτε καθησύχασαν, οὕτως πως
3 ἤρξατο τοῦ λέγειν. "Ἡμεῖς, ἄνδρες Λακεδαιμόνιοι,
παρεγενόμεθα μὲν ὑπὸ τοῦ κοινοῦ τῶν Ἀκαρνάνων
ἀπεσταλμένοι πρὸς ὑμᾶς, μετέχοντες δὲ σχεδὸν ἀεί
ποτε Μακεδόσι τῶν αὐτῶν ἐλπίδων καὶ τὴν πρεσβείαν
ταύτην κοινὴν ὑπολαμβάνομεν ἡμῖν ὑπάρχειν καὶ
4 Μακεδόσιν. ὥσπερ δὲ καὶ κατὰ τοὺς κινδύνους διὰ τὴν
ὑπεροχὴν καὶ τὸ μέγεθος τῆς Μακεδόνων δυνάμεως
ἐμπεριέχεσθαι συμβαίνει τὴν ἡμετέραν ἀσφάλειαν ἐν
ταῖς ἐκείνων ἀρεταῖς, οὕτως καὶ κατὰ τοὺς πρεσβευ-
τικοὺς ἀγῶνας ἐμπεριέχεται τὸ τῶν Ἀκαρνάνων συμ-
5 φέρον ἐν τοῖς Μακεδόνων δικαίοις. διόπερ οὐ δεῖ

also with whom you fought against Macedonia in the late war, what justifiable room for discussion is left? For by your action then your friendly relations with Antigonus and Philip were cancelled. So you must either be able to point to some act of injustice to you committed subsequently by the Aetolians or some benefit conferred on you by Macedonia, or if neither one nor the other exists, how can you, ceding to the instances of the very people whose advances you before rightly decided to reject when your hands were free, contemplate the violation of treaties, oaths, and the most solemn pledges known to men?"

Chlaeneas after speaking in these terms which seemed difficult to refute, here ended his harangue.

32. After this Lyciscus,[61] the Acarnanian envoy, coming forward at first refrained from addressing the assembly, as he saw that they were nearly all engaged in discussing the speech with each other, but when silence was restored he began to speak somewhat as follows: "We, men of Lacedaemon, have been sent to you by the Acarnanian League; and as we have nearly always made common cause with Macedonia we consider that this embassy represents Macedonia as well as our own country. And just as in battles owing to the superiority and strength of the Macedonian force their valor involves our safety, so in diplomatic contests the interests of Acarnania are involved in the rights of Macedonia. You must not therefore be surprised if the

---

[61] An otherwise unknown Acarnanian, speaking for the alliance led by King Philip. For P.'s favorable opinion of the Acarnanians, see 4.30.2–5.

θαυμάζειν ὑμᾶς, ἐὰν τὸν πλείω λόγον ὑπὲρ Φιλίππου
6 ποιώμεθα καὶ Μακεδόνων. Χλαινέας τοιγαροῦν, κατα-
στρέφων τὴν δημηγορίαν, ἀπότομόν τινα συγκεφα-
λαίωσιν ἐποιήσατο τῶν ὑπαρχόντων πρὸς ὑμᾶς δικαί-
7 ων. ἔφη γάρ, εἰ μὲν ἐπιγέγονέ τι μετὰ τὸ θέσθαι τὴν
συμμαχίαν ὑμᾶς τὴν πρὸς τούτους ἤτοι βλαβερὸν καὶ
δυσχερὲς ὑπ᾽ Αἰτωλῶν ἢ καὶ νὴ Δία φιλάνθρωπον ὑπὸ
Μακεδόνων, εἰκότως ἂν καὶ τὸ νῦν διαβούλιον ἐξ
8 ἀκεραίου σκέψεως τυγχάνειν· εἰ δὲ μηδενὸς ἐπιγεγονότος τοιούτου τὰ κατ᾽ Ἀντίγονον προφερόμενοι τὰ
πρότερον ὑφ᾽ ὑμῶν δεδοκιμασμένα πεπείσμεθα νῦν
ἡμεῖς ἀνασκευάσειν ὅρκους καὶ συνθήκας, εὐηθεστά-
9 τους πάντων ἡμᾶς ὑπάρχειν. ἐγὼ δ᾽, εἰ μὲν μηδὲν
ἐπιγέγονε κατὰ τὸν τούτου λόγον, μένει δὲ τὰ πράγματα τοιαῦτα τοῖς Ἕλλησιν οἷα πρότερον ἦν, ὅτε
πρὸς αὐτοὺς Αἰτωλοὺς ἐποιεῖσθε τὴν συμμαχίαν,
ὁμολογῶ πάντων εὐηθέστατος ὑπάρχειν καὶ ματαίους
10 μέλλειν διατίθεσθαι λόγους· εἰ δὲ τὴν ἐναντίαν
ἔσχηκε διάθεσιν, ὡς ἐγὼ σαφῶς δείξω προϊόντος τοῦ
λόγου, καὶ λίαν ἐμὲ μὲν οἴομαι φανήσεσθαί τι λέγειν
11 ὑμῖν τῶν συμφερόντων, Χλαινέαν δ᾽ ἀγνοεῖν. παρα-
γινόμεθα μὲν οὖν ὑπὲρ αὐτοῦ τούτου πεπεισμένοι δεῖν
ἡμᾶς ποιεῖσθαι τοὺς λόγους, ὑπὲρ τοῦ δεῖξαι διότι καὶ
πρέπον ὑμῖν ἐστι καὶ συμφέρον, εἰ μὲν δυνατόν, ἀκούσαντας τῆς ἐπιφερομένης τοῖς Ἕλλησι περιστάσεως
καλόν τι βουλεύσασθαι καὶ πρέπον ἑαυτοῖς, μετα-
12 σχόντας ἡμῖν τῶν ἐλπίδων· εἰ δὲ μή, τούτων τὴν
ἡσυχίαν ἔχειν κατὰ τὸ παρόν.

greater part of my speech refers to Philip and the Macedonians. Now Chlaeneas at the close of his speech summed up very abruptly the nature of the Aetolian claims on you. He said that if subsequently to your entering into alliance with the Aetolians, you had suffered any injury or offense from them, or had even met with any kindness from the Macedonians, the present meeting would be justified in considering the question afresh, but if nothing of the kind had happened, and if we Acarnanians now believe that by alleging what occurred and met with your approbation in the time of Antigonus we shall succeed in overthrowing oaths and treaties, we are the greatest simpletons in the world. Well, I allow that I am the greatest simpleton in the world and that the words I am about to address to you are idle, if, as he says, nothing has taken place subsequently, but the state of Greece is precisely the same as it was when you made the alliance with the Aetolians alone. But if the exact reverse is the case, as I shall clearly show in the course of this speech, I think you will be convinced that my advice is highly to your advantage and that Chlaeneas is wrong. We have come here then convinced that we ought to address you on this very matter and demonstrate to you that it will be both to your credit and to your interest to adopt if possible, once you have heard how serious is the danger that threatens Greece, a policy both honorable and worthy of yourselves, by joining our cause; or if that may not be so, by taking at least no active part in this dispute.

33. ἐπεὶ δ᾽ ἀνέκαθεν οὗτοι κατηγορεῖν ἐτόλμησαν τῆς Μακεδόνων οἰκίας, ἀναγκαῖον εἶναί μοι δοκεῖ πρότερον ὑπὲρ τούτων βραχέα διαλεχθέντ᾽ ἀφελέσθαι τὴν ἄγνοιαν τῶν πεπιστευκότων τοῖς εἰρημένοις.

2 Ἔφη τοιγαροῦν Χλαινέας Φίλιππον τὸν Ἀμύντου διὰ τῆς Ὀλυνθίων ἀτυχίας κύριον γενέσθαι Θετ-τα-3 λίας. ἐγὼ δὲ διὰ Φίλιππον οὐ μόνον Θετταλούς, ἀλλὰ καὶ τοὺς λοιποὺς Ἕλληνας ὑπολαμβάνω σεσῶσθαι.
4 καθ᾽ οὓς γὰρ καιροὺς Ὀνόμαρχος καὶ Φιλόμηλος καταλαβόμενοι Δελφοὺς ἀσεβῶς καὶ παρανόμως ἐγέ-νοντο κύριοι τῶν τοῦ θεοῦ χρημάτων, τότε τίς ὑμῶν οὐκ οἶδε διότι τηλικαύτην συνεστήσαντο δύναμιν, πρὸς ἣν οὐδεὶς ἔτι τῶν Ἑλλήνων ἀντοφθαλμεῖν δυνα-5 τὸς ἦν; ἀλλ᾽ ἐκινδύνευον ἅμα ταῖς εἰς τὸ θεῖον ἀσε-6 βείαις καὶ τῆς Ἑλλάδος γενέσθαι κύριοι πάσης. ἐν οἷς καιροῖς Φίλιππος ἐθελοντὴν αὑτὸν ἐπιδοὺς ἐπανεί-λετο μὲν τοὺς τυράννους, ἠσφαλίσατο δὲ τὰ κατὰ τὸ ἱερόν, αἴτιος δ᾽ ἐγένετο τοῖς Ἕλλησι τῆς ἐλευθερίας, ὡς αὐτὰ τὰ πράγματα μεμαρτύρηκε καὶ τοῖς ἐπιγε-7 νομένοις. οὐ γὰρ ὡς ἠδικηκότα Φίλιππον Θετταλούς, καθάπερ οὗτος ἐτόλμα λέγειν, ἀλλ᾽ ὡς εὐεργέτην ὄντα τῆς Ἑλλάδος, καὶ κατὰ γῆν αὐτὸν ἡγεμόνα καὶ κατὰ 8 θάλατταν εἵλοντο πάντες· οὗ πρότερον ἀνθρώπων οὐ-δεὶς ἔτυχε. νὴ Δί᾽, ἀλλὰ παρεγένετο μετὰ τῆς δυνά-9 μεως εἰς τὴν Λακωνικήν· οὐ κατά γε τὴν αὑτοῦ προαί-ρεσιν, ὡς ὑμεῖς ἴστε, καλούμενος δὲ καὶ πολλάκις

33. But since our opponents have ventured to bring against the house of Macedon accusations dating from early times, I think it incumbent on me to begin by addressing to you a few words on these matters, in order to correct the error of those who put faith in the statements made.

"Chlaeneas, then, said, that it was by means of the calamity of Olynthus that Philip, son of Amyntas, made himself master of Thessaly, whereas what I assert is that not only the Thessalians, but the rest of the Greeks owed their safety to Philip. For at the time when Onomarchus[62] and Philomelus seized on Delphi and impiously and illegally possessed themselves of the god's treasure, who among you is not aware that they established a force of such strength that none of the Greeks dared to face it; indeed, while acting thus impiously they very nearly made themselves at the same time masters of the whole of Greece. It was then that Philip voluntarily proffered his services, destroyed the tyrants, secured the temple and was the author of liberty in Greece, as actual facts have testified to posterity also. For it was not because he had injured the Thessalians, as Chlaeneas had the audacity to say, but because he was the benefactor of Greece, that they all chose him commander in chief[63] both on sea and land, an honor previously conferred on no one. But we are told that he entered Laconia[64] with his army. True, but, as you know it was not of his own choice, but it was after being frequently

---

[62] Events of the years 356–353. *RE* Onomarchos 493–505 (W. S. Ferguson) and Philomelos 2524–2525 (K. Fiehn).

[63] *StV* 403.

[64] Lyciscus is answering Chlaeneas' charge, 28.5–7.

ὀνομαζόμενος ὑπὸ τῶν ἐν Πελοποννήσῳ φίλων καὶ
10 συμμάχων μόλις αὐτὸν ἐπέδωκε. καὶ παραγενόμενος
πῶς τοῖς πράγμασιν ἐχρήσατο, ὦ Χλαινέα, σκόπει.
δυνάμενος γὰρ συγχρήσασθαι ταῖς τῶν ἀστυγειτό-
νων ὁρμαῖς πρός τε τὴν τῆς χώρας τῆς τούτων κατα-
φθορὰν καὶ τὴν τῆς πόλεως ταπείνωσιν, καὶ τοῦτο
11 πρᾶξαι μετὰ τῆς μεγίστης χάριτος, ἐπὶ μὲν τὴν τοιαύτην αἵρεσιν οὐδαμῶς αὐτὸν ἐνέδωκε, καταπληξάμε-
νος δὲ κἀκείνους καὶ τούτους ἐπὶ τῷ κοινῇ συμφέροντι
διὰ λόγου τὴν ἐξαγωγὴν ἀμφοτέρους ἠνάγκασε ποιή-
12 σασθαι περὶ τῶν ἀμφισβητουμένων, οὐχ αὑτὸν ἀποδείξας κριτὴν ὑπὲρ τῶν ἀντιλεγομένων, ἀλλὰ κοινὸν
ἐκ πάντων τῶν Ἑλλήνων καθίσας κριτήριον. ἄξιόν γε
τὸ γεγονὸς ὀνείδους καὶ προφορᾶς.

34. Πάλιν Ἀλεξάνδρῳ διότι μὲν ἀδικεῖσθαι δόξας
τὴν Θηβαίων πόλιν ἐκόλασε, τοῦτο πικρῶς ὠνείδισας,
2 ὅτι δὲ τιμωρίαν ἔλαβε παρὰ τῶν Περσῶν ὑπὲρ τῆς εἰς
ἅπαντας τοὺς Ἕλληνας ὕβρεως, οὐκ ἐποιήσω μνήμην,
3 οὐδὲ διότι μεγάλων κακῶν κοινῇ πάντας ἡμᾶς ἔλυσε,
καταδουλωσάμενος τοὺς βαρβάρους καὶ παρελόμενος
αὐτῶν τὰς χορηγίας, αἷς ἐκεῖνοι χρώμενοι κατέφθει-
ραν τοὺς Ἕλληνας, ποτὲ μὲν Ἀθηναίους καὶ τοὺς
τούτων προγόνους ἀγωνοθετοῦντες καὶ συμβάλλοντες, ποτὲ δὲ Θηβαίους, καὶ τέλος ὑπήκοον ἐποίησε τὴν
4 Ἀσίαν τοῖς Ἕλλησι. περὶ δὲ τῶν διαδεξαμένων πῶς
καὶ τολμᾶτε μνημονεύειν; ἐκεῖνοι γὰρ κατὰ τὰς τῶν
καιρῶν περιστάσεις οἷς μὲν ἀγαθῶν οἷς δὲ κακῶν
5 ἐγίνοντο παραίτιοι πολλάκις· περὶ ὧν τοῖς μὲν ἄλλοις

entreated and appealed to by his friends and allies in the Peloponnese that he reluctantly gave way. And when he arrived, pray consider, Chlaeneas, how he behaved. It was in his power to avail himself of the animosity of the neighboring peoples to devastate the territory of Sparta and humiliate the city, winning thereby profound thanks, but instead of adopting such a course he struck equal terror into the Spartans and their enemies and compelled them to their common good to settle their differences by a congress, not assuming himself the right of judging their disputes, but appointing a court of arbitration[65] selected from all the Greek states. How proper a subject for reproach and censure!

34. "Again, you have bitterly reproached Alexander for punishing Thebes when he believed that city had wronged him, but you never mentioned how he inflicted punishment on the Persians for their outrages on all the Greeks, and how he delivered us all from the greatest evils by enslaving the barbarians and depriving them of the resources they used for the destruction of the Greeks, pitting now the Athenians and now the Thebans against the ancestors of these Spartans, how in a word he made Asia subject to Greece. And as for his successors, how have you the assurance to mention them? They did indeed often, under changing circumstances, bestow benefits and inflict injuries on different people, and others might be justified in

[65] See n. on 28.7.

ἴσως ἂν ἐξείη μνησικακεῖν, ὑμῖν δ' οὐδαμῶς καθήκει
τοῦτο ποιεῖν τοῖς ἀγαθοῦ μὲν μηδενὶ μηδενὸς παραι-
6 τίοις γεγονόσι, κακῶν δὲ πολλοῖς καὶ πολλάκις. ἐπεὶ
τίνες οἱ τὸν Ἀντίγονον εἰσὶ τὸν Δημητρίου παρακα-
7 λέσαντες ἐπὶ διαιρέσει τοῦ τῶν Ἀχαιῶν ἔθνους; τίνες
δ' οἱ πρὸς τὸν Ἀλέξανδρον τὸν Ἠπειρώτην ὅρκους
ποιησάμενοι καὶ συνθήκας ἐπ' ἐξανδραποδισμῷ καὶ
8 μερισμῷ τῆς Ἀκαρνανίας; οὐχ ὑμεῖς; τίνες δὲ κατὰ
κοινὸν τοιούτους ἡγεμόνας ἐξέπεμψαν οἵους ὑμεῖς; οἵ
γε καὶ τοῖς ἀσύλοις ἱεροῖς ἐτόλμησαν προσάγειν τὰς
9 χεῖρας. ὧν Τίμαιος μὲν τό τ' ἐπὶ Ταινάρῳ τοῦ Ποσειδῶνος καὶ τὸ τῆς ἐν Λούσοις ἱερὸν Ἀρτέμιδος ἐσύ-
10 λησε, Φάρυκος δὲ καὶ Πολύκριτος, ὁ μὲν τὸ τῆς Ἥρας
ἐν Ἄργει τέμενος, ὁ δὲ τὸ τοῦ Ποσειδῶνος ἐν Μαντι-
11 νείᾳ διήρπασε. τί δαὶ Λάτταβος καὶ Νικόστρατος; οὐ
τὴν τῶν Παμβοιωτίων πανήγυριν εἰρήνης οὔσης παρ-
εσπόνδησαν, Σκυθῶν ἔργα καὶ Γαλατῶν ἐπιτελοῦντες,
ὧν οὐδὲν πέπρακται τοῖς διαδεξαμένοις.

35. Καὶ πρὸς οὐδὲν τούτων ἀπολογηθῆναι δυνάμενοι σεμνύνεσθε, διότι τὴν ἐπὶ Δελφοὺς ἔφοδον τῶν
βαρβάρων ὑπέστητε, καὶ φατὲ δεῖν διὰ ταῦτα χάριν
2 ἔχειν ὑμῖν τοὺς Ἕλληνας. ἀλλ' εἰ διὰ μίαν ταύτην
χρείαν Αἰτωλοῖς χάρις ὀφείλεται, τίνος καὶ πηλίκης
δεῖ τιμῆς ἀξιοῦσθαι Μακεδόνας, οἳ τὸν πλείω τοῦ βίου

---

66 See n. at 2.45.1.   67 Festival of the Boeotian Confed-
eracy, held at the sanctuary of Athena Itonia at Corone. M. Feyel,
Contribution à l'épigraphie béotienne (Le Puy 1942), 58–66; L.
Moretti, *Iscrizioni agonistiche greche* (Rome 1953), no. 39.

feeling resentment against them, but you Aetolians have not the least right to do so, you who have never done any good to a soul, but have done evil to many and at many times. Who, tell me, invited Antigonus the son of Demetrius to assist in dissolving the Achaean League? Who made a sworn treaty[66] with Alexander of Epirus for the enslavement and partition of Acarnania? Was it not you? Who elected and sent out such commanders as you did, men who even ventured to lay hands on inviolable sanctuaries, Timaeus having plundered those of Poseidon on Taenarus and of Artemis at Lusi, while Pharycus pillaged the holy place of Hera at Argos and Polycritus that of Poseidon in Mantinea? And what shall we say of Lattabus and Nicostratus? Did they not violate in time of peace the sanctity of the Pamboeotian festival[67]—conduct worthy of Scythians[68] or Gauls? No such crimes were ever perpetrated by Alexander's successors.

35. "While you have no defense to offer for any of these acts you pride yourselves on having resisted the attack of the barbarians on Delphi, and say that the Greeks ought to be grateful to you for this. But if thanks are due to the Aetolians for this single service, how highly should we honor the Macedonians,[69] who for the greater part of their

[68] The Scythians were proverbial for irrational brutality. See, for instance, *LXX, 2 Ma* 4.47 with the note of C. Habicht, *Jüdische Schriften aus hellenistisch-römischer Zeit* I 3 (1976), 223.

[69] The speaker sees in Macedonia a bulwark against wild peoples from the North, including the Celts. The same argument is used by Titus Flamininus in 197 in answering Aetolian demands that the Macedonian monarchy be abandoned; see 18.37.8–9.

χρόνον οὐ παύονται διαγωνιζόμενοι πρὸς τοὺς βαρ-
3 βάρους ὑπὲρ τῆς τῶν Ἑλλήνων ἀσφαλείας; ὅτι γὰρ
αἰεί ποτ᾽ ἂν ἐν μεγάλοις ἦν κινδύνοις τὰ κατὰ τοὺς
Ἕλληνας, εἰ μὴ Μακεδόνας εἴχομεν πρόφραγμα καὶ
τὰς ⟨τῶν⟩ παρὰ τούτοις βασιλέων φιλοτιμίας, τίς οὐ
4 γινώσκει; μέγιστον δὲ τούτου σημεῖον· ἅμα γὰρ τῷ
Γαλάτας καταφρονῆσαι Μακεδόνων νικήσαντας Πτολεμαῖον τὸν Κεραυνὸν ἐπικαλούμενον, εὐθέως κατα-
γνόντες τῶν ἄλλων ἧκον οἱ περὶ Βρέννον εἰς μέσην
τὴν Ἑλλάδα μετὰ δυνάμεως. ὃ πολλάκις ἂν συνέβαινε
γίνεσθαι μὴ προκαθημένων Μακεδόνων.

5   Οὐ μὴν ἀλλὰ περὶ μὲν τῶν γεγονότων ἔχων πολλὰ
6 λέγειν ἀρκεῖν ἡγοῦμαι· τῶν δὲ Φιλίππῳ πεπραγμένων
εἰς ἀσέβειαν ὠνείδισαν τὴν τοῦ ναοῦ καταφθοράν, οὐ
προσθέντες τὴν αὐτῶν ὕβριν καὶ παρανομίαν, ἣν
ἐπετελέσαντο περὶ τοὺς ἐν Δίῳ καὶ Δωδώνῃ ναοὺς καὶ
7 τὰ τεμένη τῶν θεῶν. ἐχρῆν δὲ λέγειν τοῦτο πρῶτον.
ὑμεῖς δ᾽ ἃ μὲν ἐπάθετε, τούτοις ἐξηγήσασθε, μείζω
ποιοῦντες τῶν γεγονότων, ἃ δ᾽ ἐποιήσατε πρότεροι,
8 πολλαπλάσια γεγονότα παρεσιωπήσατε, σαφῶς εἰδότες ὅτι τὰς ἀδικίας καὶ ζημίας ἅπαντες ἀεὶ τοῖς ἄρχουσι χειρῶν ἀδίκων ἐπιφέρουσι.

36. Περὶ δὲ τῶν κατ᾽ Ἀντίγονον ἕως τούτου βούλομαι ποιήσασθαι τὴν μνήμην, [ἕως] τοῦ μὴ δόξαι
καταφρονεῖν τῶν γεγονότων μηδ᾽ ἐν παρέργῳ τίθε-
2 σθαι τὴν τηλικαύτην πρᾶξιν. ἔγωγ᾽ εὐεργεσίαν μείζω
τῆς ὑπ᾽ Ἀντιγόνου γεγενημένης εἰς ὑμᾶς οὐδ᾽ ἱστο-
ρεῖσθαι νομίζω· δοκεῖ γὰρ ἔμοιγε μηδ᾽ ὑπερβολὴν

lives never cease from fighting with the barbarians for the sake of the security of Greece? For who is not aware that Greece would have constantly stood in the greatest danger, had we not been fenced by the Macedonians and the honorable ambition of their kings? The best proof of it is this. The moment that the Gauls after defeating Ptolemy Ceraunus conceived a contempt for the Macedonians, Brennus making light of all other opponents marched into the middle of Greece with his army, a thing that would often have happened if our frontiers were not protected by the Macedonians.

"I have much more to say about the past, but have said, I think, enough. Among Philip's actions they cite his destruction of the temple as an instance of impiety, but they do not add a word about the criminal outrages they committed at the temples of Dium and Dodona[70] and the precincts of the gods there. They should have mentioned these first. But you Aetolians while you tell this meeting of the evils you suffered, greatly exaggerating their gravity, are silent regarding the far more numerous evils you did to others unprovoked, well knowing that all impute the blame for injustice and injuries to those who first resort to such violence.

36. "As for the conduct of Antigonus, I will only mention it so far as to avoid seeming to make light of what happened or to regard as of minor importance such a performance as his. I do not for my part think there is an example in history of such benevolence as Antigonus showed to you. It seems to me in fact that it could not be surpassed.

[70] A reference to 4.62.1–4 (Dium) and 4.67.3–4 (Dodona).

ἐπιδέχεσθαι τὸ γεγονός. γνοίη δ' ἄν τις ἐκ τούτων.

3 ἐπολέμησε πρὸς ὑμᾶς Ἀντίγονος, καὶ μετὰ ταῦτα
παραταξάμενος ἐνίκησε· διὰ τῶν ὅπλων ἐγένετο κύρι-

4 ος τῆς χώρας ἅμα καὶ τῆς πόλεως. ὤφειλε ποιεῖν τὰ
τοῦ πολέμου· τοσοῦτον ἀπέσχε τοῦ πρᾶξαί τι καθ'
ὑμῶν δεινόν, ὡς πρὸς τοῖς ἄλλοις ἐκβαλὼν τὸν τύραννον καὶ τοὺς νόμους καὶ τὸ πάτριον ὑμῖν ἀπο-

5 κατέστησε πολίτευμα. ἀνθ' ὧν ὑμεῖς ἐν ταῖς κοιναῖς
πανηγύρεσι μάρτυρας ποιησάμενοι τοὺς Ἕλληνας
εὐεργέτην ἑαυτῶν καὶ σωτῆρα τὸν Ἀντίγονον ἀνεκη-

6 ρύξατε. τί οὖν ἐχρῆν ποιεῖν ὑμᾶς; ἐρῶ γὰρ τὸ φαινόμενον, ἄνδρες. ὑμεῖς δ' ἀνέξεσθε· ποιήσω γὰρ τοῦτο
νῦν οὐκ ἀπροσλόγως ὀνειδίσαι βουλόμενος ὑμῖν, ἀλλ'
ὑπὸ τῆς τῶν πραγμάτων περιστάσεως ἀναγκαζόμενος

7 ἐπὶ τῷ κοινῇ συμφέροντι. τί δὴ μέλλω λέγειν; ὅτι καὶ
κατὰ τὸν προγεγονότα πόλεμον οὐκ Αἰτωλοῖς, ἀλλὰ
Μακεδόσιν ἔδει συμμαχεῖν ὑμᾶς, καὶ νῦν παρακαλου-
μένους Φιλίππῳ μᾶλλον ἢ τούτοις ἑαυτοὺς προσνέ-

8-9 μειν. νὴ Δί', ἀλλὰ παραβήσεσθε τὰς συνθήκας· καὶ
πότερα δεινότερον ἂν ποιήσαιτε, τὰ κατ' ἰδίαν πρὸς
Αἰτωλοὺς ὑμῖν συγκείμενα δίκαια παριδόντες ἢ τὰ
πάντων τῶν Ἑλλήνων ἐναντίον ἐν στήλῃ γεγονότα

10 καὶ καθιερωμένα; πῶς δὲ τούτους ἀθετεῖν εὐλαβεῖσθε,
παρ' ὧν οὐδεμίαν προειλήφατε χάριν, Φίλιππον δὲ καὶ
Μακεδόνας οὐκ ἐντρέπεσθε, δι' οὓς ἔχετε καὶ τοῦ νῦν

11 βουλεύεσθαι τὴν ἐξουσίαν; ἢ τὸ μὲν τοῖς φίλοις τὰ

12 δίκαια ποιεῖν ἀναγκαῖον ἡγεῖσθε; καὶ μὴν οὐχ οὕτως

For what were the facts? Antigonus went to war with you and beat you in a pitched battle,[71] and by force of arms took possession of your territory and town. Strictly, he should have exercised the rights of war. But he was so far from treating you with any severity, that besides all the rest he did for you he expelled your tyrant[72] and reestablished the reign of law and your ancient constitution. And in return for this you proclaimed Antigonus at public festivals in the hearing of all Greece to be your savior[73] and benefactor. Now what course should you have taken afterward? I will tell you my opinion, sirs, and you must not take it ill; for I will do so not with any wish to heap pointless reproaches on you, but under the pressure of circumstances and for the general good. This is what I have to say. Both in the former war[74] you should have taken the side not of the Aetolians but of Macedonia and now that these advances are made to you you should rather join Philip than the Aetolians. But I shall be told that you will be breaking a treaty.[75] Now which is the most serious offense, to disregard the private convention you made with the Aetolians or the treaty made in the sight of all the Greeks and inscribed on a column and consecrated? Why should you have compunction about throwing over those from whom you never received any favor, but show no respect to Philip and the Macedonians to whom you owe even your power of deliberating on this occasion? Do you think it necessary to keep faith with your friends? But the piety of observing

[71] At Sellasia in 222 (2.65–69).   [72] King Cleomenes; see n. on Nabis, likewise called "tyrant," 4.81.13 .

[73] Above, 29.12.   [74] The Social War, 220–217.

[75] Of 224, *StV* 507.

ὅσιόν ἐστι τὸ τὰς ἐγγράπτους πίστεις βεβαιοῦν, ὡς
ἀνόσιον τὸ τοῖς σώσασι πολεμεῖν· ὃ νῦν Αἰτωλοὶ
πάρεισιν ὑμᾶς ἀξιοῦντες.

37. Οὐ μὴν ἀλλ' εἰρήσθω μέν μοι ταῦτα, κρινέσθω
δὲ παρὰ τοῖς φιλοτιμότερον διακειμένοις ἐκτὸς εἶναι
τῶν ἐνεστώτων. ἐπὶ δὲ τὸ συνέχον, ὡς οὗτοί φασιν,
2 ἐπάνιμεν. τοῦτο δ' ἦν, εἰ μὲν ὡμοίωται τὰ πράγματα
νῦν καὶ καθ' οὓς καιροὺς ἐποιεῖσθε τὴν πρὸς τούτους
συμμαχίαν, διότι δεῖ μένειν καὶ τὴν ὑμετέραν αἵρεσιν
3 ἐπὶ τῶν ὑποκειμένων· ταῦτα γὰρ ἐν ἀρχαῖς εἶναι· εἰ δ'
ὁλοσχερῶς ἠλλοίωται, διότι δίκαιόν ἐστι καὶ νῦν ὑμᾶς
ἐξ ἀκεραίου βουλεύεσθαι περὶ τῶν παρακελευομένων.
4 ἐρωτῶ τοιγαροῦν ὑμᾶς, ὦ Κλεόνικε καὶ Χλαινέα, τίνας
ἔχοντες συμμάχους τότε παρεκαλεῖτε τούτους εἰς τὴν
κοινοπραγίαν; ἆρ' οὐ πάντας Ἕλληνας; τίσι δὲ νῦν
5 κοινωνεῖτε τῶν ἐλπίδων, ἢ πρὸς ποίαν παρακαλεῖτε
6 τούτους συμμαχίαν; ἆρ' οὐ πρὸς τὴν τῶν βαρβάρων;
ὅμοιά γε δοκεῖ τὰ πράγμαθ' ὑμῖν ὑπάρχειν νῦν καὶ
7 πρότερον, ἀλλ' οὐ τἀναντία· τότε μὲν γὰρ ὑπὲρ ἡγεμονίας καὶ δόξης ἐφιλοτιμεῖσθε πρὸς Ἀχαιοὺς καὶ
Μακεδόνας ὁμοφύλους καὶ τὸν τούτων ἡγεμόνα Φί-
λιππον· νῦν δὲ περὶ δουλείας ἐνίσταται πόλεμος τοῖς
8 Ἕλλησι πρὸς ἀλλοφύλους ἀνθρώπους, οὓς ὑμεῖς δο-
κεῖτε μὲν ἐπισπᾶσθαι κατὰ Φιλίππου, λελήθατε δὲ

---

76 For the Romans called barbarians, see J. Deininger, *Der
politische Widerstand gegen Rom in Griechenland 217–86 v. Chr.*

a written treaty is less than the impiety of fighting against your preservers, as the Aetolians now come and ask you to do.

37. "Let what I have said on this head suffice, and let those who are disposed to be captious pronounce my words to have no bearing on the present situation. I will now revert to what my adversaries themselves speak of as the main question. And this is that if matters are now in the same state as when you made an alliance with them, you should decide to maintain your original attitude, for this, they said, was the first point, but if the situation has radically changed, you are justified now in discussing the requests made to you afresh. I ask you, therefore, Cleonicus and Chlaeneas, what allies had you when you first invited the Spartans to act with you? Were they not all Greeks? But who make common cause with you at present or what kind of alliance do you invite them to enter? Is it not an alliance with barbarians?[76] Far from being similar, the circumstances are now the reverse of what they formerly were. Then your rivals in the struggle for supremacy and renown were the Achaeans and Macedonians, peoples of your own race, and Philip was their commander. But now Greece is threatened with a war against men of a foreign race who intend to enslave[77] her, men whom you fancy you are calling in against Philip, but are calling in really against

(Berlin 1971), 23–27; A. Erskine, *Polybius and Barbarian Rome*, *Mediterraneo antico* 3 (2000) 165–182. They are again so called in 38.5 and identified by name in 38.7. See also 11.5.7.

[77] This was hardly spoken in 211, as it reflects the situation after 168, and insofar contradicts the notion that this speech is based on a genuine record.

κατὰ σφῶν αὐτῶν ἐπεσπασμένοι καὶ κατὰ πάσης
9 Ἑλλάδος. ὥσπερ γὰρ οἱ κατὰ τὰς πολεμικὰς περιστάσεις βαρυτέρας ἐπαγόμενοι φυλακὰς εἰς τὰς πόλεις
τῆς αὑτῶν δυνάμεως χάριν τῆς ἀσφαλείας ἅμα τὸν
ἀπὸ τῶν ἐχθρῶν ἀπωθοῦνται φόβον καὶ ποιοῦσιν
ὑποχειρίους σφᾶς αὐτοὺς ταῖς τῶν φίλων ἐξουσίαις,
10 τὸν αὐτὸν τρόπον καὶ νῦν Αἰτωλοὶ διανοοῦνται. βουλόμενοι γὰρ περιγενέσθαι Φιλίππου καὶ ταπεινῶσαι
Μακεδόνας, λελήθασιν αὑτοῖς ἐπισπασάμενοι τηλι-
κοῦτο νέφος ἀπὸ τῆς ἑσπέρας, ὃ κατὰ μὲν τὸ παρὸν
ἴσως πρώτοις ἐπισκοτήσει Μακεδόσι, κατὰ δὲ τὸ
συνεχὲς πᾶσιν ἔσται τοῖς Ἕλλησι μεγάλων κακῶν
αἴτιον.

38. Ἅπαντας μὲν οὖν δεῖ τοὺς Ἕλληνας προϊδέσθαι τὸν ἐπιφερόμενον καιρόν, μάλιστα δὲ Λακε-
2 δαιμονίους. ἐπεὶ τίνος χάριν ὑπολαμβάνετε τοὺς ὑμε-
τέρους προγόνους, ἄνδρες Λακεδαιμόνιοι, καθ' οὓς
καιροὺς ὁ Ξέρξης ἀπέστειλε πρεσβευτὴν πρὸς ὑμᾶς,
ὕδωρ καὶ γῆν αἰτούμενος, ἀπώσαντας εἰς τὸ φρέαρ
τὸν παραγεγονότα καὶ προσεπιβαλόντας τῆς γῆς
κελεύειν ἀπαγγεῖλαι τῷ Ξέρξῃ διότι παρὰ Λακεδαιμονίων ἔχει τὰ κατὰ τὴν ἐπαγγελίαν, ὕδωρ καὶ
3 γῆν; τίνος πάλιν ἐθελοντὴν καὶ προδήλως ἐξορμᾶν
4 ἀποθανουμένους τοὺς περὶ Λεωνίδην; ἆρ' οὐχ ἵνα
δόξωσι μὴ μόνον ⟨ὑπὲρ⟩ τῆς αὑτῶν, ἀλλὰ καὶ περὶ
τῆς τῶν ἄλλων Ἑλλήνων ἐλευθερίας προκινδυνεύειν;
5 ἄξιόν γε τοιούτων ἀνδρῶν ἀπογόνους ὑπάρχοντας,
κἄπειτα νῦν συμμαχίαν ποιησαμένους τοῖς βαρβά-

yourselves and the whole of Greece. For just as those[78] who when imperiled by war introduce into their cities garrisons stronger than their own forces for the sake of safety, repel indeed all danger from the enemy but at the same time subject themselves to the authority of their friends, so do the Aetolians contemplate doing. For in their anxiety to get the better of Philip and humiliate the Macedonians, they have without knowing it invoked such a cloud from the west[79] as may, perhaps, at first only cast its shadow on Macedonia, but in time will be the cause of great evil to all Greece.

38. "All Greeks, therefore, should foresee the approaching storm and especially the Lacedaemonians. For why do you think it was, men of Sparta, that your ancestors, at the time when Xerxes sent you an envoy[80] demanding water and earth, thrust the stranger into the well and heaped earth upon him, and bade him announce to Xerxes that he had received what was demanded, water and earth? Or why did Leonidas and his men march forth of their own will to meet certain death? Surely it was to show that they were risking their lives not for their own freedom alone, but for that of the other Greeks. It very well becomes you, the descendants of such men, to make an alli-

[78] Refers to the events at Messana (1.7.1 ff.) and Rhegium (1.7.6 ff.).

[79] The same metaphor as in Agelaus' speech in 217 (5.104.10).

[80] Those sent were, in fact, heralds, not envoys ($\pi\rho\epsilon\sigma\beta\epsilon\upsilon\tau\alpha\acute{\iota}$), and therefore considered to be untouchable (which envoys were not). *RE* Presbeia (Suppl. 13), 499–628 (D. Kienast), on 544–546. On P.'s deviation from Herodotus, see WC 2.177.

ροις, στρατεύειν μετ᾿ ἐκείνων καὶ πολεμεῖν Ἠπειρώταις, Ἀχαιοῖς, Ἀκαρνᾶσι, Βοιωτοῖς, Θετταλοῖς, σχε-
6 δὸν πᾶσι τοῖς Ἕλλησι πλὴν Αἰτωλῶν. τούτοις μὲν οὖν
ἔθος ἐστὶ ταῦτα πράττειν καὶ μηδὲν αἰσχρὸν νομίζειν,
7 εἰ μόνον πρόσεστι τὸ πλεονεκτεῖν, οὐ μὴν ὑμῖν. καὶ τί
δήποτε προσδοκᾶν δεῖ τούτους ἀπεργασομένους, ἐπεὶ
8 τὴν Ῥωμαίων προσειλήφασι συμμαχίαν; οἵ γε τῆς
Ἰλλυριῶν ἐπιλαβόμενοι ῥοπῆς καὶ βοηθείας κατὰ μὲν
θάλατταν βιάζεσθαι καὶ παρασπονδεῖν ἐπεβάλοντο
Πύλον, κατὰ δὲ γῆν ἐπολιόρκησαν μὲν τὴν Κλειτο-
9 ρίων πόλιν, ἐξηνδραποδίσαντο δὲ τὴν Κυναιθέων. καὶ
πρότερον μὲν Ἀντιγόνῳ, καθάπερ ἐπάνω προεῖπον,
ἐποιήσαντο συνθήκας οὗτοι περί τε τοῦ τῶν Ἀχαιῶν
καὶ τοῦ τῶν Ἀκαρνάνων ἔθνους, νῦν δὲ πεποίηνται
πρὸς Ῥωμαίους κατὰ πάσης τῆς Ἑλλάδος.

39. Ἃ τίς οὐκ ἂν πυθόμενος ὑπίδοιτο μὲν τὴν
Ῥωμαίων ἔφοδον, μισήσαι δὲ τὴν Αἰτωλῶν ἀπόνοιαν,
2 ὅτι τοιαύτας ἐθάρρησαν ποιήσασθαι συνθήκας; ἤδη
παρῄρηνται μὲν Ἀκαρνάνων Οἰνιάδας καὶ Νᾶσον·
κατέσχον δὲ πρῴην τὴν τῶν ταλαιπώρων Ἀντικυρέων
3 πόλιν, ἐξανδραποδισάμενοι μετὰ Ῥωμαίων αὐτήν. καὶ
τὰ μὲν τέκνα καὶ τὰς γυναῖκας ἀπάγουσι Ῥωμαῖοι,
πεισόμενα δῆλον ὅτι ἅπερ εἰκός ἐστι πάσχειν τοῖς ὑπὸ
τὰς τῶν ἀλλοφύλων πεσοῦσιν ἐξουσίας· τὰ δ᾿ ἐδάφη
4 κληρονομοῦσι τῶν ἠτυχηκότων Αἰτωλοί. καλόν γε

---

81 34.6, however the pact was not made with Antigonus but
with Alexander of Epirus, 34.7.

ance now with barbarians, to take the field with them and make war on the Epirots, Achaeans, Acarnanians, Boeotians, and Thessalians, in fact with almost all the Greeks except the Aetolians! They indeed are accustomed to act so and to think nothing disgraceful if only something is to be gained by it, but it is not so with you. And what feats do you expect they will accomplish when they have gained the alliance of Rome, the people who, when they were reinforced by the help of the Illyrians, attempted by sea to surprise and treacherously take Pylus and on land laid siege to Cleitor and sold the citizens of Cynaetha into slavery? Formerly, as I already said,[81] they made a treaty with Antigonus for the destruction of the Achaean and Acarnanian Leagues, and now they have made one with the Romans against the whole of Greece.

39. "How, when one knows of this, can one help viewing with suspicion the advance of the Romans and with detestation the unprincipled conduct of the Aetolians in venturing to make such treaties? Already they have robbed the Acarnanians of Oeniadae[82] and Nasus, and it is but the other day that they together with the Romans seized on the unhappy city of Anticyra,[83] selling its inhabitants into slavery. So the Romans are carrying *off* the women and children to suffer, of course, what those must suffer who fall into the hands of aliens, while the Aetolians divide the soil and buildings of the unfortunate people among them-

---

[82] Conquered by Laevinus in 211 and turned over to the Aetolians (Livy 26.24.15).

[83] A small town in southern Phocis, today Aspra Spitia, on the north coast of the Corinthian Gulf.

101

ταύτης τῆς συμμαχίας μετασχεῖν κατὰ προαίρεσιν,
5 ἄλλως τε καὶ Λακεδαιμονίους ὑπάρχοντας, οἵ γε Θηβαίους τοὺς κατ' ἀνάγκην ἡσυχίαν ἄγειν βουλευ-
σαμένους μόνους τῶν Ἑλλήνων κατὰ τὴν τῶν Περσῶν
ἔφοδον ἐψηφίσαντο δεκατεύσειν τοῖς θεοῖς κρατήσαντες τῷ πολέμῳ τῶν βαρβάρων.

6 Καλὸν μὲν οὖν, ὦ ἄνδρες Λακεδαιμόνιοι, καὶ πρέπον ὑμῖν ἐστι τὸ μνησθέντας μὲν τῶν προγόνων,
εὐλαβηθέντας δὲ τὴν Ῥωμαίων ἔφοδον, ὑπιδομένους
δὲ τὴν Αἰτωλῶν κακοπραγμοσύνην, τὸ δὲ μέγιστον
τῶν ἐξ Ἀντιγόνου γεγονότων μνησθέντας, ἔτι καὶ νῦν
μισοπονηρῆσαι, καὶ τὴν μὲν Αἰτωλῶν ἀποστραφῆναι
φιλίαν, Ἀχαιοῖς δὲ καὶ Μακεδόσι κοινωνῆσαι τῶν
7 αὐτῶν ἐλπίδων. εἰ δ' ἄρα πρὸς τοῦτό τινες ἀντι-
πράττουσι τῶν πλεῖον δυναμένων παρ' ὑμῖν, πρός γε
τὴν ἡσυχίαν ὁρμήσατε, καὶ μὴ μετάσχητε τῆς τούτων
ἀδικίας." . . .

40. Τὸ γὰρ τοιοῦτον ἦθος αἰεὶ βούλεται διαφυλάττειν ἡ τῶν Ἀθηναίων πόλις

2 Προθυμίαν γὰρ φίλων συμφόρως μὲν γινομένην
μεγάλην παρέχεσθαι χρείαν, ἐφελκομένην δὲ καὶ καθ-
υστεροῦσαν τελέως ἀνωφελῆ τὴν ἐπικουρίαν.

3 εἴπερ οὖν βούλονται μὴ τοῖς γράμμασι μόνον,
ἀλλὰ καὶ τοῖς ἔργοις τηρεῖν τὴν πρὸς αὐτοὺς
συμμαχίαν . . .

selves by lot. A fine alliance this for anyone to determine to join and specially for you Lacedaemonians, who decreed that when you had conquered the barbarians, the Thebans were to pay a tithe[84] to the gods for having decided under compulsion, but alone among the Greeks, to remain neutral during the Persian invasion.

"Your honor then and your dignity, men of Lacedaemon, require that you should remember who were your ancestors, that you should place yourselves on your guard against the aggression of Rome, and view with suspicion the evil designs of the Aetolians, but above all that you should bear in mind the favors conferred on you by Antigonus and still continue to be haters of wickedness, refusing the friendship of the Aetolians and throwing in your lot with the Achaeans and Macedonians. But if some of your most powerful citizens are opposed to this policy at least do all in your power to remain neutral and not participate in the iniquity of the Aetolians."

40.1 Such a character the city of Athens always tries to preserve.

40.2 Assistance willingly provided by friends is of great use, but is worthless if it comes slowly and late.

40.3 So, if they were willing to honor the alliance not only according to the letter, but by action . . .[85]

---

[84] See Lycurg. 81; D. S. 11.3.3. This was never carried out.
[85] For 40.4–6 see after 27.12.

THE HISTORIES OF POLYBIUS

41. Προθέμενος δὲ τῆς πόλεως κατὰ δύο πύργους
ποιεῖσθαι τὴν προσαγωγὴν κατὰ μὲν τούτους χελώνας κατεσκεύαζε χωστρίδας καὶ κριούς, κατὰ δὲ τὸ
μεσοπύργιον στοὰν ἐποίει μεταξὺ τῶν κριῶν παράλ-
2 ληλον τῷ τείχει. τῆς δὲ προθέσεως συντελουμένης
παραπλήσιος ἡ τῶν ἔργων ἐγίνετο πρόσοψις τῇ τοῦ
3 τείχους διαθέσει· τὰ μὲν γὰρ ἐπὶ ταῖς χελώναις κατα-
σκευάσματα πύργων ἐλάμβανε καὶ φαντασίαν καὶ
διάθεσιν ἐκ τῆς τῶν γέρρων συνθέσεως, τὸ δὲ μεταξὺ
τούτων τείχους, τῶν ἀνωτέρω γέρρων τῆς στοᾶς εἰς
4 ἐπάλξεις τῇ πλοκῇ διῃρημένων. διὰ μὲν οὖν τοῦ κάτω
μέρους τῶν πύργων οἵ τε προσχωννύντες τὰς ἀνω-
μαλίας τῶν τόπων ἐπὶ τῇ τῶν ἐσχαρίων ἐφόδῳ τὴν
5 γῆν ἐπέβαλλον ὅ τε κριὸς ἐξωθεῖτο. τὸ δὲ δεύτερον
ὑδρίας καὶ τὰς πρὸς τοὺς ἐμπυρισμοὺς εἶχε παρα-
6 σκευὰς καὶ τὰ καταπελτικὰ σὺν τούτοις. ἐπὶ δὲ τοῦ
τρίτου πλῆθος ἀνδρῶν ἐφειστήκει τῶν ἀπομαχομένων
πρὸς τοὺς κακοποιεῖν ἐπιβαλλομένους τὸν κριόν. οὗ-
7 τοι δ᾽ ἦσαν ἰσοϋψεῖς τοῖς τῆς πόλεως πύργοις. ἐκ δὲ
τῆς μεταξὺ τῶν πύργων στοᾶς ὀρύγματα διπλᾶ προσ-
8 ήγετο πρὸς τὸ μεσοπύργιον. καὶ τρεῖς ἦσαν βελο-
στάσεις λιθοβόλοις, ὧν ὁ μὲν εἷς ταλαντιαίους, οἱ δὲ
9 δύο τριακονταμναίους ἐξέβαλλον λίθους. ἀπὸ δὲ τῆς
παρεμβολῆς ὡς πρὸς τὰς χελώνας τὰς χωστρίδας
ἐπεποίηντο σύριγγες κατάστεγοι χάριν τοῦ μήτε τοὺς
προσιόντας ἐκ τῆς στρατοπεδείας μήτε τοὺς ἀπιόντας
ἀπὸ τῶν ἔργων βλάπτεσθαι μηδὲν ὑπὸ τῶν ἐκ τῆς

Siege of Echinus by Philip

41. Having decided to make his approaches to the city[86]   [211
opposite two towers, he constructed in front of each of   B.C.
them a shelter for sappers and a ram, and opposite the wall
between the towers a gallery from one ram to the other
running parallel to the wall. When the design was carried
out the appearance of the work was very similar in style to
the wall. For the superstructures on the shelters were
in appearance and arrangement like towers owing to the
fashion of the wickerwork, while the space between them
was like a wall, the upper row of wickerwork being divided into battlements by the way it was woven. From the
ground floor of the towers the men employed in leveling
the surface to enable the rollers to advance threw up earth,
and the ram was then propelled. On the second story there
were water jars and other appliances for putting out fires,
and also the catapults, while on the third, level with the
towers of the town, stood a number of men ready to engage
those who attempted to damage the ram. From the gallery
between the towers two trenches were opened and carried
toward the wall of the city. There were also three batter-
ies of ballistae of which one threw stones of a talent's
weight, and the other two stones of half that weight. From
the camp to the shelters for sappers roofed underground
passages had been constructed, so that neither those coming from the camp nor those leaving the works should be

[86] Echinus (41.11), at the north shore of the Malian gulf, opposite Nicaea. See F. Stählin, *Das hellenische Thessalien* (Stuttgart 1924), 186. In 168 Echinus honored the Roman praetor and
commander of the fleet Cn. Octavius (*AE* 1971, 450).

10 πόλεως βελῶν. ἐν ὀλίγαις δὲ τελέως ἡμέραις συνέβη
καὶ τὴν τῶν ἔργων ἐπιτελεσθῆναι συντέλειαν διὰ τὸ
τὴν χώραν ἀφθόνους ἔχειν τὰς εἰς τοῦτο τὸ μέρος

11 χορηγίας. οἱ γὰρ Ἐχιναιεῖς κεῖνται μὲν ἐν τῷ Μηλιεῖ
κόλπῳ, τετραμμένοι πρὸς μεσημβρίαν, καταντίπεραν
τῆς τῶν Θρονιέων χώρας, καρποῦνται δὲ γῆν πάμφο-
ρον. δι᾽ ἣν αἰτίαν οὐδὲν ἐνέλειπε τὸν Φίλιππον τῶν

12 πρὸς τὰς ἐπιβολάς. οὐ μὴν ἀλλά, καθάπερ εἶπον,
ἐπιτελεσθέντων τῶν ἔργων προσῆγον ἅμα τὰς τῶν
ὀρυγμάτων καὶ μηχανημάτων κατασκευάς.

42. Πόπλιος ὁ τῶν Ῥωμαίων στρατηγὸς καὶ Δωρί-
μαχος ὁ τῶν Αἰτωλῶν, τοῦ Φιλίππου πολιορκοῦντος
τὴν Ἐχιναιῶν πόλιν, καὶ τὰ πρὸς τὸ τεῖχος καλῶς
ἀσφαλισαμένου καὶ τὰ πρὸς τὴν ἐκτὸς ἐπιφάνειαν τοῦ

2 στρατοπέδου τάφρῳ καὶ τείχει ὀχυρωσαμένου, παραγενόμενοι αὐτοί, ὁ μὲν Πόπλιος στόλῳ, ὁ δὲ Δωρί-
μαχος πεζικῇ καὶ ἱππικῇ δυνάμει, καὶ προσβαλόντες
τῷ χάρακι καὶ ἀποκρουσθέντες, τοῦ Φιλίππου μᾶλλον

3 ἰσχυρῶς ἀγωνισαμένου, ἀπελπίσαντες οἱ Ἐχιναιεῖς

4 παρέδοσαν ἑαυτοὺς τῷ Φιλίππῳ. οὐ γὰρ οἷοί τε ἦσαν
οἱ περὶ τὸν Δωρίμαχον τῇ τῶν δαπανημάτων ἐνδείᾳ
ἀναγκάζειν τὸν Φίλιππον, ἐκ θαλάττης ταῦτα πορι-
ζόμενον.

5 Ὅτι τῆς Αἰγίνης ὑπὸ Ῥωμαίων ἁλούσης, οἱ Αἰγι-
νῆται συναθροισθέντες ἐπὶ τὰς ναῦς, ὅσοι μὴ διεκλά-
πησαν, ἐδέοντο τοῦ στρατηγοῦ συγχωρῆσαι σφίσι

wounded by missiles from the town. These works were entirely completed in the course of a few days, as the country round has abundance of the materials required. For Echinus is situated on the Malian Gulf, facing south, opposite the territory of Thronium, and the land is rich in every kind of produce, so that nothing was lacking for Philip's purpose. But, as I said, when the work was completed both the saps and the siege machines began to advance.

42. While Philip was besieging Echinus, and had both well secured his position on the side of the town and fortified his camp on the outer side with a trench and a wall, Publius Sulpicius,[87] the Roman proconsul, and Dorimachus,[88] the strategus of the Aetolians, appeared in person, Publius with a fleet and Dorimachus with a force of infantry and cavalry. When they attacked the entrenched camp and were repulsed, Philip having fought more vigorously, the Echinaeans lost heart and surrendered to Philip. For Dorimachus was unable to compel Philip to raise the siege by cutting off his supplies, as he got them by sea.

Aegina Occupied by the Romans

When Aegina[89] was taken by the Romans, such of the inhabitants as did not escape having been assembled on the ships begged the proconsul to allow them to send con-

[87] The consul of 211, now, in 210, proconsul (*MRR* 1.280).

[88] See 4.3.5. He was strategus for the second time in 211/10.

[89] The island was a member of the Achaean League. The Romans turned it over to the Aetolians, who sold it to Attalus of Pergamum.

πρεσβευτὰς ἐκπέμψαι πρὸς τὰς συγγενεῖς πόλεις περὶ
6 λύτρων· ὁ δὲ Πόπλιος τὸ μὲν πρῶτον πικρῶς ἀντέφη,
φάσκων, ὅτ᾽ ἦσαν αὐτῶν κύριοι, τότε <δεῖν> διαπρεσβεύεσθαι πρὸς τοὺς κρείττους περὶ σωτηρίας, μὴ
7 νῦν δούλους γεγονότας· τὸ δὲ μικρῷ πρότερον αὐτοὺς
μηδὲ λόγου καταξιώσαντας τοὺς παρ᾽ αὐτοῦ πρεσβευτάς, νῦν ὑποχειρίους γεγονότας ἀξιοῦν πρεσβεύειν
8 πρὸς τοὺς συγγενεῖς, πῶς οὐκ εὔηθες εἶναι; καὶ τότε
μὲν ἀπέπεμψε τοὺς ἐντυγχάνοντας ταῦτ᾽ εἰπών· τῇ δ᾽
ἐπαύριον συγκαλέσας ἅπαντας τοὺς αἰχμαλώτους,
Αἰγινήταις μὲν <οὐδὲν> ὀφείλειν ἔφη ποιεῖν φιλάνθρωπον, τῶν δὲ λοιπῶν Ἑλλήνων ἕνεκα συγχωρεῖν
ἔφη πρεσβεύειν περὶ τῶν λύτρων, ἐπεὶ τοῦτο παρ᾽
αὐτοῖς ἔθος ἐστίν.

VIII. RES ASIAE

43. Ὁ γὰρ Εὐφράτης τὴν μὲν ἀρχὴν λαμβάνει τῆς
συστάσεως ἐξ Ἀρμενίας, διαρρεῖ δὲ [τὸν] διὰ Συρίας
2 καὶ τῶν ἑξῆς τόπων ὡς ἐπὶ Βαβυλωνίαν. καὶ δοκεῖ μὲν
εἰς τὴν Ἐρυθρὰν ἐμβάλλειν θάλατταν, οὐ μὴν ἔστι γε
τοῦτο· ταῖς γὰρ διώρυξι ταῖς ἐπὶ τὴν χώραν ἀγομέναις
προεκδαπανᾶται πρὶν ἐκβολὴν εἰς θάλατταν πεποιῆ-
3 σθαι. διὸ καὶ συμβαίνει τὴν ὑπεναντίαν φύσιν ἔχειν

---

90 For Sulpicius' treatment of the population (42.5–8), see W.
K. Pritchett, *The Greek State at War* 5 (Berkeley 1991), 263; in the
end, nearly all of them were sold into slavery (22.8.9–10). The

voys to cities of kindred race to obtain ransom.[90] Publius at first refused very sharply, saying that they ought to have sent envoys to their betters to come and save them while they were still their own masters and not now they were slaves. That they who a short time ago had not even deigned to reply to his envoys, now when they had fallen into his power should request leave to send envoys to their kinsmen was most foolish. So at the time he dismissed those who had approached him with these words, but next day summoning all the prisoners of war, he said he was under no obligation to be lenient to the Aeginetans, but for the sake of the rest of the Greeks he would allow them to send envoys to get ransom, as such was their custom.

VIII. AFFAIRS OF ASIA

The Euphrates

43. The Euphrates[91] commences its course in Armenia and flows through Syria and the adjacent countries in the direction of Babylonia. It is supposed to fall into the Persian Gulf, but this is not the case; for the canals[92] which are carried over the country exhaust the water of the river before it can fall into the sea. So that its nature is the reverse of that of most rivers. In the case of other rivers the stream

Romans brought to warfare a new degree of brutality, not previously known in Greece.

[91] From Antiochus' expedition to the eastern satrapies. The fragment dates to 211/10. The army traveled on boats downstream.

[92] For the Mesopotamian system of canals, see *RE* Euphrates 1208–1211 (F. Weissbach).

τοῦτον τοῖς πλείστοις τῶν ποταμῶν. τοῖς μὲν γὰρ
ἄλλοις αὔξεται τὸ ῥεῦμα, καθὼς ἂν πλείους διαφέρωνται τόπους, καὶ μέγιστοι μέν εἰσι κατὰ χειμῶνα,
4 ταπεινότατοι δὲ κατὰ τὴν ἀκμὴν τοῦ θέρους· οὗτος δὲ
καὶ πλεῖστος γίνεται τῷ ῥεύματι κατὰ κυνὸς ἐπιτολὴν
καὶ μέγιστος ἐν τοῖς κατὰ Συρίαν τόποις, αἰεὶ δὲ
5 προϊὼν ἐλάττων. αἴτιον δὲ τούτων ὅτι συμβαίνει τὴν
μὲν αὔξησιν οὐκ ἐκ τῆς συρρύσεως τῶν χειμερινῶν
ὄμβρων, ἀλλ᾿ ἐκ τῆς ἀνατήξεως τῶν χιόνων ⟨γίνε-
σθαι⟩, τὴν δὲ μείωσιν διὰ τὰς ἐκτροπὰς τὰς ἐπὶ τὴν
χώραν καὶ τὸν μερισμὸν αὐτοῦ τὸν ἐπὶ τὰς ἀρδεύσεις.
6 ᾗ καὶ τότε βραδεῖαν συνέβαινε γίνεσθαι τὴν κομιδὴν
τῶν δυνάμεων, ἅτε καταγόμων μὲν ὄντων τῶν πλοίων,
ταπεινοτάτου δὲ τοῦ ποταμοῦ καὶ τελέως βραχύ τι
συνεργούσης τῆς τοῦ ῥεύματος βίας πρὸς τὸν πλοῦν.

44. Ὅτι τοὺς μὴ μετ᾿ εὐνοίας καὶ προθυμίας ἐμ-
βαίνοντας οὐδ᾿ ἐπ᾿ αὐτῶν εἰκός ἐστι τῶν ἔργων ἀλη-
θεῖς εἶναι συμμάχους

2 Καὶ ἔστιν ἀληθὲς τὸ πολλάκις ὑφ᾿ ἡμῶν εἰρημένον
ὡς οὐχ οἷόν τε περιλαβεῖν οὐδὲ συνθεάσασθαι τῇ
ψυχῇ τὸ κάλλιστον θέαμα τῶν γεγονότων, λέγω δὲ
τὴν τῶν ὅλων οἰκονομίαν, ἐκ τῶν τὰς κατὰ μέρος
πράξεις γραφόντων

45. Πολύβιος ἐν τῇ ἐνάτῃ τῶν Ἱστοριῶν καὶ ποταμόν τινα ἀναγράφει Κύαθον καλούμενον περὶ Ἀρσινόην πόλιν Αἰτωλίας.

increases the more country they traverse, they are largest in winter and lowest in the height of summer, but the Euphrates is in highest flood[93] at the rising of the Dog Star, and the stream is largest in Syria and gets smaller as it advances. The reason of this is that its rise is not due to the conflux of winter rains but to the melting of the snow, while its decrease is due to the diversion of the stream into the land and its subdivision for purposes of irrigation. So that on this occasion the conveyance of the troops was very slow, the boats being over full, while the river was at its lowest, and the force of its current only helped their progress to a very slight extent.

44.1 Those who embark (on war) without loyalty and eagerness are not likely to be true allies when it comes to action.

44.2 It is true what we have often said: that it is not possible to understand and fully appreciate the most beautiful view of the events, namely the universal history, from those who write on particular events.

45.1 Polybius mentions in Book 9 of his *Histories* a river named Cyathus near Arsinoe, a city of Aetolia.

---

[93] P.'s data here are inaccurate; better is Str. 16.1.9.

2   Ἀρσινόη, πόλις Λιβύης . . . . τὸ ἐθνικὸν Ἀρσινοί-
της, καὶ Ἀρσινοεὺς ἐπὶ τῆς Αἰτωλικῆς, ὡς Πολύβιος
ἐνάτῳ.

3   Ξυνία, Θετταλίας πόλις. Πολύβιος ἐνάτῳ. Φόρυν-
να, πόλις Θρᾴκης· Πολύβιος ἐνάτῳ.

45.2 Arsinoë,[94] city of Libya . . . the ethnic is Arsinoites, but Arsinoeus for the Aetolian city, as Polybius says in Book 9.

45.3 Xynia,[95] a city in Thessaly, as Polybius in Book 9 . . . Phorunna,[96] a city in Thrace, as Polybius 9.

---

[94] For Arsinoë in Aetolia and the river Cyathus, a tributary of the Achelous, see G. Cohen, *The Hellenistic Settlements in Europe, the Islands, and Asia Minor* (Berkeley 1995), 109–110. The city was probably founded by the Aetolians and named in honor of Arsinoë, at the time the Queen of Lysimachus, that is, before 281. Epigraphically, the city's name is attested as Arsinoeia and Arsinoea.   [95] The city has been located at Koromilia in Achaea Phthiotis, west of Melitaia. *RE* Xyniai 2174–2177 (E. Meyer). In 214/3 a territorial dispute she had with Melitaia was assigned to arbitrators by the Aetolian League: S. Ager, *Interstate Arbitration in the Greek World, 337–90 B.C.* (Berkeley 1995), no. 56; A. Magnetto, *Gli arbitrati interstatali Greci* II (Pisa 1997), no. 54.   [96] Mentioned only in P. and in Steph, Byz.

FRAGMENTA LIBRI X

I. RES ITALIAE

1. Ὄντων γὰρ ἀπὸ τοῦ πορθμοῦ καὶ τῆς Ῥηγίνων πόλεως σταδίων εἰς Τάραντα πλειόνων ἢ δισχιλίων, εἰς τέλος ἀλίμενον εἶναι συμβαίνει τὴν πλευρὰν τῆς

2 Ἰταλίας ταύτην πλὴν τῶν ἐν Τάραντι λιμένων· ἢ τέτραπται μὲν εἰς τὸ Σικελικὸν πέλαγος, νεύει δὲ πρὸς τοὺς κατὰ τὴν Ἑλλάδα τόπους, ἔχει δὲ τῶν τε βαρβάρων ἐθνῶν τὰ πολυανθρωπότατα καὶ τῶν Ἑλληνί-

3 δων πόλεων τὰς ἐπιφανεστάτας. Βρέττιοι γὰρ καὶ Λευκανοὶ καί τινα μέρη τῶν Σαυνιτῶν, ἔτι δὲ Καλαβροὶ καὶ πλείους ἕτεροι τοῦτο τὸ κλίμα νέμονται τῆς

4 Ἰταλίας· ὁμοίως δὲ καὶ τῶν Ἑλληνίδων πόλεων Ῥήγιον καὶ Καυλωνία καὶ Λοκροὶ καὶ Κρότων, ἔτι δὲ Μεταπόντιον καὶ Θούριοι ταύτην ἐπέχουσι τὴν παρα-

5 λίαν, ὥστε καὶ τοὺς ἀπὸ Σικελίας καὶ τοὺς ἀπὸ τῆς Ἑλλάδος φερομένους ἐπί τινα τόπον τῶν προειρημένων κατ᾽ ἀνάγκην ὁρμεῖν ἐν τοῖς τῶν Ταραντίνων λιμέσι, καὶ τὰς ἀμείψεις καὶ τὰς οἰκονομίας πρὸς πάντας τοὺς κατέχοντας ταύτην τὴν πλευρὰν τῆς

6 Ἰταλίας ἐν ταύτῃ ποιεῖσθαι τῇ πόλει. τεκμήραιτο δ᾽

FRAGMENTS OF BOOK X

I. AFFAIRS OF ITALY

The Recovery of Tarentum

211–210
B.C.

1. The distance from the Sicilian strait and Rhegium to Tarentum is more than two thousand stades,[1] but all this side of Italy has not a single harbor except those of Tarentum.[2] This part of Italy faces the Sicilian Sea and verges toward Greece, and it contains the most populous barbarian tribes and the most famous Greek cities, being inhabited by the Bruttians, Lucanians, a portion of the Samnites, the Calabrians, and several other tribes, while on its coast lie Rhegium, Caulonia, Locri, Croton,[3] Metapontum, and Thurii, so that those travelling either from Greece or from Sicily to any of the aforesaid places must of necessity anchor in the harbors of Tarentum, and make that city the seat of their exchange and traffic with all the inhabitants of this side of Italy. One can form some idea of the advantages

---

[1] In fact, about 2,500 stades or 290 miles.

[2] The Mare Grande, lying on the outer side of the city, and the harbor proper within the Mare Piccolo; see the map in WC 2.1.

[3] For the city's prosperity see 7.1.1.

115

ἄν τις τοῦ τόπου τὴν εὐκαιρίαν ἐκ τῆς περὶ Κροτω-
νιάτας γενομένης εὐδαιμονίας. ἐκεῖνοι γὰρ θερινοὺς
ἔχοντες ὅρμους καὶ βραχεῖάν τινα παντελῶς προσ-
αγωγήν, μεγάλην εὐδαιμονίαν δοκοῦσι περιποιήσασθαι δι᾽ οὐδὲν ἕτερον ἢ διὰ τὴν τῶν τόπων εὐφυΐαν, ἣν
οὐδὲ συγκρίνειν ἄξιόν ἐστι τοῖς Ταραντίνων λιμέσι
7 καὶ τόποις. τέτακται δὲ καὶ πρὸς τοὺς κατὰ τὸν
Ἀδρίαν λιμένας εὐφυῶς καὶ νῦν μέν, ἔτι δὲ μᾶλλον ἦν
8 πρὸ τοῦ. ἀπὸ γὰρ ἄκρας Ἰαπυγίας ἕως εἰς Σιποῦντα
πᾶς ὁ προσφερόμενος ἐκ τῶν ἀντιπέρας καὶ καθορ-
μισθεὶς πρὸς τὴν Ἰταλίαν εἰς Τάραντ᾽ ἐποιεῖτο τὴν
ὑπερβολήν, καὶ ταύτῃ συνεχρῆτο τῇ πόλει πρὸς τὰς
9 ἀλλαγὰς καὶ μεταθέσεις οἷον [εἰ] ἐμπορίῳ· οὐδέπω
γὰρ συνέβαινε τότε τὴν τῶν Βρεντεσίνων ἐκτίσθαι
10 πόλιν. διόπερ ὁ Φάβιος, ἐν μεγάλῳ τιθέμενος τὴν
ἐπιβολήν, τἆλλα παρεὶς πρὸς ταῖς εἰς τοῦτο τὸ μέρος
ἦν ἐπινοίαις.

II. RES HISPANIAE

2. Ὅτι μέλλοντες ἱστορεῖν τὰ πραχθέντα Ποπλίῳ
κατὰ τὴν Ἰβηρίαν, συλλήβδην δὲ πάσας τὰς κατὰ
τὸν βίον ἐπιτελεσθείσας αὐτῷ πράξεις, ἀναγκαῖον
ἡγούμεθα τὸ προεπιστῆσαι τοὺς ἀκούοντας ἐπὶ τὴν
2 αἵρεσιν καὶ φύσιν τἀνδρός. τῷ γὰρ σχεδὸν ἐπιφα-

---

4 The harbors on the opposite Greek coast.

of its situation from the prosperity of the people of Croton; for they, although they have but roadsteads suitable for the summer and though quite few ships put in there, have, it would seem, attained great wealth simply owing to the favorable situation of the place, which is in no way to be compared with the harbors and district of Tarentum. Tarentum is also very favorably situated with respect to the harbors of the Adriatic[4] even at the present day, and was still more so formerly. For from the extremity of Iapygia, as far as Sipontum, everyone coming from the opposite coast to put in to an Italian harbor crossed to Tarentum and used that as an emporium for the exchange and sale of merchandise, the town of Brundisium having not yet been founded.[5] So that Fabius,[6] regarding this enterprise[7] as of great moment, neglected other matters and turned his whole attention to this. . . .

II. AFFAIRS OF SPAIN

Character of Scipio

2. Now that I am about to recount Scipio's[8] exploits in Spain, and in short everything that he achieved in his life, I think it necessary to convey to my readers, in the first place, a notion of his character and natural parts. For the

---

[5] This statement is incorrect, since a Roman colony was founded there in 244. *OCD* Brundisium 263 (H. K. Lomas).

[6] The consul of 209, Quintus Fabius Maximus Verrucosus; *RE* Fabius 1814–1830 (F. Münzer).

[7] The recovery of Tarentum.

[8] The famous *Africanus*, son of the homonymous man who was killed in battle in 211. *RE* Cornelius 1462–1470 (F. Münzer).

νέστατον αὐτὸν γεγονέναι τῶν πρὸ τοῦ, ζητοῦσι μὲν
πάντες εἰδέναι τίς ποτ᾽ ἦν καὶ ἀπὸ ποίας φύσεως ἢ
τριβῆς ὁρμηθεὶς τὰς τηλικαύτας καὶ τοσαύτας ἐπετε-
3 λέσατο πράξεις, ἀγνοεῖν δὲ καὶ ψευδοδοξεῖν ἀναγ-
κάζονται διὰ τὸ τοὺς ἐξηγουμένους ὑπὲρ αὐτοῦ παρα-
4 πεπαικέναι τῆς ἀληθείας. ὅτι δ᾽ ἔστιν ὑγιὲς τὸ νυνὶ
λεγόμενον ὑφ᾽ ἡμῶν δῆλον ἔσται διὰ τῆς ἡμετέρας
ἐξηγήσεως τοῖς ἐπισημαίνεσθαι δυναμένοις τὰ κάλλι-
5 στα καὶ παραβολώτατα τῶν ἐκείνῳ πεπραγμένων. οἱ
μὲν οὖν ἄλλοι πάντες αὐτὸν ἐπιτυχῆ τινα καὶ τὸ
πλεῖον αἰεὶ παραλόγως καὶ ταὐτομάτῳ κατορθοῦντα
6 τὰς ἐπιβολὰς παρεισάγουσι, νομίζοντες ὡς ἂν εἰ θειο-
τέρους εἶναι καὶ θαυμαστοτέρους τοὺς τοιούτους
ἄνδρας τῶν κατὰ λόγον ἐν ἑκάστοις πραττόντων,
ἀγνοοῦντες ὅτι τὸ μὲν ἐπαινετόν, τὸ δὲ μακαριστὸν
εἶναι συμβαίνει τῶν προειρημένων, καὶ τὸ μὲν κοινόν
7 ἐστι καὶ τοῖς τυχοῦσι, τὸ δ᾽ ἐπαινετὸν μόνον ἴδιον
ὑπάρχει τῶν εὐλογίστων καὶ φρένας ἐχόντων ἀνδρῶν,
οὓς καὶ θειοτάτους εἶναι καὶ προσφιλεστάτους τοῖς
8 θεοῖς νομιστέον. ἐμοὶ ⟨δὲ⟩ δοκεῖ Πόπλιος Λυκούργῳ
τῷ τῶν Λακεδαιμονίων νομοθέτῃ παραπλησίαν ἐσχη-
9 κέναι φύσιν καὶ προαίρεσιν. οὔτε γὰρ Λυκοῦργον
ἡγητέον δεισιδαιμονοῦντα καὶ πάντα προσέχοντα τῇ
Πυθίᾳ συστήσασθαι τὸ Λακεδαιμονίων πολίτευμα,
οὔτε Πόπλιον ἐξ ἐνυπνίων ὁρμώμενον καὶ κληδόνων
10 τηλικαύτην περιποιῆσαι τῇ πατρίδι δυναστείαν· ἀλλ᾽

fact that he was almost the most famous man of all time makes everyone desirous to know what sort of man he was, and what were the natural gifts and the training which enabled him to accomplish so many great actions. But none can help falling into error and acquiring a mistaken impression of him, as the estimate of those who have given us their views about him is very wide of the truth.[9] That what I myself state here is sound will be evident to all who by means of my narrative are able to appreciate the most glorious and hazardous of his exploits. As for all other writers, they represent him as a man favored by fortune, who always owed the most part of his success to the unexpected and to mere chance, such men being, in their opinion, more divine and more worthy of admiration than those who always act by calculation. They are not aware that one of the two things deserves praise and the other only congratulation, the latter being common to ordinary men, whereas what is praiseworthy belongs alone to men of sound judgment and mental ability, whom we should consider to be the most divine and most beloved by the gods. To me it seems that the character and principles of Scipio much resembled those of Lycurgus, the Lacedaemonian legislator. For neither must we suppose that Lycurgus drew up the constitution of Sparta under the influence of superstition and solely prompted by the Pythia, nor that Scipio won such an empire for his country by following the suggestion of dreams and omens. But since both of them

[9] P. attacks the popular opinion that Scipio owed his successes to chance; he insists time and again that he gained them by proper calculation, but that he let people believe that he enjoyed divine favor. See, however, n. on 40.5.

ὁρῶντες ἑκάτεροι τοὺς πολλοὺς τῶν ἀνθρώπων οὔτε
⟨τὰ⟩ παράδοξα προσδεχομένους ῥᾳδίως οὔτε τοῖς
δεινοῖς τολμῶντας παραβάλλεσθαι χωρὶς τῆς ἐκ τῶν
11 θεῶν ἐλπίδος, Λυκοῦργος μὲν αἰεὶ προσλαμβανόμενος
ταῖς ἰδίαις ἐπιβολαῖς τὴν ἐκ τῆς Πυθίας φήμην εὐ-
παραδεκτοτέρας καὶ πιστοτέρας ἐποίει τὰς ἰδίας ἐπι-
12 νοίας, Πόπλιος δὲ παραπλησίως ἐνεργαζόμενος αἰεὶ
δόξας τοῖς πολλοῖς ὡς μετά τινος θείας ἐπιπνοίας
ποιούμενος τὰς ἐπιβολάς, εὐθαρσεστέρους καὶ προθυμοτέρους κατεσκεύαζε τοὺς ὑποταττομένους πρὸς τὰ
13 δεινὰ τῶν ἔργων. ὅτι δ' ἕκαστα μετὰ λογισμοῦ καὶ
προνοίας ἔπραττε, καὶ διότι πάντα κατὰ λόγον ἐξ-
έβαινε τὰ τέλη τῶν πράξεων αὐτῷ, δῆλον ἔσται διὰ
τῶν λέγεσθαι μελλόντων.

3. Ἐκεῖνος γὰρ ὅτι μὲν ἦν εὐεργετικὸς καὶ μεγα-
λόψυχος ὁμολογεῖται, διότι δ' ἀγχίνους καὶ νήπτης
καὶ τῇ διανοίᾳ περὶ τὸ προτεθὲν ἐντεταμένος, οὐθεὶς
ἂν συγχωρήσειε πλὴν τῶν συμβεβιωκότων καὶ τεθε-
2 αμένων ὑπ' αὐγὰς αὐτοῦ τὴν φύσιν. ὧν εἷς ἦν Γάιος
Λαίλιος, ἀπὸ νέου μετεσχηκὼς αὐτῷ παντὸς ἔργου καὶ
λόγου μέχρι τελευτῆς, ὁ ταύτην περὶ αὐτοῦ τὴν δόξαν
ἡμῖν ἐνεργασάμενος διὰ τὸ δοκεῖν εἰκότα λέγειν καὶ
3 σύμφωνα τοῖς ὑπ' ἐκείνου πεπραγμένοις. ἔφη γὰρ
πρώτην γεγονέναι Ποπλίου πρᾶξιν ἐπίσημον, καθ' ὃν
καιρὸν ὁ πατὴρ αὐτοῦ τὴν ἱππομαχίαν συνεστήσατο
πρὸς Ἀννίβαν περὶ τὸν Πάδον καλούμενον ποταμόν.

---

[10] Scipio's trusted companion who had been with him in Spain

saw that most men neither readily accept anything unfamiliar to them, nor venture on great risks without the hope of divine help, Lycurgus made his own scheme more acceptable and more easily believed in by invoking the oracles of the Pythia in support of projects due to himself, while Scipio similarly made the men under his command more sanguine and more ready to face perilous enterprises by instilling into them the belief that his projects were divinely inspired. That everything he did was done with calculation and foresight, and that all his enterprises fell out as he had reckoned, will be clear from what I am about to say.

3. It is generally agreed that Scipio was beneficent and magnanimous, but that he was also shrewd and discreet with a mind always concentrated on the object he had in view would be conceded by none except those who associated with him and to whom his character stood clearly revealed. One of these was Gaius Laelius,[10] who from his youth up to the end had participated in his every word and deed, and who has produced the above impression upon myself, as his account seems both probable on the face of it and in accordance with the actual performances of Scipio. For he tells us that Scipio first distinguished himself on the occasion of the cavalry engagement[11] between his father and Hannibal in the neighborhood of the Po.[12] He was at

in 209 and close to him until Scipio's death. *RE* Laelius 400–404 (F. Münzer). For other likely or possible sources see WC 2.193–196.   [11] The battle of Ticinus, 3.65.1–11. The story that Scipio there saved his father's life is dismissed as wrong by Münzer, *RE* Laelius 400 ("erwiesenermaßen unrichtig"), but defended by WC 2.199.   [12] Battle of the Ticino.

4 τότε γάρ, ὡς ἔοικεν, ἑπτακαιδέκατον ἔτος ἔχων καὶ
πρῶτον εἰς ὕπαιθρον ἐξεληλυθώς, συστήσαντος αὐτῷ
τοῦ πατρὸς διαφερόντων ἱππέων οὐλαμὸν ἀσφαλείας
χάριν, συνθεασάμενος ἐν τῷ κινδύνῳ τὸν πατέρα περι-
ειλημμένον ὑπὸ τῶν πολεμίων μετὰ δυεῖν ἢ τριῶν
ἱππέων καὶ τετρωμένον ἐπισφαλῶς, τὰς μὲν ἀρχὰς
ἐπεβάλετο παρακαλεῖν τοὺς μεθ' αὑτοῦ βοηθῆσαι τῷ
5 πατρί, τῶν δ' ἐπὶ ποσὸν κατορρωδούντων διὰ τὸ πλῆθος τῶν περιεστώτων πολεμίων, αὐτὸς εἰσελάσαι
παραβόλως δοκεῖ καὶ τολμηρῶς εἰς τοὺς περικεχυ-
6 μένους. μετὰ δὲ ταῦτα καὶ τῶν ἄλλων ἀναγκασθέντων
ἐμβαλεῖν οἱ μὲν πολέμιοι καταπλαγέντες διέστησαν,
ὁ δὲ Πόπλιος ἀνελπίστως σωθεὶς πρῶτος αὐτὸς τὸν
7 υἱὸν σωτῆρα προσεφώνησε πάντων ἀκουόντων. περι-
γενομένης δ' αὐτῷ τῆς ἐπ' ἀνδρείᾳ φήμης ὁμολογουμένης διὰ τὴν προειρημένην χρείαν, λοιπὸν ἤδη
σπανίως αὐτὸν ἐδίδου κατὰ τοὺς ὕστερον καιροὺς εἰς
τοὺς κατ' ἰδίαν κινδύνους, ὅτ' εἰς αὐτὸν ἀναρτηθεῖεν
ὑπὸ τῆς πατρίδος αἱ τῶν ὅλων ἐλπίδες· ὅπερ ἴδιόν
ἐστιν οὐ τῇ τύχῃ πιστεύοντος, ἀλλὰ νοῦν ἔχοντος
ἡγεμόνος.

4. Μετὰ δὲ ταῦτα, πρεσβύτερον ἔχων ἀδελφὸν
Λεύκιον, καὶ τούτου προσπορευομένου πρὸς τὴν ἀγο-
ρανομίαν, ἣν σχεδὸν ἐπιφανεστάτην ἀρχὴν εἶναι
2 συμβαίνει τῶν νέων παρὰ Ῥωμαίοις, ἔθους δ' ὄντος
δύο πατρικίους καθίστασθαι, τότε δὲ καὶ πλειόνων
προσπορευομένων, ἐκ πολλοῦ μὲν οὐκ ἐτόλμα μετα-
3 πορεύεσθαι τὴν αὐτὴν ἀρχὴν τἀδελφῷ· συνεγγιζού-

the time seventeen years of age, this being his first campaign, and his father had placed him in command of a picked troop of horse in order to ensure his safety, but when he caught sight of his father in the battle, surrounded by the enemy and escorted only by two or three horsemen and dangerously wounded, he at first endeavored to urge those with him to go to the rescue, but when they hung back for a time owing to the large numbers of the enemy round them, he is said with reckless daring to have charged the encircling force alone. Upon the rest being now forced to attack, the enemy were terror-struck and broke up, and Publius Scipio, thus unexpectedly delivered, was the first to salute his son in the hearing of all as his preserver. Having by this service gained a universally acknowledged reputation for bravery, later he rarely exposed his person in battle,[13] when his country reposed her hopes of success on him.—conduct characteristic not of a commander who relies on luck, but on one gifted with intelligence.

4. After this his elder brother Lucius was a candidate for the aedileship,[14] which is almost the highest office at Rome open to young men, it being the custom to elect two patricians; but there being on this occasion several patrician candidates, Publius Scipio for long did not venture to stand for the same office as his brother. But on the ap-

212 B.C.

---

[13] See 13.1 for the way he was protected in battle.

[14] The story (4.1–5.8) is full of inaccuracies and therefore cannot come from Laelius: Lucius was the younger, not the elder, of the brothers; Publius alone was aedile in 213 (not in 217). It is rather odd that P. found the story worth telling.

σης δὲ τῆς καταστάσεως, λογιζόμενος ἐκ τῆς τοῦ
πλήθους φορᾶς οὐκ εὐμαρῶς τὸν ἀδελφὸν ἐφιξόμενον
τῆς ἀρχῆς, τὴν δὲ πρὸς αὐτὸν εὔνοιαν τοῦ δήμου
θεωρῶν μεγάλην ὑπάρχουσαν, καὶ μόνως οὕτως ὑπο-
λαμβάνων κἀκεῖνον καθίξεσθαι τῆς προθέσεως, εἰ
συμφρονήσαντες ἅμα ποιήσαιντο τὴν ἐπιβολήν, ἦλ-
4 θεν ἐπί τινα τοιαύτην ἔννοιαν. θεωρῶν γὰρ τὴν μητέρα
περιπορευομένην τοὺς νεὼς καὶ θύουσαν τοῖς θεοῖς
ὑπὲρ τἀδελφοῦ καὶ καθόλου μεγάλην προσδοκίαν
5 ἔχουσαν ὑπὲρ τοῦ μέλλοντος, ἧς μόνης ἔμελεν αὐτῷ—
τὸν μὲν γὰρ πατέρα τότε πλεῖν συνέβαινεν εἰς Ἰβηρίαν στρατηγὸν καθεσταμένον ἐπὶ τὰς προειρημένας
πράξεις—οὐ μὴν ἀλλ' ἔφη πρὸς αὐτὴν ὄνειρον τεθεω-
6 ρηκέναι δὶς ἤδη τὸν αὐτόν. δοκεῖν γὰρ ἅμα τἀδελφῷ
καθεσταμένος ἀγορανόμος ἀναβαίνειν ἀπὸ τῆς ἀγορᾶς ὡς ἐπὶ τὴν οἰκίαν, ἐκείνην δὲ συναντᾶν αὐτοῖς εἰς
7 τὰς θύρας καὶ περιπτύξασαν ἀσπάσασθαι. τῆς δὲ
παθούσης τὸ γυναικεῖον πάθος καί τι προσεπι-
φθεγξαμένης "Εἰ γὰρ ἐμοὶ ταύτην ἰδεῖν γένοιτο τὴν
8 ἡμέραν" "Βούλει" φησί "μῆτερ, πεῖραν λάβωμεν;" τῆς
δὲ συγκαταθεμένης, ὡς οὐ τολμήσοντος αὐτοῦ, πρὸς
δὲ τὸν καιρὸν οἱονεὶ προσπαίζοντος—καὶ γὰρ ἦν
κομιδῇ νέος—ἠξίου τήβενναν αὐτῷ λαμπρὰν εὐθέως
9 ἑτοιμάσαι· τοῦτο γὰρ ἔθος ἐστὶ τοῖς τὰς ἀρχὰς μετα-
πορευομένοις.

5. καὶ τῇ μὲν οὐδ' ἐν νῷ τὸ ῥηθὲν ἦν, ὁ δὲ λαβὼν
πρῶτον λαμπρὰν ἐσθῆτα κοιμωμένης ἔτι τῆς μητρὸς
2 παρῆν εἰς τὴν ἀγοράν. τοῦ δὲ πλήθους καὶ διὰ τὸ

proach of the election, judging from the disposition of the
people that his brother had a poor chance of being elected,
and seeing that he himself was exceedingly popular, he
came to the conclusion that the only means by which his
brother would attain his object would be by their coming
to an agreement and both of them making the attempt, and
so he hit on the following plan. Seeing that his mother was
visiting the different temples and sacrificing to the gods on
behalf of his brother and generally exhibiting great concern about the result—he had only to concern himself with
her, his father having left for Spain, where he had been appointed to the command in the campaign I have described
—he, as a fact, told her that he had twice had the same
dream. He had dreamed that both he and his brother had
been elected to the aedileship and were going up from the
forum to their house, when she met them at the door and
fell on their necks and kissed them. She was affected by
this, as a woman would be, and exclaimed, "Would I might
see that day" or something similar. "Then would you like us
to try, mother?" he said. Upon her consenting, as she never
dreamed he would venture on it, but thought it was merely
a casual joke—for he was exceedingly young—he begged
her to get a white toga[15] ready for him at once, this being
the dress that candidates are in the habit of wearing. What
she had said had entirely gone out of her head,

5. and Scipio waiting until he received the white toga
appeared in the forum while his mother was still asleep.
The people, owing to the unexpectedness of the sight and

---

[15] The *toga candida* of Romans who were running for office.
The explanation has Greek readers in mind.

παράδοξον καὶ διὰ τὴν προϋπάρχουσαν εὔνοιαν ἐκ-
πληκτικῶς αὐτὸν ἀποδεξαμένου, καὶ μετὰ ταῦτα προ-
ελθόντος εἰς τὸν ἀποδεδειγμένον τόπον καὶ στάντος
3 παρὰ τὸν ἀδελφόν, οὐ μόνον τῷ Ποπλίῳ περιέθεσαν οἱ
πολλοὶ τὴν ἀρχήν, ἀλλὰ καὶ τἀδελφῷ δι' ἐκεῖνον, καὶ
παρῆσαν ἐπὶ τὴν οἰκίαν ἀμφότεροι γεγονότες ἀγο-
4 ρανόμοι. τῇ δὲ μητρὶ τοῦ πράγματος ἄφνω προσπεσόντος, περιχαρὴς οὖσα πρὸς τὰς θύρας ἀπήντα καὶ
5 μετὰ παραστάσεως ἠσπάζετο τοὺς νεανίσκους, ὥστε
τὸν Πόπλιον ἐκ τοῦ συμβαίνοντος δοκεῖν πᾶσι τοῖς
προακηκοόσι τῶν ἐνυπνίων μὴ μόνον κατὰ τὸν ὕπνον,
ἔτι ⟨δὲ⟩ μᾶλλον ὕπαρ καὶ μεθ' ἡμέραν διαλέγεσθαι
6 τοῖς θεοῖς. ὧν οὐδὲν ἦν ἐνύπνιον, ἀλλ' ὑπάρχων εὐεργετικὸς καὶ μεγαλόδωρος καὶ προσφιλὴς κατὰ τὴν
ἀπάντησιν συνελογίσατο τὴν τοῦ πλήθους πρὸς αὐ-
7 τὸν εὔνοιαν. λοιπὸν πρός τε τὸν τοῦ δήμου καὶ τὸν
τῆς μητρὸς καιρὸν ἁρμοσάμενος εὐστόχως οὐ μόνον
καθίκετο τῆς προθέσεως, ἀλλὰ καὶ μετά τινος ἐδόκει
8 θείας ἐπιπνοίας αὐτὸ πράττειν. οἱ γὰρ μὴ δυνάμενοι
τοὺς καιροὺς μηδὲ τὰς αἰτίας καὶ διαθέσεις ἑκάστων
ἀκριβῶς συνθεωρεῖν, ἢ διὰ φαυλότητα φύσεως ἢ δι'
ἀπειρίαν καὶ ῥᾳθυμίαν, εἰς θεοὺς καὶ τύχας ἀναφέρουσι τὰς αἰτίας τῶν δι' ἀγχίνοιαν ἐκ λογισμοῦ
⟨καὶ⟩ προνοίας ἐπιτελουμένων.
9 Ταῦτα μὲν οὖν εἰρήσθω μοι χάριν τῶν ἀκουόντων,
ἵνα μὴ συγκαταφερόμενοι ψευδῶς τῇ καθωμιλημένῃ
δόξῃ περὶ αὐτοῦ παραπέμπωσι τὰ σεμνότατα καὶ
κάλλιστα τἀνδρός, λέγω δὲ τὴν ἐπιδεξιότητα καὶ

owing to his previous popularity, received him with enthu-
siastic surprise, and afterward when he went on to the sta-
tion appointed for candidates and stood by his brother they
not only conferred the office on Publius but on his brother
too for his sake, and both appeared at their house elected
aediles. When the news suddenly reached his mother's
ears, she met them overjoyed at the door and embraced
the young men with deep emotion, so that from this circumstance all who had heard of the dreams believed that
Publius communed with the gods not only in his sleep, but
still more in reality and by day. Now it was not a matter of a
dream at all, but as he was kind and munificent and agreeable in his address he reckoned on his popularity with the
people, and so by cleverly adapting his action to the actual
sentiment of the people and of his mother he not only attained his object but was believed to have acted under a
sort of divine inspiration. For those who are incapable of
taking an accurate view of opportunities, causes, and dispositions, either from lack of natural ability or from inexperience and indolence, attribute to the gods and to fortune the causes of what is accomplished by shrewdness
and with calculation and foresight.

I have made these observations for the sake of my readers, that they may not by falsely accepting the generally
received opinion of Scipio neglect to notice his finest qualities and those most worthy of respect, I mean his clev-

10 φιλοπονίαν. ἔτι δὲ μᾶλλον ἔσται τοῦτο συμφανὲς ἐπ'
αὐτῶν τῶν πράξεων.

6. Οὐ μὴν ἀλλὰ τότε συνηθροισμένων τῶν δυνάμεων παρεκάλει μὴ καταπεπλῆχθαι τὴν προγεγενη-

2 μένην περιπέτειαν· οὐ γὰρ ταῖς ἀρεταῖς ἡττῆσθαι
Ῥωμαίους ὑπὸ Καρχηδονίων οὐδέποτε, τῇ δὲ προδο-
σίᾳ τῇ Κελτιβήρων καὶ τῇ προπετείᾳ, διακλεισθέντων
τῶν στρατηγῶν ἀπ' ἀλλήλων διὰ τὸ πιστεῦσαι τῇ

3 συμμαχίᾳ τῶν εἰρημένων. ὧν ἑκάτερα νῦν ἔφη περὶ
τοὺς πολεμίους ὑπάρχειν· χωρὶς γὰρ ἀπ' ἀλλήλων
πολὺ διεσπασμένους στρατοπεδεύειν, τοῖς τε συμμάχοις ὑβριστικῶς χρωμένους ἅπαντας ἀπηλλοτριω-

4 κέναι καὶ πολεμίους αὐτοῖς παρεσκευακέναι. διὸ καὶ
τοὺς μὲν ἤδη διαπέμπεσθαι πρὸς σφᾶς, τοὺς δὲ λοιπούς, ὡς ἂν τάχιστα θαρρήσωσι καὶ διαβάντας ἴδωσι
τὸν ποταμόν, ἀσμένως ἥξειν, οὐχ οὕτως εὐνοοῦντας
σφίσι, τὸ δὲ πλεῖον ἀμύνεσθαι σπουδάζοντας τὴν

5 Καρχηδονίων εἰς αὐτοὺς ἀσέλγειαν, τὸ δὲ μέγιστον,
στασιάζοντας πρὸς ἀλλήλους τοὺς τῶν ὑπεναντίων
ἡγεμόνας ἄθρους διαμάχεσθαι πρὸς αὐτοὺς οὐ θελή-
σειν, κατὰ μέρος δὲ κινδυνεύοντας εὐχειρώτους ὑπάρ-

6 χειν. διὸ βλέποντας εἰς ταῦτα παρεκάλει περαιοῦσθαι
τὸν ποταμὸν εὐθαρσῶς· περὶ δὲ τῶν ἑξῆς ἀνεδέχετο

7 μελήσειν αὐτῷ καὶ τοῖς ἄλλοις ἡγεμόσι. ταῦτα δ'
εἰπὼν τρισχιλίους μὲν ἔχοντα πεζοὺς καὶ πεντακοσίους ἱππεῖς Μάρκον ἀπέλειπε τὸν συνάρχοντα περὶ τὴν

erness and laboriousness. This will be still more evident from my account of his actual exploits.

6. To resume my narrative—on this occasion he assembled his soldiers and exhorted them not to be cast down by their recent reverse.[16] The Romans, he said, were never beaten by the Carthaginians owing to the superior courage of the latter, but it was all due to the treachery of the Celtiberians and to rashness, the generals having been cut off from each other owing to their trust in the alliance of that people. "Both of these disadvantages," he said, "now affect the enemy; for they are encamped at a long distance apart, and by their tyrannical treatment of their allies they have estranged them all and made them their enemies. So that some of them are already negotiating with us, while the rest, as soon as they have the courage to do it and see that we have crossed the river, will be glad to come in not so much out of affection for us as from eagerness to be avenged on the Carthaginians for their brutal conduct. But the chief point is that the enemy's commanders are on ill terms with each other and will not readily engage us with their united forces, while if they attack us separately it will be easy to overcome them." He therefore begged his soldiers to take all this into consideration and cross the river confidently. After that it would be the business of himself and the other commanders to decide what was next to be done. Having made this speech he left his colleague Marcus Silanus[17] with three thousand foot and five hun-

209
B.C.

---

[16] The catastrophe of Scipio's father and uncle in 211; *MRR* 1.274.　　[17] Marcus Iunius Silanus, sent to Spain with Scipio in 210. The command of both men was extended to 209. *RE* Iunius 1092–1093 (F. Münzer).

διάβασιν ἐφεδρεύσοντα τοῖς ἐντὸς τοῦ ποταμοῦ συμ-
μάχοις· αὐτὸς δὲ τὴν ἄλλην ἐπεραίου δύναμιν, ἄδηλον
8 πᾶσι ποιῶν τὴν αὑτοῦ πρόθεσιν. ἦν γὰρ αὐτῷ κεκρι-
μένον πράττειν ὧν μὲν εἶπε πρὸς τοὺς πολλοὺς μηδέν,
προὔκειτο δὲ πολιορκεῖν ἐξ ἐφόδου τὴν ἐν Ἰβηρίᾳ
9 Καρχηδόνα προσαγορευομένην. ὃ δὴ καὶ πρῶτον ἄν
τις λάβοι καὶ μέγιστον σημεῖον τῆς ὑφ᾽ ἡμῶν ἄρτι
10 ῥηθείσης διαλήψεως. ἔτος γὰρ ἕβδομον ἔχων πρὸς
τοῖς εἴκοσι πρῶτον μὲν ἐπὶ πράξεις αὑτὸν ἔδωκε
τελέως παρὰ τοῖς πολλοῖς ἀπηλπισμένας διὰ <τὸ>
11 μέγεθος τῶν προγεγονότων ἐλαττωμάτων, δεύτερον
δοὺς αὑτὸν τὰ μὲν κοινὰ καὶ προφαινόμενα πᾶσι
παρέλειπε, τὰ δὲ μήτε παρὰ τοῖς πολεμίοις <μήτε
παρὰ τοῖς φίλοις προσδοκηθέντα>, ταῦτ᾽ ἐπενόει καὶ
12 προετίθετο πράττειν. ὧν οὐδὲν ἦν χωρὶς ἐκλογισμῶν
τῶν ἀκριβεστάτων.

7. Ἔτι μὲν γὰρ ἀπὸ τῆς ἀρχῆς ἱστορῶν ἐν τῇ
Ῥώμῃ καὶ πυνθανόμενος ἐπιμελῶς τήν τε προδοσίαν
τῶν Κελτιβήρων καὶ τὸν διαζευγμὸν τῶν ἰδίων στρατοπέδων, καὶ συλλογιζόμενος ὅτι παρὰ τοῦτο συμβαί-
2 νει τοῖς περὶ τὸν πατέρα γενέσθαι τὴν περιπέτειαν, οὐ
κατεπέπληκτο τοὺς Καρχηδονίους οὐδ᾽ ἥττητο τῇ
3 ψυχῇ, καθάπερ οἱ πολλοί. μετὰ δὲ ταῦτα τοὺς ἐντὸς
Ἴβηρος ποταμοῦ συμμάχους ἀκούων μένειν ἐν τῇ
πρὸς αὐτοὺς φιλίᾳ, τοὺς δὲ τῶν Καρχηδονίων ἡγεμόνας στασιάζειν μὲν πρὸς σφᾶς, ὑβρίζειν δὲ τοὺς
ὑποταττομένους, εὐθαρσῶς διέκειτο πρὸς τὴν ἔξοδον,
4 οὐ τῇ τύχῃ πιστεύων, ἀλλὰ τοῖς συλλογισμοῖς. παρα-

dred horse at the ford to watch over the allies on the near
side of the river, and himself began to cross with the rest of
his forces, revealing his plan to no one. The fact was, he
had decided not to do any of the things he had publicly announced, but to invest suddenly the town in Spain to which
they had given the name of Carthage.[18] This we take as the
first and strongest confirmation of the view I have just expressed. He was now but twenty-seven years of age, and
yet he in the first place took in hand a situation pronounced
by most people as desperate owing to the serious nature of
the recent reverses, and secondly in dealing with it he put
aside the measures obvious to anyone and planned out and
decided on a course which neither his enemies <nor his
friends expected>.[19] There was nothing in all this that was
not due to most close calculation.

7. For from the very outset, having learned by careful
inquiries at Rome the facts about the treachery of the
Celtiberians and the separation of the Roman armies, and
reaching the conclusion that his father's defeat was due to
these causes, he was not in terror of the Carthaginians nor
broken in spirit like most people. When subsequently he
heard that the allies on the Roman side of the Ebro remained friendly, and that the Carthaginian commanders
had fallen out with each other and were treating their subjects tyrannically, he felt full confidence in the result of
his expedition, relying not on chance but on inference

[18] New Carthage, founded by Hasdrubal ca. 228.
[19] Reiske's supplement is clearly what the sense of the passage
requires.

γενόμενός γε μὴν εἰς τὴν Ἰβηρίαν, πάντας ἀνακινῶν
καὶ παρ᾽ ἑκάστου πυνθανόμενος τὰ περὶ τοὺς ἐναντίους, ηὕρισκε τὰς μὲν δυνάμεις τῶν Καρχηδονίων εἰς
5   τρία μέρη διῃρημένας· ὧν Μάγωνα μὲν ἐπυνθάνετο
διατρίβειν ἐντὸς Ἡρακλείων στηλῶν ἐν τοῖς Κονίοις
προσαγορευομένοις, Ἀσδρούβαν δὲ τὸν Γέσκωνος
περὶ Τάγου ποταμοῦ στόμα κατὰ τὴν Λυσιτανήν, τὸν
δ᾽ ἕτερον Ἀσδρούβαν πολιορκεῖν τινα πόλιν ἐν τοῖς
Καρπητανοῖς, οὐδένα ⟨δὲ⟩ τῶν προειρημένων ἐλάττω
6   δέχ᾽ ἡμερῶν ὁδὸν ἀπέχειν τῆς Καινῆς πόλεως. νομίζων οὖν, ἐὰν μὲν εἰς μάχην συνιέναι κρίνῃ τοῖς πολεμίοις, τὸ μὲν πρὸς πάντας ἅμα κινδυνεύειν ⟨ἐπισφα-
λὲς εἶναι⟩ τελέως καὶ διὰ τὸ προηττῆσθαι τοὺς πρὸ
αὑτοῦ καὶ διὰ τὸ πολλαπλασίους εἶναι τοὺς ὑπεναν-
7   τίους, ἐὰν δὲ πρὸς ἕνα συμβαλεῖν σπεύδῃς, κἄπειτα
τούτου φυγομαχήσαντος, ἐπιγενομένων δὲ τῶν ἄλλων
δυνάμεων, συγκλεισθῇ που, κατάφοβος ἦν μὴ ταῖς
αὐταῖς Γναΐῳ τῷ θείῳ καὶ Ποπλίῳ τῷ πατρὶ περιπέσῃ
συμφοραῖς.

8. διὸ τοῦτο μὲν τὸ μέρος ἀπεδοκίμασε, πυνθανόμενος δὲ τὴν προειρημένην Καρχηδόνα μεγίστας μὲν
χρείας παρέχεσθαι τοῖς ὑπεναντίοις, μέγιστα δὲ βλάπτειν καὶ κατὰ τὸν ἐνεστῶτα πόλεμον αὐτόν, ἐξῃτάκει
τὰ κατὰ μέρος ὑπὲρ αὐτῆς ἐν τῇ παραχειμασίᾳ ⟨διὰ⟩
2   τῶν εἰδότων. ἀκούων δὲ πρῶτον μὲν ὅτι λιμένας ἔχει
στόλῳ καὶ ναυτικαῖς δυνάμεσι μόνη σχεδὸν τῶν κατὰ
τὴν Ἰβηρίαν, ἅμα δὲ καὶ διότι πρὸς τὸν ἀπὸ τῆς
Λιβύης πλοῦν καὶ πελάγιον δίαρμα λίαν εὐφυῶς κεῖ-

from the facts. On his arrival in Spain he set everyone on
the alert and inquired from everyone about the circumstances of the enemy, and thus learned that the Carthaginian forces were divided into three bodies. Mago,[20] he
heard, was posted on this side of the pillars of Hercules in
the country of the people called Conii; Hasdrubal, son of
Gesco, was in Lusitania near the mouth of the Tagus; and
the other Hasdrubal was besieging a city in the territory of
the Carpetani: none of them being within less than ten
days' march from New Carthage. He thought, then, that if
he decided to engage the enemy it would be extremely
dangerous to risk a battle with all the three at once, both
because his predecessors had been defeated and because
the enemy were greatly superior in numbers, while if he
made a dash at one of the three and upon his declining
an engagement found himself shut in somewhere by the
other hostile forces coming up to help, he feared that he
might meet with a disaster such as befell his uncle and
father.

8. He therefore rejected any such course; and on learning that the above city, New Carthage, was of very great
service to the enemy, and a cause of great damage to himself in the present war, he made detailed inquiries about it
during the winter[21] from people acquainted with it. He
learned in the first place that it stood almost alone among
Spanish cities in possessing harbors fit for a fleet and for
naval forces, and that it was at the same time very favorably
situated for the Carthaginians to make the direct sea cross-

20 Hannibal's brother (the other Hasdrubal): Hannibal's younger brother.
21 Of 210/9.

3 ται τοῖς Καρχηδονίοις, μετὰ δὲ ταῦτα διότι καὶ τὸ τῶν
χρημάτων πλῆθος καὶ τὰς ἀποσκευὰς τῶν στρατοπέδων ἁπάσας ἐν ταύτῃ τῇ πόλει συνέβαινε τοῖς
Καρχηδονίοις ὑπάρχειν, ἔτι δὲ τοὺς ὁμήρους τοὺς ἐξ

4 ὅλης τῆς Ἰβηρίας, τὸ δὲ μέγιστον, ὅτι μάχιμοι μὲν
ἄνδρες εἴησαν εἰς χιλίους οἱ τὴν ἄκραν τηροῦντες διὰ
τὸ μηδένα μηδέποτ' ἂν ὑπολαμβάνειν ὅτι κρατούντων
Καρχηδονίων σχεδὸν ἁπάσης Ἰβηρίας ἐπινοήσει τις

5 τὸ παράπαν πολιορκῆσαι ταύτην τὴν πόλιν, τὸ δ'
ἄλλο πλῆθος ὅτι πολὺ μὲν εἴη διαφερόντως ἐν αὐτῇ,
πᾶν δὲ δημιουργικὸν καὶ βάναυσον καὶ θαλαττουργὸν
καὶ πλεῖστον ἀπέχον πολεμικῆς ἐμπειρίας, ὃ κατὰ τῆς
πόλεως ὑπελάμβανεν εἶναι, παραδόξου γενομένης ἐπι-

6 φανείας. καὶ μὴν οὐδὲ τὴν θέσιν τῆς Καρχηδόνος οὐδὲ
τὴν κατασκευὴν οὐδὲ τὴν τῆς περιεχούσης αὐτὴν

7 λίμνης διάθεσιν ἠγνόει, διὰ δέ τινων ἁλιέων τῶν
ἐνειργασμένων τοῖς τόποις ἐξητάκει διότι καθόλου
μέν ἐστι τεναγώδης ἡ λίμνη καὶ βατὴ κατὰ τὸ πλεῖστον, ὡς δ' ἐπὶ τὸ πολὺ καὶ γίνεταί τις αὐτῆς ἀπο-

8 χώρησις καθ' ἡμέραν ἐπὶ δείλην ὀψίαν. ἐξ ὧν συλλογισάμενος ὅτι καθικόμενος μὲν τῆς ἐπιβολῆς οὐ μόνον
βλάψει τοὺς ὑπεναντίους, ἀλλὰ καὶ τοῖς σφετέροις

9 πράγμασι μεγάλην ἐπίδοσιν παρασκευάσει, διαπε-
σὼν δὲ τῆς προθέσεως, ὅτι δύναται σῴζειν τοὺς ὑποταττομένους διὰ τὸ θαλαττοκρατεῖν, ἐὰν ἅπαξ ἀσφα-

10 λίσηται τὴν στρατοπεδείαν—τοῦτο δ' ἦν εὐχερὲς διὰ
τὸ μακρὰν ἀπεσπάσθαι τὰς τῶν ὑπεναντίων δυνά-

134

ing from Africa. Next he heard that the Carthaginians kept the bulk of their money and their baggage[22] in this city, as well as their hostages from the whole of Spain, and, what was of most importance, that the trained soldiers who garrisoned the citadel were only about a thousand in number, because no one dreamed that while the Carthaginians were masters of nearly the whole of Spain it would enter anyone's head to besiege the city, while the remaining population was exceedingly large but composed of craftsmen, artisans, and sailors, men very far from having any military experience. This he considered to be a thing that would tell against the city, if he appeared suddenly before it. Nor was he ignorant of the position and plan of New Carthage and of the nature of the lagoon which surrounded it, but had learned from some fishermen who plied their craft there that the whole lagoon was shallow and in most parts fordable, and that usually the water in it receded every day toward evening.[23] Taking all these facts into consideration he came to the conclusion that if he succeeded in his enterprise he would not only damage the enemy, but would much advance the Roman cause, while in the event of failure he could, since he was master of the sea, place his troops in a position of safety, once he had secured his camp—an easy matter as the forces of the enemy were at so great a distance. Abandoning, therefore, all other proj-

[22] Includes all the persons who follow the army; see n. on 1.66.7.

[23] The ebb did, in fact, occur at various times of the day.

μεις—οὕτως ἀφέμενος τῶν ἄλλων περὶ ταύτην ἐγίνετο
τὴν παρασκευὴν ἐν τῇ παραχειμασίᾳ.

9. καὶ ταύτην ἔχων τὴν ἐπιβολὴν καὶ τὴν ἡλικίαν,
ἣν ἀρτίως εἶπα, πάντας ἀπεκρύψατο χωρὶς Γαΐου
Λαιλίου, μέχρι πάλιν αὐτὸς ἔκρινε φανερὸν ποιεῖν.

2   Τούτοις δὲ τοῖς ἐκλογισμοῖς ὁμολογοῦντες οἱ συγγραφεῖς, ὅταν ἐπὶ τὸ τέλος ἔλθωσι τῆς πράξεως, οὐκ
οἶδ' ὅπως οὐκ εἰς τὸν ἄνδρα καὶ τὴν τούτου πρόνοιαν,
εἰς δὲ τοὺς θεοὺς καὶ τὴν τύχην ἀναφέρουσι τὸ γεγο-
3 νὸς κατόρθωμα, καὶ ταῦτα χωρὶς τῶν εἰκότων καὶ τῆς
τῶν συμβεβιωκότων μαρτυρίας, καὶ διὰ τῆς ἐπιστολῆς τῆς πρὸς Φίλιππον αὐτοῦ τοῦ Ποπλίου σαφῶς
ἐκτεθεικότος ὅτι τούτοις τοῖς ἐκλογισμοῖς χρησάμενος, οἷς ἡμεῖς ἀνώτερον ἐξελογισάμεθα, καθόλου τε
τοῖς ἐν Ἰβηρίᾳ πράγμασιν ἐπιβάλοιτο καὶ κατὰ μέρος τῇ τῆς Καρχηδόνος πολιορκίᾳ.

4   Πλὴν τότε γε τῷ μὲν ἐπὶ τοῦ στόλου Γαΐῳ Λαιλίῳ
δι' ἀπορρήτων ἐντειλάμενος παρήγγειλε πλεῖν ἐπὶ τὴν
5 προειρημένην πόλιν—μόνος γὰρ οὗτος αὐτῷ συνῄδει
6 τὴν ἐπιβολήν, καθάπερ ἀνώτερον εἶπον—αὐτὸς δὲ τὰς
πεζικὰς δυνάμεις ἀναλαβὼν ἐποιεῖτο τὴν πορείαν
μετὰ σπουδῆς. εἶχε δὲ τὸ μὲν τῶν πεζῶν πλῆθος εἰς
7 δισμυρίους καὶ πεντακισχιλίους, ἱππεῖς δ' εἰς δισχιλίους καὶ πεντακοσίους. ἀφικόμενος δ' ἑβδομαῖος κατεστρατοπέδευσε κατὰ τὸ πρὸς ἄρκτους μέρος τῆς
πόλεως, καὶ περιεβάλετο κατὰ μὲν τὴν ἐκτὸς ἐπιφάνειαν τῆς στρατοπεδείας τάφρον καὶ χάρακα δι-
πλοῦν ἐκ θαλάττης εἰς θάλατταν, κατὰ δὲ τὴν πρὸς

ects he spent his time while in winter quarters in preparing for this,

9. and though he had formed such a great project and was only of the age I just stated he concealed the plan from everyone except Gaius Laelius, until the time when he judged it proper to make it public.

Although authors[24] agree that he made these calculations, yet when they come to the accomplishment of his plan, they attribute for some unknown reason the success not to the man and his foresight, but to the gods and to chance, and that in spite of all probability and in spite of the testimony of those who lived with him, and of the fact that Scipio himself in his letter to Philip[25] explained clearly that it was after making the calculations which I have just recited that he undertook all his operations in Spain and particularly the siege of New Carthage.

Be that as it may, he now gave secret orders to Gaius Laelius, who commanded the fleet, to sail to that city—it was Laelius alone, as I above stated, who was aware of the project—while he himself with his land forces marched rapidly against it. He had about twenty-five thousand infantry and two thousand five hundred horse. Arriving on the seventh day[26] he encamped to the north of the city, defending the outer side of his camp by a trench and double palisade reaching from sea to sea, but erecting no defenses

[24] Among them was Silenus of Caleacte in Sicily (Livy 26.49.3); see for him *FGrH* 175. He accompanied Hannibal on his expedition. [25] Written after Scipio and Philip V had met in 190 and formed a personal relationship; F. W. Walbank, *Philip V of Macedon* (Cambridge 1940), 210–211.

[26] Somewhat doubtful given the large distance.

τὴν πόλιν ἁπλῶς οὐδέν. αὐτὴ γὰρ ἡ τοῦ τόπου φύσις
ἱκανὴν ἀσφάλειαν αὐτῷ παρεσκεύαζε.

8 Μέλλοντες δὲ καὶ τὴν πολιορκίαν καὶ τὴν ἅλωσιν
τῆς πόλεως δηλοῦν, ἀναγκαῖον ἡγούμεθ᾽ εἶναι τὸ καὶ
τοὺς παρακειμένους τόπους καὶ τὴν θέσιν αὐτῆς ἐπὶ
ποσὸν ὑποδεῖξαι τοῖς ἀκούουσι.

10. κεῖται μὲν οὖν τῆς Ἰβηρίας κατὰ μέσην τὴν
παραλίαν ἐν κόλπῳ νεύοντι πρὸς ἄνεμον λίβα· οὗ τὸ
μὲν βάθος ἐστὶς ὡς εἴκοσι σταδίων, τὸ δὲ πλάτος ἐν
ταῖς ἀρχαῖς ὡς δέκα· λαμβάνει ⟨δὲ⟩ διάθεσιν λιμένος
2 ὁ πᾶς κόλπος διὰ τοιαύτην αἰτίαν. νῆσος ἐπὶ τοῦ
στόματος αὐτοῦ κεῖται βραχὺν ἐξ ἑκατέρου τοῦ μέ-
3 ρους εἴσπλουν εἰς αὐτὸν ἀπολείπουσα. ταύτης ἀπο-
δεχομένης τὸ πελάγιον κῦμα συμβαίνει τὸν κόλπον
ὅλον εὐδίαν ἴσχειν, πλὴν ἐφ᾽ ὅσον οἱ λίβες καθ᾽
ἑκάτερον τὸν εἴσπλουν παρεισπίπτοντες κλύδωνας
4 ἀποτελοῦσι. τῶν γε μὴν ἄλλων πνευμάτων ἀκλυδώ-
νιστος ὢν τυγχάνει διὰ τὴν περιέχουσαν αὐτὸν ἤπει-
5 ρον. ἐν δὲ τῷ μυχῷ τοῦ κόλπου πρόκειται χερρονη-
σίζον ὄρος, ἐφ᾽ οὗ κεῖσθαι συμβαίνει τὴν πόλιν,
περιεχομένην θαλάττῃ μὲν ἀπ᾽ ἀνατολῶν καὶ μεσημβρίας, ἀπὸ δὲ τῶν δύσεων λίμνη προσεπιλαμβανούσῃ
6 καὶ τοῦ πρὸς ἄρκτον μέρους, ὥστε τὸν λοιπὸν τόπον
μέχρι τῆς ἐπὶ θάτερα θαλάττης, ὃς καὶ συνάπτει τὴν
πόλιν πρὸς τὴν ἤπειρον, μὴ πλέον ὑπάρχειν ἢ δυεῖν
7 σταδίων. ἡ δὲ πόλις αὐτὴ μεσόκοιλός ἐστι· κατὰ δὲ
τὴν ἀπὸ μεσημβρίας πλευρὰν ἐπίπεδον ἔχει τὴν ἀπὸ
θαλάττης πρόσοδον· τὰ δὲ λοιπὰ περιέχεται λόφοις,

at all on the side facing the town, where the nature of the ground sufficiently secured his position.

Now that I am about to narrate the siege and capture of the place, I think it behooves me to make my readers acquainted to some extent with its surroundings and actual position.[27]

10. New Carthage lies half way down the coast of Spain, in a gulf which faces southwest and is about twenty stades long and ten stades broad at the entrance. This gulf serves as a harbor for the following reason. At its mouth lies an island which leaves only a narrow passage on either side, and as this breaks the waves of the sea, the whole gulf is perfectly calm, except that the southwest wind sometimes blows in through both the channels and raises some sea. No other wind, however, disturbs it as it is quite landlocked. In the innermost nook of the gulf a hill in the form of a peninsula juts out, and on this stands the city, surrounded by the sea on the east and south and on the west by a lagoon which extends so far to the north that the remaining space, reaching as far as the sea on the other side and connecting the city with the mainland, is not more than two stades in breadth. The town itself is low in the center, and on its southern side the approach to it from the sea is level. On the other sides it is surrounded by hills, two

[27] The description (through 10.13) is correct with, however, a deviation of ca. 70 degrees, in that Polybius' north is, in fact, east-northeast. See the map in WC 2. 206 (which shows that the deviation is much more than the 45 degrees WC [2. 209] states); U. Kahrstedt, *Geschichte der Karthager* 3 (Berlin 1913), 509, n. 2, gives ca. 70 degrees.

δυσὶ μὲν ὀρεινοῖς καὶ τραχέσιν, ἄλλοις δὲ τρισὶ πολὺ
8   μὲν χθαμαλωτέροις, σπιλώδεσι δὲ καὶ δυσβάτοις· ὧν
ὁ μὲν μέγιστος ἀπὸ τῆς ἀνατολῆς αὐτῇ παράκειται,
προτείνων εἰς θάλατταν, ἐφ' οὗ καθίδρυται νεὼς
9   Ἀσκληπιοῦ. τούτῳ δ' ὁ ἀπὸ τῆς δύσεως ἀντίκειται,
παραπλησίαν θέσιν ἔχων, ἐφ' οὗ καὶ βασίλεια κατ-
εσκεύασται πολυτελῶς, ἅ φασιν Ἀσδρούβαν ποιῆσαι,
10   μοναρχικῆς ὀρεγόμενον ἐξουσίας. αἱ δὲ λοιπαὶ τρεῖς
τῶν ἐλαττόνων βουνῶν ὑπεροχαὶ τὸ πρὸς ἄρκτον
11   αὐτῆς μέρος περιέχουσι. καλεῖται δὲ τῶν τριῶν ὁ μὲν
πρὸς ἀνατολὰς νεύων Ἡφαίστου, τούτῳ δ' ὁ συνεχὴς
Ἀλήτου—δοκεῖ δ' οὗτος εὑρετὴς γενόμενος τῶν ἀργυρείων μετάλλων ἰσοθέων τετευχέναι τιμῶν—ὁ δὲ τρί-
12   τος προσαγορεύεται Κρόνου. συμβαίνει δὲ τὴν λίμνην
τῇ παρακειμένῃ θαλάττῃ σύρρουν γεγονέναι χειρο-
13   ποιήτως χάριν τῶν θαλαττουργῶν. κατὰ δὲ τὴν τοῦ
διείργοντος αὐτὰς χείλους διακοπὴν γέφυρα κατ-
εσκεύασται πρὸς τὸ καὶ τὰ ὑποζύγια καὶ τὰς ἁμάξας
ταύτῃ ποιεῖσθαι τὴν παρακομιδὴν τῶν ἐκ τῆς χώρας
ἀναγκαίων.

11. Τοιαύτης δ' ὑπαρχούσης τῆς διαθέσεως τῶν
τόπων, ἀσφαλίζεσθαι συνέβαινε τοῖς Ῥωμαίοις τὴν
στρατοπεδείαν κατὰ τὴν ἐντὸς ἐπιφάνειαν ἀκατασκεύ-
2   ως ὑπό τε τῆς λίμνης καὶ τῆς ἐπὶ θάτερα θαλάττης. τὸ
δὲ μεταξὺ τούτων διάστημα τὸ συνάπτον τὴν πόλιν
πρὸς τὴν ἤπειρον ἀχαράκωτον εἴασε, κατὰ μέσην
3   ὑπάρχον τὴν αὐτοῦ στρατοπεδείαν, εἴτε καὶ καταπλήξεως χάριν εἴτε καὶ πρὸς τὴν ἐπιβολὴν ἁρμοζόμενος,

of them lofty and rugged, and the other three, though much lower, yet craggy and difficult of access. The biggest of these hills lies on the east side of the town and juts out into the sea, and on it is built a temple of Eshmun.[28] The second is opposite it on the western side in a similar position, and on it stands a magnificent palace said to have been built by Hasdrubal when he aspired to royal power. The three other smaller eminences are to the north of the city, the most easterly being called the hill of Kousor, the next one the hill of Aletes, who is said to have received divine honors for his discovery of the silver mines, while the third is known as the hill of Baal Hammon.[29] An artificial communication has been opened between the lagoon and the neighboring sea for the convenience of shipping, and over the channel thus cut through the tongue of land that separates lagoon and sea a bridge has been built for the passage of beasts of burden and carts bringing in supplies from the country.

11. Such being the situation of the place, the Roman camp was protected on its inner side without any fortification by the lagoon and by the outer sea. The intervening space, which connects the city with the mainland and which lay in the middle of his camp, was also left untrenched by Scipio, either to intimidate the enemy or to adapt it to his own particular purpose, so that there should

[28] Since the Greek text gives the names of Greek gods (Asclepius, Hephaestus, Cronus) for their Semitic counterparts, it will not do to replace the Greek names with their Roman equivalents.

[29] These place names were probably Punic; attempts to identify their Punic equivalents are hypothetical. For their topographical locations see the map in WC 2.206.

ὅπως ἀνεμποδίστους ἔχῃ καὶ τὰς ἐξαγωγὰς καὶ τὰς
4 ἀναχωρήσεις εἰς τὴν παρεμβολήν. ὁ δὲ περίβολος τῆς
πόλεως οὐ πλεῖον εἴκοσι σταδίων ὑπῆρχε τὸ πρότερον—καίτοι γ᾽ οὐκ ἀγνοῶ διότι πολλοῖς εἴρηται τετ-
ταράκοντα· τὸ δ᾽ ἐστὶ ψεῦδος. οὐ γὰρ ἐξ ἀκοῆς ἡμεῖς,
ἀλλ᾽ αὐτόπται γεγονότες μετ᾽ ἐπιστάσεως ἀποφαινόμεθα—νῦν δὲ καὶ μᾶλλον ἔτι συνῄρηται.

5   Πλὴν ὅ γε Πόπλιος, συνάψαντος καὶ τοῦ στόλου
πρὸς τὸν δέοντα καιρόν, ἐπεβάλετο συναθροίσας τὰ
πλήθη παρακαλεῖν, οὐχ ἑτέροις τισὶ χρώμενος ἀπολογισμοῖς, ἀλλ᾽ οἷς ἐτύγχανε πεπεικὼς αὑτόν, ὑπὲρ
ὧν ἡμεῖς τὸν κατὰ μέρος ἄρτι πεποιήμεθα λόγον.
6 ἀποδείξας δὲ δυνατὴν οὖσαν τὴν ἐπιβολήν, καὶ συγ-
κεφαλαιωσάμενος τὴν ἐκ τοῦ κατορθώματος ἐλάττωσιν ⟨τῶν ὑπεναντίων, αὔξησιν⟩ δὲ τῶν σφετέρων πραγμάτων, λοιπὸν χρυσοῦς στεφάνους ἐπηγγείλατο τοῖς
πρώτοις ἐπὶ τὸ τεῖχος ἀναβᾶσι καὶ τὰς εἰθισμένας
7 δωρεὰς τοῖς ἐπιφανῶς ἀνδραγαθήσασι· τὸ δὲ τελευταῖον ἐξ ἀρχῆς ἔφη τὴν ἐπιβολὴν αὐτῷ ταύτην ὑπο-
δεδειχέναι τὸν Ποσειδῶνα παραστάντα κατὰ τὸν
ὕπνον, καὶ φάναι συνεργήσειν ἐπιφανῶς κατ᾽ αὐτὸν
τὸν τῆς πράξεως καιρὸν οὕτως ὥστε παντὶ τῷ στρατο-
8 πέδῳ τὴν ἐξ αὐτοῦ χρείαν ἐναργῆ γενέσθαι. τῶν δὲ
κατὰ τὴν παράκλησιν λόγων ἅμα μὲν ἀπολογισμοῖς
ἀκριβέσι μεμιγμένων, ἅμα δ᾽ ἐπαγγελίαις χρυσῶν
στεφάνων, ἐπὶ δὲ πᾶσι τούτοις θεοῦ προνοίᾳ, τελέως
μεγάλην ὁρμὴν καὶ προθυμίαν παρίστασθαι συνέβαινε τοῖς νεανίσκοις.

142

be no impediment to sorties from his camp and subsequent retirement into it. The circumference of the city was formerly not more than twenty stades[30]—I am quite aware that many state it to be forty, but this is not true, as I speak not from report but from my own careful observation—and at the present day it has still further shrunk.

Scipio, then, when the fleet arrived in due time, decided to call a meeting of his troops and address them, using no other arguments than those which had carried conviction to himself and which I have above stated in detail. After proving to them that the project was feasible, and pointing out briefly what loss its success would entail on the enemy and what an advantage it would be to themselves, he went on to promise gold crowns to those who should be the first to mount the wall and the usual rewards to such as displayed conspicuous courage. Finally he told them that it was Neptune[31] who had first suggested this plan to him, appearing to him in his sleep, and promising that when the time for the action came he would render such conspicuous aid that his intervention would be manifest to the whole army. The combination in this speech of accurate calculation, of the promise of gold crowns, and therewithal of confidence in the help of Providence created great enthusiasm and ardor among the soldiers.

[30] About 3800 meters and approximately right. P. has visited the scene, in 151 or later, and is a witness for this detail, while the rest of the description seems to come from a written source.

[31] Scipio predicts the god's help (creating the ebb), since he knows from reports and observation what will happen. See n. on 2.3.

12. Τῇ δ' ἐπαύριον κατὰ μὲν τοὺς ἐκ τῆς θαλάττης τόπους περιστήσας ναῦς παντοδαποῖς βέλεσιν ἐξηρτυμένας καὶ δοὺς τὴν ἐπιτροπὴν Γαΐῳ, κατὰ δὲ γῆν τοὺς εὐρωστοτάτους τῶν ἀνδρῶν εἰς δισχιλίους ὁμόσε τοῖς κλιμακοφόροις ἐπιστήσας, ἐνήρχετο τῆς πολιορ-

2 κίας κατὰ τρίτην ὥραν. ὁ δὲ Μάγων ὁ τεταγμένος ἐπὶ τῆς πόλεως τὸ μὲν τῶν χιλίων σύνταγμα διελὼν τοὺς μὲν ἡμίσεις ἐπὶ τῆς ἄκρας ἀπέλιπε, τοὺς δ' ἄλλους ἐπὶ

3 τοῦ πρὸς ἀνατολὰς λόφου παρενέβαλε· τῶν δὲ λοιπῶν τοὺς εὐρωστοτάτους περὶ δισχιλίους κατεσκευακὼς τοῖς ὑπάρχουσι κατὰ τὴν πόλιν ὅπλοις ἐπέστησε κατὰ τὴν πύλην τὴν φέρουσαν ἐπὶ τὸν ἰσθμὸν καὶ τὴν τῶν πολεμίων στρατοπεδείαν· τοῖς δὲ λοιποῖς παρήγγειλε βοηθεῖν κατὰ δύναμιν πρὸς πάντα τὰ μέρη τοῦ τεί-

4 χους. ἅμα δὲ τῷ τὸν Πόπλιον ταῖς σάλπιγξι διασημῆναι [καὶ] τὸν καιρὸν τῆς προσβολῆς, ἐξαφίησι τοὺς καθωπλισμένους ὁ Μάγων διὰ τῆς πύλης, πεπεισμένος ὅτι καταπλήξεται τοὺς ὑπεναντίους καὶ τὸ

5 παράπαν ἀφελεῖται τὴν ἐπιβολὴν αὐτῶν. προσπεσόντων δὲ τούτων ἐρρωμένως τοῖς ἐκ τοῦ στρατοπέδου κατὰ τὸν ἰσθμὸν παρατεταγμένοις ἐγίνετο μάχη λαμπρὰ καὶ παρακελευσμὸς ἐξ ἀμφοῖν ἐναγώνιος, τῶν μὲν ἐκ τοῦ στρατοπέδου, τῶν δ' ἐκ τῆς πόλεως τοῖς

6 ἰδίοις ἑκατέρων ἐπιβοώντων. τῆς δὲ διὰ τῶν βοηθούντων ἐπικουρίας οὐχ ὁμοίας ὑπαρχούσης διὰ τὸ τοῖς μὲν Καρχηδονίοις διὰ μιᾶς πύλης καὶ σχεδὸν ἀπὸ δυεῖν σταδίοιν γίνεσθαι τὴν παρουσίαν, τοῖς δὲ Ῥωμαίοις ἐκ χειρὸς καὶ κατὰ πολὺν τόπον, ἄνισος ἦν

12. Next day, encircling the city from the sea by ships furnished with all kinds of missiles under the command of Laelius, and sending forward on the land side two thousand of his strongest men together with the ladder bearers, he began the assault at about the third hour. Mago, who was in command of the place, divided his regiment of a thousand men into two, leaving half of them on the citadel and stationing the others on the eastern hill. As for the rest, he armed two thousand of the strongest with such arms as were to be found in the town, and posted them near the gate leading to the isthmus and the enemy's camp: the others he ordered to do their best to defend the whole of the wall. As soon as Scipio had given the signal for the assault by bugle, Mago sent the armed citizens out through the gate, feeling sure of striking terror into the enemy and entirely defeating their design. They delivered a vigorous assault on the Romans who had issued from the camp and were now drawn up on the isthmus, and a sharp engagement ensued, accompanied by vehement shouts of encouragement from both sides, those in the camp and those in the town respectively cheering on their own men. But as the assistance sent to either side was not equal, the Carthaginians arriving through a single gate and from a distance of nearly two stades and the Romans from close by and from several points, the battle for this reason was an un-

7 ἡ μάχη παρὰ ταύτην τὴν αἰτίαν. ὁ γὰρ Πόπλιος ἑκὼν
ἐπέστησε τοὺς αὑτοῦ παρ' αὐτὴν τὴν στρατοπεδείαν
χάριν τοῦ προκαλέσασθαι τοὺς πολεμίους πορρωτάτω, σαφῶς γινώσκων, ἐὰν διαφθείρῃ τούτους, ὄντας
οἷον εἰ στόμα τοῦ κατὰ τὴν πόλιν πλήθους, ὅτι δια-
τραπήσεται τὰ ὅλα καὶ τὴν πύλην οὐκέτι τῶν ἔνδον
8 οὐδεὶς ἐξιέναι θαρρήσει. οὐ μὴν ἀλλ' ἕως μέν τινος
ἐφάμιλλον συνέβαινε γίνεσθαι τὴν μάχην, ὡς ἐξ
ἀμφοῖν κατ' ἐκλογὴν τῶν ἀρίστων ἀνδρῶν προκεκρι-
μένων· τέλος δ' ἐξωθούμενοι τῷ βάρει διὰ τοὺς ἐκ τῆς
παρεμβολῆς προσγινομένους ἐτράπησαν οἱ παρὰ τῶν
9 Καρχηδονίων, καὶ πολλοὶ μὲν αὐτῶν ἐν τῷ τῆς μάχης
καιρῷ διεφθάρησαν καὶ κατὰ τὴν ἀποχώρησιν, οἱ δὲ
πλείους ἐν τῷ παραπίπτειν εἰς τὴν πύλην ὑφ' αὑτῶν
10 ἠλοήθησαν. οὗ συμβαίνοντος ὁ κατὰ τὴν πόλιν ὄχλος
οὕτως ἐπτοήθη πᾶς ὥστε καὶ τοὺς ἀπὸ τῶν τειχῶν
11 φεύγειν. παρ' ὀλίγον μὲν οὖν ἦλθον οἱ Ῥωμαῖοι τοῦ
συνεισπεσεῖν τότε μετὰ τῶν φευγόντων· οὐ μὴν ἀλλὰ
τάς γε κλίμακας τῷ τείχει μετ' ἀσφαλείας προσήρει-
σαν.

13. Ὁ δὲ Πόπλιος ἐδίδου μὲν αὑτὸν εἰς τὸν κίν-
2 δυνον, ἐποίει δὲ τοῦτο κατὰ δύναμιν ἀσφαλῶς· εἶχε
γὰρ μεθ' αὑτοῦ τρεῖς ἄνδρας θυρεοφοροῦντας, οἳ
παρατιθέντες τοὺς θυρεοὺς καὶ τὴν ἀπὸ τοῦ τείχους
ἐπιφάνειαν σκεπάζοντες ἀσφάλειαν αὐτῷ παρεσκεύ-
3 αζον. διὸ παρὰ τὰ πλάγια καὶ τοὺς ὑπερδεξίους
τόπους ἐπιπαριὼν μεγάλα συνεβάλλετο πρὸς τὴν
4 χρείαν· ἅμα μὲν γὰρ ἑώρα τὸ γινόμενον, ἅμα δ' αὐτὸς

equal one. For Scipio had purposely posted his men close to the camp itself in order to entice the enemy as far out as possible, well knowing that if he destroyed those who were so to speak the steel edge of the population of the town he would cause universal dejection, and none of those inside would venture out of the gate. However, for some time the battle was hotly contested, as both sides had picked out their best men. But finally, as reinforcements continued to come up from the camp, the Carthaginians were forced back, by sheer weight, and took to flight, many of them falling in the actual battle or in the retreat but the greater number being trodden down by each other in entering the gate. When this took place the city people were thrown into such panic that even the defenders of the walls fled. The Romans very nearly succeeded in entering together with the fugitives, and at any rate set up their scaling-ladders in full security.

13. Scipio took part in the battle, but consulted his safety as far as possible; for he had with him three men carrying large shields, who holding these close covered the surface exposed to the wall and thus afforded him protection. So that passing along the side of his line on higher ground he contributed greatly to the success of the day; for he could both see what was going on and being seen by all

ὑπὸ πάντων ὁρώμενος ἐνειργάζετο προθυμίαν τοῖς
5 ἀγωνιζομένοις. ἐξ οὗ συνέβαινε μηδὲν ἐλλιπὲς γίνεσθαι τῶν πρὸς τὸν κίνδυνον, ἀλλ᾽ ὁπότε τιν᾽ αὐτῷ
πρὸς τὸ προκείμενον ὁ καιρὸς ὑποδείξειε, πᾶν ἐκ
χειρὸς ἀεὶ συνηργεῖτο πρὸς τὸ δέον.

6 Ὁρμησάντων δὲ ταῖς κλίμαξι περὶ τὴν ἀνάβασιν
τῶν πρώτων τεθαρρηκότως, οὐχ οὕτως τὸ πλῆθος τῶν
ἀμυνομένων ἐπικίνδυνον ἐποίει τὴν προσβολὴν ὡς τὸ
7 μέγεθος τῶν τειχῶν. διὸ καὶ μᾶλλον ἐπερρώσθησαν οἱ
κατὰ ⟨τὰ⟩ τείχη, θεωροῦντες τὴν δυσχρηστίαν τῶν
8 συμβαινόντων. ἔνιαι μὲν γὰρ συνετρίβοντο τῶν κλιμάκων, πολλῶν ἅμα διὰ τὸ μέγεθος συνεπιβαινόντων·
ἐφ᾽ αἷς δ᾽ οἱ πρῶτοι προσβαίνοντες ἐσκοτοῦντο διὰ
τὴν εἰς ὕψος ἀνάτασιν καὶ βραχείας προσδεόμενοι
τῆς ἐκ τῶν ἀμυνομένων ἀντιπράξεως ἐρρίπτουν σφᾶς
9 αὐτοὺς ἀπὸ τῶν κλιμάκων. ὅτε δὲ καὶ δοκοὺς ἤ τι
τοιοῦτον ἐγχειρήσαιεν ἐπιρρίπτειν ἀπὸ τῶν ἐπάλξεων,
ὁμοῦ πάντες ἀπεσύροντο καὶ κατεφέροντο πρὸς τὴν
10 γῆν. οὐ μὴν ἀλλὰ τοιούτων ἀπαντωμένων οὐδὲν
ἱκανὸν ἦν πρὸς τὸ κωλύειν τὴν ἐπιφορὰν καὶ τὴν
ὁρμὴν τῶν Ῥωμαίων, ἀλλ᾽ ἔτι καταφερομένων τῶν
πρώτων ἐπέβαινον οἱ συνεχεῖς ἐπὶ τὴν ἐκλείπουσαν
11 ἀεὶ χώραν. ἤδη δὲ τῆς ἡμέρας προβαινούσης, καὶ τῶν
στρατιωτῶν τετρυμμένων ὑπὸ τῆς κακοπαθείας,
ἀνεκαλέσατο ταῖς σάλπιγξιν ὁ στρατηγὸς τοὺς προσ-
βάλλοντας.

14. Οἱ μὲν οὖν ἔνδον περιχαρεῖς ἦσαν ὡς ἀποτε-
2 τριμμένοι τὸν κίνδυνον· ὁ δὲ Πόπλιος, προσδοκῶν ἤδη

his men he inspired the combatants with great spirit. The consequence was that nothing was omitted which was necessary in the engagement, but the moment that circumstances suggested any step to him he set to work at once to do what was necessary.

When the front rank advanced confidently to mount the ladders, it was not so much the numbers of the defenders which made the assault hazardous as the great height of the wall. Those on the wall consequently plucked up courage when they saw the difficulties of the assailants. For some of the ladders broke, as owing to their height so many mounted them at the same time, while on others those who led the way grew dizzy owing to their elevated position, and a very slight resistance on the part of the besieged sufficed to make them throw themselves off the ladders. Also whenever the defenders adopted the expedient of throwing beams or suchlike things from the battlements the whole of those on the ladders would be swept off and fall to the ground. Yet in spite of all these difficulties nothing could restrain the dash and fury of the Romans, but while the first scalers were still falling the vacant places were instantly taken by the next in order. The hour, however, was now advanced, and as the soldiers were worn out by fatigue, Scipio recalled the assailants by bugle.

14. The garrison were now overjoyed at having, as they thought, repelled the danger, but Scipio, who was now

τὸν τῆς ἀμπώτεως καιρόν, κατὰ μὲν τὴν λίμνην ἡτοί-

3 μασε πεντακοσίους ἄνδρας μετὰ κλιμάκων, κατὰ δὲ
τὴν πύλην καὶ τὸν ἰσθμὸν νεαλεῖς ποιήσας τοὺς στρατιώτας καὶ παρακαλέσας προσανέδωκε κλίμακας
πλείους τῶν πρότερον, ὥστε συνεχῶς πλῆρες γενέ-

4 σθαι τὸ τεῖχος τῶν προσβαινόντων. ἅμα δὲ τῷ σημῆναι τὸ πολεμικὸν καὶ προσθέντας τῷ τείχει τὰς κλίμακας προσβαίνειν κατὰ πάντα τὰ μέρη τεθαρρηκότως
μεγάλην συνέβαινε ταραχὴν καὶ διατροπὴν γίνεσθαι

5 τῶν ἔνδον. νομίζοντες γὰρ ἀπολελύσθαι τῆς περιστάσεως, αὖθις ἀρχὴν ἑώρων λαμβάνοντα τὸν κίν-

6 δυνον ἐξ ἄλλης ὁρμῆς· ἅμα δὲ καὶ τῶν βελῶν αὐτοὺς
ἤδη λειπόντων, καὶ τοῦ πλήθους τῶν ἀπολωλότων εἰς
ἀθυμίαν ἄγοντος, δυσχερῶς μὲν ἔφερον τὸ γινόμενον,

7 οὐ μὴν ἀλλ' ἡμύνοντο δυνατῶς. κατὰ δὲ τὴν ἀκμὴν τοῦ
διὰ τῶν κλιμάκων ἀγῶνος ἤρχετο τὰ κατὰ τὴν ἄμ-

8 πωτιν, καὶ τὰ μὲν ἄκρα τῆς λίμνης ἀπέλειπε τὸ ὕδωρ
κατὰ βραχύ, διὰ δὲ τοῦ στόματος ὁ ῥοῦς εἰς τὴν
συνεχῆ θάλατταν ἄθρους ἐφέρετο καὶ πολύς, ὥστε
τοῖς ἀπρονοήτως θεωμένοις ἄπιστον φαίνεσθαι τὸ

9 γινόμενον. ὁ δὲ Πόπλιος ἔχων ἑτοίμους τοὺς καθηγε-
μόνας ἐμβαίνειν παρεκελεύετο καὶ θαρρεῖν τοὺς πρὸς

10 τὴν χρείαν ταύτην ἡτοιμασμένους· καὶ γὰρ ἦν εὖ
πεφυκώς, εἰ καὶ πρὸς ἄλλο τι, πρὸς τὸ θάρσος ἐμβαλεῖν καὶ συμπαθεῖς ποιῆσαι τοὺς παρακαλουμέ-

11 νους. τότε δὴ πειθαρχησάντων αὐτῶν καὶ διὰ τοῦ
τέλματος ἀμιλλωμένων, ἅπαν τὸ στρατόπεδον ὑπέλαβε μετά τινος θεοῦ προνοίας γίνεσθαι τὸ συμ-

waiting for the fall of the tide,[32] got ready five hundred men with ladders on the shore of the lagoon and recruited his force at the isthmus and by the gate. Then after addressing the soldiers he gave them still more ladders than before so that the whole extent of the wall was covered with escaladers. When the signal for attack was sounded and the assailants setting up the ladders against the wall mounted it everywhere in the most daring manner, the defenders were thrown into great confusion and became very despondent. They had thought they were delivered from peril, and now they saw they were menaced again by a new assault. As at the same time they had run out of ammunition and their losses were so severe as to dispirit them, they supported the assault with difficulty, but nevertheless offered a stubborn resistance. Just when the escalading attack was at its height the tide began to ebb and the water gradually receded from the edge of the lagoon, a strong and deep current setting in through the channel to the neighboring sea, so that to those who were not prepared for the sight the thing appeared incredible. But Scipio had his guides ready and bade all the men he had told off for this service enter the water and have no fear. He indeed possessed a particular talent for inspiring confidence and sympathy in his troops when he called upon them. Now when they obeyed and raced through the shallow water, it struck the whole army that it was the work of some god. So

[32] This is the help of god that Scipio had predicted (11.7).

12 βαῖνον. ἐξ οὗ καὶ μνησθέντες τῶν κατὰ τὸν Ποσειδῶ
καὶ τοῦ Ποπλίου κατὰ τὴν παράκλησιν ἐπαγγελίας,
ἐπὶ τοσοῦτο ταῖς ψυχαῖς παρωρμήθησαν ὡς συμ-
φράξαντες καὶ βιασάμενοι πρὸς τὴν πύλην ἔξωθεν
ἐπεχείρουν διακόπτειν τοῖς πελέκεσι καὶ ταῖς ἀξίναις

13 τὰς θύρας. οἱ δὲ διὰ τῶν τελμάτων ἐγγίσαντες τῷ
τείχει, καὶ καταλαβόντες ἐρήμους τὰς ἐπάλξεις, οὐ
μόνον προσέθεσαν ἀσφαλῶς τὰς κλίμακας, ἀλλὰ καὶ

14 κατέσχον ἀναβάντες ἀμαχητὶ τὸ τεῖχος, ἅτε τῶν
ἔνδον περισπωμένων μὲν περὶ τοὺς ἄλλους τόπους,
καὶ μάλιστα τοὺς κατὰ τὸν ἰσθμὸν καὶ τὴν ταύτῃ
πύλην, οὐδέποτε δ' ἂν ἐλπισάντων ἐγγίσαι τῷ τείχει

15 τοὺς πολεμίους κατὰ τὸν τῆς λίμνης τόπον, τὸ δὲ
πλεῖστον, ὑπὸ τῆς ἀτάκτου κραυγῆς καὶ τῆς συμ-
μίκτου πολυοχλίας οὐ δυναμένων οὔτ' ἀκούειν οὔτε
συνορᾶν τῶν δεόντων οὐδέν.

15. Οἱ δὲ Ῥωμαῖοι κρατήσαντες τοῦ τείχους τὸ μὲν
πρῶτον ἐπεπορεύοντο κατὰ τὴν ἐφοδείαν ἀποσύροντες
τοὺς πολεμίους, μεγάλα συμβαλλομένης αὐτοῖς τῆς

2 ὁπλίσεως πρὸς τοῦτο τὸ γένος τῆς χρείας· ἐπεὶ δ'
ἀφίκοντο πρὸς τὴν πύλην, οἱ μὲν καταβάντες δι-
έκοπτον τοὺς μοχλούς, οἱ δ' ἔξωθεν εἰσέπιπτον, οἱ δὲ
διὰ τῶν κλιμάκων βιαζόμενοι κατὰ τὸν ἰσθμόν, ἤδη
κρατοῦντες τῶν ἀμυνομένων, ἐπέβαινον ἐπὶ τὰς ἐπάλ-

3 ξεις. καὶ τέλος τὰ μὲν τείχη τούτῳ τῷ τρόπῳ κατ-
είληπτο, τὸν δὲ λόφον οἱ διὰ τῆς πύλης εἰσπορευόμε-
νοι κατελάμβανον τὸν πρὸς τὰς ἀνατολάς, τρεψάμενοι

4 τοὺς φυλάττοντας. ὁ δὲ Πόπλιος ἐπεὶ τοὺς εἰσεληλυθό-

that now remembering Scipio's reference to Neptune and the promise he made in his speech their courage was redoubled, and under cover of their shields they forced their way in dense order to the gate and began to try to cut down the doors with axes and hatchets. Meanwhile those who reached the wall through the lagoon finding the battlements deserted not only set up their ladders unmolested, but ascended them and occupied the wall without striking a blow, the defenders having been diverted to other quarters, especially to the isthmus and gate there, and having never conceived it possible that the enemy would reach the wall from the lagoon, while above all there was such disorderly shouting and such crowding and confusion that they could neither hear nor see to any effect.

15. The Romans, having once taken the wall, at first marched along it sweeping the enemy off it, the nature of their arms being very well adapted for such a service. Upon reaching the gate some of them descended and began to cut through the bolts, upon which those outside began to force their way in, while the escaladers at the isthmus had now overpowered the defense and established themselves on the battlements. Finally, when the walls had been taken in this manner, those who entered through the gate occupied the hill on the east after dislodging its defenders. When Scipio thought that a sufficient number of

τας ἀξιόχρεως ὑπελάμβανεν εἶναι, τοὺς μὲν πλείστους
ἐφῆκε κατὰ τὸ παρ' αὐτοῖς ἔθος ἐπὶ τοὺς ἐν τῇ πόλει,
παραγγείλας κτείνειν τὸν παρατυχόντα καὶ μηδενὸς
φείδεσθαι, μηδὲ πρὸς τὰς ὠφελείας ὁρμᾶν, μέχρις ἂν
5 ἀποδοθῇ τὸ σύνθημα. ποιεῖν δέ μοι δοκοῦσι τοῦτο
καταπλήξεως χάριν· διὸ καὶ πολλάκις ἰδεῖν ἔστιν ἐν
ταῖς τῶν Ῥωμαίων καταλήψεσι τῶν πόλεων οὐ μόνον
τοὺς ἀνθρώπους πεφονευμένους, ἀλλὰ καὶ τοὺς κύνας
δεδιχοτομημένους καὶ τῶν ἄλλων ζῴων μέλη παρα-
6 κεκομμένα. τότε δὲ καὶ τελέως πολὺ τὸ τοιοῦτον ἦν διὰ
7 τὸ πλῆθος τῶν κατειλημμένων. αὐτὸς δὲ περὶ χιλίους
ἔχων ὥρμησε πρὸς τὴν ἄκραν. ἐγγίσαντος δ' αὐτοῦ τὸ
μὲν πρῶτον ἐπεβάλλετο Μάγων ἀμύνεσθαι, μετὰ δὲ
ταῦτα συννοήσας βεβαίως ἤδη κατειλημμένην τὴν
πόλιν διεπέμψατο περὶ τῆς ἀσφαλείας τῆς αὐτοῦ, καὶ
8 παρέδωκε τὴν ἄκραν. οὗ γενομένου, καὶ τοῦ συνθήμα-
τος ἀποδοθέντος, τοῦ μὲν φονεύειν ἀπέστησαν, ὥρμη-
9 σαν δὲ πρὸς τὰς ἁρπαγάς. ἐπιγενομένης δὲ τῆς νυκτὸς
οἱ μὲν ἐπὶ τῆς παρεμβολῆς ἔμενον, οἷς ἦν οὕτω δια-
τεταγμένον· μετὰ δὲ τῶν χιλίων ὁ στρατηγὸς ἐπὶ τῆς
ἄκρας ηὐλίσθη, τοὺς δὲ λοιποὺς διὰ τῶν χιλιάρχων ἐκ
τῶν οἰκιῶν ἐκκαλεσάμενος ἐπέταξε συναθροίσαντας
εἰς τὴν ἀγορὰν τὰ διηρπασμένα κατὰ σημαίας ἐπὶ
10 τούτων κοιτάζεσθαι. τοὺς δὲ γροσφομάχους ἐκ τῆς
παρεμβολῆς καλέσας ἐπὶ τὸν λόφον ἐπέστησε τὸν
ἀπὸ τῶν ἀνατολῶν.
11   Καὶ τῆς μὲν κατὰ τὴν Ἰβηρίαν Καρχηδόνος τοῦτον
τὸν τρόπον ἐγένοντο κύριοι Ῥωμαῖοι·

154

troops had entered he sent most of them, as is the Roman custom, against the inhabitants of the city with orders to kill all they encountered, sparing none, and not to start pillaging until the signal was given. They do this, I think, to inspire terror, so that when towns are taken by the Romans one may often see not only the corpses of human beings, but dogs cut in half, and the dismembered limbs of other animals, and on this occasion such scenes were very many owing to the numbers of those in the place. Scipio himself, with about a thousand men, proceeded to the citadel. On his approach Mago at first attempted to resist, but afterward, when he saw that the city had undoubtedly been captured, he sent a message begging for his life and surrendered the citadel. After this, upon the signal being given, the massacre ceased and they began pillaging. At nightfall such of the Romans as had received orders to that effect, remained in the camp, while Scipio with his thousand men bivouacked in the citadel, and recalling the rest from the houses ordered them, through the tribunes, to collect the booty in the market, each maniple separately, and sleep there, keeping guard over it. Summoning also the light-armed troops from the camp he stationed them on the easternmost hill.

Such was the manner in which the Romans gained possession of Spanish Carthage.

16. εἰς δὲ τὴν ἐπαύριον ἀθροισθείσης εἰς τὴν ἀγορὰν τῆς τε τῶν στρατευομένων παρὰ τοῖς Καρχηδονίοις ἀποσκευῆς καὶ τῆς τῶν πολιτικῶν καὶ τῶν ἐργα-
στικῶν κατασκευῆς, ταῦτα μὲν ἐμέριζον οἱ χιλίαρχοι
τοῖς ἰδίοις στρατοπέδοις κατὰ τὸ παρ' αὐτοῖς ἔθος.
2 ἔστι δὲ παρὰ Ῥωμαίοις τοιαύτη τις ἡ περὶ τὰς τῶν
πόλεων καταλήψεις οἰκονομία. ποτὲ μὲν γὰρ ἑκάστης
σημαίας πρὸς τὴν πρᾶξιν ἀπομερίζονταί τινες τῶν
ἀνδρῶν κατὰ τὸ μέγεθος τῆς πόλεως, ποτὲ δὲ κατὰ
3 σημαίας μερίζουσιν αὐτούς. οὐδέποτε <δὲ> πλείους
ἀποτάττονται πρὸς τοῦτο τῶν ἡμίσεων· οἱ δὲ λοιποὶ
μένοντες κατὰ τὰς τάξεις ἐφεδρεύουσι, ποτὲ μὲν ἐκτὸς
τῆς πόλεως, ποτὲ δὲ πάλιν ἐντός, ἀεὶ πρὸς τὸ δεικνύ-
4 ειν. τῆς δὲ δυνάμεως διῃρημένης αὐτοῖς κατὰ μὲν τὸ
πλεῖον εἰς δύο στρατόπεδα Ῥωμαϊκὰ καὶ δύο τῶν
συμμάχων, τοτὲ δὲ καὶ σπανίως ἀθροιζομένων ὁμοῦ
τῶν τεττάρων, πάντες οἱ πρὸς τὴν ἁρπαγὴν ἀπομερι-
σθέντες ἀναφέρουσι τὰς ὠφελείας ἕκαστοι τοῖς ἑαυ-
5 τῶν στρατοπέδοις, κἄπειτα πραχθέντων τούτων οἱ
χιλίαρχοι διανέμουσι πᾶσιν ἴσον, οὐ μόνον τοῖς μεί-
νασιν ἐν ταῖς ἐφεδρείαις, ἀλλὰ καὶ τοῖς τὰς σκηνὰς
φυλάττουσι τοῖς τ' ἀρρωστοῦσι καὶ τοῖς ἐπί τινα
6 λειτουργίαν ἀπεσταλμένοις. περὶ δὲ τοῦ μηδένα
νοσφίζεσθαι μηδὲν τῶν ἐκ τῆς διαρπαγῆς, ἀλλὰ
τηρεῖν τὴν πίστιν κατὰ τὸν ὅρκον, <ὃν> ὀμνύουσι
πάντες, ὅταν ἀθροισθῶσι πρῶτον εἰς τὴν παρεμβο-
7 λήν, ἐξιέναι μέλλοντες εἰς τὴν πολεμίαν, ὑπὲρ τούτου
δὲ τοῦ μέρους εἴρηται πρότερον ἡμῖν διὰ πλειόνων ἐν

16. Next day the booty,[33] both the baggage of the troops in the Carthaginian service and the household stuff of the townsmen and working classes, having been collected in the market, was divided by the tribunes among the legions on the usual system. The Romans after the capture of a city manage matters more or less as follows: according to the size of the town sometimes a certain number of men from each maniple, at other times certain whole maniples are told off to collect booty, but they never thus employ more than half their total force, the rest remaining in their ranks at times outside and at times inside the city, ready for the occasion. As their armies are usually divided into two Roman legions and two legions of allies, the whole four legions being rarely massed, all those who are told off to spoil bring the booty back, each man to his own legion, and when this had been done[34] the tribunes distribute the profits equally among all, including not only those who were left behind in the protecting force, but the men who are guarding the tents, the sick, and those absent on any special service. I have already stated at some length in my chapters on the Roman state how it is that no one appropriates any part of the loot, but that all keep the oath[35] they make when first assembled in camp on setting out for a

[33] This digression on the division of booty in the Roman army (16.1–17.5) complements P.'s chapters on the Roman military system (6.19–42).

[34] The transmitted reading (πραχθέντων) seems preferable to Casaubon's emendation πραθέντων (sold).

[35] Refers to 6.33.1.

8 τοῖς περὶ τῆς πολιτείας. λοιπὸν ὅταν οἱ μὲν ἡμίσεις
τράπωνται πρὸς τὰς ἁρπαγάς, οἱ δ' ἡμίσεις διαφυλάτ-
τοντες τὰς τάξεις ἐφεδρεύωσι τούτοις, οὐδέποτε κιν-
9 δυνεύει Ῥωμαίοις τὰ ὅλα διὰ πλεονεξίαν. τῆς γὰρ
ἐλπίδος τῆς κατὰ τὴν ὠφέλειαν οὐκ ἀπιστουμένης
ἀλλήλοις, ἀλλ' ἐπ' ἴσης ἑστηκυίας τοῖς μένουσι κατὰ
τὰς ἐφεδρείας καὶ τοῖς διαρπάζουσιν, οὐδεὶς ἀπολείπει
τὰς τάξεις· ὃ μάλιστα τοὺς ἄλλους εἴωθε βλάπτειν.

17. ἐπειδὴ γὰρ οἱ πλεῖστοι τῶν ἀνθρώπων κακο-
παθοῦσι καὶ κινδυνεύουσι τοῦ κέρδους ἕνεκεν, φανερὸν ὡς, ὅταν ὁ καιρὸς οὗτος ὑποπέσῃ, δυσχερῶς εἰκὸς
ἀπέχεσθαι τοὺς ἐν ταῖς ἐφεδρείαις ἢ στρατοπεδείαις
ἀπολειπομένους διὰ τὸ [τοὺς] παρὰ τοῖς πλείστοις
2 πᾶν τὸ ληφθὲν εἶναι τοῦ κυριεύσαντος· καὶ γὰρ ἂν
ὅλως μόναρχος ἢ στρατηγὸς ἐπιμελὴς ἀναφέρειν εἰς
τὸ κοινὸν ἐπιτάξῃ τὰς ὠφελείας, ὅμως τὰ δυνατὰ
3 κρύπτεσθαι πάντες ἴδια νομίζουσι. διὸ τῶν πολλῶν
ὁρμώντων ἐπὶ τοῦτο τὸ μέρος οὐ δυνάμενοι κρατεῖν
4 κινδυνεύουσι τοῖς ὅλοις· καὶ πολλοὶ δή τινες κατορθώ-
σαντες τὰς ἐπιβολάς, καὶ ποτὲ μὲν ἐπιπεσόντες ταῖς
τῶν πολεμίων παρεμβολαῖς, ποτὲ δὲ καταλαβόμενοι
πόλεις, οὐ μόνον ἐξέπεσον, ἀλλὰ καὶ τοῖς ὅλοις
ἐσφάλησαν παρ' οὐδὲν ἢ τὴν προειρημένην αἰτίαν.
5 διὸ δεῖ περὶ μηδὲν οὕτω σπουδάζειν καὶ προνοεῖσθαι
τοὺς ἡγουμένους ὡς περὶ τοῦτο τὸ μέρος, ἵνα, καθ'
ὅσον ἐστὶ δυνατόν, ὑπάρχῃ παρὰ τοῖς πολλοῖς ἐλπὶς
ὡς ἐξ ἴσου πᾶσι τῆς ὠφελείας οὔσης, ἐάν τις ὑπο-
πίπτῃ τοιοῦτος καιρός.

campaign. So that when half of the army disperse to pillage and the other half keep their ranks and afford them protection, there is never any chance of the Romans suffering disaster owing to individual covetousness. For as all, both the spoilers and those who remain to safeguard them, have equal confidence that they will get their share of the booty, no one leaves the ranks, a thing which usually does injury to other armies.

17. For since most men endure hardship and risk their lives for the sake of gain, it is evident that whenever the chance presents itself it is not likely that those left in the protecting force or in the camp will refrain, since the rule among most people is that any man keeps whatever comes into his hands. And even if any careful king or general orders the booty to be brought in to form a common fund, yet everyone regards as his own whatever he can conceal. So that, as most of the men start pillaging, commanders cannot maintain any control and run the risk of disaster, and indeed many who have been successful in their object have, after capturing the enemy's camp or a town, not only been driven out but have met with complete disaster simply for the above reason. Commanders should therefore exercise the utmost care and foresight about this matter, so that as far as is possible the hope of equal participation in the booty when such a chance presents itself may be common to all.

6   Πλὴν οἱ μὲν χιλίαρχοι τότε περὶ τὴν τῶν λαφύρων
ἦσαν οἰκονομίαν· ὁ δὲ στρατηγὸς τῶν Ῥωμαίων, ἐπεὶ
συνήχθη τὸ τῶν αἰχμαλώτων πλῆθος, ὃ συνέβη γενέσθαι μικρῷ λεῖπον τῶν μυρίων, συνέταξε χωρισθῆναι
πρῶτον μὲν τοὺς πολιτικοὺς ἄνδρας τε καὶ γυναῖκας
καὶ τὰ τούτων τέκνα, δεύτερον δὲ τοὺς χειροτέχνας.

7 γενομένου δὲ τούτου, τοὺς μὲν πολιτικοὺς παρακαλέσας εὐνοεῖν Ῥωμαίοις καὶ μνημονεύειν τῆς εὐεργεσίας

8 ἀπέλυσε πάντας ἐπὶ τὰς ἰδίας οἰκήσεις. οὗτοι μὲν οὖν
ἅμα δακρύοντες καὶ χαίροντες ἐπὶ τῷ παραδόξῳ τῆς
σωτηρίας, προσκυνήσαντες τὸν στρατηγὸν διελύθη-

9 σας· τοῖς δὲ χειροτέχναις κατὰ τὸ παρὸν εἶπε διότι
δημόσιοι τῆς Ῥώμης εἰσί· παρασχομένοις δὲ τὴν
εὔνοιαν καὶ προθυμίαν ἑκάστοις κατὰ τὰς αὑτῶν
τέχνας ἐπηγγείλατο τὴν ἐλευθερίαν, κατὰ νοῦν χωρή-

10 σαντος τοῦ πρὸς τοὺς Καρχηδονίους πολέμου. καὶ
τούτους μὲν ἀπογράφεσθαι προσέταξε πρὸς τὸν
ταμίαν, συστήσας Ῥωμαϊκὸν ἐπιμελητὴν κατὰ τρι-
άκοντα· τὸ γὰρ πᾶν πλῆθος ἐγένετο τούτων περὶ

11 δισχιλίους. ἐκ δὲ τῶν λοιπῶν αἰχμαλώτων ἐκλέξας
τοὺς εὐρωστοτάτους καὶ τοῖς εἴδεσι καὶ ταῖς ἡλικίαις

12 ἀκμαιοτάτους προσέμιξε τοῖς αὑτοῦ πληρώμασι, καὶ
ποιήσας ἡμιολίους τοὺς πάντας ναύτας ἢ πρόσθεν
συνεπλήρωσε καὶ τὰς αἰχμαλώτους νῆας, ὥστε τοὺς
ἄνδρας ἑκάστῳ σκάφει βραχύ τι λείπειν τοῦ διπλασί-

13 ους εἶναι τοὺς ὑπάρχοντας τῶν προγενομένων· αἱ μὲν
γὰρ αἰχμάλωτοι νῆες ἦσαν ὀκτωκαίδεκα τὸν ἀριθμόν,

14 αἱ δ' ἐξ ἀρχῆς πέντε καὶ τριάκοντα. παραπλησίως δὲ

The tribunes, then, were now dealing with the booty, but the Roman commander, when the whole of the prisoners, numbering little less than ten thousand, had been collected, ordered first the citizens with their wives and children, and next the working men, to be set apart. Upon this being done, after exhorting the citizens to be well disposed to the Romans and to be mindful of the kindness shown to them, he dismissed them all to their houses. Weeping and rejoicing at one and the same time, owing to their unexpected delivery, they made obeisance to Scipio and dispersed. He told the working men that for the time being they were public slaves of Rome, but if they showed goodwill and industry in their several crafts be promised them freedom upon the war against Carthage terminating successfully. He ordered them to enroll themselves in the quaestor's office, appointing a Roman superintendent over every thirty, the whole number being about two thousand. Selecting from the other prisoners those who were strongest, finest looking, and in the prime of youth, he incorporated them with the crews of his ships, and having thus got half as many sailors again as before, he manned the captured vessels also, and made the complement of each ship nearly double what it had been, the captured vessels numbering eighteen sail and his original fleet thirty-five. He

καὶ τούτοις ἐπηγγείλατο τὴν ἐλευθερίαν, παρασχομένοις τὴν αὑτῶν εὔνοιαν καὶ προθυμίαν, ἐπειδὰν
15 κρατήσωσι τῷ πολέμῳ τῶν Καρχηδονίων. τοῦτον δὲ
χειρίσας τὸν τρόπον τὰ κατὰ τοὺς αἰχμαλώτους μεγάλην μὲν εὔνοιαν καὶ πίστιν ἐνειργάσατο τοῖς πολιτι-
κοῖς καὶ πρὸς αὑτὸν καὶ πρὸς τὰ κοινὰ πράγματα,
μεγάλην δὲ προθυμίαν τοῖς χειροτέχναις διὰ τὴν
16 ἐλπίδα τῆς ἐλευθερίας. ἡμιόλιον δὲ ποιήσας τὸ ναυτικὸν ἐκ τοῦ καιροῦ διὰ τὴν αὑτοῦ πρόνοιαν . . .

18. Μετὰ δὲ ταῦτα Μάγωνα καὶ τοὺς ἅμα τούτῳ
Καρχηδονίους ἐχώριζε. δύο μὲν γὰρ ἦσαν κατειλημ-
μένοι τῶν ἐκ τῆς γερουσίας, πέντε δὲ καὶ δέκα τῶν ἐκ
2 τῆς συγκλήτου. καὶ τούτους μὲν συνέστησε Γαΐῳ
Λαιλίῳ, συντάξας τὴν ἁρμόζουσαν ἐπιμέλειαν ποιεῖ-
3 σθαι τῶν ἀνδρῶν· ἐπὶ δὲ τούτοις τοὺς ὁμήρους προσ-
εκαλέσατο, πλείους ὄντας τῶν τριακοσίων. καὶ τοὺς
μὲν παῖδας καθ᾽ ἕνα προσαγαγόμενος καὶ καταψήσας
θαρρεῖν ἐκέλευε, διότι μετ᾽ ὀλίγας ἡμέρας ἐπόψονται
4 τοὺς αὑτῶν γονεῖς· τοὺς δὲ λοιποὺς ὁμοῦ παρεκάλεσε
πάντας θαρρεῖν καὶ γράφειν αὐτοὺς εἰς τὰς ἰδίας
5 πόλεις πρὸς αὑτῶν ἀναγκαίους πρῶτον μὲν ὅτι σῴζον-
ται καὶ καλῶς αὐτοῖς ἐστι, δεύτερον δὲ διότι θέλουσι
Ῥωμαῖοι πάντας αὐτοὺς εἰς τὴν οἰκείαν ἀποκαταστῆσαι μετ᾽ ἀσφαλείας, ἑλομένων τῶν ἀναγκαίων σφίσι
6 τὴν πρὸς Ῥωμαίους συμμαχίαν. ταῦτα δ᾽ εἰπών, καὶ
παρεσκευακὼς πρότερον ἐκ τῶν λαφύρων τὰ λυσιτελέ-
στερα πρὸς τὴν ἐπίνοιαν, τότε κατὰ γένη καὶ καθ᾽
ἡλικίαν ἑκάστοις ἐδωρεῖτο τὰ πρέποντα, ταῖς μὲν

promised these men also their liberty after the final defeat of Carthage if they displayed good will and zeal. By this treatment of the prisoners he produced in the citizens great affection and loyalty to himself and to the common cause, while the workmen were most zealous owing to their hope of being set free. Having thus by his foresight seized the opportunity of making his fleet half as large again . . .

18. After this he set apart Mago and the Carthaginians who were with him, two of them being members of the council of elders and fifteen members of the senate. He committed these[36] to the custody of Laelius, ordering him to pay them due attention. Next he invited the hostages, over three hundred in number, to visit him, and calling the children to him one by one and caressing them bade them be of good cheer, as in a few days they would see their parents. He also bade the rest take heart and asked them all to write to their relations at home, firstly, that they were safe and well, and secondly, that the Romans were willing to restore them all in safety to their homes if their relatives chose to become allies of Rome. After speaking thus, having reserved from the booty the most suitable objects for this purpose, he gave them such gifts as became their sex and age, presenting the girls with earrings and bracelets

---

[36] Mago and the representatives of the government who were with him.

παισὶ κόνους καὶ ψέλλια, τοῖς δὲ νεανίσκοις ῥαμφὰς

7 καὶ μαχαίρας. ἐκ δὲ τῶν αἰχμαλωτίδων τῆς Μανδο-
νίου γυναικός, ὃς ἦν ἀδελφὸς Ἀνδοβάλου τοῦ τῶν
Ἰλεργητῶν βασιλέως, προσπεσούσης αὐτῷ καὶ δεομένης μετὰ δακρύων ἐπιστροφὴν ποιήσασθαι τῆς
αὐτῶν εὐσχημοσύνης ἀμείνω Καρχηδονίων, συμπαθὴς γενόμενος ἤρετο τί λείπει τῶν ἐπιτηδείων αὐταῖς·

8 καὶ γὰρ ἦν ἡ γυνὴ πρεσβυτέρα καί τινα προστασίαν

9 ἀξιωματικὴν ἐπιφαίνουσα. τῆς δὲ κατασιωπώσης
ἐκάλει τοὺς πρὸς τὴν ἐπιμέλειαν τῶν γυναικῶν ἀπο-

10 τεταγμένους. ὧν παραγενομένων καὶ διασαφούντων
ὅτι πάντα τὰ δέοντα δαψιλῶς αὐταῖς παρασκευάζοιεν,
πάλιν ὁμοίως ἁψαμένης αὐτοῦ τῶν γονάτων τῆς
γυναικὸς καὶ τὸν αὐτὸν εἰπούσης λόγον, μᾶλλον ἔτι
διαπορήσας ὁ Πόπλιος, καί τινα λαβὼν ἔννοιαν ὡς
ὀλιγωρούντων καὶ ψευδῶς πρὸς τὸ παρὸν ἀποφαινο-
μένων τῶν πρὸς τὴν ἐπιμέλειαν ἀποτεταγμένων, θαρ-

11 ρεῖν ἐκέλευε τὰς γυναῖκας· αὐτὸς γὰρ ἑτέρους ἐπιστή-
σειν τοὺς φροντιοῦντας ἵνα μηδὲν αὐτὰς ἐλλείπῃ τῶν

12 ἐπιτηδείων. ἡ δ᾽ ἐπισχοῦσα μικρόν "Οὐκ ὀρθῶς" ἔφη
"στρατηγέ, τοὺς ἡμετέρους ἐκδέχῃ λόγους, εἰ νομίζεις

13 ἡμᾶς ὑπὲρ τῆς γαστρὸς δεῖσθαί σου νῦν"· καὶ τότε
λαβὼν ὁ Πόπλιος ἐν νῷ τὸ βούλημα τῆς γυναικός, καὶ
θεωρῶν ὑπὸ τὴν ὄψιν τὴν ἀκμὴν τῶν Ἀνδοβάλου
θυγατέρων καὶ πλειόνων ἄλλων δυναστῶν, ἠναγ-
κάσθη δακρῦσαι, τῆς γυναικὸς ἐν ὀλίγῳ τὴν τῆς

14 περιστάσεως ἔμφασιν ὑποδεικνυούσης. διὸ δὴ καὶ
τότε φανερὸς γενόμενος ὅτι συνῆκε τὸ ῥηθέν, καὶ

and the young men with poniards and swords. When one of the captive women, the wife of Mandonius, who was the brother of Andobales,[37] king of the Ilergetes, fell at his feet and entreated him with tears to treat them with more proper consideration than the Carthaginians had done, he was touched and asked her what they stood in need of. The lady was indeed of advanced age, and bore herself with a certain majestic dignity. Upon her making no reply he sent for the officials appointed to attend on the women. When they presented themselves and informed him that they kept the women generously supplied with all they required, the lady again clasped his knees and addressed him in the same words, upon which Scipio was still more puzzled, and conceiving the idea that the officials who attended on the women were neglecting them and had now made a false statement, he bade the ladies be of good cheer, for he said he would himself appoint other attendants who would see to it that they were in want of nothing. The old lady after some hesitation said, "General, you do not take me rightly if you think that our present petition is about our food." Scipio then understood what the lady meant, and noticing the youth and beauty of the daughters of Andobales and other princes he was forced to tears, recognizing in how few words she had pointed out to him the danger to which they were exposed. So now he made it clear to her that he had taken her meaning, and grasping

37 For Mandonius and Andobales (*Indibilis* in Livy), see n. on 3.76.6.

λαβόμενος τῆς δεξιᾶς, θαρρεῖν αὐτήν τε ταύτην ἐκέ-
15 λευε καὶ τὰς ἄλλας ὁμοίως· ποιήσεσθαι γὰρ πρόνοιαν
ὡς ἰδίων ἀδελφῶν καὶ τέκνων, συστήσεσθαι δὲ καὶ
πρὸς τὴν τούτων ἐπιμέλειαν ἀκολούθως τοῖς προειρημένοις πιστοὺς ἄνδρας.

19. Μετὰ ταῦτα παρεδίδου τοῖς ταμίαις [τὰ χρή-
2 ματα], ὅσα δημόσια κατελήφθη τῶν Καρχηδονίων. ἦν
δὲ ταῦτα πλείω τῶν ἑξακοσίων ταλάντων, ὥστε προσ-
τεθέντων τούτων οἷς παρῆν αὐτὸς ἐκ Ῥώμης ἔχων
τετρακοσίοις, τὴν ὅλην παράθεσιν αὐτῷ γενέσθαι τῆς
χορηγίας πλείω τῶν χιλίων.

3 Κατὰ δὲ τὸν καιρὸν τοῦτον νεανίσκοι τινὲς τῶν
Ῥωμαίων ἐπιτυχόντες παρθένῳ κατὰ τὴν ἀκμὴν καὶ
κατὰ τὸ κάλλος διαφερούσῃ τῶν ἄλλων γυναικῶν, καὶ
συνιδόντες φιλογύνην ὄντα τὸν Πόπλιον, ἧκον αὐτὴν
ἄγοντες καὶ παραστήσαντες ἔφασκον αὐτῷ δωρεῖ-
4 σθαι τὴν κόρην. ὁ δὲ καταπλαγεὶς καὶ θαυμάσας τὸ
κάλλος, ἰδιώτης μὲν ὢν οὐδεμίαν ἥδιον ἂν ἔφη δέξασθαι ταύτης τῆς δωρεᾶς, στρατηγὸς δ' ὑπάρχων οὐδ'
5 ὁποίαν ἧττον, ὡς μὲν ἐμοὶ δοκεῖ, τοῦτ' αἰνιττόμενος
διὰ τῆς ἀποφάσεως, διότι κατὰ μὲν τὰς ἀναπαύσεις
ἐνίοτε καὶ ῥᾳθυμίας ἐν τῷ ζῆν ἡδίστας τοῖς νέοις
ἀπολαύσεις τὰ τοιαῦτα παρέχεται καὶ διατριβάς, ἐν δὲ
τοῖς τοῦ πράττειν καιροῖς μέγιστα γίνεται καὶ κατὰ
6 σῶμα καὶ κατὰ ψυχὴν ἐμπόδια τοῖς χρωμένοις. τοῖς
μὲν οὖν νεανίσκοις ἔφη χάριν ἔχειν, τὸν δὲ τῆς παρθένου πατέρα καλέσας καὶ δοὺς αὐτὴν ἐκ χειρὸς
ἐκέλευε συνοικίζειν ᾧ ποτ' ἂν προαιρῆται τῶν πολι-

her by the right hand bade her and the rest be of good cheer, for he would look after them as if they were his own sisters and children and would accordingly appoint trustworthy men to attend on them.

19. After this he handed over to the quaestors[38] all the public funds of the Carthaginians which had been captured. There were more than six hundred talents, so that when these were added to the four hundred he had brought from Rome, the total sum at his disposal was more than a thousand talents.

It was at this time that some young Romans came across a girl of surpassing bloom and beauty, and being aware that Scipio was fond of women brought her to him and introduced her, saying that they wished to make a present of the damsel to him. He was overcome and astonished by her beauty, but he told them that had he been in a private position, no present would have been more welcome to him, but as he was the General it would be the least welcome of any, giving them to understand, I suppose, by this answer that sometimes, during seasons of repose and leisure in our life, such things afford young men most delightful enjoyment and entertainment, but that in times of activity they are most prejudicial to the body and the mind alike of those who indulge in them. So he expressed his gratitude to the young men, but called the girl's father and delivering her over to him at once bade him give her in marriage to

---

[38] The plural is inaccurate; Scipio's (single) quaestor was Gaius Flaminius, *MRR* 1.286.

THE HISTORIES OF POLYBIUS

7 τῶν. δι' ὧν καὶ τὰ τῆς ἐγκρατείας καὶ τὰ τῆς μετρι-
ότητος ἐμφαίνων μεγάλην ἀποδοχὴν ἐνειργάζετο τοῖς
ὑποταττομένοις.

8 Ταῦτα δὲ διοικησάμενος, καὶ τὰ λοιπὰ τῶν αἰχμαλώτων παραδοὺς τοῖς χιλιάρχοις, ἐξέπεμψε Γάιον τὸν
Λαίλιον ἐπὶ πεντήρους εἰς τὴν Ῥώμην, τούς τε Καρχηδονίους συστήσας καὶ τῶν ἄλλων αἰχμαλώτων
τοὺς ἐπιφανεστάτους, δηλώσοντα τοῖς ἐν τῇ πατρίδι
9 τὰ γεγονότα. τὸ γὰρ πλεῖον αὐτῶν ἤδη τὰ κατὰ τὴν
Ἰβηρίαν ἀπηλπικότων, σαφῶς ᾔδει διότι τούτων
προσαγγελθέντων αὖθις ἀναθαρρήσαντες πολλαπλασίως συνεπιλήψονται τῶν πραγμάτων.

20. Αὐτὸς δὲ χρόνον μέν τιν' ἐν τῇ Καρχηδόνι τάς
τε ναυτικὰς δυνάμεις ἐγύμναζε συνεχῶς καὶ τοῖς χιλιάρχοις ὑπέδειξε τοιοῦτόν τινα τρόπον τῆς τῶν πεζικῶν
2 στρατοπέδων γυμνασίας. τὴν μὲν πρώτην ἡμέραν
ἐκέλευσε τροχάζειν ἐπὶ τριάκοντα σταδίους ἐν τοῖς
ὅπλοις, τὴν δὲ δευτέραν πάντας ἐκτρίβειν καὶ θερα-
πεύειν καὶ κατασκοπεῖν ἐν τῷ φανερῷ τὰς πανοπλίας,
3 τῇ δ' ἑξῆς ἀναπαύεσθαι καὶ ῥᾳθυμεῖν, τῇ δὲ μετὰ
ταύτην τοὺς μὲν μαχαιρομαχεῖν ξυλίναις ἐσκυτωμέ-
ναις μετ' ἐπισφαιρῶν μαχαίραις, τοὺς δὲ τοῖς ἐσφαι-
ρωμένοις γρόσφοις ἀκοντίζειν, τῇ δὲ πέμπτῃ πάλιν
4 ἐπὶ τοὺς αὐτοὺς δρόμους καὶ τὴν ἀρχὴν ἐπανάγειν. ἵνα
δὲ μήτε τῶν πρὸς τὰς μελέτας ὅπλων μήτε τῶν πρὸς
τὴν ἀλήθειαν μηδὲν ἐλλείπῃ, τὴν πλείστην ἐποιεῖτο
5 σπουδὴν πρὸς τοὺς χειροτέχνας. κατὰ μέρος μὲν οὖν

whomever of the citizens he preferred. The self-restraint and moderation he displayed on this occasion secured him the warm approbation of his troops.

Having arranged these matters and handed over the rest of the prisoners to the tribunes, he dispatched Laelius on a quinquereme to Rome, to convey the news, placing under his charge the Carthaginians and the most distinguished among the other prisoners. For as the Romans had for the most part regarded the situation in Spain as desperate he knew that this intelligence would revive their spirits and that they would redouble their efforts to support him.

20. He himself remaining for some time in New Carthage constantly exercised his navy and instructed the tribunes to train the land forces in the following manner. He ordered the soldiers on the first day to go at the double for thirty stades in their armor. On the second day they were all to polish up, repair, and examine their arms in full view, and the third day to rest and remain idle. On the following day they were to practice, some of them sword fighting with wooden swords covered with leather and with a button on the point, while others practiced casting with javelins also having a button at the point. On the fifth day they were to begin the same course of exercise again. In order that there should be no lack of weapons for practice and for real warfare he paid particular attention to the artificers.

ἄνδρας ἐπιμελεῖς ἐφεστάκει πρὸς ταύτην τὴν χρείαν,
καθάπερ ἐπάνω προεῖπον· αὐτὸς δὲ καθ' ἡμέραν ἐπεπορεύετο, καὶ δι' αὐτοῦ τὰς χορηγίας ἑκάστοις παρ-
6 εσκεύαζε. λοιπὸν τῶν μὲν πεζικῶν στρατοπέδων κατὰ
τοὺς πρὸ τῆς πόλεως τόπους χρωμένων ταῖς μελέταις
καὶ ταῖς γυμνασίαις, τῶν δὲ ναυτικῶν δυνάμεων κατὰ
θάλατταν ταῖς ἀναπείραις καὶ ταῖς εἰρεσίαις, τῶν δὲ
κατὰ τὴν πόλιν ἀκονώντων τε καὶ χαλκευόντων καὶ
τεκταινομένων, καὶ συλλήβδην ἁπάντων σπουδαζόν-
7 των περὶ τὰς τῶν ὅπλων κατασκευάς, οὐκ ἔσθ' ὃς οὐκ
ἂν εἶπε κατὰ τὸν Ξενοφῶντα τότε θεασάμενος ἐκείνην
8 τὴν πόλιν ἐργαστήριον εἶναι πολέμου. ἐπεὶ δ' αὐτῷ
πάντα καλῶς ἐδόκει καὶ δεόντως ἐξησκῆσθαι τὰ πρὸς
τὰς χρείας, μετὰ ταῦτα ταῖς τε φυλακαῖς καὶ ταῖς τῶν
τειχῶν κατασκευαῖς ἀσφαλισάμενος τὰ κατὰ τὴν πόλιν, ἀνέζευξε καὶ τῇ πεζικῇ καὶ ναυτικῇ δυνάμει, καὶ
προῆγε ποιούμενος τὴν πορείαν ὡς ἐπὶ Ταρράκωνος,
ἔχων μεθ' αὐτοῦ καὶ τοὺς ὁμήρους.

III. RES GRAECIAE

21. Ὅτι Εὐρυλέων ὁ τῶν Ἀχαιῶν στρατηγὸς ἄτολ-
(24) 2 μος ἦν καὶ πολεμικῆς χρείας ἀλλότριος. τοῦ δὲ καιροῦ
τοῦ κατὰ τὴν διήγησιν ἐφεστακότος ἡμᾶς ἐπὶ τὴν
ἀρχὴν τῶν Φιλοποίμενος πράξεων, καθήκειν ἡγού-

---

39 In 17.9–10.   40 X. *Ages.* 1.26, slightly different X. *HG*
3.4.17.   41 Strategus of the Achaean League in 211/10. He is

As I before stated,[39] he had appointed skilled supervisors of the different sections of this branch, and he used himself to visit the workshops daily and personally distribute the materials required. So with the infantry exercising and drilling on the ground outside the town, with the fleet at sea practicing maneuvers and rowing, and with the men in the town sharpening weapons, forging brass or carpentering, in a word, with everyone busily engaged upon the preparation of weapons, no one could have helped when he saw that town saying, in the words of Xenophon,[40] that it was "a workshop of war." As soon as he considered that all the requirements of the service had been properly met, he secured the town by placing guards and repairing the wall, and setting forth with his army and navy began to advance toward Tarracon, taking the hostages with him.

III. AFFAIRS OF GREECE

Philopoemen

21. Euryleon, the strategus of the Achaeans,[41] was a timid man, without any military capacity. Now that the course of my narrative has brought me to the beginning of the achievements of Philopoemen,[42] I think it is incum-

---

mentioned only here but was in all probability the father of Xenophon, son of Euryleon, from Aegium, a *proxenos* at Delphi in 195/4 (*SIG* 585.28–29).   [42] See n. on 2.40.2 and Errington's monograph. He was born in 252. His brother Xenainetos has recently become known: a statue in his honor was set up at Megalopolis by his wife and signed by the Spartan Aenetidas, son of Antilas, who appears ca. 180/175 in an unpublished inscription as strategus of the Achaeans (*SEG* 45, 341).

μεθα, καθάπερ καὶ περὶ τῶν ἄλλων τῶν ἀξιολόγων
ἀνδρῶν τὰς ἑκάστων ἀγωγὰς καὶ φύσεις ἐπειράθημεν
ὑποδεικνύναι, καὶ περὶ τούτου ποιῆσαι τὸ παραπλή-
3   σιον. καὶ γὰρ ἄτοπον τὰς μὲν τῶν πόλεων κτίσεις τοὺς
συγγραφέας, καὶ πότε καὶ πῶς καὶ διὰ τίνων ἐκτίσθη-
σαν, ἔτι δὲ τὰς διαθέσεις καὶ περιστάσεις μετ᾽ ἀποδείξεως ἐξαγγέλλειν, τὰς δὲ τῶν τὰ ὅλα χειρισάντων
ἀνδρῶν ἀγωγὰς καὶ ζήλους παρασιωπᾶν, καὶ ταῦτα
4   τῆς χρείας μεγάλην ἐχούσης τὴν διαφοράν· ὅσῳ
γὰρ ἄν τις καὶ ζηλῶσαι καὶ μιμήσαισθαι δυνηθείη
μᾶλλον τοὺς ἐμψύχους ἄνδρας τῶν ἀψύχων κατασκευ-
ασμάτων, τοσούτῳ καὶ τὸν περὶ αὐτῶν λόγον δια-
5   φέρειν εἰκὸς <πρὸς> ἐπανόρθωσιν τῶν ἀκουόντων. εἰ
μὲν οὖν μὴ κατ᾽ ἰδίαν ἐπεποιήμεθα τὴν περὶ αὐτοῦ
σύνταξιν, ἐν ᾗ διεσαφοῦμεν καὶ τίς ἦν καὶ τίνων καὶ
τίσιν ἀγωγαῖς ἐχρήσατο νέος ὤν, ἀναγκαῖον ἦν ὑπὲρ
6   ἑκάστου τῶν προειρημένων φέρειν ἀπολογισμόν· ἐπεὶ
δὲ πρότερον ἐν τρισὶ βυβλίοις ἐκτὸς ταύτης τῆς συντάξεως τὸν ὑπὲρ αὐτοῦ πεποιήμεθα λόγον, τήν τε
παιδικὴν ἀγωγὴν διασαφοῦντες καὶ τὰς ἐπιφανεστά-
7   τας πράξεις, δῆλον ὡς ἐν τῇ νῦν ἐξηγήσει πρέπον ἂν
εἴη τῆς μὲν νεωτερικῆς ἀγωγῆς καὶ τῶν νεωτερικῶν
ζήλων κατὰ μέρος ἀφελεῖν, τοῖς δὲ κατὰ τὴν ἀκμὴν
αὐτοῦ κεφαλαιωδῶς ἐκεῖ δεδηλωμένοις ἔργοις προσθεῖναι καὶ κατὰ μέρος, ἵνα τὸ πρέπον ἑκατέρᾳ τῶν
8   συντάξεων τηρῶμεν. ὥσπερ γὰρ ἐκεῖνος ὁ τόπος,
ὑπάρχων ἐγκωμιαστικός, ἀπήτει τὸν κεφαλαιώδη καὶ
μετ᾽ αὐξήσεως τῶν πράξεων ἀπολογισμόν, οὕτως ὁ

bent on me, just as in the case of other eminent men I have
attempted to sketch their training and character, to do now
the like for him. It is indeed a strange thing that authors
should narrate circumstantially the foundations of cities,
telling us when, how, and by whom they were founded, and
detailing the precise conditions and the difficulties of the
undertaking, while they pass over in silence the previous
training and the objects of the men who directed the whole
matter, though such information is more profitable. For inasmuch as it is more possible to emulate and to imitate living men than lifeless buildings, so much more important
for the improvement of a reader is it to learn about the former. Now had I not dealt with Philopoemen in a special
work[43] in which I explain who he and his family were, and
the nature of his training when young, I should be compelled to give an account of all these matters here. Since,
however, I have formerly in three books, which do not
form part of the present work, treated of him, stating what
was his training as a boy and enumerating his most famous actions, it is evident that in the present narrative my
proper course is to omit details concerning his early training and the ambitions of his youth, but to add detail to the
summary account I there gave of the achievements of his
riper years, in order that the proper character of each work
may be preserved. For just as the former work, being in the
form of an encomium, demanded a summary and somewhat exaggerated account of his achievements, so the pres-

---

43 P.'s *Life of Philopoemen*, three books "in the form of an encomium" (so P. 21.8); see *FGrH* 173. The work is lost, but Plu-
tarch's *Life of Philopoemen*, which made use of it, is preserved.

τῆς ἱστορίας, κοινὸς ὢν ἐπαίνου καὶ ψόγου, ζητεῖ τὸν
ἀληθῆ καὶ τὸν μετ᾽ ἀποδείξεως καὶ τῶν ἑκάστοις
παρεπομένων συλλογισμῶν.

22. Φιλοποίμην τοίνυν πρῶτον μὲν ἔφυ καλῶς· ἦν
(25) γὰρ ἐξ ἀνδρῶν τῶν ἐπιφανεστάτων κατ᾽ Ἀρκαδίαν,
τραφεὶς δὲ καὶ παιδευθεὶς ὑπὸ Κλέανδρον τὸν Μαντι-
νέα, πατρικὸν μὲν αὑτῷ ξένον ὑπάρχοντα, φυγαδεύ-
οντα δὲ κατ᾽ ἐκείνους τοὺς καιρούς, ὄντα δὲ Μαντινέων
2 ἐπιφανέστατον. μετὰ δὲ ταῦτα παραγενόμενος εἰς ἡλικίαν ἐγένετο ζηλωτὴς Ἐκδήμου καὶ Δημοφάνους, οἳ
τὸ μὲν γένος ἦσαν ἐκ Μεγάλης πόλεως, φεύγοντες δὲ
τοὺς τυράννους καὶ συμβιώσαντες Ἀρκεσίλᾳ τῷ φι-
λοσόφῳ κατὰ τὴν φυγὴν ἠλευθέρωσαν μὲν τὴν αὑτῶν
πατρίδα, συστησάμενοι κατ᾽ Ἀριστοδήμου τοῦ τυράν-
3 νου πρᾶξιν, συνεπελάβοντο δὲ καὶ τῆς καταλύσεως
τοῦ Σικυωνίων τυράννου Νικοκλέους, κοινωνήσαντες
Ἀράτῳ τῆς ἐπιβολῆς· ἔτι δὲ Κυρηναίων αὐτοὺς μετα-
πεμψαμένων ἐπιφανῶς προύστησαν καὶ διεφύλαξαν
4 αὐτοῖς τὴν ἐλευθερίαν, οἷς κατὰ τὴν πρώτην ἡλικίαν
ἐπὶ πολὺ συμβιώσας διέφερε μὲν εὐθέως τῶν καθ᾽
αὑτὸν περί τε τὰς ἐν τοῖς κυνηγίοις κακοπαθείας καὶ
5 τόλμας περί τε τὰς ἐν τοῖς πολεμικοῖς, ἦν δὲ καὶ περὶ
τὸν βίον ἐπιμελὴς καὶ λιτὸς κατὰ τὴν περικοπήν,
παρειληφὼς παρὰ τῶν προειρημένων ἀνδρῶν τοιαύτας τινὰς δόξας ὡς οὐχ οἷόν τε τῶν κοινῶν προστατεῖν

---

44 Each of the two names is somewhat uncertain.
45 Born at Pitane near Pergamum, the leader of Plato's Acad-

ent history, which distributes praise and blame impartially, demands a strictly true account and one which states the ground on which either praise or blame is based.

22. Philopoemen, then, came of a good stock, his family being one of the noblest in Arcadia. He was brought up and educated under the charge of Cleander of Mantinea, an old family friend and the most distinguished of the Mantineans, but living at the time in exile. When he grew up he became an admirer of Ecdemus and Demophanes,[44] who were natives of Megalopolis, but had escaped from the oppression of the tyrants, and after being with Arcesilaus the philosopher[45] during their exile liberated their country by organizing a plot against the tyrant Aristodemus, and also took part in the overthrow of Nicocles, the tyrant of Sicyon,[46] joining Aratus in that enterprise. In addition to this, when the people of Cyrene sent for them they had championed their cause in a brilliant manner and preserved their liberty.[47] Spending much of his time with these two men in his early youth he soon came to excel all his contemporaries in endurance and courage both in the chase and in war. He was also strict in his way of living and simple in dress and other such matters, for these men had instilled into him such convictions as that it was impossible for a man who was careless about the conduct of his own

emy from the 260s until his death in 241/0. See D. L. 4.28–45 with A. A. Long, *Elenchos* 7 (1986), 429–449.

[46] In 251 overthrown after a rule of only four months.

[47] There was a short period of democracy in Cyrene after the death of its ruler Magas and before Ptolemy II (or III) recovered the Cyrenaica, shortly before or after 250. See A. Laronde, *Cyrène et la Libye hellénistique* (Paris 1987), 382.

καλῶς τὸν ὀλιγωροῦντα τῶν κατὰ τὸν ἴδιον βίον, οὔτε
μὴν ἀποσχέσθαι τῶν τῆς πατρίδος, ὅστις πολυτελέ-
στερον ζῇ τῆς κατὰ τὴν ἰδίαν ὕπαρξιν χορηγίας.

6   Πλὴν κατασταθεὶς ὑπὸ τῶν Ἀχαιῶν ἱππάρχης ἐν
τοῖς προειρημένοις καιροῖς, καὶ παραλαβὼν τὰ συν-
τάγματα τῶν ἱππέων παντὶ τρόπῳ κατεφθαρμένα καὶ
7   τὰς ψυχὰς τῶν ἀνδρῶν ἡττημένας, οὐ μόνον αὐτοὺς
ἑαυτῶν βελτίους, ἀλλὰ καὶ τῶν ὑπεναντίων κρείττους
ἐν ὀλίγῳ χρόνῳ κατεσκεύασε, πάντας εἰς ἀληθινὴν
8   ἄσκησιν καὶ ζῆλον ἐπιτευκτικὸν ἐμβιβάσας. τῶν μὲν
γὰρ ἄλλων οἱ πλεῖστοι τῶν καθισταμένων ἐπὶ τὴν
προειρημένην ἀρχήν, οἱ μὲν διὰ τὴν ἰδίαν ἀδυναμίαν
ἐν τοῖς ἱππικοῖς οὐδὲ τοῖς πλησίον τολμῶσιν οὐδὲν ὧν
9   καθήκει προστάττειν, οἱ δὲ τῆς στρατηγίας ὀρεγό-
μενοι διὰ ταύτης τῆς ἀρχῆς ἐξεριθεύονται τοὺς νέους
καὶ παρασκευάζουσιν εὔνους συναγωνιστὰς εἰς τὸ
μέλλον, οὐκ ἐπιτιμῶντες τῷ δεομένῳ, δι' οὗ τρόπου
σῴζεται τὰ κοινά, ⟨ἀλλὰ⟩ συμπεριστέλλοντες τὰς
ἁμαρτίας καὶ μικρᾷ χάριτι μεγάλα βλάπτοντες τοὺς
10 πιστεύοντας. εἰ δέ ποτε γένοιντο τῶν ἀρχόντων τινὲς
τῇ τε κατὰ σῶμα χρείᾳ δυνατοὶ πρός τε τὸ τῶν κοινῶν
ἀπέχεσθαι πρόθυμοι, πλείω κατὰ τῶν ὀλιγωρούντων
διὰ τὴν κακοζηλωσίαν ἀπεργάζονται τοὺς πεζούς, ἔτι
δὲ μᾶλλον τοὺς ἱππεῖς.

23. Ἦσαν δὲ κινήσεις, ἃς ὑπελάμβανε πρὸς πάντα
(21) καιρὸν ἁρμόζειν, αἷς ἔδει συνειθίσθαι τοὺς ἱππεῖς,

life to administer public affairs well, and that it was impossible for a man who lived more extravagantly than his own resources allowed to keep his hands off public money.

Being appointed by the Achaeans to the command of the cavalry[48] at this time and finding the regiments in every way disorganized and the men dispirited, he made them in a short time not only superior to what they had been but superior to the enemy by submitting them to a course of real training and inspiring them with such zeal as could not fail to assure success. For, as for most of the others who are appointed to this office, some of them owing to their own incapacity in horse exercise do not even dare to give any proper orders to the men they have under them, while others who treat this office as a step to that of strategus, canvass the soldiers and secure their future support, never rebuking a man who deserves it, which is the way to safeguard public interests, but screening all faults and by conferring a small favor doing infinite harm to those who trust them. And if at any time some commanders are personally efficient and are also anxious to keep their hands off public money, they manage by their unhappy ambition to do more harm to the infantry than the negligent ones, and they do still more mischief to the cavalry.

23. The movements[49] in which he thought the cavalry should be trained, as being applicable to all circumstances,

---

[48] Philopoemen held this command in 210/09.

[49] P. speaks in this chapter and the following from his own experience as *hipparch* of the Achaeans in 169/8. Earlier, Xenophon had published instructions for the cavalry commander in his *Hipparchicus* and for the individual horseman in his *On Horsemanship*.

2   αὗται· αἱ καθ' ἵππον μὲν κλίσεις ἐφ' ἡνίαν καὶ πάλιν
ἐπὶ δόρυ, πρὸς δὲ τούτοις ἀναστροφὴ καὶ μεταβολή,
3–4 κατ' οὐλαμὸν δ' ἐπιστροφὴ καὶ περισπασμός, ἔτι δ'
ἐκπερισπασμός, πρὸς δὲ τούτοις ἐξαγωγαὶ κατὰ
λόχους καὶ διλοχίας ἀφ' ἑκατέρων τῶν κεράτων μετὰ
τάχους, ποτὲ δ' ἀπὸ τῶν μέσων, καὶ συναγωγαὶ πάλιν
5   μετ' ἐποχῆς εἰς οὐλαμούς, εἰς ἴλας, εἰς ἱππαρχίας, ἐπὶ
δὲ τούτοις ἐκτάξεις ἐφ' ἑκατέρων τῶν κεράτων ἢ διὰ
παρεμβολῆς ἢ διὰ παραγωγῆς τῆς παρὰ τοὺς οὐρα-
6   γούς. τὰς μὲν γὰρ κατὰ περίκλασιν οὐ προσδεῖσθαι
μελέτης ἔφη· σχεδὸν γὰρ ὡς ἂν εἰ πορείας ἔχειν
7   διάθεσιν. ἐκ δὲ τούτου τὰς ἐπαγωγὰς τὰς ἐπὶ τοὺς
ἐναντίους καὶ τὰς ἀποχωρήσεις ἔδει συνεθίζειν ἐν
πάσαις ταῖς κινήσεσιν ἐπὶ τοσοῦτον ὥστε δεινῷ τῷ
τάχει προσάγειν, ἐφ' ὅσον συζυγοῦντας καὶ συστοι-
χοῦντας διαμένειν, ἅμα δὲ καὶ τὰ διαστήματα κατὰ
8   τοὺς οὐλαμοὺς τηρεῖν, ὡς ἱππέων λελυκότων τὴν τάξιν
τὴν ἐν οὐλαμοῖς, αἱρουμένων κινδυνεύειν, οὐδὲν ἐπι-
9   σφαλέστερον ὑπάρχον οὐδ' ἀχρειότερον. ταῦτα δ'
ὑποδείξας τοῖς τε πολλοῖς καὶ τοῖς ἀποτελείοις, αὖθις
ἐπεπορεύετο τὰς πόλεις, ἐξετάζων πρῶτον μὲν εἰ συμ-
περιφέρονθ' οἱ πολλοὶ τοῖς παραγγελλομένοις, δεύτερον δ' εἰ κρατοῦσιν οἱ κατὰ πόλεις ἄρχοντες τοῦ
10 σαφῶς καὶ δεόντως διδόναι τὰ παραγγέλματα, κρίνων
πρὸς τὴν ἀλήθειαν οὐδὲν ἀναγκαιότερον εἶναι τῆς τῶν
κατὰ μέρος ἡγεμόνων ἐμπειρίας.

    24. προκατασκευασάμενος δὲ τὰ προειρημένα τοῦ-
(22) τον τὸν τρόπον, συνῆγε τοὺς ἱππεῖς ἐκ τῶν πόλεων εἰς

were as follows. Each separate horseman must learn to wheel his horse to the left or to the right and also to wheel round and again return. In squadrons they were to learn to wheel so as to describe either a quarter, a half, or three-quarters of a circle and next to dash out at full speed from either of the wings or from the center in single or double files and then reining in to resume their formation in troops, squadrons, or regiments. Besides this they must be able to extend their line on either wing either by filling up intervals or by bringing up men from the rear. He considered that deployment by wheeling required no practice, as it was much the same thing as falling into marching order. After this they were to practice charging and retiring in every kind of formation until they could advance at a tremendous pace but without falling out of line or column, keeping at the same time the proper distances between the squadrons, as he considered that nothing was more dangerous or ineffectual than cavalry which have broken their order in squadrons and choose to engage the enemy while in this state. When he had given these instructions to the troops and the local officers, he paid a second visit to the towns to inquire in the first place if the soldiers were obeying orders, and next if the municipal magistrates were thoroughly capable of giving the words of command clearly and properly, as he considered that for actual warfare nothing was more essential than the efficiency of particular officers.

24. After thus making his preliminary preparations, he collected the cavalry from the different towns at one spot,

ἕνα τόπον, καὶ δι᾽ αὐτοῦ τὰς κινήσεις ἐπετέλει καὶ τὸν
2 ὅλον χειρισμὸν αὐτὸς ἐποιεῖτο τῆς ἐξοπλισίας, οὐ
προηγούμενος πάντων, ὅπερ οἱ νῦν ποιοῦσιν ἡγεμόνες, ὑπολαμβάνοντες ἡγεμονικὴν εἶναι τὴν πρώτην
3 χώραν. τί γὰρ ἀπειρότερον, ἅμα δ᾽ ἐπισφαλέστερον
ἄρχοντος, ⟨ὃς⟩ ὁρᾶται μὲν ὑπὸ πάντων τῶν ὑπο-
4 τεταγμένων, ὁρᾷ δ᾽ οὐδένα; οὐ γὰρ στρατιωτικῆς
ἐξουσίας, ἀλλ᾽ ἡγεμονικῆς ἐμπειρίας, ἅμα δὲ καὶ
δυνάμεως δεῖγμα δεῖ φέρειν τὸν ἱππάρχην ἐν ταῖς
ἐξοπλισίαις, ποτὲ μὲν ἐν πρώτοις, ποτὲ δ᾽ ἐν ἐσχάτοις,
5 ποτὲ δὲ κατὰ μέσους γινόμενον. ὅπερ ὁ προειρημένος
ἀνὴρ ἐποίει, παριππεύων καὶ πάντας ἐφορῶν αὐτός,
καὶ προσδιασαφῶν αὐτοῖς ἀποροῦσι καὶ διορθῶν ἐν
6 ἀρχαῖς πᾶν τὸ διαμαρτανόμενον. ἦν δὲ τὰ τοιαῦτα
τελέως βραχέα καὶ σπάνια διὰ τὴν προγεγενημένην
7 ἐν τοῖς κατὰ μέρος ἐπιμέλειαν. Δημήτριος ὁ Φαληρεὺς
ἕως λόγου τὸ τοιοῦτον ὑπέδειξε, φήσας ὅτι καθάπερ ἐν
οἰκοδομίαις, ἐὰν κατὰ μίαν πλίνθον θῆς καὶ καθ᾽ ἕνα
δόμον ἐπιμελείας τύχῃ τὸ παρατεθέν, οὕτως ἐν στρατοπέδῳ τὸ κατ᾽ ἄνδρα καὶ κατὰ λόχον ἀκριβωθὲν ὅλην
ποιεῖ τὴν δύναμιν ἰσχυράν.

25. Εἶναι γὰρ τὸ νῦν γινόμενον ὁμοιότατον τῇ περὶ
(23) 2 τὰς παρατάξεις οἰκονομίᾳ καὶ χειρισμῷ. καὶ γὰρ ἐπ᾽

---

50 Pupil of Theophrastus, Peripatetic philosopher. Cassander
of Macedon put him in charge of Athens, which he ruled from
317 to 307. Prolific writer. *FGrH* 228, F 27 for the present quotation. W. W. Fortenbaugh—E. Schütrumpf (ed.), *Demetrius of*

where he personally supervised their evolutions and directed the whole of their drill, not riding at the head of them as is done by the generals of our day, who fancy that the foremost place is the proper one for a commander. What, I should like to know, can be less practical or more dangerous than a commander's being seen by all his troops, but seeing none of them? A leader of cavalry should during exercise not display the qualifications of an ordinary soldier but his capability and power as a commander, placing himself now in front, now in the rear, and now in the center. This was what Philopoemen did, riding alongside and personally inspecting all his men, making matters clear to those who were in doubt and correcting all mistakes at the outset. Such mistakes, however, were quite trivial and rare owing to the care which had been taken previously in exercising each part in particular. Demetrius of Phaleron[50] pointed this out, if not in practice in a phrase at least, when he said that just as a building will be solid if each brick is placed rightly and every course laid with care, so in an army it is the careful instruction of each man and each unit which makes the whole force strong.

Fragment of the Speech of a Macedonian Orator

25. What is happening now[51] is exceedingly like the disposition and management of an army for battle. For in that

Phalerum: Text, Translation and Discussion (New Brunswick 2000).

[51] Probably from peace negotiations in 209. The speaker tries to drive a wedge between the Aetolians (with their Peloponnesian allies) and the Romans.

ἐκείνων προκινδυνεύει μὲν ὡς ἐπίπαν καὶ προαπόλ-
λυται τὰ κοῦφα καὶ τὰ πρακτικώτατα τῆς δυνάμεως,
τὴν δ᾽ ἐπιγραφὴν τῶν ἐκβαινόντων ἡ φάλαγξ καὶ τὰ
3 βαρέα λαμβάνει τῶν ὅπλων. νῦν δὲ παραπλησίως
προκινδυνεύουσι μὲν Αἰτωλοὶ καὶ Πελοποννησίων οἱ
τούτοις συμμαχοῦντες, ἐφεδρεύουσι δὲ Ῥωμαῖοι, φά-
4 λαγγος ἔχοντες διάθεσιν. κἂν μὲν οὗτοι πταίσαντες
καταφθαρῶσιν, ἀναστρέψαντες ἐκ τῶν πραγμάτων
5 ἀβλαβεῖς ἀπολυθήσονται Ῥωμαῖοι· νικησάντων δὲ
τούτων, ὃ μὴ δόξειε τοῖς θεοῖς, ἅμα τούτοις καὶ τοὺς
6 ἄλλους Ἕλληνας ὑφ᾽ αὑτοὺς ἐκεῖνοι ποιήσονται. Πᾶσαν γὰρ δημοκρατικὴν συμμαχίαν καὶ φιλίας πολλῆς
δεῖσθαι διὰ τὰς ἐν τοῖς πλήθεσι γινομένας ἀλογίας.

26. Ὅτι Φίλιππος ὁ βασιλεὺς Μακεδόνων μετὰ τὸ
ἐκτελέσαι τὸν τῶν Νεμέων ἀγῶνα αὖθις εἰς Ἄργος
ἐπανῆλθε καὶ τὸ μὲν διάδημα καὶ τὴν πορφύραν ἀπέ-
θετο, βουλόμενος αὑτὸν ἴσον τοῖς πολλοῖς καὶ πρᾷόν
2 τινα καὶ δημοτικὸν ὑπογράφειν. ὅσῳ δὲ τὴν ἐσθῆτα
δημοτικωτέραν περιετίθετο, τοσούτῳ τὴν ἐξουσίαν
3 ἐλάμβανε μείζω καὶ μοναρχικωτέραν. οὐ γὰρ ἔτι τὰς
χήρας ἐπείρα γυναῖκας οὐδὲ τὰς ὑπάνδρους ἠρκεῖτο
μοιχεύων, ἀλλ᾽ ἐκ προστάγματος ἦν αὐτῷ φανείη,
προσπέμψας ἐκάλει, ταῖς δὲ μὴ προχείρως συνυπ-
ακουούσαις ἐνύβριζε, κώμους ποιούμενος ἐπὶ τὰς οἰ-
4 κίας. καὶ τῶν μὲν τοὺς υἱεῖς, τῶν δὲ τοὺς ἄνδρας

----

52 Elis, Messene, and Sparta.   53 The fragment, in *ora-
tio obliqua*, probably comes from the same event as 25.1–5.

case also the first to be exposed to danger and to suffer loss are the light and most active part of the force, whereas the phalanx and the heavy-armed troops get the credit for the result. Similarly at present those who bear the brunt of the danger are the Aetolians and those Peloponnesians who are in alliance[52] with them, while the Romans, like a phalanx, hold themselves in reserve. If the former are beaten and destroyed, the Romans will get away unharmed from the struggle, but should the Aetolians be victorious, which Heaven forbid, the Romans will subjugate them as well as all the other Greeks. Every alliance with a democracy requires much goodwill because of the irrationality of the masses.[53]

Philip V

26. Philip, king of Macedon, after celebrating the Nemean games,[54] returned to Argos and laid aside his diadem and purple robe, wishing to produce the impression that he was on a level with others and a lenient and popular prince. But the more democratic the clothes he wore, the greater and more monarchlike was the license he displayed. For he no longer confined himself to attempting to seduce widows or to corrupting married women, but used to send and order any woman he chose to come to him, and insulted those who did not at once obey his behests, making noisy processions to their houses. Summoning their sons or husbands on absurd pretexts he intimidated them,

[54] While in Argos, Philip was elected president of the games (ἀγωνοθέτης) in July 209 (Livy 27.30.9; 17).

ἀνακαλούμενος ἐπὶ προφάσεσιν ἀλόγοις διέσειε, καὶ
5 πολλὴν ἀσέλγειαν ἐναπεδείκνυτο καὶ παρανομίαν. διὸ
καὶ χρώμενος τῇ κατὰ τὴν παρεπιδημίαν ἐξουσίᾳ . . .
ἀνέδην πολλοὺς ἐλύπει τῶν Ἀχαιῶν, καὶ μάλιστα τοὺς
6 μετρίους ἄνδρας. πιεζόμενοι δὲ διὰ τὸ πανταχόθεν
αὐτοῖς περιεστάναι τὸν πόλεμον ἠναγκάζοντο καρτε-
ρεῖν καὶ φέρειν τὰ παρὰ φύσιν. . . .

7 Ὅτι [Φιλίππου] οὐκ ⟨ἂν⟩ ἀγαθὰ μείζω τις σχοίη
πρὸς βασιλείαν οὐδεὶς τῶν πρότερον οὐδὲ κακὰ τού-
8 του τοῦ βασιλέως. καί μοι δοκεῖ τὰ μὲν ἀγαθὰ φύσει
περὶ αὐτὸν ὑπάρξαι, τὰ δὲ κακὰ προβαίνοντι κατὰ τὴν
ἡλικίαν ἐπιγενέσθαι, καθάπερ ἐνίοις ἐπιγίνεται γη-
9 ράσκουσι τῶν ἵππων. καίπερ ἡμεῖς οὐκ ἐν τοῖς προ-
οιμίοις, ὥσπερ τῶν λοιπῶν συγγραφέων, προφερό-
μεθα τὰς τοιαύτας διαλήψεις, ἀλλ' ἐπ' αὐτῶν τῶν
πραγμάτων ἀεὶ τὸν καθήκοντα λόγον ἁρμόζοντες
ἀποφαινόμεθα περί τε τῶν βασιλέων καὶ τῶν ἐπι-
10 φανῶν ἀνδρῶν, νομίζοντες ταύτην οἰκειοτέραν εἶναι
καὶ τοῖς γράφουσι καὶ τοῖς ἀναγινώσκουσι τὴν ἐπιση-
μασίαν.

IV. RES ASIAE

27. Ἔστι τοίνυν ἡ Μηδία κατά τε τὸ μέγεθος τῆς
χώρας ἀξιοχρεωτάτη τῶν κατὰ τὴν Ἀσίαν δυναστειῶν
καὶ κατὰ τὸ πλῆθος καὶ κατὰ τὰς ἀρετὰς τῶν ἀνδρῶν,
2 ὁμοίως δὲ καὶ τῶν ἵππων· τοῖς γὰρ ζῴοις τούτοις
σχεδὸν ἅπασαν χορηγεῖ τὴν Ἀσίαν τῷ καὶ τὰ βασι-

and on the whole behaved in a most outrageous and lawless manner. Consequently by this excessive display of license during his stay in the country he vexed many of the
Achaeans and especially the most respectable men, but
pressed as they were on all sides by war they had perforce
to put up with what was naturally offensive to them. . . .

None of the former kings possessed more of the qualities which make a good or bad ruler than Philip, and in my
opinion his good qualities were natural to him, but his defects were acquired as he advanced in age, as is the case
with some horses[55] when they grow old. I, however, do not,
like other writers, deliver such judgments at the outset,[56]
but always in dealing with actual facts employ terms suited
to the situation to convey my opinion of kings and other
prominent men, thinking that this method of indicating it
is most proper for writers and most agreeable to readers.

IV. AFFAIRS OF ASIA

Expedition of Antiochus Against Arsaces

27. Media is the most notable principality in Asia, both
in the extent of its territory and the number and excellence
of the men and also of the horses it produces. It supplies
nearly the whole of Asia with these animals, the royal herds

210
B.C.

---

[55] Again P. seems to speak from personal experience.
[56] When first introducing a character.

λικὰ συστήματα τῶν ἱπποτροφιῶν Μήδοις ἐπιτετρά-
3 φθαι ⟨διὰ τὴν τῶν τόπων⟩ εὐφυΐαν. περιοικεῖται δὲ
πόλεσιν Ἑλληνίσι κατὰ τὴν ὑφήγησιν τὴν Ἀλεξάνδρου, φυλακῆς ἕνεκεν τῶν συγκυρούντων αὐτῇ βαρ-
4 βάρων πλὴν Ἐκβατάνων. αὕτη δ' ἔκτισται μὲν ἐν τοῖς
πρὸς τὰς ἄρκτους μέρεσι τῆς Μηδίας, ἐπίκειται δὲ
τοῖς περὶ τὴν Μαιῶτιν καὶ τὸν Εὔξεινον μέρεσι τῆς
5 Ἀσίας, ἦν δὲ βασίλειον ἐξ ἀρχῆς Μήδων, πλούτῳ δὲ
καὶ τῇ τῆς κατασκευῆς πολυτελείᾳ μέγα τι παρὰ τὰς
6 ἄλλας δοκεῖ διενηνοχέναι πόλεις. κεῖται μὲν οὖν ὑπὸ
τὴν παρώρειαν τὴν παρὰ τὸν Ὀρόντην, ἀτείχιστος
οὖσα, ἄκραν δ' ἐν αὐτῇ χειροποίητον ἔχει, θαυμασίως
7 πρὸς ὀχυρότητα κατεσκευασμένην. ὑπὸ δὲ ταύτην
ἐστὶ βασίλεια, περὶ ὧν καὶ τὸ λέγειν κατὰ μέρος καὶ
8 τὸ παρασιωπᾶν ἔχει τιν' ἀπορίαν· τοῖς μὲν γὰρ αἱρου-
μένοις τὰς ἐκπληκτικὰς τῶν διηγήσεων προφέρεσθαι
καὶ μετ' αὐξήσεως ἔνια καὶ διαθέσεως εἰθισμένοις
ἐξαγγέλλειν καλλίστην ὑπόθεσιν ἡ προειρημένη πόλις ἔχει, τοῖς δ' εὐλαβῶς προσπορευομένοις πρὸς πᾶν
⟨τὸ⟩ παρὰ τὴν κοινὴν ἔννοιαν λεγόμενον ἀπορίαν
9 παρασκευάζει καὶ δυσχρηστίαν. πλὴν ἔστι γε τὰ
βασίλεια τῷ μὲν μεγέθει σχεδὸν ἑπτὰ σταδίων ἔχοντα
τὴν περιγραφήν, τῇ δὲ τῶν κατὰ μέρος κατασκευ-
ασμάτων πολυτελείᾳ μεγάλην ἐμφαίνοντα τὴν τῶν ἐξ
10 ἀρχῆς καταβαλλομένων εὐκαιρίαν. οὔσης γὰρ τῆς
ξυλείας ἁπάσης κεδρίνης καὶ κυπαριττίνης, οὐδεμίαν
αὐτῶν γεγυμνῶσθαι συνέβαινεν, ἀλλὰ καὶ τὰς δοκοὺς
καὶ τὰ φατνώματα καὶ τοὺς κίονας τοὺς ἐν ταῖς στοαῖς

for breeding being entrusted to the Medes owing to the excellence of the pastures. On its borders a ring of Greek cities was founded by Alexander[57] to protect it from the neighboring barbarians. Ecbatana[58] is an exception. This city is situated in the northern part of Media and commands that portion of Asia which borders on the Maeotis and Euxine. It had always been the royal residence of the Medes and is said to have greatly exceeded all the other cities in wealth and the magnificence of its buildings. It lies on the skirts of Mount Orontes and has no wall, but possesses an artificial citadel the fortifications of which are of wonderful strength. Beneath this stands the palace, regarding which I am in doubt if I should say something or keep silence. For to those who are disposed to recount marvelous tales and are in the habit of giving exaggerated and rhetorical reports of certain matters this city affords an admirable theme, but to such as approach with caution all statements which are contrary to ordinary conceptions it is a source of doubt and difficulty. The palace, however, is about seven stades in circumference, and by the magnificence of the separate structures in it conveys a high idea of the wealth of its original founders. For the woodwork was all of cedar and cypress, but no part of it was left exposed, and the rafters, the compartments of the ceiling, and the columns in the porticoes and colonnades were

[57] For the cities founded by Alexander, see P. M. Fraser, *Cities of Alexander the Great* (Oxford 1996). There is hardly any evidence to substantiate P.'s statement for Media and the adjoining regions.   [58] Modern Hamadan, built over the ancient city, a fact prohibiting systematic excavations. The city is mainly known from P.'s "glowing description" (P. Briant, *OCD* Ecbatana 501).

καὶ περιστύλοις, τοὺς μὲν ἀργυραῖς, τοὺς δὲ χρυσαῖς
λεπίσι περιειλῆφθαι, τὰς δὲ κεραμίδας ἀργυρᾶς εἶναι
11 πάσας. τούτων δὲ τὰ μὲν πλεῖστα συνέβη λεπισθῆναι
κατὰ τὴν Ἀλεξάνδρου καὶ Μακεδόνων ἔφοδον, τὰ δὲ
λοιπὰ κατὰ τὴν Ἀντιγόνου καὶ Σελεύκου ⟨Νικάτορος⟩
12 δυναστείαν. ὅμως δὲ κατὰ τὴν Ἀντιόχου παρουσίαν ὅ
τε ναὸς αὐτὸς ὁ τῆς Αἴνης προσαγορευόμενος ἔτι τοὺς
κίονας εἶχε τοὺς πέριξ κεχρυσωμένους, καὶ κεραμίδες
ἀργυραῖ καὶ πλείους ἐν αὐτῷ συνετέθειντο, πλίνθοι δὲ
χρυσαῖ τινες ὀλίγαι μὲν ἦσαν, ἀργυραῖ δὲ καὶ πλείους
13 ὑπέμενον. ἐκ δὲ πάντων τῶν προειρημένων τὸ χαρα-
χθὲν εἰς τὸ βασιλικὸν ἠθροίσθη νόμισμα μικρῷ λεῖπον τετρακισχιλίων ταλάντων.

28. Ἕως μὲν οὖν τούτων τῶν τόπων ἤλπισεν αὐτὸν
ἥξειν Ἀρσάκης, τὴν δ᾿ ἔρημον τὴν τούτοις πρόσ-
χωρον οὐ τολμήσειν ἔτι δυνάμει τηλικαύτῃ διεκβα-
2 λεῖν, καὶ μάλιστα διὰ τὴν ἀνυδρίαν. ἐπιπολῆς μὲν γὰρ
οὐδέν ἐστι φαινόμενον ὕδωρ ἐν τοῖς προειρημένοις
τόποις, ὑπόνομοι δὲ πλείους εἰσὶ καὶ διὰ τῆς ἐρήμου
3 φρεατίας ἔχοντες ἀγνοουμένας τοῖς ἀπείροις. περὶ δὲ
τούτων ἀληθὴς παραδίδοται λόγος διὰ τῶν ἐγχωρίων,
ὅτι καθ᾿ οὓς χρόνους Πέρσαι τῆς Ἀσίας ἐπεκράτουν,
ἔδωκαν τοῖς ἐπί τινας τόπους τῶν μὴ πρότερον ἀρδευ-
ομένων ἐπεισαγομένοις ὕδωρ πηγαῖον ἐπὶ πέντε γενε-

---

59 For Alexander's stay at Ecbatana in 330, see Arr., *An.*
3.19.5–8. A. B. Bosworth, however, persuasively rejects the report, since no other writer knows of a visit to Ecbatana and cir-

plated with either silver or gold, and all the tiles were silver. Most of the precious metals were stripped off in the invasion of Alexander and his Macedonians,[59] and the rest during the reigns of Antigonus and Seleucus Nicator, but still, when Antiochus reached the place, the temple of Aene[60] alone had the columns round it still gilded and a number of silver tiles were piled up in it, while a few gold bricks and a considerable quantity of silver ones remained. From all the objects I have mentioned coined money amounting to very nearly four thousand talents was paid into the treasury.

28. Arsaces[61] had expected Antiochus to advance as far as this region, but he did not think he would venture with such a large force to cross the adjacent desert, chiefly owing to the scarcity of water. For in the region I speak of there is no water visible on the surface, but even in the desert there are a number of underground channels communicating with wells unknown to those not acquainted with the country. About these a true story is told by the inhabitants. They say that at the time when the Persians were the rulers of Asia they gave to those who conveyed a supply of water to places previously unirrigated the right of cultivating the land for five generations, and conse-

cumstances do not allow for it. He argues that the author must have misunderstood his source (*CQ* 26 [1976], 132–136). P. does not say that the king himself visited the city.   [60] The Persian goddess Anahita, called Nanaia in inscriptions. F. Canali de Rossi, *Iscrizioni dello estremo oriente Greco* (Bonn 2004), no. 197.3, and Index, p. 353.   [61] Arsaces II, king of Parthia, 211–191. See H. H. Schmitt, *Untersuchungen zur Geschichte Antiochos' des Grossen und seiner Zeit* (Wiesbaden 1964) 63–64.

4 ἃς καρπεῦσαι τὴν χώραν· ὅθεν ἔχοντος τοῦ Ταύρου
πολλὰς καὶ μεγάλας ὑδάτων ἀπορρύσεις, πᾶσαν ἐπε-
δέχοντο δαπάνην καὶ κακοπάθειαν, ἐκ μακροῦ κατα-
σκευάζοντες τοὺς ὑπονόμους, ὥστε κατὰ τοὺς νῦν
καιροὺς μηδὲ τοὺς χρωμένους τοῖς ὕδασι γινώσκειν
τὰς ἀρχὰς τῶν ὑπονόμων πόθεν ἔχουσι τὰς ἐπιρ-
5 ρύσεις. πλὴν ὁρῶν Ἀρσάκης ἐπιβαλόμενον αὐτὸν τῇ
διὰ τῆς ἐρήμου πορείᾳ, τὸ τηνικάδε χωννύειν καὶ
6 φθείρειν ἐνεχείρησε τὰς φρεατίας. ὁ δὲ βασιλεύς,
ἐξαγγελθέντος αὐτῷ, πάλιν ἐξαπέστειλε τοὺς περὶ
Νικομήδην μετὰ χιλίων ἱππέων, οἳ καὶ καταλαβόντες
τὸν Ἀρσάκην μετὰ τῆς δυνάμεως ὑποκεχωρηκότα,
τινὰς δὲ τῶν ἱππέων φθείροντας τὰ στόματα τῶν
ὑπονόμων, τούτους μὲν ἐξ ἐφόδου τρεψάμενοι φυγεῖν
ἠνάγκασαν, αὐτοὶ δὲ πάλιν ἀνεχώρησαν ὡς τὸν Ἀντί-
7 οχον. ὁ δὲ βασιλεὺς διανύσας τὴν ἔρημον ἧκε πρὸς
τὴν Ἑκατόμπυλον προσαγορευομένην, ἣ κεῖται μὲν ἐν
μέσῃ τῇ Παρθυηνῇ, τῶν δὲ διόδων <τῶν> φερουσῶν
ἐπὶ πάντας τοὺς πέριξ τόπους ἐνταῦθα συμπιπτουσῶν
ἀπὸ τοῦ συμβαίνοντος ὁ τόπος εἴληφε τὴν προσηγορίαν.

29. Πλὴν αὐτοῦ διαναπαύσας τὴν δύναμιν, καὶ
συλλογισάμενος ὡς εἰ μὲν οἷός <τ᾽> ἦν Ἀρσάκης διὰ
μάχης κρίνεσθαι πρὸς σφᾶς, οὔτ᾽ ἂν ἐξεχώρει λιπὼν
τὴν αὑτοῦ χώραν οὔτ᾽ ἂν ἐπιτηδειοτέρους τόπους
ἐζήτει πρὸς ἀγῶνα ταῖς σφετέραις δυνάμεσι τῶν περὶ

---

62 Actually the Elburz. *RE* Tauros 39–50, for P.'s testimony 44

quently as the Taurus[62] has many large streams descending from it, people incurred great expense and trouble in making underground channels reaching a long distance, so that at the present day those who make use of the water do not know whence the channels derive their supply. Arsaces, however, when he saw that Antiochus was attempting to march across the desert, endeavored instantly to fill up and destroy the wells. The king when this news reached him sent off Nicomedes[63] with a thousand horse, who, finding that Arsaces had retired with his army, but that some of his cavalry were engaged in destroying the mouths of the channels, attacked and routed these, forcing them to fly, and then returned to Antiochus. The king having traversed the desert came to the city called Hecatompylus,[64] which lies in the center of Parthia. This city derives its name from the fact that it is the meeting place of all the roads leading to the surrounding districts.

29. Here he gave his army a rest, and now came to the conclusion that had Arsaces been able to risk a battle he would not have withdrawn from his own country and could not have chosen a place more favorable to his army for the struggle than the neighborhood of Hecatompylus. It

(W. Ruge). Map in WC 2.237. See also B. Bar-Kochva, *The Seleucid Army* (Cambridge 1976), 142–145.

[63] A Coan (29.6), probably none other than the governor of Caria for Antiochus in 201 (*I. Amyzon* 15.11 and, in his honor, 16). J. D. Grainger, *A Seleukid Prosopography and Gazetteer* (Leiden 1997), 109.

[64] "City of one hundred gates," located, after much dispute, at Shahr-i Qumis by J. Hansman and D. Stronach; see references in *OCD* Hecatompylus 673 (M. A. R. Colledge).

2 τὴν Ἑκατόμπυλον· ἐπειδὴ δ᾽ ἐκχωρεῖ, δῆλός ἐστι τοῖς
ὀρθῶς σκοπουμένοις ἐπ᾽ ἄλλης ὢν γνώμης· διόπερ
3 ἔκρινε προάγειν εἰς τὴν Ὑρκανίαν. παραγενόμενος δ᾽
ἐπὶ Ταγάς, καὶ πυνθανόμενος τῶν ἐγχωρίων τήν τε
δυσχέρειαν τῶν τόπων, οὓς ἔδει διεκβάλλειν αὐτόν,
ἕως εἰς τὰς ὑπερβολὰς διεξίκοιτο τοῦ Λάβου τὰς
νευούσας ἐπὶ τὴν Ὑρκανίαν, καὶ τὸ πλῆθος τῶν βαρβάρων τῶν κατὰ τόπους ἐφεστώτων ταῖς δυσχωρίαις
4 αὐτοῦ, προέθετο διατάττειν τὸ τῶν εὐζώνων πλῆθος
καὶ τοὺς τούτων ἡγεμόνας μερίζειν, ὡς ἑκάστους δεήσει πορεύεσθαι, ὁμοίως δὲ καὶ τοὺς λειτουργούς, οὓς
ἔδει παραπορευομένους τὸν καταλαμβανόμενον ὑπὸ
τῶν εὐζώνων τόπον εὔβατον παρασκευάζειν τῇ τῶν
5 φαλαγγιτῶν καὶ τῇ τῶν ὑποζυγίων πορείᾳ. ταῦτα δὲ
διανοηθεὶς τὴν μὲν πρώτην ἔδωκε τάξιν Διογένει,
συστήσας αὐτῷ τοξότας καὶ σφενδονήτας καὶ τῶν
ὀρείων τοὺς ἀκοντίζειν καὶ λιθάζειν δυναμένους, οἵτινες τάξιν μὲν οὐκ ἔνεμον, αἰεὶ δὲ πρὸς τὸν παρόντα
καιρὸν καὶ τόπον κατ᾽ ἄνδρα ποιούμενοι τὸν κίνδυνον
πραγματικωτάτην παρείχοντο χρείαν ἐν ταῖς δυσ-
6 χωρίαις. τούτοις δὲ συνεχεῖς Κρῆτας ἀσπιδιώτας
ἐπέταξε περὶ δισχιλίους, ὧν ἡγεῖτο Πολυξενίδας Ῥό-
διος, τελευταίους δὲ θωρακίτας καὶ θυρεοφόρους, ὧν
εἶχον τὴν ἡγεμονίαν Νικομήδης Κῷος καὶ Νικόλαος
Αἰτωλός.

---

65 The region southeast of the Caspian Sea. *RE* Hyrcania 454–
526 (E. Kiessling).   66 Modern Taq; see map in WC 2.237.

was evident then to anyone who gave proper consideration to the matter that as he was retreating he had other intentions. Antiochus therefore decided to advance into Hyrcania.[65] Upon reaching Tagae[66] and learning from the inhabitants what a difficult country he would have to pass through before reaching the pass over Mount Labus, which leads down to Hyrcania, and how great numbers of barbarians were posted at different spots where his march would be particularly hard, he decided to break up his light-armed troops into several bodies and divide their officers among them, with instructions as to the route they should take. He also resolved to break up the pioneers whose duty it was to march together with the light-armed troops and make the ground occupied by these passable for the phalanx and the pack train. Having made this plan he gave the command of the first division to Diogenes,[67] entrusting him with archers and slingers and those of the mountaineers who were expert in throwing javelins and stones, and who occupied no regular position but, whenever time and place called for it, fought singly and rendered most useful service on difficult ground. After these he placed about two thousand Cretans armed with bucklers under the command of Polyxenidas of Rhodes,[68] and lastly the light troops armed with breastplate and shield under Nicomedes of Cos and Nicolaus[69] the Aetolian.

[67] Probably the former governor of Susa (5.46.7; cf. 48.14), and of Media since 220 (5.54.12).

[68] An exile from Rhodes; twenty years later he was Antiochus' admiral and in 190 victorious in a naval battle over the Rhodian fleet. *RE* Polyxenidas 1850–1851 (Th. Lenschau).

[69] Previously in the service of Ptolemy IV: 5.61.8; 68.5.

30. Προαγόντων δὲ τούτων εἰς τὸ πρόσθεν, πολλῷ δυσχερεστέρας συνέβαινε φαίνεσθαι τὰς τῶν τόπων τραχύτητας καὶ στενότητας τῆς τοῦ βασιλέως προσ-

2 δοκίας. ἦν γὰρ τὸ μὲν ὅλον μῆκος τῆς ἀναβάσεως περὶ τριακοσίους σταδίους· ταύτης δὲ τὸ πλεῖστον μέρος ἔδει ποιεῖσθαι τῆς πορείας διὰ χαράδρας χει-μάρρου καὶ βαθείας, εἰς ἣν πολλαὶ μὲν αὐτομάτως ἐκ τῶν ὑπερκειμένων κρημνῶν πέτραι κατενηνεγμέναι καὶ δένδρα δύσβατον ἐποίουν τὴν δι᾽ αὐτῆς πορείαν, πολλὰ δ᾽ ὑπὸ τῶν βαρβάρων εἰς τοῦτο τὸ μέρος

3 συνηργεῖτο. καὶ γὰρ ἐκκοπὰς δένδρων ἐπεποίητο συνεχεῖς καὶ λίθων πλήθη μεγέθει ⟨διαφερόντων⟩ συνηθροίκεισαν· αὐτοί τε παρ᾽ ὅλην τὴν φάραγγα τὰς εὐκαίρους ὑπεροχὰς καὶ δυναμένας σφίσιν ἀσφάλειαν παρέχεσθαι κατειληφότες ἐτήρουν, ὥστ᾽, εἰ μὴ διή-μαρτον, ἐντελῶς ἂν ἐξαδυνατήσαντα τὸν Ἀντίοχον

4 ἀποστῆναι τῆς ἐπιβολῆς. ὡς γὰρ δέον τοὺς πολεμίους πάντας κατ᾽ ἀνάγκην ποιεῖσθαι δι᾽ αὐτῆς τῆς φάραγ-γος τὴν ἀνάβασιν, οὕτως παρεσκευάσαντο καὶ πρὸς

5 τοῦτο κατελάβοντο τοὺς τόπους. ἐκεῖνο δ᾽ οὐκ ἔβλεψαν ὅτι τὴν μὲν φάλαγγα ⟨καὶ⟩ τὴν ἀποσκευὴν οὐκ ἄλλως δυνατὸν ἦν, ἀλλ᾽ ὡς ἐκεῖνοι διέλαβον, ποιεῖσθαι τὴν πορείαν· πρὸς γὰρ τὰ παρακείμενα τῶν ὀρῶν οὐχ οἷόν τ᾽ ἦν τούτοις προσβαλεῖν, ἀλλὰ τοῖς ψιλοῖς καὶ τοῖς εὐζώνοις οὐκ ἀδύνατος ἦν ἡ δι᾽ αὐτῶν τῶν λευκο-

6 πέτρων ἀναβολή. ὅθεν ἅμα ⟨τῷ⟩ πρὸς τὸ πρῶτον φυλακεῖον προσμῖξαι τοὺς περὶ τὸν Διογένην, ἔξωθεν τῆς χαράδρας ποιουμένους τὴν ἀνάβασιν, ἀλλοιο-

194

30. As these separate bodies advanced they found the road much rougher and narrower than the king had expected. For the total length of the ascent was about three hundred stades, and for the greater part of this distance it was through a deep torrent bed, in which progress was rendered difficult by quantities of rock and trees that had fallen of their own accord from the precipices above, while numerous other obstacles placed there by the barbarians contributed to the result. For they had constructed a series of barricades of felled trees and had collected a quantity of huge rocks, while they themselves along the whole defile had occupied favorable positions on the heights where they fancied themselves in security. So that Antiochus would have found it perfectly impossible to execute his project had they not miscalculated: for these preparations had been made and these positions occupied under the idea that the whole enemy army must necessarily ascend through the defile itself; but they never saw that though the phalanx and pack train could not march by any other route than the one they supposed, since it was impossible for that part of the army to ascend the mountain slopes, yet it was by no means beyond the power of unburdened and light-armed troops to ascend over the bare rocks. So that as soon as Diogenes, advancing outside the defile, came in

7 τέραν ἐλάμβανε τὰ πράγματα διάθεσιν. εὐθέως γὰρ
κατὰ τὴν συμπλοκὴν αὐτοῦ τοῦ πράγματος διδάσκον-
τος, ὑπερτιθέμενοι καὶ προσβαίνοντες πρὸς τὰ πλάγια τῶν χωρίων οἱ περὶ τὸν Διογένην, ὑπερδέξιοι τῶν
πολεμίων ἐγίνοντο, καὶ χρώμενοι πυκνοῖς τοῖς ἀκον-
τίσμασι καὶ τοῖς ἐκ χειρὸς λίθοις κακῶς διετίθεσαν
τοὺς βαρβάρους, καὶ μάλιστα ταῖς σφενδόναις ἐκακο-
8 ποίουν ἐξ ἀποστήματος βάλλοντες. ὅτε δὲ τοὺς πρώτους ἐκβιασάμενοι κατάσχοιεν τὸν τούτων τόπον, ἐδί-
δοτο τοῖς λειτουργοῖς καιρὸς εἰς τὸ πᾶν τὸ πρὸ ποδῶν
ἀνακαθαίρειν καὶ λεαίνειν μετ᾽ ἀσφαλείας. ἐγίνετο δὲ
9 τοῦτο ταχέως διὰ τὴν πολυχειρίαν. οὐ μὴν ἀλλὰ τούτῳ
τῷ τρόπῳ τῶν μὲν σφενδονητῶν καὶ τοξοτῶν ἔτι δ᾽
ἀκοντιστῶν κατὰ τοὺς ὑπερδεξίους τόπους πορευομένων σποράδην, ποτὲ δὲ συναθροιζομένων καὶ κατα-
λαμβανομένων τοὺς εὐκαίρους τόπους, τῶν <δ᾽> ἀσπι-
διωτῶν ἐφεδρευόντων, καὶ παρ᾽ αὐτὴν τὴν χαράδραν
παραπορευομένων <ἐν> τάξει καὶ βάδην, οὐκ ἔμενον οἱ
βάρβαροι, πάντες δὲ λιπόντες τοὺς τόπους ἠθροίσθη-
σαν ἐπὶ τὴν ὑπερβολήν.

31. Οἱ δὲ περὶ τὸν Ἀντίοχον ἀσφαλῶς διέβησαν
τὰς δυσχωρίας τῷ προειρημένῳ τρόπῳ, βραδέως δὲ
καὶ δυσχερῶς· μόλις γὰρ ὀγδοαῖοι πρὸς τὰς κατὰ τὸν
2 Λάβον ὑπεροχὰς ἀφίκοντο. τῶν δὲ βαρβάρων συνηθροισμένων ἐκεῖ, καὶ πεπεισμένων κωλύειν τῆς ὑπερ-
βολῆς τοὺς πολεμίους, ἀγὼν συνέστη νεανικός.
ἐξεώσθησαν δ᾽ οἱ βάρβαροι διὰ τοιαύτας αἰτίας.
3 συστραφέντες γὰρ ἐμάχοντο πρὸς τοὺς φαλαγγίτας

contact with the first barbarian post, matters took a different turn. For at once upon encountering the enemy he acted as circumstances suggested and, avoiding an engagement by ascending on the enemy's flank and making a further flank movement uphill, got on higher ground, and by throwing showers of javelins and stones from the hand inflicted severe punishment on them, the greatest damage being done by the stones slung from a distance. As soon as they had forced this first post to withdraw and occupied their position the pioneers had time to clear and level the ground in front of them at their ease, a task soon accomplished owing to their large numbers. In fact, by this means, with the slingers, archers and javelineers marching along the high ground in loose order, but closing up and occupying favorable positions, and with the Cretans covering their movements and marching parallel to them close to the defile slowly and in good order, the barbarians no longer stood their ground, but abandoning their positions collected on the actual summit of the pass.

31. Antiochus traversed the worst part of the road in the manner I have described, safely but very slowly and with difficulty, only just reaching the pass of Mount Labus[70] on the eighth day. The barbarians were collected there, convinced that they would prevent the enemy from crossing, and a fierce struggle now took place, in which the barbarians were forced back for the following reason. Formed in a dense mass they fought desperately against the phalanx

[70] The pass cannot be identified.

κατὰ πρόσωπον ἐκθύμως· τῆς δὲ νυκτὸς ἔτι τῶν εὐζώνων ἐκπεριελθόντων ἐκ πολλοῦ, καὶ καταλαβομένων
⟨τοὺς⟩ ὑπερδεξίους καὶ κατὰ νώτου τόπους, ἅμα τῷ
συνιδεῖν οἱ βάρβαροι τὸ γεγονὸς εὐθέως πτοηθέντες
4 ὥρμησαν πρὸς φυγήν. ὁ δὲ βασιλεὺς τὴν μὲν ἐπὶ
πλεῖον ὁρμὴν τῶν διωκόντων παρακατέσχε μετὰ πολλῆς σπουδῆς, ἀνακαλεσάμενος ταῖς σάλπιγξι, διὰ τὸ
βούλεσθαι καταβαίνειν ἄθρους καὶ συντεταγμένους
5 εἰς τὴν Ὑρκανίαν. συστησάμενος δὲ τὴν πορείαν ὡς
ἐβούλετο καὶ παραγενόμενος ἐπὶ Τάμβρακα, πόλιν
ἀτείχιστον, ἔχουσαν δὲ βασίλεια καὶ μέγεθος, αὐτοῦ
6 κατεσκήνωσε. τῶν δὲ πλείστων πεποιημένων τὴν ἀποχώρησιν ἔκ τε τῆς μάχης καὶ τῆς περικειμένης χώρας
εἰς τὴν προσαγορευομένην Σίρυγκα πόλιν—συνέβαινε κεῖσθαι ⟨ ʼκείνην⟩ οὐ μακρὰν τῆς Τάμβρακος,
εἶναι δὲ τῆς Ὑρκανίας ὡς ἂν εἰ βασίλειον διά τε τὴν
ὀχυρότητα καὶ τὴν ἄλλην εὐκαιρίαν—ἔκρινε ταύτην
7 ἐξελεῖν μετὰ βίας. ἀναλαβὼν οὖν τὴν δύναμιν προῆγε, καὶ περιστρατοπεδεύσας ἤρχετο τῆς πολιορκίας.
8 ἦν δὲ τὸ πλεῖστον μέρος τῆς ἐπιβολῆς ἐν ταῖς
χωστρίσι χελώναις. τάφροι γὰρ ἦσαν τριτταί, πλάτος
μὲν οὐκ ἔλαττον ἔχουσαι τριάκοντα πηχῶν, βάθος δὲ
πεντεκαίδεκα· ἐπὶ δὲ τοῖς χείλεσιν ἑκάστης ἐπέκειτο
χαρακώματα διπλᾶ καὶ τελευταῖον προτείχισμα δυνα-
9 τόν. συμπλοκαὶ μὲν οὖν ἐγίνοντο συνεχεῖς ἐπὶ τῶν
ἔργων, ἐν αἷς οὐκ ἤνυον ἑκάτεροι φέροντες τοὺς
νεκροὺς καὶ τοὺς τραυματίας διὰ τὸ μὴ μόνον ὑπὲρ
γῆς, ἀλλὰ καὶ κατὰ γῆς διὰ τῶν ὀρυγμάτων ἐκ χειρὸς

face to face, but while it was still night the light-armed troops had made a wide detour and occupied the heights in their rear, and the barbarians, the moment they noticed this, were panic-stricken and took to flight. The king made every effort to restrain his men from continuing the pursuit, summoning them back by bugle call, as he wanted his army to descend into Hyrcania unbroken and in good order. Having regulated his march in the manner he wished he reached Tambrax,[71] an unwalled city, but of large size and containing a royal palace, and encamped there. Most of the enemy, both from the scene of the battle and from the surrounding country, had retreated to a town called Sirynx,[72] which was at no great distance from Tambrax, and was as it were the capital of Hyrcania owing to its strength and favorable situation, and he decided to take this city by storm. He advanced therefore with his army and encamping round it began the siege. The chief means he employed was the use of mantelets for sappers. There were three moats, each not less than thirty cubits broad and fifteen deep, and each defended at its edge by a double row of palisades, and behind all there was a strong wall. There were constant combats at the works, in which neither side could bring off their dead and wounded, as the hand-to-hand fighting took place not only on the surface of the ground

[71] Location disputed.
[72] Location uncertain.

10 γίνεσθαι τοὺς κινδύνους. οὐ μὴν ἀλλὰ τῷ πλήθει καὶ
τῇ τοῦ βασιλέως ἐνεργείᾳ ταχέως συνέβη καὶ τὰς
τάφρους χωσθῆναι καὶ τὸ τεῖχος πεσεῖν διὰ τῶν

11 ὀρυγμάτων. οὗ συμβάντος διατραπέντες οἱ βάρβαροι
τοῖς ὅλοις, καὶ τοὺς μὲν Ἕλληνας κατασφάξαντες
τοὺς ἐν τῇ πόλει, τὰ δ᾽ ἐπιφανέστατα τῶν σκευῶν

12 διαρπάσαντες, νυκτὸς ἀπεχώρησαν. ὁ δὲ βασιλεὺς
συνθεασάμενος Ὑπερβάσαν ἀπέστειλε μετὰ τῶν
μισθοφόρων· οὗ συμμίξαντος οἱ βάρβαροι ῥίψαντες

13 τὰς ἀποσκευὰς αὖθις εἰς τὴν πόλιν ἔφυγον. τῶν δὲ
πελταστῶν ἐνεργῶς βιαζομένων διὰ ⟨τοῦ⟩ πτώματος,
ἀπελπίσαντες σφᾶς αὐτοὺς παρέδοσαν.

14 Ἀχριανή, πόλις Ὑρκανίας. Πολύβιος δεκάτῳ.

15 Καλλιόπη, πόλις Παρθυαίας. Πολύβιος δεκάτῳ.

V. RES ITALIAE

32. Βουλόμενοι δ᾽ οἱ ὕπατοι κατοπτεῦσαι σαφῶς τὰ
πρὸς τὴν τῶν ὑπεναντίων στρατοπεδείαν κεκλιμένα
μέρη τοῦ λόφου, τοῖς μὲν ἐν τῷ χάρακι μένειν κατὰ

2 χώραν ἐπήγγειλαν, αὐτοὶ δὲ τῶν ἱππέων ἀναλαβόντες
ἴλας δύο καὶ γροσφομάχους μετὰ τῶν ῥαβδοφόρων
εἰς τριάκοντα προῆγον, κατασκεψόμενοι τοὺς τόπους.

3 τῶν δὲ Νομάδων εἰθισμένοι τινὲς τοῖς ἀκροβολιζομένοις καὶ καθόλου προπορευομένοις ἐκ τοῦ τῶν
ὑπεναντίων χάρακος ἐνέδρας ποιεῖν, ὑπεστάλκεισαν

but beneath it in the mines. But in spite of all, owing to superiority of numbers and the personal activity of the king, the moats were very soon filled up and the wall was undermined and fell, upon which the barbarians were thoroughly discouraged, and after killing all the Greeks in the town and pillaging all the finest things they made off by night. When the king became aware of this he sent Hyperbasas after them with the mercenaries, and the barbarians when overtaken by him threw away their baggage and fled again into the town. When the peltasts now vigorously forced their way through the breach, they surrendered in despair.

14. Achriane, a city of Hyrcania. Polybius in Book 10.

15. Calliope, a city in Parthia. Polybius in Book 10.

V. AFFAIRS OF ITALY

Death of the Consul Claudius Marcellus

32. The consuls,[73] wishing to survey accurately the side of the hill which was turned toward the enemy's camp, ordered the rest of their forces to remain in the entrenched camp, and themselves taking two troops of cavalry and about thirty velites together with their lictors advanced to reconnoiter the ground. Certain Numidians, who were in the habit of lying in ambush for skirmishers and in general for any of the enemy who advanced out of their camp, were

208
B.C.

[73] Marcus Claudius Marcellus and Titus Quinctius Crispinus, *MRR* 1.289–290. For Marcellus see n. on 8.1.7. His death happened in an ambush. P.'s criticism is similar to his criticism of young Scipio Africanus in 3.5–7.

4 κατά τινα συντυχίαν ὑπὸ τὸν λόφον. οἷς τοῦ σκοποῦ
σημήναντος ὅτι παραγίνονταί τινες κατ᾽ ἄκρον τὸν
βουνὸν ὑπερδέξιοι ᾽κείνων, ἐξαναστάντες καὶ παρὰ
πλάγια ποιησάμενοι τὴν πορείαν ἀποτέμνονται τοὺς
στρατηγοὺς καὶ διακλείουσιν ἀπὸ τῆς ἰδίας παρεμ-
5 βολῆς. καὶ τὸν μὲν Κλαύδιον εὐθέως ἐν τῇ πρώτῃ
συμπλοκῇ καί τινας ἑτέρους ἅμα τούτῳ κατέβαλον,
τοὺς δὲ λοιποὺς κατατραυματίσαντες διὰ τῶν κρη-
6 μνῶν ἠνάγκασαν ἄλλον ἄλλῃ φεύγειν. οἱ δ᾽ ἐν τῷ
στρατοπέδῳ θεωροῦντες τὸ γινόμενον οὐδαμῶς ἠδυνή-
θησαν ἐπικουρῆσαι τοῖς κινδυνεύουσιν· ἔτι γὰρ ἀνα-
βοώντων καὶ πρὸς τὸ συμβαῖνον ἐκπεπληγμένων, καὶ
τῶν μὲν χαλινούντων τοὺς ἵππους, τῶν δὲ καθοπλι-
ζομένων, πέρας εἶχε τὸ πρᾶγμα. καὶ τὸν υἱὸν τοῦ
Κλαυδίου τραυματίαν, μόλις καὶ παραδόξως τὸν κίνδυνον διαπεφευγότα.

7 Μάρκος μὲν οὖν ἀκακώτερον ἢ στρατηγικώτερον
αὑτῷ χρησάμενος τοῖς δεδηλωμένοις περιέπεσε συμ-
8 πτώμασιν· ἐγὼ δὲ παρ᾽ ὅλην τὴν πραγματείαν πολλάκις ἀναγκάζομαι περὶ τῶν τοιούτων ὑπομιμνήσκειν
τοὺς ἐντυγχάνοντας, θεωρῶν, εἰ καὶ περὶ ‹τι τῶν› τῆς
στρατηγίας μερῶν ἄλλο, καὶ περὶ τοῦτο διαμαρτάνον-
τας τοὺς ἡγεμόνας, καίτοι προδήλου τῆς ἀγνοίας
9 ὑπαρχούσης. τί γὰρ ὄφελος ἡγεμόνος ἢ στρατηγοῦ
μὴ διειληφότος διότι τῶν κατὰ μέρος κινδύνων, οἷς μὴ
συμπάσχει τὰ ὅλα, πλεῖστον ἀπέχειν δεῖ τὸν ἡγού-
10 μενον; τί δ᾽ ἀγνοοῦντος ὅτι, κἄν ποτ᾽ ἀναγκάζωσιν οἱ
καιροὶ πράττειν τι τῶν κατὰ μέρος, πολλοὺς δεῖ πρό-

by hazard hidden at the foot of the hill. Upon their lookout signaling to them that some of the enemy had appeared on the crest of the hill just above them, they rose, and marching up the slope obliquely, cut off the consuls and prevented their return to their camp. Marcellus and some others with him were cut down at the first onset, and the others were wounded and compelled to take to flight down the cliffs in different directions. The Romans in the camp, though they were spectators of what was happening, had no means of coming to the help of their comrades who were in danger. For while they were still shouting out in a state of great consternation, some of them bridling their horses and others putting on their armor, the whole affair was over. The son of Marcellus was wounded, and with great difficulty and beyond expectation escaped.

Marcellus, it must be confessed, brought this misfortune on himself by behaving not so much like a general as like a simpleton. Throughout this work I am often compelled to call the attention of my readers to such occurrences, as I observe that generals are more liable to make mistakes in this matter than in any other parts of their duty as commanders, although the error is such an obvious one. For what is the use of a general or commander who does not comprehend that he must keep himself as far away as possible from all partial encounters in which the fate of the whole army is not involved? Of what use is he if he does not know that, if circumstances at times compel commanders to undertake in person such partial encounters, they must

τερον ἀποθανεῖν τῶν συνόντων πρὶν ἢ τὸ δεινὸν ἐγ-
11 γίσαι τοῖς προεστῶσι τῶν ὅλων; δεῖ γὰρ ἐν Καρὶ τὴν
πεῖραν, ὡς ἡ παροιμία φησίν, οὐκ ἐν τῷ στρατηγῷ
12 γίνεσθαι. τὸ μὲν γὰρ λέγειν ὡς "οὐκ ἂν ᾠόμην" "τίς
γὰρ ἂν ἤλπισε τοῦτο γενέσθαι;" μέγιστον εἶναί μοι
δοκεῖ σημεῖον ἀπειρίας στρατηγικῆς καὶ βραδυτῆτος.

33. Διὸ καὶ τὸν Ἀννίβαν κατὰ πολλοὺς τρόπους
2 ἀγαθὸν ἡγεμόνα κρίνων, κατὰ τοῦτο μάλιστά τις ἂν
ἐπισημήναιτο, διότι πολλοὺς μὲν χρόνους ἐν τῇ πολε-
μίᾳ διατρίψας, πολλοῖς δὲ καιροῖς καὶ ποικίλοις χρησάμενος, ἔσφηλε μὲν τοὺς ὑπεναντίους πολλάκις ἐν
ταῖς κατὰ μέρος χρείαις διὰ τὴν ἰδίαν ἀγχίνοιαν,
ἐσφάλη δ' οὐδέποτε τοσούτους καὶ τηλικούτους ἀγῶ-
3 νας χειρίσας· τοιαύτην ἐποιεῖτο τὴν πρόνοιαν, ὡς
4 ἔοικε, περὶ τῆς ἀσφαλείας αὐτοῦ. καὶ μάλ' εἰκότως·
ἀκεραίου μὲν γὰρ καὶ σῳζομένου τοῦ προεστῶτος, κἂν
ποτε πέσῃ τὰ ὅλα, πολλὰς ἀφορμὰς ἡ τύχη δίδωσι
πρὸς τὸ πάλιν ἀνακτήσασθαι τὰς ἐκ τῶν περιπετειῶν
5 ἐλαττώσεις· πταίσαντος δέ, καθάπερ ἐν νηὶ τοῦ κυβερ-
νήτου, κἂν [τὸ νικᾶν] ἡ τύχη τοῖς πολλοῖς παραδιδῷ
κρατεῖν τῶν ἐχθρῶν, οὐδὲν ὄφελος γίνεται διὰ τὸ
πάσας ἐξηρτῆσθαι τὰς ἐλπίδας ἑκάστοις ἐκ τῶν ἡγου-
6 μένων. ταῦτα μὲν οὖν εἰρήσθω μοι πρὸς τοὺς ἢ διὰ
κενοδοξίαν ἢ μειρακιώδει <παρα>στάσει περιπίπτον-
τας τοῖς τοιούτοις ἀλογήμασιν ἢ δι' ἀπειρίαν ἢ διὰ
7 καταφρόνησιν· ἓν γὰρ ἀεί τι τῶν προειρημένων αἴτιον
γίνεται τῶν τοιούτων περιπετειῶν. . . .

sacrifice many of their men before the danger is suffered to approach the supreme commander of the whole? Let the risk be for the Carian,[74] as the proverb has it, and not for the general. And as for saying "I should never have thought it" or "Who would have expected it to happen?" that in a general is a most manifest sign of incompetence and dullness.

33. For this reason while we regard Hannibal as being a good general in very many ways, we should lay especial stress on the fact that after spending many years in a hostile country and meeting with great variety of fortune he frequently by his cleverness worsted the enemy in partial engagements, whereas he never met with disaster to himself in spite of the numerous and severe battles in which he engaged, so great was the care he took of his own safety. And very properly too; for when the commander is safe and sound, even if a total defeat takes place, Fortune furnishes many means for retrieving the loss, but if he falls, just as in the case of the pilot of a ship, even if Fortune give victory to the soldiers, it is of no service to them, as all their hopes depend upon their leaders. So much for those who fall into such errors from ostentation and childish vanity or from inexperience or contempt of the enemy. One or other of these is always the cause of such accidents.

[74] The proverb ἐν Καρὶ κινδυνεύειν focuses on persons, specifically mercenaries, considered to be of little value: *Paroemiogr.* 1.70–71; 2.404–405.

8   Οἱ δὲ καταρράκτας, οὓς εἶχον ὀλίγον ἐξωτέρω διὰ
μηχανημάτων ἀνημμένους, αἰφνίδιον καθῆκαν καὶ ἐπεβάλοντο, καὶ τούτους κατασχόντες πρὸ τοῦ τείχους
ἀνεσκολόπισαν.

VI. RES HISPANIAE

34. Κατὰ δὲ τὴν Ἰβηρίαν Πόπλιος ὁ τῶν Ῥωμαίων
στρατηγός, ποιούμενος τὴν παραχειμασίαν ἐν Ταρ-
ράκωνι, καθάπερ ἐν τοῖς πρὸ τούτων δεδηλώκαμεν,
πρῶτον μὲν τοὺς Ἴβηρας εἰς τὴν αὑτῶν φιλίαν καὶ
πίστιν ἐνεδήσατο διὰ τῆς τῶν ὁμήρων ἑκάστοις ἀπο-
2 δόσεως, λαβὼν συναγωνιστὴν ἐκ ταὐτομάτου πρὸς
τοῦτο τὸ μέρος Ἐδεκῶνα τὸν Ἐδετανῶν δυνάστην, ὃς
ἅμα τῷ προσπεσεῖν τὴν Καρχηδόνος ἅλωσιν καὶ
γενέσθαι κύριον τῆς γυναικὸς αὐτοῦ καὶ τῶν υἱῶν τὸν
Πόπλιον, εὐθέως συλλογισάμενος τὴν ἐσομένην τῶν
Ἰβήρων μεταβολὴν ἀρχηγὸς ἐβουλήθη ⟨γενέσθαι⟩
3 τῆς αὐτῆς ὁρμῆς, μάλιστα πεπεισμένος οὕτως τὴν
γυναῖκα καὶ τὰ τέκνα κομιεῖσθαι καὶ δόξειν οὐ κατ᾽
ἀνάγκην, ἀλλὰ κατὰ πρόθεσιν αἱρεῖσθαι τὰ Ῥω-
4 μαίων· ἃ καὶ συνέβη γενέσθαι. τῶν γὰρ δυνάμεων
ἄρτι διαφειμένων εἰς τὴν παραχειμασίαν παρῆν εἰς
5 τὴν Ταρράκωνα μετὰ τῶν οἰκείων καὶ φίλων. ἐλθὼν δ᾽
εἰς λόγους τῷ Ποπλίῳ ταύτην ἔφη τοῖς θεοῖς μεγίστην

---

75 At Salapia Hannibal had Marcellus buried with high honors

*Incident in Hannibal's Attempt to Capture
Salapia After the Above Event*

Suddenly letting down the portcullis which they had raised somewhat higher by mechanical means, they attacked the intruders[75] and capturing them crucified them before the wall.

VI. AFFAIRS OF SPAIN

34. In Spain Publius Scipio, the Roman commander, who, as I above stated,[76] was wintering at Tarraco, first of all secured the confidence and friendship of the Iberians by the restoration of the hostages to their respective homes, availing himself in the matter of the assistance voluntarily proffered by Edeco the prince of the Edetani,[77] who on receiving the news of the capture of New Carthage and learning that his wife and sons were in Scipio's power, at once anticipated the change that would take place in the attitude of the Iberians and desired to be leader of this movement, chiefly owing to his conviction that by this reason he would recover his wife and children and would appear to have taken the part of the Romans not under compulsion but deliberately. And this proved to be so. For just after the troops had been dispersed to their winter quarters he appeared at Tarraco with his relatives and friends. Seeking an interview with Scipio he said he gave thanks to

210–212
B.C.

but took his signet and used it in an attempt to recapture Salapia; it was foiled by the forewarned inhabitants (Livy 27.22.4–12).

[76] 20.8; the date is winter 209/8. [77] *RE* Edico 1939 (F. Münzer) and Edetani 1938–1939 (E. Hübner).

χάριν ἔχειν, ὅτι πρῶτος τῶν κατὰ τὴν χώραν δυνα-
6 στῶν ἥκει πρὸς αὐτόν. τοὺς μὲν γὰρ ἄλλους ἀκμὴν
διαπέμπεσθαι καὶ βλέπειν πρὸς Καρχηδονίους, τὰς δὲ
χεῖρας ἐκτείνειν Ῥωμαίοις· αὐτὸς δὲ παραγεγονέναι
διδοὺς οὐ μόνον αὐτόν, ἀλλὰ καὶ τοὺς φίλους καὶ
7 συγγενεῖς εἰς τὴν Ῥωμαίων πίστιν. διόπερ ἂν νομι-
σθῇ παρ' αὐτῷ φίλος καὶ σύμμαχος, μεγάλην μὲν
αὐτῷ πρὸς τὸ παρὸν ἔφη, μεγάλην δ' εἰς τὸ μέλλον
8 παρέξεσθαι χρείαν. παραυτίκα μὲν γὰρ θεασαμένους
τοὺς Ἴβηρας πρός τε τὴν φιλίαν αὐτὸν προσδεδεγμέ-
νον καὶ τετευχότα τῶν ἀξιουμένων πάντας ἐπὶ τὸ
παραπλήσιον ἥξειν, σπουδάζοντας κομίσασθαι τοὺς
9 ἀναγκαίους καὶ τυχεῖν τῆς Ῥωμαίων συμμαχίας· εἰς
δὲ τὸν μετὰ ταῦτα χρόνον προκαταληφθέντας τῇ τοιαύτῃ τιμῇ καὶ φιλανθρωπίᾳ συναγωνιστὰς ἀπροφα-
σίστους ὑπάρξειν αὐτῷ πρὸς τὰ κατάλοιπα τῶν
10 ἔργων. διόπερ ἠξίου τὴν γυναῖκα καὶ τὰ τέκνα κομίσασθαι, καὶ κριθεὶς φίλος ἐπανελθεῖν εἰς τὴν οἰκείαν,
ἵνα λαβὼν ἀφορμὴν εὔλογον ἐναποδείξηται τὴν αὐτοῦ
καὶ τῶν φίλων εὔνοιαν κατὰ δύναμιν εἴς τε τὸν
11 Πόπλιον αὐτὸν καὶ τὰ Ῥωμαίων πράγματα. Ἐδεκὼν
μὲν οὖν τοιαῦτα διαλεχθεὶς ἐπέσχεν·

35. ὁ δὲ Πόπλιος, καὶ πάλαι πρὸς τοῦτο τὸ μέρος
ἕτοιμος ὢν καὶ συλλελογισμένος παραπλήσια τοῖς
ὑπὸ τοῦ Ἐδεκῶνος εἰρημένοις, τὴν γυναῖκα καὶ τὰ
2 τέκνα παρέδωκεν αὐτῷ καὶ τὴν φιλίαν συνέθετο. πρὸς
δὲ τούτοις παρὰ τὴν συνουσίαν ποικίλως ψυχαγωγή-
σας τὸν Ἴβηρα καὶ πᾶσι τοῖς αὐτοῦ μεγάλας εἰς τὸ

Heaven that he was the first of the Spanish princes to come
to him. The others, he said, were still communicating with
Carthage and looking to that quarter, while at the same
time stretching out their hands to the Romans, but he himself had come in and put not only his own person but his
friends and relatives at the mercy of the Romans. So, if
Scipio would regard him as a friend and ally, he would be of
the greatest service to him both at present and in the future. For the Iberians at once, upon seeing that he had
been received into Scipio's friendship and that his requests
had been granted, would all come with the same object,
desirous of recovering their relatives and securing the alliance of Rome, and their affections would be so much engaged for the future by such honor and kindness that they
would unreservedly cooperate with Scipio in the rest of his
operations. He therefore begged that his wife and children
might be restored to him and that before returning to his
home he should be pronounced to be a friend, so that
he might have a plausible pretext for displaying by every
means in his power the goodwill that he himself and his
friends bore to Scipio and the Roman cause.

35. Edeco after speaking somewhat in these terms
ended his discourse, and Scipio, who had been previously
disposed to take such a course, and whose views corre-
sponded with those expressed by Edeco, returned his wife
and children and made him his friend. And not only this,
but he captivated the Spaniard by diverse means during

μέλλον ἐλπίδας ὑπογράψας, οὕτως εἰς τὴν οἰκείαν
3 ἐξαπέστειλε. τούτου τοῦ πράγματος ταχέως περιβοή-
του γενομένου πάντας συνέβη τοὺς ἐντὸς Ἴβηρος
ποταμοῦ κατοικοῦντας οἷον ἀπὸ μιᾶς ὁρμῆς ἑλέσθαι
τὰ Ῥωμαίων, ὅσοι μὴ πρότερον αὐτῶν ὑπῆρχον φίλοι.
4   Ταῦτα μὲν οὖν καλῶς κατὰ νοῦν ἐχώρει τῷ Ποπλίῳ·
5 μετὰ δὲ τὸν τούτων χωρισμὸν τὰς μὲν ναυτικὰς δυνάμεις διέλυσε, θεωρῶν οὐδὲν ἀντίπαλον ὑπάρχον κατὰ
θάλατταν, ἐκ δὲ τῶν ναυτῶν ἐκλέξας τοὺς ἐπιτηδείους
ἐπὶ τὰς σημαίας ἐμέρισε. καὶ συνηύξησε τοιούτῳ
τρόπῳ τὰς πεζικὰς δυνάμεις.
6   Ἀνδοβάλης δὲ καὶ Μανδόνιος, μέγιστοι μὲν ὄντες
δυνάσται τότε τῶν κατ' Ἰβηρίαν, ἀληθινώτατοι δὲ
Καρχηδονίων φίλοι δοξαζόμενοι, πάλαι μὲν ὑπούλως
διέκειντο καὶ καιρὸν ἐπετήρουν, ἐξ ὅτου προσποιη-
θέντες οἱ περὶ τὸν Ἀσδρούβαν ἀπιστεῖν αὐτοῖς ᾔτη-
σαν χρημάτων τε πλῆθος καὶ τὰς γυναῖκας καὶ τὰς
θυγατέρας εἰς ὁμηρείαν, καθάπερ ἐν τοῖς πρὸ τούτων
7 ἐδηλώσαμεν· τότε δὲ νομίσαντες ἔχειν εὐφυῆ καιρόν,
ἀναλαβόντες τὰς ἑαυτῶν δυνάμεις ἐκ τῆς Καρχηδονίων παρεμβολῆς νυκτὸς ἀπεχώρησαν εἴς τινας ἐρυ-
μνοὺς τόπους καὶ δυναμένους αὐτοῖς τὴν ἀσφάλειαν
8 παρασκευάζειν. οὗ γενομένου καὶ τῶν ἄλλων Ἰβήρων
συνέβη τοὺς πλείστους ἀπολιπεῖν Ἀσδρούβαν, πάλαι
μὲν βαρυνομένους ὑπὸ τῆς τῶν Καρχηδονίων ἀγερω-
χίας, τότε δὲ πρῶτον καιρὸν λαβόντας εἰς τὸ φανερὰν
ποιῆσαι τὴν αὐτῶν προαίρεσιν.
36. Ὃ δὴ καὶ περὶ πολλοὺς ἤδη γέγονε. μεγάλου

the time they spent together, and holding out high hopes of future advantage to all those with him, he sent them back to their home. The matter was soon bruited abroad, and all the Iberians on the side of the Ebro[78] who had not previously been friendly to the Romans now as with one consent embraced their cause.

These matters, then, were proceeding as well as Scipio could wish, and after the departure of the Iberians he broke up his navy, as no enemy was visible at sea, and selecting the most capable men from the crews distributed them among the maniples and thus increased his land forces.

Andobales and Mandonius[79] were at this time two of the greatest princes in Spain and were supposed to be the most trusty adherents of Carthage, but they had long been disaffected and were watching for an opportunity of revolt, ever since Hasdrubal, as I above stated, on the pretext that he mistrusted them, had demanded from them the payment of a large sum of money and the surrender of their wives and daughters as hostages. Thinking that the present time was favorable, they left the Carthaginian camp with all their forces by night and withdrew to a strong position where they would be in safety. Upon this most of the other Iberians also deserted Hasdrubal. They had long been offended by the arrogance of the Carthaginians, but this was the first opportunity they had of manifesting their inclinations.

36. The same thing has happened before to many peo-

78 North of the river.
79 The brothers were last mentioned in 10.18.7. Andobales and Hasdrubal: 9.11.3.

γὰρ ὄντος, ὡς πλεονάκις ἡμῖν εἴρηται, τοῦ κατορθοῦν
ἐν πράγμασι καὶ περιγίνεσθαι τῶν ἐχθρῶν ἐν ταῖς
ἐπιβολαῖς, πολλῷ μείζονος ἐμπειρίας προσδεῖται καὶ
2 φυλακῆς τὸ καλῶς χρήσασθαι τοῖς κατορθώμασι· διὸ
καὶ πολλαπλασίους ἂν εὕροι τις τοὺς ἐπὶ προτερημάτων γεγονότας τῶν καλῶς τοῖς προτερήμασι κε-
χρημένων. ὃ καὶ τότε περὶ τοὺς Καρχηδονίους συνέβη
3 γενέσθαι. μετὰ γὰρ τὸ νικῆσαι μὲν τὰς Ῥωμαίων
δυνάμεις, ἀποκτεῖναι δὲ τοὺς στρατηγοὺς ἀμφοτέρους, Πόπλιον καὶ Γνάϊον, ὑπολαβόντες ἀδήριτον
αὐτοῖς ὑπάρχειν τὴν Ἰβηρίαν, ὑπερηφάνως ἐχρῶντο
4 τοῖς κατὰ τὴν χώραν. τοιγαροῦν ἀντὶ συμμάχων καὶ
φίλων πολεμίους ἔσχον τοὺς ὑποταττομένους. καὶ
5 τοῦτ᾽ εἰκότως ἔπαθον· ἄλλως μὲν ⟨γὰρ ἐπειδήπερ⟩
ὑπέλαβον δεῖν κτᾶσθαι τὰς ἀρχάς, ἄλλως δὲ τηρεῖν,
οὐκ ἔμαθον διότι κάλλιστα φυλάττουσι τὰς ὑπεροχὰς
οἱ κάλλιστα διαμείναντες ἐπὶ τῶν αὐτῶν προαιρέσεων,
6 αἷς ἐξ ἀρχῆς κατεκτήσαντο τὰς δυναστείας, καίτοι γε
προφανοῦς ὄντος καὶ ἐπὶ πολλῶν ἤδη τεθεωρημένου
διότι κτῶνται μὲν ἄνθρωποι τὰς εὐκαιρίας εὖ ποιοῦντες καὶ προτεινόμενοι τὴν ἀγαθὴν ἐλπίδα τοῖς
7 πέλας, ἐπειδὰν δὲ τῶν ἐπιθυμουμένων τυχόντες κακῶς
ποιῶσι καὶ δεσποτικῶς ἄρχωσι τῶν ὑποτεταγμένων,
εἰκότως ἅμα ταῖς τῶν προεστώτων μεταβολαῖς συμ-
μεταπίπτουσι καὶ τῶν ὑποταττομένων αἱ προαιρέσεις.
ὃ καὶ τότε συνέβη τοῖς Καρχηδονίοις.

37. Ἀσδρούβας μὲν οὖν ἐν τοιαύταις περιστάσεσι
πολλὰς καὶ ποικίλας ἐποιεῖτο περὶ τῶν ἐπιφερομένων

ple. For, as I have often said, while success in policy and victory in the field are great things, it requires much more skill and caution to make a good use of such success. So that you will find that those who have won victories are far more numerous than those who have used them to advantage. This is exactly what happened to the Carthaginians at this period. For after having defeated the Roman forces and killed the two commanders Publius and Gnaeus Scipio, they regarded their position in Spain as undisputed and treated the natives in an overbearing manner. In consequence their subjects, instead of being their allies and friends, were their enemies. And quite naturally; for they fancied that there is one method by which power should be acquired and another by which it should be maintained; they had not learned that those who preserve their supremacy best are those who adhere to the same principles by which they originally established it, and this although it is evident and has been observed by many that it is by kind treatment of their neighbors and by holding out the prospect of further benefits that men acquire power, but when having attained their wish they treat their subjects ill and rule over them tyrannically it is only natural that with the change of character in the rulers the disposition of their subjects should change likewise, as actually happened now to the Carthaginians.

37. As for Hasdrubal, beset by these difficulties, he was disturbed by many and various apprehensions regarding

2 πραγμάτων ἐννοίας. ἐλύπει μὲν γὰρ αὐτὸν ἡ περὶ τὸν
Ἀνδοβάλην ἀπόστασις, ἐλύπει δὲ καὶ τὰ κατὰ τὴν
ἀντιπαραγωγὴν καὶ τὴν ἀλλοτριότητα τὴν ὑπάρχουσαν αὐτῷ πρὸς ⟨τοὺς⟩ ἄλλους στρατηγούς· ἠγωνία δὲ

3 καὶ τὴν Ποπλίου παρουσίαν. καὶ ⟨τὸ λοιπὸν⟩ ἤδη
προσδοκῶν αὐτὸν ἥξειν μετὰ τῶν δυνάμεων, θεωρῶν
δ᾽ αὐτὸν μὲν ἐγκαταλειπόμενον ὑπὸ τῶν Ἰβήρων, τοῖς
δὲ Ῥωμαίοις πάντας ὁμοθυμαδὸν προσχωροῦντας, ἐπί

4 τινας λογισμοὺς κατήντησε τοιούτους. προέθετο γὰρ
διότι δεῖ παρεσκευασμένον τὰ δυνατὰ συμβαλεῖν
πρὸς μάχην τοῖς ὑπεναντίοις, κἂν μὲν ἡ τύχη δῷ τὸ
νικᾶν, βουλεύσασθαι μετὰ ταῦτα περὶ τῶν ἑξῆς ἀσφα-

5 λῶς· ἂν δ᾽ ἀντιπίπτῃ ⟨τὰ⟩ κατὰ τὴν μάχην, ποιεῖσθαι
τὴν ἀποχώρησιν μετὰ τῶν διασῳζομένων ἐξ αὐτῆς εἰς
Γαλατίαν, κἀκεῖθεν παραλαβόντα τῶν βαρβάρων ὡς
πλείστους βοηθεῖν εἰς τὴν Ἰταλίαν καὶ κοινωνεῖν
Ἀννίβᾳ τἀδελφῷ τῶν αὐτῶν ἐλπίδων.

6 Ἀσδρούβας ⟨μὲν⟩ δὴ ταῦτα διανοηθεὶς πρὸς τούτοις ἦν· Πόπλιος δὲ προσδεξάμενος Γάιον τὸν Λαίλιον
καὶ διακούσας τῶν παραγγελλομένων ὑπὸ τῆς συγκλήτου, προῆγε τὰς δυνάμεις ἀναλαβὼν ἐκ τῆς παρα-
χειμασίας, ἀπαντώντων αὐτῷ κατὰ τὴν δίοδον τῶν

7 Ἰβήρων, ἑτοίμως καὶ προθύμως συνεξορμώντων. οἱ δὲ
περὶ τὸν Ἀνδοβάλην πάλαι μὲν διεπέμποντο πρὸς τὸν
Πόπλιον, τότε δὲ πλησιάσαντος αὐτοῦ τοῖς τόποις
ἧκον ὡς αὐτὸν ἐκ τῆς παρεμβολῆς ἅμα τοῖς φίλοις,
καὶ συμμίξαντες ἀπελογίσαντο περὶ τῆς προγεγε-
νημένης σφίσι φιλίας πρὸς Καρχηδονίους, ὁμοίως δὲ

the dangers that menaced him. To begin with he was troubled by the revolt of Andobales and next by the opposition and estrangement of the other commanders. The prospect of Scipio's arrival also caused him much anxiety. Expecting him as he did to be soon on the spot with his army, and seeing himself deserted by the Iberians, who all with one accord were joining the Romans, he more or less decided on the following course. He proposed to make all possible preparations and meet the enemy in battle. Should Fortune give him victory, he would afterward deliberate in security as to his future action, but if he met with a reverse in the battle he would retreat from the field with the survivors to Gaul and getting as many of the natives as he could to join him would pass into Italy and throw in his fortunes with his brother Hannibal.

Hasdrubal, then, having resolved on this course was making his preparations. Meanwhile Scipio, having received Gaius Laelius and heard from him the senate's orders, withdrew his troops from their winter quarters and advanced,[80] being met on his march by the Iberians who joined him with hearty alacrity. Andobales had been for long communicating with Scipio, and now that he was in the neighborhood came to him from his camp together with his friends, and when they met, justified his former friendship with the Carthaginians and likewise pointed out

[80] In spring 208.

καὶ τὰς χρείας καὶ τὴν ὅλην πίστιν ἐνεφάνιζον, ἣν
8 ἐτύγχανον ἐκείνοις παρεσχημένοι. μετὰ δὲ ταῦτα τὰς
ἀδικίας ἐξηγοῦντο καὶ τὰς ὕβρεις τὰς ἐξ ἐκείνων
9 ἀπηντημένας. διόπερ ἠξίουν τὸν Πόπλιον αὐτὸν κριτὴν γίνεσθαι τῶν λεγομένων, κἂν μὲν φανῶσιν ἀδίκως
ἐγκαλοῦντες Καρχηδονίοις, σαφῶς γινώσκειν αὐτὸν
ὡς οὐδὲ τὴν πρὸς Ῥωμαίους δύνανται τηρεῖν πίστιν·
10 ἐὰν δὲ πολλὰς ἀδικίας ἀναλογιζόμενοι κατ' ἀνάγκην
ἀφιστῶνται τῆς εὐνοίας τῆς ἐκείνων, καλὰς ἐλπίδας
ἔχειν διότι νῦν ἑλόμενοι τὰ Ῥωμαίων βεβαίως τηρή-
σουσι τὴν πρὸς αὐτοὺς εὔνοιαν.

38. Καὶ πλείω πρὸς τοῦτο τὸ μέρος αὐτῶν δια-
λεχθέντων, ἐπεὶ κατέπαυσαν τὸν λόγον, μεταλαβὼν ὁ
Πόπλιος καὶ τοῖς ὑπ' ἐκείνων εἰρημένοις ἔφη πιστεύειν, μάλιστα δὲ γινώσκειν τὴν Καρχηδονίων ὕβριν ἔκ
τε τῆς εἰς τοὺς ἄλλους Ἴβηρας καὶ μάλιστα τῆς εἰς
2 τὰς ἐκείνων γυναῖκας καὶ θυγατέρας ἀσελγείας, ἃς
αὐτὸς παρειληφὼς νῦν οὐχ ὁμήρων ἐχούσας διάθεσιν,
ἀλλ' αἰχμαλώτων καὶ δούλων, οὕτως τετηρηκέναι τὴν
πίστιν ὡς οὐδ' ἂν αὐτοὺς ἐκείνους τηρῆσαι πατέρας
3 ὑπάρχοντας. τῶν δ' ἀνθομολογησαμένων διότι παρα-
κολουθοῦσι καὶ προσκυνησάντων αὐτὸν καὶ προσ-
φωνησάντων βασιλέα ⟨πάντων⟩, οἱ μὲν παρόντες
ἐπεσημήναντο ⟨τὸ⟩ ῥηθέν, ὁ δὲ Πόπλιος ἐντραπεὶς
θαρρεῖν αὐτοῖς παρῄνει· τεύξεσθαι γὰρ ἔφη σφᾶς
4 ἁπάντων τῶν φιλανθρώπων ὑπὸ Ῥωμαίων. καὶ παραυτίκα μὲν ἐκ χειρὸς τὰς θυγατέρας ἀπέδωκε, τῇ δ'
5 ἐπαύριον ἐποιεῖτο τὰς συνθήκας πρὸς αὐτούς. ἦν δὲ τὸ

all the services he had rendered them and how loyal he had been to their cause. He next gave an account of the injuries and insults he had met with at their hands. He therefore begged Scipio to judge for himself as to his statements, and if it appeared to him that he was accusing the Carthaginians unjustly, he might be perfectly sure that he was not capable of remaining loyal to Rome. But if, taking into consideration their many acts of injustice, he had been forced to abandon his friendly attitude, Scipio might feel confident that now he had chosen the cause of Rome he would be firm in his affection.

38. Andobales spoke still further on the subject, and when he had finished Scipio in reply said that he perfectly believed his statements and himself had the clearest evidence of the tyrannical conduct of the Carthaginians in their licentious treatment of the wives and daughters of the speaker and his friends, whom he himself had found in the position not so much of hostages as of prisoners and slaves, adding that he had kept faith to them with a loyalty that not even they, their fathers, could have displayed. When they acknowledged that they agreed and did obeisance and all saluted him as king, those present applauded, and Scipio, who was much touched, exhorted them to be of good cheer, for they would meet with all kindness at the hands of the Romans. He at once handed over their daughters to them, and next day made a treaty[81] with them, the

---

[81] *StV* 540; cf. Mommsen *Staatsr.* 1.246–247.

συνέχον τῶν ὁμολογηθέντων ἀκολουθεῖν τοῖς Ῥωμαίων ἄρχουσι καὶ πείθεσθαι τοῖς ὑπὸ τούτων παραγ-
6 γελλομένοις. γενομένων δὲ τούτων ἀναχωρήσαντες εἰς
τὰς αὐτῶν παρεμβολὰς καὶ παραλαβόντες τὰς δυνάμεις, ἧκον πρὸς τὸν Πόπλιον, καὶ στρατοπεδεύσαντες
ὁμοῦ τοῖς Ῥωμαίοις προῆγον ἐπὶ τὸν Ἀσδρούβαν.

7 Ὁ δὲ τῶν Καρχηδονίων στρατηγὸς ἐτύγχανε μὲν
διατρίβων ἐν τοῖς περὶ Κασταλῶνα τόποις περὶ Βαίκυλα πόλιν οὐ μακρὰν τῶν ἀργυρείων μετάλλων·
8 πυθόμενος δὲ τὴν παρουσίαν τῶν Ῥωμαίων μετεστρα-
τοπέδευσε, καὶ λαβὼν ἐκ μὲν τῶν ὄπισθεν ποταμὸν
ἀσφαλῆ, παρὰ δὲ τὴν κατὰ πρόσωπον πλευρὰν τοῦ
χάρακος ἐπίπεδον τόπον, ὀφρὺν προβεβλημένην
ἔχοντα καὶ βάθος ἱκανὸν πρὸς ἀσφάλειαν καὶ μῆκος
πρὸς ἔκταξιν, <ἔμενεν> ἐπὶ τῶν ὑποκειμένων, προ-
9 τιθέμενος ἐπὶ τὴν ὀφρὺν ἀεὶ τὰς ἐφεδρείας. ὁ δὲ
Πόπλιος ἐγγίσας προθύμως μὲν εἶχε πρὸς τὸ διακινδυνεύειν, ἀπόρως δὲ διέκειτο, θεωρῶν τοὺς τόπους
10 εὐφυεῖς ὄντας πρὸς τὴν τῶν ἐναντίων ἀσφάλειαν. οὐ
μὴν ἀλλὰ προσανασχὼν δύ᾽ ἡμέρας καὶ διαγωνιάσας
μὴ συνεπιγενομένων τῶν περὶ τὸν Μάγωνα καὶ τὸν
τοῦ Γέσκωνος Ἀσδρούβαν πανταχόθεν αὐτὸν οἱ πολέμιοι περιστῶσιν, ἔκρινε παραβάλλεσθαι καὶ καταπειράζειν τῶν ὑπεναντίων.

39. Τὴν μὲν οὖν ἄλλην δύναμιν ἑτοιμάσας πρὸς
μάχην συνεῖχεν ἐν τῷ χάρακι, τοὺς δὲ γροσφομάχους
καὶ τῶν πεζῶν τοὺς ἐπιλέκτους ἐξαφιεὶς ἐκέλευε προσ-
βάλλειν πρὸς τὴν ὀφρὺν καὶ καταπειράζειν τῆς τῶν

essential part of the agreement being that they should follow the Roman commanders and obey their orders. After this they retired to their own camps, and taking their forces came back to Scipio, and now joining the Roman camp advanced against Hasdrubal.

The Carthaginian general was then quartered in the district of Castalon near the town of Baecula[82] not far from the silver mines. On hearing of the arrival of the Romans, he shifted his camp to a position where he had in his rear the effective protection of a river and in his front a stretch of level ground defended by a ridge and of sufficient depth for safety and sufficient width for deploying his troops. Here he remained, stationing all the time his covering force on the ridge in front of him. Scipio on approaching was eager to risk a battle, but was somewhat at a loss, as he saw how advantageous and safe the enemy's position was. But after waiting for two days he became apprehensive lest Mago and Hasdrubal, son of Gesco should come up and he should find himself surrounded by the enemy on all sides, and he therefore decided to take his chance and make an attempt on the enemy.

39. Getting the rest of his forces ready for battle he kept them inside the camp, and sending off the velites and a picked force of foot he ordered them to ascend the ridge and attack the enemy's covering force. They executed his

[82] Probably the modern town of Bailén, some fifteen kilometers northwest of Castulo. For the battle, see the map in WC 2.249. Livy 27.18.1–19.1 complements P.'s report.

2 πολεμίων ἐφεδρείας. τῶν δὲ ποιούντων τὸ παραγ-
γελθὲν εὐψύχως, τὰς μὲν ἀρχὰς ὁ τῶν Καρχηδονίων
στρατηγὸς ἐκαραδόκει τὸ συμβαῖνον· θεωρῶν δὲ διὰ
τὴν τόλμαν τῶν Ῥωμαίων τοὺς παρ' αὐτῶν πιεζομένους καὶ κακῶς πάσχοντας, ἐξῆγε τὴν δύναμιν καὶ
παρενέβαλε παρὰ τὴν ὀφρύν, πιστεύων τοῖς τόποις.

3 κατὰ δὲ τὸν καιρὸν τοῦτον ὁ Πόπλιος τοὺς μὲν εὐζώνους ἅπαντας ἐπαφῆκε, συντάξας βοηθεῖν τοῖς προκινδυνεύουσι, τοὺς δὲ λοιποὺς ἑτοίμους ἔχων, τοὺς μὲν
ἡμίσεις αὐτὸς ἔχων, περιελθὼν τὴν ὀφρὺν κατὰ τὸ

4 λαιὸν τῶν ὑπεναντίων, προσέβαλλε τοῖς Καρχηδονίοις, τοὺς δ' ἡμίσεις Λαιλίῳ δοὺς ὁμοίως παρήγγειλε

5 τὴν ἔφοδον ἐπὶ τὰ δεξιὰ μέρη τῶν πολεμίων. οὗ
συμβαίνοντος ὁ μὲν Ἀσδρούβας ἀκμὴν ἐκ τῆς στρατοπεδείας ἐξῆγε τὴν δύναμιν· τὸν γὰρ πρὸ τούτου
χρόνον ἐπέμενε πιστεύων τοῖς τόποις καὶ πεπεισμένος
μηδέποτε τολμήσειν τοὺς πολεμίους ἐγχειρεῖν αὐτοῖς·
διὸ παρὰ τὴν προσδοκίαν γεγενημένης τῆς ἐπιθέσεως

6 καθυστέρει τῆς ἐκτάξεως. οἱ δὲ Ῥωμαῖοι κατὰ κέρας
ποιούμενοι τὸν κίνδυνον, οὐδέπω τῶν πολεμίων κατ-
ειληφότων τοὺς ἐπὶ τῶν κεράτων τόπους, οὐ μόνον
ἐπέβησαν ἀσφαλῶς ἐπὶ τὴν ὀφρύν, ἀλλὰ καὶ προσ-
άγοντες ἔτι παρεμβαλλόντων καὶ κινουμένων τῶν ὑπεναντίων τοὺς μὲν αὐτῶν προσπίπτοντες ἐκ πλαγίων
ἐφόνευον, τοὺς δὲ παρεμβάλλοντας ἐξ ἐπιστροφῆς

7 φεύγειν ἠνάγκαζον. Ἀσδρούβας δὲ κατὰ τοὺς ἐξ ἀρχῆς διαλογισμούς, θεωρῶν κλινούσας καὶ διατετραμ-
μένας τὰς αὐτοῦ δυνάμεις, τὸ μὲν ψυχομαχεῖν μέχρι

order with great gallantry, and at first the Carthaginian commander remained waiting for the result. But when he saw that, owing to the dashing courage of the Romans, his men were hard pressed and in an evil plight, he led out his forces and drew them up near the ridge, relying on the strength of the position. Scipio at once dispatched the whole of his light-armed troops with orders to support the force which had commenced the attack, and having the rest of his army ready, he himself took one half of it and skirting the ridge to the left of the enemy fell upon the Carthaginians; the other half he gave to Laelius with orders to attack the enemy on their right in a similar manner. While this was happening Hasdrubal was still engaged in leading his forces out of the camp. For up to now he had waited there relying on the strength of the position and convinced that the enemy would never venture to attack him: thus, owing to the unexpectedness of the assault, he was too late in deploying his troops. The Romans fighting oh the wings, since the enemy had not yet occupied the ground on their wings, not only succeeded in safely mounting the ridge, but as the enemy were still forming up and in motion when they attacked, slaughtered some of them by falling on their flank and compelled those who were getting into formation to turn and fly. Hasdrubal, as had been his original intention, when he saw his troops giving way

8 τῆς ἐσχάτης ἐλπίδος ἀπεδοκίμαζε, λαβὼν δὲ τά τε
χρήματα καὶ τὰ θηρία, καὶ τῶν φευγόντων ὅσους
ἠδύνατο πλείστους ἐπισπασάμενος, ἐποιεῖτο τὴν ἀναχώρησιν παρὰ τὸν Τάγον ποταμὸν ὡς ἐπὶ τὰς Πυρή-
νης ὑπερβολὰς καὶ τοὺς ταύτῃ κατοικοῦντας Γαλάτας.

9 Πόπλιος δὲ τὸ μὲν ἐκ ποδὸς ἕπεσθαι τοῖς περὶ τὸν
Ἀσδρούβαν οὐχ ἡγεῖτο συμφέρειν τῷ δεδιέναι τῶν
ἄλλων στρατηγῶν ⟨τὴν⟩ ἔφοδον, τὸν δὲ χάρακα τῶν
ὑπεναντίων ἐφῆκε τοῖς αὑτοῦ στρατιώταις διαρπάζειν.

40. Εἰς δὲ τὴν ἐπαύριον συναθροίσας τὸ τῶν
αἰχμαλώτων πλῆθος, ὧν ἦσαν πεζοὶ μὲν εἰς μυρίους,
ἱππεῖς δὲ πλείους δισχιλίων, ἐγίνετο περὶ τὴν τούτων
2 οἰκονομίαν. τῶν δ' Ἰβήρων ὅσοι κατὰ τοὺς προειρημένους τόπους Καρχηδονίοις τότε συνεμάχουν, ἧκον
ἐγχειρίζοντες σφᾶς αὑτοὺς εἰς τὴν Ῥωμαίων πίστιν,
κατὰ δὲ τὰς ἐντεύξεις βασιλέα προσεφώνουν τὸν
3 Πόπλιον. πρῶτον μὲν οὖν ἐποίησε τοῦτο καὶ προσ-
εκύνησε πρῶτος Ἐδεκών, μετὰ δὲ τοῦτον οἱ περὶ τὸν
Ἀνδοβάλην. τότε μὲν οὖν ἀνεπιστάτως αὐτὸν παρέ-
4 δραμε τὸ ῥηθέν· μετὰ δὲ τὴν μάχην ἁπάντων βασιλέα
προσφωνούντων, εἰς ἐπίστασιν ἤγαγε τὸν Πόπλιον τὸ
5 γινόμενον. διὸ καὶ συναθροίσας τοὺς Ἴβηρας βασιλι-
κὸς μὲν ἔφη βούλεσθαι καὶ λέγεσθαι παρὰ πᾶσι καὶ
ταῖς ἀληθείαις ὑπάρχειν, βασιλεύς γε μὴν οὔτ' ⟨εἶ-
ναι⟩ θέλειν οὔτε λέγεσθαι παρ' οὐδενί. ταῦτα δ' εἰπὼν
6 παρήγγειλε στρατηγὸν αὐτὸν προσφωνεῖν. ἴσως μὲν
οὖν καὶ τότε δικαίως ἄν τις ἐπεσημήνατο τὴν μεγαλοψυχίαν τἀνδρός, ᾗ κομιδῇ νέος ὢν καὶ τῆς τύχης αὐτῷ

and in disorder, declined to fight it out to the death, but taking his money and his elephants and drawing off after him as many of the fugitives as he could, retreated along the River Tagus in the direction of the pass over the Pyrenees and of the Gauls who inhabited that part of the country. Scipio did not think it advisable to follow Hasdrubal, as he was afraid of being attacked by the other generals, but gave the enemy's camp up to his soldiers to plunder.

40. Next day collecting the prisoners, of whom there were about ten thousand foot and more than two thousand horse, he occupied himself with their disposal. The Iberians in the districts I spoke of who were still allies of the Carthaginians now came in to submit to the Romans, and on meeting Scipio saluted him as king.[83] Edeco was the first who had done this and made obeisance to him, and he had been followed by Andobales. On that occasion Scipio had paid no great attention and did not particularly notice the appellation, but when after the battle all addressed him as king, the matter gave him pause. He therefore assembled the Iberians and told them that he wished to be called kingly by them and actually to be kingly, but that he did not wish to be king or to be called so by any one. After saying this he ordered them to call him general. Perhaps even on this occasion one would be justified in noting with admiration Scipio's greatness of mind, in view of the fact that though he was still quite young and fortune had fa-

[83] Scipio so saluted a third time, after the salutations by Edeco and Andobales.

συνεκδραμούσης ἐπὶ τοσοῦτον ὥστε πάντας τοὺς ὑποταττομένους ἐξ αὐτῶν ἐπί τε ταύτην κατενεχθῆναι τὴν
διάληψιν καὶ τὴν ὀνομασίαν, ὅμως ἐν ἑαυτῷ διέμεινε
καὶ παρῃτεῖτο τὴν τοιαύτην ὁρμὴν καὶ φαντασίαν.

7 πολὺ δὲ μᾶλλον ἄν τις θαυμάσειε τὴν ὑπερβολὴν τῆς
περὶ τὸν ἄνδρα μεγαλοψυχίας, βλέψας εἰς τοὺς ἐσχά-
τους τοῦ βίου καιρούς, ἡνίκα πρὸς τοῖς κατὰ τὴν
Ἰβηρίαν ἔργοις κατεστρέψατο μὲν Καρχηδονίους, καὶ
τὰ πλεῖστα καὶ κάλλιστα μέρη τῆς Λιβύης ἀπὸ τῶν
Φιλαίνου βωμῶν ἕως Ἡρακλείων στηλῶν ὑπὸ τὴν τῆς
πατρίδος ἐξουσίαν ἤγαγε, κατεστρέψατο δὲ τὴν Ἀσίαν καὶ τοὺς τῆς Συρίας βασιλεῖς, καὶ τὸ κάλλιστον
καὶ μέγιστον μέρος τῆς οἰκουμένης ὑπήκοον ἐποίησε
Ῥωμαίοις, ἔλαβε δὲ καιροὺς εἰς τὸ περιποιήσασθαι
δυναστείαν βασιλικὴν ἐν οἷς ἐπιβάλοιτο καὶ βουλη-
8 θείη τόποις τῆς οἰκουμένης. ταῦτα γὰρ οὐ μόνον
ἀνθρωπίνην φύσιν, ἀλλὰ καὶ θειοτέραν, εἰ θέμις εἰ-
9 πεῖν, ὑπερφρονεῖν ἂν ἐποίησεν. Πόπλιος ⟨δὲ⟩ τοσοῦτον ὑπερέθετο μεγαλοψυχίᾳ τοὺς ἄλλους ἀνθρώπους ὡς οὐ μεῖζον ἀγαθὸν εὔξασθαί τις τοῖς θεοῖς
⟨οὐ⟩ τολμήσειε, λέγω δὲ βασιλείας, τοῦτ' ἐκεῖνος
πολλάκις ὑπὸ τῆς τύχης αὐτῷ δεδομένον ἀπηξίωσε,
καὶ περὶ πλείονος ἐποιήσατο τὴν πατρίδα καὶ τὴν

---

84 P. contradicts his emphatic earlier statement that Scipio
owed his achievements not to Fortune but to his prudence and
foresight, e. g., 10.2.3; 5.8.

85 It is indeed tempting to see in these words a reference to the
time after the Third Punic War (so A. Aymard, *Études d'histoire*

vored him so highly that all who were subject to him were
prompted to form this estimate of him[84] and bestow on
him the name of king of their own accord, he still kept his
head and declined to profit by their enthusiasm and accept
this splendid title. But much more must we admire this exceptional greatness of mind when we look at the close of
his life, at the period when in addition to his exploits in
Spain he had destroyed the power of Carthage and subjected[85] to the dominion of his country the largest and
finest part of Libya from the altars of Philaenus to the pillars of Heracles,[86] when he had reduced Asia and overthrown the kings of Syria[87] and had made the greatest and
richest part of the world subject to Rome, and had the opportunity of attaining royal power in whatever part of the
world he chose to attempt it. Such success indeed might
have made not only a man, but if it is permitted to say so,
even a god overweening. And yet Scipio so far excelled all
other men in greatness of mind, that when kingship, the
greatest blessing[88] for which any man would dare to pray to
the gods, was often offered to him by fortune, he refused it,
and valued more highly his country and his own loyalty to

ancienne [Paris 1967], 392–393, a reprint of a paper of 1954); a
different opinion in WC 2.253.

[86] The Carthaginian realm is described with these same words
in 3.39.2.

[87] The Seleucids, in fact only Antiochus III, despite the plural,
in 190. Publius Scipio is given credit, although his brother Lucius
was in charge and Publius only his deputy.

[88] This verdict is somewhat surprising coming from a man im-
bued with the tradition of Greek republicanism. See the com-
ments of K. Welwei, *Könige und Königtum im Urteil des Polybios*
(Diss. Cologne 1963), 126–132.

ταύτης πίστιν τῆς περιβλέπτου καὶ μακαριστῆς ‹βα-
10 σιλείας›. πλὴν τότε γε διαλέξας ἐκ τῶν αἰχμαλώτων
τοὺς Ἴβηρας, τούτους μὲν ἀπέλυσε χωρὶς λύτρων
πάντας εἰς τὰς ἑαυτῶν πατρίδας, τῶν δ' ἵππων τριακοσίους κελεύσας ἐκλέξαι τοῖς περὶ τὸν Ἀνδοβάλην
11 τοὺς λοιποὺς διέδωκε τοῖς ἀνίπποις. καὶ τὸ λοιπὸν ἤδη
μεταλαβὼν τὴν τῶν Καρχηδονίων στρατοπεδείαν διὰ
τὴν τῶν τόπων εὐφυΐαν, αὐτὸς μὲν ἔμενε καραδοκῶν
τοὺς καταλειπομένους τῶν Καρχηδονίων στρατηγούς,
ἐπὶ δὲ τὰς ὑπερβολὰς τῶν Πυρηναίων ὀρέων ἐξαπέ-
12 στειλε τοὺς τηρήσοντας τὸν Ἀσδρούβαν. μετὰ δὲ
ταῦτα, τῆς ὥρας ἤδη συναπτούσης, ἀνεχώρησε μετὰ
τῆς δυνάμεως εἰς Ταρράκων', ἐν τούτοις τοῖς τόποις
ποιεῖσθαι τὴν παραχειμασίαν.

VII. RES GRAECIAE

41. Οἱ μὲν Αἰτωλοί, προσφάτως ἐπηρμένοι ταῖς
ἐλπίσιν ἐπὶ τῇ Ῥωμαίων καὶ τῇ τοῦ βασιλέως Ἀττάλου παρουσίᾳ, πάντας ἐξέπληττον καὶ πᾶσιν ἐπέκειν-
το κατὰ γῆν, οἱ δὲ περὶ τὸν Ἄτταλον καὶ Πόπλιον
2 κατὰ θάλατταν. διόπερ ἧκον Ἀχαιοὶ μὲν παρακαλοῦντες τὸν Φίλιππον βοηθεῖν· οὐ γὰρ μόνον τοὺς Αἰτωλοὺς ἠγωνίων, ἀλλὰ καὶ τὸν Μαχανίδαν διὰ τὸ προ-
καθῆσθαι μετὰ τῆς δυνάμεως ἐπὶ τοῖς τῶν Ἀργείων

---

89 Regent of Sparta since ca. 211, perhaps as tutor of King

her than the thing which is the object of universal admiration and envy. To resume my narrative, on the present occasion he picked out the Iberians from the prisoners and left them all free to return to their own countries without ransom, and ordering Andobales to choose for himself three hundred of the horses, he distributed the rest among those who had none. After this he transferred his army to the Carthaginian camp owing to its favorable position, and, while he remained there himself, waiting to see the movements of the other Carthaginian generals, he dispatched a force to the pass over the Pyrenees to observe the movements of Hasdrubal. Subsequently, as the season was now advanced, he retired with his army to Tarraco to pass the winter in that district.

VII. AFFAIRS OF GREECE

Action of Philip

41. The Aetolians, whose hopes had recently risen high owing to the arrival of the Romans and King Attalus, were terrorizing and threatening everyone by land while the Romans and Attalus were doing the same by sea. The Achaeans therefore came to Philip to beg for his help, for they were not only in dread of the Aetolians but of Machanidas,[89] as he was hovering with his army on the

208/7
B.C.

Lycurgus' son Pelops. He continued Lycurgus' policy as an enemy of Macedonia and caused Philip's Achaean allies serious trouble. *RE* Machanidas 142–143 (V. Ehrenberg). P. Cartledge, in Cartledge-Spawforth, *Hellenistic and Roman Sparta* (London 1989), 65–67.

3 ὅροις. Βοιωτοὶ ⟨δὲ⟩ δεδιότες τὸν στόλον τῶν ὑπεναντίων, ἡγεμόνα καὶ βοήθειαν ᾔτουν. φιλοπονώτατά γε
μὴν οἱ τὴν Εὔβοιαν κατοικοῦντες ἠξίουν ⟨ἔχειν⟩ τινὰ
πρόνοιαν τῶν πολεμίων. παραπλήσια δ᾽ Ἀκαρνᾶνες
4 παρεκάλουν. ἦν δὲ καὶ παρ᾽ Ἠπειρωτῶν πρεσβεία.
προσήγγελτο δὲ καὶ Σκερδιλαΐδαν καὶ Πλευρᾶτον
ἐξάγειν τὰς δυνάμεις· ἔτι δὲ τοὺς προσορῶντας τῇ
Μακεδονίᾳ Θρᾷκας, καὶ μάλιστα τοὺς Μαιδούς, ἐπιβολὰς ἔχειν ὡς ἐμβαλοῦντας ἐπὶ Μακεδονίαν, ἐὰν
βραχύ τι μόνον ὁ βασιλεὺς τῆς οἰκείας ἀποσπασθῇ.
5 προκατελάμβανον δὲ καὶ τὰ περὶ Θερμοπύλας στενὰ
τάφροις καὶ χάρακι καὶ φυλακαῖς βαρείαις Αἰτωλοί,
πεπεισμένοι συγκλείειν τὸν Φίλιππον καὶ καθόλου
κωλύειν παραβοηθεῖν τοῖς ἐντὸς Πυλῶν συμμάχοις.
6 δοκεῖ δέ μοι τὰς τοιαύτας περιστάσεις εὐλόγως ἄν
τις ἐπισημήνασθαι καὶ συνεφιστάνειν τοὺς ἀναγινώσκοντας, ἐν αἷς πεῖρα καὶ βάσανος ἀληθινὴ γίνεται
κατὰ τάς ⟨τε ψυχικὰς ὁρμὰς καὶ τὰς⟩ σωματικὰς
7 δυνάμεις τῶν ἡγεμόνων. καθάπερ ⟨γὰρ⟩ ἐν ταῖς κυνη-
γεσίαις τὰ ζῷα τότε διάδηλα γίνεται κατὰ τὴν ἀλκὴν
καὶ τὴν δύναμιν, ὅταν τὸ δεινὸν αὐτὰ περιστῇ πανταχόθεν, τὸν αὐτὸν τρόπον συμβαίνει καὶ ἐπὶ τῶν
ἡγουμένων. ὃ δὴ τότε μάλιστα συνιδεῖν ἦν γινόμενον
8 ὑπὸ τοῦ Φιλίππου· τὰς μὲν γὰρ πρεσβείας ἀπέλυσε
πάσας, ἑκάστοις τὰ δυνατὰ ποιήσειν ἐπαγγειλάμενος,
τῷ ⟨δὲ⟩ πολέμῳ πανταχόθεν ἐπεῖχε, καραδοκῶν πῇ
καὶ πρὸς τίνα πρῶτον δεήσει ποιεῖσθαι τὴν ὁρμήν.

42. προσπεσόντος δ᾽ αὐτῷ κατὰ τὸν καιρὸν τοῦτον

Argive frontier. The Boeotians, who were afraid of the enemy's fleet, begged for a commander and for succor, but
the inhabitants of Euboea were the most energetic of all in
their instances to Philip to take precautions against the enemy. The Acarnanians made the same request, and there
was also an embassy from Epirus. Information had been
received that Scerdilaidas and Pleuratus[90] were setting
their forces in motion, and also that the Thracians on the
Macedonian frontier, and especially the Maedi,[91] intended
to invade Macedonia if the king were drawn away however
so little from his native country. The Aetolians also had occupied the pass of Thermopylae, fortifying it with a palisade and trench and strongly garrisoning it, feeling sure
that they thus shut out Philip and prevented him from
coming to help his allies beyond the pass. It seems to me
that it is only reasonable to bring into relief and prominently before the eyes of my readers those occasions on
which the mental and physical capacities of commanders
are really tried and put to the test. For just as in the chase
the courage and power of wild beasts is then fully revealed,
when they are exposed to danger on all sides, so is it with
commanders, as was manifest then from Philip's action. He
dismissed all the embassies after promising each to do
what was in his power and devoted his whole attention to
the war, waiting to see in what direction and against whom
in the first place he should act.

42. Upon news reaching him at this time that Attalus

90 The son of the Illyrian Scerdilaidas.
91 Thracians who often raided Macedonia. *RE* Maidoi 541 and
Thrake 434 (B. Lenk).

τοὺς περὶ τὸν Ἄτταλον διάραντας καὶ προσορμή-
σαντας τῇ Πεπαρήθῳ κατεσχηκέναι τὴν χώραν, τούτοις μὲν ἐξαπέστειλε τοὺς παραφυλάξοντας τὴν

2 πόλιν, εἰς δὲ Φωκέας καὶ τοὺς κατὰ τὴν Βοιωτίαν
τόπους Πολυφάνταν ἐξέπεμψε μετὰ συμμέτρου δυνάμεως, εἰς δὲ Χαλκίδα καὶ τὴν ἄλλην Εὔβοιαν Μένιπ-
πον, ἔχοντα πελταστὰς χιλίους, Ἀγριᾶνας πεντακοσί-

3 ους. αὐτὸς δὲ προῆγε ποιούμενος τὴν πορείαν εἰς
Σκοτοῦσαν, παραπλησίως δὲ καὶ τοῖς Μακεδόσιν εἰς

4 ταύτην τὴν πόλιν παρήγγειλεν ἀπαντᾶν. πυθόμενος δὲ
τοὺς περὶ τὸν Ἄτταλον εἰς Νίκαιαν καταπεπλευκέναι,
τῶν δ᾽ Αἰτωλῶν τοὺς ἄρχοντας εἰς Ἡράκλειαν ἀθροί-
ζεσθαι χάριν τοῦ κοινολογηθῆναι πρὸς ἀλλήλους
ὑπὲρ τῶν ἐνεστώτων, ἀναλαβὼν τὴν δύναμιν ἐκ τῆς
Σκοτούσης ὥρμησε σπεύδων καταταχῆσαι καὶ πτοή-

5 σας διασῦραι τὴν σύνοδον αὐτῶν. τοῦ μὲν οὖν συλ-
λόγου καθυστέρει, τὸν δὲ σῖτον φθείρας καὶ παρελόμενος τῶν περὶ τὸν Αἰνιᾶνα κόλπον κατοικούντων

6 ἐπανῆλθε. καὶ τὴν μὲν δύναμιν ἐν τῇ Σκοτούσῃ πάλιν
ἀπέλειπε, μετὰ δὲ τῶν εὐζώνων καὶ τῆς βασιλικῆς
ἴλης εἰς Δημητριάδα καταλύσας ἔμενε, καραδοκῶν

7 ⟨τὰς⟩ τῶν ἐναντίων ἐπιβολάς. ἵνα δὲ μηδὲν αὐτὸν
λανθάνῃ τῶν πραττομένων, διεπέμψατο πρὸς Πεπαρη-
θίους καὶ πρὸς τοὺς ἐπὶ τῆς Φωκίδος, ὁμοίως δὲ καὶ
πρὸς τοὺς ἐπὶ τῆς Εὐβοίας, καὶ παρήγγειλε διασαφεῖν

92 Today Skopelos, island north of Euboea, controlled by King
Philip. *RE* Peparethos 551–558 (R. Herbst).

had crossed and anchored off Peparethus[92] and occupied its country districts, he dispatched a force to protect the town against them; to Phocis and Boeotia and that neighborhood he sent Polyphantas with an adequate number of troops, and to Calchis and the rest of Euboea Menippus with a thousand peltasts and five hundred Agrianians; he himself marched upon Scotussa,[93] and ordered the Macedonians also to meet him at that town. Hearing now that Attalus had put in at Nicaea and that the Aetolian magistrates were about to meet at Heraclea to discuss the situation, he took the force he had with him from Scotusa and made for Heraclea[94] with the object of arriving in time to frighten and disperse their meeting. He arrived too late for the meeting, but after destroying or carrying off the crops of the inhabitants round the Gulf of Aenus,[95] he returned. Leaving his main force again in Scotusa he halted and remained at Demetrias[96] with the royal troop of horse and his light-armed troops, waiting for the enemy to reveal their plans. So that nothing that was going on should escape his notice he sent to the Peparethians, and to his commanders in Phocis and Euboea, ordering them to inform

[93] City in the Pelasgiotis. Stählin (9.41.1), 109–111. An important document, recently found: *SEG* 43.321.

[94] Heraclea Trachinia, founded by Sparta in 426, became Aetolian in 280. Stählin (9.41.1), 206–209.

[95] The Malian Gulf.

[96] Opposite modern Volos. The city was founded in 294 by King Demetrius Poliorcetes as a second, Greek, residence of the kings of Macedonia. F. Stählin, E. Meyer, A. Heidner, *Pagasai und Demetrias* (Berlin 1934) and the series *DEMETRIAS* of the German Archaeological Institute, Bonn, since 1976.

αὐτῷ πάντα τὰ γινόμενα διὰ τῶν πυρσῶν ἐπὶ τὸ
8 Τίσαιον. τοῦτο δ᾽ ἐστὶ τῆς Θετταλίας ὄρος, εὐφυῶς
κείμενον πρὸς τὰς τῶν προειρημένων τόπων περι-
φάσεις.

43. Τοῦ δὲ κατὰ τὰς πυρσείας γένους, μεγίστας δὴ
παρεχομένου χρείας ἐν τοῖς πολεμικοῖς, ἀνεργάστου
πρότερον ὑπάρχοντος, χρήσιμον εἶναί μοι δοκεῖ τὸ μὴ
παραδραμεῖν, ἀλλὰ ποιήσασθαι περὶ αὐτοῦ τὴν ἁρ-
2 μόζουσαν μνήμην. ὅτι μὲν οὖν ὁ καιρὸς ἐν πᾶσι
μεγάλην ἔχει μερίδα πρὸς τὰς ἐπιβολάς, μεγίστην δ᾽
ἐν τοῖς πολεμικοῖς, παντὶ δῆλον· τῶν δὲ πρὸς τοῦτο
συναγωνισμάτων πλείστην ἔχουσι δύναμιν οἱ πυρ-
3 σοί. ⟨δηλοῦσι γὰρ⟩ τίνα μὲν ἄρτι γέγονε, τινὰ δ᾽
ἀκμὴν ἐνεργεῖται, καὶ δυνατόν ἐστι γινώσκειν, ᾧ
μέλει, ποτὲ μὲν ἡμερῶν τριῶν ἢ τεττάρων ὁδὸν ἀπ-
4 έχοντι, ποτὲ δὲ καὶ πλειόνων. ὥστ᾽ ἀεὶ τοῖς δεομένοις
πράγμασιν ἐπικουρίας παράδοξον γίνεσθαι τὴν βοή-
5 θειαν διὰ τῆς τῶν πυρσῶν ἀπαγγελίας. τὸν μὲν ⟨οὖν⟩
πρὸ τούτου χρόνον ἁπλῆς γινομένης τῆς πυρσείας
κατὰ τὸ πλεῖστον αὐτὴν ἀνωφελῆ συνέβαινε γίνεσθαι
6 τοῖς χρωμένοις. διὰ γὰρ συνθημάτων ὡρισμένων ἔδει
τὴν χρείαν συντελεῖν· τῶν δὲ πραγμάτων ἀορίστων
ὑπαρχόντων τὰ πλεῖστα διέφυγε τὴν τῶν πυρσῶν
7 χρείαν, οἷον ἐπ᾽ αὐτῶν τῶν νῦν εἰρημένων. ὅτι μὲν οὖν

---

97 Until the advent of modern technology, fire signaling and
the use of carrier pigeons were the fastest ways of communicating
over long distances in antiquity. This digression is motivated by

him of everything by fire signals direct to Mount Tisaeum, a mountain in Thessaly favorably situated for commanding a view of the above places.

Fire Signaling

43. I think that as regards the system of signaling by fire,[97] which is now of the greatest possible service in war but was formerly undeveloped, it will be of use not to pass it over but to give it a proper discussion. It is evident to all that in every matter, and especially in warfare, the power of acting at the right time contributes very much to the success of enterprises, and fire signals are the most efficient of all the devices which aid us to do this. For they show what has recently occurred and what is still in the course of being done, and by means of them anyone who cares to do so even if he is at a distance of three, four, or even more days' journey can be informed. So that it is always surprising how help can be brought by means of fire messages when the situation requires it. Now in former times, as fire signals were simple beacons, they were for the most part of little use to those who used them. For the service had to be performed by signals previously determined upon, and as facts are indefinite, most of them defied communication by fire signals. To take the case I just mentioned, it was possible for those who had agreed on this to convey information that a fleet had arrived at

Philip's use of it from Demetrias to Peparethus. The same method was already used in 361/0 for a message sent to Peparethus for Alexander of Pherae besieging the island (Polyaen. 6.2.2; cf. Diod. Sic. 15.95).

εἰς Ὠρεὸν καὶ Πεπάρηθον ἢ Χαλκίδα πάρεστι στό-
λος, δυνατὸν ἦν διασαφεῖν τοῖς περὶ τούτου συνθε-
8 μένοις· ὅτι δὲ μεταβάλλονταί τινες τῶν πολιτῶν ἢ
προδιδόασιν, ἢ φόνος ἐν τῇ πόλει γέγονεν, ἤ τι τῶν
τοιούτων, ἃ δὴ συμβαίνει μὲν πολλάκις, πρόληψιν δ'
9 ἔχειν πάντων ἀδύνατον—μάλιστα δὲ τὰ παραδόξως
γινόμενα τῆς ἐκ τοῦ καιροῦ συμβουλίας καὶ ἐπικουρίας προσδεῖται—τὰ τοιαῦτα πάντα διέφυγε τὴν τῶν
10 πυρσῶν χρείαν. περὶ ὧν γὰρ οὐκ ἐνεδέχετο προνοηθῆ-
ναι, περὶ τούτων οὐδὲ σύνθημα ποιήσασθαι δυνατόν.

44. Αἰνείας δὲ βουληθεὶς διορθώσασθαι τὴν τοιαύτην ἀπορίαν, ὁ τὰ περὶ τῶν Στρατηγικῶν ὑπομνήματα συντεταγμένος, βραχὺ μέν τι προεβίβασε, τοῦ
γε μὴν δέοντος ἀκμὴν πάμπολυ τὸ κατὰ τὴν ἐπίνοιαν
2 ἀπελείφθη. γνοίη δ' ἄν τις ἐκ τούτων. φησὶ γὰρ δεῖν
τοὺς μέλλοντας ἀλλήλοις διὰ τῶν πυρσῶν δηλοῦν τὸ
κατεπεῖγον ἀγγεῖα κατασκευάσαι κεραμεᾶ, κατά τε τὸ
πλάτος καὶ κατὰ τὸ βάθος ἰσομεγέθη πρὸς ἀκρίβειαν·
εἶναι δὲ μάλιστα τὸ μὲν βάθος τριῶν πηχῶν, τὸ δὲ
3 πλάτος πήχεος. εἶτα παρασκευάσαι φελλοὺς βραχὺ
κατὰ πλάτος ἐνδεεῖς τῶν στομάτων, ἐν δὲ τούτοις
μέσοις ἐμπεπηγέναι ‹βακτηρίας διῃρημένας εἰς› ἴσα
μέρη τριδάκτυλα, καθ' ἕκαστον δὲ μέρος εἶναι περι-
4 γραφὴν εὔσημον. ἐν ἑκάστῳ δὲ μέρει γεγράφθαι τὰ
προφανέστατα καὶ καθολικώτατα τῶν ἐν τοῖς πολεμι-
5 κοῖς συμβαινόντων, οἷον εὐθέως ἐν τῷ πρώτῳ, διότι
"πάρεισιν ἱππεῖς εἰς τὴν χώραν," ἐν δὲ τῷ δευτέρῳ
6 διότι "πεζοὶ βαρεῖς," ἐν δὲ τῷ τρίτῳ "ψιλοί," τούτων δ'

Oreus, Peparethus, or Chalcis, but when it came to some of the citizens having changed sides or having been guilty of treachery or a massacre having taken place in the town, or anything of the kind, things that often happen, but cannot all be foreseen—and it is chiefly unexpected occurrences which require instant consideration and help—all such matters defied communication by fire signal. For it was quite impossible to have a preconcerted code for things which there was no means of foretelling.

44. Aeneas,[98] the author of the work on strategy, wishing to find a remedy for the difficulty, advanced matters a little, but his device still fell far short of our requirements, as can be seen from this description of it. He says that those who are about to communicate urgent news to each other by fire signal should procure two earthenware vessels of exactly the same width and depth, the depth being some three cubits and the width one. Then they should have corks made a little narrower than the mouths of the vessels and through the middle of each cork should pass a rod graduated in equal sections of three fingerbreadths, each clearly marked off from the next. In each section should be written the most evident and ordinary events that occur in war, e.g., on the first "Cavalry arrived in the country," on the second "Heavy infantry," on the third

98 For Aeneas Tacticus see n. on 1.7.4. In his work *How to Survive under Siege* 7.4, he mentions fire signaling but refers to a fuller account (not preserved) in another treatise. See Whitehead's commentary, pp. 111–113.

ἐξῆς "πεζοὶ μεθ᾽ ἱππέων," εἶτα "πλοῖα," μετὰ δὲ ταῦτα
"σῖτος," ‹καὶ› κατὰ τὸ συνεχὲς οὕτω, μέχρις ἂν ἐν
πάσαις γραφῇ ταῖς χώραις τὰ μάλιστ᾽ ἂν ἐκ τῶν
εὐλόγων προνοίας τυγχάνοντα καὶ συμβαίνοντα κατὰ

7 τοὺς ἐνεστῶτας καιροὺς ἐκ τῶν πολεμικῶν. τούτων δὲ
γενομένων ἀμφότερα κελεύει τρῆσαι τὰ ἀγγεῖα πρὸς
ἀκρίβειαν, ὥστε τοὺς αὐλίσκους ἴσους εἶναι καὶ κατ᾽
ἴσον ἀπορρεῖν· εἶτα πληρώσαντας ὕδατος ἐπιθεῖναι
τοὺς φελλοὺς ἔχοντας ‹τὰς› βακτηρίας, κἄπειτα τοὺς

8 αὐλίσκους ἀφεῖναι ῥεῖν ἅμα. τούτου δὲ συμβαίνοντος
δῆλος ὡς ἀνάγκη πάντων ἴσων καὶ ὁμοίων ὄντων, καθ᾽
ὅσον ἂν ἀπορρέῃ τὸ ὑγρόν, κατὰ τοσοῦτον τοὺς φελλοὺς καταβαίνειν καὶ τὰς βακτηρίας κρύπτεσθαι κατὰ

9 τῶν ἀγγείων. ὅταν δὲ τὰ προειρημένα γένηται κατὰ
τὸν χειρισμὸν ἰσοταχῆ καὶ σύμφωνα, τότε κομίσαν-
τας ἐπὶ τοὺς τόπους, ἐν οἷς ἑκάτεροι μέλλουσι συντη-

10 ρεῖν τὰς πυρσείας, ἑκάτερον θεῖναι τῶν ἀγγείων. εἶτ᾽
ἐπὰν ἐμπέσῃ τι τῶν ἐν τῇ βακτηρίᾳ γεγραμμένων,
πυρσὸν ἆραι κελεύει, καὶ μένειν, ἕως ἂν ἀνταίρωσιν οἱ
συντεταγμένοι· γενομένων δὲ φανερῶν ἀμφοτέρων
ἅμα τῶν πυρσῶν καθελεῖν. εἶτ᾽ εὐθέως ἀφεῖναι τοὺς

11 αὐλίσκους ῥεῖν. ὅταν δὲ καταβαίνοντος τοῦ φελλοῦ
καὶ τῆς βακτηρίας ἔλθῃ τῶν γεγραμμένων ὃ βούλει
δηλοῦν κατὰ τὸ χεῖλος τοῦ τεύχους, ἆραι κελεύει τὸν

12 πυρσόν· τοὺς δ᾽ ἑτέρους ἐπιλαβεῖν εὐφέως τὸν αὐλί-
σκον, καὶ σκοπεῖν τί κατὰ τὸ χεῖλός ἐστι τῶν ἐν τῇ

13 βακτηρίᾳ γεγραμμένων· ἔσται δὲ τοῦτο τὸ δηλού-
μενον πάντων ἰσοταχῶς παρ᾽ ἀμφοτέροις κινουμένων.

236

"Light-armed infantry," next "Infantry and cavalry," next "Ships," next "Corn," and so on until we have entered in all the sections the chief contingencies of which, at the present time, there is a reasonable probability in war time. Next he tells us to bore holes in both vessels of exactly the same size, so that they allow exactly the same escape. Then we are to fill the vessels with water and put on the corks with the rods in them and allow the water to flow through the two apertures. When this is done it is evident that, the conditions being precisely similar, in proportion as the water escapes the two corks will sink and the rods will disappear into the vessels. When by experiment it is seen that the rapidity of escape is in both cases exactly the same, the vessels are to be conveyed to the places in which both parties are to look after the signals and deposited there. Now whenever any of the contingencies written on the rods occurs he tells us to raise a torch and to wait until the corresponding party raise another. When both the torches are clearly visible the signaler is to lower his torch and at once allow the water to escape through the aperture. Whenever, as the corks sink, the contingency you wish to communicate reaches the mouth of the vessel he tells the signaler to raise his torch and the receivers of the signal are to stop the aperture at once and to note which of the messages written on the rods is at the mouth of the vessel. This will be the message delivered, if the apparatus works at the same pace in both cases.

45. Ταῦτα δὲ βραχὺ μέν τι τῆς διὰ τῶν συνθημάτων πυρσείας ἐξήλλαχεν, ἀκμὴν δ' ἐστὶν ἀόριστα.

2 δῆλον γὰρ [ἔσται] ὡς οὔτε προϊδέσθαι τὰ μέλλοντα πάντα δυνατὸν οὔτε προϊδόμενον εἰς τὴν βακτηρίαν γράψαι· λοιπὸν ὁπόταν ἐκ τῶν καιρῶν ἀνυπονόητά τινα συμβαίνῃ, φανερὸν ὡς οὐ δύναται δηλοῦσθαι

3 κατὰ ταύτην τὴν ἐπίνοιαν. καὶ μὴν οὐδ' αὐτῶν τῶν ἐν τῇ βακτηρίᾳ γεγραμμένων οὐδέν ἐστιν ὡρισμένον. πόσοι γὰρ ἥκουσιν ἱππεῖς ἢ πόσοι πεζοὶ καὶ ποῦ τῆς χώρας καὶ πόσαι νῆες καὶ πόσος σῖτος, οὐχ οἷόν τε

4 διασαφῆσαι· περὶ γὰρ ὧν ἀδύνατον γνῶναι πρὶν ἢ γενέσθαι, περὶ τούτων οὐδὲ συνθέσθαι πρὸ τοῦ δυνα

5 τόν. τὸ δὲ συνέχον ἐστὶ τοῦτο· πῶς γὰρ ἄν τις βουλεύσαιτο περὶ τοῦ βοηθεῖν μὴ γινώσκων πόσοι πάρεισι τῶν πολεμίων ἢ ποῦ; πῶς δὲ θαρρῆσαι πάλιν ἢ τοὐναντίον ἢ καθόλου διανοηθείη τι μὴ συνεὶς πόσαι νῆες ἢ πόσος σῖτος ἥκει παρὰ τῶν συμμάχων;

6 Ὁ δὲ τελευταῖος ⟨τρόπος⟩, ἐπινοηθεὶς διὰ Κλεοξένου καὶ Δημοκλείτου, τυχὼν δὲ τῆς ἐξεργασίας δι' ἡμῶν, ⟨πάντῃ πάντως⟩ μέν ἐστιν ὡρισμένος καὶ πᾶν τὸ κατεπεῖγον δυνάμενος ἀκριβῶς διασαφεῖν, κατὰ δὲ τὸν χειρισμὸν ἐπιμελείας δεῖ καὶ παρατηρήσεως ἀκρι

7 βεστέρας. ἔστι δὲ τοιοῦτος. τὸ τῶν στοιχείων πλῆθος ἑξῆς δεῖ λαμβάνοντας διελεῖν εἰς πέντε μέρη κατὰ πέντε γράμματα. λείψει δὲ τὸ τελευταῖον ἑνὶ στοιχείῳ·

8 τοῦτο δ' οὐ βλάπτει πρὸς τὴν χρείαν. μετὰ δὲ ταῦτα πλατεῖα παρεσκευάσθαι πέντε τοὺς μέλλοντας ἀποδιδόναι τὴν πυρσείαν ἀλλήλοις ἑκατέρους καὶ γράψαι

45. This is a slight advance on beacons with a preconcerted code, but it is still quite indefinite. For it is evident
that it is neither possible to foresee all contingencies, or
even if one did to write them on the rod. So that when circumstances produce some unexpected event, it is evident
that it cannot be conveyed by this plan. Again none of the
things written on the rod are defined statements, for it is
impossible to indicate how many infantry are coming and
to what part of the country, or how many ships or how
much corn. For it is impossible to agree beforehand about
things of which one cannot be aware before they happen.
And this is the vital matter; for how can anyone consider
how to render assistance if he does not know how many of
the enemy have arrived, or where? And how can anyone be
of good cheer or the reverse, or in fact think of anything at
all, if he does not understand how many ships or how much
corn has arrived from the allies?

The most recent method, devised by Cleoxenus and
Democleitus[99] and perfected by myself, is quite definite
and capable of dispatching with accuracy every kind of urgent messages, but in practice it requires care and exact attention. It is as follows:[100] We take the alphabet and divide
it into five parts, each consisting of five letters. There is one
letter less in the last division, but this makes no practical
difference. Each of the two parties who are about to signal
to each other must now get ready five tablets and write one
division of the alphabet on each tablet, and then come to

---

[99] Otherwise unknown, possibly contemporaries of P.

[100] Graphic in WC 2.260. The system allows better communication by using the full alphabet.

9 τῶν μερῶν ἑξῆς εἰς ἕκαστον πλατεῖον, κἄπειτα συνθέσθαι πρὸς αὑτοὺς διότι τοὺς μὲν πρώτους ἀρεῖ
πυρσοὺς ὁ μέλλων σημαίνειν ἅμα καὶ δύο καὶ μενεῖ
10 μέχρις ἂν ὁ ἕτερος ἀνταίρῃ. τοῦτο δ' ἔσται χάριν τοῦ
διὰ ταύτης τῆς πυρσείας ἑαυτοῖς ἀνθομολογήσασθαι
11 διότι προσέχουσι. καθαιρεθέντων δὲ τούτων λοιπὸν
⟨ὁ⟩ σημαίνων ἀρεῖ μὲν τοὺς πρώτους ἐκ τῶν εὐωνύμων, διασαφῶν τὸ πλατεῖον ποῖον δεήσει σκοπεῖν,
οἷον ἐὰν μὲν τὸ πρῶτον, ἕν', ἂν δὲ τὸ δεύτερον, δύο,
12 καὶ κατὰ λόγον οὕτω· τοὺς δὲ δευτέρους ἐκ τῶν δεξιῶν
κατὰ τὸν αὐτὸν λόγον, ποῖον δεήσει γράμμα τῶν ἐκ
τοῦ πλατείου γράφειν αὖ τὸν ἀποδεχόμενον τὴν πυρσείαν.

46. Ὅταν δὲ ταῦτα συνθέμενοι χωρισθῶσιν, ἑκάτερον ἐπὶ τοῦ τόπου δεήσει πρῶτον μὲν διόπτραν ἔχειν
δύ' αὐλίσκους ἔχουσαν, ὥστε τοῦ μέλλοντος ἀντιπυρ-
σεύειν τῷ μὲν τὸν δεξιὸν τόπον, τῷ δὲ τὸν εὐώνυμον
2 δύνασθαι θεωρεῖν. παρὰ δὲ τὴν διόπτραν ἑξῆς ὀρθὰ
3 δεῖ τὰ πλατεῖα πεπηγέναι, παραπεφράχθαι δὲ καὶ τὸν
δεξιὸν καὶ τὸν εὐώνυμον τόπον ἐπὶ δέκα πόδας, τὸ δὲ
βάθος ὡς ἀνδρόμηκες, ⟨εἰς⟩ τὸ τοὺς πυρσοὺς αἰρομέ-
νους μὲν παρὰ ταῦτα τὴν φάσιν ἀκριβῆ ποιεῖν, καθαι-
4 ρουμένους δὲ τὴν κρύψιν. τούτων δ' ἑτοιμασθέντων
παρ' ἀμφοτέροις, ὅταν βούλῃ δηλῶσαι λόγου χάριν
διότι "τῶν στρατιωτῶν τινες εἰς ἑκατὸν ἀποκεχωρή-
κασι πρὸς τοὺς ὑπεναντίους," πρῶτον δεῖ διαλέξαι
τῶν λέξεων, ὅσαι δι' ἐλαχίστων γραμμάτων δύνανται
5 ταὐτὸ δηλοῦν, οἷον ἀντὶ τοῦ προειρημένου "Κρῆτες

an agreement that the man who is going to signal is in the
first place to raise two torches and wait until the other re-
plies by doing the same. This is for the purpose of conveying to each other that they are both at attention. These
torches having been lowered the dispatcher of the message will now raise the first set of torches on the left side
indicating which tablet is to be consulted, i.e., one torch if
it is the first, two if it is the second, and so on. Next he will
raise the second set on the right on the same principle to
indicate what letter of the tablet the receiver should write
down.

46. Upon their separating after coming to this understanding each of them must first have on the spot a telescope[101] with two tubes, so that with the one he can observe the space on the right of the man who is going to
signal back and with the other that on the left. The tablets
must be set straight up in order next the telescope, and
there must be a screen before both spaces, as well the right
as the left, ten feet in length and of the height of a man so
that by this means the torches may be seen distinctly when
raised and disappear when lowered. When all has been
thus got ready on both sides, if the signaler wants to convey, for instance, that about a hundred of the soldiers have
deserted to the enemy, he must first of all choose words
which will convey what he means in the smallest number
of letters, e.g., instead of the above "Cretans a hundred de-

---

[101] Just concentrating the vision on the desired point without
magnifying.

ἑκατὸν ἀφ᾽ ἡμῶν ηὐτομόλησαν." νῦν γὰρ τὰ μὲν
γράμματ᾽ ἐστὶν ἐλάττω τῶν ἡμίσεων, διασαφεῖται δὲ

6 ταὐτόν. τούτου δὲ γραφέντος εἰς πινάκιον, οὕτω δηλω-
θήσεται τοῖς πυρσοῖς. πρῶτον δ᾽ ἐστὶ γράμμα τὸ

7 κάππα· τοῦτο δ᾽ ἐστὶν ἐν τῇ δευτέρᾳ μερίδι καὶ τῷ
δευτέρῳ πλατείῳ. δεήσει δὲ καὶ πυρσοὺς ἐκ τῶν εὐωνύμων δύ᾽ αἴρειν, ὥστε τὸν ἀποδεχόμενον γινώσκειν ὅτι

8 δεῖ τὸ δεύτερον πλατεῖον ἐπισκοπεῖν. εἶτ᾽ ἐκ τῶν δεξιῶν ἀρεῖ πέντε, διασαφῶν ὅτι κάππα· τοῦτο γὰρ πέμ-
πτον ἐστὶ τῆς δευτέρας μερίδος, ὃ δεήσει γράφειν εἰς

9 τὸ πινάκιον τὸν ἀποδεχόμενον τοὺς πυρσούς. <εἶτα
τέτταρας ἐκ τῶν εὐωνύμων, ἐπεὶ> τὸ ῥῶ τῆς τετάρτης
ἐστὶ μερίδος. εἶτα δύο πάλιν ἐκ τῶν δεξιῶν· δεύτερον
<γάρ> ἐστι τῆς τετάρτης. ἐξ οὗ τὸ ῥῶ γράφει [ὁ

10 δεχόμενος τοὺς πυρσούς]· καὶ τὰ λοιπὰ τὸν αὐτὸν
τρόπον. προδηλοῦται μὲν οὖν πᾶν τὸ προσπῖπτον
ὡρισμένων κατὰ ταύτην τὴν ἐπίνοιαν,

47. πολλοὶ δὲ γίνονθ᾽ οἱ πυρσοὶ διὰ τὸ δεῖν ὑπὲρ
ἑκάστου γράμματος διττὰς ποιεῖσθαι τὰς πυρσείας.

2 οὐ μὴν ἀλλ᾽ ἐάν τις εὐτρεπῆ ποιήσῃ τὰ πρὸς τὸ

3 πρᾶγμα, δύναται γίνεσθαι τὸ δέον. καθ᾽ ἑκατέραν δὲ
τὴν ἐπίνοιαν προμελετᾶν δεῖ τοὺς χειρίζοντας, ἵνα τῆς
χρείας γινομένης ἀδιαπτώτως δύνωνται διασαφεῖν

4 ἀλλήλοις. πηλίκην δὲ συμβαίνει φαίνεσθαι τὴν διαφορὰν ἐπὶ τῶν αὐτῶν πραγμάτων πρῶτον λεγομένων
καὶ πάλιν κατὰ συνήθειαν γινομένων, ἐκ πολλῶν

5 εὐχερὲς τῷ βουλομένῳ καταμαθεῖν. πολλὰ γὰρ οὐ
μόνον τῶν δυσχερῶν, ἀλλὰ καὶ τῶν ἀδυνάτων εἶναι

serted us," for thus the letters are less than one half in number, but the same sense is conveyed. Having jotted this down on a writing tablet he will communicate it by the torches as follows: The first letter is *kappa*. This being in the second division is on tablet number two, and, therefore, he must raise two torches on the left, so that the receiver may know that he has to consult the second tablet. He will now raise five torches on the right, to indicate that it is *kappa*, this being the fifth letter in the second division, and the receiver of the signal will note this down on his writing tablet. The dispatcher will then raise four torches on the left as *rho* belongs to the fourth division, and then two on the right, *rho* being the second letter in this division. The receiver writes down *rho* and so forth. This device enables any news to be definitely conveyed.

47. Many torches, of course, are required, as the signal for each letter is a double one. But if all is properly prepared for the purpose, what is required can be done whichever system we follow. Those engaged in the work must have had proper practice, so that when it comes to putting it in action they may communicate with each other without the possibility of a mistake. From many instances it is easy for all who wish it to learn how great the difference is between the same thing when it is first heard of and when it has become a matter of habit. For many things which appear at the beginning to be not only difficult but impossi-

δοκούντων κατὰ τὰς ἀρχάς, μετὰ ταῦτα χρόνου καὶ
6 συνηθείας τυχόντα ῥᾷστα πάντων ἐπιτελεῖται. τοῦ δὲ
τοιούτου λόγου παραδείγματα μὲν πολλὰ καὶ ἕτερα
πρὸς πίστιν, ἐναργέστατον δὲ τὸ γινόμενον ἐπὶ τῆς
7 ἀναγνώσεως. ἐπὶ γὰρ ἐκείνης, εἴ τις παραστησάμενος
ἄνθρωπον ἄπειρον μὲν καὶ ἀσυνήθη γραμματικῆς,
τἆλλα δ᾽ ἀγχίνουν, κἄπειτα παιδάριον ἕξιν ἔχον
παραστήσας καὶ δοὺς βυβλίον κελεύοι λέγειν τὰ
8 γεγραμμένα, δῆλον ὡς οὐκ ἂν δύναιτο πιστεῦσαι διότι
⟨δεῖ⟩ πρῶτον ἐπὶ τὰς ὄψεις τὰς ἑνὸς ἑκάστου τῶν
γραμμάτων ἐπιστῆσαι τὸν ἀναγινώσκοντα, δεύτερον
ἐπὶ τὰς δυνάμεις, τρίτον ἐπὶ τὰς πρὸς ἄλληλα συμ-
πλοκάς, ὧν ἕκαστον ποσοῦ χρόνου τινὸς δεῖται.
9 διόπερ ὅταν ἀνεπιστάτως θεωρῇ τὸ παιδάριον ὑπὸ τὴν
ἀναπνοὴν ἑπτὰ καὶ πέντε στίχους συνεῖρον, οὐκ ἂν
εὐχερῶς δύναιτο πιστεῦσαι διότι πρότερον οὗτος οὐκ
10 ἀνέγνωκε τὸ βυβλίον· εἰ δὲ καὶ τὴν ὑπόκρισιν καὶ τὰς
διαιρέσεις, ἔτι δὲ δασύτητας καὶ ψιλότητας δύναιτο
11 συσσῴζειν, οὐδὲ τελέως. διόπερ οὐκ ἀποστατέον οὐδενὸς τῶν χρησίμων διὰ τὰς προφαινομένας δυσχε-
ρείας, προσακτέον δὲ τὴν ἕξιν, ᾗ πάντα τὰ καλὰ
γίνεται θηρατὰ τοῖς ἀνθρώποις, ἄλλως τε καὶ περὶ τῶν
τοιούτων, ἐν οἷς πολλάκις κεῖται τὸ συνέχον τῆς
σωτηρίας.

12 Ταῦτα μὲν οὖν κατὰ τὴν ἐξ ἀρχῆς ἐπαγγελίαν
προήχθημεν εἰπεῖν. ἔφαμεν γὰρ πάντα τὰ θεωρήματα
καθ᾽ ἡμᾶς ἐπὶ τοσοῦτον εἰληφέναι τὰς προκοπάς,
ὥστε τῶν πλείστων τρόπον τινὰ μεθοδικὰς εἶναι τὰς

ble are performed quite easily after time and practice. There are many other examples which confirm this, but the clearest of all is the case of reading. Here if we put side by side a man who is ignorant and unpracticed in letters, but generally intelligent, and a boy who is accustomed to read, give the boy a book and order him to read it, the man will plainly not be able to believe that a reader must first of all pay attention to the form of each letter, then to its sound value, next to the combinations of the different letters, each of which things requires a considerable amount of time. So when he sees that the boy without hesitation reels off five or seven lines in a breath he will not find it easy to believe that he never read the book before, and he will absolutely refuse to believe this if the reader should be able to observe the action, the pauses, and the rough and smooth breathings. We should not, therefore, abandon anything useful owing to the difficulties which show themselves at the outset,[102] but we must call in the aid of habit, through which all good things fall into the hands of men, and more especially when the matter is one on which our preservation mainly depends.

In offering these observations I am acting up to the promise I originally made at the outset of this Olympiad. For I stated that in our time all arts and sciences have so much advanced that knowledge of most of them may be

[102] Refers to 9.2.5.

13 ἐπιστήμας. διὸ καὶ τοῦτο γίνεται τῆς δεόντως ἱστορίας συντεταγμένης ὠφελιμώτατον.

11.7.1 Καὶ πολλὰ μὲν αὐτὸν κατοιμώξας ὅτι παρὰ
μικρὸν ἔλθοι τοῦ λαβεῖν τὸν Ἄτταλον ὑποχείριον.

VIII. RES ASIAE

48. Οἱ δ' Ἀπασιάκαι κατοικοῦσι μὲν ἀνὰ μέσον
Ὄξου καὶ Τανάιδος, ὧν ὁ μὲν εἰς τὴν Ὑρκανίαν
ἐμβάλλει θάλατταν, ὁ δὲ Τάναϊς ἐξίησιν εἰς τὴν Μαιῶτιν λίμνην· εἰσὶ δ' ἑκάτεροι κατὰ τὸ μέγεθος πλωτοί.
2 καὶ δοκεῖ θαυμαστὸν εἶναι πῶς οἱ Νομάδες περαιού-
μενοι τὸν Ὄξον εἰς τὴν Ὑρκανίαν ἔρχονται πεζῇ μετὰ
3 τῶν ἵππων. εἰσὶ δὲ δύο λόγοι περὶ τούτου τοῦ πράγματος, ὁ μὲν ἐπιεικής, ὁ δ' ἕτερος παράδοξος, οὐ μὴν
4 ἀδύνατος. ὁ γὰρ Ὄξος ἔχει μὲν ἐκ τοῦ Καυκάσου τὰς
πηγάς, ἐπὶ πολὺ δ' αὐξηθεὶς ἐν τῇ Βακτριανῇ, συρ-
ρεόντων εἰς αὐτὸν ὑδάτων, φέρεται διὰ πεδιάδος χώ-
5 ρας πολλῷ καὶ θολερῷ ῥεύματι. παραγενόμενος δ' εἰς
τὴν ἔρημον ἐπί τινας πέτρας ἀπορρῶγας ἐξωθεῖ τὸ
ῥεῦμα τῇ βίᾳ διὰ τὸ πλῆθος καὶ τὴν καταφορὰν τῶν
ὑπερκειμένων τόπων ἐπὶ τοσοῦτον ὥστε τῆς πέτρας ἐν
τοῖς κάτω μέρεσι πλεῖον ἢ στάδιον ἀφάλλεσθαι τὴν
6 καταφορὰν αὐτοῦ. διὰ δὴ τούτου τοῦ τόπου φασὶ τοὺς
Ἀπασιάκας παρ' αὐτὴν τὴν πέτραν ὑπὸ τὴν κατα-

[103] For the reasons to put this fragment here, see WC 2.277–
278.   [104] A Scythian people, probably Sacas.

said to have been reduced to a system. This is, then, one of the most useful parts of a history properly written.

11.7.1 He bewailed his ill luck in having narrowly missed taking Attalus prisoner.[103]

VIII. AFFAIRS OF ASIA

The River Oxus

48. The Apasiacae[104] inhabit the district between the Oxus[105] and Tanaïs,[106] the former of which rivers falls into the Hyrcanian Sea, while the Tanaïs falls into the Palus Maeotis.[107] Both are large enough to be navigable, and it is considered marvelous how the nomads passing the Oxus on foot with their horses reach Hyrcania. There are two stories regarding this, one reasonably probable and the other very surprising, but yet not impossible. The Oxus, I should say, rises in the Caucasus,[108] but in traversing Bactria greatly increases in volume owing to the number of tributaries it receives, and henceforth runs through the plain with a strong and turbid current. Reaching in the desert a certain precipice it projects its stream, owing to the volume of the current and the height of the fall, so far from the crest of the cataract that in falling it leaps to a distance of more than a stade from the bottom of the precipice. It is in this place that they say the Apasiacae pass dry-

[105] The Amu-darya. *RE* Oxus 2006–2017 (A. Herrmann).

[106] Usually the Don, but here the Syr-darya. *RE* IX Iaxartes 1181–1189, esp. 1184 (A. Herrmann).　　　[107] The Sea of Azov.

[108] P. means the Pamir or Hindu Kush, the name having been transferred there after the expedition of Alexander the Great. *RE* Kaukasos 59–62, esp. 60–61 (A. Herrmann).

φορὰν τοῦ ποταμοῦ πεζεύειν μετὰ τῶν ἵππων εἰς τὴν
7 Ὑρκανίαν. ὁ δ᾽ ἕτερος λόγος ἐπιεικεστέραν ἔχει τοῦ
πρόσθεν τὴν ἀπόφασιν. τοῦ γὰρ ὑποκειμένου τόπου
μεγάλους ἔχοντος πλαταμῶνας, εἰς οὓς καταρράττει,
τούτους φασὶ τῇ βίᾳ τοῦ ῥεύματος ἐκκοιλαίνοντα καὶ
διαρρηγνύντα κατὰ βάθος ὑπὸ γῆν φέρεσθαι τόπον
8 οὐ πολύν, εἶτ᾽ ἀναφαίνεσθαι πάλιν. τοὺς δὲ βαρβάρους διὰ τὴν ἐμπειρίαν κατὰ τὸν διαλείποντα τόπον
ποιεῖσθαι τὴν δίοδον ἐπὶ τῶν ἵππων εἰς τὴν Ὑρκανίαν.
. . .

49. Γενομένης δὲ τῆς προσαγγελίας διότι συμβαίνει τὸν μὲν Εὐθύδημον μετὰ τῆς δυνάμεως εἶναι
περὶ Ταπουρίαν, μυρίους δ᾽ ἱππεῖς προκαθίζεσθαι
φυλάττοντας <τὰς> περὶ τὸν Ἄριον ποταμὸν δια-
βάσεις, ἔκρινε τὴν πολιορκίαν ἀπογνοὺς ἔχεσθαι τῶν
2 προκειμένων. ἀπέχοντος δὲ τοῦ ποταμοῦ τριῶν ἡμερῶν ὁδόν, ἐπὶ μὲν ἡμέρας δύο σύμμετρον ἐποιήσατο
τὴν πορείαν, τῇ δὲ τρίτῃ μετὰ τὸ δειπνῆσαι τοῖς
ἄλλοις ἅμα τῷ φωτὶ ποιεῖσθαι παρήγγειλε τὴν ἀνα-
3 ζυγήν, αὐτὸς δ᾽ ἀναλαβὼν τοὺς ἱππέας καὶ τοὺς εὐζώνους, ἅμα δὲ πελταστὰς μυρίους, προῆγε νυκτός,
4 πορείᾳ χρώμενος ἐνεργῷ. τοὺς γὰρ ἱππεῖς ἐπυνθάνετο

---

109 A Greek from Magnesia in Ionia (P. Bernard, *Fouilles d'Ai Khanoum*, IV [Paris 1985], 131–133), the second king of Bactria, formerly a Seleucid satrapy. He ruled from ca. 225 to the 180s (A. K. Narain, *The Indo-Greeks* [Oxford 1957], 18–29. G. Woodcock, *The Greeks in India* [London 1966], 70–73). His striking portrait on coins: A. D. H. Bivar, "The Bactrian Coinage of Euthy-

shod with their horses to Hyrcania, skirting the precipice under the waterfall. There is more reasonable probability in the second account than in the first. They say there are at the foot of the cataract large slabs of rock on which the river falls, and by the force of the current hollows out and pierces these rocks for some depth and flows underground for a short distance, after which it comes to the surface again. The barbarians are acquainted with this and cross to Hyrcania on horseback at the place where the river thus interrupts its course.

Campaign of Antiochus in Bactria

49. When the news came that Euthydemus[109] with his army was before Tapuria, and that ten thousand cavalry were in his front guarding the ford of the river Arius,[110] Antiochus decided to abandon the siege and deal with the situation. The river being at a distance of three days' march, he marched at a moderate pace for two days, but on the third day he ordered the rest of his army to break up their camp at daylight while he himself with his cavalry, his light-armed infantry, and ten thousand peltasts advanced during the night marching quickly. For he had heard that

208
B.C.

demus and Demetrius," *NC* 1951, 22–39, and pl. III. The bibliography on the Greeks in Bactria and India (*CAH*, 2nd. ed., vol. 8, 1989, 569–577) already listed 168 titles, and many more have been published since. M. Sidky, *The Greek Kingdom of Bactria* (Lanham 2000), 159–180: Antiochus the Great and Euthydemus (with a good map of Bactria and the surrounding areas on p. 146). O. Coloru, *Da Alessandro a Menandro: il regno Greco di Battriana* (Pisa 2009).   110 The Hari-rud or Tedzhen.

τῶν ὑπεναντίων τὰς μὲν ἡμέρας ἐφεδρεύειν παρὰ τὸ
χεῖλος τοῦ ποταμοῦ, τὰς δὲ νύκτας ὑποχωρεῖν πρός
τινα πόλιν οὐκ ἔλαττον εἴκοσι σταδίων <διέχουσαν>.
διανύσας δὲ νύκτωρ τὴν καταλειπομένην ὁδόν, ἅτε
5 τῶν πεδίων ἱππασίμων ὑπαρχόντων, ἔφθασε περαι-
ώσας τὸν ποταμὸν ἅμα τῷ φωτὶ τὸ πλεῖστον μέρος
6 τῆς μεθ᾽ ἑαυτοῦ δυνάμεως. οἱ δὲ τῶν Βακτριανῶν
ἱππεῖς, σημηνάντων αὐτοῖς τῶν σκοπῶν τὸ γεγονός,
ἐξεβοήθουν, καὶ κατὰ πορείαν συνέμισγον τοῖς ὑπ-
7 εναντίοις. ὁ δὲ βασιλεύς, θεωρῶν ὅτι δεῖ δέξασθαι τὴν
πρώτην ἐπιφορὰν τῶν πολεμίων, παρακαλέσας τοὺς
περὶ αὐτὸν εἰθισμένους κινδυνεύειν τῶν ἱππέων δισχιλίους, τοῖς μὲν ἄλλοις παρήγγειλε κατὰ σημαίας
καὶ κατ᾽ οὐλαμοὺς αὐτοῦ παρεμβαλεῖν καὶ λαμβάνειν
8 ἑκάστους τὰς εἰθισμένας τάξεις, αὐτὸς δὲ μετὰ τῶν
προειρημένων ἱππέων ἀπαντήσας συνέβαλε τοῖς πρώ-
9 τοις ἐπιφερομένοις τῶν Βάκτρων. δοκεῖ δὲ κατὰ τοῦτον
τὸν κίνδυνον Ἀντίοχος ἀγωνίσασθαι διαπρεπέστατα
10 τῶν μεθ᾽ αὑτοῦ. πολλοὶ μὲν οὖν ἀμφοτέρων διεφθάρησαν, ἐπεκράτησαν δὲ τῆς πρώτης ἱππαρχίας οἱ μετὰ
τοῦ βασιλέως· τῆς δὲ δευτέρας καὶ τρίτης ἐπιφερο-
11 μένης ἐπιέζοντο καὶ κακῶς ἀπήλλαττον. κατὰ δὲ τὸν
καιρὸν τοῦτον, τῶν πλείστων ἱππέων ἐκτεταγμένων
ἤδη, Παναίτωλος ἐπαγαγεῖν παραγγείλας τὸν μὲν
βασιλέα καὶ τοὺς μετ᾽ αὐτοῦ κινδυνεύοντας ἐδέξατο,
τοὺς δὲ τῶν Βακτριανῶν ἐπιφερομένους ἀτάκτως ἐκ
12 μεταβολῆς προτροπάδην ἠνάγκασε φυγεῖν. ἐκεῖνοι
μὲν οὖν, τῶν περὶ τὸν Παναίτωλον αὐτοῖς ἐπικειμένων,

the enemy's horse kept guard during the day on the river bank, but retired at night to a town as much as twenty stades away. Having completed the remainder of the distance during the night, as the plain is easy to ride over, he succeeded in getting the greater part of his forces across the river by daylight. The Bactrian cavalry, when their scouts had reported this, came up to attack and engaged the enemy while still on the march. The king, seeing that it was necessary to stand the first charge of the enemy, called on two thousand of his cavalry who were accustomed to fight round him and ordered the rest to form up on the spot in squadrons and troops and all place themselves in their usual order, while he himself with the force I spoke of met and engaged the Bactrians who were the first to charge. In this affair it seems that Antiochus himself fought more brilliantly than any of those with him. There were severe losses on both sides, but the king's cavalry repulsed the first Bactrian regiment. When, however, the second and third came up they were in difficulties and had the worst of it. It was now, when most of the cavalry were in position, that Panaetolus[111] ordered his men to advance, and joining the king and those who were fighting round him, compelled those Bactrians who were pursuing in disorder to turn rein and take to headlong flight. The Bactrians, now hard pressed by Panaetolus, never stopped until they

[111] Mentioned in 5.61.5 and 62.2, another deserter from Ptolemy IV during the Fourth Syrian War.

οὐ πρότερον ἔστησαν ἕως οὗ συνέμιξαν τοῖς περὶ τὸν
13 Εὐθύδημον, τοὺς πλείστους ἀπολωλεκότες αὐτῶν· οἱ
δὲ τοῦ βασιλέως ἱππεῖς, πολλοὺς μὲν φονεύσαντες,
πολλοὺς ⟨δὲ⟩ ζωγρίᾳ λαβόντες, ἀνεχώρουν. καὶ τότε
14 μὲν αὐτοῦ παρὰ τὸν ποταμὸν ηὐλίσθησαν· ἐν δὲ τούτῳ
τῷ κινδύνῳ τὸν μὲν ἵππον συμβαίνει . . . ἀποθανεῖν
τραυματισθέντα . . . , αὐτὸν δὲ πληγέντα διὰ τοῦ
στόματος ἀποβαλεῖν τινας τῶν ὀδόντων, καθόλου δὲ
φήμην ἐπ᾽ ἀνδρείᾳ περιποιήσασθαι τότε μάλιστα.
15 γενομένης δὲ τῆς μάχης ταύτης ὁ μὲν Εὐθύδημος
καταπλαγεὶς ἀνεχώρησε μετὰ τῆς δυνάμεως εἰς πόλιν
Ζαριάσπαν τῆς Βακτριανῆς.

joined Euthydemus after losing most of their men. The royal cavalry, after killing many of the enemy and making many prisoners, withdrew, and at first encamped on the spot near the river. In this battle Antiochus' horse was transfixed and killed, and he himself received a wound in the mouth and lost several of his teeth, having in general gained a greater reputation for courage on this occasion than on any other. After the battle Euthydemus was terror-stricken and retired with his army to a city in Bactria called Zariaspa.[112]

[112] Better known under the name Bactra, today Balkh in northern Afghanistan, the royal residence. *RE* Zariaspa 2327–2328 (H.Treidler).

FRAGMENTA LIBRI XI

I. EX PROOEMIO

1a. Ἴσως δέ τινες ἐπιζητοῦσι πῶς ἡμεῖς οὐ προγραφὰς ἐν ταύτῃ τῇ βίβλῳ, καθάπερ οἱ πρὸ ἡμῶν,
ἀλλὰ καὶ προεκθέσεις καθ᾽ ἑκάστην ὀλυμπιάδα πεποι-
2 ήκαμεν τῶν πράξεων. ἐγὼ δὲ κρίνω χρήσιμον μὲν
εἶναι καὶ τὸ τῶν προγραφῶν γένος· καὶ γὰρ εἰς ἐπίστασιν ἄγει τοὺς ἀναγινώσκειν θέλοντας καὶ συνεκ-
καλεῖται καὶ παρορμᾷ πρὸς τὴν ἀνάγνωσιν τοὺς ἐντυγχάνοντας, πρὸς δὲ τούτοις πᾶν τὸ ζητούμενον
3 ἑτοίμως ἔνεστιν εὑρεῖν διὰ τούτου· θεωρῶν δὲ διὰ
πολλὰς αἰτίας καὶ τὰς τυχούσας ὀλιγωρούμενον καὶ
φθειρόμενον τὸ τῶν προγραφῶν γένος, οὕτως καὶ διὰ
4 ταῦτα πρὸς τοῦτο τὸ μέρος κατηνέχθην· τῆς γὰρ
προεκθέσεως οὐ μόνον ἰσοδυναμούσης ⟨πρὸς⟩ τὴν
προγραφήν, ἀλλὰ καὶ πλεῖόν τι δυναμένης, ἅμα δὲ καὶ
χώραν ἐχούσης ἀσφαλεστέραν διὰ τὸ συμπεπλέχθαι
5 τῇ πραγματείᾳ, τούτῳ μᾶλλον ἐδοκιμάσαμεν χρῆσθαι
τῷ μέρει παρ᾽ ὅλην τὴν σύνταξιν πλὴν ἐξ τῶν πρώτων
βυβλίων· ἐν ἐκείνοις ⟨δὲ⟩ προγραφὰς ἐποιησάμεθα
διὰ τὸ μὴ λίαν ἐναρμόζειν ἐν αὐτοῖς τὸ τῶν προ-
εκθέσεων γένος.

254

FRAGMENTS OF BOOK XI

I. FROM THE PREFACE

1a. Some will perhaps inquire why in this work I do not, like former authors, write prologues[1] but simply give a summary of the events in each Olympiad. I indeed regard a prologue as a useful kind of thing, since it fixes the attention of those who wish to read the work and stimulates and encourages readers in their task, besides which by this means any matter that we are in search of can be easily found. But as I saw that for various fortuitous reasons prologues are held in little regard and get destroyed, I was led to adopt the other alternative. For an introductory summary is not only of equal value to a prologue but even of somewhat greater, while at the same time it occupies a surer position, as it forms an integral part of the work. I, therefore, decided to employ this method throughout except in the first six books to which I wrote prologues, because in their case previous summaries are not very suitable.

[1] The (lost) introductions to the first six books. Thereafter, P. switched to summaries, comparable to a table of contents. These are not prefixed to the scroll or the codex, but integral parts of the text and therefore less prone to getting lost.

II. RES ITALIAE

1. Ἀλλὰ πολὺ ῥᾳδιεστέραν καὶ συντομωτέραν συνέβη γενέσθαι τὴν Ἀσδρούβου παρουσίαν εἰς Ἰταλίαν.
Διόπερ ὡς οὐδέποτε μᾶλλον ὀρθὴ καὶ περίφοβος ἡ
τῶν Ῥωμαίων πόλις ἐγεγόνει, καραδοκοῦσα τὸ συμβησόμενον. . . .

2 Ἀσδρούβᾳ δὲ τούτων μὲν ἤρεσκεν οὐδέν, τῶν δὲ
πραγμάτων οὐκέτι διδόντων ἀναστροφὴν διὰ τὸ θεωρεῖν τοὺς πολεμίους ἐκτεταγμένους καὶ προσάγοντας,
ἠναγκάζετο παρατάττειν τοὺς Ἴβηρας καὶ τοὺς μετ'
3 αὐτοῦ γεγονότας Γαλάτας. προθέμενος δὲ τὰ θηρία
τὸν ἀριθμὸν ὄντα δέκα, καὶ τὸ βάθος αὐξήσας τῶν
τάξεων, καὶ ποιήσας ἐν βραχεῖ χώρῳ τὴν ὅλην δύναμιν, πρὸς δὲ τούτοις μέσον αὐτὸν θεὶς τῆς παρατάξεως
κατὰ τὴν τῶν θηρίων προστασίαν, ἐποιεῖτο τὴν ἔφοδον ἐπὶ τὰ λαιὰ τῶν πολεμίων, προδιειληφὼς ὅτι δεῖ
4 κατὰ τὸν παρόντα κίνδυνον νικᾶν ἢ θνήσκειν. ὁ μὲν
οὖν Λίβιος ἀντεπῄει τοῖς πολεμίοις σοβαρῶς καὶ
5 συμβαλὼν ταῖς αὑτοῦ δυνάμεσιν ἐμάχετο γενναίως· ὁ
δὲ Κλαύδιος ἐπὶ τοῦ δεξιοῦ κέρατος τεταγμένος προάγειν μὲν εἰς τοὔμπροσθεν καὶ περικερᾶν τοὺς ὑπεναντίους οὐκ ἐδύνατο διὰ τὰς προκειμένας δυσχωρίας,
αἷς πεπιστευκὼς Ἀσδρούβας ἐποιήσατο τὴν ἐπὶ τὰ
6 λαιὰ τῶν πολεμίων ἔφοδον. ἀπόρως δὲ διακείμενος ἐπὶ
τῷ μηδὲν πράττειν, ὑπ' αὐτοῦ ⟨τοῦ⟩ συμβαίνοντος

II. AFFAIRS OF ITALY

Hasdrubal's Expedition

1. Hasdrubal's arrival[2] in Italy was much easier and   207 B.C.
more rapid than was expected.

Rome had never been in such a state of excitement and
dismay, awaiting the result. . . .

None of these things were agreeable to Hasdrubal, but
as circumstances did not admit of delay, for he saw the
Romans already in battle order[3] and advancing, he was
obliged to draw up his Iberians and the Gauls who were
with him. Stationing his elephants, ten in number, in front,
he increased the depth of his line, making the front of his
whole army very narrow, and then taking up his position in
the center behind the elephants, fell upon the enemy's left,
having determined either to conquer or die in this battle.
Livius[4] advanced to meet the enemy's attack in an imposing fashion, and on encountering them with his army
fought gallantly. Claudius,[5] who was stationed on the right
wing, could not advance and outflank the enemy owing to
the difficult character of the ground in front of him, relying
on which Hasdrubal had attacked the Roman left, but
when he found himself thus at a loss owing to his forced in-

[2] In spring 207. For the full meaning of the sentence, see Livy
27.39.6. For the main events and sources for 207, see *MRR* 1.294.

[3] The battle took place at the end of June close to the river
Metaurus which empties into the Adriatic between Rimini and
Ancona, not far from Sena Gallica (Sinigaglia). The exact site of
the battle has not been determined.

[4] Marcus Livius Salinator, one of the consuls.

[5] Gaius Claudius Nero, the other consul.

7 ἔμαθεν ὃ δέον ἦν πράττειν. διὸ καὶ παραδεξάμενος
ἀπὸ τῶν δεξιῶν τοὺς αὑτοῦ στρατιώτας κατὰ τὸν
ὄπισθεν τόπον τῆς μάχης, καὶ τὸ λαιὸν ὑπεράρας τῆς
ἰδίας παρεμβολῆς, προσέβαλε κατὰ κέρας τοῖς Καρ-
8 χηδονίοις ἐπὶ τὰ θηρία. καὶ μέχρι μὲν [οὖν] τούτων
ἀμφίδοξος ἦν ἡ νίκη. οἵ τε γὰρ ἄνδρες ἐφαμίλλως
ἐκινδύνευον ἀμφότεροι διὰ τὸ μήτε τοῖς Ῥωμαίοις
ἐλπίδα καταλείπεσθαι σωτηρίας, εἰ σφαλεῖεν μήτε
τοῖς Ἴβηρσι καὶ Καρχηδονίοις· τά τε θηρία κοινὴν
9 ἀμφοῖν παρείχοντο τὴν χρείαν ἐν τῇ μάχῃ· μέσα γὰρ
ἀπειλημμένα καὶ συνακοντιζόμενα διετάραττε καὶ τὰς
10 τῶν Ῥωμαίων καὶ τὰς τῶν Ἰβήρων τάξεις. ἅμα δὲ τῷ
τοὺς περὶ τὸν Κλαύδιον προσπεσεῖν κατ' οὐρὰν τοῖς
πολεμίοις ἄνισος ἦν ἡ μάχη, τῶν μὲν κατὰ πρόσωπον,
11 τῶν δὲ κατὰ νώτου τοῖς Ἴβηρσι προσκειμένων. ἐξ οὗ
καὶ συνέβη τοὺς πλείστους τῶν Ἰβήρων ἐν αὐτῷ τῷ
12 τῆς μάχης καιρῷ κατακοπῆναι. τῶν δὲ θηρίων τὰ μὲν
ἓξ ἅμα τοῖς ἀνδράσιν ἔπεσε, τὰ δὲ τέτταρα διωσάμενα
τὰς τάξεις ὕστερον ἑάλω μεμονωμένα καὶ ψιλὰ τῶν
Ἰνδῶν.

2. Ἀσδρούβας δὲ καὶ τὸν πρὸ τούτου χρόνον καὶ
κατὰ τὸν ἔσχατον καιρὸν ἀνὴρ ἀγαθὸς γενόμενος, ἐν
χειρῶν νόμῳ κατέστρεψε τὸν βίον· ⟨ὃν⟩ οὐκ ἄξιον
2 ἀνεπισήμαντον παραλιπεῖν. ὅτι μὲν ἀδελφὸς ἦν Ἀννίβου κατὰ φύσιν, καὶ διότι χωριζόμενος εἰς τὴν
Ἰταλίαν τούτῳ ⟨τὰς⟩ κατὰ τὴν Ἰβηρίαν πράξεις
ἐνεχείρισε, ταῦτα μὲν ἐν ⟨τοῖς πρὸ τούτων⟩ ἡμῖν
3 ⟨δεδήλωται⟩. παραπλησίως δὲ καὶ διότι πολλοῖς μὲν

action, circumstances suggested to him what ought to be done. Having therefore collected his men from the right wing in the rear of the field he passed round the left of the Roman battle line and attacked the Carthaginians in flank where the elephants were. Up to now the victory had been disputed, for the men fought on both sides with equal bravery, as there was no hope of safety either for the Romans if defeated or for the Spaniards and Carthaginians. The elephants too had been of equal service to both sides in the battle; for as they were shut in between the two armies and tormented by missiles, they threw both the Roman and the Spanish ranks into confusion. But as soon as Claudius fell on the enemy from behind, the battle became unequal, as the Spaniards were now attacked both in front and rear. In consequence they were most of them cut to pieces on the battlefield. Of the elephants six were killed with their drivers and the other four having forced their way through the ranks were captured afterward alone and abandoned by their Indians.

2. Hasdrubal,[6] who was always a brave man both in former times and at this his last hour, fell in the thick of the fight, and it would not be just to take leave of this commander without a word of praise. I have already stated that he was Hannibal's own brother, and that Hannibal on quitting Spain entrusted him with the management of affairs there, and I also told in a previous book how in his many

---

[6] The whole chapter praises Hasdrubal as an able and brave commander. P. also gives him credit for the fact that, while he was careful not to expose himself as long as there was hope, he sought death when none was left.

χρησάμενος ἀγῶσι πρὸς Ῥωμαίους, πολλαῖς δὲ καὶ
ποικίλαις περιστάσεσι παλαίσας διὰ τὸ <στασιάζειν
πρὸς αὐτοὺς ἀεὶ> τοὺς ἐπαποστελλομένους ἐκ Καρχηδόνος εἰς Ἰβηρίαν στρατηγούς, ἐν πᾶσι τοῖς εἰρημένοις καιροῖς ἀξίως μὲν τοῦ πατρὸς Βάρκα, καλῶς δὲ
καὶ γενναίως τὰς περιπετείας καὶ τὰς ἐλαττώσεις
διετέλει φέρων, καὶ ταῦτα διὰ τῶν πρὸ τοῦ συντάξεων
4 δεδηλώκαμεν. περὶ δὲ τῶν τελευταίων ἀγώνων νῦν
ἐροῦμεν, καθὸ μάλιστα πέφηνεν ἡμῖν ἄξιος ἐπιστά-
5 σεως εἶναι καὶ ζήλου. τοὺς γὰρ πλείστους ἰδεῖν ἔστι
τῶν στρατηγῶν καὶ τῶν βασιλέων, ἐπειδὰν συνιστῶν-
ται τοὺς ὑπὲρ τῶν ὅλων ἀγῶνας, τὰ μὲν ἐκ τῶν
κατορθωμάτων ἔνδοξα καὶ λυσιτελῆ συνεχῶς λαμβάνοντας ὑπὸ τὴν ὄψιν, καὶ πολλάκις ἐφιστάνοντας
καὶ διαλογιζομένους πῶς ἑκάστοις χρήσονται, κατὰ
6 λόγον σφίσι χωρησάντων τῶν πραγμάτων, τὰ δ' ἐκ
τῶν ἀποπτωμάτων οὐκέτι πρὸ ὀφθαλμῶν τιθεμένους,
οὐδ' ἐν νῷ λαμβάνοντας πῇ καὶ τί πρακτέον ἑκάστοις
ἐστὶ κατὰ τὰς περιπετείας. καίτοι τὸ μὲν ἕτοιμόν ἐστι,
7 τὸ δὲ πολλῆς δεῖται προνοίας. τοιγαροῦν οἱ πλεῖστοι
διὰ τὴν αὑτῶν ἀγεννίαν καὶ τὴν ἐν τούτοις ἀβουλίαν
αἰσχρὰς μὲν ἐποίησαν τὰς ἥττας, εὐγενῶς πολλάκις
ἠγωνισμένων τῶν στρατιωτῶν, κατήσχυναν δὲ τὰς
πρὸ τούτου πράξεις, ἐπονείδιστον δὲ σφίσι τὸν κατα-
8 λειπόμενον ἐποίησαν βίον. διότι <δὲ> πολλοὶ τῶν
ἡγουμένων περὶ τοῦτο τὸ μέρος σφάλλονται, καὶ διότι
μεγίστην ἐν τούτοις ἔχει διαφορὰν ἀνὴρ ἀνδρός, εὐχερὲς τῷ βουλομένῳ καταμαθεῖν· πολλὰ γὰρ ὑπο-

encounters with the Romans and in his frequent struggles
with adverse circumstances, owing ‹to the constant wran-
gling between those›[7] who were sent to cooperate with
him in Spain from Carthage, he constantly bore disaster
and defeat with spirit and courage and in a manner worthy
of his father Barcas. I will now say for what reason in this
his final struggle he seems to me to have been worthy of
our respect and emulation. For we see that most generals
and kings, when they undertake a critical struggle, constantly keep before their eyes the glory and profit that will
accrue from success, and while they devote their attention
and consideration to the manner in which they will manage
everything if all goes in their favor, do not envisage the
consequences of mischance or consider at all how they
should behave and what they should do in the event of disaster, although the one thing is simple enough and the
other requires the greatest foresight. Consequently most
of them, owing to their lack of spirit and their helplessness
in such a case, make defeat shameful, and although their
soldiers have often fought bravely, cast disgrace on their
former exploits and make the rest of their life a reproach to
them. Anyone who wishes can easily see that many commanders err in this respect and that there is here the greatest difference between one man and another, as past his-

[7] B-W's plausible supplement.

δείγματα τῶν τοιούτων πεποίηκεν ὁ προγεγονὼς χρό-
9 νος. Ἀσδρούβας δ', ἕως μὲν ἦν ἐλπὶς ἐκ τῶν κατὰ
λόγον τοῦ δύνασθαι πράττειν ἄξιόν τι τῶν προβεβιωμένων, οὐδενὸς μᾶλλον προενοεῖτο κατὰ τοὺς κινδύ-
10 νους ὡς τῆς αὑτοῦ σωτηρίας· ἐπεὶ δὲ πάσας ἀφελο-
μένη τὰς εἰς τὸ μέλλον ἐλπίδας ἡ τύχη συνέκλεισε
πρὸς τὸν ἔσχατον καιρόν, οὐδὲν παραλιπὼν οὔτε περὶ
τὴν παρασκευὴν οὔτε κατὰ τὸν κίνδυνον πρὸς τὸ
νικᾶν, οὐχ ἧττον πρόνοιαν εἶχε καὶ τοῦ σφαλεὶς τοῖς
ὅλοις ὁμόσε χωρῆσαι τοῖς παροῦσι καὶ μηδὲν ὑπομεῖναι τῶν προβεβιωμένων ἀνάξιον.
11   Ταῦτα μὲν οὖν ἡμῖν εἰρήσθω περὶ τῶν ἐν πράγμασιν ἀναστρεφομένων, ἵνα μήτε προπετῶς κινδυ-
νεύοντες σφάλλωσι τὰς τῶν πιστευσάντων ἐλπίδας
μήτε φιλοζωοῦντες παρὰ τὸ δέον αἰσχρὰς καὶ ἐπονει-
δίστους ποιῶσι τὰς αὑτῶν περιπετείας·
       3. Ῥωμαῖοι δὲ τῇ μάχῃ κατορθώσαντες παραυτίκα
μὲν τὸν χάρακα διήρπαζον τῶν ὑπεναντίων, καὶ πολλοὺς μὲν τῶν Κελτῶν ἐν ταῖς στιβάσι κοιμωμένους
2 διὰ τὴν μέθην κατέκοπτον ἱερείων τρόπον· συνῆγον δὲ
καὶ τὴν λοιπὴν τῶν αἰχμαλώτων λείαν, ἀφ' ἧς εἰς τὸ
δημόσιον ἀνήχθη πλείω τῶν τριακοσίων ταλάντων.
3 ἀπέθανον δὲ τῶν μὲν Καρχηδονίων κατὰ τὴν μάχην
σὺν τοῖς Κελτοῖς οὐκ ἐλάττους μυρίων, τῶν δὲ Ῥωμαίων περὶ δισχιλίους. ἑάλωσαν δὲ καὶ ζωγρίᾳ τινὲς
τῶν ἐνδόξων Καρχηδονίων, οἱ δὲ λοιποὶ κατεφθάρη-
4 σαν. τῆς δὲ φήμης ἀφικομένης εἰς τὴν Ῥώμην τὴν μὲν
ἀρχὴν ἠπίστουν τῷ λίαν βούλεσθαι τοῦτο γενόμενον

tory affords so many examples of the fact. But Hasdrubal, as long as there was a reasonable hope of his being able to accomplish something worthy of his past, was more careful of nothing in action than of his own safety, but when fortune had robbed him of the last shred of hope and forced him to face the last extremity, though he neglected nothing in his preparations for the struggle or in the battle itself that might contribute to victory, nevertheless he took thought how if he met with total defeat he might confront that contingency and suffer nothing unworthy of his past.

What I have said here may serve to warn all who direct public affairs neither by rashly exposing themselves to cheat the hopes of those who trust in them nor by clinging to life when duty forbids it to add to their own disasters disgrace and reproach.

3. The Romans now, having won the battle, at once pillaged the enemy's camp, and butchered like sacrificial animals many of the Gauls whom they found drunk and asleep on their litter beds. They then collected the rest of the prisoners and from this part of the booty more than three hundred talents were realized for the treasury. Not fewer than ten thousand Carthaginians and Gauls fell in the battle, while the Roman loss amounted to two thousand.[8] Some of the Carthaginians of distinction were captured and the rest were slain. When the news arrived in Rome they at first refused to believe it, just because they

[8] The figure of two thousand Romans killed in the battle is not necessarily in contradiction with Livy's statement that eight thousand Romans and allies were lost (27.49.7).

5 ἰδεῖν· ἐπειδὴ δὲ καὶ πλείους ἧκον, οὐ μόνον τὸ γεγονός, ἀλλὰ καὶ ⟨τὰ⟩ κατὰ μέρος διασαφοῦντες, τότε
δὴ χαρᾶς ὑπερβαλλούσης ἦν ἡ πόλις πλήρης, καὶ
πᾶν μὲν τέμενος ἐκοσμεῖτο, πᾶς δὲ ναὸς ἔγεμε
6 πελάνων καὶ θυμάτων, καθόλου δ' εἰς τοιαύτην εὐελ-
πιστίαν παρεγένοντο καὶ θάρσος ὥστε πάντας τὸν
Ἀννίβαν, ὃν μάλιστα πρότερον ἐφοβήθησαν, τότε
μηδ' ἐν Ἰταλίᾳ νομίζειν παρεῖναι.

III. RES GRAECIAE

Ὁ δὲ φαντασίαν μὲν ἔχειν ἔφη τοὺς εἰρημένους
λόγους, τὴν δ' ἀλήθειαν οὐ τοιαύτην εἶναι, τὸ δ'
ἐναντίον. . . .

(5)   4. ""Ὅτι μὲν οὔτε Πτολεμαῖος ὁ βασιλεὺς οὔθ' ἡ τῶν
Ῥοδίων πόλις οὔθ' ἡ τῶν Βυζαντίων καὶ Χίων καὶ
Μυτιληναίων ἐν παρέργῳ τίθενται τὰς ὑμετέρας, ὦ
ἄνδρες Αἰτωλοί, διαλύσεις, ἐξ αὐτῶν τῶν πραγμάτων
2 ὑπολαμβάνω τοῦτ' εἶναι συμφανές. οὐ γὰρ νῦν πρῶτον οὐδὲ δεύτερον ποιούμεθα πρὸς ὑμᾶς τοὺς ὑπὲρ τῆς
εἰρήνης λόγους, ἀλλ' ἐξ ὅτου τὸν πόλεμον ἐνεστή-
σασθε, προσεδρεύοντες καὶ πάντα καιρὸν θεραπεύ-
οντες οὐ διαλείπομεν ὑπὲρ τούτων ποιούμενοι πρὸς
3 ὑμᾶς μνήμην, κατὰ μὲν τὸ παρὸν τῆς ὑμετέρας καὶ
Μακεδόνων στοχαζόμενοι καταφθορᾶς, πρὸς δὲ τὸ

---

9 Fragment of a speech, perhaps from the same occasion as
4.1–6 and 10. See WC 2.16–17.

had been so very eager to see this happen, but when more messengers arrived not only announcing the fact, but adding details, then indeed the city was full of exceeding great joy, every holy place was decorated, and every temple was filled with offerings and victims. In a word they became so sanguine and confident that it seemed to everyone that Hannibal whom they had formerly so much dreaded was not now even in Italy.

III. AFFAIRS OF GREECE

He said[9] that the speech was full of imagination, but that the truth was not this but rather the reverse. . . .

Speech of an Ambassador

4. "I consider, men of Aetolia,[10] that the facts themselves demonstrate that neither King Ptolemy nor Rhodes nor Byzantium nor Chios nor Mytilene make light of coming to terms with you. For this is not the first or the second time that we make proposals to you for peace, but from the date at which you opened hostilities we have never ceased to mention the matter to you, entreating you to entertain it and availing ourselves gladly of every occasion, having before our eyes the ruin brought by the war on yourselves

[10] The speaker addresses an Aetolian assembly. His name is given in the margin of F 2 as Thrasycrates, a Rhodian according to Schweighaeuser's suggestion. This name, however, is not attested at Rhodes (*LGPN* 1.226) and is in general as rare as Thrasycles is common. The speaker pleads for peace and does not seem to be associated with either side.

μέλλον καὶ περὶ τῶν σφετέρων πατρίδων καὶ περὶ τῶν
4 ἄλλων Ἑλλήνων προνοούμενοι. καθάπερ γὰρ ἐπὶ τοῦ
πυρός, ὅταν ὑφάψῃ τις ἅπαξ τὴν ὕλην, οὐκέτι τὸ
λοιπὸν ἐπὶ τῇ τούτου προαιρέσει γίνεται τὸ συμβαῖνον, ἀλλ᾽ ᾗ ποτ᾽ ἂν τύχῃ λαμβάνει τὴν νομήν, τὸ
πλεῖον τοῖς ἀνέμοις κυβερνώμενον καὶ τῇ τῆς ὑποκειμένης ὕλης διαφθορᾷ, καὶ πολλάκις ἐπ᾽ αὐτὸν τὸν
5 ἐμπρήσαντα πρῶτον ὥρμησε παραλόγως, τὸν αὐτὸν
τρόπον [καὶ] ὁ πόλεμος ὑπό τινων ὅταν ἅπαξ ἐκκαθῇ,
τοτὲ μὲν αὐτοὺς τούτους πρώτους ἀπόλλυσι, ποτὲ δὲ
φέρεται φθείρων ἀδίκως πᾶν τὸ παραπεσόν, αἰεὶ και-
νοποιούμενος καὶ προσφυόμενος, ὥσπερ ὑπ᾽ ἀνέμων,
6 ὑπὸ τῆς τῶν πλησιαζόντων ἀγνοίας. διόπερ, ὦ ἄνδρες
Αἰτωλοί, νομίσαντες καὶ τοὺς νησιώτας πανδημεὶ καὶ
τοὺς τὴν Ἀσίαν κατοικοῦντας Ἕλληνας παρόντας
ὑμῶν δεῖσθαι τὸν μὲν πόλεμον ἆραι, τὴν δ᾽ εἰρήνην
ἑλέσθαι, διὰ τὸ καὶ πρὸς σφᾶς ἀνήκειν τὰ γινόμενα,
σωφρονήσαντες ἐντράπητε καὶ πείσθητε τοῖς παρα-
7 καλουμένοις. καὶ γὰρ εἰ κατά τινα τύχην ἐπολεμεῖτε
πόλεμον ἀλυσιτελῆ μέν, ἐπειδὴ παντὶ πολέμῳ τοῦτο
παρέπεται κατὰ τὸ πλεῖστον, ἔνδοξον δὲ καὶ κατὰ τὴν
ἐξ ἀρχῆς ὑπόθεσιν καὶ κατὰ τὴν τῶν ἀποβαινόντων
ἐπιγραφήν, ἴσως ἄν τις ὑμῖν ἔσχε συγγνώμην, φιλο-
8 τίμως διακειμένοις. εἰ δὲ πάντων αἴσχιστον καὶ πολλῆς ἀδοξίας πλήρη καὶ βλασφημίας, ἆρ᾽ οὐ μεγάλης
9 προσδεῖται τὰ πράγματ᾽ ἐπιστάσεως; ῥηθήσεται γὰρ
τὸ δοκοῦν μετὰ παρρησίας· ὑμεῖς δ᾽, ἂν εὖ φρονῆτε,
10 μεθ᾽ ἡσυχίας ἀνέξεσθε. πολλῷ γάρ ἐστιν ἄμεινον

and the Macedonians, and taking thought for the future safety of our own countries and the rest of Greece. For, as with fire, once we have set the fuel alight the consequences are not at our discretion, but it spreads wherever chance directs it, guided chiefly by the wind and by the rapidity with which the fuel it feeds on is consumed, often strangely enough turning on the very man who lit it, so it is with war. Once it has been kindled by anyone, at times it destroys in the first place its authors and at times advances blindly, bringing unmerited destruction on everything it meets with, ever revived and ever blown anew into a blaze, as if by winds, by the folly of those who come near it. Therefore, men of Aetolia, we beg you, as if the whole of the islanders and all the Greeks who inhabit Asia Minor were present here and were entreating you to put a stop to the war and decide for peace—for the matter concerns them as much as ourselves—to come to your senses and relent and agree to our request. Now if it so chanced that you were engaged in a war, unprofitable indeed, as every war for the most part is, but glorious in the motive of its inception and in the splendor of its results, you might perhaps be pardoned for acting from ambitious motives. But if it is a war most shameful and full of dishonor and reproach, does not the situation call for deep consideration? We will state our opinion frankly, and you, if you are wise, will listen to it calmly. For it is far better to be reproached and saved in

ὀνειδισθέντας ἐν καιρῷ σωθῆναι μᾶλλον ἢ πρὸς χάριν ἀκούσαντας μετ᾽ ὀλίγον ἀπολέσθαι μὲν αὑτούς,
ἀπολέσαι δὲ καὶ τοὺς λοιποὺς Ἕλληνας.

(6)   5. Λάβετε τοίνυν πρὸ ὀφθαλμῶν τὴν αὑτῶν ἄγνοιαν. φατὲ μὲν γὰρ πολεμεῖν ὑπὲρ τῶν Ἑλλήνων πρὸς
Φίλιππον, ἵνα σῳζόμενοι μὴ ποιῶσι τούτῳ τὸ προσταττόμενον, πολεμεῖτε δ᾽ ἐπ᾽ ἐξανδραποδισμῷ καὶ
2   καταφθορᾷ τῆς Ἑλλάδος. ταῦτα γὰρ αἱ συνθῆκαι
λέγουσιν ὑμῶν αἱ πρὸς Ῥωμαίους, αἳ πρότερον μὲν ἐν
τοῖς γράμμασιν ὑπῆρχον, νῦν δ᾽ ἐν τοῖς πράγμασι
3   θεωροῦνται γινόμεναι. καὶ τότε μὲν αὐτὰ τὰ γράμματα
τὴν αἰσχύνην ὑμῖν ἐπέφερε, νῦν δὲ διὰ τῶν ἔργων ὑπὸ
4   τὴν ὄψιν τοῦτο γίνεται πᾶσι καταφανές. λοιπὸν ὁ μὲν
Φίλιππος ὄνομα γίνεται καὶ πρόσχημα τοῦ πολέμου·
πάσχει γὰρ οὐδὲν δεινόν· τούτῳ δὲ συμμάχων ὑπαρχόντων Πελοποννησίων τῶν πλείστων, Βοιωτῶν,
Εὐβοέων, Φωκέων, Λοκρῶν, Θετταλῶν, Ἠπειρωτῶν,
κατὰ τούτων πεποίησθε τὰς συνθήκας ἐφ᾽ ᾧ τὰ μὲν
5   σώματα καὶ τἄπιπλα Ῥωμαίων ὑπάρχειν, τὰς δὲ πόλεις
6   καὶ τὴν χώραν Αἰτωλῶν. καὶ κυριεύσαντες μὲν αὐτοὶ
πόλεως οὔτ᾽ ἂν ὑβρίζειν ὑπομείναιτε τοὺς ἐλευθέρους
οὔτ᾽ ἐμπιπράναι τὰς πόλεις, νομίζοντες ὠμὸν εἶναι τὸ
7   τοιοῦτο καὶ βαρβαρικόν· συνθήκας δὲ πεποίησθε τοιαύτας, δι᾽ ὧν ἅπαντας τοὺς ἄλλους Ἕλληνας ἐκδότους
δεδώκατε τοῖς βαρβάροις εἰς τὰς αἰσχίστας ὕβρεις
8   καὶ παρανομίας. καὶ ταῦτα πρότερον μὲν ἠγνοεῖτο·
νυνὶ δὲ διὰ τῆς Ὠρειτῶν καὶ τῶν ταλαιπώρων Αἰγι-

time, than to listen to pleasant words and a little after to be ruined yourselves and to ruin the rest of the Greeks.

5. "Consider, then, the errors you have committed. You say that you are fighting with Philip for the sake of the Greeks, that they may be delivered and may refuse to obey his commands; but as a fact you are fighting for the enslavement and ruin of Greece. This is the story your treaty[11] with the Romans tells, a treaty formerly existing merely in writing, but now seen to be carried out in actual fact. Previously the words of the treaty alone involved you in disgrace, but now when it is put in action this becomes evident to the eyes of all. Philip, then, is but the nominal pretext of the war; he is in no kind of danger; but as he has for allies[12] most of the Peloponnesians, the Boeotians, the Euboeans, the Phocians, the Locrians, the Thessalians, and Epirots, you made the treaty against them all, the terms being that their persons and personal property should belong to the Romans and their cities and lands to the Aetolians. Did you capture a city yourselves you would not allow yourselves to outrage freemen or to burn their towns, which you regard as a cruel proceeding and barbarous; but you have made a treaty by which you have given up to the barbarians[13] all the rest of the Greeks to be exposed to atrocious outrage and violence. This was not formerly understood, but now the case of the people

---

[11] The alliance with Rome (*StV* 536), because of its stipulations and its execution, was deeply resented in Greece.

[12] The members of the alliance forged by Antigonus Doson in 224: *StV* 507.

[13] For the Romans called barbarians see n. on 9.37.6.

νητῶν ἅπασι γεγόνατε καταφανεῖς, τῆς τύχης ὥσπερ
ἐπίτηδες ἐπὶ τὴν ἐξώστραν ἀναβιβαζούσης τὴν ὑμε-
9 τέραν ἄγνοιαν. ἡ μὲν οὖν ἀρχὴ τοῦ πολέμου καὶ τὰ
νῦν ἤδη συμβαίνοντα τοιαῦτ᾽ ἐστί· τὸ δὲ τέλος, ἂν
ὅλως πάντα κατὰ νοῦν ὑμῖν χωρήσῃ, ποῖόν τι δεῖ
προσδοκᾶν; ἆρ᾽ οὐ κακῶν ἀρχὴν μεγάλων ἅπασι τοῖς
Ἕλλησιν;

(7)   6. ὅτι γάρ, ἂν Ῥωμαῖοι τὸν ἐν Ἰταλίᾳ πόλεμον
ἀποτρίψωνται—τοῦτο δ᾽ ἐστὶν ἐν ὀλίγῳ, συγκεκλει-
μένου τῆς Βρεττίας εἰς πάνυ βραχεῖς τόπους Ἀννί-
2 βου—λοιπὸν ὅτι πάσῃ τῇ δυνάμει τὴν ὁρμὴν ἐπὶ τοὺς
κατὰ τὴν Ἑλλάδα τόπους ποιήσονται, λόγῳ μὲν Αἰτωλοῖς βοηθήσοντες κατὰ Φιλίππου, τῇ δ᾽ ἀληθείᾳ
πᾶσαν ὑφ᾽ ἑαυτοὺς ποιησόμενοι, καὶ λίαν ⟨ὑπολαμ-
3 βάνω⟩ τοῦτ᾽ εἶναι καταφανές. ἐάν τε καλῶς προθῶνται
ποιεῖν Ῥωμαῖοι κυριεύσαντες, ἐκείνων ἔσεσθαι καὶ
τὴν χάριν καὶ τὴν ἐπιγραφήν, ἐάν τε κακῶς, τῶν
αὑτῶν ὑπάρξειν καὶ τὰς ὠφελίας ἐκ τῶν ἀπολλυμένων
4 καὶ τὴν ἐξουσίαν ⟨τῶν⟩ σῳζομένων. ὑμεῖς δὲ τότε τοὺς
θεοὺς ἐπικαλέσεσθε μάρτυρας, ὅταν μήτε τῶν θεῶν
βούληται μήτε τῶν ἀνθρώπων ἔτι δύνηται βοηθεῖν
ὑμῖν μηδείς.

5   Ἴσως μὲν οὖν ἐξ ἀρχῆς ἔδει πάντα προορᾶσθαι·
6 τοῦτο γὰρ ἦν ὑμῖν πρέπον· ἐπειδὴ δὲ πολλὰ διαφεύγει
τῶν μελλόντων τὴν ἀνθρωπίνην πρόνοιαν, νῦν γε δέον
ἂν εἴη, διὰ τούτων τῶν πραγμάτων συνεωρακότας τὸ
συμβαῖνον, βέλτιον βουλεύεσθαι περὶ τοῦ μέλλοντος.
7 οὐ μὴν ἀλλ᾽ ἡμεῖς γε κατὰ τὸ παρὸν οὐδὲν ἀπολελοί-

of Oreus[14] and that of the unhappy Aeginetans have exposed you to all, Fortune having of set purpose as it were mounted your infatuation on the stage. Such was the beginning of this war, such are already its consequences, and what must we expect its end to be, if all falls out entirely as you wish? Surely the beginning of terrible disaster to all the Greeks.

6. For it is only too evident, I think, that the Romans if they get the war in Italy off their hands—and this will be very shortly, as Hannibal is now confined in quite a small district of Bruttium[15]—will next throw themselves with their whole strength on Grecian lands on the pretext that they are helping the Aetolians against Philip, but really with the intention of conquering the whole country. Should the Romans, when they have subjected us, determine to treat us kindly, the credit and thanks will be theirs; but if they treat us ill it is they who will acquire the spoil of those they destroy and sovereignty over the survivors, and you will then call the gods to witness when neither any god will be still willing, nor any man still able to help you.

"Possibly you should have foreseen all the consequences from the beginning, but as much of the future escapes human foresight, it should be your duty now at last, when these occurrences have opened your eyes to facts, to take better counsel for the future. As for ourselves we pro-

[14] A city in northern Euboea, conquered by the Roman Sulpicius Galba because of the treachery of Philip's Illyrian commander. The plunder fell to the Romans, the city to the Aetolians. For Aegina see nn. on 9.42.5.

[15] True only if the speech was given some time after the battle at the Metaurus (which is far from certain).

παμεν τῶν ἁρμοζόντων ἢ λέγειν ἢ πράττειν τοῖς
ἀληθινοῖς φίλοις, καὶ περὶ τοῦ μέλλοντος τὸ δοκοῦν
8 μετὰ παρρησίας εἰρήκαμεν· ὑμᾶς δ' ἀξιοῦμεν καὶ
παρακαλοῦμεν μήθ' αὑτοῖς φθονῆσαι μήτε τοῖς ἄλλοις Ἕλλησι τῆς ἐλευθερίας καὶ τῆς σωτηρίας."

9 Τούτου δὲ ποιήσαντος διατροπήν τινα τοῖς πολλοῖς, ὡς ἐδόκει, μετὰ τοῦτον εἰσῆλθον οἱ παρὰ τοῦ
Φιλίππου πρέσβεις, οἳ τοὺς μὲν κατὰ μέρος λόγους
ὑπερέθεντο, δύο δ' ἔφασαν ἥκειν ἔχοντες ἐντολάς,
10 αἱρουμένων μὲν τῶν Αἰτωλῶν τὴν εἰρήνην ἑτοίμως
δέχεσθαι ‹μὴ βουλομένων ... › τοὺς θεοὺς καὶ τοὺς
πρεσβευτὰς τοὺς παρόντας ἀπὸ τῆς Ἑλλάδος ἐπι-
μαρτυραμένους χωρίζεσθαι διότι τῶν μετὰ ταῦτα
συμβησομένων τοῖς Ἕλλησιν Αἰτωλούς, ἀλλ' οὐ Φίλιππον αἴτιον δεήσει νομίζειν. . . .[1]

2 7. Ὅτι Φίλιππος πορευθεὶς ἐπὶ τὴν Τριχωνίδα
λίμνην καὶ παραγενόμενος εἰς τὸν Θέρμον, ἔνθ' ἦν
ἱερὸν Ἀπόλλωνος, ὅσα πρότερον ἀπέλιπε τῶν ἀνα-
θημάτων, τότε πάλιν ἅπαντα διελωβήσατο, κακῶς μὲν
3 πρὸ τοῦ, κακῶς δὲ τότε χρώμενος τῷ θυμῷ· τὸ γὰρ
τοῖς ἀνθρώποις ὀργιζόμενον εἰς τὸ θεῖον ἀσεβεῖν τῆς
πάσης ἀλογιστίας ἐστὶ σημεῖον. . . .

4 Ἑλλόπιον, πόλις Αἰτωλίας. Πολύβιος ιαʹ.

5 Φύταιον, πόλις Αἰτωλίας. Πολύβιος ἑνδεκάτῳ.

---

[1] F 11.7.1 has been placed after 10.47.13.

---

16 Lake Agrinion. Philip came perhaps by the same route as in
218; see map in WC 1.542.

test that on the present occasion we have neglected nothing which it is proper for true friends to say or do, and we have frankly stated our opinion about the future. To conclude we beg and entreat you not to grudge to yourselves and to the rest of the Greeks the blessings of liberty and security."

This speech appears to have made a considerable impression on the people, and after the speaker the ambassadors from Philip entered. Leaving the discussion of details over for the present they said they had come with two imperative messages. If the Aetolians elected for peace the king readily consented, but if not, the ambassadors were bidden to take their leave after calling to witness the gods and the embassies from the rest of Greece that the Aetolians and not Philip must be considered responsible for what might happen afterward to the Greeks. . . .

Philip at Thermus

7. Philip, marching toward Lake Trichonis,[16] reached Thermus where there was a temple of Apollo and now mutilated all the statues which he had spared on the former occasion,[17] acting wrongly both then and now in giving way to his passion. For it is the height of unreasonableness to be guilty of impiety to the gods because one is angry with men. . . .

7.4 Ellopium, a city of Aetolia. Polybius in Book 11.

7.5 Phytaeum, a city of Aetolia. Polybius in Book 11.[18]

[17] In 218. For similar behavior of King Prusias II at Pergamum in 155, see 32.15.3–9 (where P. refers to Philip at Thermus).

[18] For possible locations of these two towns, see WC 1.543–545.

8. Ὅτι τριῶν ὄντων τρόπων, καθ᾽ οὓς ἐφίενται
πάντες στρατηγίας οἱ κατὰ λόγον αὐτῇ προσιόντες,
πρώτου μὲν διὰ τῶν ὑπομνημάτων καὶ τῆς ἐκ τούτων
2 κατασκευῆς, ἑτέρου δὲ τοῦ μεθοδικοῦ καὶ τῆς παρὰ
τῶν ἐμπείρων ἀνδρῶν παραδόσεως, τρίτου δὲ τοῦ διὰ
τῆς ἐπ᾽ αὐτῶν τῶν πραγμάτων ἕξεως καὶ τριβῆς,
3 πάντων ἦσαν τούτων ἀνεννόητοι οἱ τῶν Ἀχαιῶν στρατηγοὶ ἁπλῶς. . . .

4   Τοῖς γὰρ πλείστοις ὑπεγεγόνει τις ζῆλος οὐκ εὐτυ-
χὴς ἐκ τῆς τῶν ἄλλων ἀλαζονείας καὶ τῆς ἀκαιρίας·
5 ἐσπούδαζον γὰρ τὰς ἀκολουθίας καὶ τὰς ἐσθῆτας
διαφερόντως, καί τις ἦν περὶ τοὺς πλείστους καλλω-
6 πισμός, ὑπερέχων τὴν ἐκ τοῦ βίου χορηγίαν. ὅπλων δ᾽
οὐδὲ τὸν ἐλάχιτον ἐποιοῦντο λόγον. . . .

7   Οἱ γὰρ πολλοὶ τὰ μὲν ἔργα τῶν εὐτυχούντων οὐδὲ
πειρῶνται μιμεῖσθαι, τὰ δὲ πάρεργα ζηλοῦντες μετὰ
βλάβης ἐκθεατρίζουσι τὴν ἑαυτῶν ἀκρισίαν. . . .

9. Μεγάλα μὲν γὰρ ἔφη τὴν λαμπρότητα συμβάλ-
λεσθαι πρὸς ἔκπληξιν τῶν ὑπεναντίων, πολλὰ δὲ
συνεργεῖν τὴν ἐκ τῆς ἐπισκευῆς ἁρμογὴν τῶν ὅπλων
2 εἰς τὴν χρείαν. γίνεσθαι δ᾽ ἂν μάλιστα τὸ δέον, εἰ τὴν
μὲν ἐπιμέλειαν, ἣν νῦν ποιοῦνται περὶ τὸν ἱματισμόν,
ταύτην ποιήσαιντο περὶ τῶν ὅπλων, τὴν δὲ πρότερον
ὀλιγωρίαν περὶ τῶν ὅπλων παρ᾽ αὐτοῖς ὑπάρχουσαν,
3 ταύτην μετενέγκαιεν ἐπὶ τὰς ἐσθῆτας· οὕτως γὰρ ἅμα

---

19 P. has already criticized several strategi for incompetence:
Aratus the Younger in 4.60.2, Euryleon in 10.21.1.

The Achaean Strategi and Philopoemen

8. There are three ways in which those who aim at acquiring the art of generalship may reasonably hope to do so, first by studying histories and availing themselves of the lessons contained in them, secondly by following the systematic instruction of experienced men, and thirdly by the habit and experience acquired in actual practice, and in all three the present Achaean strategi were absolutely unversed[19]. . . .

Most of them displayed an unhappy emulation of the inopportune pretentiousness of others. They were particularly careful about their retinues and their dress, generally exhibiting a dandyism much in excess of what their fortunes permitted, while as to their arms they paid not the least attention to them. . . .

Most men do not even attempt to imitate the essential characteristics of those who are favored by fortune, but by striving to copy them in unessentials make a damaging display of their own want of judgment. . . .

9. Philopoemen[20] told them that the brightness of their arms and armor would contribute much to intimidate the enemy, and that it was also of great importance in battle that arms should fit well.[21] What was required[22] could be best done by bestowing on their arms the care they now devote to their dress, and transferring to the latter the lack of attention they formerly exhibited to their arms. For by

[20] Federal strategus in 208/7.   [21] For alternative meanings of the phrase, see WC 2.281.   [22] Paragraphs 2 to 7 make Philopoemen's point that soldiers ought to give greater care to their weapons and equipment than to their dress.

τούς τε κατ᾽ ἰδίαν βίους ὠφελήσεσθαι καὶ τὰ κοινὰ
πράγμαθ᾽ ὁμολογουμένως αὐτοὺς δυνήσεσθαι σῴζειν.
4 διόπερ ἔφη δεῖν τὸν εἰς ἐξοπλισίαν ἢ στρατείαν ἐκπο-
ρευόμενον, ὅτε μὲν τὰς κνημῖδας περιτίθεται, σκοπεῖν
ὅπως ἀραρυῖαί τε καὶ στίλβουσαι τῶν ὑποδεσμῶν
5 καὶ κρηπίδων ὑπάρχωσιν αὗται μᾶλλον, ὅταν δὲ τὴν
ἀσπίδα καὶ <τὸν> θώρακα καὶ τὸ κράνος διαλαμβάνῃ,
περιβλέπειν ἵνα τῆς χλαμύδος καὶ τοῦ χιτῶνος καθ-
6 αρειότερα ταῦθ᾽ ὑπάρχῃ καὶ πολυτελέστερα· παρ᾽ οἷς
γὰρ τὰ πρὸς ἐπιφάνειαν αἱρετώτερά [ἐστι] τῶν πρὸς
τὴν χρείαν, παρὰ τούτοις αὐτόθεν εὐθέως προφανὲς
7 εἶναι τὸ συμβησόμενον ἐν τοῖς κινδύνοις. καθόλου δ᾽
ἠξίου διαλαμβάνειν ὡς ὁ μὲν ἐν τοῖς ἱματίοις καλ-
λωπισμὸς γυναικός ἐστι, καὶ ταύτης οὐ λίαν σώφρο-
νος, ἡ δ᾽ ἐν τοῖς ὅπλοις πολυτέλεια καὶ σεμνότης
ἀνδρῶν ἀγαθῶν, προαιρουμένων ἑαυτοὺς καὶ τὰς πα-
8 τρίδας ἐνδόξως σῴζειν. πάντες δ᾽ οἱ παρόντες οὕτως
ἀπεδέξαντο τὰ ῥηθέντα καὶ τὸν νοῦν τῆς παρακλήσεως ἐθαύμασαν, ὡς καὶ παραχρῆμα μὲν ἐκπορευ-
όμενοι τὸ βουλευτήριον εὐθέως ἐνεδείκνυντο <τοὺς>
κεκαλλωπιμένους καὶ διακλίνειν ἐνίους ἠνάγκαζον τῆς
9 ἀγορᾶς, ἔτι δὲ μᾶλλον ἐν ταῖς ἐξοπλισίαις καὶ στρα-
τείαις παρετήρουν σφᾶς αὐτοὺς ἐν τοῖς προειρημένοις.

10. Οὕτως εἷς λόγος εὐκαίρως ῥηθεὶς ὑπ᾽ ἀνδρὸς
ἀξιοπίστου πολλάκις οὐ μόνον ἀποτρέπει τῶν χειρί-
στων, ἀλλὰ καὶ παρορμᾷ πρὸς τὰ κάλλιστα τοὺς
2 ἀνθρώπους. ὅταν δὲ καὶ τὸν ἴδιον βίον ἀκόλουθον

this means they would both benefit their private fortunes, and as all would acknowledge, enable themselves to save the state. Therefore he said that a man on starting for a review or a campaign should in putting on his greaves[23] take more care to see that they fit well and look shiny than he does about his shoes and boots, and again, when he handles his shield, breastplate, and helmet, see to it that they are cleaner and smarter than his chlamys and chiton. For when a man gives the preference over serviceable things to superficial things it is on the face of it evident what will happen to him in a battle. He begged them to regard general daintiness in dress as being fit for a woman and not for a very modest woman, while the richness and distinction of armor is suited to brave men who are determined to save gloriously both themselves and their country. All present applauded his speech so much and so admired the spirit of his advice, that at once on issuing from the council chamber they pointed to such as were dressed like dandies, and compelled some of them to retire from the marketplace, and henceforth in their military exercises and campaigns they paid much more attention to these matters.

10. So true is it that a single word spoken in season by a man of authority not only deters his hearers from what is worst, but urges them on to what is best. And when the speaker can reinforce his advice by the example of a life

[23] Plu. *Phil*. 9.2, and Paus. 8.50.1, both using a lost passage of P., report that Philopoemen introduced heavier armor and the corresponding phalanx tactics after the Macedonian fashion. Similar practices were introduced elsewhere at the time.

εἰσφέρηται τοῖς εἰρημένοις ὁ παρακαλῶν, ἀνάγκη
λαμβάνειν τὴν πρώτην πίστιν τὴν παραίνεσιν. ὃ δὴ
περὶ ἐκεῖνον τὸν ἄνδρα μάλιστ᾽ ἄν τις ἴδοι γινόμενον.
3 κατά τε γὰρ τὴν ἐσθῆτα καὶ τὴν σίτησιν ἀφελὴς καὶ
λιτὸς ἦν, ὁμοίως δὲ καὶ περὶ τὰς τοῦ σώματος θεραπείας, ἔτι δὲ καὶ τὰς ἐντεύξεις, εὐπερίκοπτος καὶ
4 ἀνεπίφθονος· περί γε μὴν τοῦ παρ᾽ ὅλον τὸν βίον
ἀληθεύειν μεγίστην ἐποιήσατο σπουδήν. τοιγάρτοι
βραχέα καὶ τὰ τυχόντ᾽ ἀποφαινόμενος μεγάλην ἐγκα-
τέλειπε πίστιν τοῖς ἀκούουσι· παράδειγμα γὰρ ἐν
5 πᾶσι τὸν ἴδιον βίον εἰσφερόμενος οὐ πολλῶν ἐποίει
6 προσδεῖσθαι λόγων τοὺς ἀκούοντας. διὸ καὶ πολλάκις
λόγους μακροὺς καὶ δοκοῦντας ὑπὸ τῶν ἀντιπολι-
τευομένων δεόντως εἰρῆσθαι δι᾽ ὀλίγων ῥημάτων τῇ
πίστει καὶ ταῖς ἐννοίαις τῶν πραγμάτων ὁλοσχερῶς
ἐξέβαλε.

7   Πλὴν τότε συντελεσθέντος τοῦ διαβουλίου πάντες
ἐπανῆγον ἐπὶ τὰς πόλεις, τά τε ῥηθέντα καὶ τὸν ἄνδρα
διαφερόντως ἀποδεδεγμένοι, καὶ νομίζοντες οὐδ᾽ ἂν
8 παθεῖν οὐδὲν δεινὸν ἐκείνου προεστῶτος. ὁ δὲ Φιλοποίμην εὐθέως ἐπεπορεύετο τὰς πόλεις, ἐνεργῶς καὶ
9 μετὰ σπουδῆς ποιούμενος τὴν ἔφοδον. κἄπειτα συναγαγὼν τοὺς ὄχλους ἅμα μὲν ⟨ἐγύμναζεν ἅμα δὲ⟩
συνέταττε καὶ τέλος οὐδ᾽ ὅλους ὀκτὼ μῆνας χρησάμενος τῇ τοιαύτῃ παρασκευῇ καὶ μελέτῃ συνῆγε τὰς
δυνάμεις εἰς Μαντίνειαν, διαγωνιούμενος πρὸς τὸν
τύραννον ὑπὲρ τῆς ἁπάντων Πελοποννησίων ἐλευθερίας.

which follows it, it is impossible not to give the fullest credit to his words. And this, we see, was especially true of Philopoemen.[24] For in his dress and living he was plain and simple, and alike in the care he bestowed on his person and in his conversation he was marked by fine restraint and quite unassuming. Through his whole life he was most scrupulous in always speaking the truth, and therefore a few ordinary words from his lips inspired complete trust in the hearers; for since in everything the example of his own life supported his advice, they did not require many words from him. Consequently on many occasions by his credit and his insight into affairs he completely overthrew in a few sentences long speeches of his adversaries which had appeared to be very plausible.

To resume—after the close of the council all returned to their cities completely approving of the speech and the speaker, and convinced that with him as a leader no calamity could overtake them. Philopoemen now at once went the round of the cities, visiting and inspecting each with the greatest diligence and care. Afterward collecting their forces he trained and drilled them, and finally after spending less than eight months[25] on these preparations he collected his army at Mantinea, to enter on the struggle against the tyrant[26] for the liberty of the whole Peloponnese.

[24] He practices what he teaches.

[25] Counting from his entry into office in autumn 208, this would be ca. June 207.

[26] Machanidas; see n. on 10.41.2. He once made a dedication to Eileithyia at Delphi (*SIG* 551).

11. Ὁ δὲ Μαχανίδας κατατεθαρρηκώς, καὶ νομίζων ὡς ἂν εἰ κατ᾽ εὐχὴν αὐτῷ γίνεσθαι τὴν τῶν Ἀχαιῶν ὁρμήν, ἅμα τῷ γνῶναι διότι συνηθροισμένοι τυγ-

2 χάνουσιν εἰς τὴν Μαντίνειαν, παρακαλέσας ἐν Τεγέᾳ τοὺς Λακεδαιμονίους τὰ πρέποντα τοῖς καιροῖς, εὐθέως εἰς τὴν ἐπιοῦσαν, ἄρτι τῆς ἡμέρας ἐπιφαινούσης, προῆγεν ὡς ἐπὶ τὴν Μαντίνειαν, τῆς μὲν φάλαγγος

3 καθηγούμενος τῷ δεξιῷ κέρατι, τοὺς δὲ μισθοφόρους ἐξ ἑκατέρου τοῦ μέρους τῆς πρωτοπορείας παραλλήλους ἄγων, ἐπὶ δὲ τούτοις ζεύγη πλῆθος ὀργάνων καὶ

4 βελῶν κομίζοντα καταπελτικῶν. κατὰ δὲ τὸν αὐτὸν καιρὸν Φιλοποίμην εἰς τρία μέρη διῃρηκὼς τὴν δύναμιν ἐξῆγεν ἐκ τῆς Μαντινείας, κατὰ μὲν ⟨τὴν⟩ ἐκ τοῦ Ποσειδῶνος ἱεροῦ φέρουσαν τοὺς Ἰλλυριοὺς καὶ θωρακίτας, ἅμα δὲ τὸ ξενικὸν ἅπαν καὶ τοὺς εὐζώνους, κατὰ δὲ τὴν ἑξῆς ὡς πρὸς τὰς δύσεις τοὺς φαλαγγίτας, ἔτι δὲ κατὰ τὴν ἐχομένην τοὺς πολιτικοὺς

5 ἱππεῖς. τοῖς μὲν οὖν εὐζώνοις κατελάβετο πρώτοις τὸν λόφον τὸν πρὸ τῆς πόλεως, ὃς ἀνατείνων ἱκανὸν ὑπὲρ τὴν ὁδὸν κεῖται τὴν Ξενίδα καὶ τὸ προειρημένον ἱερόν· τοὺς δὲ θωρακίτας συνάπτων ἐπὶ τὴν μεσημβρίαν κατέστησε. τούτοις δὲ συνεχεῖς τοὺς Ἰλλυριοὺς παρ-

6 ενέβαλε. μετὰ δὲ τούτους ἐπὶ τὴν αὐτὴν εὐθεῖαν τὴν φάλαγγα κατὰ τέλη σπειρηδὸν ἐν διαστήμασιν ἐπέστησε παρὰ τὴν τάφρον τὴν φέρουσαν ἐπὶ τοῦ Ποσειδίου διὰ μέσου τοῦ τῶν Μαντινέων πεδίου καὶ συνάπτουσαν τοῖς ὄρεσι τοῖς συντερμονοῦσι τῇ τῶν

7 Ἐλισφασίων χώρᾳ. πρὸς μὲν τούτοις ἐπὶ τὸ δεξιὸν

The Defeat and Death of Machanidas

11. Machanidas, filled with confidence and regarding the attack of the Achaeans almost as a godsend, as soon as he heard that they were concentrated at Mantinea, addressed the Lacedaemonians at Tegea in terms suitable to the occasion, and at once on the next day shortly after daybreak began to advance on Mantinea. He himself led the right wing of the phalanx, and placed the mercenaries in parallel columns on each side of the van with wagons behind them charged with a quantity of engines and missiles for catapults. At the same time Philopoemen, dividing his army into three parts, led it out of Mantinea,[27] taking by the road that starts from the temple of Poseidon the Illyrians and cuirassed infantry, together with all his mercenaries and light-armed troops, by the next road to the west the phalanx, and by the next the Achaean cavalry. He first of all occupied with his light-armed troops the hill in front of the city which rises at a considerable height above the road called Xenis and the above temple, and next to them on the south he placed the cuirassed infantry, with the Illyrians adjacent to them. Next to these on the same straight line he stationed the phalanx in several divisions at a certain distance from each other along the ditch that runs toward the temple of Poseidon through the plain of Mantinea and is contiguous with a range of hills forming the boundary of the territory of Elisphasia. Then next the phalanx on his

[27] For the battle, just a little south of the city, and for the topographical points mentioned, see map in WC 2.284.

κέρας ἐπέστησε τοὺς Ἀχαϊκοὺς ἱππεῖς, ὧν Ἀρισταί-
νετος ἡγεῖτο Δυμαῖος· κατὰ δὲ τὸ λαιὸν αὐτὸς εἶχε τὸ
ξενικὸν ἅπαν ἐν ἐπαλλήλοις τάξεσιν.

12. Ἅμα δὲ τῷ σύνοπτον ἤδη καλῶς εἶναι παρα-
γενομένην τὴν τῶν ὑπεναντίων δύναμιν ἐπιπορευόμενος τὰ συστήματα τῶν φαλαγγιτῶν παρεκάλει
βραχέως μέν, ἐμφαντικῶς δὲ τοῦ παρόντος κινδύνου.
2 τὰ μὲν οὖν πλεῖστα τῶν λεγομένων ἀσαφῆ συνέβαινε
γίνεσθαι· διὰ γὰρ τὴν πρὸς αὐτὸν εὔνοιαν καὶ πίστιν
τῶν ὄχλων εἰς τοιαύτην ὁρμὴν καὶ προθυμίαν παρέστη τὸ πλῆθος ὥστε παραπλησίαν ἐνθουσιασμῷ τὴν
ἀντιπαράκλησιν γίνεσθαι τῶν δυνάμεων, ἄγειν καὶ
3 θαρρεῖν αὐτὸν παρακελευομένων· τοῦτο μέντοι παράπαν ἐπιμελῶς ἐπειρᾶτο διασαφεῖν, ὅτε λάβοι καιρόν,
ὅτι τοῖς μὲν ὑπὲρ αἰσχρᾶς καὶ ἐπονειδίστου δουλείας,
τοῖς δ᾽ ὑπὲρ ἀειμνήστου καὶ λαμπρᾶς ἐλευθερίας συν-
έστηκεν ὁ παρὼν κίνδυνος.

4 Ὁ δὲ Μαχανίδας τὸ μὲν πρῶτον ὑπέδειξεν ὡς
ὀρθίᾳ τῇ φάλαγγι προσμίξων πρὸς τὸ δεξιὸν τῶν
πολεμίων· ἐπεὶ δ᾽ ἐπλησίασε, λαβὼν σύμμετρον ἀπό-
στημα περιέκλα τὴν δύναμιν ἐπὶ δόρυ, καὶ παρεκτεί-
νας ἴσον ἐποίησε τὸ παρ᾽ αὐτοῦ δεξιὸν τῷ τῶν Ἀχαιῶν
εὐωνύμῳ, τοὺς δὲ καταπέλτας πρὸ πάσης ἐπέστησε
5 τῆς δυνάμεως ἐν διαστήμασιν. ὁ δὲ Φιλοποίμην θεα-

---

28 An error for Aristaenus; R. M. Errington, *Philopoemen* (Oxford 1969), 276–279. Aristaenus was the son of Timocades and a
citizen of Dyme. The Achaeans dedicated a statue of his at Delphi

right wing he posted the Achaean cavalry under the command of Aristaenetus[28] of Dyme. On the left wing under his own command were all the mercenaries in close order.

12. As soon as the enemy were well in view he rode along the divisions of the phalanx and addressed them in a few brief words,[29] pointing out the importance of the coming battle. Most of what he said was not distinctly heard, because, owing to the soldiers' affection for him and reliance on him, such was their ardor and zeal that they responded to his address by what was almost a transport of enthusiasm, exhorting him to lead them on and be of good heart. The general tenor, however, of what he attempted to point out to them whenever he got the chance, was that in the present battle the enemy were fighting for shameful and ignominious slavery[30] and they themselves for imperishable and glorious liberty.

Machanidas at first looked as if he were about to charge the enemy's right with his phalanx in column, but on approaching, when he found himself at the proper distance he wheeled to the right, and deploying into line made his own right wing equal in extent to the Achaean left, placing his catapults at certain intervals in front of his whole army. Philopoemen, seeing that Machanidas' plan was by shoot-

(*FD* III 3.122), the Roman general Titus Flamininus set up another at Corinth (*ISE* 37), and the city of Aptera in Crete made him a *proxenos* (*IC* 2.23, no. 6 F, where he is called a son of Damocades). In the beginning he cooperated with Philopoemen but later favored Rome and became his opponent.

[29] This speech is discussed by B. Dreyer, *ZPE* 140 (2002), 33–39.   [30] Because Machanidas, like Nabis before him, was widely considered to be a tyrant.

σάμενος αὐτοῦ τὴν ἐπιβολήν, ὅτι τοῖς καταπέλταις
ἐπενόει βαλὼν εἰς τὰς σπείρας τῶν φαλαγγιτῶν τραυ-
ματίζειν τοὺς ἄνδρας καὶ θόρυβον ἐμποιεῖν τοῖς ὅλοις,

6 οὐκέτι χρόνον ἔδωκεν οὐδ' ἀνατροφήν, ἀλλὰ διὰ τῶν
Ταραντίνων ἐνεργῶς ἐχρῆτο τῇ καταρχῇ τοῦ κινδύνου
κατὰ τοὺς περὶ τὸ Ποσείδιον τόπους, ὄντας ἐπιπέδους

7 καὶ πρὸς ἱππικὴν εὐφυεῖς χρείαν. ὁ δὲ Μαχανίδας
ὁρῶν τὸ γινόμενον ἠναγκάζετο ποιεῖν τὸ παραπλήσιον καὶ συναφεῖναι τοὺς παρ' αὐτοῦ Ταραντίνους.

13. Τὸ μὲν οὖν πρῶτον αὐτῶν τούτων ἀνδρώδης ἦν
ἡ σύμπτωσις· κατὰ βραχὺ δὲ προσγινομένων τοῖς
πιεζομένοις τῶν εὐζώνων, ἐν πάνυ βραχεῖ χρόνῳ συνέβη ⟨τὸ⟩ παρ' ἑκατέρων ξενικὸν ἀναμὶξ γενέσθαι,

2 πάντῃ δὲ τούτων συμπλοκῆς ἀθρόως καὶ κατ' ἄνδρα
γινομένης ἐπὶ πολὺν χρόνον πάρισος ἦν ὁ κίνδυνος
οὕτως ὥστε τὰς λοιπὰς δυνάμεις, καραδοκούσας καθ'
ὁποτέρων ὁ κονιορτὸς τραπήσεται, μὴ δύνασθαι συμβαλεῖν διὰ ⟨τὸ⟩ μένειν ἀμφοτέρους ἐπὶ πολὺ διακατ-

3 έχοντας ἐν τῇ μάχῃ τὸν ἐξ ἀρχῆς τόπον. χρόνου δὲ
γινομένου κατίσχυον καὶ τῷ πλήθει καὶ ταῖς εὐχειρί-
αις διὰ τὴν ἕξιν οἱ παρὰ τοῦ τυράννου μισθοφόροι.

4-5 τοῦτο δ' εἰκότως καὶ τὸ παράπαν εἴωθε γίνεσθαι. ὅσῳ
γὰρ συμβαίνει τοὺς ἐν ταῖς δημοκρατίαις ὄχλους
προθυμοτέρους ὑπάρχειν ἐν τοῖς πολεμικοῖς ἀγῶσι
τῶν τοῖς τυράννοις πολιτικῶν ὑποταττομένων, τοσούτῳ τὰ παρὰ τοῖς μονάρχοις ξενικὰ τῶν ἐν ταῖς
δημοκρατίαις μισθοφορούντων εἰκὸς ὑπεράγειν καὶ

6 διαφέρειν. ὥσπερ γὰρ ἐπ' ἐκείνων οἷς μὲν ὑπὲρ ἐλευ-

ing at the divisions of the phalanx to wound the men and throw the whole force into disorder, gave him not a moment's leisure, but vigorously opened the attack with his Tarentines[31] in the neighborhood of the temple of Poseidon where the ground was flat and suitable for cavalry. Machanidas, when he saw this, was obliged to do likewise and order his own Tarentines to charge at the same time.

13. At first the Tarentines alone were engaged, fighting gallantly, but as the light-armed infantry gradually came up to the support of those who were hard pressed, in quite a short time the mercenaries on both sides were mixed up. They were fighting all over the field, in a confused crowd and man to man. For long the struggle was so equally balanced that the rest of the army, who were waiting to see to which side the cloud of dust was carried, could not make this out, since both long remained occupying their original positions. But after some time the tyrant's mercenaries prevailed by their superior numbers and skill, for they were well trained. This is generally what is liable to happen, since by as much as the civic force of a democracy is more courageous in action than the subjects of a tyrant, by so much will a despot's mercenaries in all probability excel those who serve for hire in a democracy. For as in the former case one side is fighting for freedom and the other for

[31] See n. on 4.77.7.

θερίας ἐστίν, οἷς δ᾽ ὑπὲρ δουλείας ὁ κίνδυνος, οὕτως
ἐπὶ τῶν μισθοφόρων οἷς μὲν ὑπὲρ ὁμολογουμένης
ἐπανορθώσεως, ⟨οἷς δ᾽⟩ ὑπὲρ προδήλου βλάβης γίνε-
7 ται φιλοτιμία. δημοκρατία μὲν γάρ, ἐπανελομένη τοὺς
ἐπιβουλεύσαντας, οὐκέτι μισθοφόροις τηρεῖ τὴν ἑαυτῆς ἐλευθερίαν· τυραννὶς δ᾽ ὅσῳ μειζόνων ἐφίεται,
8 τοσούτῳ πλειόνων προσδεῖται μισθοφόρων. πλείονας
γὰρ ἀδικοῦσα πλείονας ἔχει καὶ τοὺς ἐπιβουλεύοντας.
ἡ δὲ τῶν μονάρχων ἀσφάλεια τὸ παράπαν ἐν τῇ τῶν
ξένων εὐνοίᾳ κεῖται καὶ δυνάμει.

14. Διὸ δὴ καὶ τότε συνέβαινε τὸ παρὰ τῷ Μαχανίδᾳ ξενικὸν οὕτως ἐκθύμως ἀγωνίζεσθαι καὶ βιαίως
ὥστε μηδὲ τοὺς ἐφεδρεύοντας τοῖς ξένοις Ἰλλυριοὺς
καὶ θωρακίτας δύνασθαι τὴν ἔφοδον αὐτῶν ὑπομεῖναι,
πάντας δ᾽ ἐκπιεσθέντας φεύγειν προτροπάδην ὡς ἐπὶ
τῆς Μαντινείας, ἀπεχούσης τῆς πόλεως ἑπτὰ στα-
2 δίους. ἐν ᾧ δὴ καιρῷ τὸ παρ᾽ ἐνίοις ἀπορούμενον τότε
παρὰ πᾶσιν ὁμολογούμενον ἐγένετο καὶ συμφανές,
ὅτι πλεῖστα τῶν κατὰ πόλεμον συντελουμένων ⟨παρὰ
τὴν τῶν ἡγουμένων⟩ ἐμπειρίαν καὶ πάλιν ἀπειρίαν
3 ἐπιτελεῖται. μέγα μὲν γὰρ ἴσως καὶ τὸ προτερήματος
ἀρχὴν λαβόντα προσθεῖναι τἀκόλουθον, πολὺ δὲ μεῖζον τὸ σφαλέντα ταῖς πρώταις ἐπιβολαῖς μεῖναι παρ᾽
αὑτὸν καὶ συνιδεῖν τὴν τῶν εὐτυχούντων ἀκρισίαν καὶ
4 συνεπιθέσθαι τοῖς τούτων ἁμαρτήμασιν. ἰδεῖν γοῦν
ἔστι πολλάκις τοὺς μὲν ἤδη δοκοῦντας πεπροτερη-
κέναι μετ᾽ ὀλίγον τοῖς ὅλοις ἐσφαλμένους, τοὺς δ᾽
ἐν ἀρχαῖς δόξαντας ἐπταικέναι πάλιν ἐκ μεταβολῆς

slavery, so in the case of the mercenaries the one force is fighting for manifest improvement in their situation and the other for evident damage to their own; since a democracy when it has destroyed those who conspire against it no longer requires mercenaries to protect its freedom, but a tyranny, the more ambitious its aims, requires all the more mercenaries. For since it injures more people it has the more conspiring against it, and in general it may be said that the safety of despots depends on the affection and strength of their foreign soldiers.

14. So it was at present also. The mercenaries of Machanidas fought with such desperate courage and force that the Illyrians and cuirassed troops who supported the mercenaries could not resist the attack, but all gave way and fled in disorder toward Mantinea, which was seven stades distant.[32] This occasion afforded evidence sufficient to convince all of what some have doubted, the fact that most results in war are due to the skill or the reverse of the commanders. It is perhaps a great feat to follow up initial success, but it is a much greater one upon meeting with reverse at the outset to keep coolheaded, to be able to detect any lack of judgment on the part of the victors and take advantage of their errors. Indeed we often see those who already seem to have gained the day totally worsted very shortly afterward, and those who at first seemed to have

[32] Almost one and a half kilometers.

παρὰ τὴν αὐτῶν ἀγχίνοιαν τὰ ὅλα παραδόξως κατωρ-
5 θωκότας. ὃ δὴ καὶ τότε προφανῶς ἐδόκει περὶ τοὺς
6 ἡγεμόνας ἀμφοτέρους γεγονέναι. τοῦ γὰρ ξενικοῦ
παντὸς ἐγκεκλικότος τοῖς Ἀχαιοῖς καὶ παραλελυμένου
τοῦ λαιοῦ κέρως, ὁ μὲν Μαχανίδας ἀφέμενος τοῦ
μένειν ἐπὶ τῶν ὑποκειμένων, καὶ τοὺς μὲν κατὰ κέρας
ὑπεραίρειν τοῖς δὲ κατὰ πρόσωπον ἀπαντᾶν καὶ πει-
7 ρᾶσθαι τῶν ὅλων, τούτων μὲν οὐδὲν ἔπραξεν, ἀκρατῶς
δὲ καὶ μειρακιωδῶς συνεκχυθεὶς τοῖς ἑαυτοῦ μισθοφόροις ἐπέκειτο τοῖς φεύγουσιν, ὥσπερ οὐκ αὐτὸν τὸν
φόβον ἱκανὸν ὄντα τοὺς ἅπαξ ἐγκλίναντας ἄχρι τῶν
πυλῶν συνδιώκειν.

15. Ὁ δὲ τῶν Ἀχαιῶν στρατηγὸς ἕως μὲν τοῦ
δυνατοῦ διακατεῖχε τοὺς μισθοφόρους, ἐπ' ὀνόματος
2 καλῶν καὶ παροξύνων τοὺς ἡγεμόνας· ἐπεὶ δ' ἑώρα
τούτους ἐκβιαζομένους, οὐ πτοηθεὶς ἔφευγεν οὐδ' ἀθυ-
μήσας ἀπέστη . . ., ἀλλ' ὑποστείλας αὐτὸν ὑπὸ τὸ τῆς
φάλαγγος κέρας, ἅμα τῷ παραπεσεῖν τοὺς διώκοντας
καὶ γενέσθαι τὸν τόπον ἔρημον, καθ' ὃν ὁ κίνδυνος ἦν,
εὐθέως τοῖς πρώτοις τέλεσι τῶν φαλαγγιτῶν ἐπ' ἀσπίδα κλίνων, προῆγε μετὰ δρόμου, τηρῶν τὰς τάξεις.
3 καταλαβόμενος δὲ τὸν ἐκλειφθέντα τόπον ὀξέως, ἅμα
μὲν ἀπετέτμητο τοὺς διώκοντας, ἅμα δ' ὑπερδέξιος
4 ἐγεγόνει τοῦ τῶν πολεμίων κέρατος. καὶ τοὺς μὲν
φαλαγγίτας αὐτοῦ παρεκάλει θαρρεῖν καὶ μένειν, ἕως
5 ἂν παραγγείλῃ ποιεῖσθαι τὴν ἐπαγωγὴν ἀναμίξ· Πο-
λυαίνῳ δ' ἐπέταξε τῷ Μεγαλοπολίτῃ τοὺς περιλειπο-
μένους καὶ τοὺς διακεκλικότας τὴν φυγὴν Ἰλλυριοὺς

lost it unexpectedly turn the tables and restore the situation by their dexterity. This was very clearly illustrated by the conduct of both the two commanders on the present occasion. For when the whole Achaean mercenary force gave way and their left wing was broken, Machanidas, instead of keeping to his original intention to outflank the enemy on one side and by a direct attack on the other to strike a decisive blow, did neither, but with childish lack of self-control rushed forward to join his own mercenaries and fall upon the fugitives, as if terror alone were not sufficient to drive them as far as the gate once they had given way.

15. The Achaean commander did his best to rally the mercenaries, calling on their leaders by name and encouraging them, but when he saw that they were forced back he neither fled in dismay, nor lost heart and gave up hope, but posting himself on the wing of his phalanx, and waiting till the pursuers had passed by and left the ground on which the action had taken place clear, he at once had the first section of the phalanx make a left turn and advanced at the double but without breaking his ranks, and rapidly occupying the ground which the enemy had abandoned, both cut off the pursuers and at the same time outflanked the Spartan wing. He exhorted the men of his phalanx to be of good heart and wait until he gave the order for a general charge. He commanded Polyaenus[33] of Megalopolis to collect rapidly all those of the Illyrians, cuirassed infantry, and

---

[33] The name is not certain.

καὶ θωρακίτας καὶ μισθοφόρους συναθροίσαντι μετὰ
σπουδῆς ἐφεδρεύειν τῷ κέρατι τῆς φάλαγγος καὶ
τηρεῖν τὴν ἐπάνοδον τῶν ἐκ διώγματος ἀναχωρούν-
6 των. οἱ δὲ Λακεδαιμόνιοι χωρὶς παραγγέλματος, ἐπαρθέντες ταῖς διανοίαις ἐπὶ τῷ τῶν εὐζώνων προτερή-
ματι, καταβαλόντες τὰς σαρίσας ὥρμησαν ἐπὶ τοὺς
7 ὑπεναντίους. ὅτε δὲ κατὰ τὴν ἐπαγωγὴν προάγοντες
ἧκον ἐπὶ τὸ τῆς τάφρου χεῖλος, τὰ μὲν οὐκέτι διδόντος
τοῦ καιροῦ μεταμέλειαν ὥστ᾽ ἐν χερσὶν ὄντας τῶν
πολεμίων ἀναστρέφειν, τὰ δὲ καὶ τῆς τάφρου κατα-
φρονήσαντες διὰ τὸ τὴν κατάβασιν ἔχειν ἐκ πολλοῦ
καὶ μήθ᾽ ὕδωρ κατὰ τὸ θέρος ἐν αὐτῇ μήτε τιν᾽ ἀγρίαν
ὕλην ὑπάρχειν, ὥρμησαν ἀνεπιστάτως διὰ ταύτης.

16. Ὁ δὲ Φιλοποίμην ἅμα τῷ παραπεσεῖν κατὰ τῶν
ὑπεναντίων τὸν ἐκ πολλῶν χρόνων ἑωραμένον ὑπ᾽
αὐτοῦ καιρόν τότε πᾶσιν ἐπάγειν τοῖς φαλαγγίταις
2 καταβαλοῦσι τὰς σαρίσας παρήγγειλε. τῶν δ᾽ Ἀχαιῶν ὁμοθυμαδὸν καὶ μετὰ καταπληκτικῆς κραυγῆς
ποιησαμένων τὴν ἔφοδον, οἱ μὲν προδιαλελυκότες τὰς
τάξεις τῶν Λακεδαιμονίων ἐν τῇ τῆς τάφρου κατα-
<βάσει πάλιν ἀνα>βαίνοντες πρὸς ὑπερδεξίους τοὺς
3 πολεμίους ἀποδειλιάσαντες ἐτρέποντο· τὸ δὲ πολὺ
πλῆθος ἐν αὐτῇ τῇ τάφρῳ διεφθείρετο, τὸ μὲν ὑπὸ τῶν
4 Ἀχαιῶν, τὸ δ᾽ ὑπὸ τῶν ἰδίων. συνέβαινε δὲ τὸ προειρημένον οὐκ αὐτομάτως οὐδ᾽ ἐκ τοῦ καιροῦ, διὰ δὲ
τὴν ἀγχίνοιαν τοῦ προεστῶτος, <ὃς> εὐθέως προεβά-
5 λετο τὴν τάφρον. ὁ δὲ Φιλοποίμην οὐ φυγομαχῶν, ὥς
τινες ὑπελάμβανον, ἀλλὰ καὶ λίαν ἀκριβῶς καὶ στρα-

mercenaries who were left behind or had evaded the pursuit, and to support the wing of the phalanx and wait for the return of the pursuers. The Lacedaemonian phalanx now, without orders but elated by the success of the light-armed troops, leveled their spears and charged the enemy. When in charging they reached the edge of the ditch, partly because they had no longer time to change their minds and retrace their steps as they were at close quarters with the enemy, and partly since they made light of the ditch as its descent was gentle and it had neither water nor bushes in the heat of the summer,[34] they dashed through it without hesitating.

16. When he saw that the chance of smiting the enemy that had so long been present to his mind had at length arrived, Philopoemen ordered the whole phalanx to level their spears and charge. When the Achaeans, like one man and with a loud cheer that cast terror into their foes, rushed on them, those of the Lacedaemonians who had broken their ranks and descended into the ditch, lost courage as they mounted the bank to meet the enemy above their heads and took to flight. The greater number of them perished in the ditch itself, killed either by the Achaeans or by each other. And this result was not due to chance or to momentary luck, but to the sagacity of the commander in at once protecting his men by the ditch. This he did not with the desire to avoid an encounter as was supposed by some, but calculating everything accurately like the expert

---

[34] Causabon's brilliant emendation of τέλος to θέρος is confirmed by *P. Rylands* I 60, col. IV 38 κατὰ [τὸ θ]έρος.

THE HISTORIES OF POLYBIUS

τηγικῶς ἕκαστα συλλογισάμενος, ὅτι παραγενόμενος
ὁ Μαχανίδας, εἰ μὲν προσάξει τὴν δύναμιν οὐ προ-
ϊδόμενος τὴν τάφρον, οὕτω συμβήσεται παθεῖν αὐτῷ
τὴν φάλαγγα ⟨τὸ⟩ προειρημένον νῦν, γινόμενον δὲ
6 τότ᾽ ἐπὶ τῆς ἀληθείας· εἰ δὲ συλλογισάμενος τὴν
δυσχρηστίαν τῆς τάφρου, κἄπειτα μεταμεληθεὶς καὶ
δόξας ἀποδειλιᾶν, ἐκ παρατεταγμένων ἀπολύσει καὶ
μακρὰν αὐτὸν ἐν πορείᾳ διδόναι μέλλει, διότι χωρὶς
ὁλοσχεροῦς ἀγῶνος αὐτῷ μὲν τὸ νικᾶν, ἐκείνῳ δὲ
7 τἀναντία περιέσται. πολλοῖς γὰρ ἤδη τοῦτο συμβέβηκεν, οἵτινες παραταξάμενοι μέν, οὐκ ἀξιόχρεως
ἔκριναν σφᾶς αὐτοὺς εἶναι τοῖς ὑπεναντίοις ἀγωνί-
8 ζεσθαι, τινὲς μὲν διὰ τόπους, οἱ δὲ διὰ πλῆθος, οἱ δὲ
δι᾽ ἄλλας αἰτίας, μακρὰν ἑαυτοὺς δόντες ἐν πορείᾳ,
κατὰ τὴν ἀπόλυσιν δι᾽ αὐτῶν τῶν οὐραγούντων ἤλπι-
σαν οἱ μὲν προτερήσειν, οἱ δ᾽ ἀσφαλῶς ἀπολυθήσεσθαι
9 τῶν πολεμίων. ἐν οἷς δὴ καὶ μέγιστα συμβαίνει τοὺς
ἡγουμένους.

17. Πλὴν ὅ γε Φιλοποίμην οὐ διεψεύσθη τῇ προνοίᾳ τοῦ συντελεσθησομένου· τροπὴν ⟨γὰρ⟩ ἰσχυρὰν
2 συνέβαινε γίνεσθαι τῶν Λακεδαιμονίων. συνορῶν δὲ
τὴν φάλαγγα νικῶσαν καὶ τὰ ὅλα καλῶς αὐτῷ προχω-
ροῦντα καὶ λαμπρῶς, ἐπὶ τὸ καταλειπόμενον ὥρμησε
τῆς ὅλης ἐπιβολῆς· τοῦτο δ᾽ ἦν τὸ μὴ διαφυγεῖν τὸν
3 Μαχανίδαν. εἰδὼς οὖν αὐτὸν κατὰ ⟨τὴν⟩ τοῦ διώγματος παράπτωσιν ἀποτετμημένον ἐν τοῖς πρὸς τὴν
πόλιν μέρεσι τῆς τάφρου μετὰ τῶν ἰδίων μισθοφόρων,
4 ἐκαραδόκει τὴν τούτου παρουσίαν. ὁ δὲ Μαχανίδας,

general he was and foreseeing that if Machanidas, when he came up, led his force forward without reckoning on the ditch, the phalanx would suffer the fate which I have just described and which on that occasion it did suffer in reality, whereas if the tyrant took into consideration the difficulty presented by the ditch, and changing his mind, seemed to shirk an encounter, breaking up his formation and exposing himself in long marching order, he would then without a general engagement himself secure victory while Machanidas would suffer defeat. This has already happened to many, who after drawing up in order of battle, judging[35] that they were not equal to engaging the enemy, either owing to their position or owing to their inferiority in numbers or for any other reason, have exposed themselves in a long marching column, hoping as they retired to succeed, by the sole aid of their rearguard, either in getting the better of the enemy or in making good their escape. This is a most frequent cause of error on the part of commanders.

17. But Philopoemen was by no means deceived in his anticipation of what the result would be; for the Lacedaemonians were completely routed. When he saw his phalanx victorious and everything going on splendidly for himself he turned his mind to the remainder of his project, which was to prevent the escape of Machanidas. Knowing that in his unwise pursuit he had been cut off together with his mercenaries on the side of the ditch lying nearest the town, he was waiting for his reappearance. Machanidas on

[35] *P. Rylands* I 60, col. VI 58 gives the true reading for what was a lacuna before.

συνθεωρήσας κατὰ τὴν ἀπόλυσιν τὴν ἀπὸ τοῦ διώγματος φεύγουσαν τὴν αὑτοῦ δύναμιν, καὶ συλλογισάμενος διότι προπέπτωκε καὶ διέψευσται τῆς ὅλης
ἐλπίδος, εὐθέως ἐπειρᾶτο συστραφεὶς μεθ' ὧν εἶχε
περὶ αὑτὸν ξένων, ἄθρους διαπεσεῖν διὰ τῶν ἐσκε-
5 δασμένων καὶ διωκόντων. εἰς ἃ καὶ συνορῶντες ἔνιοι
συνέμενον αὐτῷ τὰς ἀρχάς, ταύτην ἔχοντες τὴν ἐλ-
6 πίδα τῆς σωτηρίας. ὡς δὲ παραγενόμενοι συνεῖδον
τοὺς Ἀχαιοὺς τηροῦντας τὴν ἐπὶ τῆς τάφρου γέφυραν,
τότε δὴ πάντες ἐξαθυμήσαντες ἀπέρρεον ἀπ' αὐτοῦ,
7 καὶ καθ' ἑαυτὸν ἕκαστος ἐπορίζετο τὴν σωτηρίαν. καθ'
ὃν δὴ καιρὸν ὁ τύραννος ἀπογνοὺς τὴν διὰ τῆς γεφύρας ὁδὸν παρήλαυνε παρὰ τὴν τάφρον, ἐνεργῶς διάβασιν ζητῶν.

18. Ὁ δὲ Φιλοποίμην, ἐπιγνοὺς τὸν Μαχανίδαν ἀπό
τε τῆς πορφυρίδος καὶ τοῦ περὶ τὸν ἵππον κόσμου,
τοὺς μὲν περὶ τὸν Ἀναξίδαμον ἀπολείπει, παρακαλέσας τηρεῖν ἐπιμελῶς τὴν δίοδον καὶ μηδενὸς φείδεσθαι τῶν μισθοφόρων διὰ τὸ τούτους εἶναι τοὺς συν-
2 αὐξοντας αἰεὶ τὰς ἐν τῇ Σπάρτῃ τυραννίδας· αὐτὸς δὲ
παραλαβὼν Πολύαινον τὸν Κυπαρισσέα καὶ Σιμίαν,
οἷς ἐχρῆτο τότε παρασπισταῖς, ἐκ τοῦ πέραν τῆς
τάφρου τὴν ἀντιπαραγωγὴν ἐποιεῖτο τῷ τυράννῳ καὶ
3 τοῖς μετ' αὐτοῦ· δύο γὰρ ἦσαν οἱ τότε τῷ Μαχανίδᾳ
συμμίξαντες, Ἀρηξίδαμος καὶ τῶν μισθοφόρων εἷς.
4 ἅμα δὲ τῷ τὸν Μαχανίδαν κατά τινα τόπον εὔβατον
τῆς τάφρου, προσθέντα τοὺς μύωπας, βίᾳ τὸν ἵππον
ἐπάγειν καὶ διαπερᾶν, συναγαγὼν ἐκ μεταβολῆς ὁ

observing when he had desisted from the pursuit that his troops were in flight, and on realizing that he had advanced too far and thereby lost the day, at once attempted to make the mercenaries he had round him close up and force their way in a compact body through the scattered ranks of the pursuers. Some of them with this end in view remained with him at first, hoping thus to get off safe, but when they got up to the ditch and saw that the Achaeans were holding the bridge over it, they all lost heart and dropped off from him, each attempting to save himself as best he could. Meanwhile the tyrant, despairing of making his way across the bridge, rode along the ditch trying with all his might to find a crossing.

18. Recognizing Machanidas by his purple cloak and the trappings of his horse, Philopoemen left Anaxidamus[36] with orders to guard the passage carefully and spare none of the mercenaries, as they were the men who had always maintained the power of the Spartan tyrants. Taking with him Polyaenus of Cyparissia and Simias,[37] who acted at the time as his aides-de-camp, he followed the tyrant and those with him—there were two who had joined him, Arexidamus and one of the mercenaries—along the opposite side of the ditch. When Machanidas, on reaching a place where the ditch was easily passable, set spurs to his

[36] Unknown.
[37] Unknown.

Φιλοποίμην αὐτῷ καὶ πατάξας τῷ δόρατι καιρίως, καὶ
προσενεγκὼν τῷ σαυρωτῆρι πληγὴν ἄλλην ἐκ δια-
5 λήψεως, ἐν χειρῶν νόμῳ διέφθειρε τὸν τύραννον. τὸ δὲ
παραπλήσιον ἐγίνετο καὶ περὶ τὸν Ἀρηξίδαμον ὑπὸ
τῶν παρίππων. ὁ δὲ τρίτος ἀπογνοὺς τὴν διάβασιν
διέφυγε τὸν κίνδυνον κατὰ τὸν τῶν προειρημένων
6 φόνον. πεσόντων δ᾽ ἀμφοτέρων, εὐθέως οἱ περὶ τὸν
Σιμίαν, σκυλεύσαντες τοὺς νεκροὺς καὶ συναφελόντες
ἅμα τοῖς ὅπλοις τὴν τοῦ τυράννου κεφαλήν, ἠπείγοντο
7 πρὸς τοὺς διώκοντας, σπεύδοντες ἐπιδεῖξαι τοῖς
ὄχλοις τὴν ἀπώλειαν τοῦ τῶν ὑπεναντίων ἡγεμόνος
χάριν τοῦ πιστεύσαντας ἔτι μᾶλλον ἀνυπόπτως καὶ
τεθαρρηκότως ποιήσασθαι τὸν ἐπιδιωγμὸν τῶν ὑπ-
8 εναντίων ἕως τῆς Τεγεατῶν πόλεως. ὃ καὶ μεγάλα
συνεβάλετο πρὸς τὴν ὁρμὴν τῶν ὄχλων· οὐ γὰρ
ἥκιστα διὰ τούτων τῆς μὲν Τεγέας ἐξ ἐφόδου κύριοι
κατέστησαν, ταῖς δ᾽ ἐχομέναις παρὰ τὸν Εὐρώταν
ἐστρατοπέδευον, κρατοῦντες ἤδη τῶν ὑπαίθρων ἀναμ-
9 φισβητήτως. καὶ πολλῶν χρόνων οὐ δυνάμενοι τοὺς
πολεμίους ἐκ τῆς οἰκείας ἀπώσασθαι, τότε πᾶσαν
10 ἀδεῶς ἐπόρθουν αὐτοὶ τὴν Λακωνικήν, τῶν μὲν ἰδίων
οὐ πολλοὺς ἀπολωλεκότες ἐν τῇ μάχῃ, τῶν δὲ Λακεδαιμονίων ἀπεκτακότες μὲν οὐκ ἐλάττους τῶν τετρακισχιλίων, ζωγρίᾳ δ᾽ εἰληφότες ἔτι πλείους τούτων,
ὁμοίως δὲ καὶ τῆς ἀποσκευῆς κεκυριευκότες ἁπάσης
καὶ τῶν ὅπλων.

horse and forced it across, Philopoemen turned to meet him. Giving him a mortal wound with his spear and adding yet another thrust with the lower end of it, he slew the tyrant hand to hand.[38] Arexidamus[39] suffered the same fate at the hands of the two officers who rode with Philopoemen, and after the death of the two the third man, despairing of crossing, sought safety in flight. When both had fallen Simias and his companion stripped the bodies and taking the armor and the head of the tyrant hastened back to the pursuers, eager to show to their men those proofs of the death of the enemy's commander, so that believing the evidence of their eyes they might with increased confidence and fearlessness continue the pursuit of the enemy as far as Tegea. And the sight did as a fact much contribute to the spirit of the soldiers; for it was chiefly owing to this that they captured Tegea by storm, and a few days after were encamped on the banks of the Eurotas, already in undisputed command of the country. For many years they had been unable to repulse the enemy from their own land, and now they themselves fearlessly pillaged Laconia, having suffered little loss in the battle, but having not only slain as many as four thousand Lacedaemonians but captured a still greater number and made themselves masters of all the baggage and arms.

[38] The deed was celebrated by a statue the Achaeans erected at Delphi which showed Philopoemen in the posture of striking his enemy: *FD* III 1.47 with Plu. *Philop*.10.8 and G. Daux, *BCH* 90 (1966), 285–291.

[39] Unknown.

IV. RES ITALIAE

19a. Ὅτι φησὶν ὁ Πολύβιος, τί γὰρ ὄφελός ἐστι τοῖς ἀναγινώσκουσι διεξιέναι πολέμους καὶ μάχας
(18a) καὶ πόλεων ἐξανδραποδισμοὺς καὶ πολιορκίας, εἰ μὴ τὰς αἰτίας ἐπιγνώσονται, παρ' ἃς ἐν ἑκάστοις οἱ μὲν
2 κατώρθωσαν, οἱ δ' ἐσφάλησαν; τὰ γὰρ τέλη τῶν πράξεων ψυχαγωγεῖ μόνον τοὺς ἀκούοντας, αἱ δὲ πρόσθεν διαλήψεις τῶν ἐπιβαλλομένων ἐξεταζόμεναι
3 δεόντως ὠφελοῦσι τοὺς φιλομαθοῦντας. μάλιστα δὲ πάντων ὁ κατὰ μέρος χειρισμὸς ἑκάστων ἐπιδεικνύμενος ἐπανορθοῖ τοὺς συνεφιστάνοντας. . . .

19. Τίς οὐκ ἂν ἐπισημήναιτο τὴν ἡγεμονίαν καὶ τὴν ἀρετὴν καὶ τὴν δύναμιν ἐν τοῖς ὑπαίθροις τἀνδρός,
2 βλέψας εἰς τὸ μῆκος τούτου τοῦ χρόνου, καὶ συνεπιστήσας αὐτὸν ἐπί τε τὰς καθόλου καὶ τὰς κατὰ μέρος μάχας καὶ πολιορκίας καὶ πόλεων μεταβολὰς καὶ περιστάσεις καιρῶν, ἐπί τε τὴν περιοχὴν τῆς ὅλης
3 ἐπιβολῆς καὶ πράξεως, ἐν ᾗ συνεχῶς Ἀννίβας ἑκκαίδεκα πολεμήσας ἔτη Ῥωμαίοις κατὰ τὴν Ἰταλίαν οὐδέποτε διέλυσε τὰς δυνάμεις ἐκ τῶν ὑπαίθρων, ἀλλὰ συνέχων ὑφ' αὑτόν, ὥσπερ ἀγαθὸς κυβερνήτης, ἀστασίαστα διετήρησε τοσαῦτα πλήθη καὶ πρὸς αὑτὸν καὶ πρὸς ἄλληλα, καίπερ οὐχ οἷον ὁμοεθνέσιν, ἀλλ' οὐδ'
4 ὁμοφύλοις χρησάμενος στρατοπέδοις. εἶχε γὰρ Λίβυας, Ἴβηρας, Λιγυστίνους, Κελτούς, Φοίνικας, Ἰτα-

---

40 Complements and varies 9.22–26.11; the assessment of

IV. AFFAIRS OF ITALY

19a. What is the use of recounting to our readers wars and battles and the sieges and captures of cities, if they are not likewise informed of the causes to which in each case success or failure was due? For the results of actions merely fascinate readers, but the previous decisions of those responsible, when the inquiry is properly conducted, is of benefit to students. Most salutary of all to those who give due attention to it is an exposition of the detailed management of each particular question.

Hannibal

19. No one can withhold admiration for Hannibal's generalship,[40] courage, and power in the field, who considers the length of this period, and carefully reflects on the major and minor battles, on the sieges he undertook, on defections of cities from one side to the other, on the difficulties that at times faced him, and in a word on the whole scope of his design and its execution, a design in the pursuit of which, having constantly fought the Romans for sixteen years, he never broke up his forces and dismissed them from the field, but holding them together under his personal command, like a good ship's captain, kept such a large army free from sedition toward him or among themselves, and this although his regiments were not only of different nationalities but of different races. For he had with him Africans, Spaniards, Ligurians, Celts, Phoeni-

Hannibal's character is here followed by his evaluation as a commander.

THE HISTORIES OF POLYBIUS

λούς, Ἕλληνας, οἷς οὐ νόμος, οὐκ ἔθος, οὐ λόγος, οὐχ
ἕτερον οὐδὲν ἦν κοινὸν ἐκ φύσεως πρὸς ἀλλήλους.
5 ἀλλ᾽ ὅμως ἡ τοῦ προεστῶτος ἀγχίνοια τὰς τηλικαύτας
καὶ τοιαύτας διαφορὰς ἑνὸς ἐποίει προστάγματος
ἀκούειν καὶ μιᾷ πείθεσθαι γνώμῃ, καίπερ οὐχ ἁπλῆς
οὔσης τῆς περιστάσεως, ἀλλὰ καὶ ποικίλης, καὶ πολλάκις μὲν αὐτοῖς λαμπρᾶς ἐπιπνεούσης τῆς τύχης,
6 ποτὲ δὲ τοὐναντίον. ἐξ ὧν εἰκότως ἄν τις θαυμάσειε
τὴν τοῦ προεστῶτος δύναμιν ἐν τούτῳ τῷ μέρει, καὶ
θαρρῶν εἴπειεν ὡς εἴπερ ποιησάμενος τὴν ἀρχὴν ἐπ᾽
ἄλλα μέρη τῆς οἰκουμένης ἐπὶ τελευταίους ἦλθε Ῥω-
7 μαίους, οὐδὲν ἂν τῶν προτεθέντων αὐτὸν διέφυγε. νῦν
δ᾽, ἐφ᾽ οὓς ἔδει τελευταίους ἐλθεῖν, ἀπὸ τούτων ἀρξά-
μενος, ἐν τούτοις ἐποιήσατο καὶ τὴν ἀρχὴν τῶν πράξεων καὶ τὸ τέλος.

V. RES HISPANIAE

20. Οἱ μὲν οὖν περὶ τὸν Ἀσδρούβαν, ἀθροίσαντες
τὴν στρατιὰν ἐκ τῶν πόλεων, ἐν αἷς ἐποιοῦντο τὴν
παραχειμασίαν, προῆλθον, καὶ κατεστρατοπέδευσαν
οὐ μακρὰν ἀπὸ τῆς πόλεως τῆς προσαγορευομένης
Ἰλίπας, βαλόμενοι τὸν χάρακα πρὸς ταῖς ὑπωρείαις,
καὶ προθέμενοι πεδία πρὸς ἀγῶνα καὶ μάχην εὐφυῆ.
2 πλῆθος δὲ πεζῶν μὲν εἶχον εἰς ἑπτὰ μυριάδας, ἱππεῖς
δὲ τετρακισχιλίους, θηρία δὲ δυσὶ πλείω τῶν τρι-

300

cians, Italians, and Greeks, peoples who neither in their laws, customs, or language, nor in any other respect had anything naturally in common. But, nevertheless, the ability of their commander forced men so radically different to give ear to a single word of command and yield obedience to a single will. And this he did not under simple conditions but under very complicated ones, the gale of fortune blowing often strongly in their favor and at other times against them. Therefore we cannot but justly admire Hannibal in these respects and pronounce with confidence that had he begun with the other parts of the world and finished with the Romans none of his plans would have failed to succeed. But as it was, commencing with those whom he should have left to the last, his career began and finished in this field.

V. AFFAIRS OF SPAIN

The Defeat of Hasdrubal, Son of Gisco, by Publius Scipio

20. Hasdrubal, collecting his forces from the towns in which they had passed the winter, advanced and encamped not far from the town called Ilipa,[41] entrenching himself just under the hills with a level space in front favorably situated for giving battle. He had about seventy thousand infantry, four thousand horse, and thirty-two ele-

206 B.C.

---

[41] A village on the Guadalquivir, fourteen kilometers north of Seville. *RE* Ilipa 1066 (A. Schulten). For the site of the battle, see H. H. Scullard, *JRS* 26 (1936), 19–23 and pl. VI.

3 ἄκοντα· Πόπλιος δὲ Μάρκον μὲν Ἰούνιον ἐξαπέστειλε
πρὸς Κολίχαντα, παραληψόμενον τὰς ἑτοιμασθείσας
αὐτῷ παρὰ τούτου δυνάμεις· αὗται δ' ἦσαν πεζοὶ μὲν
4 τρισχίλιοι, ἱππεῖς δὲ πεντακόσιοι· τοὺς δὲ λοιποὺς
συμμάχους αὐτὸς παρελάμβανε, προάγων καὶ ποιού-
5 μενος τὴν πορείαν ἐπὶ τὸ προκείμενον. ἐγγίσας δὲ τῷ
Κασταλῶνι καὶ τοῖς περὶ Βαίκυλα τόποις, καὶ συμ-
μίξας ἐνθάδε τῷ Μάρκῳ καὶ ταῖς παρὰ τοῦ Κολίχαν-
τος δυνάμεσιν, εἰς πολλὴν ἀπορίαν ἐνέπιπτε περὶ τῶν
6 ἐνεστώτων. χωρὶς γὰρ τῶν συμμάχων οὐκ ἀξιόχρεοι
<παρ>ῆσαν αἱ Ῥωμαϊκαὶ δυνάμεις αὐτῷ πρὸς τὸ δια-
κινδυνεύειν· τὸ δ' ἐπὶ τοῖς συμμάχοις ἔχοντας τὰς
ἐλπίδας ὑπὲρ τῶν ὅλων κινδυνεύειν ἐπισφαλὲς ἐδόκει
7 καὶ λίαν εἶναι παράβολον. οὐ μὴν ἀλλὰ διαπορήσας,
ὑπὸ δὲ τῶν πραγμάτων συγκλειόμενος, ἐπὶ τὸ συγ-
χρῆσθαι κατηνέχθη τοῖς Ἴβηρσιν οὕτως ὥστε φαντασίαν μὲν παρασκευάζειν τοῖς ὑπεναντίοις, τὸν δ'
8 ἀγῶνα ποιεῖσθαι διὰ τῶν ἰδίων στρατοπέδων. ταῦτα
δὲ προθέμενος ἀνέζευξε μετὰ πάσης τῆς δυνάμεως,
ἔχων πεζοὺς μὲν εἰς τετρακισμυρίους καὶ πεντακισ-
9 χιλίους, ἱππεῖς δὲ περὶ τρισχιλίους. ἐγγίσας δὲ τοῖς
Καρχηδονίοις καὶ γενόμενος σύνοπτος ἐστρατοπέ-
δευσε περί τινας γεωλόφους καταντικρὺ τῶν πολεμίων.

21. Μάγων δὲ νομίσας εὐφυῆ καιρὸν ἐπιθέσθαι
καταστρατοπεδεύουσι τοῖς Ῥωμαίοις, ἀναλαβὼν τὸ
πλεῖστον μέρος τῶν ἰδίων ἱππέων καὶ Μασαννάσαν
μετὰ τῶν Νομάδων, ἤλαυνε πρὸς τὴν παρεμβολήν,

phants. Scipio sent off Marcus Junius[42] to Colichas[43] to take over the forces that the latter had got ready for him, which consisted of three thousand foot and five hundred horse. The rest of the allies he took with himself and advanced marching to encounter the enemy. When he drew near Castalon and the neighborhood of Baecula and there joined Marcus and the troops sent by Colichas, he found the situation a very embarrassing one. For without the allies the Roman troops at his disposal were not sufficient for him to risk a battle, while it seemed to him dangerous, and far too risky, to rely on the support of the allies in what promised to be a decisive engagement. However, though he hesitated, he found himself forced by circumstances and was reduced to employing the Spaniards, using them for the purpose of impressing the enemy by an imposing show but leaving the actual fighting to his own legions. With this purpose he left with his whole army, consisting of about forty-five thousand foot and three thousand horse. When he got near the Carthaginians and was in full sight of them he encamped on certain low hills opposite to the enemy.

21. Mago,[44] thinking it a favorable occasion to attack the Romans as they were forming their camp, took most of his own cavalry and Massanissa[45] with his Numidians and charged the camp, being convinced that he would find

[42] M. Iunius Silanus, since 210 with Scipio in Spain. In 207 he defeated and captured the Carthaginian general Hanno. *RE* Iunius 1092–1093 (F. Münzer).

[43] Culchas in Livy, a Spanish dynast.

[44] Hannibal's youngest brother. *RE* Mago 499–505 (V. Ehrenberg).   [45] See n. on 9.25.4.

2 πεπεισμένος ἀφυλακτοῦντα λήψεσθαι τὸν Πόπλιον. ὁ
δὲ πάλαι προορώμενος τὸ μέλλον, ὑπό τινα βουνὸν
ὑπεστάλκει τοὺς ἱππεῖς, ἴσους ⟨τοῖς⟩ τῶν Καρχηδο-
3 νίων· ὧν ἀνυπονοήτως ἐμπεσόντων πολλοὶ μὲν ἐν ταῖς
ἀρχαῖς ἀναστρέφοντες διὰ τὸ παράδοξον τῆς ἐπιφανείας ⟨τῆς⟩ ἄφνω τῶν ἱππέων ἀπέπεσον, οἱ δὲ λοιποὶ
4 συμβάλλοντες τοῖς πολεμίοις ἐμάχοντο γενναίως. τῇ
δὲ παρὰ τῶν καταβαινόντων ἐν τοῖς Ῥωμαϊκοῖς ἱππεῦσιν εὐχειρίᾳ δυσχρηστούμενοι καὶ πολλοὺς ἀπολλύν-
τες οἱ Καρχηδόνιοι, βραχὺ προσαντισχόντες ἐνέκλι-
5 ναν. καὶ τὸ μὲν πρῶτον ἐν τάξει τὴν ἀναχώρησιν
ἐποιοῦντο, τῶν δὲ Ῥωμαίων ἐγκειμένων αὐτοῖς λύσαν-
τες τὰς ἴλας κατέφυγον ὑπὸ τὴν αὐτῶν παρεμβολήν.
6 οἱ μὲν οὖν Ῥωμαῖοι τούτου γενομένου θαρραλεώτερον
διέκειντο πρὸς τὸν κίνδυνον, οἱ δὲ Καρχηδόνιοι τοὐ-
7 ναντίον. οὐ μὴν ἀλλὰ ταῖς ἑξῆς ἐπί τινας ἡμέρας τάς
τε δυνάμεις ἐκτάξαντες ἐν τῷ μεταξὺ πεδίῳ ⟨καὶ⟩ διὰ
τῶν ἱππέων καὶ διὰ τῶν εὐζώνων ἀκροβολισμοὺς ποιησάμενοι καὶ καταπειράσαντες ἀλλήλων, ὥρμησαν
ἐπὶ τὸ κρίνειν τὰ ὅλα.

22. Κατὰ δὲ τὸν καιρὸν τοῦτον δυσὶ δοκεῖ κεχρῆ-
2 σθαι στρατηγήμασιν ὁ Πόπλιος. θεωρῶν γὰρ τὸν
Ἀσδρούβαν ὀψὲ ποιούμενον τὰς ἐξαγωγάς, καὶ μέσους Λίβυας, τὰ δὲ θηρία προτιθέμενον ἑκατέρων τῶν
κεράτων, αὐτὸς εἰωθὼς τῇ μὲν ὥρᾳ προσανατείνειν,
3 τοὺς δὲ Ῥωμαίους μέσους ἀντιτάττειν τοῖς Λίβυσι,
τοὺς δ᾽ Ἴβηρας ἐπὶ τῶν κεράτων παρεμβάλλειν, ᾗ
προέθετο κρίνειν ἡμέρᾳ, τἀναντία τοῖς προειρημένοις

Scipio off his guard. Scipio, however, had long foreseen what would happen, and had stationed his cavalry, who were equal in number to those of the Carthaginians, under a hill. Surprised by this unexpected attack many of the Carthaginians as they wheeled sharply round at the unexpected sight, lost their seats, but the rest met the enemy and fought bravely. Thrown, however, into difficulties by the dexterity with which the Roman horsemen dismounted, and losing many of their numbers, the Carthaginians gave way after a short resistance. At first they retired in good order, but when the Romans pressed them hard, the squadrons broke up and they took refuge under their own camp. After this the Romans displayed greater eagerness to engage and the Carthaginians less. However, for several days following they drew up their forces on the level ground between them, and after trying their strength by skirmishing with their cavalry and light infantry, finally resolved on a decisive action.

22. On this occasion we see Scipio employing two different stratagems. Observing that Hasdrubal always brought his troops out of camp at a late hour and drew them up with the Libyans in the center and the elephants in front of the two wings, and having himself been in the habit of delaying until a still later hour and of opposing his Romans to the Libyans in the center and stationing the Spaniards on his wings, he acted on the day on which he

ποιήσας μεγάλα συνήργησε ταῖς σφετέραις δυνάμεσι
πρὸς τὸ νικᾶν, οὐκ ὀλίγα δ' ἠλάττωσε τοὺς πολεμίους.

4 ἅμα γὰρ τῷ φωτὶ διαπεμψάμενος τοὺς ὑπηρέτας παρήγγειλε πᾶσι τοῖς χιλιάρχοις καὶ τοῖς στρατιώταις
ἀριστοποιησαμένους καὶ καθοπλισαμένους ἐξάγειν

5 πρὸ τοῦ χάρακος. γενομένου δὲ τούτου καὶ προθύμως
πειθαρχησάντων διὰ τὴν ὑπόνοιαν τοῦ μέλλοντος,
τοὺς μὲν ἱππεῖς καὶ τοὺς εὐζώνους προαπέστειλε,
συντάξας ἐγγίζειν τῇ παρεμβολῇ τῶν ὑπεναντίων καὶ

6 προσακροβολίζεσθαι θρασέως, αὐτὸς δὲ τοὺς πεζοὺς
ἔχων ἄρτι τῆς κατὰ τὸν ἥλιον ἀνατολῆς ἐπιφαινομέ-
νης προῆγε, καὶ παραγενόμενος εἰς μέσον τὸ πεδίον
παρενέβαλε, τάττων ἐναντίως ἢ πρόσθεν· μέσους μὲν
γὰρ ἐτίθει τοὺς Ἴβηρας, ἐπὶ δὲ τῶν κεράτων τὰ τῶν

7 Ῥωμαίων. τοῖς δὲ Καρχηδονίοις, ἄφνω συνεγγιζόντων πρὸς τὸν χάρακα τῶν ἱππέων, ἅμα δὲ καὶ τῆς
ἄλλης δυνάμεως ἐκταττομένης ἐν ὄψει, μόλις ἐδόθη

8 καιρὸς εἰς τὸ καθοπλίσασθαι. διόπερ ἠναγκάσθησαν
οἱ περὶ τὸν Ἀσδρούβαν ἔτι νήστεις ἔχοντες τοὺς
ἄνδρας ἀπαρασκεύως ἐκ τοῦ καιροῦ τοὺς μὲν ἱππεῖς
καὶ τοὺς εὐζώνους ἐπαφιέναι τοῖς ἱππεῦσι τῶν ὑπεναντίων εἰς τὰ πεδία, τὰς δὲ πεζικὰς δυνάμεις παρατάττειν, οὐ πολὺ τῆς παρωρείας ἐν τοῖς ἐπιπέδοις ποιού-

9 μενοι τὴν ἔκταξιν, καθάπερ ἦν ἔθος αὐτοῖς. ἕως μὲν
οὖν τινος ἔμενον οἱ Ῥωμαῖοι τὴν ἡσυχίαν ἔχοντες·
ἐπειδὴ δὲ τὸ μὲν τῆς ἡμέρας προύβαινε, τῶν δ' εὐζώνων ἄκριτος ἦν καὶ πάρισος ἡ συμπλοκὴ διὰ τὸ
τοὺς πιεζομένους καταφεύγοντας ὑπὸ τὰς ἰδίας φά-

had decided to deliver the decisive battle in a precisely opposite manner, and thus much contributed to the victory of his own army and the discomfiture of the enemy. For as soon as it was light he sent a message by his aides-de-camp to all the tribunes and soldiers to take their morning meal and arm themselves and march out of the camp. When this was done, all showing great zeal in carrying out the order, as they suspected what was in the wind, he sent on the cavalry and light infantry with orders to get close up to the enemy's camp and shoot at him boldly, while he himself with his infantry advanced just as the sun was rising, and when he reached the middle of the plain, formed in order of battle, disposing his troops in an order contrary to that which he had previously used, as he placed the Spaniards in the center and the Romans on the wings. The Carthaginians, upon the enemy's cavalry coming suddenly up to their camp and the rest of his army forming up in full view, scarcely had time to arm themselves. So that Hasdrubal, with his men still fasting, was obliged on the spur of the moment and without any preparation to send off his own cavalry and light infantry to engage those of the enemy on the plain and to draw up his heavy infantry on the level ground at no great distance from the foot of the hill, as was his usual practice. For a certain time the Romans remained inactive, but when, as the day advanced, there was no decisive advantage on either side in the engagement of the light-armed troops, those who were hard pressed al-

10 λαγγας ἐκ μεταβολῆς κινδυνεύειν, τὸ τηνικαῦτα δὲ
διαδεξάμενος ὁ Πόπλιος διὰ τῶν διαστημάτων ἐν ταῖς
σημαίαις εἴσω τοὺς ἀκροβολιζομένους, καὶ μερίσας
ἐφ' ἑκάτερον κέρας ὀπίσω τῶν παρατεταγμένων, πρῶτον μὲν τοὺς γροσφομάχους, ἐπὶ δὲ τούτοις ἐπιβάλλει
τοὺς ἱππεῖς, τὰς μὲν ἀρχὰς μετωπηδὸν ποιούμενος τὴν
11 ἔφοδον· ἀποσχὼν δὲ περὶ <τετρα>στάδιον τῶν ὑπεναντίων, τοὺς μὲν Ἴβηρας τηροῦντας τὰς τάξεις τὸν
αὐτὸν τρόπον ποιεῖσθαι τὴν ἐπαγωγὴν <ἐκέλευσε,
τοῖς δὲ κέρασι> παρήγγειλε, τῷ μὲν δεξιῷ τὰς σημαίας καὶ τὰς ἴλας ἐπιστρέφειν ἐπὶ δόρυ, τῷ δ' εὐωνύμῳ τἀναντία.

23. καὶ λαβὼν αὐτὸς μὲν ἀπὸ τοῦ δεξιοῦ, Λεύκιος δὲ
Μάρκιος καὶ Μάρκος Ἰούνιος ἀπὸ τῶν εὐωνύμων τρεῖς
ἴλας ἱππέων τὰς ἡγουμένας, καὶ πρὸ τούτων γροσφομάχους τοὺς εἰθισμένους καὶ τρεῖς σπείρας—τοῦτο
δὲ καλεῖται τὸ σύνταγμα τῶν πεζῶν παρὰ Ῥωμαίοις
2 κοόρτις—πλὴν οἱ μὲν ἐπ' ἀσπίδα περικλάσαντες τούτους, οἱ δ' ἐπὶ δόρυ, προῆγον ὀρθίους ἐπὶ τοὺς πολεμίους, ἐνεργῆ ποιούμενοι τὴν ἔφοδον, ἀεὶ τῶν ἑξῆς
3 ἐπιβαλλόντων καὶ κατὰ περίκλασιν ἑπομένων. ἐπεὶ δὲ
τούτους μὲν οὐ πολὺ συνέβαινε τῶν πολεμίων ἀπέχειν, τοὺς δ' Ἴβηρας ἐν τῇ κατὰ πρόσωπον πλευρᾷ
τόπον ἱκανὸν ἔτι διεστάναι τῷ βάδην ποιεῖσθαι τὴν
ἐπαγωγήν, προσέβαλλον τοῖς κέρασιν ἀμφοτέροις
ἅμα τοῖς τῶν ὑπεναντίων ὀρθίαις ταῖς Ῥωμαϊκαῖς
4 δυνάμεσι κατὰ τὴν ἐξ ἀρχῆς πρόθεσιν. αἱ δὲ μετὰ
ταῦτα κινήσεις, δι' ὧν συνέβαινε τοὺς ἑπομένους,

ways retreating to the shelter of their respective phalanxes and then issuing forth again to resume the combat, Scipio receiving the skirmishers through the intervals between his maniples distributed them on his wings behind his infantry, placing the velites in front with the horse behind them. At first he made a direct frontal advance, but when at a distance of four stades[46] from the enemy he ordered the Spaniards to continue advancing in the same order ⟨and directed the maniples⟩ and cavalry on the right wing to wheel to the right and those of the left wing to wheel to the left.

23. Then taking, himself from the right wing and Lucius Marcius[47] and Marcus Junius from the left, the leading three troops of horse and in front of them the usual number of velites and three maniples (this body of infantry the Romans call a cohort), they advanced straight on the enemy at a rapid pace, wheeling in the one case to the left and in the other to the right, the rear ranks always following the direction of the front ones. When they were not far away from the enemy, while the Spaniards, who continued their direct advance, were still at some distance, as they were marching slowly, he fell, as he had originally intended, directly on both wings of the enemy with the Roman forces in columns. The subsequent movements, which enabled the rear ranks to get into the same line as

---

[46] The mss. give "one stade," which has been emended by B-W to ⟨τετρα⟩στάδιον (four stades), as Livy 28.14.13 has *quingentos passus*.

[47] Legate under Scipio; *MRR* 1. 300. For the difficult passage 22.11–23.2, see WC 2.301–302.

ἐπιπαρεμβάλλοντας ⟨ἐπὶ⟩ τὴν αὐτὴν εὐθεῖαν τοῖς
ἡγουμένοις, συγκαθίστασθαι τοῖς πολεμίοις εἰς τὴν
μάχην, τὴν ἐναντίαν εἶχον διάθεσιν ἀλλήλαις, καὶ
καθόλου τὸ δεξιὸν κέρας τῷ λαιῷ ⟨καὶ⟩ κατὰ μέρος οἱ
5 πεζοὶ τοῖς ἱππεῦσιν. οἱ μὲν γὰρ ἐπὶ τοῦ δεξιοῦ κέρως
ἱππεῖς μετὰ τῶν εὐζώνων, ἐκ δόρατος ἐπιπαρεμβάλ-
λοντες, ὑπερκερᾶν ἐπειρῶντο τοὺς πολεμίους, οἱ δὲ
6 πεζοὶ τοὐναντίον ἐξ ἀσπίδος παρενέβαλλον· τῶν δὲ
κατὰ τὸ λαιὸν οἱ μὲν ἐν ταῖς σπείραις ἐκ δόρατος, οἱ δ᾽
7 ἱππεῖς μετὰ τῶν γροσφομάχων ἐξ ἡνίας. ἐγεγόνει μὲν
οὖν ἐκ τῶν ἱππέων καὶ τῶν εὐζώνων ἀμφοτέρων τῶν
κεράτων ἐκ ταύτης τῆς κινήσεως τὸ δεξιὸν εὐώνυμον.
8 οὐ μικρὸν λόγον θέμενος ὁ στρατηγὸς τοῦ μείζονος
ἐποιήσατο πρόνοιαν, τοῦ κατὰ τὴν ὑπερκέρασιν, ὀρ-
9 θῶς λογιζόμενος· εἰδέναι μὲν γὰρ δεῖ τὸ γινόμενον,
χρῆσθαι δὲ ταῖς πρὸς τὸν καιρὸν ἁρμοζούσαις κινήσεσιν.

24. Ἐκ δὲ τῆς τούτων συμπλοκῆς τὰ μὲν θηρία διὰ
τῶν γροσφομάχων καὶ τῶν ἱππέων ἀκοντιζόμενα
καὶ διαταραττόμενα πανταχόθεν ἔπασχε μὲν κακῶς,
ἔβλαπτε δ᾽ οὐδὲν ἧττον τοὺς φίλους ἢ τοὺς πολεμίους·
φερόμενα γὰρ εἰκῇ τοὺς ὑποπεσόντας ἐξ ἀμφοῖν αἰεὶ
2 διέφθειρε. τῆς δὲ πεζικῆς δυνάμεως τὰ μὲν κέρατα τῶν
Καρχηδονίων ἐθραύετο, τὸ δὲ μέσον τὸ κατὰ τοὺς
Λίβυας, ὅπερ ἦν χρησιμώτατον, εἰς τέλος ἄπρακτον
3 ἦν· οὔτε γὰρ παραβοηθεῖν ἠδύναντο τοῖς ἐπὶ τῶν
κεράτων, λιπόντες τὸν ἴδιον τόπον διὰ τὴν τῶν Ἰβήρων ἔφοδον, οὔτε μένοντες ἐπὶ τῶν ὑποκειμένων ἐνερ-

the leading ones and place themselves in a position to attack the enemy, were in contrary directions both as regards the right and left wings and as regards the infantry and cavalry. For the cavalry and light infantry on the right wing wheeling to the right attempted to outflank the enemy, while the heavy infantry wheeled to the left. On the left wing the maniples wheeled to the right and the cavalry and velites to the left. The consequence of this was that the right of the cavalry and light-armed troops on both wings had become their left. But the general, regarding this as of small importance, devoted his intention to the really important object—outflanking the enemy—and he estimated rightly, for a general should, of course, know the actual course of events, but employ those movements which are suited to an emergency.

24. In consequence of this attack the elephants, assailed by the missiles of the cavalry and velites and harassed on every side, were suffering much, and doing as much damage to their own side as to the enemy. For in their wild rush they destroyed all, friend or foe, who came in their way. As for the infantry the wings of the Carthaginians were broken, and the center, where stood the Libyans, the flower of the army, was of no service, as they could neither leave their original position to help those on the wings, for fear of attack by the Spaniards, nor, remain-

γεῖν τι τῶν δεόντων οἷοί τ᾽ ἦσαν διὰ τὸ μὴ συνιέναι
τοὺς κατὰ πρόσωπον πολεμίους αὐτοῖς εἰς τὰς χεῖρας.
4 οὐ μὴν ἀλλὰ χρόνον μὲν τινα διηγωνίζοντο τὰ κέρατα
γενναίως διὰ τὸ περὶ τῶν ὅλων ἑκατέροις συνεστάναι
5 τὸν κίνδυνον. ἤδη δὲ τοῦ καύματος ἐφεστῶτος κατὰ
τὴν ἀκμήν, οἱ μὲν Καρχηδόνιοι παρελύοντο διὰ τὸ μὴ
πεποιῆσθαι τὴν ἔξοδον κατὰ τὴν ἰδίαν προαίρεσιν,
6 κεκωλῦσθαι δὲ τῆς ἁρμοζούσης παρασκευῆς, οἱ δὲ
Ῥωμαῖοι καὶ τῇ δυνάμει καὶ ταῖς εὐψυχίαις καθυπερ-
εῖχον, καὶ μάλιστα τῷ τοῖς χρησιμωτάτοις πρὸς τοὺς
ἀχρειοτάτους τῶν πολεμίων συμβεβληκέναι διὰ τὴν
7 τοῦ στρατηγοῦ πρόνοιαν. τὰς μὲν οὖν ἀρχὰς οἱ περὶ
τὸν Ἀσδρούβαν κατὰ πόδα πιεζούμενοι τὴν ἀναχώρησιν ἐποιοῦντο, μετὰ δὲ ταῦτα κλίναντες ἀθρόοι πρὸς
τὴν παρώρειαν ἀπεχώρουν· ἐγκειμένων δὲ τῶν Ῥωμαίων βιαιότερον ἔφευγον εἰς τὸν χάρακα προτροπάδην.
8 εἰ μὲν οὖν μὴ θεός αὐτοῖς τις συνεπελάβετο τῆς
σωτηρίας, παραχρῆμ᾽ ἂν ἐξέπεσον ἐκ τῆς παρεμ-
9 βολῆς. ἐπιγενομένης δὲ κατὰ τὸν ἀέρα συστροφῆς
ἐξαισίου, καὶ καταρραγέντος ὄμβρου λάβρου καὶ
συνεχοῦς, μόλις εἰς τὴν αὐτῶν στρατοπεδείαν ἀνεκο-
μίσθησαν οἱ Ῥωμαῖοι. . . .

10   Ἰλούργεια, πόλις Ἰβηρίας, Πολύβιος ἑνδεκάτη
(Steph. Byz.).

11   Τὸ δὲ τετηκὸς καὶ συνερρυηκὸς ἀργύριον καὶ χρυ-
σίον ἀναζητοῦντες ὑπὸ τοῦ πυρὸς πλεῖστοι Ῥωμαίων
διεφθάρησαν. . . .

24a. Ὅτι πάντων εὐδαιμονιζόντων τὸν Πόπλιον

ing where they were, could they operate effectively, as the enemy in front of them would not come to blows. The wings, however, kept up a gallant struggle for some time, as each side was aware that all depended on the result of this battle. But when the heat of the day was at its height, the Carthaginians grew faint, as they had not left their camp on their own initiative and had been prevented from preparing themselves properly, while the Romans began to exhibit superior strength and spirit, chiefly because, owing to the foresight of their commander, their choicest troops encountered here the least efficient of the enemy. At first Hasdrubal's men, yielding to the pressure, retired step by step, but later they gave way in a body and retreated to the foot of the hill, and when the Romans pushed their attack home with more violence they fled in rout to their camp. Had not some deity interposed to save them they would have been at once driven out of their entrenchments, but now arose an unprecedented disturbance in the heavens, and such heavy and continuous torrents of rain fell, that the Romans with difficulty made their way back to their own camp. . . .

Ilourgia,[48] a city of Spain. Polybius in Book 11.

Many of the Romans perished by fire in their search for the molten masses of silver and gold[49]. . . .

24a. When everyone congratulated Scipio on having

---

[48] The town Ilorci (Plin. *HN* 3.9), modern Lorqui on the Segura. The town defected from the Romans after the catastrophe of the brothers Scipio in 211 and was now reconquered by the younger Scipio (Livy 28.19.1–20.7).

[49] At Astapa, modern Estepa, near Osuna (Livy 28.23.4). *RE* Ostippo 1665 (A. Schulten).

μετὰ τὸ τοὺς Καρχηδονίους ἐξελάσαι τῆς Ἰβηρίας,
καὶ παρακαλούντων ἀναπαύεσθαι καὶ ῥᾳθυμεῖν, ἐπεὶ
πέρας ἐπιτέθεικε τῷ πολέμῳ, μακαρίζειν αὐτοὺς ἔφη
2 διότι τοιαύτας ἔχουσι τὰς ἐλπίδας, αὐτὸς δὲ νῦν καὶ
μάλιστα βουλεύεσθαι τίνα τρόπον ἄρξηται τοῦ πρὸς
3 Καρχηδονίους πολέμου· τὸν μὲν γὰρ πρὸ τούτου χρόνον Καρχηδονίους Ῥωμαίοις πεπολεμηκέναι, νυνὶ δὲ
τὴν τύχην παραδεδωκέναι καιρὸν εἰς τὸ Ῥωμαίους
Καρχηδονίοις ἐξενεγκεῖν πόλεμον. . . .
4 Ὅτι ὁ Πόπλιος διαλεχθεὶς τῷ Σόφακι, ἅτε δὴ πρὸς
τοῦτο τὸ μέρος εὐφυὴς ὑπάρχων, οὕτω φιλανθρώπως
ὡμίλησε καὶ ἐπιδεξίως ὥστε τὸν Ἀσδρούβαν εἰπεῖν
ταῖς ὕστερον ἡμέραις πρὸς τὸν Σόφακα διότι φοβερώ-
τερος αὐτῷ Πόπλιος πέφηνε κατὰ τὴν ὁμιλίαν ἤπερ ἐν
τοῖς ὅπλοις. . . .

25. Ὅτι στάσεως γενομένης τινῶν ἐν τῷ στρατοπέδῳ τῷ Ῥωμαϊκῷ, ὁ Πόπλιος, καίπερ ἤδη πεῖραν
εἰληφὼς τῶν πραγμάτων ἐφ᾽ ἱκανόν, ὅμως οὐδέποτε
μᾶλλον εἰς ἀπορίαν ἧκε καὶ δυσχρηστίαν. καὶ τοῦτ᾽
2 ἔπασχε κατὰ λόγον· καθάπερ ⟨γὰρ⟩ ἐπὶ τῶν σωμάτων
τὰς μὲν ἐκτὸς αἰτίας τοῦ βλάπτειν, λέγω δ᾽ οἷον
ψύχους, καύματος, κόπου, τραυμάτων, καὶ πρὶν γίνεσθαι φυλάξασθαι δυνατὸν καὶ γενομέναις εὐμαρὲς
βοηθῆσαι, τὰ δ᾽ ἐξ αὐτῶν τῶν σωμάτων γινόμενα
3 φύματα καὶ νόσους δυσχερὲς μὲν προϊδέσθαι, δυσχερὲς δὲ γενομένοις βοηθεῖν, τὸν αὐτὸν δὴ τρόπον καὶ

---

50 King of the Masaesyli; his realm was in modern Oran and
Algiers, with the capital Siga. *RE* Syphax 1472–1477 (P. Habel).

driven the Carthaginians out of Spain and entreated him to rest and take his ease, as he had put an end to the war, he said he considered them happy in having such hopes, but that for his own part now especially the time had come when he had to consider how he should begin the war against Carthage; for up to now the Carthaginians had been making war on the Romans, but now chance had given the Romans the opportunity of making war on the Carthaginians.

Scipio, who was highly gifted in this respect, spoke to Syphax[50] with such urbanity and adroitness that Hasdrubal[51] afterward said to Syphax that Scipio had seemed to him to be more formidable in his conversation than on the field of battle. . . .

Mutiny in the Roman Army

25. When a sedition broke out among some of the soldiers in the Roman camp, Scipio, though he had by this time gained considerable practical experience, never found himself in such difficulty and perplexity. And this was only to be expected. For just as in the case of our bodies external causes of injury, such as cold, extreme heat, fatigue, and wounds, can be guarded against before they happen and easily remedied when they do happen, but growths and illnesses which originate in the body itself can with difficulty be foreseen and with difficulty be cured when they happen, we should assume the same to be true

[51] At the residence of Syphax the two commanders met accidentally and shared the same couch at dinner. Scipio tried to win Syphax as an ally, Hasdrubal to keep him as such. Livy 28.17.10–18.12. See n. on F 184.

315

περὶ πολιτείας καὶ περὶ στρατοπέδων διαληπτέον.

4 πρὸς μὲν γὰρ τὰς ἔξωθεν ἐπιβουλὰς καὶ πολέμους πρόχειρος ὁ τρόπος τῆς παρασκευῆς καὶ βοηθείας

5 τοῖς ἐφιστάνουσι, πρὸς δὲ τὰς ἐν αὐτοῖς γενομένας ἀντιπολιτείας καὶ στάσεις καὶ ταραχὰς δύσχρηστος ἡ βοήθεια καὶ μεγάλης ἐπιδεξιότητος καὶ διαφερούσης

6 ἀγχινοίας δεομένη· πλὴν ἑνὸς παραγγέλματος, ὃ πᾶσιν ἁρμόσει, ⟨δεῖ⟩ καὶ στρατοπέδοις καὶ πόλεσι

7 καὶ σώμασιν, ὡς ἐμὴ δόξα. τοῦτο δ' ἐστὶ τὸ μηδέποτ' ἐᾶν ἐπὶ πολὺ ῥαθυμεῖν καὶ σχολάζειν περὶ μηδὲν τῶν προειρημένων, ἥκιστα δ' ἐν ταῖς εὐροίαις τῶν πρα-

8 γμάτων καὶ ἐν ταῖς δαψιλείαις τῶν ἐπιτηδείων. πλὴν ὅ γε Πόπλιος, ἅτε διαφερόντως ἐπιμελὴς ὤν, καθάπερ ἐξ ἀρχῆς εἶπον, ἔτι δ' ἀγχίνους καὶ πρακτικός, συν-αθροίσας τοὺς χιλιάρχους τοιάνδε τινὰ τῶν ἐνεστώ-

9 των εἰσηγεῖτο λύσιν. ἔφη γὰρ δεῖν ἀναδέξασθαι τοῖς στρατιώταις τὴν τῶν ὀψωνίων ἀπόδοσιν· χάριν δὲ τοῦ πιστεύεσθαι τὴν ἐπαγγελίαν, τὰς ἐπιτεταγμένας εἰσ-φορὰς ταῖς πόλεσι πρότερον εἰς τὴν τοῦ παντὸς στρατοπέδου χορηγίαν ταύτας νῦν ἀθροίζειν ἐπι-φανῶς καὶ μετὰ σπουδῆς, ὡς πρὸς τὴν διόρθωσιν τῶν

10 ὀψωνίων γινομένης τῆς παρασκευῆς· τοὺς δὲ χιλιάρ-χους τοὺς αὐτοὺς πάλιν πορευθέντας ἀξιοῦν καὶ παρα-καλεῖν μετατίθεσθαι τὴν ἄγνοιαν καὶ κομίζεσθαι τὰς σιταρχίας, παραγινομένους ὡς αὐτόν, ἄν τε κατὰ μέρη βούλωνται τοῦτο ποιεῖν ἄν θ' ὁμοῦ πάντες.

11 γενομένου δὲ τούτου τὸ λοιπὸν ἤδη παρ' αὐτὸν τὸν καιρὸν ἔφη δεῖν βουλεύεσθαι τί δέον ἐστὶ πράττειν.

of a state or an army. As for plots and wars from outside, it is easy, if we are on the watch, to prepare to meet them and to find a remedy, but in the case of intestine opposition, sedition, and disturbance it is a difficult task to hit on a remedy, a task requiring great adroitness and exceptional sagacity. There is one rule, however, which in my opinion is equally applicable to armies, cities, and to the body, and that is never to allow any of them to remain long indolent and inactive and especially when they enjoy prosperity and plenty. Scipio, as I said originally, was exceptionally painstaking and at the same time very sagacious and practical, and he now summoned the tribunes[52] and laid before them the following plan for relieving the present situation. He said they should undertake to pay the men their arrears, and in order to secure credence for this promise, collect at once publicly and energetically the contributions formerly imposed on the cities for the maintenance of the whole army, making it evident that the measure was taken to adjust the irregularity of payment. He begged the same officers to return to their troops and urge them to retrieve their error and present themselves before him to receive their pay either singly or in a body. When this had been done he said it would be time to consult what further action the circumstances demanded.

[52] Refers to the seven tribunes sent by Scipio to the camp at Sucro and to their return (Livy 28.25.3–7).

26. Οὗτοι μὲν οὖν ταῦτα διανοηθέντες ἐγίνοντο περὶ
2 τὴν τῶν χρημάτων ἐπιμέλειαν· . . . . τῶν
δὲ χιλιάρχων διασαφούντων τὰ δεδογμένα, γνοὺς ὁ
Πόπλιος ἀνεκοινοῦτο τῷ συνεδρίῳ τί δέον ἐστὶ ποιεῖν.
3 ἔδοξεν οὖν αὐτοῖς, ἡμέραν διασαφήσαντας εἰς ἣν
δεήσει παρεῖναι, πρὸς μὲν τὸ πλῆθος διαλύεσθαι, τοὺς
δ' αἰτίους κολάζειν πικρῶς· οὗτοι δ' ἦσαν εἰς πέντε καὶ
4 τριάκοντα τὸν ἀριθμόν. τῆς δ' ἡμέρας ἐπελθούσης,
καὶ παραγενομένων τῶν ἀποστατῶν ἐπί τε τὰς δια-
5 λύσεις καὶ τὴν κομιδὴν τῶν ὀψωνίων, τοῖς μὲν χιλιάρχοις τοῖς πρεσβεύσασι συνέταξε δι' ἀπορρήτων ὁ
Πόπλιος ἀπαντᾶν τοῖς ἀποστάταις καὶ διελομένους
ἕκαστον πέντε τῶν ἀρχηγῶν τῆς στάσεως εὐθέως
κατὰ τὴν ἀπάντησιν φιλανθρωπεῖν καὶ καλεῖν ὡς
αὑτούς, μάλιστα μὲν πρὸς κατασκήνωσιν· οἳ δ' ἂν μὴ
δύνωνται τοῦτο, πρός γε δεῖπνον καὶ τοιαύτην συν-
6 ουσίαν. τῷ δὲ μεθ' αὑτοῦ στρατοπέδῳ παρήγγειλε πρὸ
ἡμερῶν τριῶν ἐφόδια παρεσκευάσθαι κατὰ πλείω
χρόνον ὡς ἐπὶ τὸν Ἀνδοβάλην αὐτῶν μετὰ Μάρκου
7 πορευομένων. ὃ καὶ θαρραλεωτέρους αὐτοὺς ἀκούσαντας ἐποίησε τοὺς ἀποστάτας· ἐν αὑτοῖς γὰρ ὑπέλαβον
ἔσεσθαι τὴν πλείστην ἐξουσίαν, ἐπειδὰν συμμίξωσι
τῷ στρατηγῷ τῶν ἄλλων στρατοπέδων κεχωρισμέ-
νων.

27. Συνεγγιζόντων δ' αὐτῶν τῇ πόλει, τοῖς μὲν
ἄλλοις στρατιώταις εἰς τὴν ἐπαύριον ἅμα τῷ φωτὶ
παρηγγέλλετο μετὰ τῆς παρασκευῆς ἐξάγειν, τοῖς δὲ
2 χιλιάρχοις καὶ τοῖς ἐπάρχοις, ὅταν ἐκπορευομένοις

26. The officers with this object in view applied themselves to collecting the money.[53] . . . When the tribunes communicated the decision[54] to Scipio he, on hearing of it, laid before the council his views as to what should be done. It was decided to fix a day for the soldiers to present themselves and then come to terms with the rank and file, but to punish severely the authors of the mutiny, who numbered about five and thirty. When the day arrived and the mutineers came to make terms and receive their pay, Scipio gave secret instructions to the tribunes who had been on the mission to him to meet the mutineers and each attaching to himself five of the ringleaders, at once upon meeting them make professions of friendship and invite them to their quarters, if possible to lodge there, but if that were impossible to take supper and similar entertainment afterward. Three days previously he had ordered the army he had with him to furnish themselves with provisions for a considerable time on the pretext that they were marching under Marcus against Andobales.[55] This, when it reached their ears, gave the mutineers increased confidence, as they thought that they themselves would be masters of the situation when they met their general after the other legions had taken their departure.

27. When they were approaching the town he ordered the other soldiers to march out at daybreak next day with all their baggage, the tribunes and prefects upon their issu-

[53] It is evident from Livy 28.25.15 that a good deal is missing.

[54] The intention of the mutineers to appear in full force before Scipio was mentioned in the lacuna after 26.1 (Livy 28.25.15).

[55] The reason for naming him here becomes clear in 29.3.

<πρὸ τῆς πόλεως συμβαίνῃ παραγίνεσθαι>, μετὰ
τοῦτο τὸ πρῶτον τὰς μὲν ἀποσκευὰς ἀποτιθέναι, τοὺς
δὲ στρατιώτας κατέχειν ἐν τοῖς ὅπλοις ἐπὶ τῆς πύλης,
κἄπειτα διελεῖν σφᾶς ἐφ᾽ ἑκάστην τῶν πυλῶν καὶ
3 φροντίζειν ἵνα μηδεὶς ἐκπορεύηται τῶν ἀποστατῶν. οἱ
δὲ πρὸς τὴν ἀπάντησιν ἀποτεταγμένοι, συμμίξαντες
τοῖς παραγινομένοις πρὸς αὐτούς, ἀπῆγον μετὰ φιλανθρωπίας τοὺς ἐν ταῖς αἰτίαις κατὰ τὸ συντεταγμέ-
4 νον. τούτοις μὲν οὖν ὑπ᾽ αὐτὸν τὸν καιρὸν ἐρρήθη
συλλαβεῖν τοὺς πέντε καὶ τριάκοντ᾽ ἄνδρας, ἐπειδὰν
δειπνήσωσι, δήσαντάς <τε> τηρεῖν, μηδενὸς ἔτι τῶν
ἔνδον ἐκπορευομένου πλὴν τοῦ διασαφήσοντος τῷ
5 στρατηγῷ παρ᾽ ἑκάστου τὸ γεγονός. πραξάντων δὲ
τῶν χιλιάρχων τὸ συνταχθέν, εἰς τὴν ἐπιοῦσαν ὁ
στρατηγὸς ἅμα τῷ φωτὶ θεωρῶν τοὺς παραγινομένους
ἠθροισμένους εἰς τὴν ἀγοράν, συνεκάλει τὴν ἐκκλη-
6 σίαν. πάντων δὲ συντρεχόντων κατὰ τὸν ἐθισμὸν ἅμα
τῷ σημῆναι, καὶ μετεώρων ὄντων ταῖς διανοίαις <οἷ-
όν> ποτ᾽ ὄψονται τὸν στρατηγὸν καὶ τί ποτ᾽ ἀκούσον-
7 ται περὶ τῶν ἐνεστώτων, πρὸς μὲν τοὺς ἐπὶ τῶν πυλῶν
χιλιάρχους ὁ Πόπλιος διεπέμψατο, κελεύων αὐτοὺς
ἄγειν τοὺς στρατιώτας ἐν τοῖς ὅπλοις καὶ περιστῆναι
τὴν ἐκκλησίαν, αὐτὸς δὲ προπορευθεὶς ἐξέστησε ταῖς
διανοίαις πάντας εὐθέως κατὰ τὴν πρώτην φαντασίαν·
8 ἔτι γὰρ ὑπολαμβάνοντες αὐτὸν ἀσθενῶς ἔχειν οἱ πολλοί, κἄπειτα παρὰ τὴν προσδοκίαν αἰφνιδίως ἐρρωμέ-
νον θεασάμενοι κατὰ τὴν ἐπίφασιν κατεπλάγησαν.

28. Οὐ μὴν ἀλλ᾽ οὕτω πως ἤρξατο τῶν λόγων. ἔφη

ing ‹from the city to be present›, then make them first deposit their baggage and halt them under arms at the gate, afterward distributing them to guard all the gates and to see that none of the mutineers got out. Those tribunes who had been told off to meet the mutineers, when they encountered them as they advanced toward them, cordially received the most culpable of them, as had been arranged, and led them off. Orders had been given to them to arrest at once after supper the thirty-five and secure them bound, not allowing any of those inside to go out except the messenger sent by each to inform the general that the thing had been done. The tribunes acted on these orders, and next morning Scipio, seeing that the newly arrived soldiers were collected in the marketplace, summoned an assembly. When they all, as they were in the habit of doing, ran to obey the summons with their curiosity fully aroused as to how the general would look, and what they would be told about the present situation, Scipio sent to the tribunes at the gates ordering them to bring their men under arms and surround the assembly. When he advanced and presented himself his appearance at once struck them all with amazement. For most of them still supposed him to be in feeble health, and now when contrary to their expectation they suddenly saw him looking well they were dumbfounded by the apparition.

28. He began to speak somewhat as follows. He said

THE HISTORIES OF POLYBIUS

γὰρ θαυμάζειν τίνι δυσαρεστήσαντες ἢ ποίαις ἐλπίσιν ἐπαρθέντες ἐπεβάλοντο ποιεῖσθαι τὴν ἀπόστασιν.

2 τρεῖς γὰρ αἰτίας εἶναι, δι' ἃς τολμῶσι στασιάζειν ἄνθρωποι πρὸς πατρίδα καὶ τοὺς ἡγουμένους, ὅταν <τοῖς> προεστῶσι μέμφωνταί τι καὶ δυσχεραίνωσιν, ἢ τοῖς ὑποκειμένοις πράγμασι δυσαρεστῶσιν, ἢ καὶ νὴ

3 Δία μειζόνων ὀρεχθῶσι καὶ καλλιόνων ἐλπίδων. "ἐρωτῶ δὲ τί τούτων ὑμῖν ὑπῆρξεν; ἐμοὶ δῆλον ὅτι δυσηρεστήσασθε, διότι τὰς σιταρχίας ὑμῖν οὐκ ἀπεδίδουν·

4 ἀλλὰ τοῦτ' ἐμὸν μὲν οὐκ ἦν ἔγκλημα· κατὰ γὰρ τὴν

5 ἐμὴν ἀρχὴν οὐδὲν ὑμῖν ἐνέλειπε τῶν ὀψωνίων· εἰ δ' ἄρ' ἦν ἐκ τῆς Ῥώμης, διότι τὰ πάλαι προσοφειλόμενα νῦν

6 οὐ διωρθοῦτο—πότερον οὖν ἐχρῆν ἀποστάτας γενομένους τῆς πατρίδος καὶ πολεμίους τῆς θρεψάσης οὕτως ἐγκαλεῖν ἢ παρόντας λέγειν μὲν περὶ τούτων πρὸς ἐμέ, παρακαλεῖν δὲ τοὺς φίλους συνεπιλαβέσθαι καὶ βοη-

7 θεῖν ὑμῖν; δοκῶ γάρ, ἢν τοῦτο βέλτιον. τοῖς μὲν γὰρ μισθοῦ παρά τισι στρατευομένοις ἔστιν ὅτε συγγνώμην δοτέον ἀφισταμένοις τῶν μισθοδοτῶν, τοῖς δ' ὑπὲρ ἑαυτῶν πολεμοῦσι καὶ γυναικῶν ἰδίων καὶ

8 τέκνων οὐδαμῶς συγχωρητέον· ἔστι γὰρ παραπλήσιον ὡς ἂν εἴ τις ὑπὸ γονέως ἰδίου φάσκων εἰς ἀργυρίου λόγον ἀδικεῖσθαι παρείη μετὰ τῶν ὅπλων,

9 ἀποκτενῶν τοῦτον παρ' οὗ τὸ ζῆν αὐτὸς ἔλαβε. νὴ Δί' ἀλλ' ἐγὼ τὰς μὲν κακοπαθείας ὑμῖν καὶ τοὺς κινδύνους πλείους ἢ τοῖς ἄλλοις ἐπέταττον, τὰ δὲ λυσιτελῆ καὶ

10 τὰς ὠφελείας ἑτέροις μᾶλλον ἐμέριζον· ἀλλ' οὔτε τολμᾶτε τοῦτο λέγειν οὔτε τολμήσαντες δύναισθ' ἂν ἀπο-

he wondered what grievance or what expectations had induced them to make this revolt. For there were three reasons which make men venture to revolt against their country and their officers. Either they find fault and are displeased with those in command, or they are dissatisfied with their actual situation, or indeed they entertain hopes of some improvement in their fortunes. "Which of these, I ask you," he said, "existed in your case? Evidently you were displeased with me because I did not pay what was due to you. But that was no fault of mine, for since I myself have been in command, you have been always paid in full. But if you have a grievance against Rome because your old arrears were not made good, was it the proper method of complaint to revolt against your country and take up arms against her who nourished you? Should you not rather have come and spoken to me about the matter, and begged your friends to take up your cause and help you? Yes, that, I think, would have been far better. Mercenary troops may indeed sometimes be pardoned for revolting against their employers, but no pardon can be extended to those who are fighting for themselves and their wives and children. For that is just as if a man who said he had been wronged by his own father in money matters were to take up arms to kill him who was the author of his life. Great Heavens! can you say that I imposed more hardship and danger on you than on others but bestowed on others a larger share of profit and booty? Neither will you dare to say so, nor could

11 δεῖξαι. τί οὖν ἐστιν, ἐφ᾽ ᾧ δυσαρεστούμ·νοι κατὰ τὸ
παρὸν ἡμῖν τὰς ἀποστάσεις ἐποιήσασθε; τοῦτ᾽ ἤδη
βούλομαι πυθέσθαι· δοκῶ μὲν γὰρ οὐδὲν οὔτ᾽ ἐρεῖν
οὔτ᾽ ἐπινοήσειν ὑμῶν οὐδένα.

29. καὶ μὴν οὐδὲ τοῖς ὑποκειμένοις ἀσχάλλοντες·
πότε γὰρ εὔροια πραγμάτων μείζων; πότε δὲ πλείω
προτερήματα γέγονε τῇ Ῥώμῃ; πότε δὲ τοῖς στρατευ-
2 ομένοις μείζους ἐλπίδες ἢ νῦν; ἀλλ᾽ ἴσως ⟨ἐρεῖ⟩ τις
τῶν ἀπηλπικότων ὅτι πλείω τὰ λυσιτελῆ τὰ παρὰ τοῖς
ἐχθροῖς προυφαίνετο καὶ μείζους ἐλπίδες καὶ βεβαι-
3 ότεραι· παρὰ τίσι δὴ τούτοις; ἢ παρ᾽ Ἀνδοβάλῃ καὶ
Μανδονίῳ; καὶ τίς ὑμῶν οὐκ οἶδε διότι πρότερον μὲν
οὗτοι παρασπονδήσαντες Καρχηδονίους πρὸς ἡμᾶς
ἀπέστησαν, νῦν δὲ πάλιν ἀθετήσαντες τοὺς ὅρκους
καὶ ⟨τὴν⟩ πίστιν ἐχθροὺς ἡμῖν σφᾶς αὐτοὺς ἀναδεδεί-
4 χασι; καλόν γε τούτοις πιστεύσαντας πολεμίους γενέ-
5 σθαι τῆς ἑαυτῶν πατρίδος. οὐ μὴν οὐδ᾽ ἐν αὑτοῖς
εἴχετε τὰς ἐλπίδας ὡς κρατήσοντες τῆς Ἰβηρίας· οὐδὲ
γὰρ μετ᾽ Ἀνδοβάλου ταχθέντες ἱκανοὶ πρὸς ἡμᾶς ἦτε
6 διακινδυνεύειν, μή τι καὶ καθ᾽ ἑαυτοὺς ταττόμενοι. τί
οὖν ἦν ᾧ προσείχετε; πυθέσθαι γὰρ ἂν βουλοίμην
ὑμῶν. εἰ μὴ νὴ Δία ταῖς ἐμπειρίαις τῶν νῦν προχει-
ρισθέντων ἡγεμόνων καὶ ταῖς ἀρεταῖς πιστεύοντες ἢ
καὶ ταῖς ῥάβδοις καὶ τοῖς πελέκεσι τοῖς προηγου-
7 μένοις αὐτῶν· ὑπὲρ ὧν οὐδὲ λέγειν πλείω καλόν. ἀλλ᾽
οὐκ ἔστι τούτων, ὦ ἄνδρες, οὐδέν· οὐδ᾽ ἂν ἔχοιθ᾽ ὑμεῖς
δίκαιον οὐδὲ τοὐλάχιστον εἰπεῖν οὔτε πρὸς ἡμᾶς οὔτε
8 πρὸς τὴν πατρίδα. διόπερ ἐγὼ περὶ ὑμῶν πρός τε τὴν

you prove it if you did. What is it then with which you are so dissatisfied at present as to revolt against me? I should very much like to know; for my opinion is that there is not one of you who will be able to tell me any grievance or think of any.

29. Nor is it that you are discontented with your present situation. When was everything so abundant, when had Rome enjoyed more success, when had her soldiers brighter hopes than now? But perhaps one of the more despondent among you will tell me that with the enemy there would be more profit for you and greater and more certain expectations! Who are these enemies? Are they Andobales and Mandonius?[56] Who among you is not aware that, to begin with, they revolted to us after betraying Carthage and now again, breaking their oaths and pledges to us, have proclaimed themselves our enemies? A fine thing truly to rely on these men and become enemies of your own country! Again you could not hope to conquer Spain by your own arms, for you were not a match for me even if you joined Andobales' army, much less by yourselves. What then was in your minds? I should very much like to learn that from you. Unless indeed the fact was that you relied on the skill and valor of the leaders you have just appointed[57] or on the fasces and axes that are carried before them, about which it is disgraceful even to speak further. No, my men, it was nothing of the sort, and you could not give the slightest reason to justify yourselves in my eyes or in those of your country. I, therefore, will plead for you to

[56] See n. on 3.76.6. Both also in 10.18.7.
[57] The two leaders elected by the mutineers (Livy 28.24.13–14).

Ῥώμην καὶ πρὸς αὐτὸν ἀπολογήσομαι, τὰ παρὰ
πᾶσιν ἀνθρώποις ὁμολογούμενα δίκαια προθέμενος.

9 ταῦτα δ᾽ ἐστὶ διότι πᾶς ὄχλος εὐπαραλόγιστος ὑπάρχει καὶ πρὸς πᾶν εὐάγωγος. ὅθεν αἰεὶ τὸ παραπλήσιον
πάθος συμβαίνει περί τε τοὺς ὄχλους καὶ τὴν θάλατ-

10 ταν. καθάπερ γὰρ κἀκείνης ἡ μὲν ἰδία φύσις ἐστὶν
ἀβλαβὴς τοῖς χρωμένοις καὶ στάσιμος, ὅταν δ᾽ εἰς
αὐτὴν ἐμπέσῃ τὰ πνεύματα βίᾳ, τοιαύτη φαίνεται τοῖς
χρωμένοις οἷοί τινες ἂν ὦσιν οἱ κυκλοῦντες αὐτὴν

11 ἄνεμοι, τὸν αὐτὸν τρόπον καὶ τὸ πλῆθος ἀεὶ καὶ
φαίνεται καὶ γίνεται πρὸς τοὺς χρωμένους οἵους ἂν

12 ἔχῃ προστάτας καὶ συμβούλους. διὸ κἀγὼ νῦν καὶ
πάντες οἱ προεστῶτες τοῦ στρατοπέδου πρὸς μὲν ὑμᾶς
διαλυόμεθα καὶ πίστιν δίδομεν ἐφ᾽ ᾧ μὴ μνησικα-

13 κήσειν. πρὸς δὲ τοὺς αἰτίους ἀκαταλλάκτως διακεί-
μεθα, κολάζειν αὐτοὺς ἀξίως καὶ τῶν εἰς τὴν πατρίδα
καὶ τῶν εἰς ἡμᾶς ἡμαρτημένων."

30. Ἀκμὴν δὲ ταῦτ᾽ ἔλεγε καὶ κύκλῳ μὲν οἱ στρατιῶται περιεστῶτες ἐν τοῖς ὅπλοις ἀπὸ παραγγέλματος συνεψόφησαν ταῖς μαχαίραις τοὺς θυρεούς,
ἅμα δὲ τούτοις δεδεμένοι γυμνοὶ . . . οἱ τῆς στάσεως

2 αἴτιοι γεγονότες εἰσήγοντο. τῷ δὲ πλήθει τοιοῦτον
παρέστη δέος ὑπό τε τοῦ πέριξ φόβου καὶ τῶν κατὰ
πρόσωπον δεινῶν, ὥστε τῶν μὲν μαστιγουμένων, τῶν
δὲ πελεκιζομένων μήτε τὴν ὄψιν ἀλλοιῶσαι μήτε
φωνὴν προέσθαι μηδένα, μένειν δὲ πάντας ἀχανεῖς,

3 ἐκπεπληγμένους πρὸς τὸ συμβαῖνον. οἱ μὲν οὖν ἀρχη-
γοὶ τῶν κακῶν αἰκισθέντες εἵλκοντο διὰ μέσων, ἀπηλ-

Rome and to myself, using a plea universally acknowledged among men: and that is that all multitudes are easily misled and easily impelled to every excess, so that a multitude is ever liable to the same vicissitudes as the sea. For as the sea is by its own nature harmless to those who voyage on it and quiet, but when winds fall violently upon it seems to those who have dealings with it to be of the same character as the winds that happen to stir it, so a multitude ever appears to be and actually is to those who deal with it of the same character as the leaders and counselors it happens to have. Therefore I, too, on the present occasion and all the superior officers of the army consent to be reconciled with you and engage to grant you amnesty But with the guilty parties we refuse to be reconciled and have decided to punish them for their offenses against their country and ourselves."

30. Hardly had he finished speaking when the men who stood round him in arms upon a signal given clashed their swords against their bucklers, and at the same time the authors of the mutiny were brought in bound and naked. The multitude of mutineers were so thoroughly cowed by fear of the surrounding force and the terror that looked them in the face, that while some of their leaders were being scourged and others beheaded none of them either changed his countenance or uttered a word, but all remained dumbfounded, smitten with astonishment and dread. After the authors of the evil had thus been put to death with contumely, their bodies were dragged through

λαγμένοι τοῦ ζῆν· οἱ δὲ λοιποὶ παρὰ μὲν τοῦ στρατηγοῦ καὶ τῶν ἄλλων ἀρχόντων κατὰ κοινὸν ἔλαβον τὰς
4 πίστεις ἐφ᾽ ᾧ μηδένα μηδενὶ μνησικακήσειν, αὐτοὶ δὲ
καθ᾽ ἕνα προϊόντες ὤμνυον τοῖς χιλιάρχοις ἦ μὴν
πειθαρχήσειν τοῖς παραγγελλομένοις ὑπὸ τῶν ἀρχόντων καὶ μηδὲν ὑπεναντίον φρονήσειν τῇ Ῥώμῃ.
5   Πόπλιος μὲν οὖν, μεγάλων κινδύνων ἀρχὴν φυομέ-
νων καλῶς διορθωσάμενος, πάλιν ἀποκατέστησε τὰς
οἰκείας δυνάμεις εἰς τὴν ἐξ ἀρχῆς διάθεσιν. . . .
31. Ὁ δὲ Πόπλιος συναθροίσας εὐθέως ἐν αὐτῇ τῇ
Καρχηδόνι τὰς δυνάμεις εἰς ἐκκλησίαν ἔλεγε περί τε
τῆς Ἀνδοβάλου τόλμης καὶ τῆς εἰς αὐτοὺς ἀθεσίας,
2 καὶ πολλὰ πρὸς τοῦτο τὸ μέρος ἐνεγκάμενος παρώξυνε
τοὺς πολλοὺς πρὸς τὴν ⟨κατὰ⟩ τῶν προειρημένων
3 δυναστῶν ὁρμήν. ἐπὶ δὲ τούτοις ἐξηριθμήσατο τοὺς
προγεγενημένους αὐτοῖς ἀγῶνας πρὸς Ἴβηρας ὁμοῦ
καὶ πρὸς Καρχηδονίους, στρατηγούντων Καρχηδο-
4 νίων, ἐν οἷς ἀεὶ νικῶντας οὐ καθήκειν ἔφη νυνὶ διαπορεῖν, μήποτε πρὸς αὐτοὺς Ἴβηρας Ἀνδοβάλου
5 στρατηγοῦντος μαχόμενοι λειφθῶσι. διόπερ οὐδὲ
προσδέξασθαι συναγωνιστὴν Ἰβήρων οὐδένα καθάπαξ ἔφη, δι᾽ αὐτῶν δὲ Ῥωμαίων συστήσασθαι τὸν
6 κίνδυνον, ἵνα φανερὸν γένηται πᾶσιν ὡς οὐκ Ἴβηρσι
Καρχηδονίους καταπολεμησάμενοι, καθάπερ ἔνιοί
φασιν, ἐξεβάλομεν ἐξ Ἰβηρίας, ἀλλὰ καὶ Καρχηδονίους καὶ Κελτίβηρας ταῖς Ῥωμαίων ἀρεταῖς καὶ τῇ
7 σφετέρᾳ γενναιότητι νενικήκαμεν. ταῦτα δ᾽ εἰπὼν ὁμο-

the troops, and the rest of the mutineers received from the general and other officers a common assurance that no one would remember their past faults. Advancing singly, they took their oath to the tribunes that they would obey the orders of their officers and be guilty of no disloyalty to Rome.

Scipio then by successfully nipping in the bud what might have proved a great danger restored his forces to their original discipline.

The Revolt of Andobales and Its Suppression

31. Scipio, calling a meeting of his troops in New Carthage itself, addressed them on the subject of the daring design of Andobales and his perfidy toward them. Dealing at length with this topic he thoroughly aroused the passions of the soldiers against these princes.[58] Enumerating in the next place all the battles in which they had previously encountered the Spaniards and Carthaginians together under the command of the Carthaginians he told them that as they had in all cases won the day, they should not now have a shadow of apprehension lest they should be beaten by the Spaniards alone under Andobales. He had therefore not consented to call in the aid of a single Spaniard, but was going to give battle with his Romans alone, that it might be evident to all that it was not due to the help of the Spaniards that they had crushed the Carthaginians and driven them out of Spain, but that they had conquered both the Carthaginians and Celtiberians by Roman valor and their own brave effort. Having said this he exhorted

[58] Both had certainly just been mentioned in a passage now lost.

νοεῖν παρῄνει καὶ θαρροῦντας, εἰ καὶ πρὸς ἄλλον τινά,
καὶ πρὸς τοῦτον ἰέναι τὸν κίνδυνον. περὶ δὲ τοῦ νικᾶν
αὐτὸς ἔφη μετὰ τῶν θεῶν ποιήσασθαι τὴν καθήκου-
8 σαν πρόνοιαν. τῷ δὲ πλήθει τοιαύτη παρέστη προθυμία καὶ θάρσος ὥστε παραπλησίους εἶναι πάντας ἐκ
τῆς ἀπόψεως τοῖς ὁρῶσι τοὺς πολεμίους καὶ μέλλου-
σιν ὅσον οὔπω πρὸς αὐτοὺς διακινδυνεύειν.

32. Τότε μὲν οὖν ταῦτ' εἰπὼν διαφῆκε τὴν ἐκκλησίαν. τῇ δ' ἐπαύριον ἀναζεύξας προῆγε, καὶ παραγενηθεὶς ἐπὶ τὸν Ἴβηρα ποταμὸν δεκαταῖος καὶ περαιωθεὶς τῇ τετάρτῃ μετὰ ταύτην προσεστρατοπέδευσε
τοῖς ὑπεναντίοις, λαβὼν αὐλῶνά τινα μεταξὺ τῆς
2 αὑτοῦ καὶ τῶν πολεμίων στρατοπεδείας. τῇ δ' ἑξῆς εἰς
τὸν προειρημένον αὐλῶνα προσέβαλέ τινα θρέμματα
τῶν παρεπομένων τῷ στρατοπέδῳ, συντάξας ἑτοίμους
ἔχειν τοὺς ἱππεῖς τῷ Γαΐῳ, τοὺς ⟨δὲ⟩ γροσφομάχους
3 ἐπέταξε τῶν χιλιάρχων τισὶ παρασκευάζειν. ταχὺ δὲ
τῶν Ἰβήρων ἐπιπεσόντων ἐπὶ τὰ θρέμματ' ἐξαφῆκε
τῶν γροσφομάχων τινάς. γινομένης δὲ διὰ τούτων
συμπλοκῆς καὶ προσβοηθούντων ἑκατέροις πλειόνων,
συνέστη μέγας ἀκροβολισμὸς τῶν πεζῶν περὶ τὸν
4 αὐλῶνα. τοῦ δὲ καιροῦ παραδιδόντος εὐλόγους ἀφορμὰς πρὸς ἐπίθεσιν, ἔχων ὁ Γάιος ἑτοίμους τοὺς ἱππεῖς
κατὰ τὸ συνταχθὲν ἐπεβάλετο τοῖς ἀκροβολιζομένοις,
ἀποτεμόμενος ἀπὸ τῆς παρωρείας, ὥστε τοὺς πλείους
αὐτῶν κατὰ τὸν αὐλῶνα σκεδασθέντας ὑπὸ τῶν ἱπ-
5 πέων διαφθαρῆναι. γενομένου δὲ τούτου, παροξυνθέν-
τες οἱ βάρβαροι, καὶ διαγωνιάσαντες μὴ διὰ τὸ προ-

them to be of one mind, and if ever they marched to a battle in a spirit of confidence, to do so now. As for victory he himself with the aid of the gods would take the proper steps to secure it. His words produced such zeal and confidence in the troops, that in appearance they grew all of them like men who had the enemy before their eyes and were about to do battle with them at that instant.

32. After making this speech he dismissed the meeting. Next day he set out on the march. He reached the Ebro on the tenth day[59] and crossing it took up on the fourth day after this a position[60] in front of the enemy, leaving a valley between his own camp and theirs. On the following day he drove into this valley some of the cattle that followed the army, ordering Laelius to hold his cavalry in readiness and some of the tribunes to prepare the velites for action. Very soon, upon the Spaniards throwing themselves on the cattle, he sent some of the velites against them, and the engagement which ensued developed, as reinforcements came up from each side, into a sharp infantry skirmish round the valley. The opportunity was now an excellent one for attacking, and Laelius, who, as he had been ordered, was holding his cavalry in readiness, charged the enemy's skirmishers, cutting them off from the hillside, so that most of them scattered about the valley and were cut down by the horsemen. Upon this the barbarians were irritated, and being in extreme anxiety lest it should be

[59] An exaggeration (as in 10.9.7), since the distance is more than three hundred miles from New Carthage.

[60] North of the Ebro; the location has not been determined.

ἡττῆσθαι δόξωσι καταπεπλῆχθαι τοῖς ὅλοις, ἐξῆγον
ἅμα τῷ φωτὶ καὶ παρέταττον εἰς μάχην ἅπασαν τὴν
6 δύναμιν. ὁ δὲ Πόπλιος ἕτοιμος μὲν ἦν πρὸς τὴν
χρείαν, θεωρῶν δὲ τοὺς Ἴβηρας ἀλογίστως συγκατα-
βαίνοντας εἰς τὸν αὐλῶνα καὶ τάττοντας οὐ μόνον
τοὺς ἱππεῖς, ἀλλὰ καὶ τοὺς πεζοὺς ἐν τοῖς ἐπιπέδοις,
ἐπέμενε, βουλόμενος ὡς πλείστους ταύτῃ χρήσασθαι
7 τῇ παρεμβολῇ, πιστεύων μὲν καὶ τοῖς ἱππεῦσι τοῖς
ἰδίοις, ἔτι δὲ μᾶλλον τοῖς πεζοῖς, διὰ ‹τὸ κατὰ› τὰς ἐξ
ὁμολόγου καὶ συστάδην μάχας τόν τε καθοπλισμὸν
καὶ τοὺς ἄνδρας τοὺς παρ' αὐτοῦ πολὺ διαφέρειν τῶν
Ἰβήρων.

33. Ἐπεὶ δ' ἔδοξε τὸ δέον αὐτῷ γίνεσθαι, πρὸς μὲν
τοὺς ἐν τῇ παρωρείᾳ τεταγμένους τῶν πολεμίων ἀντέ-
ταττε . . . πρὸς δὲ τοὺς εἰς τὸν αὐλῶνα καταβεβηκότας
ἄθρους ἄγων ἐκ τῆς παρεμβολῆς ἐπὶ τέτταρας κοόρτις
2 προσέβαλε τοῖς πεζοῖς τῶν ὑπεναντίων. κατὰ δὲ τὸν
καιρὸν τοῦτον καὶ Γάιος Λαίλιος, ἔχων τοὺς ἱππεῖς,
προῆγε διὰ τῶν λόφων τῶν ἀπὸ τῆς παρεμβολῆς ἐπὶ
τὸν αὐλῶνα κατατεινόντων, καὶ προσέβαλλε τοῖς τῶν
Ἰβήρων ἱππεῦσι κατὰ νώτου, καὶ συνεῖχε τούτους ἐν
τῇ πρὸς αὐτὸν μάχῃ. λοιπὸν οἱ μὲν πεζοὶ τῶν ὑπ-
3 εναντίων, ἐρημωθέντες τῆς τῶν ἱππέων χρείας, οἷς
πιστεύσαντες εἰς τὸν αὐλῶνα κατέβησαν, ἐπιεζοῦντο
καὶ κατεβαροῦντο τῇ μάχῃ, οἱ δ' ἱππεῖς τὸ παραπλή-
4 σιον ἔπασχον· ἀπειλημμένοι γὰρ ἐν στενῷ καὶ δυσχρηστούμενοι πλείους ὑφ' αὑτῶν ἢ τῶν πολεμίων
διεφθείροντο, τῶν μὲν ἰδίων πεζῶν ἐκ πλαγίου προσ-

thought that this reverse at the outset had created general
terror among them, they marched out in full force as soon
as day dawned and drew up in order of battle. Scipio was
ready for the emergency, but noticing that the Spaniards
had the imprudence to descend *en masse* into the valley
and to draw up not only their cavalry but their infantry on
the level ground, he bided his time wishing that as many as
possible of them should take up this position. He had great
confidence in his own horse and still greater in his infantry,
because in a pitched battle hand-to-hand they were much
superior to the Spaniards both as regards their armament
and as regards the quality of the men.

33. When he thought that conditions were as he desired
he opposed his velites to the enemy who were drawn up at
the foot of the hill, and himself advancing from his camp
with four cohorts in close order against those who had
come down into the valley fell upon the enemy's infantry.
Simultaneously Gaius Laelius with the cavalry advanced
along the ridges which descended from the camp to the
valley and took the Spanish cavalry in the rear, keeping
them confined to defending themselves from him. In the
long run the enemy's infantry, thus deprived of the services
of the cavalry, relying on whose support they had come
down into the valley, found themselves hard pressed and in
difficulties. The cavalry suffered no less; for confined as
they were in a narrow space and incapacitated from action,
more of them destroyed each other than were destroyed

κειμένων αὐτοῖς, τῶν δὲ πολεμίων τῶν πεζῶν κατὰ
πρόσωπον, τῶν δ' ἱππέων κατὰ νώτου περιεστώτων.
5 τοιαύτης δὲ γενομένης τῆς μάχης οἱ μὲν εἰς τὸν
αὐλῶνα καταβάντες σχεδὸν ἅπαντες διεφθάρησαν, οἱ
6 δ' ἐν τῇ παρωρείᾳ διέφυγον. οὗτοι δ' ἦσαν εὔζωνοι,
τρίτον δὲ μέρος τῆς ἁπάσης δυνάμεως, μεθ' ὧν καὶ τὸν
Ἀνδοβάλην συνέβη διασωθέντα φυγεῖν εἴς τι χωρίον
ὀχυρόν.
7   Πόπλιος δέ, συντέλειαν ἐπιτεθεικὼς τοῖς κατὰ τὴν
Ἰβηρίαν ἔργοις, παρῆν εἰς τὸν Ταρράκωνα ⟨μετὰ⟩
μεγίστης χαρᾶς, κάλλιστον θρίαμβον καὶ καλλίστην
8 νίκην τῇ πατρίδι κατάγων. σπεύδων δὲ μὴ καθυστε-
ρεῖν τῆς ἐν τῇ Ῥώμῃ καταστάσεως τῶν ὑπάτων, πάντα τὰ κατὰ τὴν Ἰβηρίαν διατάξας καὶ παραδοὺς τὸ
στρατόπεδον τοῖς περὶ τὸν Ἰούνιον καὶ Μάρκιον, αὐτὸς ἀπέπλευσε μετὰ Γαΐου καὶ τῶν ἄλλων φίλων εἰς
τὴν Ῥώμην.

VI. RES ASIAE

34. Καὶ γὰρ αὐτὸς ἦν ὁ Εὐθύδημος Μάγνης, πρὸς
ὃν ἀπελογίζετο φάσκων ὡς οὐ δικαίως αὐτὸν Ἀντί-

---

61 A lacuna follows, in which some of the events recorded in
Livy 28.34.1 ff. would have been narrated.

62 The word is used here metaphorically: P. does not say that
Scipio actually celebrated a triumph after the campaign in Spain.
As a *privatus cum imperio* he was not qualified.

63 For 205; Scipio was elected.   64 For Iunius see n. on
20.3; for L. Marcius Septimius, legatus in 206, see *MRR* 1.300.

by the enemy, their own infantry pressing on their flank, the enemy's infantry on their front and his cavalry hovering round their rear. Such being the conditions of the battle nearly all those who had come down into the valley were cut to pieces, those on the hill escaping. The latter were light-armed infantry forming the third part of the whole army, and Andobales in their company succeeded in saving his life and escaping to a strong place.[61]

Having thus completely executed his task in Spain Scipio reached Tarraco full of joy, taking home as a gift to his country a splendid triumph[62] and a glorious victory. He was anxious not to arrive in Rome too late for the consular elections,[63] and after regulating everything in Spain and handing over his army to Junius Silanus and Marcius[64] he sailed to Rome with Laelius and his other friends.

VI. AFFAIRS OF ASIA

The Situation in Bactria

34. For Euthydemus[65] himself was a native of Magnesia, and he now, in defending himself to Teleas, said that

206–205
B.C.

[65] P. continues where he left off in 10.49.15. The year is 206. Teleas, a citizen of Magnesia like Euthydemus, was sent by Antiochus to negotiate after a long and ineffective siege. A recent find from eastern Bactria dates from Euthydemus' reign and focuses on him and his son. It is a Greek epigram with a dedication to Hestia, found at Kuliab in Tajikistan. The dedicant, a certain Heliodotus, asks the goddess to preserve, with Tyche, Euthydemus, "the greatest of all kings," and his son Demetrius, "the famous victor" (Καλλίνικος). Published with rich commentary by G. Rougemont and P. Bernard, *JS* 2004, 333–356, and figs. 26–27.

2 οχος ἐκ τῆς βασιλείας ἐκβαλεῖν σπουδάζει· γεγονέναι
γὰρ οὐκ αὐτὸς ἀποστάτης τοῦ βασιλέως, ἀλλ᾽ ἑτέρων
ἀποστάντων ἐπανελόμενος τοὺς ἐκείνων ἐκγόνους,

3 οὕτως κρατῆσαι τῆς Βακτριανῶν ἀρχῆς. καὶ πλείω δὲ
πρὸς ταύτην τὴν ὑπόθεσιν διαλεχθεὶς ἠξίου τὸν Τηλέαν μεσιτεῦσαι τὴν διάλυσιν εὐνοϊκῶς, παρακαλέ-
σαντα τὸν Ἀντίοχον μὴ φθονῆσαι τῆς ὀνομασίας

4 αὐτῷ τῆς τοῦ βασιλέως ⟨καὶ⟩ προστασίας, ὥς γ᾽ ἐὰν
μὴ συγχωρῇ τοῖς ἀξιουμένοις, οὐδετέρῳ τῆς ἀσφα-

5 λείας ὑπαρχούσης· πλήθη γὰρ οὐκ ὀλίγα παρεῖναι
τῶν Νομάδων, δι᾽ ὧν κινδυνεύειν μὲν ἀμφοτέρους,
ἐκβαρβαρωθήσεσθαι δὲ τὴν χώραν ὁμολογουμένως,

6 ἐὰν ἐκείνους προσδέχωνται. ταῦτα δ᾽ εἰπὼν ἐξαπέ-

7 στειλε τὸν Τηλέαν πρὸς τὸν Ἀντίοχον. ὁ δὲ βασιλεύς,
πάλαι περιβλεπόμενος λύσιν τῶν πραγμάτων, πυθόμενος ταῦτα παρὰ τοῦ Τηλέου, προθύμως ὑπήκουσε

8 πρὸς τὰς διαλύσεις διὰ τὰς προειρημένας αἰτίας. τοῦ
δὲ Τηλέου προσανακάμψαντος καὶ πολλάκις πρὸς
ἀμφοτέρους, τέλος Εὐθύδημος ἐξέπεμψε Δημήτριον

9 τὸν υἱὸν βεβαιώσοντα τὰς ὁμολογίας· ὃν ὁ βαιλεὺς
ἀποδεξάμενος, καὶ νομίσας ἄξιον εἶναι τὸν νεανίσκον
βασιλείας καὶ κατὰ τὴν ἐπιφάνειαν καὶ κατὰ τὴν
ἔντευξιν ⟨καὶ⟩ προστασίαν, πρῶτον μὲν ἐπηγγείλατο
δώσειν αὐτῷ μίαν τῶν ἑαυτοῦ θυγατέρων· δεύτερον δὲ

10 συνεχώρησε τῷ πατρὶ τὸ τῆς βασιλείας ὄνομα. περὶ
δὲ τῶν λοιπῶν ἐγγράπτους ποιησάμενος ὁμολογίας
καὶ συμμαχίαν ἔνορκον, ἀνέζευξε σιτομετρήσας δαψι-

Antiochus was not justified in attempting to deprive him of his kingdom, as he himself had never revolted against the king, but after others[66] had revolted he had possessed himself of the throne of Bactria by destroying their descendants. After speaking at some length in the same sense he begged Teleas to mediate between them in a friendly manner and bring about a reconciliation, entreating Antiochus not to grudge him the name and state of king, as if he did not yield to this request, neither of them would be safe; for considerable hordes of Nomads[67] were approaching, and this was not only a grave danger to both of them, but if they consented to admit them, the country would certainly relapse into barbarism. After speaking thus he dispatched Teleas to Antiochus. The king, who had long been on the lookout for a solution of the question when he received Teleas' report, gladly consented to an accommodation owing to the reasons above stated. Teleas went backward and forward more than once to both kings, and finally Euthydemus sent off his son Demetrius[68] to ratify the agreement. Antiochus, on receiving the young man and judging him from his appearance, conversation, and dignity of bearing to be worthy of royal rank, in the first place promised to give him one of his daughters in marriage[69] and next gave permission to his father to style himself king. After making a written treaty concerning other points and entering into a sworn alliance, Antiochus took his departure,

[66] This refers to Diodotus, who defected from his Seleucid overlord and whose son Diodotus II had later been overthrown by Euthydemus. [67] Known under the collective name of Sacas. [68] He later became his father's successor and ruled ca. 190–170, conquering parts of India.

[69] It is not known whether the marriage took place.

λῶς τὴν δύναμιν, προσλαβὼν καὶ τοὺς ὑπάρχοντας
11 ἐλέφαντας τοῖς περὶ τὸν Εὐθύδημον. ὑπερβαλὼν δὲ
τὸν Καύκασον καὶ κατάρας εἰς τὴν Ἰνδικήν, τήν τε
φιλίαν ἀνενεώσατο τὴν πρὸς τὸν Σοφαγασῆνον τὸν
12 βασιλέα τῶν Ἰνδῶν, καὶ λαβὼν ἐλέφαντας, ὥστε
γενέσθαι τοὺς ἅπαντας εἰς ἑκατὸν καὶ πεντήκοντ᾽, ἔτι
δὲ σιτομετρήσας πάλιν ἐνταῦθα τὴν δύναμιν, αὐτὸς
μὲν ἀνέζευξε μετὰ τῆς στρατιᾶς, Ἀνδροσθένην δὲ τὸν
Κυζικηνὸν ἐπὶ τῆς ἀνακομιδῆς ἀπέλιπε τῆς γάζης τῆς
13 ὁμολογηθείσης αὐτῷ παρὰ τοῦ βαιλέως. διελθὼν δὲ
τὴν Ἀραχωσίαν καὶ περαιωθεὶς τὸν Ἐρύμανθον ποταμόν, ἧκε διὰ τῆς Δραγγηνῆς εἰς τὴν Καρμανίαν, οὗ
καὶ συνάπτοντος ἤδη τοῦ χειμῶνος ἐποιήσατο τὴν
14 παραχειμασίαν. τὸ μὲν οὖν πέρας τῆς εἰς τοὺς ἄνω
τόπους στρατείας Ἀντιόχου τοιαύτην ἔλαβε τὴν συντέλειαν, δι᾽ ἧς οὐ μόνον τοὺς ἄνω σατράπας ὑπηκόους
ἐποιήσατο τῆς ἰδίας ἀρχῆς, ἀλλὰ καὶ τὰς ἐπιθαλατ-
τίους πόλεις καὶ τοὺς ἐπὶ τάδε τοῦ Ταύρου δυνάστας,
15 καὶ συλλήβδην ἠσφαλίσατο τὴν βασιλείαν, καταπλη-
ξάμενος τῇ τόλμῃ καὶ φιλοπονίᾳ πάντας τοὺς ὑποτατ-
16 τομένους· διὰ γὰρ ταύτης τῆς στρατείας ἄξιος ἐφάνη
τῆς βασιλείας οὐ μόνον τοῖς κατὰ τὴν Ἀσίαν, ἀλλὰ
καὶ τοῖς κατὰ τὴν Εὐρώπην.

---

70 See n. on 10.48.4. The crossing brought him into the Kabul
valley.

71 This alliance is styled as being a renewal of the treaty of 305/
302 that Seleucus I had concluded with Chandragupta (Sandro-

serving out generous rations of corn to his troops and adding to his own the elephants belonging to Euthydemus. Crossing the Caucasus[70] he descended into India and renewed his alliance with Sophagasenus the Indian king.[71] Here he procured more elephants, so that his total force of them amounted now to a hundred and fifty, and after a further distribution of corn to his troops, set out himself with his army, leaving Androsthenes of Cyzicus to collect the sum of money which the king had agreed to pay. Having traversed Arachosia[72] and crossed the river Erymanthus[73] he reached Carmania through Drangene, and there, as winter was now at hand, he took up his quarters.[74] Such was the final result of Antiochus' expedition[75] into the interior, an expedition by which he not only brought the upper satraps under his rule, but also the maritime cities and the princes this side of Taurus. In a word[76] he put his kingdom in a position of safety, overawing all subject to him by his courage and industry. It was this expedition, in fact, which made him appear worthy of his throne not only to the inhabitants of Asia, but to those of Europe likewise.

kottos). On this see A. Mehl, *Seleukos Nikator und sein Reich* (Louvain 1986), 170–181; cf. Megasthenes, *FGrH* 715 T 2.

[72] The area south and west of the Hindu-kush. It soon was conquered by Demetrius, the son of Euthydemus, who founded *Demetrias* in Arachosia: V. Tscherikower (10.31.14), 103.

[73] The modern river Helmand.   [74] Winter 206/5.

[75] The so-called *Anabasis*, on which see R. M. Errington, *CAH* (2nd ed.) 8 1989, 249–250. Soon after its end Antiochus began to be called "the Great" (Μέγας); see J. Ma, *Antiochus III and the Cities of Western Asia Minor* (Oxford 1999), 272–276.

[76] P.'s assessment is somewhat too positive: there were few lasting results from this campaign.

FRAGMENTA LIBRI XII

I. RES AFRICAE

1. Πολύβιος . . . Βυζακίδα χώραν εἶναί φησι περὶ τὰς Σύρτεις ἐν δωδεκάτῳ· "σταδίων μὲν οὖσα τὴν περίμετρον δισχιλίων, τῷ σχήματι περιφερής."

2 Ἵππων, Λιβύης πόλις. Πολύβιος δωδεκάτῳ.

3 Σίγγα, πόλις Λιβύης ὡς Πολύβιος δωδεκάτῳ.

4 Τάβρακα, πόλις Λιβύης. Πολύβιος δωδεκάτῳ.

5 Χαλκεῖα, πόλις Λιβύης· ὁ πολυίστωρ ἐν Λιβυκῶν τρίτῳ, ὡς Δημοσθένης· ᾧ μεμφόμενος Πολύβιος ἐν τῷ δωδεκάτῳ ὧδε γράφει· "ἀγνοεῖ δὲ μεγάλως καὶ περὶ τῶν Χαλκείων· οὐδὲ γὰρ πόλις ἐστίν, ἀλλὰ χαλκουργεῖα."

---

1 *RE* Byzacium 1114–1116 (H. Dessau). Among cities of that region are Hadrumetum, Leptis Minor, and Thapsus. The same "perimeter" is given in Plin. *NH* 5.24. See J. Desanges, pp. 226–229 of his edition of Pliny's Book 5, *Les Belles Lettres* (Paris 1980).

2 Hippo is probably Hippo regius (as opposed to Hippo diarrythus), since it occurs first for the year 205 in Livy 29.3.7. *RE* Hippo 2627 (H. Dessau).   3 Σίγγα (Singa) is almost certainly an error for Σίγα (Siga), Syphax's residence; see n. on 11.24a.4. *RE* Siga 2274–2275 (H. Dessau).

4 This is modern Tabarka, west of Carthage in Numidia, but

FRAGMENTS OF BOOK XII

I. AFFAIRS OF AFRICA

1.1 Polybius says in Book 12 that Byzacium[1] is a region close to the Syrtes, its circumference is two thousand stades and its form round.

1.2 Hippo, a city of Libya.[2] Polybius in Book 12.

1.3 Singa, a city of Libya,[3] as Polybius ⟨says⟩ in Book 12.

1.4 Tabraka, a city of Libya.[4] Polybius in Book 12.

1.5 Chalkeia, a city of Libya. The Polyhistor[5] in Book 3 of *Libyka,* and so Demosthenes. Whom Polybius reprimands saying in Book 12: "He is completely ignorant also about τὰ Χαλκεῖα, because this is no city, but copper mines."

close to the border of the later Roman province Africa. *RE* Thabraka 1178–1179 (H. Treidler).

5 The author is Alexander "Polyhistor" of Miletus, the fragment *FGrH* 273 F 46. Alexander lived in the first century, came to Rome as a prisoner of war, and was awarded Roman citizenship by the dictator Sulla. *RE* Alexandros 1449–1452 (Ed. Schwartz). "Demosthenes" is probably an error for Timosthenes, admiral of Ptolemy II, who wrote on the geography of Africa (so A. Geier at *RE* Timosthenes 1321–1322 [F. Gisinger]). See, however, F. Jacoby, *FGrH* 699 (Demosthenes) F 17.

I. DE LOTO

2. Τὰ παραπλήσια τοῖς περὶ τὸν Ἡρόδοτον ἱστορεῖ περὶ τοῦ ἐν Λιβύῃ καλουμένου λωτοῦ αὐτόπτης γενόμενος ὁ Μεγαλοπολίτης Πολύβιος ἐν τῇ ιβ΄ τῶν ἱστο-
2 ριῶν λέγων οὕτως· "Ἔστι δὲ τὸ δένδρον ὁ λωτὸς οὐ μέγα, τραχὺ δὲ καὶ ἀκανθῶδες, ἔχει δὲ φύλλον χλωρὸν παραπλήσιον τῇ ῥάμνῳ, μικρὸν βαθύτερον καὶ
3 πλατύτερον. ὁ δὲ καρπὸς τὰς μὲν ἀρχὰς ὅμοιός ἐστι καὶ τῇ χρόᾳ καὶ τῷ μεγέθει ταῖς λευκαῖς μυρτίσι ταῖς
4 τετελειωμέναις, αὐξανόμενος δὲ τῷ μὲν χρώματι γίνεται φοινικοῦς, τῷ δὲ μεγέθει ταῖς γογγύλαις ἐλαίαις
5 παραπλήσιος, πυρῆνα δὲ ἔχει τελέως μικρόν. ἐπὰν δὲ πεπανθῇ, συνάγουσι, καὶ τὸν μὲν τοῖς οἰκέταις μετὰ χόνδρου κόψαντες σάττουσιν εἰς ἀγγεῖα, τὸν δὲ τοῖς ἐλευθέροις ἐξελόντες τὸν πυρῆνα συντιθέασιν ὡσαύ-
6 τως, καὶ σιτεύονται τοῦτον. ἔστι δὲ τὸ βρῶμα παραπλήσιον σύκῳ καὶ φοινικοβαλάνῳ, τῇ δὲ εὐωδίᾳ βέλ-
7 τιον. γίνεται δὲ καὶ οἶνος ἐξ αὐτοῦ βρεχομένου καὶ τριβομένου δι' ὕδατος, κατὰ μὲν τὴν γεῦσιν ἡδὺς καὶ ἀπολαυστικός, οἰνομέλιτι χρηστῷ παραπλήσιος, ᾧ
8 χρῶνται χωρὶς ὕδατος. οὐ δύναται δὲ πλέον δέκα μένειν ἡμερῶν· διὸ καὶ ποιοῦσι κατὰ βραχὺ πρὸς τὴν χρείαν. ποιοῦσι δὲ καὶ ὄξος ἐξ αὐτῶν."

II. TIMAEI DE AFRICA ET CORSICA ERRORES

3. Τὴν μὲν τῆς χώρας ἀρετὴν πᾶς ἄν τις θαυ-
2 μάσειε, τὸν δὲ Τίμαιον εἴποι τις ἂν οὐ μόνον ἀνιστό-

I. THE LOTUS[6]

2. Polybius in the twelfth book of his histories gives from personal observation the same account as Herodotus of the so-called lotus of Africa.[7] He says: "The lotus is not a large tree, but it is rough and thorny. Its leaf is green and resembles that of the blackthorn, but is rather wider and flatter. The fruit at first both in color and in size resembles the white myrtle berry when fully grown, but as it grows it becomes purple in color and about the size of a round olive. The stone is quite small. They gather it when ripe and, after pounding with groats what is meant for the slaves, pack it in jars. They remove the stones from the portion meant for freemen and store it in the same way and on this they feed. The food rather resembles figs or dates, but has a better aroma. Wine is also made from it by moistening it and crushing it in water. This wine is sweet and of an agreeable flavor, resembling very good mead, and they drink it unwatered. It does not, however, keep for more than ten days, so that they make it in small quantities when required. They also make vinegar from it."

II. MISTAKES OF TIMAEUS CONCERNING AFRICA AND CORSICA

3. No one can help admiring the richness of the country, and one is inclined to say that Timaeus[8] was not only

---

[6] From Athenaeus 14.651 D.   [7] Written from personal experience, therefore in all likelihood after 146. This is the *Zizyphus lotus*, different from other kinds. *RE* Lotos, 1: Lotosbaum 1526–1530 (A. Steier). Other descriptions are Hdt. 2.96 and 4.177, and Thphr. *HP* 4.3.1–4, but it is P. who gives the best description.   [8] See n. on 1.5.1.

ρητον γεγονέναι περὶ τῶν κατὰ τὴν Λιβύην, ἀλλὰ καὶ
παιδαριώδη καὶ τελέως ἀσυλλόγιστον καὶ ταῖς ἀρχαί-
αις φήμαις ἀκμὴν ἐνδεδεμένον, ἃς παρειλήφαμεν, ὡς
ἀμμώδους πάσης καὶ ξηρᾶς καὶ ἀκάρπου καθυπαρ-
3   χούσης τῆς Λιβύης. ὁ δ' αὐτὸς λόγος καὶ περὶ τῶν
ζῴων. τό τε γὰρ τῶν ἵππων καὶ τῶν βοῶν καὶ προβάτων, ἅμα δὲ τούτοις αἰγῶν πλῆθος τοσοῦτόν ἐστι κατὰ
τὴν χώραν ὅσον οὐκ οἶδ' εἰ δύναιτ' ἂν εὑρεθῆναι κατὰ
4   τὴν λοιπὴν οἰκουμένην, διὰ τὸ πολλὰ τῶν κατὰ Λιβύην ἐθνῶν τοῖς μὲν ἡμέροις μὴ χρῆσθαι καρποῖς,
ἀπὸ δὲ τῶν θρεμμάτων καὶ σὺν τοῖς θρέμμασιν ἔχειν
5   τὸν βίον. καὶ μὴν τὸ τῶν ἐλεφάντων καὶ λεόντων καὶ
παρδάλεων πλῆθος καὶ τὴν ἀλκήν, ἔτι δὲ βουβάλων
κάλλος καὶ στρουθῶν μεγέθη, τίς οὐχ ἱστόρησεν; ὧν
κατὰ μὲν τὴν Εὐρώπην τὸ παράπαν οὐδέν ἐστιν, ἡ δὲ
6   Λιβύη πλήρης ἐστὶ τῶν προειρημένων. περὶ ὧν οὐδὲν
ἱστορήσας Τίμαιος ὥσπερ ἐπίτηδες τἀναντία τοῖς
κατ' ἀλήθειαν ὑπάρχουσιν ἐξηγεῖται.

7   Καθάπερ δὲ καὶ περὶ τῶν κατὰ Λιβύην ἀπεσχε-
δίακεν, οὕτως καὶ περὶ τῶν κατὰ τὴν νῆσον τὴν προσ-
8   αγορευομένην Κύρνον. καὶ γὰρ ὑπὲρ ἐκείνης μνημο-
νεύων ἐν τῇ δευτέρᾳ βύβλῳ φησὶν αἶγας ἀγρίας καὶ
πρόβατα καὶ βοῦς ἀγρίους ὑπάρχειν ἐν αὐτῇ πολλούς,
ἔτι δ' ἐλάφους καὶ λαγὼς καὶ λύκους καί τινα τῶν ἄλλων ζῴων, καὶ τοὺς ἀνθρώπους περὶ ταῦτα διατρίβειν
κυνηγετοῦντας καὶ τὴν ὅλην τοῦ βίου διαγωγὴν ἐν
9   τούτοις ἔχειν. κατὰ δὲ τὴν προειρημένην νῆσον οὐχ
οἷον αἶξ ἄγριον ἢ βοῦς, ἀλλ' οὐδὲ λαγὼς οὐδὲ λύκος

unacquainted with Africa but that he was childish and entirely deficient in judgment, and was still fettered by the ancient report handed down to us that the whole of Africa is sandy, dry, and unproductive. The same holds good regarding the animals. For the number of horses, oxen, sheep, and goats in the country is so large that I doubt if so many could be found in the rest of the world, because many of the African tribes make no use of cereals but live on the flesh of their cattle and among their cattle. Again, all are aware of the numbers and strength of the elephants, lions, and panthers in Africa, of the beauty of its antelopes, and the size of its ostriches, creatures that do not exist at all in Europe while Africa is full of them. Timaeus has no information[9] on this subject and seems of set purpose to tell the exact opposite of the actual facts.

Regarding Corsica, too, he makes the same kind of random statements as in the case of Africa. In the account he gives of it in his second book he tells us that there are many wild goats, sheep, and cattle in it, as well as deer, hares, wolves, and certain other animals, and that the inhabitants spend their time in hunting those animals, this being their sole occupation. The fact is that in this island not only is there not a single wild goat or wild ox, but there are not

[9] P., for his part, seems to write from personal experience (as in 2.1), that is, probably after 146.

οὐδ' ἔλαφος οὐδ' ἄλλο τῶν τοιούτων ζῴων οὐδέν ἐστι,
πλὴν ἀλωπέκων καὶ κυνίκλων καὶ προβάτων ἀγρίων.
10 ὁ δὲ κύνικλος πόρρωθεν μὲν ὁρώμενος εἶναι δοκεῖ λαγὼς μικρός, ὅταν δ' εἰς τὰς χεῖρας λάβῃ τις, μεγάλην
ἔχει διαφορὰν καὶ κατὰ τὴν ἐπιφάνειαν καὶ κατὰ τὴν
βρῶσιν· γίνεται δὲ τὸ πλεῖον μέρος κατὰ γῆς.
   4. δοκεῖ γε μὴν πάντ' εἶναι τὰ ζῷα κατὰ τὴν νῆσον
2 ἄγρια διὰ τοιαύτην αἰτίαν. οὐ δύνανται κατὰ τὰς
νομὰς συνακολουθεῖν οἱ ποιμαίνοντες τοῖς θρέμμασι
διὰ τὸ σύνδενδρον καὶ κρημνώδη καὶ τραχεῖαν εἶναι
τὴν νῆσον· ἀλλ' ὅταν βούλωνται συναθροῖσαι, κατὰ
τοὺς εὐκαίρους τόπους ἐφιστάμενοι τῇ σάλπιγγι συγ-
καλοῦσι τὰ ζῷα, καὶ πάντα πρὸς τὴν ἰδίαν ἀδιαπτώ-
3 τως συντρέχει σάλπιγγα. λοιπὸν ὅταν τινὲς προσ-
πλεύσαντες πρὸς τὴν νῆσον αἶγας ἢ βοῦς θεάσωνται
νεμομένας ἐρήμους, κἄπειτα βουληθῶσι καταλαβεῖν,
οὐ προσίεται τὰ ζῷα διὰ τὴν ἀσυνήθειαν, ἀλλὰ φεύ-
4 γει. ὅταν δὲ καὶ συνιδὼν ὁ ποιμὴν τοὺς ἀποβαίνοντας
σαλπίσῃ, προτροπάδην ἅμα φέρεται καὶ συντρέχει
πρὸς τὴν σάλπιγγα. διὸ φαντασίαν ἀγρίων ποιεῖ·
ὑπὲρ ὧν Τίμαιος κακῶς καὶ παρέργως ἱστορήσας
5 ἐσχεδίασε. τὸ δὲ τῇ σάλπιγγι πειθαρχεῖν οὐκ ἔστι
θαυμάσιον· καὶ γὰρ κατὰ τὴν Ἰταλίαν οἱ τὰς ὗς
6 τρέφοντες οὕτω χειρίζουσι τὰ κατὰ τὰς νομάς. οὐ γὰρ
ἕπονται κατὰ πόδας οἱ συοφορβοὶ τοῖς θρέμμασιν,
ὥσπερ παρὰ τοῖς Ἕλλησιν, ἀλλὰ προηγοῦνται φω-
νοῦντες τῇ βυκάνῃ κατὰ διάστημα, τὰ δὲ θρέμματα
7 κατόπιν ἀκολουθεῖ καὶ συντρέχει πρὸς τὴν φωνήν, καὶ

even any hares, wolves, deer, or similar animals, with the exception of foxes, rabbits, and wild sheep. The rabbit when seen from a distance looks like a small hare, but when captured it differs much from a hare both in appearance and taste. It lives for the most part under the ground

4. All the animals in the island, however, seem to be wild for the following reason. The shepherds are not able to follow their cattle as they graze, owing to the island being thickly wooded, rough, and precipitous, but when they want to collect the herds they take up their position on suitable spots and call them in by trumpet, all the animals without fail responding to their own trumpet. So that when people touching at the island see goats and oxen grazing by themselves and then attempt to catch them, the animals will not approach them, being unused to them, but take to flight. When the shepherd sees the strangers disembarking and sounds his trumpet the herd starts off at full speed to respond to the call. For this reason the animals give one the impression of being wild, and Timaeus, after inadequate and casual inquiry, made this random statement. It is by no means surprising that the animals should obey the call of the trumpet; for in Italy those in care of swine manage matters in the same way in pasturing them. The swineherd does not follow behind the animals as in Greece but goes in front and sounds a horn at intervals, the animals following him and responding to the call. They have

τηλικαύτη γίνεται συνήθεια τοῖς ζῴοις πρὸς τὴν ἰδίαν
βυκάνην ὥστε θαυμάζειν καὶ δυσπαραδέκτως ἔχειν
8 τοὺς πρώτους ἀκούσαντας. διὰ γὰρ τὴν πολυχειρίαν
καὶ τὴν λοιπὴν χορηγίαν μεγάλα συμβαίνει τὰ συβό-
σια κατὰ τὴν Ἰταλίαν ὑπάρχειν, καὶ μάλιστα τὴν
Γαλατίαν, ὥστε τὴν μίαν τοκάδα χιλίους ἐκτρέφειν ὗς,
9 ποτὲ δὲ καὶ πλείους. διὸ καὶ κατὰ γένη ποιοῦνται καὶ
καθ’ ἡλικίαν τὰς ἐκ τῶν νυκτερευμάτων ἐξαγωγάς.
10 ὅθεν εἰς τὸν αὐτὸν τόπον προαγομένων καὶ πλειόνων
συστημάτων οὐ δύνανται ταῦτα κατὰ γένη τηρεῖν,
ἀλλά γε συμπίπτει κατά τε τὰς ἐξελασίας καὶ νομὰς
11 ἀλλήλοις, ὁμοίως δὲ κατὰ τὰς προσαγωγάς. ἐξ ὧν
αὐτοῖς ἐπινενόηται πρὸς τὸ διακρίνειν, ὅταν συμπέσῃ,
12 χωρὶς κόπου καὶ πραγματείας τὸ κατὰ βυκάνην. ἐπειδὰν γὰρ τῶν νεμόντων ὁ μὲν ἐπὶ τοῦτο τὸ μέρος
προάγῃ φωνῶν, ὁ δ’ ἐφ’ ἕτερον ἀποκλίνας, αὐτὰ δι’
αὑτῶν χωρίζεται τὰ θρέμματα καὶ κατακολουθεῖ ταῖς
ἰδίαις βυκάναις μετὰ τοιαύτης προθυμίας ὥστε μὴ
δυνατὸν εἶναι βιάσασθαι μηδὲ κωλῦσαι μηδενὶ τρόπῳ
13 τὴν ὁρμὴν αὐτῶν. παρὰ δὲ τοῖς Ἕλλησι κατὰ τοὺς
δρυμούς, ἐπειδὰν ἀλλήλοις συμπέσῃ διώκοντα τὸν
καρπόν, ὁ πλείονας ἔχων χεῖρας καὶ κατευκαιρήσας
περιλαβὼν τοῖς ἰδίοις θρέμμασιν ἀπάγει τὰ τοῦ πλη-
14 σίον. ποτὲ δὲ κλέπτης ὑποκαθίσας ἀπήλασεν, οὐδ’
ἐπιγινώσκοντος τοῦ περιάγοντος πῶς ἀπέβαλε, διὰ
τὸ μακρὰν ἀποσπᾶσθαι τὰ κτήνη τῶν περιαγόντων,
ἁμιλλώμενα περὶ τὸν καρπόν, ὅταν ἀκμὴν ἄρχηται
ῥεῖν. πλὴν ταῦτα μὲν ἐπὶ τοσοῦτον.

learned so well to answer to their own horn that those who hear of this for the first time are astonished and loath to believe it. For owing to the large laboring population and the general abundance of food the herds of swine in Italy are very large, especially in Gallia, so that a thousand pigs[10] and sometimes even more are reared from one sow. They, therefore, drive them out from their night quarters in different troops according to their breed and age. Thus when several troops are driven on to the same place they cannot keep the different classes apart, but they get mixed either when they are being driven out, or when they are feeding, or when they are on the way home. They, therefore, invented the horn call to separate them when they get mixed without trouble or fuss. For when one of the swineherds advances in one direction sounding the horn and another turns off in another direction, the animals separate of their own accord and follow the sound of their own horn with such alacrity that it is impossible by any means to force them back or arrest their course. In Greece, on the contrary, when different herds meet each other in the thickets in their search for acorns, whoever has more hands with him and has the opportunity includes his neighbor's swine with his own and carries them off, or at times a robber will lie in wait and drive some off without the man in charge of them knowing how he has lost them, as the swine become widely separated from their conductors in their race for the acorn when the fruit just begins to fall. But this is enough on this subject.[11]

[10] Some kind of misunderstanding.

[11] The contents of chapters 3 and 4 deviated from narrating history, and P. may finally have become aware of that.

III. DE ALIIS TIMAEI ERRORIBUS

4a. Ὅτι διασύρας ὁ Πολύβιος τὸν Τίμαιον ἐν
πολλοῖς αὖθίς φησι· Τίς ἂν ἔτι δοίη συγγνώμην ⟨ἐπὶ⟩
τοῖς τοιούτοις ἁμαρτήμασιν ἄλλως τε καὶ Τιμαίῳ τῷ
προσφυομένῳ τοῖς ἄλλοις πρὸς τὰς τοιαύτας παρωνυ-
2 χίας; ἐν αἷς Θεοπόμπου μὲν κατηγορεῖ διότι Διονυσίου ποιησαμένου τὴν ἀνακομιδὴν ἐκ Σικελίας εἰς
Κόρινθον ἐν μακρᾷ νηί, Θεόπομπός φησιν ἐν στρογ-
γύλῃ παραγενέσθαι τὸν Διονύσιον, Ἐφόρου δὲ πάλιν
3 ἄγνοιαν καταψεύδεται, φάσκων λέγειν αὐτὸν ὅτι Διο-
νύσιος ὁ πρεσβύτερος παρελάμβανε τὴν ἀρχὴν ἐτῶν
εἴκοσι τριῶν ὑπάρχων, δυναστεῦσαι δὲ τετταράκοντα
καὶ δύο, μεταλλάξαι δὲ τὸν βίον προσλαβὼν τοῖς
4 ἑξήκοντα τρία· τοῦτο γὰρ οὐδεὶς ἂν εἴπειε δήπου τοῦ
συγγραφέως εἶναι τὸ διάπτωμα, τοῦ δὲ γραφέως ὁμο-
5 λογουμένως· ἢ γὰρ δεῖ τὸν Ἔφορον ὑπερβεβηκέναι
τῇ μωρίᾳ καὶ τὸν Κόροιβον καὶ τὸν Μαργίτην, εἰ μὴ
δυνατὸς ἦν συλλογίζεσθαι διότι τὰ τετταράκοντα καὶ
δύο προσθέντα τοῖς εἴκοσι καὶ τρισὶν ἑξήκοντα
6 γίνεται καὶ πέντε· ἢ τούτου μηδαμῶς ἂν πιστευθέντος
ὑπὲρ Ἐφόρου φανερὸν ὅτι τὸ μὲν ἁμάρτημα . . . ἐστι
τοῦ γραφέως, τὸ δὲ Τιμαίου φιλεπίτιμον καὶ φιλέγ-
κλημον οὐδεὶς ἂν ἀποδέξαιτο.

4b. Καὶ μὴν ἐν τοῖς περὶ Πύρρου πάλιν φησὶ τοὺς
Ῥωμαίους ἔτι νῦν ὑπόμνημα ποιουμένους τῆς κατὰ τὸ

---

12 See n. on 8.9.1. References are to Theopompus, FGrH 115
F 341, and to Timaeus, FGrH 566 F 116–117.

III. OTHER ERRORS
MADE BY TIMAEUS

4a. Who could continue to pardon such faults, especially when committed by Timaeus who is so fond of caviling at similar blemishes in others? For instance, he accuses Theopompus[12] of stating that Dionysius was conveyed from Sicily to Corinth in a merchant ship, whereas he really travelled in a warship, and again he falsely accuses Ephorus[13] of making a blunder because he tells us that the elder Dionysius began to reign at the age of twenty-three, reigned for forty-two years, and died at the age of sixty-three. For surely no one could say that the mistake here was the author's, but it is obviously the scribe's. Either Ephorus must have surpassed Coroebus[14] and Margites[15] in stupidity if he could not reckon that forty-two added to twenty-three make sixty-five, or as nobody would believe this of Ephorus, the mistake is evidently due to the scribe. No one, however, could approve of Timaeus' love of caviling and faultfinding.[16]

4b. Again in his account of Pyrrhus he tells us that the Romans still commemorate their disaster at Troy by shoot-

[13] See nn. on 4.20.5 and 5.33.2. P. refers to Ephorus, *FGrH* 70 F 218, and Timaeus 566 F 110.

[14] A Phrygian not paying heed to Cassandra, proverbial for a fool.

[15] A moron, hero of a humorous poem with that title, edited and translated by M. L. West, in the *Homeric Hymns, Homeric Apocrypha, Lives of Homer* (Loeb 496).

[16] This habit earned Timaeus the nickname *Epitimaeus* (ἐπι-τίμαιος), "fault-finder" (Ister at Ath. 6.272 b; Diod. Sic. 5.1.3).

Ἴλιον ἀπωλείας ἐν ἡμέρᾳ τινὶ κατακοντίζειν ἵππον
πολεμιστὴν πρὸ τῆς πόλεως ἐν τῷ Κάμπῳ καλουμένῳ
διὰ τὸ τῆς Τροίας τὴν ἅλωσιν διὰ τὸν ἵππον γενέσθαι
τὸν δούριον προσαγορευόμενον, πρᾶγμα πάντων παι-
2 δαριωδέστατον· οὕτω μὲν γὰρ δεήσει πάντας τοὺς
3 βαρβάρους λέγειν Τρώων ἀπογόνους ὑπάρχειν· σχεδὸν γὰρ πάντες, εἰ δὲ μή γ᾽, οἱ πλείους, ὅταν ἢ πολεμεῖν μέλλωσιν ἐξ ἀρχῆς ἢ διακινδυνεύειν πρός τινας
ὁλοσχερῶς, ἵππῳ προθύονται καὶ σφαγιάζονται, ση-
μειούμενοι τὸ μέλλον ἐκ τῆς τοῦ ζῴου πτώσεως.

4c. ὁ δὲ Τίμαιος περὶ τοῦτο τὸ μέρος τῆς ἀλογίας
οὐ μόνον ἀπειρίαν, ἔτι δὲ μᾶλλον ὀψιμαθίαν δοκεῖ μοι
πολλὴν ἐπιφαίνειν, ὅς γε, διότι θύουσιν ἵππον, εὐθέως
ὑπέλαβε τοῦτο ποιεῖν αὐτοὺς διὰ τὸ τὴν Τροίαν ἀφ᾽
ἵππου δοκεῖν ἑαλωκέναι.

2 Πλὴν ὅτι γε κακῶς ἱστόρηκε καὶ τὰ περὶ τὴν
Λιβύην καὶ τὰ περὶ τὴν Σαρδόνα, καὶ μάλιστα τὰ
3 κατὰ τὴν Ἰταλίαν, ἐκ τούτων ἐστὶ συμφανές, καὶ
καθόλου διότι τὸ περὶ τὰς ἀνακρίσεις μέρος ἐπι-
σέσυρται παρ᾽ αὐτῷ τελέως· ὅπερ ἐστὶ κυριώτατον τῆς
4 ἱστορίας. ἐπειδὴ γὰρ αἱ μὲν πράξεις ἅμα πολλαχῇ
συντελοῦνται, παρεῖναι δὲ τὸν αὐτὸν ἐν πλείοσι τόποις
κατὰ τὸν αὐτὸν καιρὸν ἀδύνατον, ὁμοίως γε μὴν οὐδ᾽
αὐτόπτην γενέσθαι πάντων τῶν κατὰ τὴν οἰκουμένην
τόπων καὶ τῶν ἐν τοῖς τόποις ἰδιωμάτων τὸν ἕνα δυ-
5 νατόν, καταλείπεται πυνθάνεσθαι μὲν ὡς παρὰ πλείστων, πιστεύειν δὲ τοῖς ἀξίοις πίστεως, κριτὴν δ᾽ εἶναι
τῶν προσπιπτόντων μὴ κακόν.

ing on a certain day a warhorse[17] before the city in the Campus Martius, because the capture of Troy was due to the wooden horse—a most childish statement. For at that rate we should have to say that all barbarian tribes were descendants of the Trojans, since nearly all of them, or at least the majority, when they are entering on a war or on the eve of a decisive battle sacrifice a horse, divining the issue from the manner in which it falls.

4c. Timaeus in dealing with the foolish practice seems to me to exhibit not only ignorance but pedantry in supposing that in sacrificing a horse they do so because Troy was said to have been taken by means of a horse.

But from all this it is evident that the account he gives of Africa, of Sardinia, and especially of Italy, is inaccurate, and we see that generally the task of investigation[18] has been entirely scamped by him, and this is the most important part of history. For since many events occur at the same time in different places, and one man cannot be in several places at one time, nor is it possible for a single man to have seen with his own eyes every place in the world and all the peculiar features of different places, the only thing left for an historian is to inquire from as many people as possible, to believe those worthy of belief and to be an adequate critic of the reports that reach him.

[17] Refers to Timaeus, *FGrH* 566 F 36. There was in fact an annual sacrifice of a horse but of very different significance; see WC 2.327–328.

[18] P. accuses Timaeus, here and in 4d, of not doing, or of doing sloppily, the necessary research.

4d. Ἐν ᾧ γένει μεγίστην ἐπίφασιν ἕλκων Τίμαιος
2 πλεῖστον ἀπολείπεσθαί μοι δοκεῖ τῆς ἀληθείας· τοσοῦτο γὰρ ἀπέχει τοῦ δι᾽ ἑτέρων ἀκριβῶς τὴν ἀλήθειαν
ἐξετάζειν ὡς οὐδὲ τούτων ὧν αὐτόπτης γέγονε καὶ ἐφ᾽
οὓς αὐτὸς ἥκει τόπους, οὐδὲ περὶ τούτων οὐδὲν ὑγιὲς
3 ἡμῖν ἐξηγεῖται. τοῦτο δ᾽ ἔσται δῆλον, ἐὰν ἐν τοῖς κατὰ
τὴν Σικελίαν δείξωμεν αὐτὸν ἀγνοοῦντα περὶ ὧν ἀπο-
4 φαίνεται· σχεδὸν γὰρ οὐ πολλῶν ἔτι προσδεήσει
λόγων ὑπέρ γε τῆς ψευδολογίας, ἐὰν ἐν οἷς ἔφυ καὶ
ἐτράφη τόποις, καὶ τούτων ἐν τοῖς ἐπιφανεστάτοις [ἐν
τούτοις] ἀγνοῶν εὑρεθῇ καὶ παραπαίων τῆς ἀληθείας.
5 φησὶ τοιγαροῦν τὴν Ἀρέθουσαν κρήνην τὴν ἐν ταῖς
Συρακούσαις ἔχειν τὰς πηγὰς ἐκ τοῦ κατὰ Πελο-
πόννησον διά τε τῆς Ἀρκαδίας καὶ διὰ τῆς Ὀλυμπίας
6 ῥέοντος [ποταμοῦ] Ἀλφειοῦ· ἐκεῖνον γὰρ δύντα κατὰ
γῆς <καὶ> τετρακισχιλίους σταδίους ὑπὸ τὸ Σικελικὸν
ἐνεχθέντα πέλαγος ἀναδύνειν ἐν ταῖς Συρακούσαις,
7 γενέσθαι δὲ τοῦτο δῆλον ἐκ τοῦ κατά τινα χρόνον
οὐρανίων ὄμβρων ῥαγέντων κατὰ τὸν τῶν Ὀλυμπίων
καιρὸν καὶ τοῦ ποταμοῦ τοὺς κατὰ τὸ τέμενος ἐπι-
8 κλύσαντος τόπους, ὄνθου τε πλῆθος ἀναβλύζειν τὴν
Ἀρέθουσαν ἐκ τῶν κατὰ τὴν πανήγυριν θυομένων
βοῶν καὶ φιάλην χρυσῆν ἀναβαλεῖν, ἣν ἐπιγνόντες
εἶναι τῆς ἑορτῆς ἀνείλοντο.

354

4d. In this respect Timaeus, while making a great parade of accuracy, is, in my opinion, wont to be very short of the truth. So far is he from accurate investigation of the truth by questioning others that not even about matters he has seen with his own eyes and places he has actually visited does he tell us anything trustworthy. This will become evident if we can show that in talking of Sicily he makes mistaken statements. For we may almost say that no further evidence of his inaccuracy is required, if as regards the country where he was born and bred and the most celebrated spots in it we find him mistaken and widely diverging from the truth. He tells us, then, that the fountain of Arethusa[19] in Syracuse derives its source from the river Alpheius in the Peloponnese which runs through Arcadia and past Olympia. This river, he says, diving into the earth and travelling four thousand stades[20] under the Sicilian Sea reappears in Syracuse. This, he adds, is proved by the fact that once upon a time after heavy rains at the season of the Olympian festival, when the river had flooded the sanctuary, Arethusa threw up a quantity of dung from the beasts sacrificed at the festival and even a gold bowl which they recognized as coming from the festival and made away with.

[19] P. refers to Timaeus, *FGrH* 566 F 41 b. The myth of an association between this fountain and the Alpheius in Elis is widely recorded.

[20] Not to be taken seriously, and much too high.

IV. DE TIMAEI ERRORIBUS
COMMISSIS DE REBUS LOCRENSIUM

5. Ἐμοὶ δὴ συμβαίνει καὶ παραβεβληκέναι πλεο
νάκις εἰς τὴν τῶν Λοκρῶν πόλιν καὶ παρεσχῆσθαι
2 χρείας αὐτοῖς ἀναγκαίας· καὶ γὰρ τῆς εἰς Ἰβηρίαν
στρατείας αὐτοὺς παραλυθῆναι συνέβη δι' ἐμὲ καὶ
τῆς εἰς Δαλματεῖς, ἣν ὤφειλον κατὰ θάλατταν ἐκ
3 πέμπειν Ῥωμαίοις κατὰ τὰς συνθήκας. ἐξ ὧν καὶ
κακοπαθείας καὶ κινδύνου καὶ δαπάνης ἱκανῆς τινος
ἀπολυθέντες πᾶσιν ἡμᾶς ἡμείψαντο τοῖς τιμίοις καὶ
φιλανθρώποις· διόπερ ὀφείλω μᾶλλον εὐλογεῖν Λο
4 κροὺς ἢ τοὐναντίον. ἀλλ' ὅμως οὐκ ὤκνησα καὶ λέγειν
καὶ γράφειν ὅτι τὴν ὑπ' Ἀριστοτέλους παραδιδομένην
ἱστορίαν περὶ τῆς ἀποικίας ἀληθινωτέραν εἶναι συμ
5 βαίνει τῆς ὑπὸ Τιμαίου λεγομένης. σύνοιδα γὰρ τοῖς
ἀνθρώποις ὁμολογοῦσιν ὅτι παραδόσιμος αὐτοῖς
ἐστιν αὕτη περὶ τῆς ἀποικίας ἡ φήμη παρὰ πατέρων,
ἣν Ἀριστοτέλης εἴρηκεν, οὐ Τίμαιος. καὶ τούτων γε
6 τοιαύτας ἔφερον ἀποδείξεις. πρῶτον μὲν ὅτι πάντα τὰ
διὰ προγόνων ἔνδοξα παρ' αὐτοῖς ἀπὸ τῶν γυναικῶν,
οὐκ ἀπὸ τῶν ἀνδρῶν ἐστιν, οἷον εὐθέως εὐγενεῖς παρὰ
σφίσι νομίζεσθαι τοὺς ἀπὸ τῶν ἑκατὸν οἰκιῶν λεγο
7 μένους· ταύτας δ' εἶναι τὰς ἑκατὸν οἰκίας τὰς προκρι
θείσας ὑπὸ τῶν Λοκρῶν πρὶν ἢ τὴν ἀποικίαν ἐξελθεῖν,

---

21 *OCD* Locri Epizephyrii 879 (H. K. Lomas). *RE* Lokroi
1289–1363 (W. Oldfather).

IV. ERRORS OF TIMAEUS
ABOUT LOCRI

5. I happen to have paid several visits to Locri[21] and to have rendered the Locrians important services. It was indeed through me that they were excused from serving in the Spanish[22] and Dalmatian[23] campaigns, in both of which they were required by the terms of their treaty to send aid to the Romans by sea. In consequence they were relieved from considerable hardship, danger, and expense, and in return conferred on me all kinds of honors and favors; so that I ought rather to speak well of the Locrians than the reverse. But nevertheless I have not hesitated to affirm both in speech and writing that the account we have received from Aristotle[24] about the foundation of the colony is truer than that given by Timaeus. For I know that the Locrians[25] themselves confess that the tradition handed down to them by their fathers concerning the colony is that given by Aristotle and not that of Timaeus. And of this they adduce the following proofs. First of all that at Locri all ancestral nobility is derived from women, not from men, as, for example, those are considered noble among them who are said to be of the "hundred houses." These "hundred houses" were those distinguished by the Locrians as the leading families before the colony was sent

[22] Either the one against the Lusitanians which began in 154 or the one against the Celtiberians starting in 153 (*MRR* 1.450 and 452, respectively).

[23] In all likelihood of 156/5 (*MRR* 1.447).

[24] Probably in one of his 158 *Constitutions* of Greek states.

[25] These are the metropolitan Locrians in Greece.

ἐξ ὧν ἔμελλον οἱ Λοκροὶ κατὰ τὸν χρησμὸν κληροῦν
8 τὰς ἀποσταλησομένας παρθένους εἰς Ἴλιον. τούτων
δή τινας τῶν γυναικῶν συνεξᾶραι μετὰ τῆς ἀποικίας,
ὧν τοὺς ἀπογόνους ἔτι νῦν εὐγενεῖς νομίζεσθαι καὶ
9 καλεῖσθαι τοὺς ἀπὸ τῶν ἑκατὸν οἰκιῶν. πάλιν ὑπὲρ
τῆς φιαληφόρου παρ᾽ αὐτοῖς λεγομένης τοιαύτη τις
10 ἱστορία παραδέδοτο, διότι καθ᾽ ὃν καιρὸν τοὺς Σικελοὺς ἐκβάλοιεν τοὺς κατασχόντας τὸν τόπον τοῦτον
τῆς Ἰταλίας, ὧν καὶ ταῖς θυσίαις προηγεῖτο τῶν
ἐνδοξοτάτων καὶ τῶν εὐγενεστάτων ὑπάρχων παῖς,
αὐτοὶ καὶ πλείω τῶν Σικελικῶν ἐθῶν παραλαβόντες
διὰ τὸ μηδὲν αὐτοῖς πάτριον ὑπάρχειν καὶ τοῦτο
11 διαφυλάττοιεν ἀπ᾽ ἐκείνων, αὐτὸ δὲ τοῦτο διορθώ-
σαιντο, τὸ μὴ παῖδα ποιεῖν ἐξ αὐτῶν τὸν φιαληφόρον,
ἀλλὰ παρθένον, διὰ τὴν ἀπὸ τῶν γυναικῶν εὐγένειαν.

6. Συνθῆκαι δὲ πρὸς μὲν τοὺς κατὰ τὴν Ἑλλάδα
Λοκροὺς οὔτ᾽ ἦσαν οὔτ᾽ ἐλέγοντο παρ᾽ αὐτοῖς γεγονέναι, πρὸς μέντοι Σικελοὺς πάντες εἶχον ἐν παρα-
2 δόσει. περὶ ὧν ἔλεγον διότι, καθ᾽ ὃν καιρὸν ἐκ τῆς
πρώτης παρουσίας καταλάβοιεν Σικελοὺς κατέχοντας
ταύτην τὴν χώραν, ἐν ᾗ νῦν κατοικοῦσι, καταπλα-
γέντων αὐτοὺς ἐκείνων καὶ προσδεξαμένων διὰ τὸν
3 φόβον, ὁμολογίας ποιήσαιντο τοιαύτας, ἦ μὴν εὐνοή-
σειν αὐτοῖς καὶ κοινῇ τὴν χώραν ἕξειν, ἕως ἂν ἐπιβαί-

26 In order to expiate the crime of the Locrian Aias against
Cassandra, the Locrians used to send one or two virgins to Ilion, to
serve at the temple of Athena, as an oracle from Delphi had or-

out, the families from which the Locrians, as the oracle ordered, were to select by lot the virgins[26] they had to send to Troy. Some women belonging to these families left with the colony, and it is their descendants who are still considered noble and called "of the hundred houses." Again, as regards the virgin ministrant they call the Phialephorus the tradition is much as follows. At the time they expelled the Sicels[27] who had occupied this site in Italy, at whose sacrifices the procession was led by a boy of one of the most celebrated and noble families, the Locrians adopted several of the Sicelian rites, as they had no inherited ritual, retaining among others this particular one, but making merely this change in it that they did not appoint one of their boys to be Phialephorus, but one of their virgins, because nobility among them was derived from women.

6. As for treaties with the Locrians of Greece proper there were none, and none were ever said to have existed, but all knew of the tradition of one with the Sicels. About this they said that when on their first arrival they found the Sicels in occupation of the place they now dwell in, and the Sicels being terror-struck at their arrival received them out of fear, they made a solemn compact[28] to the effect that they would be their friends and share the country with

dered. The custom is first attested by Aen. Tact. 31.24 in the fourth century, thereafter often and with variants. See the famous inscription concerning these Locrian maidens, *IG* IX 1² 706; text, commentary, and bibliography also in *StV* 472. It dates to the early third century.   [27] For their presence on the mainland opposite Sicily, see Th. 6.2.4.

[28] The following story has parallels in various parts of the ancient world.

νωσι τῇ γῇ ταύτῃ καὶ τὰς κεφαλὰς ἐπὶ τοῖς ὤμοις
4 φορῶσι. τοιούτων δὲ τῶν ὅρκων γινομένων φασὶ τοὺς
Λοκροὺς εἰς μὲν τὰ πέλματα τῶν ὑποδημάτων ἐμβα-
λόντας γῆν, ἐπὶ δὲ τοὺς ὤμους σκόρδων κεφαλὰς
ἀφανεῖς ὑποθεμένους οὕτως ποιήσασθαι τοὺς ὅρκους,
5 κἄπειτα τὴν μὲν γῆν ἐκβαλόντας ἐκ τῶν ὑποδημάτων,
τὰς δὲ κεφαλὰς τῶν σκόρδων ἀπορρίψαντας μετ’ οὐ
πολὺ καιροῦ παραπεσόντος ἐκβαλεῖν τοὺς Σικελοὺς ἐκ
6 τῆς χώρας. ταῦτα μὲν οὖν λέγεται παρὰ Λοκροῖς. . . .

7 Τίμαιος δ’ ὁ
Ταυρομενίτης ἐν τῇ
ἐνάτῃ τῶν ἱστοριῶν,
"οὐκ ἦν" φησὶ "πάτριον
τοῖς Ἕλλησιν ὑπὸ
ἀργυρωνήτων τὸ
παλαιὸν διακονεῖσθαι,"
γράφων οὕτως·
"Καθόλου δὲ ᾐτιῶντο
8 τὸν Ἀριστοτέλη
διημαρτηκέναι τῶν
Λοκρικῶν ἐθῶν· οὐδὲ
γὰρ κεκτῆσθαι νόμον
εἶναι τοῖς Λοκροῖς."

Τίμαιος δ’ ὁ
Ταυρομενίτης
ἐκλαθόμενος αὑτοῦ—
ἐλέγχει δ’ αὐτὸν εἰς
τοῦτο Πολύβιος ὁ
Μεγαλοπολίτης διὰ τῆς
δωδεκάτης τῶν
ἱστοριῶν—οὐκ εἶναι
ἔφη σύνηθες τοῖς
Ἕλλησι δούλους
κτᾶσθαι.

6a. Ἐκ τούτων ἄν τις συλλογιζόμενος Ἀριστοτέλει
πρόσσχοι μᾶλλον ἢ Τιμαίῳ· καὶ μὴν τὸ συνεχὲς
2 τούτῳ τελέως ἄτοπον· τὸ γὰρ ὑπολαμβάνειν, καθάπερ

them as long as they trod on this earth and wore heads on their shoulders. When they were taking the oath they say that the Locrians had put some earth into the soles of their shoes and had concealed on their shoulders under their dress some heads of garlic: in this state they took the oath, but subsequently emptying their shoes of the earth and throwing away the heads of garlic, they very shortly afterward, when the occasion presented itself, expelled the Sicels from the country. Such is the account given by the Locrians.[29] . . .

(1) Timaeus of Tauromenium in the ninth book of his *Histories*, says: "It was not the Greek custom to be served by purchased slaves," adding "They accused Aristotle in general of having misunderstood the Locrian customs, for (they said) the law did not permit the Locrians even to possess them." [Athen. 6.264c]	(2) Timaeus of Tauromenium forgetting himself—he is confuted by Polybius in the twelfth book of his *Histories*— says it was once not the custom for the Greeks to possess slaves. [Athen. 6.272a]

6a. The inference from all this is that we should rely on Aristotle rather than on Timaeus. And what follows this is quite peculiar. For it is foolish to suppose, as he hints, that

[29] Timaeus' polemic against Aristotle and that of Polybius against Timaeus cannot be elucidated by short notes. See WC 2.337–339.

ἐκεῖνος ὑποδείκνυσιν, ὡς οὐκ εἰκὸς ἦν τοὺς οἰκέτας
τῶν Λακεδαιμονίοις συμμαχησάντων τὴν τῶν κυρίων
εὔνοιαν ἀναφέρειν πρὸς τοὺς ἐκείνων φίλους εὔηθες·
3 οὐ γὰρ μόνον τὰς εὐνοίας, ἀλλὰ καὶ τὰς ξενίας καὶ τὰς
συγγενείας τῶν δεσποτῶν οἱ δουλεύσαντες, ὅταν εὐτυ-
χήσωσι παραδόξως καὶ χρόνος ἐπιγένηται, πειρῶνται
προσποιεῖσθαι καὶ συνανανεοῦσθαι τῶν κατὰ φύσιν
4 ἀναγκαίων μᾶλλον, αὐτῷ τούτῳ σπουδάζοντες τὴν
προγεγενημένην περὶ αὐτοὺς ἐλάττωσιν καὶ τὴν ἀδο-
ξίαν ἐξαλείφειν, τῷ βούλεσθαι τῶν δεσποτῶν ἀπόγο-
νοι μᾶλλον ἐπιφαίνειν ἤπερ ἀπελεύθεροι.

6b. τοῦτο δὲ μάλιστα περὶ τοὺς Λοκροὺς εἰκός ἐστι
γεγονέναι· πολὺ γὰρ ἐκτοπίσαντες ἐκ τῶν συνειδότων
καὶ προσλαβόντες συνεργὸν τὸν χρόνον, οὐχ οὕτως
ἄφρονες <ἦσαν> ὥστε ταῦτ᾽ ἐπιτηδεύειν, δι᾽ ὧν ἔμελλον ἀνανέωσιν ποιεῖσθαι τῶν ἰδίων ἐλαττωμάτων,
2 ἀλλὰ μὴ τοὐναντίον δι᾽ ὧν ἐπικαλύψειν ταῦτα. διὸ καὶ
τὴν ὀνομασίαν τῇ πόλει τὴν ἀπὸ τῶν γυναικῶν εἰκότως ἐπέθεσαν καὶ τὴν οἰκειότητα τὴν κατὰ τὰς γυναῖκας προσεποιήθησαν, ἔτι δὲ τὰς φιλίας καὶ τὰς συμμαχίας τὰς προγονικὰς τὰς ἀπὸ τῶν γυναικῶν
3 ἀνενεοῦντο. ᾗ καὶ τὸ τοὺς Ἀθηναίους πορθῆσαι τὴν
χώραν αὐτῶν οὐδέν ἐστι σημεῖον ψευδῆ λέγειν τὸν
4 Ἀριστοτέλην· εὐλόγου γὰρ ὄντος ἐκ τῶν προειρημένων, εἰ καὶ δεκάκις ἦσαν οἰκέται, τοῦ προσπεποιῆ-
σθαι τὴν τῶν Λακεδαιμονίων φιλίαν τοὺς ἐξάραντας
ἐκ τῶν Λοκρῶν καὶ κατασχόντας εἰς τὴν Ἰταλίαν,
εὔλογος γίνεται καὶ [ἡ] τῶν Ἀθηναίων ἀλλοτριότης ἡ

it was improbable that the slaves of those who had been the allies of the Lacedaemonians should adopt the friendly feelings of their masters for the friends of those masters. Men, indeed, who have once been slaves when they meet with unexpected good fortune[30] attempt with the passing of time to affect and reproduce not only the likings but the friendships and relationships of their masters, taking more pains to do so than those actually connected by blood, and hope to wipe out their former inferiority and disrepute by this very effort to appear rather as descendants than as freedmen of their late masters.

6b. And in the case of the Locrians this is especially likely to have happened. For as they had removed to a great distance from those acquainted with their past and had lapse of time on their side, they would not have been so foolish as to behave in a manner likely to revive the memory of their defects, but would have so conducted themselves as to cover these defects. They, therefore, naturally named their city after the women and pretended to be related to other Locrians on the female side, renewing also those ancestral friendships and alliances which were derived from the women. For this reason too the fact that the Athenians[31] ravaged their country is no proof that Aristotle's statements are not correct, For, as it was to be expected from what I have said, that even had they been slaves ten times over these men who set sail from Locri and landed in Italy would have affected to be friends of the Lacedaemonians, it was only to be expected also that the Athenians would be hostile to the whole pack of these

30 When they are freed.
31 Their general Laches in 426 (Th. 3.103.3).

πρὸς <πάντας> τοὺς προειρημένους, οὐχ <οὕτως> ἐξ-
5 εταζόντων τὸ γένος ὡς τὴν προαίρεσιν. νὴ Δί᾽ ἀλλὰ
πῶς αὐτοὶ μὲν ἐξαπέστελλον οἱ Λακεδαιμόνιοι τοὺς
ἀκμάζοντας εἰς τὴν πατρίδα τεκνοποιίας χάριν, τοὺς
δὲ Λοκροὺς τὸ παραπλήσιον οὐκ εἴων ποιεῖν; ἕκαστα
6 δὲ τούτων οὐ μόνον κατὰ τὸ πιθανόν, ἀλλὰ καὶ κατὰ
7 τὴν ἀλήθειαν μεγάλην ἔχει διαφοράν. οὔτε γὰρ κωλύειν τοὺς Λοκροὺς ἔμελλον, αὐτοὶ τὸ ὅμοιον ποιοῦντες—ἄτοπον γάρ—οὐδὲ μὴν κελευόντων αὐτῶν οἱ
Λοκροὶ πάντως ποιήσειν ἐκείνοις τὸ παραπλήσιον.
8 παρὰ μὲν γὰρ τοῖς Λακεδαιμονίοις καὶ πάτριον ἦν καὶ
σύνηθες τρεῖς ἄνδρας ἔχειν τὴν γυναῖκα καὶ τέτταρας,
τοτὲ δὲ καὶ πλείους ἀδελφοὺς ὄντας, καὶ τὰ τέκνα
τούτων εἶναι κοινά, καὶ γεννήσαντα παῖδας ἱκανοὺς
ἐκδόσθαι γυναῖκά τινι τῶν φίλων καλὸν καὶ σύνηθες.
9 διόπερ οἱ Λοκροὶ μήτε ταῖς ἀραῖς ὄντες ἔνοχοι μήτε
τοῖς ὅρκοις, <οἷς> ὤμοσαν οἱ Λακεδαιμόνιοι μὴ πρότερον εἰς τὴν οἰκείαν ἐπανήξειν πρὶν ἢ τὴν Μεσσήνην
κατὰ κράτος ἑλεῖν, τῆς μὲν κατὰ τὸ κοινὸν ἐξαπο-
10 στολῆς εὐλόγως οὐ μετέσχον, κατὰ δὲ μέρος τὰς
ἐπανόδους ποιούμενοι καὶ σπανίως ἔδοσαν ἀναστροφὴν ταῖς γυναιξὶ πρὸς οἰκέτας γενέσθαι συνηθεστέ-
ρας ἢ πρὸς τοὺς ἐξ ἀρχῆς ἄνδρας, ταῖς δὲ παρθένοις
καὶ μᾶλλον· ὃ καὶ τῆς ἐξαναστάσεως αἴτιον γέγονεν.

---

[32] The origin of the so-called *Partheniai*, who were later sent
out from Sparta and founded Tarentum; Str. 6.3.2. *RE* Partheniai
1884–1886 (H. Schaefer).

Locrians, not so much from consideration of their ancestry as in view of their sympathies. But how again, it may be objected, could the Spartans who had once sent home those in the prime of life to beget children[32] have refused permission to the Locrians to do the same thing? Not only the probabilities, however, in each case but the facts differ considerably. For the Spartans did not want to prevent the Locrians from acting as they had acted themselves—this would have been strange indeed—nor were the Locrians prepared at the bidding of the Spartans to act in precisely the same manner as the latter had acted. For among the Lacedaemonians it was a hereditary custom and quite usual for three or four men to have one wife or even more if they were brothers,[33] the offspring being the common property of all, and when a man had begotten enough children, it was honorable and quite usual for him to give his wife to one of his friends. Therefore the Locrians, who were not subject to the same curse as the Spartans, nor bound by an oath such as the Spartans had taken that they would not return home before storming Messene, did not, as readily can be explained, imitate the Spartans in a general dispatch of men home, but returning home singly and at rare intervals allowed their wives to become more intimate with their slaves than with their original husbands, and allowed their maidens still greater latitude, which was the cause of the emigration.[34]

[33] This is the only evidence for polyandry in Sparta, but not necessarily untrue.

[34] Which led to the foundation of Locri.

(8)   7. Ὅτι πολλὰ ἱστορεῖ ψευδῆ ὁ Τίμαιος, καὶ δοκεῖ
τὸ παράπαν οὐκ ἄπειρος ὢν οὐδενὸς τῶν τοιούτων, ὑπὸ
δὲ τῆς φιλονεικίας ἐπισκοτούμενος, ὅταν ἅπαξ ἢ ψέ-
γειν ἢ τοὐναντίον ἐγκωμιάζειν τινὰ πρόθηται, πάντων
ἐπιλανθάνεται καὶ πολύ τι τοῦ καθήκοντος παρεκ-

2   βαίνει. πλὴν ταῦτα μὲν ἡμῖν ὑπὲρ Ἀριστοτέλους εἰρήσθω πῶς καὶ τίσι προσέχων τοιαύτην ἐποιήσατο τὴν

3   περὶ τῶν Λοκρῶν ἐξήγησιν· τὰ δὲ λέγεσθαι μέλλοντα
περὶ Τιμαίου καὶ τῆς ὅλης συντάξεως αὐτοῦ καὶ
καθόλου περὶ τοῦ καθήκοντος τοῖς πραγματευομένοις

4   ἱστορίαν τοιάνδε τινὰ λήψεται τὴν ἀπάντησιν. ὅτι μὲν
οὖν ἀμφότεροι κατὰ τὸν εἰκότα λόγον πεποίηνται τὴν
ἐπιχείρησιν, καὶ διότι πλείους εἰσὶ πιθανότητες ἐν τῇ
κατ᾽ Ἀριστοτέλην ἱστορίᾳ, δοκῶ, πᾶς ἄν τις ἐκ τῶν
εἰρημένων ὁμολογήσειεν· ἀληθὲς μέντοι γε καὶ καθ-

5   άπαξ διαστεῖλαι περί τινος οὐδὲν ἔστιν ἐν τούτοις. οὐ
μὴν ἀλλ᾽ ἔστω τὸν Τίμαιον εἰκότα λέγειν μᾶλλον. διὰ
ταύτην οὖν τὴν αἰτίαν δεήσει πᾶν ῥῆμα καὶ πᾶσαν
φωνὴν ἀκούειν καὶ μόνον οὐ θανάτου κρίσιν ὑπέχειν

6   τοὺς ἐν ταῖς ἱστορίαις ἧττον εἰκότα λέγοντας; οὐ
δήπου. τοῖς μὲν γὰρ κατ᾽ ἄγνοιαν ψευδογραφοῦσιν
ἔφαμεν δεῖν διόρθωσιν εὐμενικὴν καὶ συγγνώμην ἐξ-
ακολουθεῖν, τοῖς δὲ κατὰ προαίρεσιν ἀπαραίτητον
κατηγορίαν.

(9)   8. Ἢ δεικτέον οὖν τὸν Ἀριστοτέλην κατὰ τὸν ἄρτι
λόγον τὰ περὶ Λοκρῶν εἰρηκότα χάριτος ἢ κέρδους ἢ
διαφορᾶς ἕνεκεν ἢ μηδὲ τολμῶντας τοῦτο λέγειν ὁμο-
λογητέον ἀγνοεῖν καὶ παραπαίειν τοὺς τοιαύτῃ χρω-

7. Timaeus frequently makes false statements. He appears to me not to be in general uninformed about such matters, but his judgment to be darkened by prejudice; and when he once sets himself to blame or praise anyone he forgets everything and departs[35] very widely from his duty as a historian. Let it suffice, however, on behalf of Aristotle that I have shown how and relying on what authority he composed his account of Locri. But what I am now about to say concerning Timaeus and his work as a whole, and in general about the duty incumbent on those who occupy themselves with history, will meet objections more or less as follows. That both authors have aimed at reaching probability, but that there is more probability in Aristotle's account, I think everyone will avow after what I have said. It is not however, I shall be told, possible to pronounce absolutely about the truth of anything in this matter. Well! I am even ready to concede that Timaeus' account is more probable. But is this a reason why a historical writer whose statements seem less probable must submit to listen to every term of contumely and almost to be put on trial for his life? Surely not. For those, as I said, who make false statements owing to error should meet with kind correction and forgiveness, but those who lie deliberately deserve an implacable accuser.

8. We have, then, either to show that Aristotle, in making the statements I have just reproduced about Locri, did so for the sake of currying favor or for gain or from some self-interested motive, or if we do not venture to maintain

[35] Is not P. doing just the same in these chapters?

μένους ἀπεχθείᾳ καὶ πικρίᾳ κατὰ τῶν πέλας οἷα

2 κέχρηται Τίμαιος κατ' Ἀριστοτέλους. φησὶ γὰρ αὐτὸν
εἶναι θρασύν, εὐχερῆ, προπετῆ, πρὸς δὲ τούτοις κατα-
τετολμηκέναι τῆς τῶν Λοκρῶν πόλεως, εἰπόντα τὴν
ἀποικίαν αὐτῶν εἶναι δραπετῶν, οἰκετῶν, μοιχῶν,

3 ἀνδραποδιστῶν. καὶ ταῦτα λέγειν αὐτόν φησιν οὕτως
ἀξιοπίστως ὥστε δοκεῖν ἕνα τῶν ἐστρατηγηκότων
ὑπάρχειν καὶ τοὺς Πέρσας ἐν ταῖς Κιλικίαις πύλαις
ἄρτι παρατάξει νενικηκότα διὰ τῆς αὐτοῦ δυνάμεως,

4 ἀλλ' οὐ σοφιστὴν ὀψιμαθῆ καὶ μισητὸν ὑπάρχοντα
καὶ τὸ πολυτίμητον ἰατρεῖον ἀρτίως ἀποκεκλεικότα,
πρὸς δὲ τούτοις εἰς πᾶσαν αὐλὴν καὶ σκηνὴν ἐμ-
πεπηδηκότα, πρὸς δὲ γαστρίμαργον, ὀψαρτυτήν, ἐπὶ

5 στόμα φερόμενον ἐν πᾶσι. δοκεῖ δή μοι τὰ τοιαῦτα
μόλις ⟨ἂν⟩ ἄνθρωπος ἀγύρτης καὶ προπετὴς ἐπὶ δι-
καστηρίου ῥιψολογῶν ἀνεκτὸς φανῆναι· μέτριος μὲν

6 γὰρ οὐ δοκεῖ. συγγραφεὺς δὲ κοινῶν πράξεων καὶ
προστάτης ἱστορίας ἀληθινὸς οὐδ' ἂν αὐτὸς ἐν αὑτῷ
διανοηθῆναι μή τι δὴ καὶ γράφειν τολμῆσαι τοιοῦτον.

(10) 9. Σκεψώμεθα δὴ καὶ τὴν αὐτοῦ τοῦ Τιμαίου προαίρεσιν, καὶ τὰς ἀποφάσεις συγκρίνωμεν ἐκ παρα-
θέσεως, ἃς πεποίηται περὶ τῆς αὐτῆς ἀποικίας, ἵνα
γνῶμεν πότερος ἄξιος ἔσται τῆς τοιαύτης κατηγορίας.

2 φησὶ τοιγαροῦν κατὰ τὴν αὐτὴν βύβλον, οὐκέτι κατὰ

---

36 At Issus 333, Alexander's victory over Darius III.

37 Aristotle's father, Nicomachus, was a doctor.

38 Refers to the courts of the tyrant Hermias at Atarneus in

this we must confess that those are wrong and at fault who exhibit to others such animosity and bitterness as Timaeus does to Aristotle He calls him arrogant, reckless, and headstrong, and adds that he had the effrontery to attack the city of Locri by stating that the colony consisted of runaway slaves, lackeys, adulterers, and kidnappers. And all this, he says, is told with such an assumption of trustworthiness that one would take him for one of those back from the campaign who had just by his own power defeated the Persians in a pitched battle[36] at the Cilician gates, and not for a pedantic and detestable sophist who had just locked up his precious surgeon's shop.[37] Besides this he says he had forced his way into every court[38] and general's tent and was a glutton and epicure catering for his mouth in everything. I think that surely such language could scarcely be tolerated even from the lips of some unscrupulous knave making random accusations in a law court; for we must avow that he goes beyond all bounds. But no chronicler of public affairs, no really leading historian,[39] would ever dare to entertain such thoughts, much less to put them in writing.

9. Let us now look at Timaeus' own deliberate statement, and compare with Aristotle's the account he himself gives of this identical colony,[40] so that we may discover which of the two deserves such an accusation. He tells us, then, in the same book, that he investigated the history of

Asia Minor and of King Philip II. Aristotle is treated by Timaeus as a parasite and flatterer of the mighty, a κόλαξ.

[39] P. seems to think, besides himself, of Ephorus; see n. on 4.20.5.

[40] P. returns to Locri.

τὸν αὐτὸν εἰκότα λόγον χρώμενος τοῖς ἐλέγχοις, ἀλλ᾽
ἀληθινῶς αὐτὸς ἐπιβαλὼν εἰς τοὺς κατὰ τὴν Ἑλλάδα
3 Λοκρούς, ἐξετάζειν τὰ περὶ τῆς ἀποικίας. τοὺς δὲ
πρῶτον μὲν ἐπιδεικνύειν αὐτῷ συνθήκας ἐγγράπτους,
ἔτι καὶ νῦν διαμενούσας, πρὸς τοὺς ἐξαπεσταλμένους,
αἷς ὑπογεγράφθαι τὴν ἀρχὴν τοιαύτην "ὡς γονεῦσι
4 πρὸς τέκνα." πρὸς δὲ τούτοις εἶναι δόγματα, καθ᾽ ἃ
πολιτείαν ὑπάρχειν ἑκατέροις παρ᾽ ἑκατέροις. καθόλου διακούοντας τὴν Ἀριστοτέλους ἐξήγησιν περὶ
τῆς ἀποικίας θαυμάζειν τὴν ἰταμότητα τοῦ συγγρα-
5 φέως. μεταβὰς δὲ πάλιν ἐπὶ τοὺς ἐν Ἰταλίᾳ Λοκροὺς
εὑρίσκειν ἀκολούθους καὶ τοὺς νόμους φησὶ τοὺς παρ᾽
αὐτοῖς καὶ τοὺς ἐθισμοὺς οὐ τῇ τῶν οἰκετῶν ῥᾳδιουρ-
6 γίᾳ, τῇ δὲ τῶν ἐλευθέρων ἀποικίᾳ· πάντως γὰρ καὶ
τοῖς ἀνδραποδισταῖς ἐπιτίμια τετάχθαι παρ᾽ αὐτοῖς,
ὁμοίως τοῖς μοιχοῖς, τοῖς δραπέταις· ὧν οὐδὲν ἂν
ὑπάρχειν, εἰ συνῄδεισαν αὐτοῖς ἐκ τοιούτων πεφυκόσι.

10. Πρῶτον δὴ διαπορῆσαί τις ἂν πρὸς τίνας τῶν
(11) Λοκρῶν παραγενόμενος ἐπυνθάνετο περὶ τούτων. εἰ
2 μὲν γὰρ συνέβαινε, καθάπερ τοὺς ἐν Ἰταλίᾳ Λοκρούς,
οὕτω καὶ τοὺς κατὰ τὴν Ἑλλάδα μίαν πόλιν ἔχειν,
τάχ᾽ ἂν οὐκ ἔδει διαπορεῖν, ἀλλ᾽ ἦν ἂν εὐθεώρητον·
3 ἐπεὶ δὲ δύ᾽ ἔθνη Λοκρῶν ἐστι, πρὸς ποτέρους ἦλθε καὶ
πρὸς ποίας πόλεις τῶν ἑτέρων, καὶ παρὰ τίσιν εὗρε
τὰς συνθήκας ἀναγεγραμμένας; οὐδὲν γὰρ ἡμῖν δια-
4 σαφεῖται τούτων. καίτοι διότι τοῦτ᾽ ἴδιόν ἐστι Τιμαίου
καὶ ταύτῃ παρημίλληται τοὺς ἄλλους συγγραφέας
καὶ καθόλου τῇδέ πῃ τῆς ἀποδοχῆς . . .—λέγω δὲ κατὰ

the colony, no longer applying the test of mere probability, but personally visiting the Locrians in Greece proper. He states that in the first place they showed him a written treaty, still preserved between them and the emigrants, with the following phrase[41] at the outset, "As parents to children." In addition there were decrees[42] that citizens of either town were citizens of the other. When they heard Aristotle's account of the colony they expressed astonishment at that author's recklessness. Passing over in his argument to the Italian Locri he says he found their laws and customs also were such as beseemed not a pack of rascally slaves but a colony of freemen. For certainly there were penalties fixed in their code for kidnappers as well as for adulterers and runaway slaves, which would not have been the case had they been aware that they themselves sprang from such men.

10. In the first place we are in doubt as to which of the Greek Locrians he visited for the purpose of inquiry. For if the Greek Locrians, like the Italian, were confined to one city we should perhaps not entertain any doubt, but the matter would be perspicuous. But since there are two sets[43] of Locrians in Greece proper, we ask to which he went and to which of their cities and in whose possession he found the inscribed treaty; for he gives us no information on the subject. And yet Timaeus' special boast, the thing in which he outvies other authors and which is the main cause of the reputation he enjoys, is, as I suppose we

---

[41] It rings false.   [42] Such decrees are indeed common; see W. Gawantka, *Isopolitie. Ein Beitrag zur Geschichte der zwischenstaatlichen Beziehungen in der griechischen Antike* (Munich 1975).   [43] The western and the eastern Locrians.

τὴν ἐν τοῖς χρόνοις καὶ ταῖς ἀναγραφαῖς ἐπίφασιν
τῆς ἀκριβείας καὶ τὴν περὶ τοῦτο τὸ μέρος ἐπιμέ-
5 λειαν—δοκῶ, πάντες γινώσκομεν. διὸ καὶ θαυμάζειν
ἐστὶν ἄξιον πῶς οὔτε τὸ τῆς πόλεως ὄνομα, παρ' οἷς
εὗρεν, οὔτε ⟨τὸν⟩ τόπον, ἐν ᾧ συμβαίνει τὴν συνθήκην
ἀναγεγράφθαι, διεσάφησεν ἡμῖν, οὔτε τοὺς ἄρχοντας
τοὺς δείξαντας αὐτῷ τὴν ἀναγραφὴν καὶ πρὸς οὓς
ἐποιεῖτο τὸν λόγον, ἵνα μηδενὶ διαπορεῖν ἐξῇ ⟨μηδέν⟩,
ἀλλ' ὡρισμένου τοῦ τόπου καὶ τῆς πόλεως ἐνῇ τοῖς
6 ἀμφισβητοῦσιν εὑρεῖν τὴν ἀκρίβειαν. ὁ δὲ πάντα
ταῦτα παραλελοιπὼς δῆλός ἐστι συνειδὼς αὑτῷ κατὰ
πρόθεσιν ἐψευσμένῳ. διότι γὰρ τῶν τοιούτων ἐπιλαβόμενος οὐδὲν ἂν παρέλειπε Τίμαιος, ἀλλ' ἀπρίξ, τὸ
δὴ λεγόμενον, ἀμφοῖν τοῖν χεροῖν ἐπέφυ, προφανὲς ἐκ
7 τούτων. ὁ γὰρ πρὸς τὴν Ἐχεκράτους πίστιν ἀπερει-
σάμενος ἐπ' ὀνόματος, πρὸς ὅν φησι περὶ τῶν ἐν
Ἰταλίᾳ Λοκρῶν ποιήσασθαι τοὺς λόγους καὶ παρ' οὗ
8 πυθέσθαι περὶ τούτων, καὶ προσεξειργασμένος, ἵνα
μὴ φανῇ τοῦ τυχόντος ἀκηκοώς, ὅτι συνέβαινε τὸν
τούτου πατέρα πρεσβείας κατηξιῶσθαι πρότερον ὑπὸ
9 Διονυσίου, ἢ πού γ' ἂν οὗτος δημοσίας ἀναγραφῆς
ἐπιλαβόμενος ἢ παραδοσίμου στήλης παρεσιώπησεν;

11. ὁ γὰρ τὰς συγκρίσεις ποιούμενος ἀνέκαθεν τῶν
ἐφόρων πρὸς τοὺς βασιλεῖς τοὺς ἐν Λακεδαίμονι καὶ
τοὺς ἄρχοντας τοὺς Ἀθήνησι καὶ τὰς ἱερείας τὰς ἐν

all know, his display of accuracy in the matter of dates and public records, and the care he devotes to such matters. So it is most surprising that he has not informed us of the name of the city where he found the treaty or the exact spot in which it is inscribed, or who were the magistrates who showed him this document and with whom he spoke, so that no cause of perplexity would be left, but the place and the city being identified, those in doubt would have the means of discovering the exact truth. The fact that he neglects to inform us on all these points is a clear proof[44] that he knew he was deliberately lying. For that, had Timaeus got hold of such information, he would not have let a word of it escape, but, as the phrase is, would have held on to it tight with both hands, is evident from the following consideration. Would the writer who mentions Echecrates[45] by name as the man on whom he depends, having consulted him about the Italian Locrians and obtained this information, the writer who, not to appear to have heard all this from a person of no importance, takes the pains to tell us that the father of this Echecrates had formerly been deemed worthy of employment as envoy by Dionysius—would such a writer, I ask, if he had got hold of a public record or a commemorative inscription, have held his tongue about it?

11. For this is the author who compares the dates of the ephors with those of the kings in Lacedaemon from the earliest times, and the lists of Athenian archons[46] and

---

[44] Not so.   [45] Not clearly identified.

[46] See A. Chaniotis, *Historie und Historiker in den griechischen Inschriften* (Stuttgart 1988) for the use of lists of magistrates, priests, victors, etc. for chronological purposes, esp. 186–219.

Ἄργει παραβάλλων πρὸς τοὺς ὀλυμπιονίκας, καὶ τὰς
ἁμαρτίας τῶν πόλεων περὶ τὰς ἀναγραφὰς τὰς τούτων
ἐξελέγχων, παρὰ τρίμηνον ἐχούσας τὸ διαφέρον, οὗ-
2 τός ἐστι. καὶ μὴν ὁ τὰς ὀπισθοδόμους στήλας καὶ τὰς
ἐν ταῖς φλιαῖς τῶν νεῶν προξενίας ἐξευρηκὼς Τίμαιός
3 ἐστιν. ὃν οὔθ᾽ ὑπάρχον τι τῶν τοιούτων ἀγνοεῖν οὔθ᾽
εὑρόντα παραλιπεῖν πιστευτέον οὔτε ψευσαμένῳ συγ-
4 γνώμην δοτέον οὐδαμῶς· πικρὸς γὰρ γεγονὼς καὶ
ἀπαραίτητος ἐπιτιμητὴς τῶν πέλας εἰκότως ἂν καὶ
ὑπὸ τῶν πλησίον αὐτὸς ἀπαραιτήτου τυγχάνοι κατ-
5 ηγορίας. οὐ μὴν ἀλλὰ προφανῶς ἐν τούτοις ἐψευσμέ-
νος, μεταβὰς ἐπὶ τοὺς ἐν Ἰταλίᾳ Λοκροὺς πρῶτον μέν
φησι τήν τε πολιτείαν καὶ τὰ λοιπὰ φιλάνθρωπα τοῖς
Λοκροῖς ἀμφοτέροις . . . Ἀριστοτέλη καὶ Θεόφραστον
6 κατεψεῦσθαι τῆς πόλεως. ἐγὼ δ᾽ οὐκ ἀγνοῶ μὲν ὅτι καὶ
ταύτῃ τῆς πραγματείας ἀναγκασθήσομαι παρεκβαί-
νειν, διοριζόμενος καὶ διαβεβαιούμενος περὶ τούτων·
7 οὐ μὴν ἀλλὰ διὰ ταύτην τὴν αἰτίαν εἰς ἕνα τόπον
ὑπερεθέμην τὸν περὶ Τιμαίου λόγον, ἵνα μὴ πολλάκις
ἀναγκάζωμαι τοῦ καθήκοντος ὀλιγωρεῖν. . . .

(11a)   Ὅτι Τίμαιός φησι μέγιστον ἁμάρτημα περὶ τὴν
8 ἱστορίαν εἶναι τὸ ψεῦδος· διὸ καὶ παραινεῖ τούτοις, οὓς
ἂν ἐξελέγξῃ διεψευσμένους ἐν τοῖς συγγράμμασιν,
ἕτερόν τι ζητεῖν ὄνομα τοῖς βυβλίοις, πάντα δὲ μᾶλλον ἢ καλεῖν ἱστορίαν. . . .

priestesses of Hera at Argos with those of the victors at Olympia, and who convicts cities of inaccuracy in these records, there being a difference of three months. Yes, and it is Timaeus who discovered the inscriptions[47] at the back of buildings and lists of proxeni on the jambs of temples. We cannot then believe that he would have missed any such thing had it existed, or omitted to mention it had he found it,[48] nor can we in any way excuse his mendacity. Himself a most bitter and implacable critic[49] of others he can but expect to meet with implacable criticism at the hands of others. Next, having been obviously guilty of untruth in regard to this matter, he passes to the Italian Locrians and tells us in the first place that he found the constitution and general culture of both these Locrians and those in Greece to be the same, but that Aristotle and Theophrastus had falsely accused the Italian town. I am quite aware that here too I shall be compelled to digress from my main subject, in order to put my case more clearly and further fortify it, but as a fact I deferred to one place my discussion of Timaeus just because I do not wish to be obliged frequently to neglect my main task. . . .

Timaeus says that the worst vice of history is falsehood. So he advises those whom he convicts of falsehood in their works to find another name for their book and call it anything but history. . . .

[47] Timaeus discovered and used inscriptions. The most famous list of *proxenoi* is the one from Delphi, *SIG* 585, covering those elected year by year from 197 to 148, no less than 135 individuals.   [48] Timaeus assures us in fact that he had found it (9.3).   [49] The wording shows that P. alludes to Timaeus' nickname (n. on 4a.6) .

(7) 12. Καθάπερ γὰρ ἐπὶ τῶν κανόνων, κἂν ἐλάττων ᾖ τῷ μήκει κἂν τῷ πλάτει ταπεινότερος, μετέχῃ δὲ τῆς τοῦ κανόνος ἰδιότητος, κανόνα φησὶ δεῖν προσαγορεύειν ὅμως, ὅταν ⟨δὲ⟩ τῆς εὐθείας καὶ τῆς πρὸς ταύτην οἰκειότητος ἐκπέσῃ, πάντα μᾶλλον δεῖν ἢ

2 κανόνα καλεῖν, τὸν αὐτὸν τρόπον καὶ τῶν συγγραμμάτων ὅσα μὲν ἂν ἢ κατὰ τὴν λέξιν ἢ κατὰ τὸν χειρισμὸν ἢ κατ' ἄλλο τι διαμαρτάνηται τῶν ἰδίων μερῶν, ἀντέχηται δὲ τῆς ἀληθείας, προσίεσθαί φησι τὸ τῆς ἱστορίας ὄνομα τὰς βύβλους, ὅταν δὲ ταύτης

3 παραπέσῃ, μηκέτι καλεῖσθαι δεῖν ἱστορίαν. ἐγὼ δὲ διότι μὲν ἡγεῖσθαι δεῖ τῶν τοιούτων συγγραμμάτων τὴν ἀλήθειαν ὁμολογῶ, καὶ κατὰ τὴν πραγματείαν αὐτός που κέχρημαι λέγων οὕτως, ὅτι, καθάπερ ἐμψύχου σώματος τῶν ὄψεων ἐξαιρεθεισῶν ἀχρειοῦται τὸ ὅλον, οὕτως ἐξ ἱστορίας ἐὰν ἄρῃς τὴν ἀλήθειαν, τὸ καταλειπόμενον αὐτῆς ἀνωφελὲς γίνεται διήγημα.

4 Δύο μέντοι τρόπους ἔφαμεν εἶναι ψεύδους, ἕνα μὲν
5 τὸν κατ' ἄγνοιαν, ἕτερον δὲ τὸν κατὰ προαίρεσιν, καὶ τούτων δεῖν τοῖς μὲν κατ' ἄγνοιαν παραπαίουσι τῆς ἀληθείας διδόναι συγγνώμην, τοῖς δὲ κατὰ προαίρεσιν ἀκαταλλάκτως ἔχειν.

(12a) Τούτων δ' ἡμῖν ὁμολογουμένων, αὐτοῦ τούτου τοῦ
6 ψεύδους μεγάλην ὑπολαμβάνω διαφορὰν εἶναι τοῦ κατ' ἄγνοιαν γινομένου καὶ τοῦ κατὰ προαίρεσιν, καὶ τὸ μὲν ἐπιδέχεσθαι συγγνώμην καὶ διόρθωσιν εὐμενικήν, τὸ δ' ἀπαραιτήτου δικαίως ἂν τυγχάνειν κατηγο-

12. Timaeus says, that as a rule which is defective in length and breadth but possesses the essential quality of a rule must still be called a rule, but when it has no approach to straightness or any quality akin to straightness, must be called anything rather than a rule, so in the case of historical works, when they are defective in style, treatment, or any other particular quality but still strive to ascertain the truth they may claim to be styled histories, but when they fall away from the truth have no longer any claim to this name. I quite agree with him that truth is the leading quality in such books, and somewhere in the course of this work I made the same statement,[50] writing as follows, that as in the case of a living body if the eyes are put out the whole becomes useless, so if you take away truth from history what remains is but an unprofitable fable.

I said, however, that there are two kinds of falsehood, one the consequence of ignorance and the other deliberate, and that we should accord pardon to those who fall away from the truth owing to ignorance, but should refuse to forgive deliberate lying.

This point being settled I affirm that the difference is very wide between such falsehood as is the result of ignorance and such as is deliberate, the one admitting of pardon and kindly correction but the other deserving impla-

[50] 1.14.6.

7 ρίας· ᾧ γένει μάλιστ' ἂν εὕροι τις ἔνοχον αὐτὸν ὄντα
τὸν Τίμαιον· διότι δ' ἐστὶ τοιοῦτος σκοπεῖν ἤδη πάρεστιν.

12a. Ἐπὶ τῶν ἀθετούντων τὰς ὁμολογίας προφερό-
(12b) μεθα ταύτην τὴν παροιμίαν "Λοκροὶ τὰς συνθήκας."
τοῦτο δέ τις ἐξεύρηκεν ὅτι καὶ παρὰ τοῖς συγγραφεῦσι
καὶ παρὰ τοῖς ἄλλοις ἀνθρώποις ὁμολογούμενόν ἐστι,
2 διότι κατὰ τὴν τῶν Ἡρακλειδῶν ἔφοδον συνθεμένων
τῶν Λοκρῶν τοῖς Πελοποννησίοις πολεμίους πυρσοὺς
αἴρειν, ἐὰν συμβῇ τοὺς Ἡρακλείδας μὴ κατὰ τὸν
Ἰσθμόν, ἀλλὰ κατὰ τὸ Ῥίον ποιεῖσθαι τὴν διάβασιν,
χάριν τοῦ προαισθομένους φυλάξασθαι τὴν ἔφοδον
3 αὐτῶν, οὐ ποιησάντων δὲ τῶν Λοκρῶν, πᾶν δὲ τοὐναντίον φιλίους ἀράντων πυρσούς, ὅτε παρῆσαν, τοὺς μὲν
Ἡρακλείδας συνέβη μετ' ἀσφαλείας χρῆσθαι τῇ δια-
βάσει, τοὺς δὲ Πελοποννησίους κατολιγωρήσαντας
λαθεῖν παραδεξαμένους εἰς τὴν οἰκείαν τοὺς ὑπεναντίους παρασπονδηθέντας ὑπὸ τῶν Λοκρῶν.

12b. . . . κατηγορεῖν καὶ θειασ‹μὸν δια›σύρειν τῶν
(12c) ὀνειρωττόντων καὶ δαιμονώντων ἐν τοῖς ὑπομνήμασιν·
ὅσοι γε μὴν αὐτοὶ πολλὴν τῆς τοιαύτης ἐμπεποίηνται
φλυαρίας, τοὺς τοιούτους ἀγαπᾶν ἂν δέοι μὴ τυγχάνοντας κατηγορίας, μηδ' ὅτι καὶ τῶν ἄλλων αὐτοὺς
2 κατατρέχειν· ὃ συμβέβηκε περὶ Τίμαιον. ἐκεῖνος γὰρ
κόλακα μὲν εἶναί φησι τὸν Καλλισθένην τοιαῦτα
γράφοντα καὶ πλεῖστον ἀπέχειν φιλοσοφίας, κόρδαξί
τε προσέχοντα καὶ κορυβαντιώσαις γυναιξί· δικαίως
δ' αὐτὸν ὑπ' Ἀλεξάνδρου τετευχέναι τιμωρίας δι-

cable condemnation. And one finds that Timaeus himself
is a chief sinner in this respect, as I will now prove.

12a. We use this proverb about those who set agreements at naught, "The Locrians and the pact," [51] and the
origin of this is that, as both authors and other people
agree, on the occasion of the invasion of the Heracleidae
the Locrians[52] had promised the Peloponnesians to raise
war signals in case it happened that the Heracleidae tried
to cross by Rhion and not to pass the Isthmus, so that due
warning might be given and measures taken to prevent
their invasion. The Locrians, however, did not do this, but
on the contrary raised friendly signals when the Heracleidae arrived, so that they made the crossing in safety,
and the Peloponnesians, thus betrayed by the Locrians
and neglecting to take any precautions, before they were
aware of it had permitted their foes to enter their country.

12b. We should indeed reprove and ridicule the frenzy
of those authors who dream dreams and in their works
write like men possessed. But those who indulge freely
themselves in this kind of foolery should, far from accusing
others, be only too glad if they escape blame themselves.
Such is the case with Timaeus. He calls Callisthenes[53] a
flatterer for writing in the manner he does, and says he is
very far from being a philosopher, paying attention as he
does to crows and frenzied women. He adds that Alexander was very right in punishing him, as he had corrupted

[51] Supply "violated" (the phrase was proverbial: *Paroemiogr.*
1.116).

[52] Here the western Locrians on the mainland; cf. *Paroemiogr.*
1.114.

[53] See n. on 4.33.2.

εφθαρκότα τὴν ἐκείνου ψυχὴν καθ᾽ ὅσον οἷός τ᾽ ἦν·
3 καὶ Δημοσθένην μὲν καὶ τοὺς ἄλλους ῥήτορας τοὺς
κατ᾽ ἐκεῖνον τὸν καιρὸν ἀκμάσαντας ἐπαινεῖ καί φησι
τῆς Ἑλλάδος ἀξίους γεγονέναι, διότι ταῖς Ἀλεξάνδρου τιμαῖς ταῖς ἰσοθέοις ἀντέλεγον, τὸν δὲ φιλό-
σοφον αἰγίδα καὶ κεραυνὸν περιθέντα θνητῇ φύσει
δικαίως αὐτὸν ὑπὸ τοῦ δαιμονίου τετευχέναι τούτων
ὧν ἔτυχεν.

13. Ὅτι Τίμαιός φησι Δημοχάρην ἡταιρηκέναι μὲν
τοῖς ἄνω μέρεσι τοῦ σώματος, οὐκ εἶναι δ᾽ ἄξιον τὸ
ἱερὸν πῦρ φυσᾶν, ὑπερβεβηκέναι δὲ τοῖς ἐπιτηδεύμασι τὰ Βότρυος ὑπομνήματα καὶ τὰ Φιλαινίδος καὶ
τῶν ἄλλων ἀναισχυντογράφων· ταύτην δὲ τὴν λοιδο-
2 ρίαν καὶ τὰς ἐμφάσεις οὐχ οἷον ἄν τις διέθετο πεπαι-
δευμένος ἀνήρ, ἀλλ᾽ οὐδὲ τῶν ἀπὸ τέγους ἀπὸ τοῦ
3 σώματος εἰργασμένων οὐδείς. ὁ δ᾽ ἵνα πιστὸς φανῇ
κατὰ τὴν αἰσχρολογίαν καὶ τὴν ὅλην ἀναισχυντίαν,
καὶ προσκατέψευσται τἀνδρός, κωμικόν τινα μάρτυρα
4 προσεπισπασάμενος ἀνώνυμον. πόθεν δ᾽ ἐγὼ κατα-
στοχάζομαι τοῦτο; πρῶτον μὲν ἐκ τοῦ καὶ πεφυκέναι
καὶ τεθράφθαι καλῶς Δημοχάρην, ἀδελφιδοῦν ὄντα
5 Δημοσθένους, δεύτερον ἐκ τοῦ μὴ μόνον στρατηγίας
αὐτὸν ἠξιῶσθαι παρ᾽ Ἀθηναίοις, ἀλλὰ καὶ τῶν ἄλλων

---

54 In propagating the story that Alexander was the son of Zeus,
which originated with the king's visit to the oracle of Ammon
(*FGrH* 324 F 14).

55 On this question see C. Habicht, *Gottmenschentum und
griechische Städte*, 2nd ed. (Munich 1970), 28–36 and 246–250,

his mind[54] as far as he could. He praises Demosthenes and the other orators who flourished at the time and says they were worthy of Greece because they opposed the conferment of divine honors[55] on Alexander, while the philosopher who invested a mortal with aegis and thunderbolt was justly visited by heaven with the fate that befell him.

13. Timaeus tells us that Demochares[56] had been guilty of such impurity that he was not a fit person to blow the sacrificial flame, and that in his practices he had been more shameless than the works of Botrys, Philaenis, and other obscene writers.[57] Scurrilous assertions of this kind are such as not only no man of culture, but not even any of the inmates of a brothel would make. But Timaeus, in order that he may gain credit for his filthy accusations and his utter lack of decency, has libeled Demochares still further by dragging in the evidence of a comic poet of no repute. You will ask on what grounds I infer that Timaeus is guilty of falsehood? First and foremost because Demochares was of good birth and breeding, being the nephew of Demosthenes, and secondly because the Athenians deemed him worthy not only of the office of strategus, but of other distinctions, to none of which could he have successfully as-

also E. Badian, in H. J. Dell (ed.), *Ancient Macedonian Studies in Honor of Charles F. Edson* (Thessaloniki 1981), 54–59.

[56] Nephew of Demosthenes, active politician and historian. His son Laches requested in 270 from the council of Athens that he be honored posthumously (Plu. M*oralia* 851 D-F). The remains of his work in *FGrH* 75. See Timaeus, *FGrH* 566 T 2. G. Marasco, *Democare di Leuconoe* (Florence 1984).

[57] Bothrys of Messana and Philainis of uncertain provenance (Leucas or Samos) were both authors of obscene works.

τιμῶν, ὧν οὐδὲν ἂν αὐτῷ συνεξέδραμε τοιαύταις ἀτυ-
6 χίαις παλαίοντι. διὸ καὶ δοκεῖ μοι Τίμαιος οὐχ οὕτως
Δημοχάρους κατηγορεῖν ὡς Ἀθηναίων, εἰ τοιοῦτον
ἄνδρα προῆγον καὶ τοιούτῳ τὴν πατρίδα καὶ τοὺς
7 ἰδίους βίους ἐνεχείριζον. ἀλλ᾽ οὐκ ἔστι τούτων οὐδέν.
οὐ γὰρ ἂν Ἀρχέδικος ὁ κωμῳδιογράφος ἔλεγε ταῦτα
8 μόνος περὶ Δημοχάρους, ὡς Τίμαιός φησιν, ἀλλὰ
πολλοὶ μὲν ἂν τῶν Ἀντιπάτρου φίλων, καθ᾽ οὗ πεπαρ-
ρησίασται πολλὰ καὶ δυνάμενα λυπεῖν οὐ μόνον
αὐτὸν Ἀντίπατρον, ἀλλὰ καὶ τοὺς ἐκείνου διαδόχους
καὶ φίλους γεγονότας, πολλοὶ δὲ τῶν ἀντιπεπολιτευ-
9 μένων, ὧν ἦν καὶ Δημήτριος ὁ Φαληρεύς. οὐ 'κεῖνος οὐ
τὴν τυχοῦσαν πεποίηται κατηγορίαν ἐν ταῖς ἱστορίαις, φάσκων αὐτὸν γεγονέναι τοιοῦτον προστάτην
τῆς πατρίδος καὶ ἐπὶ τούτοις σεμνύνεσθαι κατὰ τὴν
πολιτείαν, ἐφ᾽ οἷς ἂν καὶ τελώνης σεμνυνθείη βάναυ-
10 σος. ἐπὶ γὰρ τῷ πολλὰ καὶ λυσιτελῶς πωλεῖσθαι κατὰ
τὴν πόλιν καὶ δαψιλῆ τὰ πρὸς τὸν βίον ὑπάρχειν
11 πᾶσιν, ἐπὶ τούτοις φησὶ μεγαλαυχεῖν αὐτόν· καὶ διότι
κοχλίας αὐτομάτως βαδίζων προηγεῖτο τῆς πομπῆς
αὐτῷ, σίαλον ἀναπτύων, σὺν δὲ τούτοις ὄνοι διεπέμποντο διὰ τοῦ θεάτρου, διότι δὴ πάντων τῶν τῆς Ἑλλάδος καλῶν ἡ πατρὶς παρακεχωρηκυῖα τοῖς ἄλλοις
ἐποίει Κασσάνδρῳ τὸ προσταττόμενον, ἐπὶ τούτοις
12 αὐτὸν οὐκ αἰσχύνεσθαί φησιν. ἀλλ᾽ ὅμως οὔτε Δημήτριος οὔτ᾽ ἄλλος οὐδεὶς εἰρήκει περὶ Δημοχάρους
τοιοῦτον οὐδέν.

pired had he had such shameful acts to combat. Timaeus, therefore, seems to me to accuse not so much Demochares as the Athenians for advancing such a man and entrusting their country and their lives and properties to him. But not a word of all this can be true. For in that case not only Archedicus, the comic poet,[58] would, as Timaeus asserts, have said this about Demochares, but many of the friends of Antipater also, against whom Demochares had ventured to say much calculated to vex not only Antipater himself but his successors and former friends. The same accusations would have been brought also by many of Demochares' political adversaries, among whom was Demetrius of Phaleron.[59] Demochares in his history brings accusations by no means trivial against Demetrius, telling us that the statesmanship on which he prided himself was such as a vulgar farmer of taxes would pride himself on, his boast having been that the market in the town was plentifully supplied and cheap, and that there was abundance of all the necessities of life for everybody. He tells us that a snail moved by machinery went in front of his procession, spitting out saliva, and that donkeys were marched through the theater, to show, forsooth, that the country had yielded up to others all the glory of Greece and obeyed the behests of Cassander. Of all this he says he was in no wise ashamed. But yet neither Demetrius nor anyone else said anything of the sort about Demochares.

[58] Athenian, son of Naucritus of Lamptrae. Member of the oligarchic regime of the years 322–318, speaker of two extant decrees. A friend of Antipater and follower of Phocion. C. Habicht, "The Poet Archedikos of Lamptrai," *Hesperia* 62 (1993), 253–256. For the broader context, the same, *Athens from Alexander to Antony* (Cambridge, MA 1997), 36–66.   [59] See n. on 10.24.7.

14. ἐξ ὧν ἐγώ, βεβαιοτέραν τὴν τῆς πατρίδος
ἡγούμενος μαρτυρίαν ἢ τὴν Τιμαίου πικρίαν, θαρρῶν
ἀποφαίνομαι μηδενὶ τὸν Δημοχάρους βίον ἔνοχον
2 εἶναι τῶν τοιούτων κατηγορημάτων. καίπερ εἰ κατ᾽
ἀλήθειαν ὑπῆρχέ τι τοιοῦτον ἀτύχημα περὶ Δημοχάρην, ποῖος καιρὸς ἢ ποία πρᾶξις ἠνάγκασε Τίμαιον
3 ταῦτα κατατάττειν εἰς τὴν ἱστορίαν; καθάπερ γὰρ οἱ
νοῦν ἔχοντες, ἐπὰν ἀμύνασθαι κρίνωσι τοὺς ἐχθρούς,
οὐ τοῦτο πρῶτον σκοποῦνται τί παθεῖν ἄξιός ἐστιν ὁ
4 πλησίον, ἀλλὰ τί ποιεῖν αὐτοῖς πρέπει, τοῦτο μᾶλλον
. . . οὕτως καὶ περὶ τῶν λοιδοριῶν, οὐ τί τοῖς ἐχθροῖς
ἀκούειν ἁρμόζει, τοῦτο πρῶτον ἡγητέον, ἀλλὰ τί
λέγειν ἡμῖν πρέπει, τοῦτ᾽ ἀναγκαιότατον λογιστέον.
5 περὶ δὲ τῶν πάντα μετρούντων ταῖς ἰδίαις ὀργαῖς καὶ
φιλοτιμίαις ἀνάγκη πάνθ᾽ ὑποπτεύειν ἐστὶ καὶ πᾶσι
6 διαπιστεῖν πέρα τοῦ δέοντος λεγομένοις. διὸ δὴ καὶ
νῦν ἡμεῖς μὲν εἰκότως ἂν δόξαιμεν ἀθετεῖν τοῖς ὑπὸ
7 Τιμαίου κατὰ Δημοχάρους εἰρημένοις· ἐκεῖνος δ᾽ ἂν
οὐκ εἰκότως τυγχάνοι συγγνώμης οὐδὲ πίστεως ὑπ᾽
οὐδενὸς διὰ τὸ προφανῶς ἐν ταῖς λοιδορίαις ἐκπίπτειν
τοῦ καθήκοντος διὰ τὴν ἔμφυτον πικρίαν.

15. Καὶ γὰρ οὐδὲ ταῖς κατ᾽ Ἀγαθοκλέους ἔγωγε
λοιδορίαις, εἰ καὶ πάντων γέγονεν ἀσεβέστατος, εὐ-
2 δοκῶ. λέγω δ᾽ ἐν τούτοις, ἐν οἷς ἐπὶ καταστροφῇ τῆς
ὅλης ἱστορίας φησὶ γεγονέναι τὸν Ἀγαθοκλέα κατὰ
τὴν πρώτην ἡλικίαν κοινὸν πόρνον, ἕτοιμον τοῖς
ἀκρατεστάτοις, κολοιόν, τρίορχην, πάντων τῶν βου-
3 λομένων τοῖς ὄπισθεν ἔμπροσθεν γεγονότα. πρὸς δὲ

14. From which, regarding the testimony of his country as more trustworthy than Timaeus' spite, I pronounce with confidence that the life of Demochares was guiltless of all such offenses. And even if, as a fact, Demochares had the misfortune to be guilty of any such thing, what circumstance or what event compelled Timaeus to record it in his history? For just as men of sense when they meditate revenge on their enemies do not examine in the first place what others deserve to suffer, but rather how it becomes themselves to act, so when we bring reproaches we must not in the first place consider what is fitting for our enemies to hear, but regard it as of the greatest importance to determine what is proper for ourselves to speak. And in the case of writers who measure everything by the standard of their own passions and jealousies, we must suspect all their statements and refuse credit to them when extravagant. So that in the present case I may claim to be justified in rejecting the slanders of Timaeus concerning Demochares, whereas this author can claim neither pardon nor credit from anyone, as he has in his reproaches so obviously let himself be carried beyond the bounds of decency by the spitefulness which was engrained in him.

15. Nor can I approve the terms in which he speaks of Agathocles,[60] even if that prince were the most impious of men. I allude to the passage at the end of his history in which he says that Agathocles in his early youth was a common prostitute, ready to yield himself to the most debauched, a jackdaw, a buzzard,[61] who would right about face to anyone who wished it. And in addition to this he

60 See n. on 1.7.2. He was born in 360/59 and died in 289/8.
61 Literally "a man with three testicles."

τούτοις, ὅτ' ἀπέθανε, τὴν γυναῖκά φησι κατακλαι-
ομένην αὐτὸν οὕτως θρηνεῖν· "Τί δ' οὐκ ἐγὼ σέ; τί δ'

4 οὐκ ἐμὲ σύ;" ἐν γὰρ τούτοις πάλιν οὐ μόνον ἄν τις
ἐπιφθέγξαιτο τὰ καὶ περὶ Δημοχάρους, ἀλλὰ καὶ τὴν

5 ὑπερβολὴν θαυμάσειε τῆς πικρίας. ὅτι γὰρ ἐκ φύσεως
ἀνάγκη μεγάλα προτερήματα γεγονέναι περὶ τὸν
Ἀγαθοκλέα, τοῦτο δῆλόν ἐστιν ἐξ αὐτῶν ὧν ὁ Τίμαιος

6 ἀποφαίνεται. εἰ γὰρ εἰς τὰς Συρακούσας παρεγενήθη
φεύγων τὸν τροχόν, τὸν καπνόν, τὸν πηλόν, περὶ ἔτη

7 τὴν ἡλικίαν ὀκτωκαίδεκα γεγονώς, καὶ μετά τινα χρόνον ὁρμηθεὶς ἀπὸ τοιαύτης ὑποθέσεως κύριος μὲν
ἐγενήθη πάσης Σικελίας, μεγίστους δὲ κινδύνους
περιέστησε Καρχηδονίοις, τέλος ἐγγηράσας τῇ δυνα-
στείᾳ κατέστρεψε τὸν βίον βασιλεὺς προσαγορευ-

8 όμενος, ἆρ' οὐκ ἀνάγκη μέγα τι γεγονέναι χρῆμα καὶ
θαυμάσιον τὸν Ἀγαθοκλέα καὶ πολλὰς ἐσχηκέναι
ῥοπὰς καὶ δυνάμεις πρὸς τὸν πραγματικὸν τρόπον;

9 ὑπὲρ ὧν δεῖ τὸν συγγραφέα μὴ μόνον τὰ πρὸς διαβολὴν κυροῦντα καὶ κατηγορίαν ἐξηγεῖσθαι τοῖς ἐπιγινομένοις, ἀλλὰ καὶ τὰ πρὸς ἔπαινον ἥκοντα περὶ τὸν

10 ἄνδρα· τοῦτο γὰρ ἴδιόν ἐστι τῆς ἱστορίας. ὁ δ' ἐπεσκο-
τημένος ὑπὸ τῆς ἰδίας πικρίας τὰ μὲν ἐλαττώματα
δυσμενικῶς καὶ μετ' αὐξήσεως ἡμῖν ἐξήγγελκε, τὰ δὲ

11 κατορθώματα συλλήβδην παραλέλοιπεν, ἀγνοῶν ὅτι
τὸ ψεῦδος οὐχ ἧττόν ἐστι περὶ τοὺς τὰ γεγονότα
⟨κρύπτοντας ἢ περὶ τοὺς τὰ μηδέποτε γεγονότα⟩ γρά-

12 φοντας ἐν ταῖς ἱστορίαις. ἡμεῖς δὲ τὸ μὲν ἐπιμετρεῖν

says that on his death his wife lamenting him called out in her wail, "What did I not do to you? What did you not do to me?" In this instance we are not only inclined to repeat the protest we made in the case of Demochares, but we are positively astonished by the excess of rancor displayed. For that Agathocles had great natural advantages is evident from Timaeus' own account of him. For if at the age of eighteen he reached Syracuse, escaping from the wheel, the kiln, and the clay,[62] and in a short time, starting from such small beginnings, became master of the whole of Sicily, exposed the Carthaginians to extreme peril, and having grown old in his sovereign position, died with the title of king,[63] must not Agathocles have had something great and wonderful in him, and must he not have been qualified for the conduct of affairs by peculiar mental force and power? Regarding all this a historian should lay before posterity not only such matters as tend to confirm slanderous accusations, but also what redounds to the credit of this prince; for such is the proper function of history. But Timaeus, blinded by his own malice, has chronicled with hostility and exaggeration the defects of Agathocles and has entirely omitted to mention his shining qualities, being unaware that it is just as mendacious for a writer ‹to conceal› what did occur ‹as to report what did not occur.›[64] I myself,[65] while refraining in order to spare him from giving

---

[62] The family belonged in fact to the upper class and seems to have owned a ceramic business.   [63] He took the title at the end of the fourth century, following the successors of Alexander.

[64] B-W's restoration, accepted by Paton and Pédech.

[65] The sentence "defies satisfactory translation," WC 2.362; see the various proposals he listed.

τῆς ἀπεχθείας αὐτοῦ χάριν ἀφήκαμεν, τὰ δ᾽ οἰκεῖα τῆς προθέσεως αὐτῶν οὐ παρελείψαμεν. . . .

16. Νεανίσκων δυεῖν περί τινος οἰκέτου διαφερο-
μένων συνέβαινε παρὰ μὲν τὸν ἕτερον καὶ πλείω
2 χρόνον γεγονέναι τὸν παῖδα, τὸν δ᾽ ἕτερον ἡμέραις
δυσὶ πρότερον εἰς τὸν ἀγρὸν ἐλθόντα μὴ παρόντος τοῦ
δεσπότου μετὰ βίας εἰς οἶκον ἀπηχέναι τὸν δοῦλον,
3 κἄπειτα τὸν ἕτερον αἰσθόμενον ἐλθεῖν ἐπὶ τὴν οἰκίαν,
καὶ λαβόντ᾽ ἀπάγειν ἐπὶ τὴν ἀρχήν, καὶ φάναι δεῖν
4 κύριον αὐτὸν εἶναι διδόντα τοὺς ἐγγυητάς· κελεύειν
γὰρ τὸν Ζαλεύκου νόμον τοῦτον δεῖν κρατεῖν τῶν
ἀμφισβητουμένων ἕως τῆς κρίσεως παρ᾽ οὗ τὴν ἀγω-
5 γὴν συμβαίνει γίνεσθαι. τοῦ δ᾽ ἑτέρου κατὰ τὸν αὐτὸν
νόμον παρ᾽ αὑτοῦ φάσκοντος γεγονέναι τὴν ἀγω-
γήν—ἐκ γὰρ τῆς οἰκίας τῆς ἐκείνου τὸ σῶμα πρὸς τὴν
6 ἀρχὴν ἥκειν ἀπαγόμενον—τοὺς προκαθημένους ἄρχοντας διαποροῦντας ὑπὲρ τοῦ πράγματος ἐπισπάσα-
7 σθαι καὶ συμμεταδοῦναι τῷ κοσμοπόλιδι. τὸν δὲ δια-
στείλασθαι τὸν νόμον, φήσαντα παρὰ τούτων τὴν
ἀγωγὴν αἰεὶ γίνεσθαι, παρ᾽ οἷς ἂν ἔσχατον ἀδήριτον
8 ᾖ χρόνον τινὰ γεγονὸς τὸ διαμφισβητούμενον· ἐὰν δὲ
τις ἀφελόμενος βίᾳ παρά τινος ἀπαγάγῃ πρὸς αὑτόν,
κἄπειτα παρὰ τούτου τὴν ἀγωγὴν ὁ προϋπάρχων
9 ποιῆται δεσπότης, οὐκ εἶναι ταύτην κυρίαν. τοῦ δὲ
νεανίσκου δεινοπαθοῦντος καὶ μὴ φάσκοντος εἶναι

---

66 Half-legendary lawgiver of Locri in the seventh century. *RE* Zaleukos 2298–2301 (H. von Fritz). The function of the story in

full expression to my hostility to Timaeus, have omitted nothing essential to the object I had in view. . . .

16. There was a dispute at Locri between two young men about a slave. The slave had been with one of them for a considerable time, and the other, two days before, had come in the absence of the master to the latter's country place and had forcibly carried off the slave to his own house. The other young man, when he heard of it, came to the house, seized on the slave, and led him before the magistrates, to whom he maintained that upon his giving proper sureties, the boy ought to remain in his possession. For he said the law of Zaleucus[66] enjoins that in cases of disputed ownership the party from whom the property had been taken away or abducted should remain in possession until the trial. The other claimant contended that according to the same law the abduction had been from him; for it was from his house that the slave had been taken and carried before the court. The presiding magistrates were in doubt about the point and calling in the cosmopolis[67] submitted it to him. The cosmopolis defined the law as meaning that the abduction always was from the party who had last been in undisputed possession of the property for a certain time. If anyone forcibly deprives another of property and carries it off to his own house, and if then the former owner comes and takes it away from him, this is not abduction within the meaning of the law. When the young man upon this felt aggrieved and asserted that such was

this context is not altogether clear, except as part of the discussion on Locri that began in chapter 5.

[67] Probably the chief magistrate.

τοῦ νομοθέτου ταύτην τὴν προαίρεσιν, παρακαλέσα-
σθαι φασι τὸν κοσμόπολιν, εἴ τι βούλεται λέγειν ὑπὲρ
10 τῆς γνώμης κατὰ τὸν Ζαλεύκου νόμον. τοῦτο δ᾽ ἐστὶ
καθισάντων τῶν χιλίων καὶ βρόχων κρεμασθέντων
11 λέγειν ὑπὲρ τῆς τοῦ νομοθέτου γνώμης· ὁπότερος δ᾽
ἂν αὐτῶν φανῇ τὴν προαίρεσιν ἐπὶ τὸ χεῖρον ἐκδεχό-
μενος, τὸν τοιοῦτον διὰ τῆς ἀγχόνης ἀπόλλυσθαι βλε-
12 πόντων τῶν χιλίων. ταῦτα προτείναντος τοῦ κοσμο-
πόλιδος, τὸν νεανίσκον εἰπεῖν φασιν ἄνισον εἶναι τὴν
συνθήκην· τῷ μὲν γὰρ ἔτη δύ᾽ ἢ τρία καταλείπεσθαι
13 τοῦ ζῆν· συνέβαινε γὰρ εἶναι τὸν κοσμόπολιν οὐ πολὺ
λεῖπον τῶν ἐνενήκοντ᾽ ἐτῶν· αὐτῷ δὲ τοῦ βίου τὸ
14 πλεῖον ἐκ τῶν εὐλόγων ἔτι μένειν. ὁ μὲν οὖν νεανίσκος
οὕτως εὐτραπελευσάμενος ἐξέλυσε τὴν σπουδήν, οἱ δ᾽
ἄρχοντες ἔκριναν τὴν ἀγωγὴν κατὰ τὴν τοῦ κοσμο-
πόλιδος γνώμην.

V. DE CALLISTHENIS IMPERITIA IN
NARRANDIS REBUS MILITARIBUS

17. Ἵνα δὲ μὴ δόξωμεν τῶν τηλικούτων ἀνδρῶν
καταξιοπιστεῖσθαι, μνησθησόμεθα μιᾶς παρατάξεως,
ἣν ἅμα μὲν οἵαν ἐπιφανεστάτην εἶναι συμβέβηκεν,
ἅμα δὲ τοῖς καιροῖς οὐ μακρὰν ἀπηρτῆσθαι, τὸ δὲ
2 μέγιστον, παρατετευχέναι τὸν Καλλισθένη. λέγω δὲ
περὶ τῆς ἐν Κιλικίᾳ γενομένης Ἀλεξάνδρῳ πρὸς Δα-

---

68 The Council of the Thousand.   69 In any event, more
than 170 years earlier; the battle took place in November 333.

390

not the intention of the lawgiver, they say that the cosmopolis invited him to state his case according to the law of Zaleucus. This is that the two disputants should speak before the "thousand"[68] on the subject of the lawgiver's meaning, each with a halter round his neck, and whichever of them appeared to interpret the law worst, should be hanged in the presence of the thousand. Upon the cosmopolis making this offer, the young man said that the bargain was not a fair one. For one of them had only two or three years left to live, the cosmopolis being very nearly ninety years of age. whereas he himself in all likelihood had the most of his life still before him. Thus the young man's ready wit relaxed the gravity of the court, but the magistrates followed the opinion of the cosmopolis in defining abduction.

V. INCAPACITY OF CALLISTHENES IN WRITING OF MILITARY MATTERS

17. In order that I may not seem to insist arbitrarily on the acceptance of my criticism of such famous writers, I will take one battle and a very celebrated one, a battle which took place at no very distant date[69] and, what is most important, one at which Callisthenes himself was present. I mean Alexander's battle with Darius in Cilicia.[70] Callis-

[70] At Issus. The main preserved description is that of Arr., *An*. 2.7.1–11.10, with A. B. Bosworth, *A Historical Commentary on Arrian's History of Alexander* 1 (Oxford 1980), 198–219. What Callisthenes said is known only from P., whose "criticism . . . shows P. at his worst" (WC 2.364) and is called "oberflächlich und kleinlich" by Beloch, *Gr. Gesch*. III² 2, 355.

ρεῖον, ἐν ᾗ φησὶ μὲν Ἀλέξανδρον ἤδη διαπεπορεῦσθαι
τὰ στενὰ καὶ τὰς λεγομένας ἐν τῇ Κιλικίᾳ Πύλας,
Δαρεῖον δὲ χρησάμενον τῇ διὰ τῶν Ἀμανίδων λεγομένων Πυλῶν πορείᾳ κατᾶραι μετὰ τῆς δυνάμεως εἰς
3 Κιλικίαν· πυθόμενον δὲ παρὰ τῶν ἐγχωρίων προάγειν
τὸν Ἀλέξανδρον ὡς ἐπὶ Συρίαν, ἀκολουθεῖν, καὶ συν-
εγγίσαντα τοῖς στενοῖς στρατοπεδεῦσαι παρὰ τὸν
4 Πίναρον ποταμόν. εἶναι δὲ τοῦ μὲν τόπου τὸ διάστημ᾽
οὐ πλείω τῶν τεττάρων καὶ δέκα σταδίων ἀπὸ θαλάτ-
5 της ἕως πρὸς τὴν παρώρειαν· διὰ δὲ τούτου φέρεσθαι
τὸν προειρημένον ποταμὸν ἐπικάρσιον, ἀπὸ μὲν τῶν
ὀρῶν εὐθέως ἐκρήγματα τῶν πλευρῶν, διὰ δὲ τῶν
ἐπιπέδων ἕως εἰς θάλατταν ἀποτόμους ἔχοντα καὶ
6 δυσβάτους λόφους. ταῦτα δ᾽ ὑποθέμενος, ἐπεὶ συνεγ-
γίζοιεν οἱ περὶ τὸν Ἀλέξανδρον ἐξ ὑποστροφῆς ἐπ᾽
αὐτοὺς ἀναχωροῦντες, κρῖναί φησι Δαρεῖον καὶ τοὺς
ἡγεμόνας τὴν μὲν φάλαγγα τάξαι πᾶσαν ἐν αὐτῇ τῇ
στρατοπεδείᾳ, καθάπερ ἐξ ἀρχῆς εἶχε, χρήσασθαι δὲ
τῷ ποταμῷ προβλήματι διὰ τὸ παρ᾽ αὐτὴν ῥεῖν τὴν
7 στρατοπεδείαν. μετὰ δὲ ταῦτά φησι τοὺς μὲν ἱππεῖς
τάξαι παρὰ θάλατταν, τοὺς δὲ μισθοφόρους ἑξῆς
τούτοις παρ᾽ αὐτὸν τὸν ποταμόν, ἐχομένους τούτων
τοὺς πελταστὰς συνάπτοντας τοῖς ὄρεσι.

18. πῶς δὲ προέταξε τούτους πρὸ τῆς φάλαγγος,
τοῦ ποταμοῦ ῥέοντος παρ᾽ αὐτὴν τὴν στρατοπεδείαν,
δυσχερὲς κατανοῆσαι, καὶ ταῦτα τῷ πλήθει τοσούτων
2 ὑπαρχόντων. τρισμύριοι μὲν γὰρ ἱππεῖς ὑπῆρχον, ὡς
αὐτὸς ὁ Καλλισθένης φησί, τρισμύριοι δὲ μισθο-

thenes tells us that Alexander had already passed the nar-
rows and the so-called Cilician gates, while Darius had
marched through the pass known as the Gates of Amanus
and had descended with his army into Cilicia. On learning
from the natives that Alexander was advancing in the direction of Syria he followed him up, and when he approached the pass, encamped on the banks of the river
Pinarus. The distance, he says, from the sea to the foot of
the hills is not more than fourteen stades, the river running obliquely across this space, with gaps in its banks just
where it issues from the mountains, but in its whole course
through the plain as far as the sea passing between steep
hills difficult to climb. Having given this sketch of the
country, he tells us that Darius and his generals, when Alexander turned and marched back to meet them, decided
to draw up the whole phalanx in the camp itself in its original position, the river affording protection, as it ran close
past the camp. After this he says they drew up the cavalry
along the seashore, the mercenaries next them at the brink
of the river, and the peltasts next the mercenaries in a line
reaching as far as the mountains.

18. It is difficult to understand how they posted all
these troops in front of the phalanx, considering that the
river ran close past the camp, especially in view of their
numbers, for, as Callisthenes himself says, there were
thirty thousand cavalry and thirty thousand mercenaries,

φόροι· πόσου δ᾽ εἶχον οὗτοι τόπου χρείαν, εὐχερὲς
3 καταμαθεῖν. πλεῖστον μὲν γὰρ ἱππέων τάττεται βάθος
ἐπ᾽ ὀκτὼ πρὸς ἀληθινὴν χρείαν, καὶ μεταξὺ τῶν ἰλῶν
ἑκάστης ἴσον ὑπάρχειν δεῖ διάστημα τοῖς μετώποις
πρὸς τὸ ταῖς ἐπιστροφαῖς δύνασθαι καὶ τοῖς περι-
4 σπασμοῖς εὐχρηστεῖν. ἐξ ὧν τὸ στάδιον ὀκτακοσίους
λαμβάνει, τὰ δὲ δέκα τοὺς ὀκτακισχιλίους, τὰ δὲ
τέτταρα τρισχιλίους διακοσίους, ὥστ᾽ ἀπὸ τῶν μυρίων χιλίων διακοσίων πεπληρῶσθαι τὸν τῶν τετταρεσ-
5 καίδεκα σταδίων τόπον. ἐὰν δὲ πάντας ἐκτάττῃ τοὺς
τρισμυρίους, βραχὺ λείπει τοῦ τριφαλαγγίαν ἐπάλ-
6 ληλον εἶναι τῶν ἱππέων αὐτῶν. εἰς ποῖον οὖν τόπον
ἐτάττετο τὸ τῶν μισθοφόρων πλῆθος; εἰ μὴ νὴ Δία
κατόπιν τῶν ἱππέων. ἀλλ᾽ οὔ φησιν, ἀλλὰ συμπεπτω-
7 κέναι τούτους τοῖς Μακεδόσι κατὰ τὴν ἐπαγωγήν. ἐξ
ὧν ἀνάγκη ποιεῖσθαι τὴν ἐκδοχὴν διότι τὸ μὲν ἥμισυ
τοῦ τόπου τὸ παρὰ θάλατταν ἡ τῶν ἱππέων ἐπεῖχε
τάξις, τὸ δ᾽ ἥμισυ τὸ πρὸς τοῖς ὄρεσιν ἡ τῶν μισθο-
8 φόρων. ἐκ δὲ τούτων εὐσυλλόγιστον πόσον ὑπῆρχε τὸ
βάθος τῶν ἱππέων καὶ ποῖον ἔδει τόπον ἀπέχειν τὸν
9 ποταμὸν ἀπὸ τῆς στρατοπεδείας. μετὰ δὲ ταῦτα συνεγγιζόντων τῶν πολεμίων φησὶ τὸν Δαρεῖον, αὐτὸν
κατὰ μέσην ὑπάρχοντα τὴν τάξιν, καλεῖν τοὺς μισθοφόρους ἀπὸ τοῦ κέρατος πρὸς αὐτόν. πῶς δὲ λέγεται
10 τοῦτο, διαπορεῖν ἔστι· τῶν γὰρ μισθοφόρων ἀνάγκη
καὶ τῶν ἱππέων τὴν συναφὴν κατὰ μέσον ὑπάρχειν
τὸν τόπον, ὥστ᾽ ἐν αὐτοῖς ὢν τοῖς μισθοφόροις ὁ
Δαρεῖος ποῦ καὶ πρὸς τί καὶ πῶς ἐκάλει τοὺς μισθο-

and it is easy to calculate how much space was required to hold them. For in a regular engagement cavalry should be at the most eight deep, and between each troop there must be a space equal in length to the front of a troop so that there may be no difficulty in wheeling and facing round. Thus a stade will hold eight hundred horse, ten stades eight thousand, and four stades three thousand two hundred, so that eleven thousand two hundred horse would fill a space of fourteen stades. If the whole force of thirty thousand were drawn up the cavalry alone would very nearly suffice to form three such bodies, one placed close behind the other. Where, then, were the mercenaries posted, unless indeed they were drawn up behind the cavalry? This he tells us was not so, as they were the first to meet the Macedonian attack. We must, then, of necessity, understand that the cavalry occupied that half of the space which was nearest to the sea and the mercenaries the half nearest the hills, and from this it is easy to reckon what was the depth of the cavalry and how far away from the camp the river must have been. After this he tells us that on the approach of the enemy, Darius, who was half way down the line, called the mercenaries himself from the wing to come to him. It is difficult to see what he means by this. For the mercenaries and cavalry must have been in touch just in the middle of the field, so that how, why, and where could Darius, who was actually among the mercenaries,

11 φόρους; τὸ δὲ τελευταῖον φησι τοὺς ἀπὸ τοῦ δεξιοῦ
κέρατος ἱππεῖς ἐπαγαγόντας ἐμβαλεῖν τοῖς περὶ τὸν
Ἀλέξανδρον, τοὺς δὲ γενναίως δεξαμένους ἀντεπάγειν
12 καὶ ποιεῖν μάχην ἰσχυράν. ὅτι δὲ ποταμὸς ἦν ἐν μέσῳ,
καὶ ποταμὸς οἷον ἀρτίως εἶπεν, ἐπελάθετο.

19. Τούτοις δ' ἐστὶ παραπλήσια τὰ κατὰ τὸν
Ἀλέξανδρον. φησὶ γὰρ αὐτὸν ποιήσασθαι τὴν εἰς τὴν
Ἀσίαν διάβασιν, πεζῶν μὲν ἔχοντα τέτταρας μυριάδας, ἱππεῖς δὲ τετρακισχιλίους καὶ πεντακοσίους,
2 μέλλοντι δ' εἰς Κιλικίαν ἐμβάλλειν ἄλλους ἐλθεῖν ἐκ
Μακεδονίας πεζοὺς μὲν πεντακισχιλίους, ἱππεῖς δ'
3 ὀκτακοσίους. ἀφ' ὧν εἴ τις ἀφέλοι τρισχιλίους μὲν
πεζούς, τριακοσίους δ' ἱππεῖς, ἐπὶ τὸ πλεῖον ποιῶν
τὴν ἀπουσίαν πρὸς τὰς γεγενημένας χρείας, ὅμως
πεζοὶ μὲν ἀπολειφθήσονται τετρακισμύριοι δισχίλιοι,
4 ⟨πεντακισχίλιοι δ' ἱππεῖς⟩. τούτων οὖν ὑποκειμένων,
φησὶ τὸν Ἀλέξανδρον πυθέσθαι τὴν Δαρείου παρουσίαν εἰς Κιλικίαν ἑκατὸν ἀπέχοντα σταδίους ἀπ'
5 αὐτοῦ, διαπεπορευμένον ἤδη τὰ στενά· διόπερ ἐξ ὑποστροφῆς πάλιν ποιεῖσθαι τὴν πορείαν διὰ τῶν στε-
νῶν, ἄγοντα πρῶτον μὲν τὴν φάλαγγα, μετὰ δὲ ταῦτα
6 τοὺς ἱππεῖς, ἐπὶ πᾶσι τὸ σκευοφόρον. ἅμα δὲ τῷ
πρῶτον εἰς τὰς εὐρυχωρίας ἐκπεσεῖν, διασκευάζεσθαι
παραγγείλαντα πᾶσιν ἐπιπαρεμβαλεῖν τὴν φάλαγγα,
καὶ ποιῆσαι τὸ βάθος αὐτῆς ἐπὶ τριάκοντα καὶ δύο,
μετὰ δὲ ταῦτα πάλιν εἰς ἑκκαίδεκα, τὸ δὲ τελευταῖον,
7 ἐγγίζοντα τοῖς πολεμίοις, εἰς ὀκτώ. ταῦτα δ' ἐστὶ
μείζω τῶν προειρημένων ἀλογήματα. τοῦ γὰρ σταδίου

call them to come to him? Lastly, he says that the cavalry from the right wing advanced and attacked Alexander's cavalry, who received their charge bravely and delivering a counter charge fought stubbornly. He forgets that there was a river between them and such a river as he has just described.

19. Very similar are his statements about Alexander. He says that when he crossed to Asia he had forty thousand foot and four thousand five hundred horse, and that when he was on the point of invading Cilicia he was joined by a further force of five thousand foot and eight hundred horse. Suppose we deduct from this total three thousand foot and three hundred horse, making a liberal allowance for losses incurred in previous operations, there still remain forty-two thousand foot and five thousand horse. Assuming these numbers, he tells us that when Alexander heard the news of Darius' arrival in Cilicia he was a hundred stades away and had already traversed the pass. In consequence he turned and marched back through the pass with the phalanx in front, followed by the cavalry, and last of all the baggage train. Immediately on issuing into the open country he re-formed his order, passing to all the word of command to form into phalanx, making it at first thirty-two deep, changing this subsequently to sixteen deep, and finally as he approached the enemy to eight deep. These statements are even more absurd than his for-

λαμβάνοντος ἄνδρας ἐν τοῖς πορευτικοῖς διαστήμασιν, ὅταν εἰς ἑκκαίδεκα τὸ βάθος ὦσι, χιλίους
ἑξακοσίους, ἑκάστου τῶν ἀνδρῶν ἐξ πόδας ἐπέχοντος,
8 φανερὸν ὅτι τὰ δέκα στάδια λήψεται μυρίους ἑξακισ-
9 χιλίους, τὰ δ' εἴκοσι τοὺς διπλασίους. ἐκ δὲ τούτων
εὐθεώρητον ὅτι καθ' ὃν καιρὸν ἐποίησε τὴν δύναμιν
Ἀλέξανδρος ἑκκαίδεκα τὸ βάθος, ἀναγκαῖον ἦν εἴκοσι
σταδίων ὑπάρχειν τὸ τοῦ τόπου διάστημα καὶ περιτ-
τεύειν ἔτι τοὺς μὲν ἱππεῖς πάντας, τῶν δὲ πεζῶν
μυρίους.

20. Μετὰ δὲ ταῦτά φησι μετωπηδὸν ἄγειν τὴν
δύναμιν, ἀπέχοντα τῶν πολεμίων περὶ τετταράκοντα
2 σταδίους. τούτου δὲ μεῖζον ἀλόγημα δυσχερὲς ἐπι-
νοῆσαι· ποῦ γὰρ ἂν εὕροι τις τοιούτους τόπους, ἄλλως
τε καὶ κατὰ Κιλικίαν, ὥστ' ἐπὶ σταδίους εἴκοσι μὲν τὸ
πλάτος τετταράκοντα δὲ τὸ μῆκος μετωπηδὸν ἄγειν
3 φάλαγγα σαρισοφόρον; τοσαῦτα γάρ ἐστιν ἐμπόδια
πρὸς τὴν τοιαύτην τάξιν καὶ χρείαν, ἅ τις οὐδ' ἂν
ἐξαριθμήσαιτο ῥαδίως. ἐν δὲ τῶν ὑπ' αὐτοῦ Καλλισθένους λεγομένων ἱκανὸν ὑπάρχει πρὸς πίστιν·
4 τοὺς γὰρ ἀπὸ τῶν ὀρῶν χειμάρρους καταφερομένους
τοσαῦτά φησι ποιεῖν ἐκρήγματα κατὰ τὸ πεδίον ὥστε
καὶ τῶν Περσῶν κατὰ τὴν φυγὴν διαφθαρῆναι λέ-
5 γουσι τοὺς πλείστους ἐν τοῖς τοιούτοις κοιλώμασι. νὴ
Δί', ἀλλ' ἕτοιμος ἐβούλετ' εἶναι πρὸς τὴν τῶν πολε-
6 μίων ἐπιφάνειαν. τί δ' ἀνετοιμότερον φάλαγγος ἐν
μετώπῳ διαλελυμένης καὶ διεσταμένης; πόσῳ γὰρ ἐκ
πορευτικῆς ἀγωγῆς ἁρμοζούσης παρατάξαι ῥᾷον ἢ

mer ones. For with the proper intervals for marching order, a stade, when the men are sixteen deep, will hold sixteen hundred, each man being at a distance of six feet[71] from the next. It is evident, then, that ten stades will hold sixteen thousand men and twenty stades twice as many. From all this it is quite plain that when Alexander made his army sixteen deep the line necessarily extended for twenty stades, and this left all the cavalry and ten thousand of the infantry over.

20. After this he says that Alexander led on his army in an extended line, being then at a distance of about forty stades from the enemy. It is difficult to conceive anything more absurd than this. Where, especially in Cilicia, could one find an extent of ground where a phalanx with its long spears could advance for forty stades in a line twenty stades long? The obstacles indeed to such a formation and such a movement are so many that it would be difficult to enumerate them all, a single one mentioned by Callisthenes himself being sufficient to convince us of its impossibility. For he tells us that the torrents descending from the mountains have formed so many clefts in the plain that most of the Persians in their flight are said to have perished in such fissures. But. it may be said, Alexander wished to be prepared for the appearance of the enemy. And what can be less prepared than a phalanx advancing in line but broken and disunited? How much easier indeed it would have been to develop from proper marching order into order of battle than to straighten out and prepare for action on thickly wooded and fissured ground a broken line with nu-

---

[71] See J. Kromayer, in J. Kromayer—G. Veith, *Heerwesen und Kriegführung der Griechen und Römer* (Munich 1928), 135–136.

διαλελυμένην ἐν μετώπῳ καὶ διεσπασμένην δύναμιν
ἐπὶ τὴν αὐτὴν εὐθεῖαν ἀγαγεῖν καὶ συστῆσαι πρὸς
7 μάχην ἐν τόποις ὑλώδεσι καὶ περικεκλασμένοις; διόπερ οὐδὲ παρὰ μικρὸν ἦν κρεῖττον ἄγειν διφαλαγ-
γίαν ἢ τετραφαλαγγίαν ἁρμόζουσαν, ᾗ καὶ τόπον
πορείας εὑρεῖν οὐκ ἀδύνατον, καὶ τὸ παρατάξαι ταχέως ῥᾴδιόν γε, δυνάμενον διὰ τῶν προδρόμων ἐκ
8 πολλοῦ γινώσκειν τὴν τῶν πολεμίων παρουσίαν. ὁ δὲ
χωρὶς τῶν ἄλλων οὐδὲ τοὺς ἱππεῖς προέθετο, μετωπηδὸν ἄγων τὴν δύναμιν ἐν τόποις ἐπιπέδοις, ἀλλ᾽ ἐξ
ἴσου ποιεῖ τοῖς πεζοῖς.

21. Τὸ δὲ δὴ πάντων μέγιστον· ἤδη γὰρ σύνεγγυς
ὄντα τοῖς πολεμίοις αὐτὸν εἰς ὀκτὼ ποιῆσαί φησι τὸ
2 βάθος. ἐξ οὗ δῆλον ὅτι κατ᾽ ἀνάγκην ἐπὶ τετταράκοντα σταδίους ἔδει γενέσθαι τὸ μῆκος τῆς φάλαγ-
3 γος. εἰ δ᾽ ὅλως συνήσπισαν κατὰ τὸν ποιητὴν οὕτως
ὥστε συνερεῖσαι πρὸς ἀλλήλους, ὅμως εἴκοσι στα-
4 δίων ἔδει τὸν τόπον ὑπάρχειν. αὐτὸς δέ φησι λείπειν
5 τῶν δεκατεττάρων σταδίων . . . καὶ τούτου μέρος μέν
τι πρὸς θαλάττῃ τοὺς ἡμίσεας ἐπὶ τοῦ δεξιοῦ· . . . ἔτι
δὲ τὴν ὅλην τάξιν ἀπὸ τῶν ὁρῶν ἱκανὸν τόπον ἀφεστάναι πρὸς τὸ μὴ τοῖς πολεμίοις ὑποπεπτωκέναι τοῖς
6 κατέχουσι τὰς παρωρείας. ἴσμεν γὰρ ὃ ποιεῖ πρὸς
τούτους ἐπικάμπιον.

Ὑπολειπόμεθα καὶ νῦν ἡμεῖς τοὺς μυρίους πεζούς,
7 πλείους ὄντας τῆς ἐκείνου προθέσεως. ὥστ᾽ ἐκ τούτων
ἕνδεκα σταδίους ἐπὶ τὸ πλεῖον ἀπολείπεσθαι τὸ τῆς

merous gaps in it? It would, therefore, have been considerably better to form a proper double or quadruple phalanx, for which it was not impossible to find marching room and which it would have been quite easy to get into order of battle expeditiously enough, as he was enabled through his scouts to receive in good time warning of the approach of the enemy. But, other things apart, Alexander did not even, according to Callisthenes, send his cavalry on in front when advancing in line over flat ground, but apparently placed them alongside the infantry.

21. But here is the greatest of all his mistakes. He tells us that Alexander, on approaching the enemy, made his line eight deep. It is evident then that now the total length of the line must have been forty stades. And even if they closed up so that, as described by Homer,[72] they actually jostled each other, still the front must have extended over twenty stades. But he tells us that there was only a space of less than fourteen stades, and as half of the cavalry were on the left near the sea and half on the right, the room available for the infantry is still further reduced. Add to this that the whole line must have kept at a considerable distance from the mountains so as not to be exposed to attack by those of the enemy who held the foothills. We know that he did as a fact draw up part of his force at an angle to oppose these latter.

I omit to reckon here also[73] the ten thousand infantry more than his purpose required. So the consequence is that the length of the line must have been, according to

[72] *Il*. 13.131–133 = 16.215–217.
[73] The reference is to 19.9, but either the omissions by the epitomator or faults in the text make the passage very obscure.

φάλαγγος μῆκος κατ' αὐτὸν τὸν Καλλισθένην, ἐν οἷς
ἀνάγκη τοὺς τρισμυρίους καὶ δισχιλίους ἐπὶ τρι-
8 άκοντα τὸ βάθος ὑπάρχειν συνησπικότας. ὁ δέ φησιν
9 εἰς ὀκτὼ τεταγμένων γενέσθαι τὴν μάχην. τὰ δὲ τοιαῦτα τῶν ἁμαρτημάτων οὐδ' ἀπολογίαν ἐπιδέχεται· τὸ
γὰρ ἀδύνατον ἐν πράγμασιν αὐτόθεν ἔχει τὴν πίστιν.
10 διόπερ ὅταν καὶ τὰ κατ' ἄνδρα διαστήματα καὶ τὸ
πᾶν τοῦ τόπου μέγεθος ὡρισμένον ὑποθῶσι καὶ τὸν
ἀριθμὸν τῶν ἀνδρῶν, ἀναπολόγητον γίνεται τὸ ψεῦδος.

22. Τὰ μὲν γὰρ ἅμα τούτοις ἀλογήματα μακρὸν ἂν
2 εἴη λέγειν πάντα πλὴν τελέως ὀλίγων. φησὶ γὰρ τὸν
Ἀλέξανδρον σπουδάζειν κατὰ τὴν τάξιν, ἵνα κατὰ τὸν
Δαρεῖον αὐτὸν ποιήσηται τὴν μάχην· ὁμοίως δὲ κατὰ
μὲν ἀρχὰς καὶ τὸν Δαρεῖον αὐτὸν βούλεσθαι κατὰ τὸν
3 Ἀλέξανδρον, ὕστερον δὲ μετανοῆσαι. πῶς δ' ἐπέ-
γνωσαν ἀλλήλους οὗτοι ποῦ τῆς ἰδίας δυνάμεως ἔχουσι τὴν τάξιν, ἢ ποῦ μετέβη πάλιν ὁ Δαρεῖος, ἁπλῶς
4 οὐδὲν λέγεται. πῶς δὲ προσανέβη πρὸς τὴν ὀφρὺν τοῦ
ποταμοῦ φαλαγγιτῶν τάξις, ἀπότομον οὖσαν καὶ βα-
5 τώδη; καὶ γὰρ τοῦτο παρὰ λόγον. Ἀλεξάνδρῳ μὲν οὖν
οὐκ ἐποιστέον τὴν τοιαύτην ἀτοπίαν ⟨διὰ τὸ πᾶσιν⟩
ὁμολογουμένην παραλαμβάνεσθαι περὶ αὐτοῦ τὴν ἐν
τοῖς πολεμικοῖς ἐμπειρίαν καὶ τριβὴν ἐκ παιδός, τῷ δὲ
6 συγγραφεῖ μᾶλλον, ὃς διὰ τὴν ἀπειρίαν οὐδὲ τὸ δυνατὸν καὶ τὸ μὴ δυνατὸν ἐν τοῖς τοιούτοις δύναται
7 διευκρινεῖν. περὶ μὲν οὖν Ἐφόρου καὶ Καλλισθένους
ταῦθ' ἡμῖν εἰρήσθω.

Callisthenes himself, eleven stades at the most, and in this space thirty-two thousand men must have stood closely packed and thirty deep, whereas he tells us that in the battle they were eight deep. Now for such mistakes we can admit no excuse. For when the actual facts show a thing to be impossible we are instantly convinced that it is so. Thus when a writer gives definitely, as in this case, the distance from man to man, the total area of the ground, and the number of men, he is perfectly inexcusable in making false statements.

22. It would be too long a story to mention all the other absurdities of his narrative, and it will suffice to point out a few. He tells us that Alexander in drawing up his army was most anxious to be opposed to Darius in person, and that Darius also at first entertained the same wish, but afterward changed his mind. But he tells us absolutely nothing as to how each learned at what point in his own line the other was stationed, or whereabouts Darius then took up his new position. And how, we ask, did a phalanx of heavy-armed men manage to mount the bank of the river which was steep and overgrown with brambles? This, too, is inexplicable. Such an absurdity cannot be attributed to Alexander, as it is universally acknowledged that from his childhood he was well versed and trained in the art of war. We should rather attribute it to the writer, who is so ignorant as to be unable to distinguish the possible from the impossible in such matters. Let this suffice for Ephorus[74] and Callisthenes.

[74] Nothing of his discussion of the battle survives.

VI. DE TIMAEO HISTORICO

23. Ὅτι κατὰ τοῦ Ἐφόρου Τίμαιος πλείστην πεποίηται καταδρομήν, αὐτὸς ὢν δυσὶν ἁμαρτήμασιν
2 ἔνοχος, τῷ μὲν ὅτι πικρῶς κατηγορεῖ τῶν πέλας ἐπὶ
τούτοις οἷς αὐτὸς ἔνοχός ἐστι, τῷ δὲ διότι καθόλου
διέφθαρται τῇ ψυχῇ, τοιαύτας ἀποφάσεις ἐκτιθέμενος
ἐν τοῖς ὑπομνήμασι καὶ τοιαύτας ἐντίκτων δόξας τοῖς
3 ἐντυγχάνουσι. πλὴν εἰ τὸν Καλλισθένην θετέον εἰκότως κολασθέντα μεταλλάξαι τὸν βίον, τί χρὴ πάσχειν
Τίμαιον; πολὺ γὰρ ἂν δικαιότερον τούτῳ νεμεσῆσαι
4 τὸ δαιμόνιον ἢ Καλλισθένει. ἐκεῖνος μὲν οὖν ἀποθεοῦν
Ἀλέξανδρον ἐβουλήθη, Τίμαιος δὲ μείζω ποιεῖ Τιμο-
5 λέοντα τῶν ἐπιφανεστάτων θεῶν, καὶ Καλλισθένης
μὲν ἄνδρα τοιοῦτον, ὃν πάντες μεγαλοφυέστερον ἢ
κατ' ἄνθρωπον γεγονέναι τῇ ψυχῇ συγχωροῦσιν,
6 οὗτος δὲ Τιμολέοντα τὸν οὐχ οἷον δόξαντά τι πεπρα-
χέναι μεγαλεῖον, ἀλλ' οὐδ' ἐπιβαλόμενον, μίαν δ' ἐν
τῷ βίῳ γραμμὴν διανύσαντα, καὶ ταύτην οὐδὲ σπου-
δαίαν τρόπον τινὰ πρὸς τὸ μέγεθος τῆς οἰκουμένης,
7 λέγω δὲ τὴν ἐκ τῆς πατρίδος εἰς Συρακούσας. ἀλλά
μοι δοκεῖ πεισθῆναι Τίμαιος ὡς, ἂν Τιμολέων, πεφι-
λοδοξηκὼς ἐν αὐτῇ Σικελίᾳ, καθάπερ ἐν ὀξυβάφῳ,
σύγκριτος φανῇ τοῖς ἐπιφανεστάτοις τῶν ἡρώων, κἂν
αὐτὸς ὑπὲρ Ἰταλίας μόνον καὶ Σικελίας πραγμα-
τευόμενος εἰκότως παραβολῆς ἀξιωθῆναι τοῖς ὑπὲρ
τῆς οἰκουμένης καὶ τῶν καθόλου πράξεων πεποιη-
8 μένοις τὰς συντάξεις. περὶ μὲν οὖν Ἀριστοτέλους καὶ

VI. THE FAULTS OF TIMAEUS

23. Timaeus, while vehemently attacking Ephorus, is himself guilty of two grave faults, the first being that he thus bitterly accuses others of the sins he himself is guilty of, and the second that he shows an utterly depraved mind in publishing such statements in his works and engendering such notions in his readers. If, indeed, we must admit that Callisthenes deserved to perish as he did under torture, what fate did Timaeus merit? For the wrath of the gods would have fallen on him with much more justice than on Callisthenes. Callisthenes wished to deify Alexander, but Timaeus makes Timoleon[75] greater than the most illustrious gods; Callisthenes spoke of a man whose soul, as all admit, had something in it greater than human, Timaeus of Timoleon who not only never seems to have achieved anything great, but never even to have attempted to do so, and in his whole life accomplished but one move and that by no means important considering the greatness of the world, the move from his country to Syracuse.[76] The fact, in my opinion, is that Timaeus was sure that if Timoleon, who had sought fame in a mere teacup, as it were, Sicily, could be shown to be worthy of comparison with the most illustrious heroes, he himself, who treated only of Italy and Sicily, could claim comparison with writers whose works dealt with the whole world and with universal history. I have now said enough to defend Aristotle, Theo-

---

[75] See n. on 4a.2 and R. Talbert, *Timoleon and the Revival of Greek Sicily, 344–317 B.C.* (Cambridge 1974). While Timaeus' praise of Timoleon was perhaps excessive, P.'s criticism of the man is mean.   [76] In 344.

Θεοφράστου καὶ Καλλισθένους, ἔτι δ᾿ Ἐφόρου καὶ
Δημοχάρους, ἱκανὰ ταῦθ᾿ ἡμῖν ἐστι πρὸς τὴν Τιμαίου
καταδρομήν, ὁμοίως δὲ καὶ πρὸς τοὺς ἀφιλοτίμως
πεπεισμένους ἀληθεύειν τὸν συγγραφέα τοῦτον.

24. Ὅτι διαπορεῖν ἔστι περὶ τῆς αἱρέσεως Τιμαίου.
φησὶ γὰρ τοὺς ποιητὰς καὶ συγγραφέας διὰ τῶν
ὑπεράνω πλεονασμῶν ἐν τοῖς ὑπομνήμασι διαφαίνειν
2 τὰς ἑαυτῶν φύσεις. λέγων τὸν μὲν ποιητὴν ἐκ τοῦ
δαιτρεύειν πολλαχοῦ τῆς ποιήσεως ὡς ἂν εἰ γαστρίμαργον παρεμφαίνειν, τὸν δ᾿ Ἀριστοτέλην, ὀψαρτύ-
οντα πλεονάκις ἐν τοῖς συγγράμμασιν, ὀψοφάγον
3 εἶναι καὶ λίχνον. τὸν αὐτὸν τρόπον ἐπιφαίνεσθαι τὴν
φύσιν⟩ τοῦ Διονυσίου τοῦ τυράννου, κλινοκοσμοῦντος
καὶ τὰς τῶν ὑφασμάτων ἰδιότητας καὶ ποικιλίας ἐξερ-
4 γαζομένου συνεχῶς ⟨ἀλλ᾿⟩ ἀνάγκη τὴν ἀκόλουθον
ποιεῖσθαι διάληψιν ⟨περὶ Τιμαίου⟩ καὶ δυσαρεστεῖ-
5 σθαι ⟨τούτῳ⟩ κατὰ τὴν προαίρεσιν. οὗτος γὰρ ἐν μὲν
ταῖς τῶν πέλας κατηγορίαις πολλὴν ἐπιφαίνει δεινό-
τητα καὶ τόλμαν, ἐν δὲ ταῖς ἰδίαις ἀποφάσεσιν
ἐνυπνίων καὶ τεράτων καὶ μύθων ἀπιθάνων καὶ συλλήβδην δεισιδαιμονίας ἀγεννοῦς καὶ τερατείας γυναι-
6 κώδους ἐστὶ πλήρης. οὐ μὴν ἀλλὰ διότι γε συμβαίνει
διὰ τὴν ἀπειρίαν καὶ κακοκρισίαν πολλοὺς ἐνίοτε
καθάπερ εἰ παρόντας τρόπον τινὰ μὴ παρεῖναι καὶ
βλέποντας μὴ βλέπειν ἐκ τῶν εἰρημένων τε νῦν καὶ
τῶν Τιμαίῳ συμβεβηκότων γέγονε φανερόν.

25. Ὅτι περὶ τοῦ ταύρου τοῦ χαλκοῦ τοῦ παρὰ

phrastus, Callisthenes, Ephorus, and Demochares from the attacks of Timaeus, and to convince those who believe him to be unprejudiced and truthful not to place implicit reliance on all he says.

24. We must entertain considerable doubt about the proclivities of Timaeus. For he tells us that poets and authors reveal their real natures in their works by dwelling excessively on certain matters. Homer, he says, is constantly feasting his heroes, and this indicates that he was more or less of a glutton. Aristotle frequently gives recipes for cookery in his works, so he must have been an epicure and a lover of dainties. In the same way Dionysius the tyrant revealed his effeminate tastes by his interest in bed hangings and the constant study he devoted to varieties and peculiarities of different woven work. We are driven then to form our opinion of Timaeus on the same principle and to take an unfavorable view of his own tendencies. For while he exhibits great severity and audacity in accusing others, his own pronouncements are full of dreams, prodigies, incredible tales, and to put it shortly, craven superstition and womanish love of the marvelous. Be this as it may, it is made evident from what I have just said and from this case of Timaeus that owing to ignorance and a defect of judgment many men are at times as it were absent when present and blind with their eyes open.

25. There was a brazen bull which Phalaris[77] made in

---

[77] Tyrant of Agrigentum around the middle of the sixth century, the prototype of a cruel man. Pi. *Pythian* 1.95–96 (from the year 476) already speaks of his brazen bull; the story is as famous as it is obscure. P.'s polemic rests on the assumption that Timaeus had denied the existence of such a bull (which he had not). *RE* Phalaris 1649–1652 (Th. Lenschau).

Φαλάριδος κατασκευασθέντος ἐν Ἀκράγαντι, εἰς ὃν
ἐνεβίβαζεν ἀνθρώπους, κἄπειτα πῦρ ὑποκαίων ἐλάμβανε τιμωρίαν παρὰ τῶν ὑποταττομένων τοιαύτην

2   ὥστ' ἐκπυρουμένου τοῦ χαλκοῦ τὸν μὲν ἄνθρωπον
παντανόθεν παροπτώμενον καὶ περιφλεγόμενον δια-
φθείρεσθαι, κατὰ δὲ τὴν ὑπερβολὴν τῆς ἀλγηδόνος,
ὁπότ' ἀναβοήσειε, μυκηθμῷ παραπλήσιον τὸν ἦχον
ἐκ τοῦ κατασκευάσματος προσπίπτειν τοῖς ἀκούουσι.

3   τούτου δὲ τοῦ ταύρου κατὰ τὴν ἐπικράτειαν Καρχηδονίων μετενεχθέντος ἐξ Ἀκράγαντος εἰς Καρχηδόνα,
καὶ τῆς θυρίδος διαμενούσης περὶ τὰς συνωμίας, δι'
ἧς συνέβαινε καθίεσθαι τοὺς ἐπὶ τὴν τιμωρίαν, καὶ
ἑτέρας αἰτίας, δι' ἣν ἐν Καρχηδόνι κατεσκευάσθη
τοιοῦτος ταῦρος, οὐδαμῶς δυναμένης εὑρεθῆναι τὸ

4   παράπαν, ὅμως Τίμαιος ἐπεβάλετο καὶ τὴν κοινὴν
φήμην ἀνασκευάζειν καὶ τὰς ἀποφάσεις τῶν ποιητῶν
καὶ συγγραφέων ψευδοποιεῖν, φάσκων μήτ' εἶναι τὸν
ἐν Καρχηδόνι ταῦρον ἐξ Ἀκράγαντος μήτε γεγονέναι

5   τοιοῦτον ἐν τῇ προειρημένῃ πόλει· καὶ πολλοὺς δή
τινας εἰς τοῦτο τὸ μέρος διατέθειται λόγους.

Κατὰ τῆς Τιμαίου τί ποτε δεῖ λέγειν ὄνομα καὶ
ῥῆμα; πάντα γὰρ ἐπιδέχεσθαί μοι δοκεῖ τὰ πικρότατα

6   τὸ γένος, οἷς ἐκεῖνος κέχρηται κατὰ τῶν πλησίον. ὅτι
μὲν οὖν ἐστι φιλαπεχθὴς καὶ ψεύστης καὶ τολμηρός,
σχεδὸν ἱκανῶς ἐκ τῶν προειρημένων ὑπεδείχθη· διότι
δ' ἀφιλόσοφός ἐστι καὶ συλλήβδην ἀνάγωγος συγ-
γραφεύς, ἐκ τῶν λέγεσθαι μελλόντων ἔσται συμφα-

7   νές. ἐν γὰρ τῇ μιᾷ καὶ εἰκοστῇ βύβλῳ, καὶ ταύτης ἐπὶ

Agrigentum, and in it he shut up men and afterward lighting fire beneath it used to take such dreadful revenge on his subjects that as the brass grew red and the man inside perished roasted and scorched, when he screamed in the extremity of his agony, the sound when it reached the ears of those present resembled, owing to the way the thing was constructed, the lowing of a bull. This bull during the Carthaginian domination was taken from Agrigentum to Carthage, and though the door at the joint of its shoulder blades through which the victims were lowered into it, was still preserved,[78] and though no reason at all can be found why such a bull should have been made in Carthage, yet Timaeus attempts to demolish the common story and to give the lie to the statements of poets and authors, asserting that neither the bull that was in Carthage came from Agrigentum, nor had there ever been such a bull in Agrigentum, and entering into quite a long disquisition on this subject.

What terms are we to use in speaking of Timaeus? For to me it seems that all the most bitter phrases of the kind he applies to others are appropriate to himself. That he was quarrelsome, mendacious, and headstrong has been, I trust, sufficiently proved by what I have already said, but what I am about to add will make it evident that he was no philosopher and in general a man of no education. For in his twenty-first book,[79] near the end. he says, in the course

---

[78] F. Jacoby argued that P. must have seen it, after it was returned from Carthage by Scipio Aemilianus in 146, which would date this passage later. WC 2.382, changing his earlier view, agrees.   [79] An error for Book 26 or 27: F. Jacoby, *FGrH* 566, Commentary, vol. III B. 1, p. 545.

τελευτῇ, λέγει κατὰ τὴν τοῦ Τιμολέοντος παράκλησιν
ταῦτα, διότι τῆς γῆς τῆς ὑπὸ τῷ κόσμῳ κειμένης εἰς
τρία μέρη διῃρημένης, καὶ τῆς μὲν Ἀσίας, τῆς δὲ
8 Λιβύης, τῆς δ᾽ Εὐρώπης προσαγορευομένης. ταῦτα
γὰρ οὐχ οἷον Τίμαιον εἰρηκέναι τίς ἂν πιστεύσειεν,
9 ἀλλ᾽ οὐδὲ τὸν λεγόμενον Μαργίτην ἐκεῖνον. τίς γὰρ
οὕτως ἐστὶν ἀδαής, οὐ λέγω τῶν πρὸς ὑπομνήμασι
γεγονότων . . .

25a. Ὅτι περὶ Τιμαίου φησὶν ὁ Πολύβιος ὁ Μεγα-
λοπολίτης· Καθάπερ γὰρ ἐκ τῶν παροιμιῶν ἱκανὸν
εἶναί φασι σταλαγμὸν ἕνα τοῦ μεγίστου τεύχους εἰς
τὸ γνῶναι τὸ πᾶν ἔγχυμα, τὸν αὐτὸν τρόπον καὶ περὶ
2 τῶν ὑποκειμένων χρὴ διαλαμβάνειν· ἐπειδὰν γὰρ ἓν ἢ
δεύτερον εὑρεθῇ ψεῦδος ἐν τοῖς συγγράμμασι, καὶ
τοῦτο γεγονὸς ᾖ κατὰ προαίρεσιν, δῆλον ὡς οὐδὲν ἂν
ἔτι βέβαιον οὐδ᾽ ἀσφαλὲς γένοιτο τῶν ὑπὸ τοῦ τοι-
3 ούτου συγγραφέως λεγομένων. ἵνα δὲ καὶ τοὺς φιλοτιμότερον διακειμένους μεταπείσωμεν, ῥητέον ἂν εἴη
περὶ τῆς αἱρέσεως αὐτοῦ καὶ μᾶλλον τῆς κατὰ τὰς
δημηγορίας καὶ τὰς παρακλήσεις, ἔτι δὲ τοὺς πρε-
σβευτικοὺς λόγους, καὶ συλλήβδην πᾶν <τὸ> τοιοῦτο
γένος, ἃ σχεδὸν ὡς κεφάλαια τῶν πράξεών ἐστι καὶ
4 συνέχει τὴν ὅλην ἱστορίαν· διότι γὰρ ταῦτα παρ᾽
ἀλήθειαν ἐν τοῖς ὑπομνήμασι κατατέταχε Τίμαιος,
καὶ τοῦτο πεποίηκε κατὰ πρόθεσιν, τίς οὐ παρακο-
5 λουθεῖ τῶν ἀνεγνωκότων; οὐ γὰρ τὰ ῥηθέντα γέγρα-
φεν, οὐδ᾽ ὡς ἐρρήθη κατ᾽ ἀλήθειαν, ἀλλὰ προθέμενος
ὡς δεῖ ῥηθῆναι, πάντας ἐξαριθμεῖται τοὺς ῥηθέντας

410

of Timoleon's address to his troops, "The earth lying under the universe being divided into three parts named Asia, Africa, and Europe." No one would credit that, I will not say Timaeus but, even the celebrated Margites[80] had said such a thing. For who is such an ignoramus, I do not speak of those who undertake to write history but . . .

25a. As the proverb tells us that a single drop from the largest vessel suffices to tell us the nature of the whole contents, so we should regard the subject now under discussion. When we find one or two false statements in a book and they prove to be deliberate ones, it is evident that not a word written by such an author is any longer certain and reliable. But to convince those also who are disposed to champion him I must speak of his principle, above all[81] in composing public speeches,[82] harangues to soldiers, the discourses of ambassadors, and, in a word, all utterances of the kind, which, as it were, sum up events and hold the whole history together. Can anyone who reads these help noticing that Timaeus has untruthfully reported them in his work, and has done so of set purpose? For he has not set down the words spoken nor the sense of what was really said, but having made up his mind as to what ought to have

80 See n. on 4a.5.

81 For keeping transmitted μᾶλλον instead of emending, see WC 2.385.

82 P. lists certain types and states that all such speeches in Timaeus are fictive products of Timaeus' imagination.

λόγους καὶ τὰ παρεπόμενα τοῖς πράγμασιν οὕτως ὡς
ἂν εἴ τις ἐν διατριβῇ πρὸς ὑπόθεσιν ἐπιχειροίη . . .
ὥσπερ ἀπόδειξιν τῆς ἑαυτοῦ δυνάμεως ποιούμενος,
ἀλλ᾽ οὐκ ἐξήγησιν τῶν κατ᾽ ἀλήθειαν εἰρημένων.

25b. Ὅτι τῆς ἱστορίας ἰδίωμα τοῦτ᾽ ἐστὶ τὸ πρῶτον
μὲν αὐτοὺς τοὺς κατ᾽ ἀλήθειαν εἰρημένους, οἷοί ποτ᾽
ἂν ὦσι, γνῶναι λόγους, δεύτερον τὴν αἰτίαν πυνθάνεσθαι, παρ᾽ ἣν ἢ διέπεσεν ἢ κατωρθώθη τὸ πρα-
2 χθὲν ἢ ῥηθέν· ἐπεὶ ψιλῶς λεγόμενον αὐτὸ τὸ γεγονὸς
ψυχαγωγεῖ μέν, ὠφελεῖ δ᾽ οὐδέν· προστεθείσης δὲ τῆς
3 αἰτίας ἔγκαρπος ἡ τῆς ἱστορίας γίνεται χρῆσις. ἐκ
γὰρ τῶν ὁμοίων ἐπὶ τοὺς οἰκείους μεταφερομένων
καιροὺς ἀφορμαὶ γίνονται καὶ προλήψεις εἰς τὸ προϊδέσθαι τὸ μέλλον, καὶ ποτὲ μὲν εὐλαβηθῆναι, ποτὲ δὲ
μιμούμενον τὰ προγεγονότα θαρραλεώτερον ἐγχειρεῖν
4 τοῖς ἐπιφερομένοις· ὁ δὲ καὶ τοὺς ῥηθέντας λόγους καὶ
τὴν αἰτίαν παρασιωπῶν, ψευδῆ δ᾽ ἀντὶ τούτων ἐπιχειρήματα καὶ διεξοδικοὺς λέγων λόγους, ἀναιρεῖ τὸ τῆς
ἱστορίας ἴδιον· ὃ μάλιστα ποιεῖ Τίμαιος· καὶ διότι
τούτου τοῦ γένους ἐστὶ πλήρη τὰ βυβλία παρ᾽ αὐτῷ,
πάντες γινώσκομεν.

25c. Ἴσως δ᾽ οὖν ἄν τις ἐναπορήσειε πῶς τοιοῦτος
ὢν οἷον ἡμεῖς ὑποδείκνυμεν τοιαύτης παρ᾽ ἐνίοις ἀπο-
2 δοχῆς τέτευχε καὶ πίστεως. τούτου δ᾽ ἐστὶν αἴτιον
διότι πλεοναζούσης αὐτῷ κατὰ τὴν πραγματείαν τῆς
κατὰ τῶν ἄλλων ἐπιτιμήσεως καὶ λοιδορίας οὐκ ἐκ
τῆς αὑτοῦ θεωρεῖται πραγματείας οὐδ᾽ ἐκ τῶν ἰδίων

412

been said, he recounts all these speeches and all else that follows upon events like a man in a school of rhetoric attempting to speak on a given subject, and shows off his oratorical power, but gives no report of what was actually spoken.

25b. The peculiar function of history is to discover, in the first place, the words actually spoken, whatever they were, and next to ascertain the reason why what was done or spoken led to failure or success. For the mere statement of a fact may interest us but is of no benefit to us: but when we add the cause of it, study of history becomes fruitful. For it is the mental transference of similar circumstances to our own times that gives us the means of forming presentiments of what is about to happen, and enables us[83] at certain times to take precautions and at others by reproducing former conditions to face with more confidence the difficulties that menace us. But a writer who passes over in silence the speeches made and the causes of events and in their place introduces false rhetorical exercises and discursive speeches, destroys the peculiar virtue of history. And of this Timaeus especially is guilty, and we all know that his work is full of blemishes of the kind.

25c. Perhaps, therefore, some might wonder how, being such as I have proved him to be, he meets with such acceptance and credit from certain people. The reason of this is that, as throughout his whole work he is so lavish of faultfinding and abuse, they do not form their estimate of him from his own treatment of history and his own state-

[83] P. insists that the study of history can be helpful to the statesman in guiding him to avoid, or to imitate, actions of the past.

ἀποφάσεων, ἀλλ᾽ ἐκ τῆς τῶν πέλας κατηγορίας, πρὸς
ὃ γένος καὶ πολυπραγμοσύνην δοκεῖ μοι καὶ φύσιν
3 προσενέγκασθαι διαφέρουσαν· παραπλήσιον γὰρ δή
τι τοιοῦτο συμβέβηκε καὶ Στράτωνι τῷ φυσικῷ· καὶ
γὰρ ἐκεῖνος ὅταν ἐγχειρήσῃ τὰς τῶν ἄλλων δόξας
διαστέλλεσθαι καὶ ψευδοποιεῖν, θαυμάσιός ἐστιν·
ὅταν δ᾽ ἐξ αὑτοῦ τι προφέρηται καί ⟨τι⟩ τῶν ἰδίων
ἐπινοημάτων ἐξηγῆται, παρὰ πολὺ φαίνεται τοῖς ἐπι-
4 στήμοσιν εὐηθέστερος αὑτοῦ καὶ νωθρότερος. καί μοι
δοκεῖ παντάπασιν ὅμοιόν τι γίνεσθαι περὶ τοὺς γρά-
5 φοντας τῷ περὶ τὸν ὅλον ἡμῶν βίον συμβαίνοντι· καὶ
γὰρ ἐν τούτῳ τὸ μὲν ἐπιτιμῆσαι τοῖς πέλας ἐστὶ
ῥᾴδιον, τὸ δ᾽ αὑτὸν ἀναμάρτητον παρέχεσθαι χαλε-
πόν, καὶ σχεδὸν ὡς ἔπος εἰπεῖν ἴδοι τις ἂν τοὺς
προχειρότατα τοῖς πέλας ἐπιτιμῶντας πλεῖστα περὶ
τὸν ἴδιον βίον ἁμαρτάνοντας.

25d. Τῷ δὲ Τιμαίῳ καὶ ἕτερόν τι χωρὶς τῶν προγε-
γραμμένων συμβέβηκεν· ἀποκαθίσας γὰρ Ἀθήνησι
σχεδὸν ἔτη πεντήκοντα καὶ πρὸς τοῖς τῶν προγεγονότων ὑπομνήμασι γενόμενος ὑπέλαβε τὰς μεγίστας
ἀφορμὰς ἔχειν πρὸς τὴν ἱστορίαν, ἀγνοῶν, ὥς γ᾽ ἐμοὶ
2 δοκεῖ. ἐχούσης γάρ τι παραπλήσιον τῆς ἱστορίας καὶ
τῆς ἰατρικῆς διὰ τὸ κατὰ τὰς ὁλοσχερεῖς διαφορὰς
ἑκατέραν αὐτῶν ὑπάρχειν τριμερῆ, παραπλησίους εἶναι συμβαίνει καὶ τὰς τῶν ἐπιβαλλομένων ἐπ᾽ αὐτὰς
3 διαθέσεις· οἷον εὐθέως τῆς ἰατρικῆς, ἑνὸς μὲν μέρους
αὐτῆς ὑπάρχοντος λογικοῦ, τοῦ δ᾽ ἑξῆς διαιτητικοῦ,
τοῦ δὲ τρίτου χειρουργικοῦ καὶ φαρμακευτικοῦ, γέ-

ments, but from the accusations he brings against others, for which kind of thing he seems to me to have possessed remarkable industry and a peculiar talent. It was much the same with Strato,[84] the writer on physical science. He also, when he undertakes to set forth and refute the views of others, is admirable, but when he produces anything original and explains his own notions, he seems to men of science much more simpleminded and dull than they took him to be. I think that the same is the case with literature as with our life in general; for here too it is very easy to find fault with others, but it is difficult to behave faultlessly oneself, and one notices as a rule that those who are readiest to blame others err most in the conduct of their own life.

25d. Besides the above-mentioned faults another thing remains to be noticed about Timaeus. Having lived for nearly fifty years in Athens with access to the works of previous writers, he considered himself peculiarly qualified to write history, making herein, I think, a great mistake. For as medicine and history[85] have this point of resemblance, that each of them may be roughly said to consist of three parts, so there is the same difference in the dispositions of those who enter on these callings. To begin with, as there are three parts of medicine, first the theory of disease, next dietetics, and thirdly surgery and pharmaceu-

[84] Of Lampsacus, head of the Peripatetic School after Theophrastus; he died about 270. D. L. 5.58–64. *OCD* Straton 1448–1449 (D. J. Furley).

[85] For the passage d.2–d.6, see, above all, H. von Staden, *Herophilus. The Art of Medicine in Early Alexandria* (Cambridge 1989), 127–129, T 56 (text and translation).

415

νους . . . ὁλοσχερῶς. ε.....μαι τῶι καταψεύδεσθαι τοῦ
4 ἐπιτηδεύματος . . . τὸ δὲ λογικόν, ὃ δὴ πλεῖστον ἀπὸ
τῆς Ἀλεξανδρείας ἄρχεται παρὰ τῶν Ἡροφιλείων καὶ
Καλλιμαχείων ἐκεῖ προσαγορευομένων, τοῦτο μέρος
μέν τι κατέχει τῆς ἰατρικῆς, κατὰ δὲ τὴν ἐπίφασιν καὶ
τὴν ἐπαγγελίαν τοιαύτην ἐφέλκεται φαντασίαν ὥστε
5 δοκεῖν μηδένα τῶν ἄλλων κρατεῖν τοῦ πράγματος· οὓς
ὅταν ἐπὶ τὴν ἀλήθειαν ἀπαγαγὼν ἄρρωστον ἐγχει-
ρίσῃς, τοσοῦτον ἀπέχοντες εὑρίσκονται τῆς χρείας
ὅσον [καὶ] οἱ μηδὲν ἀνεγνωκότες ἁπλῶς ἰατρικὸν ὑπό-
μνημα· οἷς ἤδη τινὲς τῶν ἀρρώστων ἐπιτρέψαντες
αὐτὸς διὰ τὴν ἐν λόγῳ δύναμιν οὐδὲν ἔχοντες δεινὸν
6 τοῖς ὅλοις πολλάκις ἐκινδύνευσαν. εἰσὶ γὰρ ἀληθῶς
ὅμοιοι τοῖς ἐκ βυβλίου κυβερνῶσιν· ἀλλ᾽ ὅμως οὗτοι
μετὰ φαντασίας ἐπιπορευόμενοι τὰς πόλεις, ἐπειδὰν
ἀθροίσωσι τοὺς ὄχλους ⟨μόνον οὐ καλοῦντες⟩ ἐπ᾽
ὀνόματος, τοὺς ἐπ᾽ αὐτῶν τῶν ἔργων ἀληθινὴν πεῖραν
δεδωκότας αὐτῶν εἰς τὴν ἐσχάτην ἄγουσιν ἀπορίαν
καὶ καταφρόνησιν παρὰ τοῖς ἀκούουσι, τῆς τοῦ λόγου
πιθανότητος καταγωνιζομένης πολλάκις τὴν ἐπ᾽ αὐ-
7 τῶν τῶν ἔργων δοκιμασίαν. τὸ δὲ τρίτον, τὸ τὴν
ἀληθινὴν προσφερόμενον ἕξιν ἐν ἑκάστοις τῶν ἐπιτηδευμάτων, οὐ μόνον ὑπάρχει σπάνιον, ἀλλὰ καὶ πολλάκις ὑπὸ τῆς στωμυλίας καὶ τόλμης ἐπισκοτεῖται διὰ
τὴν τῶν πολλῶν ἀκρισίαν.

---

86 The Greek text in the following section is badly damaged.

tics[86], the study of the theory of disease, which is derived chiefly from the schools of Herophilus[87] and Callimachus[88] at Alexandria, is indeed an integral part of medicine, but as regards the ostentation and pretensions of its professors they give themselves such an air of superiority that one would think no one else was master of the subject. Yet when you make them confront reality by entrusting a patient to them you find them just as incapable of being of any service as those who have never read a single medical treatise. Not a few invalids indeed who had nothing serious the matter with them have before now come very near losing their lives by entrusting themselves to these physicians, impressed by their rhetorical powers. For really they are just like pilots who steer by the book. But nevertheless these men visit different towns with great parade, and when they have collected a crowd, they reduce those who in actual practice have given clear proof of themselves to confusion, virtually singling them out by name, the persuasiveness of their eloquence often prevailing against the testimony of practical experience. The third branch,[89] which is concerned with producing general skill in each professional treatment, is not only rare but is often cast into the shade by gabble and audacity owing to people's general lack of judgment.

[87] Of Chalcedon, ca. 330–260. At Alexandria he performed dissection on cadavers and even vivisectional experiments on convicted criminals. *OCD* Herophilus 699 (H. v. Staden) and von Staden's book on Herophilus (25d.2).

[88] Member of Herophilus' School. *OCD* Callimachus 277–278 (H. von Staden).

[89] Surgery and pharmaceutics (d3).

25e. τὸν αὐτὸν δὴ τρόπον καὶ τῆς πραγματικῆς
ἱστορίας ὑπαρχούσης τριμεροῦς, τῶν δὲ μερῶν αὐτῆς
ἑνὸς μὲν ὄντος τοῦ περὶ τὴν ἐν τοῖς ὑπομνήμασι
πολυπραγμοσύνην καὶ τὴν παράθεσιν τῆς ἐκ τούτων
ὕλης, ἑτέρου δὲ τοῦ περὶ τὴν θέαν τῶν πόλεων καὶ τῶν
τόπων περί τε ποταμῶν καὶ λιμένων καὶ καθόλου τῶν
κατὰ γῆν καὶ κατὰ θάλατταν ἰδιωμάτων καὶ διαστημάτων, τρίτου δὲ τοῦ περὶ τὰς πράξεις τὰς πολιτικάς,
2 παραπλησίως ἐφίενται μὲν ταύτης πολλοὶ διὰ τὴν
προγεγενημένην περὶ αὐτῆς δόξαν, προσφέρονται δὲ
πρὸς τὴν ἐπιβολὴν οἱ μὲν πλεῖστοι τῶν γραφόντων
ἁπλῶς δίκαιον οὐδὲν πλὴν εὐχέρειαν καὶ τόλμαν
3 καὶ ῥᾳδιουργίαν, παραπλήσιον τοῖς φαρμακοπώλαις
δοξοκοποῦντες καὶ πρὸς χάριν λέγοντες ἀεὶ τὰ πρὸς
τοὺς καιροὺς ἕνεκα τοῦ πορίζειν τὸν βίον διὰ τούτων·
4 περὶ ὧν οὐκ ἄξιον πλείω ποιεῖσθαι λόγον. ἔνιοι δὲ τῶν
δοκούντων εὐλόγως προσάγειν πρὸς τὴν ἱστορίαν,
καθάπερ οἱ λογικοὶ τῶν ἰατρῶν ἐνδιατρίψαντες ταῖς
βυβλιοθήκαις καὶ καθόλου τὴν ἐκ τῶν ὑπομνημάτων
περιποιησάμενοι πολυπειρίαν πείθουσιν αὑτοὺς ὡς
ὄντες ἱκανοὶ πρὸς τὴν ἐπιβολήν, καὶ τοῖς ἐκτὸς ἀρ-
κούντως δοκοῦσι προσφέρεσθαι, . . . μέρος, ὡς ἐμοὶ
5 δοκεῖ, πρὸς τὴν ⟨πραγματικὴν⟩ ἱστορίαν· τὸ γὰρ
ἐποπτεῦσαι τὰ πρότε⟨ρον ὑπομνήματα⟩ πρὸς ⟨μὲν τὸ
γνῶναι⟩ τὰς τῶν ἀρχαίων διαλήψεις καὶ τὰς ἐννοίας
⟨ἃς πρὶν⟩ εἶχον ὑπὲρ ἐνίων, τόπων, ἐθνῶν, πολιτειῶν,
πράξεων, ⟨ἔτι δὲ⟩ πρὸς τὸ ⟨συνεῖναι⟩ τὰς ἑκάστων
περιστάσεις καὶ τύχας, αἷς κέχρηνται κατὰ τοὺς ἀνω-

25e. In the same fashion political history too consists of three parts, the first being the industrious study of memoirs and a comparison of their contents, the second the survey of cities, places, rivers, harbors, and in general all the peculiar features of land and sea and the distances of one place from another, and the third being political activity; and just as in the case of medicine, to which likewise many aspire owing to the high opinion in which it has been held, but most of them bring to the task absolutely no proper qualification except recklessness, audacity, and roguery, courting popularity like apothecaries, and always saying whatever they regard as opportune in order to curry favor for the sake of getting a living by this means. Concerning these it is not worthwhile to speak at length. Some of those again who appear to be justified in undertaking the composition of history, just like the theoretical doctors, after spending a long time in libraries and becoming deeply learned in memoirs, persuade themselves that they are adequately qualified for the task, seeming indeed to outsiders to contribute sufficient for the requirements of systematic history,[90] but, in my own opinion, contributing only a part. For it is true that looking through old memoirs is of service for knowledge of the views of the ancients and the notions people formerly had about some places,[91] nations, states, and events, and also for understanding the circumstances and chances which beset each nation in former

---

[90] There is a lacuna in the Greek after προσφέρεσθαι; the translation gives the sense of the missing words.

[91] The reading ἐνίων of the mss. is guaranteed by 5.8.2.

6 τέρω χρόνους, εὔχρηστόν ἐστι· συνεφίστησι γὰρ τὰ
προγεγονότα πρὸς τὸ μέλλον ἡμᾶς οἰκείως, ἐάν τις
7 ὑπὲρ ἑκάστων ἀληθινῶς ἱστορῇ τὰ παρεληλυθότα· τό
γε μὴν ἀπ' αὐτῆς ταύτης ⟨τῆς⟩ δυνάμεως ὁρμηθέντα
πεπεῖσθαι γράφειν τὰς ἐπιγινομένας πράξεις καλῶς,
ὃ πέπεισται Τίμαιος, τελέως εὔηθες καὶ παραπλήσιον
ὡς ἂν εἴ τις τὰ τῶν ἀρχαίων ζωγράφων ἔργα θεασάμενος ἱκανὸς οἴοιτο ζωγράφος εἶναι καὶ προστάτης
τῆς τέχνης.

25f. Δῆλον ⟨δ'⟩ ἔσται τὸ λεγόμενον ἔτι μᾶλλον ἐκ
τῶν ἐπιφερομένων, οἷον εὐθέως ἐκ τῶν συμβεβηκότων
Ἐφόρῳ κατὰ τόπους τινὰς τῆς ἱστορίας. ἐκεῖνος γὰρ
ἐν τοῖς πολεμικοῖς τῶν μὲν κατὰ θάλατταν ἔργων ἐπὶ
ποσὸν ὑπόνοιαν ἐσχηκέναι μοι δοκεῖ, τῶν δὲ κατὰ γῆν
2 ἀγώνων ἄπειρος εἶναι τελέως. τοιγαροῦν ὅταν μὲν
πρὸς τὰς περὶ Κύπρον ναυμαχίας καὶ τὰς περὶ Κνίδον
ἀτενίσῃ τις, αἷς ἐχρήσανθ' οἱ βασιλέως στρατηγοὶ
πρὸς Εὐαγόραν τὸν Σαλαμίνιον καὶ πάλιν πρὸς Λακεδαιμονίους θαυμάζειν τὸν συγγραφέα καὶ κατὰ τὴν
δύναμιν καὶ κατὰ τὴν ἐμπειρίαν ⟨εἰκὸς⟩ καὶ πολλὰ
τῶν χρησίμων ἀπενέγκασθαι πρὸς τὰς ὁμοίας περι-
3 στάσεις· ὅταν δὲ τὴν περὶ Λεῦκτρα μάχην ἐξηγῆται
Θηβαίων καὶ Λακεδαιμονίων ἢ τὴν ἐν Μαντινείᾳ
πάλιν τῶν αὐτῶν τούτων, ἐν ᾗ καὶ μετήλλαξε τὸν βίον
Ἐπαμινώνδας, ἐν τούτοις ἐὰν ἐπὶ τὰ κατὰ μέρος ἐπιστήσας τις θεωρῇ τὰς ἐκτάξεις καὶ μετατάξεις τὰς
κατ' αὐτοὺς τοὺς κινδύνους, γελοῖος φαίνεται καὶ παν-

times. For past events make us pay particular attention to the future, that is to say if we really make thorough inquiry in each case into the past. But to believe, as Timaeus did, that relying upon the mastery of material alone one can write well the history of subsequent events is absolutely foolish, and is much as if a man who had seen the works of ancient painters fancied himself to be a capable painter and a master of that art.

25f. What I say will be made plainer by the instances I am about to adduce, as, for example, in the first place, from what happened to Ephorus in certain parts of his history. Ephorus seems to me in dealing with war to have a certain notion of naval warfare, but he is entirely in the dark about battles on land. When, therefore, we study attentively his accounts of the naval battles near Cyprus[92] and Cnidus[93] in which the Persian king's commanders were engaged with Euagoras of Salamis, and on the second occasion with the Lacedaemonians, we are compelled to admire this writer for his descriptive power and knowledge of tactics, and we carry away much information useful for similar circumstances. But when he describes the battle of Leuctra[94] between the Thebans and Lacedaemonians, or that at Mantinea[95] between the same peoples, the battle in which Epaminondas lost his life, if we pay attention to every detail and look at the formation and reformation of the armies during the actual battle, he provokes our laughter

[92] The war between Euagoras of Salamis and the Persians from 391 to 381.   [93] The victory of the Athenian Conon over the Spartan fleet under Peisander in 394.

[94] The victory of Epaminondas over King Cleombrotus of Sparta in 371.   [95] Epaminondas' victory in 362.

4 τελῶς ἄπειρος καὶ ἀόρατος τῶν τοιούτων ὤν. ὁ μὲν οὖν
ἐν τοῖς Λεύκτροις κίνδυνος ἁπλοῦς γεγονὼς καὶ καθ᾽
ἕν τι μέρος τῆς δυνάμεως οὐ λίαν ἐκφανῆ ποιεῖ τὴν
τοῦ συγγραφέως ἀπειρίαν· ὁ δὲ περὶ τὴν Μαντίνειαν
τὴν μὲν ἔμφασιν ἔχει ποικίλην καὶ στρατηγικήν, ἔστι
δ᾽ ἀνυπόστατος καὶ τελέως ἀδιανόητος τῷ συγγραφεῖ.
5 τοῦτο δ᾽ ἔσται δῆλον, ἐάν τις τοὺς τόπους ὑποθέμενος
ἀληθινῶς ἐπιμετρῇ τὰς κινήσεις τὰς ὑπ᾽ αὐτοῦ δηλου-
6 μένας. τὸ δ᾽ αὐτὸ συμβαίνει καὶ Θεοπόμπῳ καὶ μάλι-
7 στα Τιμαίῳ, περὶ οὗ νῦν ὁ λόγος· οὗ μὲν γὰρ ἂν ὑπὲρ
τῶν τοιούτων κεφαλαιώδη ποιήσωνται τὴν ὑπόθεσιν,
διαλανθάνουσιν, οὗ δ᾽ ἂν βουληθῶσι διαθέσθαι καὶ
συνυποδεῖξαί τι τῶν κατὰ μέρος, τοιοῦτοι φαίνονται
καὶ πάντως οἷος Ἔφορος.

25g. Ὅτι οὔτε περὶ τῶν κατὰ πόλεμον συμβαινόντων δυνατόν ἐστι γράψαι καλῶς τὸν μηδεμίαν
ἐμπειρίαν ἔχοντα τῶν πολεμικῶν ἔργων οὔτε περὶ τῶν
ἐν ταῖς πολιτείαις τὸν μὴ πεπειραμένον τῶν τοιούτων
2 πράξεων καὶ περιστάσεων. λοιπὸν οὔτ᾽ ἐμπείρως ὑπὸ
τῶν βυβλιακῶν οὔτ᾽ ἐμφαντικῶς οὐδενὸς γραφομένου
συμβαίνει τὴν πραγματείαν ἄπρακτον γίνεσθαι τοῖς
ἐντυγχάνουσιν· εἰ γὰρ ἐκ τῆς ἱστορίας ἐξέλοι τις τὸ
δυνάμενον ὠφελεῖν ἡμᾶς, τὸ λοιπὸν αὐτῆς ἄζηλον καὶ
3 ἀνωφελὲς γίνεται παντελῶς. ἔτι δὲ περὶ τῶν πόλεων
καὶ τόπων ὅταν ἐπιβάλωνται γράφειν τὰ κατὰ μέρος,
ὄντες ἀτριβεῖς τῆς τοιαύτης ἐμπειρίας, δῆλον ὡς
ἀνάγκη συμβαίνειν τὸ παραπλήσιον, καὶ πολλὰ μὲν
ἀξιόλογα παραλείπειν, περὶ πολλῶν δὲ ποιεῖσθαι

and seems perfectly inexperienced in such things and never to have seen a battle. It is true that the battle of Leuctra, a simple affair in which only one part of the army was engaged, does not make the writer's ignorance very conspicuous, but while the battle of Mantinea has the appearance of being described with much detail and military science, the description is quite imaginary, and the battle was not in the least understood by the writer. This becomes evident if we get a correct idea of the ground and then number the movements he describes as being carried out on it. The same is the case with Theopompus, and more especially with Timaeus of whom we are now speaking. For where they give a summary account of such matters, their errors escape notice, but when they wish to describe and point out the nature of any detailed movement they are both seen to be exactly like Ephorus.

25g. It is neither possible for a man with no experience of warlike operations to write well about what happens in war, nor for one unversed in the practice and circumstances of politics to write well on that subject.[96] So that as nothing written by mere students of books is written with experience or vividness, their works are of no practical utility to readers. For if we take from history all that can benefit us, what is left is quite contemptible and useless. Again, when they attempt to write about cities and places in some detail without having any experience of such work, clearly the result must be very similar, many things worthy of mention being omitted and many things not worth speaking of being treated at great length. This is

[96] P., on the other hand, has experience both in war and in politics.

4 πολὺν λόγον οὐκ ἀξίων ὄντων· ὃ δὴ συμβαίνει μάλιστα Τιμαίῳ διὰ τὴν ἀορασίαν.

25h. Ὅτι Τίμαιός φησιν ἐν τῇ τριακοστῇ καὶ
τετάρτῃ βύβλῳ "πεντήκοντα συνεχῶς ἔτη διατρίψας
Ἀθήνησι ξενιτεύων" καὶ πάσης ὁμολογουμένως ἄπειρος ἐγένετο πολεμικῆς χρείας, ἔτι δὲ καὶ τῆς τῶν
2 τόπων θέας. λοιπὸν ὅταν εἴς τι τῶν μερῶν τούτων
ἐμπέσῃ κατὰ τὴν ἱστορίαν, πολλὰ μὲν ἀγνοεῖ καὶ
ψεύδεται· κἄν ποτε δὲ τῆς ἀληθείας ἐπιψαύσῃ, παρα-
πλήσιός ἐστι τοῖς ζωγράφοις τοῖς ἀπὸ τῶν <ἀνα-
σεσ>αγμένων θυλάκων ποιουμένοις τὰς ὑπογραφάς·
3 καὶ γὰρ ἐπ’ ἐκείνων ἡ μὲν ἐκτὸς ἐνίοτε γραμμὴ σῴζεται, τὸ δὲ τῆς ἐμφάσεως καὶ τῆς ἐνεργείας τῶν ἀλη-
θινῶν ζῴων ἄπεστιν, ὅπερ ἴδιον ὑπάρχει τῆς ζωγρα-
φικῆς τέχνης. τὸ δ’ αὐτὸ συμβαίνει καὶ περὶ Τίμαιον
καὶ καθόλου τοὺς ἀπὸ ταύτης τῆς βυβλιακῆς ἕξεως
4 ὁρμωμένους· ἡ γὰρ ἔμφασις τῶν πραγμάτων αὐτοῖς
ἄπεστι διὰ τὸ μόνον ἐκ τῆς αὐτοπαθείας τοῦτο γίνεσθαι τῆς τῶν συγγραφέων· ὅθεν οὐκ ἐντίκτουσιν ἀλη-
θινοὺς ζήλους τοῖς ἀκούουσιν οἱ μὴ δι’ αὐτῶν πεπο-
5 ρευμένοι τῶν πραγμάτων. ᾗ καὶ τοιαύτας ᾤοντο δεῖν
ἐν τοῖς ὑπομνήμασιν ὑπάρχειν ἐμφάσεις οἱ πρὸ ἡμῶν
ὥσθ’, ὅτε μὲν ὑπὲρ πολιτικῶν ὁ λόγος εἴη πραγμάτων,
ἐπιφθέγγεσθαι διότι κατ’ ἀνάγκην ὁ γράφων πεπολί-
τευται καὶ πεῖραν ἔσχηκε τῶν ἐν τούτῳ τῷ μέρει
συμβαινόντων, ὅτε δὲ περὶ πολεμικῶν, ὅτι πάλιν
ἐστράτευκε καὶ κεκινδύνευκε, καὶ μὴν ὅτε περὶ βιωτικῶν, ὅτι τέτραφε τέκνα καὶ μετὰ γυναικὸς ἔζηκε. τὸ

often the case with Timaeus owing to the fact that he does not write from the evidence of his eyes.

25h. In his thirty-fourth book Timaeus says,[97] "Living away from home at Athens for fifty years continuously," and admittedly having no experience of active service in war or any personal acquaintance with places. So that, when he meets with such matters in his history, he is guilty of many errors and misstatements, and if he ever comes near the truth he resembles those painters who make their sketches from stuffed bags.[98] For in their case the outlines are sometimes preserved but we miss that vividness and animation of the real figures which the graphic art is especially capable of rendering. The same is the case with Timaeus and in general with all who approach the work in this bookish mood. We miss in them the vividness of facts, as this impression can only be produced by the personal experience of the author. Those, therefore, who have not had experience of public life do not succeed in arousing the interest of their readers. Hence our predecessors considered that historical memoirs should possess such vividness as to make one exclaim when the author deals with political affairs that he necessarily had taken part in politics and had experience of what is wont to happen in the political world, when he deals with war that he had been in the field and risked his life, and when he deals with private life that he had reared children and lived with a wife,[99] and

---

[97] The quotation probably ended with ξενιτεύων (see *FGrH* 566 F 34).

[98] Stuffed dummies for the artist's preliminary work (WC 2.396).

[99] This is as good as a statement that P. was married himself.

δὲ παραπλήσιον καὶ ⟨περὶ⟩ τῶν ἄλλων τοῦ βίου
6 μερῶν· ὃ παρὰ μόνοις εἰκὸς εὑρίσκεσθαι τῶν συγγραφέων τοῖς δι᾽ αὑτῶν πεπορευμένοις τῶν πραγμάτων
καὶ τοῦτο τὸ μέρος περιπεποιημένοις τῆς ἱστορίας.
πάντων μὲν οὖν οἷον αὐτουργὸν γενέσθαι καὶ δρά-
στην δυσχερὲς ἴσως, τῶν μέντοι μεγίστων καὶ κοινο-
τάτων ἀναγκαῖον.

25i. ὅτι δὲ τὸ λεγόμενον οὐκ ἀδύνατον, ἱκανὸν
ὑπόδειγμα πρὸς πίστιν ὁ ποιητής, παρ᾽ ᾧ πολὺ τὸ τῆς
2 τοιαύτης ἐμφάσεως ἴδοι τις ἂν ὑπάρχον. ἐξ ὧν πᾶς ἂν
εἰκότως συγκατάθοιτο τρίτον εἶναι μέρος τῆς ἱστορίας καὶ τρίτην ἔχειν τάξιν τὴν ἐκ τῶν ὑπομνημάτων
3 πολυπραγμοσύνην. ὡς δ᾽ ἀληθές ἐστι τὸ νυνὶ λεγόμενον καὶ ἐκφανέστατον γένοιτ᾽ ἂν ἐπί τε τῶν συμ-
βουλευτικῶν καὶ παρακλητικῶν, ἔτι δὲ πρεσβευτικῶν
4 λόγων, οἷς κέχρηται Τίμαιος. ὀλίγοι μὲν γὰρ καιροὶ
πάντας ἐπιδέχονται διαθέσθαι τοὺς ἐνόντας λόγους,
οἱ δὲ πλεῖστοι βραχεῖς [καὶ] τινας τῶν ὑπόντων, καὶ
τούτων τινὰς μὲν οἱ νῦν, ἄλλους δ᾽ οἱ προγεγονότες,
καὶ τινὰς μὲν Αἰτωλοὶ προσίενται, τινὰς δὲ Πελο-
5 ποννήσιοι, τινὰς δ᾽ Ἀθηναῖοι. καὶ τὸ μὲν ματαίως καὶ
ἀκαίρως [καὶ] πρὸς πάντα πάντας διεξιέναι τοὺς ἐνόντας λόγους, ὃ ποιεῖ Τίμαιος πρὸς πᾶσαν ὑπόθεσιν
εὑρεσιλογῶν, τελέως ἀνάληθες καὶ μειρακιῶδες καὶ
διατριβικόν—ἅμα καὶ πολλοῖς ἀποτυχίας αἴτιον ἤδη
τοῦτο γέγονε καὶ καταφρονήσεως—τὸ δὲ τοὺς ἁρμό-
ζοντας καὶ καιρίους ἀεὶ λαμβάνειν, τοῦτ᾽ ἀναγκαῖον.
6 ἀστάτου δὲ τῆς χρείας οὔσης καὶ πόσοις καὶ ποίοις

so regarding the other parts of life. This quality can naturally only be found in those who have been through affairs themselves and have acquired this sort of historical knowledge. It is difficult, perhaps, to have taken a personal part and been one of the performers in every kind of event, but it is necessary to have had experience of the most important and those of commonest occurrence.

25i. That what I say is not unattainable is sufficiently evidenced by Homer, in whose works we find much of this kind of vividness. From these considerations I suppose everyone would now agree that industry in the study of documents is only a third part of history and only stands in the third place. How true what I have just said is will be most clear from the speeches, political, exhortatory, and ambassadorial, introduced by Timaeus. There are few occasions which admit of setting forth all possible arguments, most admitting only of those few brief arguments which occur to one, and even of these there are certain which are appropriate to contemporaries, others to men of former times, others again to Aetolians, others to Peloponnesians and others to Athenians. But, without point or occasion, to recite[100] all possible arguments for everything, as Timaeus, with his talent for invention, does on every subject, is perfectly untrue to facts, and a mere childish sport—to do it has even in many cases been the cause of actual failure and exposed many to contempt—the necessary thing being to choose on every occasion suitable and opportune arguments. But since there is no fixed rule as to which and how

[100] The sense must be something like "to expand a speech so as to include every possible argument . . . " (WC 2.398).

τῶν ἐνόντων χρηστέον, ἀλλοιοτέρου τινὸς δεῖ ζήλου
καὶ παραγγέλματος, εἰ μέλλομεν μὴ βλάπτειν, ἀλλ'
7 ὠφελεῖν τοὺς ἀναγινώσκοντας. ἔστι μὲν οὖν ὁ καιρὸς
ἐν πᾶσι δυσπαράγγελτος, οὐ μὴν ἀδύνατος εἰς ὑπόνοιαν ἀχθῆναι διὰ τῶν ἐκ τῆς αὐτοπαθείας καὶ τριβῆς
8 θεωρημάτων· ἐπὶ δὲ τοῦ παρόντος μάλιστ' ἂν ὑπονοη-
θείη τὸ λεγόμενον ἐκ τούτων. εἰ γὰρ οἱ συγγραφεῖς
ὑποδείξαντες τοὺς καιροὺς καὶ τὰς ὁρμὰς καὶ διαθέσεις τῶν βουλευομένων, κἄπειτα τοὺς κατ' ἀλήθειαν
ῥηθέντας λόγους ἐκθέντες διασαφήσαιεν ἡμῖν τὰς
αἰτίας, δι' ἃς ἢ κατευστοχῆσαι συνέβη τοὺς εἰπόντας
ἢ διαπεσεῖν, γένοιτ' ἄν τις ἔννοια τοῦ πράγματος
ἀληθινή, καὶ δυναίμεθ' ἂν ἅμα μὲν διακρίνοντες, ἅμα
δὲ μεταφέροντες ἐπὶ τὰ παραπλήσια κατευστοχεῖν ἀεὶ
9 τῶν προκειμένων. ἀλλ' ἔστιν, οἶμαι, τὸ μὲν αἰτιο-
λογεῖν δυσχερές, τὸ δὲ ῥησικοπεῖν <ἐν> τοῖς βυβλίοις
ῥάδιον καὶ τὸ μὲν ὀλίγα καιρίως εἰπεῖν καὶ τούτου
παραγγελίαν εὑρεῖν ὀλίγοις ἐφικτόν, τὸ δὲ πολλὰ
διαθέσθαι καὶ ματαίως τῶν ἐν μέσῳ κειμένων καὶ
κοινόν.

25k. Ἵνα δὲ καὶ περὶ ταῦτα βεβαιωσώμεθα τὴν
ἀπόφασιν τὴν ὑπὲρ Τιμαίου, καθάπερ καὶ τὴν ὑπὲρ
τῆς ἀγνοίας, ἔτι δὲ τῆς ἑκουσίου ψευδογραφίας, βραχέα προοισόμεθα τῶν ὁμολογουμένων αὐτοῦ λόγων
2 ἐπ' ὀνόματος.— ὅτι τῶν δεδυναστευκότων ἐν Σικελίᾳ

many of the possible arguments should be used on a particular occasion, there is need of an unusual degree of attention and clearly of principle if we mean to do good rather
than harm to our readers. Now it is difficult to convey by
precept what is opportune or not in all instances, but it is
not impossible to be led to a notion of it by reasoning from
our personal experience in the past. For the present the
best way of conveying my meaning is as follows. If writers,
after indicating to us the situation and the motives and inclinations of the people who are discussing it report in the
next place what was actually said and then make clear to us
the reasons why the speakers either succeeded or failed,
we shall arrive at some true notion of the actual facts, and
we shall be able, both by distinguishing what was successful from what was not and by transferring our impression
to similar circumstances, to treat any situation that faces us
with hope of success.[101] But, I fear,[102] it is difficult to assign causes, and very easy to invent phrases in books, and
while it is given only to a few to say a few words at the right
time and to discover the rules governing this, it is a common accomplishment and open to anyone to compose long
speeches to no purpose.

25k. In confirmation of my charge against Timaeus on
this count also, besides that of his mistakes and his deliberate falsification of the truth, I shall give some short ex-
tracts from speeches acknowledged to be his, giving names
and dates. Of those who were in power in Sicily after the

[101] For a similar statement see 25b.2–3.

[102] This introduces the conclusion of what has been called
"this confused and clumsy formulation of how the historian deals
with the problem of speeches" (WC 2.399).

μετὰ Γέλωνα τὸν ἀρχαῖον πραγματικωτάτους ἄνδρας
παρειλήφαμεν Ἑρμοκράτην, Τιμολέοντα, Πύρρον τὸν
Ἠπειρώτην, οἷς ἥκιστ᾽ ἂν δέοι περιάπτειν μειρακιώ-
3 δεις καὶ διατριβικοὺς λόγους. ὁ δέ φησιν ἐν τῇ μιᾷ καὶ
εἰκοστῇ βύβλῳ, καθ᾽ ὃν καιρὸν Εὐρυμέδων παραγενόμενος εἰς Σικελίαν παρεκάλει τὰς πόλεις εἰς τὸν κατὰ
τῶν Συρακοσίων πόλεμον, τότε τοὺς Γελῴους κάμνοντας τῷ πολέμῳ διαπέμψασθαι πρὸς τοὺς Καμαριναί-
4 ους ὑπὲρ ἀνοχῶν· τῶν δὲ προθύμως δεξαμένων, μετὰ
ταῦτα πρεσβεύειν ἑκατέρους πρὸς τοὺς ἑαυτῶν συμμάχους καὶ παρακαλεῖν ἄνδρας ἐκπέμψαι πιστούς,
οἵτινες εἰσελθόντες εἰς Γέλαν βουλεύσονται περὶ δια-
5 λύσεως καὶ τῶν κοινῇ συμφερόντων. παραγενομένων
δὲ τῶν συνέδρων, καὶ <τοῦ> διαβουλίου προτεθέντος
τοιούτοις τισὶ χρώμενον εἰσάγει λόγοις τὸν Ἑρμο-
6 κράτην. ἐπαινέσας γὰρ ὁ προειρημένος ἀνὴρ τοὺς
Γελῴους καὶ τοὺς Καμαριναίους, πρῶτον μὲν ὡς
αὐτῶν ποιησάντων τὰς ἀνοχάς, δεύτερον ὅτι τοῦ περὶ
διαλύσεως γενέσθαι λόγους αἴτιοι καθεστήκασι, τρίτον ὅτι προνοηθεῖεν τοῦ μὴ βουλεύεσθαι τὰ <πλήθη
περὶ τῶν δι>αλύσεων, ἀλλὰ <τοὺς προεστῶ>τας τῶν
πολιτῶν <τοὺς> σαφῶς εἰδότας τίνα διαφορὰν ὁ πόλε-
7 μος ἔχει τῆς εἰρήνης, μετὰ δὲ ταῦτα δύ᾽ ἢ τρία λαβὼν
ἐπιχειρήματα πραγματικά, λοιπόν <φησιν> αὐτοὺς

103 Of Gela, since 485 ruler of Syracuse and of large parts of
Sicily, in 480 victorious over the Carthaginians at Himera. He died
in 478.

elder Gelo,[103] we have always accepted as a fact that the most capable rulers were Hermocrates,[104] Timoleon,[105] and Pyrrhus of Epirus,[106] and these are the last to whom one should attribute childish and idle speeches. But Timaeus in his twenty-first book[107] says that at the time when Eurymedon came to Sicily and was urging the towns to pursue the war against Syracuse, the Geleans, who were suffering by the war, sent to Camarina begging for a truce. The people of Camarina gladly consented, and upon this both cities sent embassies to their allies begging them to dispatch trustworthy commissioners to Gela to discuss terms of peace and the general interests of all concerned. When, on the arrival of these commissioners, and the conference[108] had opened he represents Hermocrates as speaking[109] somewhat as follows. This statesman, after praising the people of Gela and Camarina first of all for having themselves made the truce, secondly for being the originators of the negotiations, and thirdly for seeing to it that the terms of peace were not discussed by the multitude but by the leading citizens who knew well the difference between war and peace, after this introduces one or two practical reflections and then says that they them-

[104] Of Syracuse, statesman active 424–407 and next to the Spartan Gylippus instrumental in the defense of Syracuse against the Athenians in 415–413.

[105] P.'s judgment here is very different from that in 23e.6.

[106] The illustrious king of Epirus. *RE* Pyrrhos 108–165 (D. Kienast).   [107] This seems to be a mistake for "twelfth book"; the date of the event is 424.   [108] This is the so-called peace conference, on which see Th. 4.59–64.

[109] P. does not mention Hermocrates' speech in Th. 4.59–64.

ἐπιστήσαντας μαθεῖν ἡλίκην ὁ πόλεμος διαφορὰν
ἔχει τῆς εἰρήνης, μικρῷ πρότερον εἰρηκὼς ὅτι κατ᾽
\<αὐτὸ τοῦτο\> χάριν ἔχει τοῖς Γελῴοις τὸ μὴ γίνεσθαι
τοὺς λόγους \<ἐν τοῖς πολλοῖς ἀλλ᾽\> ἐν συνεδρίῳ

8 καλῶς γινώσκοντι τὰς τοιαύτας περιπετείας. ἐξ ὧν ὁ
Τίμαιος οὐ μόνον τῆς πραγματικῆς ἂν δόξειεν ἀπολείπεσθαι δυνάμεως, ἀλλὰ καὶ τῶν ἐν ταῖς διατριβαῖς

9 ἐπι\<χειρήσεων οὐκ ὀλίγον\> ἐλαττοῦσθαι. πάντες γὰρ
δήπουθεν οἴονται δεῖν τὰς ἀποδείξεις φέρειν τῶν
ἀγνοουμένων καὶ τῶν ἀπιστουμένων παρὰ τοῖς ἀκρο-
αταῖς, περὶ δὲ τῶν ἤδη γινωσκομένων ματαιότατον
εἶναι πάντων καὶ παιδαριωδέστατον τὸ καθευρεσι-

10 λογεῖν . . . . μενον ἢ τὸ γινωσκόμενον. ὁ
δὲ χωρὶς τῆς ὅλης παραπτώσεως τοῦ \<διατε\>θεῖσθαι
τὸ πλεῖστον μέρος τοῦ λόγου πρὸς τὰ καθάπαξ μὴ
προσδεόμενα λόγου καὶ λήμμασι κέχρηται τοιούτοις,

11 οἷς τὸν μὲν Ἑρμοκράτην τίς ἂν κεχρῆσθαι πιστεύ-
σειε, τὸν συναγωνισάμενον μὲν Λακεδαιμονίοις τὴν ἐν
Αἰγὸς ποταμοῖς ναυμαχίαν, αὐτανδρὶ δὲ χειρωσάμε-
νον τὰς Ἀθηναίων δυνάμεις καὶ τοὺς στρατηγοὺς
κατὰ Σικελίαν, ἀλλ᾽ οὐδὲ μειράκιον τὸ τυχόν;

26. ὅς γε πρῶτον μὲν οἴεται δεῖν ἀναμνησθῆναι
τοὺς συνέδρους διότι τοὺς κοιμωμένους τὸν ὄρθρον ἐν
μὲν τῷ πολέμῳ διεγείρουσιν αἱ σάλπιγγες, κατὰ δὲ

2 τὴν εἰρήνην οἱ ὄρνιθες. μετὰ δὲ ταῦτα τὸν Ἡρακλέα
φησὶ τὸν μὲν Ὀλυμπίων ἀγῶνα θεῖναι καὶ τὴν ἐκε-
χειρίαν δεῖγμα ποιούμενον τῆς αὐτοῦ προαιρέσεως,
ὅσοις δ᾽ ἐπολέμησε, τούτους πάντας βεβλαφέναι κατὰ

selves must now give ear to him and learn how much war differs from peace, and this after having just said that he was thankful to the Geloans for this very thing that the discussion was not held by the multitude but in a council well acquainted with such changes. From this it appears that Timaeus was not only deficient in practical sense, but does not even attain the level of the themes we hear in schools of rhetoric. For there all, I suppose, think they ought to give their hearers proofs of things of which they are ignorant or which they disbelieve, but that to think up arguments in speaking of what our hearers already know is most foolish and childish. . . . Apart from his general mistake in devoting the greater part of the speech to a matter that does not require a single word, he employs such arguments as none could believe to have been used by, I will not say that Hermocrates who took part with the Lacedaemonians in the battle of Aegospotami[110] and captured the whole Athenian army with its generals in Sicily but, by any ordinary schoolboy.

26. In the first place he thinks it proper to remind the council that men are aroused in the morning in war time by the trumpet and in peace by the crowing of cocks. After this he tells them that Heracles founded the Olympian games[111] and truce as a proof of his real preference, and that he had injured all those he fought with under compul-

[110] An error of P., since Hermocrates was killed two years before.

[111] Some traditions put the foundation of the festival earlier than 776, among them one of Dorian origin crediting Heracles with it. *RE* Herakles (Suppl. 3), 916–917 (O. Gruppe).

τὴν ἀνάγκην καὶ κατ' ἐπιταγήν, ἑκουσίως δὲ παραί-
3 τιον οὐδενὶ γεγονέναι κακοῦ τῶν ἀνθρώπων. ἑξῆς δὲ
τούτοις παρὰ μὲν τῷ ποιητῇ τὸν Δία παρεισάγεσθαι
δυσαρεστούμενον τῷ Ἄρει καὶ λέγοντα

> ἔχθιστος δέ μοί ἐσσι θεῶν, οἳ Ὄλυμπον
> ἔχουσιν· αἰεὶ γάρ τοι ἔρις τε φίλη πόλεμοί τε
> μάχαι τε.[1]

4 ὁμοίως δὲ καὶ τὸν φρονιμώτατον τῶν ἡρώων λέγειν

> ἀφρήτωρ, ἀθέμιστος, ἀνέστιός ἐστιν ἐκεῖνος ὃς
> πολέμου ἔραται ἐπιδημίου ὀκρυόεντος.[2]

5 ὁμογνωμονεῖν δὲ τῷ ποιητῇ καὶ τὸν Εὐριπίδην, ἐν οἷς
φησιν,

> εἰρήνα βαθύπλουτε,
> καλλίστα μακάρων θεῶν,
> ζῆλός μοι σέθεν, ὡς χρονίζεις.
> δέδοικα δὲ μὴ πρὶν ὑπερβάλῃ με γῆρας,
> πρὶν σὰν χαρίεσσαν προσιδεῖν ὥραν
> καὶ καλλιχόρους ἀοιδὰς
> φιλοστεφάνους τε κώμους.[3]

6 ἔτι δὲ πρὸς τούτοις ὁμοιότατον εἶναί φησι τὸν μὲν
πόλεμον τῇ νόσῳ, τὴν δ' εἰρήνην τῇ ὑγιείᾳ· τὴν μὲν

sion and by order, but that he had done no evil to any man
of his own free will. Next he says that Homer represents
Zeus as displeased with Ares and saying

> Of all the gods who tread the spangled skies,
> Thou most unjust, most odious in our eyes!
> Inhuman discord is thy dire delight,
> The waste of slaughter, and the rage of fight;[112]

that similarly the wisest of his heroes says

> Cursed is the man, and void of law and right,
> Unworthy property, unworthy light,
> Unfit for public rule, or private care,
> That wretch, that monster, who delights in war;[113]

and that Euripides expresses the same opinion as Homer
in these verses:

> O Peace, loaded with riches, of the blest
> Gods thou art far the loveliest.
> So long thou tarriest, I am fain,
> And fear lest age o'ertake me ere
> I look upon thy features fair
> > Once again,
> See them dancing in a ring,
> > As they sing,
> See the wreaths upon their brows,
> As they troop from the carouse.[114]

In addition to this Hermocrates is made to say that war
very much resembles sickness and peace is very like

---

[112] Hom. *Il.* 5.890–891. The translations are Pope's.
[113] Hom. *Il.* 9.63–64.   [114] Eur. F 453 Kannicht.

γὰρ καὶ τοὺς κάμνοντας ἀναλαμβάνειν, ἐν ᾧ δὲ καὶ
7 τοὺς ὑγιαίνοντας ἀπόλλυσθαι. καὶ κατὰ μὲν τὴν εἰρήνην τοὺς πρεσβυτέρους ὑπὸ τῶν νέων θάπτεσθαι κατὰ
8 φύσιν, ἐν δὲ τῷ πολέμῳ τἀναντία, τὸ δὲ μέγιστον ἐν
μὲν τῷ πολέμῳ μηδ᾽ ἄχρι τῶν τειχῶν εἶναι τὴν ἀσφάλειαν, κατὰ δὲ τὴν εἰρήνην μέχρι τῶν τῆς χώρας ὅρων,
9 καὶ τούτοις ἕτερα παραπλήσια. θαυμάζω δὴ τίσι ποτ᾽
ἂν ἄλλοις ἐχρήσατο λόγοις ἢ προφοραῖς μειράκιον
ἄρτι γενόμενον περὶ διατριβὰς καὶ <τὰς> ἐκ τῶν ὑπομνημάτων πολυπραγμοσύνας καὶ βουλόμενον παραγ-
γελματικῶς ἐκ τῶν παρεπομένων τοῖς προσώποις ποιεῖσθαι τὴν ἐπιχείρησιν· δοκεῖ γὰρ <οὐχ ἑτ>έροις,
ἀλλὰ τούτοις οἷς Τίμαιος Ἑρμοκράτην κεχρῆσθαί
φησι.

26a. Τί δὲ πάλιν ὅταν ὁ Τιμολέων ἐν τῇ αὐτῇ
βύβλῳ παρακαλῶν τοὺς Ἕλληνας πρὸς τὸν ἐπὶ τοὺς
Καρχηδονίους κίνδυνον, καὶ μόνον οὐκ ἤδη μελλόντων συνάγειν εἰς τὰς χεῖρας τοῖς ἐχθροῖς πολλαπλα-
σίοις οὖσι, πρῶτον μὲν ἀξιοῖ μὴ βλέπειν αὐτοὺς πρὸς
τὸ πλῆθος τῶν ὑπεναντίων, ἀλλὰ πρὸς τὴν ἀνανδρίαν;
2 καὶ γὰρ τῆς Λιβύης ἁπάσης συνεχῶς οἰκουμένης καὶ
πληθυούσης ἀνθρώπων, ὅμως ἐν ταῖς παροιμίαις,
ὅταν περὶ ἐρημίας ἔμφασιν βουλώμεθα ποιῆσαι,
λέγειν ἡμᾶς "ἐρημότερα τῆς Λιβύης," οὐκ ἐπὶ τὴν
ἐρημίαν φέροντας τὸν λόγον, ἀλλ᾽ ἐπὶ τὴν ἀνανδρίαν
3 τῶν κατοικούντων. καθόλου δέ, φησί, τίς ἂν φοβηθείη
τοὺς ἄνδρας, οἵτινες τῆς φύσεως τοῦτο τοῖς ἀνθρώποις
δεδωκυίας ἴδιον παρὰ τὰ λοιπὰ τῶν ζῴων, λέγω δὲ τὰς

health, for peace restores even the sick and in war even the healthy perish. In peace again we are told that the old are buried by the young as is natural, while in war it is the reverse, and that above all in war there is no safety even up to the walls, but in peace there is safety as far as the boundaries of the land, and a number of similar things. I wonder what other words or expressions would be used by a boy lately come to the schools and the curious study of memoirs who wished to compose a declamatory essay made up of all that was consonant with the character of certain historical personages. The style of it would probably be no other than that of the speech Timaeus puts into the mouth of Hermocrates.

26a. And what shall we say again when Timoleon[115] in the same book exhorting the Greeks to do battle with the Carthaginians, almost at the moment that they are about to encounter an enemy largely outnumbering them, first bids them not to consider the numbers of their foes but their cowardice. For, he says, although the whole of Libya is thickly populated and full of men, yet when we wish to convey an impression of solitude we use the proverbial phrase "more desert than Libya,"[116] not referring to its solitude but to the cowardice of the inhabitants. "In general," he says, "how can we be afraid of men who having received from nature in distinction from other animals the gift of

115 For Timoleon's speech at this occasion, see D. S. 16.79.2.
116 See Hdt. 2.32.4 for desert parts of Libya.

χεῖρας, ταύτας παρ᾽ ὅλον τὸν βίον ἐντὸς τῶν χιτώνων
4 ἔχοντες ἀπράκτους περιφέρουσι; τὸ δὲ μέγιστον ὅτι
καὶ ὑπὸ τοῖς χιτωνίσκοις, φησί περιζώματα φοροῦσιν,
ἵνα μηδ᾽ ὅταν ἀποθάνωσιν ἐν ταῖς μάχαις φανεροὶ
γένωνται τοῖς ὑπεναντίοις. . . .

26b. Ὅτι Γέλωνος ἐπαγγελλομένου τοῖς Ἕλλησι
δισμυρίοις πεζοῖς, διακοσίαις δὲ ναυσὶ καταφράκτοις
βοηθήσειν, ἐὰν αὐτῷ τῆς ἡγεμονίας ἢ τῆς κατὰ γῆν ἢ
τῆς κατὰ θάλατταν παραχωρήσωσι, φασὶ τοὺς προκαθημένους ἐν Κορίνθῳ τῶν Ἑλλήνων πραγματικώ-
τατον ἀπόκριμα δοῦναι τοῖς παρὰ τοῦ Γέλωνος πρε-
2 σβευταῖς· ἐκέλευον γὰρ ὡς ἐπίκουρον ἔρχεσθαι τὸν
Γέλωνα μετὰ τῶν δυνάμεων, τὴν δ᾽ ἡγεμονίαν ἀνάγκη
τὰ πράγματα περιθήσειν τοῖς ἀρίστοις τῶν ἀνδρῶν·
3 τοῦτο δ᾽ ἐστὶν οὐ καταφευγόντων ἐπὶ τὰς Συρακοσίων
ἐλπίδας, ἀλλὰ πιστευόντων αὐτοῖς καὶ προκαλουμέ-
νων τὸν βουλόμενον ἐπὶ τὸν τῆς ἀνδρείας ἀγῶνα καὶ
4 τὸν περὶ τῆς ἀρετῆς στέφανον. ἀλλ᾽ ὅμως Τίμαιος εἰς
ἕκαστα τῶν προειρημένων τοσούτους ἐκτείνει λόγους
καὶ τοιαύτην ποιεῖται σπουδὴν περὶ τοῦ τὴν μὲν Σικελίαν μεγαλομερεστέραν ποιῆσαι τῆς συμπάσης Ἑλλάδος, τὰς δ᾽ ἐν αὐτῇ πράξεις ἐπιφανεστέρας καὶ
καλλίους τῶν κατὰ τὴν ἄλλην οἰκουμένην, τῶν δ᾽
ἀνδρῶν τῶν μὲν σοφίᾳ διενηνοχότων σοφωτάτους
τοὺς ἐν Σικελίᾳ, τῶν δὲ πραγματικῶν ἡγεμονικω-
5 τάτους καὶ θειοτάτους τοὺς ἐκ Συρακουσῶν, ὥστε μὴ
καταλιπεῖν ὑπερβολὴν τοῖς μειρακίοις τοῖς ἐν ταῖς
διατριβαῖς καὶ τοῖς <περι>πάτοις πρὸς τὰς παρα-

hands, hold them for the whole of their life idle inside their tunics, and above all wear drawers under their tunics that they may not even when killed in battle be exposed to the view of their enemies?"[117] . . .

26b. When Gelo[118] promised to send to the assistance of the Greeks twenty thousand infantry and two hundred warships, if they would grant him the command either on land or at sea, they say that the representatives of Greece sitting in council at Corinth gave a reply to Gelo's envoys which was much to the point. They bade Gelo with his forces come as an auxiliary, but as for the command actual circumstances would of necessity invest the most capable men with it. These are by no means the words of men resting their sole hope on Syracuse, but of men relying on themselves and inviting anyone who wished to do so to join in the contest and win the prize of valor. But Timaeus, in commenting on all this, is so long-winded and so obviously anxious to manifest that Sicily was more important than all the rest of Greece—the events occurring in Sicily being so much more magnificent and more noble than those anywhere else in the world, the sagest of men distinguished for wisdom coming from Sicily and the most capable and wonderful leaders being those from Syracuse—that no boy in a school of rhetoric who is set to write a eulogy of

[117] What followed in the lacuna cannot be guessed.

[118] Different is the story as told by Hdt. 7.157–162: it has Greek ambassadors coming to Syracuse and requesting Gelo's assistance, not Gelo offering assistance to the Greeks on his own.

δόξους ἐπιχειρήσεις, ὅταν ἢ Θερσίτου λέγειν ἐγκώ-
μιον ἢ Πηνελόπης πρόθωνται ψόγον ἤ τινος ἑτέρου
τῶν τοιούτων.

26c. Λοιπὸν ἐκ τούτων διὰ τὴν ὑπερβολὴν τῆς
παραδοξολογίας οὐκ εἰς σύγκρισιν, ἀλλ᾽ εἰς καταμώ-
κησιν ἄγει καὶ τοὺς ἄνδρας καὶ τὰς πράξεις ὧν βούλεται προΐστασθαι, καὶ σχεδὸν εἰς τὸ παραπλήσιον
ἐμπίπτει τοῖς περὶ τοὺς ἐν Ἀκαδημείᾳ λόγους ⟨πρὸς⟩
2   τὸν προχειρότατον λόγον ἠσκηκόσι. καὶ γὰρ ἐκείνων
τινὲς βουλόμενοι περί τε τῶν προφανῶς καταληπτῶν
εἶναι δοκούντων καὶ περὶ τῶν ἀκαταλήπτων εἰς ἀπορίαν ἄγειν τοὺς προσδιαλεγομένους τοιαύταις χρῶνται παραδοξολογίαις καὶ τοιαύτας εὐποροῦσι πιθανότητας ὥστε διαπορεῖν εἰ δυνατόν ἐστι τοὺς ἐν Ἀθήναις
ὄντας ὀσφραίνεσθαι τῶν ἑψομένων ᾠῶν ἐν Ἐφέσῳ καὶ
διστάζειν μή πως, καθ᾽ ὃν καιρὸν ἐν Ἀκαδημείᾳ δια-
λέγονται περὶ τούτων, οὐχ ὕπαρ, ἀλλ᾽ ὄναρ ἐν οἴκῳ
3   κατακείμενοι τούτους διατίθενται τοὺς λόγους. ἐξ ὧν
διὰ τὴν ὑπερβολὴν τῆς παραδοξολογίας εἰς διαβολὴν
ἤχασι τὴν ὅλην αἵρεσιν, ὥστε καὶ τὰ καλῶς ἀπορού-
4   μενα παρὰ τοῖς ἀνθρώποις εἰς ἀπιστίαν ἦχθαι. καὶ
χωρὶς τῆς ἰδίας ἀστοχίας καὶ τοῖς νέοις τοιοῦτον
ἐντετόκασι ζῆλον, ὥστε τῶν μὲν ἠθικῶν καὶ πραγματικῶν λόγων μηδὲ τὴν τυχοῦσαν ἐπίνοιαν ποιεῖσθαι
⟨συμβαίνει⟩, δι᾽ ὧν ὄνησις τοῖς φιλοσοφοῦσι, περὶ δὲ

Thersites or a censure of Penelope[119] or of any other character of this kind could surpass him in the paradoxes he ventures on.

26c. The consequence of this is that, owing to this excessive addiction to paradox, he does not induce us to consider and compare, but exposes to ridicule the men and the actions he is championing, and comes very near falling into the same vicious habit as those who in the discussions of the Academy[120] have trained themselves in extreme readiness of speech, For some of these philosophers, too, in their effort to puzzle the minds of those with whom they are arguing about the comprehensible and incomprehensible, resort to such paradoxes and are so fertile in inventing plausibilities that they wonder whether or not it is possible for those in Athens to smell eggs being roasted in Ephesus, and are in doubt as to whether all the time they are discussing the matter in the Academy they are not lying in their beds at home and composing this discourse in a dream and not in reality. Consequently from this excessive love of paradox they have brought the whole sect into disrepute, so that people have come to disbelieve in the existence of legitimate subjects of doubt. And apart from their own purposelessness they have implanted such a passion in the minds of our young men, that they never give even a thought to ethical and political questions which really

[119] There were indeed eulogies of the ugly antihero and defamations of the model wife; see *RE* Thersites 2455–2471 (K. Gebhard), and *RE* Penelope 460–493 (E. Wüst).

[120] P. attacks the profound skepticism of leading members of the School, including his contemporary Carneades. P. heard him speak at Rome in 155 (33.2, from Gellius).

τὰς ἀνωφελεῖς καὶ παραδόξους εὑρεσιλογίας κενοδο-
ξοῦντες κατατρίβουσι τοὺς βίους.

26d. Τὸ δ' αὐτὸ καὶ Τιμαίῳ συμβέβηκε περὶ τὴν
ἱστορίαν καὶ τοῖς τούτου ζηλωταῖς· παραδοξολόγος
γὰρ ὢν καὶ φιλόνεικος περὶ τὸ προτεθὲν τοὺς μὲν
πολλοὺς καταπέπληκται τοῖς λόγοις, ἠνάγκακε δ'
αὑτῷ ⟨προσέχειν⟩ διὰ τὴν ἐπίφασιν τῆς ἀληθινο-
λογίας, τινὰς δὲ καὶ προσκέκληται καὶ μετ' ἀποδεί-
2 ξεως δοκεῖ πείσειν. καὶ μάλιστα ταύτην γ'
ἐνείργασται τὴν δόξαν ἐκ τῶν περὶ τὰς ἀποικίας καὶ
3 κτίσεις καὶ συγγενείας ἀποφάσεων· ἐν γὰρ τούτοις
τηλικαύτην ἐπίφασιν ποιεῖ διὰ τῆς ἀκριβολογίας καὶ
τῆς πικρίας τῆς ἐπὶ τῶν ἐλέγχων, οἷς χρῆται κατὰ τῶν
πέλας, ὥστε δοκεῖν τοὺς ἄλλους συγγραφέας ἅπαντας
συγκεκοιμῆσθαι τοῖς πράγμασι καὶ κατεσχεδιακέναι
τῆς οἰκουμένης, αὐτὸν δὲ μόνον ἐξητακέναι τὴν ἀκρίβειαν καὶ διευκρινηκέναι τὰς ἐν ἑκάστοις ἱστορίας, ἐν
4 οἷς πολλὰ μὲν ὑγιῶς λέγεται, πολλὰ δὲ καὶ ψευδῶς. οὐ
μὴν ἀλλ' οἱ πλείω χρόνον συντραφέντες αὐτοῦ τοῖς
πρώτοις ὑπομνήμασιν, ἐν οἷς αἱ περὶ τῶν προειρημένων εἰσὶ συντάξεις, ὅταν ἅπασαν συνταξαμένῳ τὴν
ὑπερβολὴν τῆς ἐπαγγελίας ἀποπιστεύσωσι, κἄπειτά
τις αὐτοῖς ἀποδεικνύῃ τὸν Τίμαιον, ἐν οἷς πικρότατός
ἐστι κατὰ τῶν πέλας, αὐτὸν ἔνοχον ὄντα, καθάπερ
ἡμεῖς ἀρτίως ἐπὶ τῶν Λοκρῶν καὶ τῶν ἑξῆς παραπαί-
5 οντα συνεστήσαμεν, δυσέριδες γίνονται καὶ φιλόνει-
κοι καὶ δυσμετάθετοι, καὶ σχεδὸν ὡς ἔπος εἰπεῖν οἱ
φιλοπονώτατα προσεδρεύσαντες τοῖς ὑπομνήμασιν

benefit students of philosophy, but spend their lives in the vain effort to invent useless paradoxes.

26d. Timaeus and his admirers are in the same case as regards history. For being given to paradox and contentiously defending every statement, he overawes most people by his language, compelling them to belief by the superficial appearance of veracity, while some he has won over and seems likely to carry conviction by the proofs he produces. He is most successful in creating this impression when he makes statements about colonies, the foundation of towns and family history. For here he makes such a fine show owing to his affectation of accuracy and the bitter tone in which he confutes others that one would think all writers except himself had dozed over events and made mere random shots at what was befalling the world, while he alone had tested the accuracy of everything and submitted to careful scrutiny the various stories in which there is much that is genuine and much that is false. But, as a fact, when those who have made themselves by long study familiar with the earlier part of his work, in which he treats of the subjects I mentioned, have come to rely fully on his excessive professions of accuracy, and when after this someone proves to them that Timaeus is himself guilty of the very faults he bitterly reproaches in others, committing errors such as I have just above[121] exhibited in the cases of the Locrians and others; then, I say, they become the most captious of critics, disposed to contest every statement, difficult to shake; and that I might almost say is the only

[121] 5.1–11; 12a.1–3; and 16.1–14.

αὐτοῦ τοῦτ' ἀποφέρονται τὸ λυσιτελὲς ἐκ τῆς ἀναγνώ-
6 σεως. οἵ γε μὴν ταῖς δημηγορίαις προσσχόντες αὐτοῦ
καὶ καθόλου τοῖς διεξοδικοῖς λόγοις μειρακιώδεις καὶ
διατριβικοὶ καὶ τελέως ἀναλήθεις γίνονται διὰ τὰς
ἄρτι ῥηθείσας αἰτίας.

27a. Λοιπὸν δὲ τὸ πραγματικὸν αὐτῷ μέρος τῆς
ἱστορίας ἐκ πάντων σύγκειται τῶν ἁμαρτημάτων, ὧν
2 τὰ πλεῖστα διελήλύθαμεν· τὴν δ' αἰτίαν τῆς ἁμαρτίας
νῦν ἐροῦμεν, ἥτις οὐκ ἔνδοξος μὲν φανεῖται τοῖς πλείστοις, ἀληθινωτάτη δ' εὑρεθήσεται τῶν Τιμαίου κατ-
3 ηγορημάτων. δοκεῖ μὲν γὰρ καὶ τὴν ἐμπειρικὴν περὶ
ἕκαστα δύναμιν καὶ τὴν ἐπὶ τῆς πολυπραγμοσύνης
ἕξιν παρεσκευάσθαι καὶ συλλήβδην φιλοπόνως
4 προσεληλυθέναι πρὸς τὸ γράφειν τὴν ἱστορίαν, ἐν
ἐνίοις δ' οὐδεὶς οὔτ' ἀπειρότερος οὔτ' ἀφιλοπονώτερος
φαίνεται γεγονέναι τῶν ἐπ' ὀνόματος συγγραφέων.
δῆλον δ' ἔσται τὸ λεγόμενον ἐκ τούτων.

27. δυεῖν γὰρ ὄντων κατὰ φύσιν ὡς ἂν εἴ τινων
ὀργάνων ἡμῖν, οἷς πάντα πυνθανόμεθα καὶ πολυ-
πραγμονοῦμεν, ἀκοῆς καὶ ὁράσεως, ἀληθινωτέρας δ'
οὔσης οὐ μικρῷ τῆς ὁράσεως κατὰ τὸν Ἡράκλειτον—
ὀφθαλμοὶ γὰρ τῶν ὤτων ἀκριβέστεροι μάρτυρες—
2 τούτων Τίμαιος τὴν ἡδίω μέν, ἥττω δὲ τῶν ὁδῶν
3 ὥρμησε πρὸς τὸ πολυπραγμονεῖν. τῶν μὲν γὰρ διὰ
τῆς ὁράσεως εἰς τέλος ἀπέστη, τῶν δὲ διὰ τῆς ἀκοῆς
ἀντεποιήσατο. καὶ ταύτης <δι>μερ<οῦς> οὔσης τινός,
τοῦ μὲν διὰ τῶν ὑπομνημάτων . . . τὸ δὲ περὶ τὰς

benefit which the most diligent students of his history get from their reading. Those on the other hand who model themselves on his speeches and in general on his more verbose passages become for the reasons I give above childish, scholastic, and quite unveracious.

27a. The political part of his history, then, is a tissue of all the faults, most of which I have described. I will now deal with the prime cause of his errors, a cause which most people will not be inclined to admit, but it will be found to be the truest cause of accusation to be brought against him. He seems to me to have acquired both a talent for detailed research and a competence based on inquiry, and in fact generally speaking to have approached the task of writing history in a painstaking spirit, but in some matters we know of no author of repute who seems to have been less experienced and less painstaking. What I am saying will be clearer from the following considerations.

27. Nature has given us two instruments, as it were,[122] by the aid of which we inform ourselves and inquire about everything. These are hearing and sight, and of the two sight is much more veracious according to Heracleitus.[123] "The eyes are more accurate witnesses than the ears," he says. Now, Timaeus enters on his inquiries by the pleasanter of the two roads, but the inferior one. For he entirely avoids employing his eyes and prefers to employ his ears. Now the knowledge derived from hearing being of two sorts, Timaeus diligently pursued the one, the reading of

---

[122] I render ὄργανα "instruments" not "organs" as Polybius justifies his use of the word, which is, however, quite commonly used of the bodily organs by Aristotle [W.R.P.].

[123] F 6 Marcovich. A common notion, to be found in many ancient writers.

ἀνακρίσεις ῥᾳθύμως ἀνεστράφη, καθάπερ ἐν τοῖς

4 ἀνώτερον ἡμῖν δεδήλωται. δι' ἣν δ' αἰτίαν ταύτην
ἔσχε τὴν αἵρεσιν εὐχερὲς καταμαθεῖν· ὅτι τὰ μὲν ἐκ
τῶν βυβλίων δύναται πολυπραγμονεῖσθαι χωρὶς κινδύνου καὶ κακοπαθείας, ἐάν τις αὐτὸ τοῦτο προνοηθῇ
μόνον ὥστε λαβεῖν ἢ πόλιν ἔχουσαν ὑπομνημάτων

5 πλῆθος ἢ βυβλιοθήκην που γειτνιῶσαν. λοιπὸν κατα-
κείμενον ἐρευνᾶν δεῖ τὸ ζητούμενον καὶ συγκρίνειν
τὰς τῶν προγεγονότων συγγραφέων ἀγνοίας ἄνευ

6 πάσης κακοπαθείας. ἡ δὲ πολυπραγμοσύνη πολλῆς
μὲν προσδεῖται ταλαιπωρίας καὶ δαπάνης, μέγα δέ τι
συμβάλλεται καὶ μέγιστόν ἐστι μέρος τῆς ἱστορίας.

7 δῆλον δὲ τοῦτ' ἐστὶν ἐξ αὐτῶν τῶν τὰς συντάξεις
πραγματευομένων. ὁ μὲν γὰρ Ἔφορός φησιν, εἰ δυνατὸν ἦν αὐτοὺς παρεῖναι πᾶσι τοῖς πράγμασι, ταύτην

8 ἂν διαφέρειν πολὺ τῶν ἐμπειριῶν· ὁ δὲ Θεόπομπος
τοῦτον μὲν ἄριστον ἐν τοῖς πολεμικοῖς τὸν πλείστοις
κινδύνοις παρατετευχότα, τοῦτον δὲ δυνατώτατον ἐν
λόγῳ τὸν πλείστων μετεσχηκότα πολιτικῶν ἀγώνων.

9 τὸν αὐτὸς δὲ τρόπον συμβαίνειν ἐπ' ἰατρικῆς καὶ
10 κυβερνητικῆς. ἔτι δὲ τούτων ἐμφαντικώτερον ὁ ποιη-
τὴς εἴρηκε περὶ τούτου τοῦ μέρους. ἐκεῖνος γὰρ βουλόμενος ὑποδεικνύειν ἡμῖν οἷον δεῖ τὸν ἄνδρα τὸν
πραγματικὸν εἶναι, προθέμενος τὸ τοῦ Ὀδυσσέως
πρόσωπον λέγει πως οὕτως·

ἄνδρα μοι ἔννεπε, Μοῦσα, πολύτροπον, ὃς μάλα
πολλὰ πλάγχθη,

446

books, as I have above pointed out, but was very remiss in his use of the other, the interrogation of living witnesses. It is easy enough to perceive what caused him to make this choice. Inquiries from books may be made without any danger or hardship, provided only that one takes care to have access to a town rich in documents or to have a library near at hand. After that one has only to pursue one's researches in perfect repose and compare the accounts of different writers without exposing oneself to any hardship. Personal inquiry, on the contrary, requires severe labor and great expense, but is exceedingly valuable and is the most important part of history. This is evident from expressions used by historians themselves. Ephorus, for example, says[124] that if we could be personally present at all transactions such knowledge would be far superior to any other. Theopompus says[125] that the man who has the best knowledge of war is he who has been present at the most battles, that the most capable speaker is he who has taken part in the greatest number of debates, and that the same holds good about medicine and navigation. Homer has been still more emphatic on this subject than these writers. Wishing to show us what qualities one should possess in order to be a man of action he says:

The man for wisdom's various arts renowned,
Long exercised in woes, O muse, resound,
Wandering from clime to clime;[126]

[124] *FGrH* 70 F 110. For Ephorus see nn. on 4.20.5 and 5.33.2.
[125] *FGrH* 115 F 342. For Theopompus see n. on 8.9.1, and M. Flower, *Theopompus of Chios: History and Rhetoric in the Fourth Century B.C.* (Oxford 1994).
[126] Hom. *Od.* 1.1–3. The translations are Pope's.

11 καὶ προβάς,

> πολλῶν δ' ἀνθρώπων ἴδεν ἄστεα καὶ νόον ἔγνω,
> πολλὰ δ' ὅγ' ἐν πόντῳ πάθεν ἄλγεα ὃν κατὰ
>   θυμόν,

καὶ ἔτι

> ἀνδρῶν τε πτολέμους ἀλεγεινά τε κύματα πείρων.

28. Δοκεῖ δέ μοι καὶ τὸ τῆς ἱστορίας πρόσχημα
2 τοιοῦτον ἄνδρα ζητεῖν. ὁ μὲν οὖν Πλάτων φησὶ τότε
τἀνθρώπεια καλῶς ἕξειν, ὅταν ἢ οἱ φιλόσοφοι βασι-
3 λεύσωσιν ἢ οἱ βασιλεῖς φιλοσοφήσωσι· κἀγὼ δ' ἂν
εἴποιμι διότι τὰ τῆς ἱστορίας ἕξει τότε καλῶς, ὅταν ἢ
οἱ πραγματικοὶ τῶν ἀνδρῶν γράφειν ἐπιχειρήσωσι
4 τὰς ἱστορίας, μὴ καθάπερ νῦν παρέργως, νομίσαντες
δὲ καὶ τοῦτ' εἶναι σφίσι τῶν ἀναγκαιοτάτων καὶ καλ-
λίστων, ἀπερίσπαστοι ... παράσχωνται πρὸς τοῦτο
5 τὸ μέρος κατὰ τὸν βίον, ἢ οἱ γράφειν ἐπιβαλλόμενοι
τὴν ἐξ αὐτῶν τῶν πραγμάτων ἕξιν ἀναγκαίαν ἡγή-
σωνται πρὸς τὴν ἱστορίαν. πρότερον δ' οὐκ ἔσται
6 παῦλα τῆς τῶν ἱστοριογράφων ἀγνοίας. ὧν Τίμαιος
οὐδὲ τὴν ἐλαχίστην πρόνοιαν θέμενος, ἀλλὰ κατα-
βιώσας ἐν ἑνὶ τόπῳ ξενιτεύων, καὶ σχεδὸν ὡς εἰ κατὰ
πρόθεσιν ἀπειπάμενος καὶ τὴν ἐνεργητικὴν τὴν περὶ
τὰς πολεμικὰς καὶ πολιτικὰς πράξεις καὶ τὴν ἐκ τῆς
πλάνης καὶ θέας αὐτοπάθειαν, οὐκ οἶδ' ὅπως ἐκφέρε-
7 ται δόξαν ὡς ἕλκων τὴν τοῦ συγγραφέως προστασίαν. καὶ διότι τοιοῦτός ἐστιν αὐτὸν ἀνθομολογού-

and further on

>   Observant strayed,
> Their manners noted, and their states surveyed:
> On stormy seas unnumbered toils he bore;[127]

and again—

>   In scenes of death by tempest and by war.[128]

28. It appears to me that the dignity of history also demands such a man. Plato[129] tells us that human affairs will then go well when either philosophers become kings or kings study philosophy, and I would say that it will be well with history either when men of action undertake to write history, not as now happens in a perfunctory manner, but when in the belief that this is a most necessary and most noble thing they apply themselves all through their life to it with undivided attention, or again when would-be authors regard a training in actual affairs as necessary for writing history. Before this be so the errors of historians will never cease. Timaeus never gave a moment's thought to this, but though he spent all his life in exile in one single place,[130] though he almost seems to have deliberately denied himself any active part in war or politics or any personal experience gained by travel and observation, yet, for some unknown reason, he has acquired the reputation of being a leading author. That such is the character of Timaeus can

---

[127] Hom. *Od.* 1.3–4; 8.183.
[128] Hom. *Od.* 8.183.
[129] Plato, *Rep.* 5.473c–e; the sentence was already famous in antiquity.
[130] Athens.

8 μενον εὐχερὲς παραστῆσαι τὸν Τίμαιον. κατὰ γὰρ τὸ
προοίμιον τῆς ἕκτης βύβλου φησί τινας ὑπολαμβάνειν διότι τινὸς μείζονος δεῖται φύσεως καὶ φιλοπο-
νίας καὶ παρασκευῆς τὸ τῶν ἐπιδεικτικῶν λόγων γένος
ἢ τὸ τῆς ἱστορίας· ταύτας δὲ τὰς δόξας πρότερον μὲν

9 Ἐφόρῳ φησὶ προσπεσεῖν, οὐ δυνηθέντος δ' ἱκανῶς
ἐκείνου πρὸς τοὺς ταῦτα λέγοντας ἀπαντῆσαι, πει-
ρᾶται συγκρίνειν αὐτὸς ἐκ παραβολῆς τὴν ἱστορίαν

10 τοῖς ἐπιδεικτικοῖς λόγοις, πρᾶγμα ποιῶν πάντων
ἀτοπώτατον, πρῶτον μὲν τὸ καταψεύσασθαι τοῦ συγγραφέως. ὁ γὰρ Ἔφορος παρ' ὅλην τὴν πραγματείαν
θαυμάσιος ὢν καὶ κατὰ τὴν φράσιν καὶ κατὰ τὸν
χειρισμὸν καὶ κατὰ τὴν ἐπίνοιαν τῶν λημμάτων, δει-
νότατός ἐστιν ἐν ταῖς παρεκβάσεσι καὶ ταῖς ἀφ' αὑτοῦ
γνωμολογίαις, καὶ συλλήβδην ὅταν που τὸν ἐπι-

11 μετροῦντα λόγον διατίθηται· κατὰ δέ τινα συντυχίαν
εὐχαριστότατα καὶ πιθανώτατα περὶ τῆς συγκρίσεως

12 εἴρηκε τῆς τῶν ἱστοριογράφων καὶ λογογράφων. ὁ δ'
ἵνα μὴ δόξῃ κατακολουθεῖν Ἐφόρῳ, πρὸς τῷ κατεψεῦσθαι ᾽κείνου καὶ τῶν λοιπῶν ⟨ἅμα⟩ κατέγν⟨ωκε·
τὰ γὰρ παρ'⟩ ἄλλων δεόντως κεχειρισμένα μακρῶς
καὶ ἀσαφῶς καὶ τρόπῳ παντὶ χεῖρον ἐξηγούμενος
οὐδένα τῶν ζώντων ὑπέλαβε τοῦτο παρατηρήσειν.

28a. οὐ μὴν ἀλλὰ βουλόμενος αὔξειν τὴν ἱστορίαν
πρῶτον μὲν τηλικαύτην εἶναί φησι διαφορὰν τῆς
ἱστορίας πρὸς τοὺς ἐπιδεικτικοὺς λόγους, ἡλίκην ἔχει
τὰ κατ' ἀλήθειαν ᾠκοδομημένα καὶ κατεσκευασμένα
τῶν ἐν ταῖς σκηνογραφίαις φαινομένων τόπων καὶ

easily be shown from his own avowal. For in the preface to his sixth book[131] he says that some suppose that greater talent, more industry, and more previous training are required for declamatory than for historical writing. Such opinions, he says, formerly incurred Ephorus' disapproval, but as that writer could give no satisfactory answer to those who held them, he himself attempts to institute a comparison between history and declamatory writing, a most surprising thing to do, firstly in that his statement about Ephorus is false. For Ephorus, while throughout his whole work he is admirable[132] in his phraseology, method, and the originality of his thought, is most eloquent in his digressions and in the expression of his personal judgment, whenever, in fact, he allows himself to enlarge on any subject, and it so happens that his remarks on the difference between historians and speechwriters are peculiarly charming and convincing. But Timaeus, in order not to seem to be copying Ephorus, besides making a false statement about him has at the same time condemned all other historians. For dealing with matters, treated by others correctly, at inordinate length, in a confused manner, and in every respect worse, he thinks that not a living soul will notice this.

28a. Actually in order to glorify history he says that the difference between it and declamatory writing is as great as that between real buildings or furniture and the views and compositions we see in scene paintings. In the second

---

[131] *FGrH* 566 F 7.

[132] For praise of Ephorus, see also 5.33.2.

2   διαθέσεων· δεύτερον αὐτὸ τὸ συναθροῖσαί φησι τὴν
παρασκευὴν τὴν πρὸς τὴν ἱστορίαν μεῖζον ἔργον
εἶναι τῆς ὅλης πραγματείας τῆς περὶ τοὺς ἐπιδεικτι-
3   κοὺς λόγους· αὐτὸς γοῦν τηλικαύτην ὑπομεμενηκέ-
⟨ναι⟩ δαπάνην καὶ κακοπάθειαν τοῦ συναγαγεῖν τὰ
παρὰ Κυρνίων ὑπομνήματα καὶ πολυπραγμονῆσαι τὰ
Λιγύων ἔθη καὶ Κελτῶν, ἅμα δὲ τούτοις Ἰβήρων,
ὥστε μήτ' ἂν αὐτὸς ἐλπίσαι μήτ' ἂν ἑτέρους ἐξηγου-
4   μένους πιστευθῆναι περὶ τούτων. ἡδέως δέ τις ἂν
ἔροιτο τὸν συγγραφέα πότερον ὑπολαμβάνει μείζονος
δεῖσθαι δαπάνης καὶ κακοπαθείας τὸ καθήμενον ἐν
ἄστει συνάγειν ὑπομνήματα καὶ πολυπραγμονεῖν τὰ
Λιγύων ἔθη καὶ Κελτῶν ἢ τὸ πειραθῆναι τῶν πλεί-
5   στων ἐθνῶν καὶ τόπων αὐτόπτην γενέσθαι. τί δ' αὖ τὸ
πυνθάνεσθαι τὰς παρατάξεις καὶ πολιορκίας, ἔτι δὲ
ναυμαχίας, τῶν παρατετυχηκότων τοῖς κινδύνοις, ἢ τὸ
πεῖραν λαβεῖν τῶν δεινῶν καὶ τῶν ἅμα τούτοις συμ-
6   βαινόντων ἐπ' αὐτῶν τῶν ἔργων; ἐγὼ μὲν γὰρ οὐκ
οἴομαι τηλικαύτην διαφορὰν ἔχειν τὰ κατ' ἀλήθειαν
οἰκοδομήματα τῶν ἐν ταῖς σκηνογραφίαις τόπων, οὐδὲ
τὴν ἱστορίαν τῶν ἐπιδεικτικῶν λόγων, ἡλίκην ἐπὶ
πασῶν τῶν συντάξεων τὴν ἐξ αὐτουργίας καὶ τὴν ἐξ
αὐτοπαθείας ἀπόφασιν τῶν ἐξ ἀκοῆς καὶ διηγήματος
7   γραφομένων· ἧς εἰς τέλος ἄπειρος ὢν εἰκότως ὑπέλαβε τὸ πάντων ἐλάχιστον καὶ ῥᾷστον εἶναι ⟨μέγι-
στον καὶ χαλεπώτατον⟩ τοῖς πραγματευομένοις ⟨τὴν⟩
ἱστορίαν, λέγω δὲ τὸ συνάγειν ὑπομνήματα καὶ πυνθάνεσθαι παρὰ τῶν εἰδότων ἕκαστα τῶν πραγμάτων.

place he says that the mere collection of the material required for a history is a more serious task than the complete course of study of the art of declamatory speaking. He himself, he tells us, had incurred such expense and been put to so much trouble in collecting his notes from Assyria[133] and inquiring into the manners and customs of the Ligurians, Celts, and Iberians that he could not hope that either his own testimony or that of others to this would be believed. One would like to ask this writer whether he thinks that to sit in town collecting notes and inquiring into the manners and customs of the Ligurians and Celts involves more trouble and expense than an attempt to see the majority of places and peoples with one's own eyes. Which again is most troublesome, to inquire from those present at the engagements the details of battles by land and sea and of sieges, or to be present at the actual scene and experience oneself the dangers and vicissitudes of battle? In my opinion the difference between real buildings and scene paintings or between history and declamatory speechmaking is not so great as is, in the case of all works, the difference between an account founded on participation, active or passive, in the occurrences and one composed from report and the narratives of others. But Timaeus, having no experience of the former proceeding, naturally thinks that what is really of smallest importance and easiest is most important and difficult, I mean the collection of documents and inquiry from those personally

133 The true reading is beyond recovery.

8 καίτοι γε περὶ τοῦτο τὸ μέρος ἀνάγκη μεγάλα διαψεύ-
δεσθαι τοὺς ἀπείρους· πῶς γὰρ οἷόν τε καλῶς ἀνακρῖναι περὶ παρατάξεως ἢ πολιορκίας ἢ ναυμαχίας;
πῶς δὲ συνεῖναι τῶν ἐξηγουμένων τὰ κατὰ μέρος
9 ἀνεννόητον ὄντα τῶν προειρημένων; οὐ γὰρ ἔλαττον
ὁ πυνθανόμενος τῶν ἀπαγγελλόντων συμβάλλεται
πρὸς τὴν ἐξήγησιν· ἡ γὰρ τῶν παρεπομένων τοῖς
πράγμασιν ὑπόμνησις αὐτὴ χειραγωγεῖ τὸν ἐξηγού-
10 μενον ἐφ' ἕκαστα τῶν συμβεβηκότων· ὑπὲρ ὧν ὁ μὲν
ἄπειρος οὔτ' ἀνακρῖναι τοὺς παραγεγονότας ἱκανός
ἐστιν οὔτε συμπαρὼν γνῶναι τὸ γινόμενον, ἀλλὰ κἂν
παρῇ, τρόπον τινὰ παρὼν ⟨οὐ πάρεστιν⟩.

acquainted with the facts. And even in this task men of no experience are sure to be frequently deceived. For how is it possible to examine a person properly about a battle, a siege, or a sea fight, or to understand the details of his narrative, if one has no clear ideas about these matters? For the inquirer contributes to the narrative as much as his informant, since the suggestions of the person who follows the narrative guide the memory of the narrator to each incident, and these are matters in which a man of no experience is neither competent to question those who were present at an action, nor when present himself to understand what is going on, but even if present he is in a sense not present.

FRAGMENTA LIBRI XIII

I. RES GRAECIAE

1. Ὅτι Αἰτωλοὶ διά τε τὴν συνέχειαν τῶν πολέμων καὶ διὰ τὴν πολυτέλειαν τῶν βίων ἔλαθον οὐ μόνον ἄλλους, ἀλλὰ καὶ σφᾶς αὐτοὺς κατάχρεοι γενηθέντες.
2 διόπερ οἰκείως διακείμενοι πρὸς καινοτομίαν τῆς οἰκείας πολιτείας εἵλοντο νομογράφους Δωρίμαχον καὶ
3 Σκόπαν, θεωροῦντες τούτους κατά τε τὰς προαιρέσεις κινητικοὺς ὑπάρχοντας καὶ κατὰ τὰς οὐσίας ἐνδεδεμένους εἰς πολλὰ τῶν βιωτικῶν συναλλαγμάτων. οἳ καὶ παραλαβόντες τὴν ἐξουσίαν ταύτην ἔγραψαν νόμους. . . .[1]

1a. Ὅτι Ἀλέξανδρος ὁ Αἰτωλὸς νομοθετοῦντος Δωριμάχου καὶ Σκόπα ἀντέλεγε τοῖς γραφομένοις, ἐκ πολλῶν ἐπιδεικνύμενος ὅτι παρ᾽ οἷς ἔφυ τοῦτο τὸ φυτόν, οὐδέποτε κατέληξε πρότερον ἢ μεγάλοις κακοῖς περιβαλεῖν τοὺς ἅπαξ αὐτῷ χρησαμένους·
2 διόπερ ἠξίου μὴ μόνον πρὸς τὸ παρὸν ἀποβλέπειν, εἰ

---

[1] We must understand χρεῶν ἀποκοπαί, the canceling of debts.

FRAGMENTS OF BOOK XIII

I. AFFAIRS OF GREECE

The Aetolians

1. The Aetolians, owing to the long continuance of hos- 205 B.C.
tilities and owing to their extravagant way of living, became
deeply in debt before anyone else or even they themselves
were aware of it. Being therefore naturally fond of making
innovations in their own constitution they chose Dorimachus and Scopas[1] to draw up laws, as they saw that both of
these men had revolutionary tendencies and that their fortunes were compromised in many private financial transactions. Having been invested with this authority they
drafted laws. . . .

la. Alexander of Aetolia,[2] during the legislation of Dorimachus and Scopas, opposed their proposal, showing
from many instances that where this weed[3] once took root
it never stopped its growth until it had inflicted the greatest disaster on those who had once introduced it. He
begged them therefore not to keep their eyes only on their

---

[1] See n. on 4.3.5. [2] J. D. Grainger, *Aitolian Prosopo-
graphical Studies* (Leiden 2000), 90, no. 12.

[3] The canceling of debts. Alexander opposes it, being, in P.'s
words, "the richest man of all Greeks" (21.26.9).

κουφισθήσονται τῶν ἐνεστώτων συναλλαγμάτων, ἀλ-
3 λὰ καὶ πρὸς τὸ μέλλον· ἄτοπον γὰρ εἶναι πολεμοῦντας
μὲν καὶ τὸ πνεῦμα προΐεσθαι χάριν τῆς τῶν τέκνων
ἀσφαλείας, βουλευομένους δὲ μηδένα ποιεῖσθαι λόγον τοῦ μετὰ ταῦτα χρόνου. . . .

2. Ὅτι Σκόπας ὁ τῶν Αἰτωλῶν ⟨νομογράφος⟩
στρατηγὸς ἀποτυχὼν τῆς ἀρχῆς, ἧς χάριν ἐτόλμα
γράφειν τοὺς νόμους, μετέωρος ἦν εἰς τὴν Ἀλεξάνδρειαν, ταῖς ἐκεῖθεν ἐλπίσι πεπεισμένος ἀναπλη-
ρώσειν τὰ λείποντα τοῦ βίου καὶ τὴν τῆς ψυχῆς πρὸς
2 τὸ πλεῖον ἐπιθυμίαν, οὐκ εἰδὼς ὅτι, καθάπερ ἐπὶ τῶν
ὑδρωπικῶν οὐδέποτε ποιεῖ παῦλαν οὐδὲ κόρον τῆς
ἐπιθυμίας ἡ τῶν ἔξωθεν ὑγρῶν παράθεσις, ἐὰν μὴ τὴν
ἐν αὐτῷ τῷ σώματι διάθεσιν ὑγιάσῃ τις, τὸν αὐτὸν
τρόπον οὐδὲ τὴν πρὸς τὸ πλεῖον ἐπιθυμίαν οἷόν τε
κορέσαι μὴ οὐ τὴν ἐν τῇ ψυχῇ κακίαν λόγῳ τινὶ
διορθωσάμενον. ἐμφανέστατον δὲ τοῦτο συνέβη γενέσθαι περὶ τὸν ἄνδρα τοῦτον, ὑπὲρ οὗ νῦν ὁ λόγος.
3 τούτῳ γὰρ εἰς Ἀλεξάνδρειαν ἀφικομένῳ πρὸς ταῖς ἐκ
τῶν ὑπαίθρων ὠφελείαις, ὧν ἦν αὐτὸς κύριος διὰ τὸ
πιστεύεσθαι περὶ τῶν ὅλων, καὶ τῆς ἡμέρας ἑκάστης
ὀψώνιον ἐξέθηκεν ὁ βασιλεὺς αὐτῷ μὲν δεκαμναιαῖον,
τοῖς δ' ἐπί τινος ἡγεμονίας μετ' αὐτὸν τεταγμένοις
4 μναιαῖον. ἀλλ' ὅμως οὐκ ἠρκεῖτο τούτοις, ὃς τὸ πρότε-
5 ρον προσκαρτερῶν τῷ πλείονι διετέλεσε, μέχρι διὰ
τὴν ἀπληστίαν καὶ παρ' αὐτοῖς τοῖς διδοῦσι φθονη-
θεὶς τὸ πνεῦμα προσέθηκε τῷ χρυσίῳ. . .

present relief from the obligations they had incurred but to look to the future too. For it was, he said, strange indeed that on the battlefield they should give even their lives for the sake of their children's safety, but in the council chamber should take no thought for future times. . . .

2. Scopas, the ⟨lawgiver⟩ of the Aetolians, when he failed to obtain the office, for the sake of which he had ventured to draft these laws, turned eagerly toward Alexandria for help, convinced that if his expectations in that quarter were realized he would repair his damaged fortunes and satisfy his soul's longing for gain. He was unaware that as in the case of a dropsy the thirst of the sufferer never ceases and is never allayed by the administration of liquids from without, unless we cure the morbid condition of the body itself, so it is impossible to satiate the greed for gain, unless we correct by reasoning the vice inherent in the soul. The most conspicuous case of this was that of the very man of whom we are now speaking. For when he reached Alexandria,[4] in addition to the profit he drew from the force in the field which had been placed absolutely at his disposal, the king assigned him personally a daily pay of ten minae, while those serving under him in any command received one mina each. Still he was not satisfied with this, but from the very first was so devoted to gain that at the end, arousing by his insatiate greed the aversion of those even who ministered to it, he sacrificed his life for money.

[4] He came as a mercenary captain, as other Aetolians (Theodotus, Nicolaus) before him, or as the Acarnanian Aristomenes (C. Habicht, *Hermes* 85 [1957], 501–504), who about that time became chancellor of the Ptolemaic empire. Scopas was soon appointed commander in chief.

3. Ἐγένετο περὶ τὴν τοιαύτην κακοπραγμοσύνην,
ἣν δὴ βασιλικὴν μὲν οὐδαμῶς οὐδεὶς ἂν εἶναι φήσειεν, ἀναγκαίαν δὲ βούλονται λέγειν ἔνιοι πρὸς τὸν
πραγματικὸν τρόπον διὰ τὴν νῦν ἐπιπολάζουσαν

2 κακοπραγμοσύνην. οἱ μὲν γὰρ ἀρχαῖοι πολύ τι τοῦ
τοιούτου μέρους ἐκτὸς ἦσαν· τοσοῦτο γὰρ ἀπηλλο-
τρίωντο τοῦ κακομηχανεῖν περὶ τοὺς φίλους χάριν τοῦ
τῷ τοιούτῳ συναύξειν τὰς σφετέρας δυναστείας, ὥστ᾽

3 οὐδὲ τοὺς πολεμίους ᾑροῦντο δι᾽ ἀπάτης νικᾶν, ὑπολαμβάνοντες ⟨οὐδὲν⟩ οὔτε λαμπρὸν οὐδὲ μὴν βέβαιον
εἶναι τῶν κατορθωμάτων, ἐὰν μή τις ἐκ τοῦ προφανοῦς
μαχόμενος ἡττήσῃ ταῖς ψυχαῖς τοὺς ἀντιταττομένους.

4 διὸ καὶ συνετίθεντο πρὸς σφᾶς μήτ᾽ ἀδήλοις βέλεσι
μήθ᾽ ἐκηβόλοις χρήσασθαι κατ᾽ ἀλλήλων, μόνην δὲ
τὴν ἐκ χειρὸς καὶ συστάδην γινομένην μάχην ἀλη-

5 θινὴν ὑπελάμβανον εἶναι κρίσιν πραγμάτων. ᾗ καὶ
τοὺς πολέμους ἀλλήλοις προύλεγον καὶ τὰς μάχας,
ὅτε πρόθοιντο διακινδυνεύειν, καὶ τοὺς τόπους, ⟨εἰς⟩

6 οὓς μέλλοιεν ἐξιέναι παραταξόμενοι. νῦν δὲ καὶ φαύ-
λου φασὶν εἶναι στρατηγοῦ τὸ προφανῶς τι πράττειν

7 τῶν πολεμικῶν. βραχὺ δέ τι λείπεται παρὰ Ῥωμαίοις
ἴχνος ἔτι τῆς ἀρχαίας αἱρέσεως περὶ τὰ πολεμικά· καὶ
γὰρ προλέγουσι τοὺς πολέμους καὶ ταῖς ἐνέδραις
σπανίως χρῶνται καὶ τὴν μάχην ἐκ χειρὸς ποιοῦνται

8 καὶ ⟨συ⟩στάδην. ταῦτα μὲν οὖν εἰρήσθω πρὸς τὸν

Philip's Treacherous Policy

3. Philip became addicted to that kind of treacherous dealings which no one indeed would say in any way became a king but which some maintain to be necessary in practical politics, owing to the present prevalence of treachery. The ancients, as we know, were far removed from such malpractices. For so far were they from plotting mischief against their friends with the purpose of aggrandizing their own power, that they would not even consent to get the better of their enemies by fraud, regarding no success as brilliant or secure unless they crushed the spirit of their adversaries in open battle. For this reason they entered into a convention[5] among themselves to use against each other neither secret missiles nor those discharged from a distance, and considered that it was only a hand-to-hand battle at close quarters which was truly decisive. Hence they preceded war by a declaration, and when they intended to do battle gave notice of the fact and of the spot to which they would proceed and array their army. But at the present they say it is a sign of poor generalship to do anything openly in war. Some slight traces, however, of the ancient principles of warfare survive among the Romans. For they make declaration of war, they very seldom use ambuscades, and they fight hand-to-hand at close quarters. These reflections are occasioned by the excessive

[5] Concluded between Eretria and Chalcis, at war with each other over the Lelantian fields in the seventh century. See *StV* 102, where other testimonies, from Strabo, Herodotus, and Thucydides, are quoted.

461

ἐπιπολάζοντα νῦν ὑπὲρ τὸ δέον ἐν τῇ κακοπραγμο-
σύνῃ ζῆλον περὶ τοὺς ἡγουμένους ἔν τε ταῖς πολιτι-
καῖς καὶ πολεμικαῖς οἰκονομίαις.

4. Ὁ δὲ Φίλιππος Ἡρακλείδῃ μέν, καθάπερ ὑπόθεσιν δούς, ἐπέταξε φροντίζειν πῶς ἂν κακοποιήσαι
2 καὶ διαφθείραι τὰς τῶς Ῥοδίων νῆας, εἰς δὲ τὴν
Κρήτην πρεσβευτὰς ἐξαπέστειλε τοὺς ἐρεθιοῦντας καὶ
3 παρορμήσοντας ἐπὶ τὸν κατὰ τῶν Ῥοδίων πόλεμον. ὁ
δ᾽ Ἡρακλείδης, ἄνθρωπος εὖ πεφυκὼς πρὸς τὸ κακόν,
ἑρμαῖον ἡγησάμενος τὴν ἐπιταγήν, καὶ διανοηθεὶς
ἄττα δήποτ᾽ οὖν παρ᾽ αὑτῷ, μετά τινα χρόνον ὥρμησε
4 καὶ παρῆν καταπλέων εἰς τὴν Ῥόδον. συνέβαινε δὲ
τὸν Ἡρακλείδην τοῦτον τὸ μὲν γένος ἀνέκαθεν εἶναι
Ταραντῖνον, πεφυκέναι δ᾽ ἐκ βαναύσων καὶ χειρο-
τεχνῶν ἀνθρώπων, μεγάλα δ᾽ ἐσχηκέναι προτερήματα
5 πρὸς ἀπόνοιαν καὶ ῥᾳδιουργίαν· πρῶτον μὲν γὰρ
ἀναφανδὸν τῷ σώματι παρεκέχρητο κατὰ τὴν πρώτην
ἡλικίαν, εἶτ᾽ ἀγχίνους ὑπῆρχε καὶ μνήμων, καὶ πρὸς
μὲν τοὺς ταπεινοτέρους καταπληκτικώτατος καὶ τολ-
μηρότατος, πρὸς δὲ τοὺς ὑπερέχοντας κολακικώτατος.
6 οὗτος ἀρχῆθεν μὲν ἐκ τῆς πατρίδος ἐξέπεσε δόξας
τὸν Τάραντα πράττειν Ῥωμαίοις, οὐ πολιτικὴν ἔχων
δύναμιν, ἀλλ᾽ ἀρχιτέκτων ὑπάρχων καὶ διά τινας
ἐπισκευὰς τῶν τειχῶν κύριος γενόμενος τῶν κλειδῶν

---

6 "Presumably Greeks" says WC 2.417, but not necessarily, as
οἱ ἡγούμενοι by the time P. writes means the Romans and their
representatives in the East. P. may have Romans such as Quintus

prevalence among our present leaders[6] both in the conduct of public affairs and in that of war of a keenness for double dealing.

4. Philip, as if giving Heracleides[7] a proper subject for the exercise of his talents, ordered him to think of the best means of damaging and destroying the navy of Rhodes, and at the same time sent envoys to Crete to provoke the Cretans and arouse their enthusiasm for the war against Rhodes. Heracleides, a born mischief-maker, thinking this commission a godsend and forming some kind of scheme in his mind, waited a little and then set out on his voyage and appeared at Rhodes. This Heracleides was of Tarentine origin, his parents were vulgar mechanics and he possessed advantages admirably qualifying him to be a daredevil and arrant knave. For, to begin with, in his early years he had openly prostituted his person, but later he showed great sharpness and an excellent memory, and while he was a terrible bully and most bold-faced in dealing with his inferiors he was most obsequious to his superiors. He was originally expelled from his native town as he was suspected of a design of betraying Tarentum to the Romans, not that he had any political power, but because he was an architect and owing to some repairs they were making in the wall had been entrusted with the keys of the gate lead-

Marcius Philippus in mind, who treacherously deceived King Perseus in 172 and offended by his behavior even some Roman senators, *RE* Marcius 1575 (F. Münzer).

7 In Philip's service after he was exiled from Tarentum (4.6), in 209 at the latest. He may be the same Heracleides who was Philip's military representative in Phocis in 209 (*SIG* 552). Rhodes was at war against some Cretan states, whose patron was Philip.

7 τῆς πύλης τῆς ἐπὶ τὸ μεσόγαιον φερούσης· κατα-
φυγὼν δὲ πρὸς Ῥωμαίους, καὶ πάλιν ἐκεῖθεν γράφων
καὶ διαπεμπόμενος εἰς τὸν Τάραντα καὶ πρὸς Ἀννίβαν, ἐπεὶ καταφανὴς ἐγένετο, προαισθόμενος τὸ μέλ-
8 λον αὖθις ἔφυγε πρὸς τὸν Φίλιππον. παρ' ᾧ τοιαύτην
περιεποιήσατο πίστιν καὶ δύναμιν ὥστε τοῦ κατα-
στραφῆναι τὴν τηλικαύτην βασιλείαν σχεδὸν αἰτιώ-
τατος γεγονέναι. . . .

5. Διαπιστοῦντες δ' οἱ πρυτάνεις ἤδη τῷ Φιλίππῳ
διὰ τὴν περὶ τὰ Κρητικὰ κακοπραγμοσύνην, καὶ τὸν
Ἡρακλείδην ὑπώπτευον ἐγκάθετον εἶναι.

2 Ὁ δ' εἰσελθὼν ἀπελογίζετο τὰς αἰτίας, δι' ἃς πε-
φευγὼς εἴη τὸν Φίλιππον

3 Πᾶν γὰρ βουληθῆναι τὸν Φίλιππον ἀναδέξασθαι ἢ
καταφανῆ γενέσθαι Ῥοδίοις τὴν ἐν τούτοις αὐτοῦ
προαίρεσιν. ἧ καὶ τὸν Ἡρακλείδην ἀπέλυσε τῆς ὑπο-
ψίας. . . .

4 Καί μοι δοκεῖ μεγίστην θεὸν τοῖς ἀνθρώποις ἡ
φύσις ἀποδεῖξαι τὴν ἀλήθειαν καὶ μεγίστην αὐτῇ
5 προσθεῖναι δύναμιν. πάντων γοῦν αὐτὴν καταγωνι-
ζομένων, ἐνίοτε καὶ πασῶν τῶν πιθανοτήτων μετὰ τοῦ
ψεύδους ταττομένων, οὐκ οἶδ' ὅπως αὐτὴ δι' αὑτῆς εἰς
6 τὰς ψυχὰς εἰσδύεται τῶν ἀνθρώπων, καὶ ποτὲ μὲν
παραχρῆμα δείκνυσι τὴν αὑτῆς δύναμιν, ποτὲ δὲ καὶ
πολὺν χρόνον ἐπισκοτισθεῖσα, τέλος αὐτὴ δι' ἑαυτῆς
ἐπικρατεῖ καὶ καταγωνίζεται τὸ ψεῦδος, ὡς συνέβη
γενέσθαι περὶ τὸν Ἡρακλείδην τὸν παρὰ τοῦ Φιλίππου τοῦ βασιλέως εἰς Ῥόδον ἀφικόμενον. . .

ing to the interior. He then took refuge with the Romans, but later when he was detected in sending letters and messages from the Roman camp to Tarentum and to Hannibal, he foresaw what would be the result and this time sought safety with Philip, at whose court he acquired such credit and power that he was almost the chief instrument of the ruin of that mighty kingdom. . . .

5. The prytaneis[8] of Rhodes, who already distrusted Philip owing to his treacherous conduct in the Cretan question, suspected that Heracleides also was involved. . . .

He appeared before them and offered an explanation of the reasons why he had deserted Philip.

"Philip," he said, "would put up with anything rather than that his design in this matter should be revealed to the Rhodians." By this means he also freed Heracleides from suspicion. . . .

In my opinion Nature has proclaimed to men that Truth is the greatest of gods and has invested her with the greatest power. At least when all are trying to suppress her and all probabilities are on the side of falsehood, she somehow finds her own means of penetrating into the hearts of men and sometimes shows her power at once, sometimes after being darkened for years at last by her own force prevails and crushes falsehood, as happened in the case of Heracleides, King Philip's messenger to Rhodes. . .

---

[8] The highest magistrates at Rhodes, five in number, serving for six months as a committee. *RE* Prytanis (Suppl. 13), 730–816 (F. Gschnitzer), for Rhodes 766–769. Full story in Polyaen. 5.17.2: Heracleides came to Rhodes pretending to seek asylum from Philip; he duped the Rhodians, burned thirteen ship sheds with the triremes, and made his escape.

465

7   Ὅτι Δαμοκλῆς ὁ μετὰ Πυθίωνος πεμφθεὶς κατ-
άσκοπος πρὸς Ῥωμαίους ὑπηρετικὸν ἦν σκεῦος εὐ-
φυὲς καὶ πολλὰς ἔχον ἀφορμὰς εἰς πραγμάτων οἰκονομίαν. . . .

6. Ὁ δὲ τῶν Λακεδαιμονίων τύραννος Νάβις, ἔτος
ἤδη τρίτον ἔχων τὴν ἀρχήν, ὁλοσχερὲς μὲν οὐδὲν
ἐπεβάλλετο πράττειν οὐδὲ τολμᾶν διὰ τὸ πρόσφατον
εἶναι τὴν ὑπὸ τῶν Ἀχαιῶν ἧτταν τοῦ Μαχανίδου,

2   καταβολὴν δ' ἐποιεῖτο καὶ θεμέλιον ὑπεβάλλετο πολυ-
3   χρονίου καὶ βαρείας τυραννίδος. διέφθειρε γὰρ τοὺς
λοιποὺς ἄρδην ἐκ τῆς Σπάρτης, ἐφυγάδευσε δὲ τοὺς
κατὰ πλέον πλούτῳ διαφέροντας ἢ δόξῃ προγονικῇ,
τὰς δὲ τούτων οὐσίας καὶ γυναῖκας διεδίδου τῶν
ἄλλων τοῖς ἐπιφανεστάτοις καὶ τοῖς μισθοφόροις.

4   οὗτοι δ' ἦσαν ἀνδροφόνοι καὶ παρασχίσται, λωπο-
δύται, τοιχωρύχοι. καθόλου γὰρ τοῦτο τὸ γένος ἠθροί-
ζετο πρὸς αὐτὸν ἐπιμελῶς ἐκ τῆς οἰκουμένης, οἷς
ἄβατος ἦν ἡ θρέψασα δι᾽ ἀσέβειαν καὶ παρανομίαν.

5   ὧν προστάτην καὶ βασιλέα αὐτὸν ἀναδείξας, καὶ
χρώμενος δορυφόροις καὶ σωματοφύλαξι τούτοις, δῆλον ἔμελλε πολυχρόνιον ἔχειν τὴν ἐπ᾽ ἀσεβείᾳ φήμην

6   καὶ δυναστείαν. ὅς γε χωρὶς τῶν προειρημένων οὐκ
ἐξηρκεῖτο φυγαδεύειν τοὺς πολίτας, ἀλλ᾽ οὐδὲ τοῖς
φεύγουσιν οὐδεὶς τόπος ἦν ἀσφαλὴς οὐδὲ καταφυγὴ

7   βέβαιος. τοὺς μὲν γὰρ ἐν ταῖς ὁδοῖς ἐπαποστέλλων

---

9 Both unknown, as is also the person who sent them.
10 See n. on 4.81.13. He followed Machanidas in 207 and ruled

Damocles, who was sent with Pythion[9] as a spy to Rome, was a handy tool, full of resources in the management of affairs.

Nabis, Tyrant of Sparta

6. Nabis, tyrant of the Lacedaemonians,[10] who had now been in power for over two years, had not yet ventured to attempt any important enterprise, the defeat of Machanidas by the Achaeans being so recent, but was occupied in laying the foundations of a lasting and oppressive tyranny. For he utterly exterminated those of the royal houses[11] who survived in Sparta, and banishing those citizens who were distinguished for their wealth and illustrious ancestry, gave their property and wives to the chief of his own supporters and to his mercenaries, who were for the most part murderers, rippers, highwaymen, and burglars. For such kind of people flocked sedulously to his court from all over the world, people who dared not set foot in their own countries owing to their crimes against God and man. As he constituted himself their protector and king, and employed these men as satellites and members of his bodyguard, it was evident that his rule would long be memorable for its wickedness. Besides the abuses I have mentioned, not content with banishing the citizens, he left no place safe for them in their exile and no refuge secure. For he sent men after some to slay them on their journey and

until 191. Officially king and probably a member of the house of the Eurypontids, but usually called tyrant.

[11] Some definition of λοιπούς has obviously dropped out.

8 ἀνήρει, τοὺς δ' ἐκ τῶν τόπων ἐπανάγοντας ἐφόνευε. τὸ
δὲ τελευταῖον ἐν ταῖς πόλεσι τὰς σύνεγγυς οἰκίας,
ὅπου τις τυγχάνοι κατοικῶν τῶν φυγάδων, μισθού-
μενος δι' ἀνυπονοήτων ἀνθρώπων, εἰς ταύτας εἰσέπεμ-
πε Κρῆτας, οἵτινες ῥήγματα ποιοῦντες ἐν τοῖς τοίχοις
καὶ διὰ τῶν ὑπαρχουσῶν θυρίδων τοξεύοντες τοὺς μὲν
ἑστῶτας τῶν φυγάδων, τοὺς δ' ἀνακειμένους ἐν ταῖς
9 ἰδίαις οἰκίαις διέφθειρον, ὥστε μήτε τόπον εἶναι
μηδένα φύξιμον μήτε καιρὸν ἀσφαλῆ τοῖς ταλαι-
10 πώροις Λακεδαιμονίοις. καὶ δὴ τῷ τοιούτῳ τρόπῳ τοὺς
μὲν πλείστους αὐτῶν ἠφάνισε.

7. κατεσκευάσατο δὲ καί τινα μηχανήν, εἰ μηχανὴν
2 ταύτην χρὴ λέγειν. ἦν γὰρ εἴδωλον γυναικεῖον, πολυ-
τελέσιν ἱματίοις ἠμφιεσμένον, κατὰ δὲ τὴν μορφὴν εἰς
ὁμοιότητα τῇ τοῦ Νάβιδος γυναικὶ διαφόρως ἀπειρ-
3 γασμένον. ὁπότε δέ τινας τῶν πολιτικῶν ἀνακαλέσαι-
το, βουλόμενος εἰσπρᾶξαι χρήματα, τὰς μὲν ἀρχὰς
4 διετίθετο λόγους πλείονας καὶ φιλανθρώπους, ὑπο-
δεικνύων μὲν τὸν ὑπὸ τῶν Ἀχαιῶν ἐπικρεμάμενον τῇ
χώρᾳ καὶ τῇ πόλει φόβον, διασαφῶν δὲ τὸ πλῆθος
τῶν μισθοφόρων τὸ τρεφόμενον τῆς ἐκείνων ἀσφα-
5 λείας χάριν, ἔτι δὲ τὰς εἰς τοὺς θεοὺς καὶ τὰς κοινὰς
τῆς πόλεως δαπάνας. εἰ μὲν οὖν ἐντρέποιντο διὰ τῶν
τοιούτων λόγων, εἶχεν ἀποχρώντως αὐτῷ πρὸς τὸ
6 προκείμενον· εἰ δέ τινες ἐξαρνούμενοι διωθοῖντο τὴν
ἐπιταγήν, ἐπεφθέγγετο λόγον τοιοῦτον "ἴσως ἐγὼ μὲν
οὐ δύναμαί σε πείθειν, Ἀπῆγαν μέντοι ταύτην δοκῶ
σε πείσειν"· τοῦτο δ' ἦν ὄνομα τῇ γυναικὶ τοῦ Νάβι-

killed others as they were returning from exile. Finally, in the towns, renting through unsuspected agents the houses next door to those in which the exiles resided, he introduced Cretans into them, who breaking down the walls and shooting through the existing windows slew the exiles in their own houses either when standing or reposing, so that for the unhappy Spartans there was no place to fly to and no moment at which their lives were safe. It was by these means that he destroyed the greater number of them.

7. He had also constructed a machine,[12] if one can call such a thing a machine. It was in fact an image of a woman richly dressed and was a very good likeness of the wife of Nabis. Whenever he summoned any of the citizens before him with the design of extracting money from him he would begin by addressing him in kind terms, pointing out the danger to which the city and country were exposed from the Achaeans and calling attention to the number of the mercenaries he was obliged to maintain to ensure the safety of his subjects, as well as to the amount spent on religious ceremonies and the public outlay of the city. If they yielded to these arguments it was sufficient for his purpose. But if anyone refused and objected to pay the sum imposed, he would continue somewhat as follows: "Very possibly I shall not be able to persuade you, but I think this Apega[13] of mine may do so"—this being his wife's name—

---

[12] The story seems to be a legend spun out of what Nabis' wife did according to 18.17.1–5. [13] As Adolf Wilhelm saw, in all likelihood Apia, the daughter of Aristomachus II, tyrant of Argos (*IG* IV 1² 621; *LGPN* III A. 48–49). There is no name "Apega" attested for the entire Peloponnese.

7 δος. καὶ τοῦτ᾽ ἔλεγε, καὶ παρῆν ὁ μικρῷ πρότερον
8 ἔλεγον εἴδωλον. καὶ δεξιωσάμενος, ἐπειδὰν ἐκ τῆς
καθέδρας ἀνέστησε τὴν γυναῖκα καὶ περιέπτυξε ταῖς
9 χερσί, προσήγετο κατὰ βραχὺ πρὸς τὰ στέρνα. τοὺς
δὲ πήχεις εἶχε καὶ τὰς χεῖρας πλήρεις σιδηρῶν γόμ-
φων ὑπὸ τοῖς ἱματίοις, ὁμοίως καὶ κατὰ τοὺς μαστούς.
10 ὅταν προσήρεισε ταῖς χερσὶ πρὸς τὰ νῶτα τῆς γυναικός, κἄπειτα διὰ τῶν ὀργάνων ἑλκόμενον ἐπέτεινε καὶ
προσῆγε πρὸς τοὺς μαστοὺς κατ᾽ ἐλάχιστον, πᾶσαν
11 ἠνάγκαζε φωνὴν προΐεσθαι τὸν πιεζόμενον. καὶ πολλοὺς δή τινας τῷ τοιούτῳ τρόπῳ διέφθειρε τῶν ἐξαρ-
νουμένων.

8. Καὶ τὰ λοιπὰ δ᾽ ἦν τούτοις ὅμοια καὶ σύστοιχα
2 κατὰ τὴν ἀρχήν. ἐκοινώνει μὲν γὰρ τοῖς Κρησὶ τῶν
κατὰ θάλατταν λῃστειῶν· εἶχε δὲ καθ᾽ ὅλην τὴν Πελο-
πόννησον ἱεροσύλους, ὁδοιδόκους, φονέας, οἷς μερί-
της γινόμενος τῶν ἐκ τῆς ῥᾳδιουργίας λυσιτελῶν
ὁρμητήριον καὶ καταφυγὴν παρείχετο τούτοις τὴν
3 Σπάρτην. πλὴν κατά γε τοὺς καιροὺς τούτους ξένοι
τῶν ἀπὸ τῆς Βοιωτίας εἰς τὴν Λακεδαίμονα παρεπιδη-
μήσαντες ἐψυχαγώγησάν τινα τῶν τοῦ Νάβιδος ἱππο-
κόμων ὥστε συναποχωρῆσαι μεθ᾽ ἑαυτῶν ἔχοντα λευ-
κὸν ἵππον, ὃς ἐδόκει γενναιότατος εἶναι τῶν ἐκ τῆς
4 τυραννικῆς ἱπποστάσεως. τούτου δὲ πεισθέντος καὶ
πράξαντος τοῦ προειρημένου, καταδιώξαντες οἱ παρὰ
τοῦ Νάβιδος εἰς τὴν Μεγάλην πόλιν καὶ καταλαβόντες τὸν μὲν ἵππον εὐθὺς ἀπῆγον καὶ τὸν ἱπποκόμον,
οὐδενὸς ἀντιποιουμένου, μετὰ δὲ ταῦτα καὶ τοῖς ξένοις

and even as he spoke in came the image I have described. When the man offered her his hand he made the woman rise from her chair and taking her in his arms drew her gradually to his bosom.[14] Both her arms and hands as well as her breasts were covered with iron nails concealed under her dress. So that when Nabis rested his hands on her back and then by means of certain springs drew his victim toward her and increasing the pressure brought him at all in contact with her breasts he made the man thus embraced say anything and everything. Indeed by this means he killed a considerable number of those who denied him money.

8. The rest of his conduct during his rule was similar and on a level with this. For he participated in the acts of piracy of the Cretans,[15] and through the whole of the Peloponnese he had plunderers of temples, highwaymen, and assassins, the profits of whose misdeeds he shared and allowed them to make Sparta their base of operations and their refuge. But in one case some foreign soldiers from Boeotia who were paying a visit to Sparta tried to induce one of Nabis' grooms to leave with them, bringing away a white horse supposed to be the best bred animal in the tyrant's stables. Upon the groom consenting and doing as they wished, Nabis' men pursued them as far as Megalopolis and catching them there at once took away the horse and the groom, no one offering any objection. When, in the next place, they tried to lay hands on the foreigners,

14 The epitomator has so compressed the story that the exact working of the mechanism does not become clear.

15 The Cretans were notorious for piracy.

5 ἐπέβαλον τὰς χεῖρας. οἱ δὲ Βοιωτοὶ τὸ μὲν πρῶτον
ἠξίουν ἄγειν αὐτοὺς ἐπὶ τὴν ἀρχήν· οὐδενὸς δὲ προσ-
6 έχοντος ἀνεβόα τις τῶν ξένων "βοήθεια." συνδραμόν-
των δὲ τῶν ἐγχωρίων καὶ μαρτυρομένων τοὺς ἄνδρας
ἐπανάγειν ἐπὶ τὴν ἀρχήν, ἠναγκάσθησαν προιέμενοι
7 τοὺς ἀνθρώπους οἱ παρὰ τοῦ Νάβιδος ἀπελθεῖν. ὁ δὲ
πάλαι ζητῶν ἀφορμὰς ἐγκλημάτων καὶ πρόφασιν εὔλογον διαφορᾶς, τότε λαβόμενος ταύτης εὐθέως ἤλαυνε τὰ Προαγόρου θρέμματα καί τινων ἑτέρων. ἐξ ὧν
ἐγένετο ⟨κατ⟩αρχὴ τοῦ πολέμου.

II. RES ASIAE

9. Λάβαι, ὡς Σάβαι, Χαττηνίας πόλις. Πολύβιος
τρισκαιδεκάτῳ. τὸ ἐθνικὸν Λαβαῖος ὡς Σαβαῖος. τῆς
αὐτῆς χώρας ἀμφότεραι· ἡ γὰρ Χαττηνία τῶν Γερραίων ἐστὶ χώρα.

2 Χαττηνία, χώρα τρίτη Γερραίων. Πολύβιος ιγʹ.
"ἔστι δ᾽ ἡ Χαττηνία τἄλλα μὲν λυπρά, κώμαις δὲ καὶ
πύργοις διεσκεύασται διὰ τὴν εὐκαιρίαν τῶν Γερραί-
3 ων· οὗτοι γὰρ αὐτὴν νέμονται." ἔστι δὲ τῆς Ἐρυθρᾶς
θαλάσσης. . . .

4 Οἱ δὲ Γερραῖοι ἀξιοῦσι τὸν βασιλέα μὴ καταλῦσαι

---

16 "He is unknown, but probably a Megalopolitan" (WC
2.421). In fact, a Pr(o)agoras of Megalopolis is mentioned in an
honorary document from Delphi, *FD* III 1.17; for the archon's
date, see J. Scholten, *The Politics of Plunder* . . . (Berkeley 2000),
244. The war is between Sparta and Megalopolis.

the Boeotians at first demanded to be brought before the magistrates, and when no one paid any attention to their request, one of them called out "Help." Upon this the populace collected and protested that the men should be brought before the magistrates, and now Nabis' men were compelled to release their prisoners and take their departure. Nabis had been long on the lookout for some pretended grievance and a specious pretext for a rupture, and taking hold of this at once raided the cattle of Proagoras[16] and some others. This was the origin of the war.

II. AFFAIRS OF ASIA

Chattenia and the Gerraeans

9. Labae, like Sabae, city of Chattenia.[17] Polybius Book 13. Their ethnic is Labaeus like Sabaeus. Both are of the same area, since Chattenia belongs to the territory of the Gerraeans.[18]

Chattenia in the Persian Gulf is the third district belonging to the Gerraeans. It is a poor district in other respects, but villages and towers have been established in it for the convenience of the Gerraeans who cultivate it. . . .

The Gerraeans begged the king[19] not to abolish the

[17] The land of the Gerraeans. Neither Labae nor Sabae is identified.

[18] People on the western (Arabian) coast of the Persian Gulf. Their capital was Gerrha, an important place for trade by caravan and by ship. *RE* Gerrha 1270–1272 (J. Tkac). M. P. Charlesworth, *Trade-Routes and Commerce of the Roman Empire* (Cambridge 1924), 67–68.   [19] King Antiochus came to Gerrha on his return from Bactria. See also Plin. *HN* 12.35.

τὰ παρὰ τῶν θεῶν αὐτοῖς δεδομένα, τοῦτ᾽ ἔστιν ἀΐδιον
εἰρήνην καὶ ἐλευθερίαν. ὁ δὲ ἑρμηνευθείσης οἱ τῆς
ἐπιστολῆς ἔφη συγχωρεῖν τοῖς ἀξιουμένοις. . . .

5   Κυρωθείσης δὲ τῆς ἐλευθερίας τοῖς Γερραίοις
ἐστεφάνωσαν παραχρῆμα τὸν Ἀντίοχον τὸν βασιλέα
πεντακοσίοις ἀργυρίου ταλάντοις, χιλίοις δὲ λιβανω-
τοῦ καὶ διακοσίοις τῆς λεγομένης στακτῆς. καὶ ἐποίει
τὸν πλοῦν ἐπὶ Τύλον τὴν νῆσον καὶ ἐποίει τὸν ἀπό-
πλουν ἐπὶ Σελευκείας. ἦσαν δὲ τὰ ἀρώματα ἐν τῇ
Ἐρυθρᾷ θαλάττῃ.

10. Βάδιζα, πόλις τῆς Βρεττίας, Πολύβιος τρισκαιδεκάτῳ.

2   Λαμπέτεια, πόλις Βρεττίας, Πολύβιος τρισκαιδεκάτῳ.

3   Ἔστι γὰρ καὶ Ταμέση πόλις τῆς Ἰταλίας καὶ
ποταμός. Πολύβιος δ᾽ ἐν τῷ ιγ´ Τεμέσειαν τὴν πόλιν
καλεῖ.

4   Ἀλλαρία, πόλις τῆς Κρήτης, Πολύβιος τρισκαιδεκάτῃ. τὸ ἐθνικὸν Ἀλλαριάτης, ὡς αὐτός φησιν.

5   Ἰλαττία, πόλις Κρήτης, Πολύβιος τρισκαιδεκάτῳ.

6   Σίβυρτος, πόλις Κρήτης. τὸ ἐθνικὸν Σιβύρτιος, ὡς
Πολύβιος ἐν τρισκαιδεκάτῳ.

7   Ἀδράνη, πόλις Θρᾴκης . . . Πολύβιος δὲ διὰ τοῦ η
τὴν μέσην λέγει ἐν τρισκαιδεκάτῃ, Ἀδρήνη.

---

[20] Oil of myrrh or cinnamon.   [21] The island of Bahrain.
Seleucia is the city on the Tigris, the eastern capital of the
Seleucids. RE Seleukeia 1149–1184 (M. Streck).

gifts the gods had bestowed on them, perpetual peace and freedom. The king, when the letter had been interpreted to him, said that he granted their request. . . .

When their freedom had been established, the Gerraeans passed a decree honoring Antiochus with the gift of five hundred talents of silver, a thousand talents of frankincense, and two hundred talents of the so-called stacte.[20] He then sailed to the island of Tylus[21] and left for Seleucia. The spices were from the Persian Gulf.

10.1 Badiza, city among the Bruttii,[22] Polybius Book 13.

10.2 Lampetia, city among the Bruttii,[23] Polybius Book 13.

10.3 Tamese is a city and a river in Italy. Polybius in Book 13 calls the city Temesia.[24]

10.4 Allaria, a city in Crete.[25] Polybius Book 13. The ethnic is Allariates as he himself says.

10.5 Ilattia, a city in Crete.[26] Polybius Book 13.

10.6 Sibyrtos, a city in Crete.[27] The ethnic is Sibyrtios as Polybius says in Book 13.

10.7 Adrane, a city in Thracia.[28] . . . Polybius, however, calls her Adrene in Book 13.

---

[22] Probably Livy's Baesidiae, 30.19.10, site unknown.

[23] Clampetia in Livy 29.38.1, modern Amantia.

[24] *RE* Temesa 459–460 (H. Philipp). Events in 10.1–3 are from those in Italy in 205 or 204.   [25] A decree of the city from ca. 203/2 shows it under King Philip's control; see K. Rigsby, *Asylia. Territorial Inviolability in the Hellenistic World* (Berkeley 1996), 312, no. 151. See further *IC* 2, pp. 1–8.

[26] Not otherwise known.   [27] In fact Sybrita, which also granted Teos inviolability ca. 203/2; Rigsby (10.4), 301, no. 141. See also *IC* 2, pp. 289–298.   [28] Mentioned by Theopompus, *FGrH* 115 F 360; its site is unknown.

8   Ἄρειον πεδίον . . . ἔστι καὶ Θρᾴκης ἔρημον πεδίον
χαμαιοετῆ δένδρα ἔχον, ὡς Πολύβιος τρισκαιδεκάτῃ.

9   Δίγηροι, ἔθνος Θρᾴκιον, Πολύβιος ιγ΄.

10   Καβύλη, πόλις Θρᾴκης οὐ πόρρω τῆς τῶν Ἀστῶν
χώρας. Πολύβιος τρισκαιδεκάτῃ.

11   Μελίτουσσα, πόλις Ἰλλυρίας. Πολύβιος τρισκαιδεκάτῳ.

10.8 Areion Pedion.[29] . . . There is also in Thracia a barren plain *(Eremon Pedion)* with narrow trees, Polybius Book 13.

10.9 Digeroi, a Thracian people,[30] Polybius Book 13.

10.10 Cabyle, a Thracian city,[31] not far from the land of the Asti, Polybius Book 13.

10.11 Melitussa, a city in Illyria, Polybius Book 13.

[From the place-names quoted from this book it seems that it dealt chiefly with the war in Bruttium against Hannibal just before he left Italy with Cretan affairs and with a war waged by Philip in Thrace.]

[29] "Plain of Ares," unknown.

[30] These are the *Digerri* of Plin. *HN* 4.40. *RE* Digerri 484 (E. Oberhummer).

[31] Founded by Philip II, who settled criminals there; evidence in Theopompus, *FGrH* 115 F 220 and *RE* Kabyle 1455–1456 (E. Oberhummer). The Asti are a Thracian people, their center was Bizye, today Vize. On the Asti see A. Avram, *CRAI* 2003, 1190–1193.

FRAGMENTA LIBRI XIV

I. EX PROOEMIO

1a. Ὅτι φησὶν ὁ Πολύβιος περὶ ἑαυτοῦ καὶ περὶ τῆς τῶν βίβλων ὑποθετικῆς ἐξηγήσεως· Ἴσως μὲν οὖν ἐπὶ πάσαις ταῖς ὀλυμπιάσιν αἱ προεκθέσεις τῶν πράξεων εἰς ἐπίστασιν ἄγουσι τοὺς ἐντυγχάνοντας καὶ διὰ τὸ πλῆθος καὶ διὰ τὸ μέγεθος τῶν γεγονότων, ὡς ἂν ὑπὸ μίαν σύνοψιν ἀγομένων τῶν ἐξ ὅλης τῆς οἰκουμένης

2 ἔργων· οὐ μὴν <ἀλλὰ> τὰ κατὰ ταύτην τὴν ὀλυμπιάδα μάλιστα νομίζω συνεπιστήσειν τοὺς ἀναγινώσκοντας διὰ τὸ πρῶτον μὲν τοὺς κατὰ τὴν Ἰταλίαν καὶ Λιβύην πολέμους ἐν τούτοις τοῖς χρόνοις εἰληφέναι τὴν συν- τέλειαν· ὑπὲρ ὧν τίς οὐκ ἂν ἱστορῆσαι βουληθείη ποία τις ἡ καταστροφὴ καὶ τί τὸ τέλος αὐτῶν ἐγένετο;

3 φύσει γὰρ πάντες ἄνθρωποι, κἂν ὁλοσχερῶς <παρα>δέχωνται τὰ κατὰ μέρος ἔργα καὶ λόγους,

4 ὅμως ἑκάστων τὸ τέλος ἱμείρουσι μαθεῖν· πρὸς δὲ τούτοις συμβαίνει καὶ τὰς προαιρέσεις τῶν βασιλέων ἐκφανεστάτας γεγονέναι κατὰ τοὺς αὐτοὺς χρόνους· ἃ γὰρ πρότερον ἐλέγετο περὶ αὐτῶν, τότε σαφῶς ἐπ- εγνώσθη πάντα παρὰ πᾶσι καὶ τοῖς μηδ᾽ ὅλως ἐθέ-

5 λουσι πολυπραγμονεῖν. διὸ καὶ βουλόμενοι κατ᾽ ἀξίαν

FRAGMENTS OF BOOK XIV

I. FROM THE PREFACE

1a. Perhaps it is true that in all Olympiads the introductory survey of events arrests the attention of the reader, owing to their number and importance, the actions of the whole world being brought under one point of view. But I think the events of this Olympiad[1] will have a peculiar power of doing this. For in the first place it was during this Olympiad that the wars in Italy and Africa were brought to an end, wars the final outcome of which who will not be curious to learn? For everyone naturally, although he may completely accept our account of particular actions and speeches, still always longs to know the end. Besides this, the political tendencies of the kings[2] were clearly revealed during these years. For all that had been hitherto a matter of gossip about them now became clearly known to everyone, even to those who were not at all disposed to be curious. For this reason, as I wish to give such an account of the

---

[1] Ol. 144 = 204/200.

[2] P. seems to think primarily of the so-called secret pact between Antiochus the Great and Philip V, on which he will speak at 15.20.2–6.

τῶν ἔργων ποιήσασθαι τὴν ἐξήγησιν, οὐ τὰς ἐκ τῶν
δυεῖν ἐτῶν πράξεις κατατετάχαμεν εἰς μίαν βύβλον,
καθάπερ ἐν τοῖς πρὸ τούτων ἀποδεδώκαμεν.

II. RES A SCIPIONE IN
AFRICA GESTAE

1. Οἱ μὲν οὖν ὕπατοι περὶ ταύτας ἐγίνοντο τὰς
2 πράξεις, ὁ δὲ Πόπλιος ἐν τῇ Λιβύῃ κατὰ τὴν παραχειμασίαν πυνθανόμενος ἐξαρτύειν στόλον τοὺς Καρχηδονίους, ἐγίνετο μὲν καὶ περὶ ταύτην τὴν παρασκευήν, οὐχ ἧττον δὲ καὶ περὶ τὴν τῆς Ἰτύκης
3 πολιορκίαν. οὐ μὴν οὐδὲ τῆς κατὰ τὸν Σόφακα τελέως
ἐλπίδος ἀφίστατο, διεπέμπετο δὲ συνεχῶς διὰ τὸ μὴ
πολὺ ἀφεστάναι τὰς δυνάμεις ἀλλήλων, πεπεισμένος
μετακαλέσειν αὐτὸν ἀπὸ τῆς τῶν Καρχηδονίων συμ-
4 μαχίας. οὐ γὰρ ἀπεγίνωσκε καὶ τῆς παιδίσκης αὐτὸν
ἤδη κόρον ἔχειν, δι' ἣν εἵλετο τὰ Καρχηδονίων, καὶ
καθόλου τῆς πρὸς τοὺς Φοίνικας φιλίας διά τε τὴν
φυσικὴν τῶν Νομάδων ἀψικορίαν καὶ διὰ τὴν πρός τε
5 τοὺς θεοὺς καὶ τοὺς ἀνθρώπους ἀθεσίαν. ὧν δὲ περὶ
πολλὰ τῇ διανοίᾳ καὶ ποικίλας ἔχων ἐλπίδας ὑπὲρ τοῦ
μέλλοντος διὰ τὸ καταρρωδεῖν τὸν ἔξω κίνδυνον τῷ
πολλαπλασίους εἶναι τοὺς ὑπεναντίους, ἐπελάβετό
6 τινος ἀφορμῆς τοιαύτης. τῶν γὰρ διαπεμπομένων
πρὸς τὸν Σόφακά τινες ἀνήγγειλαν αὐτῷ διότι συμ-

---

3 Of 203; *MRR* 1.310.   4 Last mentioned 11.24a.4.

facts as their importance deserves, I have not comprised the events of two years in one book as was my practice in previous cases.

II. SCIPIO IN AFRICA

1. The consuls,[3] then, were engaged in these matters, but Publius Scipio, who was in winter quarters in Africa, hearing that the Carthaginians were getting a fleet ready, occupied himself in making his own naval preparations, but continued to prosecute nonetheless the siege of Utica. Nor did he entirely abandon his hope of winning over Syphax,[4] but sent frequent messages to him, their armies being at no great distance from each other, feeling sure of inducing him to abandon the Carthaginian alliance. He thought it indeed not at all unlikely that he had already grown tired of the girl[5] for whose sake he had chosen the cause of the Carthaginians, and tired generally of his friendship for Phoenicians, as Scipio well knew the natural tendency of the Numidians to grow disgusted with what pleased them and how lightly they always break their faith to gods and men alike. At present his mind was much distracted and agitated by various apprehensions, as he feared a battle in the open country owing to the enemy's superiority in numbers, and he gladly availed himself of the following occasion when it offered itself. Some of his messengers to Syphax reported that the Carthagin-

204–203
B.C.

---

[5] Sophoniba. Her father was Hasdrubal, son of Gisgo. She was engaged to Massanissa but married to Syphax. *RE* Sophoniba 1099–1100 (U. Kahrstedt), L.-M. Günther, *Studia Phoenicia* 16 (*Festschrift W. Huß*), 2009, 289–309.

βαίνει τοὺς μὲν Καρχηδονίους ἐκ παντοδαπῶν ξύλων
καὶ φυλλάδος ἄνευ γῆς ἐν τῇ παραχειμασίᾳ κατ-
7 εσκευακέναι τὰς σκηνάς, τῶν δὲ Νομάδων τοὺς μὲν ἐξ
ἀρχῆς ἐκ καλάμων, τοὺς δ᾽ ἐ<πι>συναγομένους ἐκ τῶν
πόλεων κατὰ τὸ παρὸν ἐξ αὐτῆς τῆς φυλλάδος σκηνο-
ποιεῖσθαι, τοὺς μὲν ἐντός, τοὺς δὲ πλείους αὐτῶν ἐκτὸς
8 τῆς τάφρου καὶ τοῦ χάρακος. νομίσας οὖν ὁ Πόπλιος
παραδοξοτάτην μὲν τοῖς πολεμίοις, πραγματικωτάτην
δὲ σφίσιν εἶναι τὴν διὰ τοῦ πυρὸς ἐπιβολήν, ἐγένετο
9 περὶ ταύτην τὴν κατασκευήν. ὁ δὲ Σόφαξ ἐν ταῖς πρὸς
τὸν Πόπλιον διαποστολαῖς ἀεί πως ἐπὶ ταύτην κατ-
ήντα τὴν γνώμην ὅτι δέοι Καρχηδονίους μὲν ἐκ τῆς
Ἰταλίας ἀπαλλάττεσθαι, Ῥωμαίους δὲ παραπλησίως
ἐκ τῆς Λιβύης, τὰ δὲ μεταξὺ τούτων ἔχειν ἀμφοτέρους
10 ὡς τότε κατεῖχον. ὧν ὁ Πόπλιος ἀκούων ἐν τοῖς πρὸ
τοῦ χρόνοις οὐδαμῶς ἀνείχετο· τότε δὲ τῷ Νομάδι
βραχεῖαν ἔμφασιν ἐποιήσατο διὰ τῶν ἀποστελλομένων ὡς οὐκ ἀδυνάτου τῆς ἐπιβολῆς οὔσης, ἧς ἐπι-
11 βάλλεται. δι᾽ οὗ συνέβη τὸν Σόφακα κουφισθέντα
12 πολλαπλασίως ἐπιρρωσθῆναι πρὸς τὴν ἐπιπλοκήν. οὗ
γινομένου πλείους ἦσαν οἱ διαπεμπόμενοι καὶ πλεο-
νάκις· ἔστι δ᾽ ὅτε καί τινας ἡμέρας ἔμενον παρ᾽
13 ἀλλήλοις ἀπαρατηρήτως. ἐν αἷς ὁ Πόπλιος ἀεί τινας
μὲν τῶν πραγματικῶν, οὓς δὲ καὶ στρατιωτικῶν,
ῥυπῶντας καὶ ταπεινούς, εἰς δουλικὰς ἐσθῆτας δια-
σκευάζων, μετὰ τῶν ἀποστελλομένων ἐξέπεμπε χάριν
τοῦ τὰς προσόδους καὶ τὰς εἰσόδους τὰς εἰς ἑκατέραν
τὴν παρεμβολὴν ἀσφαλῶς ἐξερευνῆσαι καὶ κατοπτεῦ-

ians in their winter camp had made their huts from all kinds of wood and branches without any mixture of earth, that the first Numidians to arrive had constructed theirs with reeds, while the others who kept joining the army from the cities had used nothing but branches for the present, some of them being encamped inside but most outside the trench and palisade. Scipio, therefore, thinking that an attempt to fire the camp would be a complete surprise for the enemy and very serviceable to himself, began to take the necessary measures. Syphax in his communications with Scipio always kept harking back to the opinion that the Carthaginians ought to evacuate Italy and the Romans do the same as regards Africa, each nation continuing to occupy the points they held between these two countries. Scipio had previously refused entirely to listen to this proposal, but he now ordered his messengers to throw out slight hints to the Numidian prince that the attainment of this end was not beyond the bounds of possibility. Syphax was very much relieved in consequence and became much more disposed than he had been to engage in parleys, the consequence being that the messengers became more numerous and their visits more frequent, some of them at times spending several days in the hostile camp without any objection being made. Scipio on such occasions used to send in the company of his envoys certain expert observers and certain of his officers, looking mean and dirty fellows, disguised as they were in the habit of slaves, with the object of exploring and inspecting undisturbed the ap-

14 σαι. δύο γὰρ ἦσαν στρατοπεδεῖαι, μία μὲν ἦν
Ἀσδρούβας εἶχε μετὰ πεζῶν τρισμυρίων καὶ τρισ-
χιλίων ἱππέων, ἄλλη δὲ περὶ δέκα σταδίους ἀφεστῶ-
σα ταύτης, ἡ τῶν Νομάδων, ἱππεῖς μὲν εἰς μυρίους
15 ἔχουσα, πεζοὺς δὲ περὶ πεντακισμυρίους. ἡ δὴ καὶ
μᾶλλον εὐέφοδος ἦν καὶ τὰς σκηνὰς εἶχε τελέως
εὐφυεῖς πρὸς ἐμπυρισμὸν διὰ ⟨τὸ⟩ τοὺς Νομάδας, ὡς
ἀρτίως εἶπον, μὴ διὰ ξύλων μηδὲ διὰ γῆς, ἁπλῶς δὲ
κάνναις καὶ καλάμοις χρῆσθαι πρὸς τὰς σκηνοποιίας.

2. Ἐπειδὴ δὲ τὰ μὲν τῆς ἐαρινῆς ὥρας ὑπέφαινεν
ἤδη, τῷ δὲ Σκιπίωνι πάντα διηρεύνητο πρὸς τὴν
προειρημένην ἐπιβολὴν τὰ κατὰ τοὺς ὑπεναντίους,
2 τὰς μὲν νῆας καθεῖλκε καὶ μηχανὰς κατεσκεύαζε ταύταις ὡς πολιορκήσων ἐκ θαλάττης τὴν Ἰτύκην, τοῖς δὲ
3 πεζοῖς, οὖσιν ὡς δισχιλίοις, κατελάβετο πάλιν τὸν
ὑπὲρ τὴν πόλιν κείμενον λόφον, καὶ τοῦτον ὠχυροῦτο
4 καὶ διετάφρευε πολυτελῶς, τοῖς μὲν ὑπεναντίοις ποιῶν
φαντασίαν ὡς τοῦτο πράττων τῆς πολιορκίας ἕνεκα,
τῇ δ' ἀληθείᾳ βουλόμενος ἐφεδρεύειν τοῖς κατὰ τὸν
τῆς πράξεως καιρόν, ἵνα μὴ τῶν στρατοπέδων ἐκ τῆς
παρεμβολῆς χωρισθέντων οἱ τὴν Ἰτύκην παραφυλάτ-
τοντες στρατιῶται τολμήσαιεν ἐξελθόντες ἐκ τῆς
πόλεως ἐγχειρεῖν τῷ χάρακι διὰ τὸ σύνεγγυς εἶναι,
5 καὶ πολιορκεῖν τοὺς φυλάττοντας. ταῦτα δὲ παρασκευ-
αζόμενος ἅμα διεπέμπετο πρὸς τὸν Σόφακα, πυνθανόμενος, ἐὰν συγχωρῇ τοῖς παρακαλουμένοις, εἰ καὶ τοῖς
Καρχηδονίοις ἔσται ταῦτα κατὰ νοῦν καὶ μὴ πάλιν

proaches and the entrances of both camps. For there were two of them, one occupied by Hasdrubal with thirty thousand foot and three thousand horse, and another at a distance of ten stades belonging to the Numidians and containing about ten thousand horse and fifty thousand foot.[6] The latter was the easiest to attack and the huts very suitable for setting on fire, since the Numidians, as I just said, used neither wood nor earth for their huts, but only reeds and matting.

2. As soon as there were signs of the approach of spring, Scipio having now completed all the inquiries necessary for the above design against the enemy, launched his ships and constructed siege machines to place on them as if he were about to blockade Utica from the sea. With his infantry, who numbered about two thousand, he again occupied the hill situated above the town and spared no expense in fortifying this hill and digging a moat round it, giving the enemy the idea that he did so for the purpose of the siege, but in reality desiring to secure himself from possible danger on the day of his enterprise; for he feared lest when his legions had left their camp the garrison of Utica might venture on a sortie, and falling on the camp, which was close by, besiege the force left to defend it. While making these preparations he sent a message to Syphax to inquire, on the supposition that the proposed terms met with his own approval, if they would also be agreeable to the Carthaginians and if they could be trusted not to say again that

6 These numbers are much inflated; other authors give smaller ones.

ἐκεῖνοι φήσουσι βουλεύσεσθαι περὶ τῶν συγχωρου-
6 μένων. ἅμα δὲ τούτοις προσενετείλατο τοῖς πρεσβευταῖς μὴ πρότερον ὡς αὑτὸν ἀπιέναι πρὶν ἢ λαβεῖν
7 ἀπόκρισιν ὑπὲρ τούτων. ὧν ἀφικομένων διακούσας ὁ
Νομὰς ἐπείσθη διότι πρὸς τὸ συντελεῖν ἐστι τὰς
διαλύσεις ὁ Σκιπίων, ἔκ τε τοῦ φάναι τοὺς πρέσβεις
μὴ πρότερον ἀπαλλαγήσεσθαι πρὶν ἢ λαβεῖν παρ᾽
αὐτοῦ τὰς ἀποκρίσεις, ἔκ τε τοῦ διευλαβεῖσθαι τὴν
8 τῶν Καρχηδονίων συγκατάθεσιν. διὸ καὶ πρὸς μὲν
τὸν Ἀσδρούβαν ἐξ αὐτῆς ἔπεμπε, διασαφῶν τὰ γινόμενα καὶ παρακαλῶν δέχεσθαι τὴν εἰρήνην, αὐτὸς δὲ
ῥᾳθύμως διῆγε, καὶ τοὺς ἐπισυναγομένους Νομάδας
9 ἐκτὸς εἴα τῆς παρεμβολῆς αὐτοῦ κατασκηνοῦν. ὁ δὲ
Πόπλιος κατὰ μὲν τὴν ἐπίφασιν ἐποίει τὸ παραπλήσιον, κατὰ δὲ τὴν ἀλήθειαν ⟨ἐν⟩ τοῖς μάλιστα
10 περὶ τὰς παρασκευὰς ἦν. ἐπειδὴ δὲ παρὰ μὲν τῶν
Καρχηδονίων τῷ Σόφακι διεσαφήθη συντελεῖν τὰ
κατὰ τὰς συνθήκας, ὁ δὲ Νομὰς περιχαρὴς ὢν εἶπε
τοῖς πρεσβευταῖς ὑπὲρ τούτων, εὐθέως οἱ πρέσβεις
ἀπῄεσαν εἰς τὴν ἰδίαν παρεμβολήν, μηνύσοντες τῷ
11 Ποπλίῳ τὰ πραχθέντα παρὰ τοῦ βασιλέως. ὧν ἀκούσας ὁ τῶν Ῥωμαίων στρατηγὸς αὖθις ἐκ ποδὸς ἔπεμπε πρέσβεις, δηλώσοντας τῷ Σόφακι διότι συμβαίνει
τὸν μὲν Πόπλιον εὐδοκεῖν καὶ σπουδάζειν ὑπὲρ τῆς
εἰρήνης, τοὺς δ᾽ ἐν τῷ συνεδρίῳ διαφέρεσθαι καὶ
12 φάναι διαμένειν ἐπὶ τῶν ὑποκειμένων· οἳ καὶ παρα-
13 γενόμενοι διεσάφησαν ταῦτα τῷ Νομάδι. τὴν δ᾽ ἀπο-
στολὴν ταύτην ὁ Σκιπίων ἐποιήσατο χάριν τοῦ μὴ

they would further consider before accepting what he was ready to concede. He also instructed his envoys not to return to him before receiving an answer to this question. When they arrived and Syphax had received the message, he felt convinced that Scipio was determined to conclude the treaty, both because the envoys had told him they would not return without an answer and because of the anxiety shown to make sure of the consent of the Carthaginians. So he sent off at once to Hasdrubal informing him of what had occurred and begging him to accept peace, while he himself passed his time at his ease and allowed the Numidians who kept on joining him to encamp outside his fortified camp. Scipio pretended to do the same, but as a fact was making every possible preparation for his attack. When Syphax had once been instructed by the Carthaginians to conclude the peace, and overjoyed at this, spoke to the envoys on the matter, they at once left for their own camp to tell Scipio the result of the king's action. The Roman commander, on hearing of it, lost no time in sending other envoys to announce to Syphax that Scipio approved of peace and was earnestly working for it,[7] but that members of the council were of a different opinion, maintaining that matters should rest as they were. The envoys went to Syphax and informed him to this effect. Scipio dispatched this embassy in order not to appear to have broken the

---

[7] A lie, as Scipio was spying and preparing a surprise attack while pretending to negotiate. This is very similar to what Quintus Marcius Philippus did to King Perseus in 172 and considered to be offensive (see n. on 13.3.8).

δόξαι παρασπονδεῖν, ἐὰν ἔτι μενούσης τῆς ὑπὲρ τῶν διαλύσεων ἐπικηρυκείας πρὸς ἀλλήλους πράξῃ τι τῶν
14 πολεμικῶν ἔργων. γενομένης δὲ τῆς ἀπορρήσεως ταύτης ἅπαν τὸ γινόμενον ἀνεπίληπτον ἕξειν ὑπέλαβε τὴν προαίρεσιν.

3. Ὁ δὲ Σόφαξ ταῦτα διακούσας ἔφερε μὲν δυσχερῶς διὰ τὸ προκατηλπικέναι περὶ τῶν διαλύσεων, συνῄει δὲ πρὸς τὸν Ἀσδρούβαν εἰς λόγους, καὶ διεσάφει τὰ παρὰ τῶν Ῥωμαίων αὐτῷ προσαγγελλόμενα.
2 περὶ ὧν πολλὰ διαπορήσαντες ἐβουλεύοντο πῶς σφίσι καθήκει χρῆσθαι τοῖς ἑξῆς πράγμασι, πλεῖστον ἀπέχοντες ταῖς ἐννοίαις καὶ ταῖς ἐπιβολαῖς τοῦ μέλ-
3 λοντος· περὶ φυλακῆς μὲν γὰρ ἢ τοῦ πείσεσθαί τι δεινὸν οὐδ' ἡντινοῦν εἶχον πρόληψιν, περὶ δὲ τοῦ δρᾶσαί τι καὶ προκαλέσασθαι τοὺς πολεμίους εἰς ὁμαλὸν τόπον πολλή τις ἦν αὐτῶν ὁρμὴ καὶ προθυμία.
4 Πόπλιος δὲ κατὰ τὸν καιρὸν τοῦτον τοῖς μὲν πολλοῖς ὑπεδείκνυε διά τε τῆς παρασκευῆς καὶ τῶν παραγ-
5 γελμάτων ὡς κατὰ τῆς Ἰτύκης ἔχων πρᾶξιν, τῶν δὲ χιλιάρχων τοὺς ἐπιτηδειοτάτους καὶ πιστοτάτους καλέσας περὶ μέσον ἡμέρας ἐξέθηκε τὴν ἐπιβολήν, καὶ παρήγγειλε δειπνοποιησαμένους καθ' ὥραν ἐξάγειν τὰ στρατόπεδα πρὸ τοῦ χάρακος, ἐπειδὰν κατὰ τὸν ἐθισμὸν οἱ σαλπιγκταὶ σημαίνωσιν ἅμα πάντες·
6 ἔστι γὰρ ἔθος Ῥωμαίοις κατὰ τὸν τοῦ δείπνου καιρὸν τοὺς βυκανητὰς καὶ σαλπιγκτὰς πάντας σημαίνειν παρὰ τὴν τοῦ στρατηγοῦ σκηνήν, χάριν τοῦ τὰς νυκτερινὰς φυλακὰς κατὰ τὸν καιρὸν τοῦτον ἵστασθαι

truce if, while formal negotiations for peace were still in progress, he committed any hostile act. But after having made this declaration he considered that whatever happened no one could find fault with his conduct.

3. Syphax, on hearing this, was no little vexed as he had made up his mind that peace was assured, but he now met Hasdrubal and communicated to him the message he had received from the Romans. After much discussion of it they fell to considering how they should now deal with the situation, being very far both in their apprehensions and designs from any suspicion of what was actually about to happen. For they never had the least thought of taking any precaution for their security or of the likelihood of any disaster, but they were very eager and anxious to take some active steps and to challenge the enemy to battle on level ground. Scipio, in the meanwhile, by his preparations and the orders he issued gave his soldiery to understand that he was about to make an attempt to seize Utica by surprise, but summoning the ablest and most trusty of his tribunes about midday, and disclosing his plan ordered them to get their supper early and then lead the legions out of the camp, after the trumpeters had all sounded the retreat as usual. For it is the custom among the Romans at supper time for the trumpeters and buglers to sound their instruments outside the general's tent as a signal that it is time to set the night-watches at their several stations. After this,

7 κατὰ τοὺς ἰδίους τόπους. μετὰ δὲ ταῦτα τοὺς κατασκόπους ἀνακαλεσάμενος, οὓς ἐτύγχανε διαπεμπόμενος εἰς τὰ τῶν πολεμίων στρατόπεδα, συνέκρινε καὶ
διηρεύνα τὰ λεγόμενα περί τε τῶν προσβάσεων καὶ
τῶν εἰσόδων τῶν εἰς τὰς παρεμβολάς, χρώμενος ἐπι-
κριτῇ τῶν λεγομένων καὶ συμβούλῳ Μασαννάσᾳ διὰ
τὴν τῶν τόπων ἐμπειρίαν.

4. Ἐπειδὴ δὲ πάντ' ἦν εὐτρεπῆ τὰ πρὸς τὴν χρείαν
αὐτῷ τὴν ἐνεστῶσαν, ἀπολιπὼν τοὺς ἱκανοὺς καὶ τοὺς
ἐπιτηδείους ἐπὶ τῆς παρεμβολῆς, ἀναλαβὼν τὰς δυνάμεις προῆγεν ἄρτι ληγούσης τῆς πρώτης φυλακῆς·
περὶ γὰρ ἑξήκοντα σταδίους ἀπεῖχον οἱ πολέμιοι.

2 συνεγγίσας δὲ τοῖς πολεμίοις περὶ τρίτην φυλακὴν
λήγουσαν, Γαΐῳ μὲν Λαιλίῳ καὶ Μασαννάσᾳ τοὺς
ἡμίσεις ἀπονείμας τῶν στρατιωτῶν καὶ πάντας τοὺς
Νομάδας ἐπέταξε ποιεῖσθαι τὴν προσβολὴν πρὸς τὸν

3 τοῦ Σόφακος χάρακα, παρακαλέσας ἄνδρας ἀγαθοὺς
γενέσθαι καὶ μηδὲν εἰκῇ πράττειν, σαφῶς εἰδότας ὅτι,
καθ' ὅσον ἐμποδίζει καὶ κωλύει τὰ τῆς ὁράσεως τὸ
σκότος, κατὰ τοσοῦτον δεῖ συνεκπληροῦν τῇ διανοίᾳ

4 καὶ τῇ τόλμῃ τὰς νυκτερινὰς ἐπιβολάς· αὐτὸς δὲ τὴν
λοιπὴν στρατιὰν ἀναλαβὼν ἐποιεῖτο τὴν ὁρμὴν ἐπὶ
τὸν Ἀσδρούβαν. ἦν δ' αὐτῷ συλλελογισμένον μὴ
πρότερον ἐγχειρεῖν, ἕως ἂν οἱ περὶ τὸν Λαίλιον πρῶ-

5 τοι τὸ πῦρ ἐμβάλωσι τοῖς πολεμίοις. οὗτος μὲν τοιαύτας ἔχων ἐπινοίας βάδην ἐποιεῖτο τὴν πορείαν· οἱ
δὲ περὶ τὸν Λαίλιον εἰς δύο μέρη σφᾶς αὐτοὺς διελόν-

6 τες ἅμα προσέβαλλον τοῖς πολεμίοις. τῆς δὲ τῶν

calling the spies whom he used to send to the enemy's camps, he questioned them closely and compared the accounts they gave of the approaches and entrances of the camps, letting Massanissa[8] decide, and following his advice owing to his personal knowledge of the ground.

4. When all was in readiness for his present enterprise, he left a sufficient body of troops suitable for the purpose to guard the camp and advanced with the rest of his army just at the end of the first watch, the enemy being at a distance of sixty stades. When toward the end of the third watch he approached them he placed half of his legionaries and all the Numidians under the command of Gaius Laelius[9] and Massanissa with orders to attack the camp of Syphax, exhorting them to behave like brave men and to do nothing rashly, as they well knew that the more the darkness in night attacks hinders and impedes the sight, the more must one supply the place of actual vision by skill and daring. He himself, with the rest of his army, advanced to attack Hasdrubal. He had made up his mind not to deliver his attack before Laelius had set fire to the other hostile camp, and, therefore, this being his purpose, marched at a slow pace. Laelius and Massanissa dividing their forces into two attacked the enemy simultaneously. The huts hav-

---

[8] In 206 still with the Carthaginians in Spain (Livy 28.13.6), now in Scipio's camp.

[9] See n. on 10.3.2.

σκηνῶν διαθέσεως οἷον ἐπίτηδες πρὸς ἐμπυρισμὸν
κατεσκευασμένης, καθάπερ ἀνώτερον εἶπον, ὡς οἱ
προηγούμενοι τὸ πῦρ ἐνέβαλλον, κατανεμηθὲν εἰς τὰς
πρώτας σκηνὰς εὐθέως ἀβοήθητον ἐποίει τὸ κακὸν διά
τε τὴν συνέχειαν τῶν σκηνῶν καὶ διὰ τὸ πλῆθος τῆς
7   ὑποκειμένης ὕλης. ὁ μὲν οὖν Λαίλιος ἔχων ἐφεδρείας
τάξιν ἔμενεν· ὁ δὲ Μασαννάσας εἰδὼς τοὺς τόπους,
καθ᾽ οὓς ἔμελλον οἱ φεύγοντες τὸ πῦρ ποιήσασθαι τὴν
ἀποχώρησιν, ἐν τούτοις ἐπέστησε τοὺς αὑτοῦ στρα-
8   τιώτας. τῶν δὲ Νομάδων οὐδεὶς ἁπλῶς συνυπώπτευσε
τὸ γινόμενον, οὐδ᾽ αὐτὸς ὁ Σόφαξ, ἀλλ᾽ ὡς αὐτομάτως
ἐμπεπρησμένου τοῦ χάρακος, ταύτην ἔσχον τὴν δι-
9   άληψιν. ὅθεν ἀνυπονοήτως οἱ μὲν ἐκ τῶν ὕπνων, οἱ δ᾽
ἀκμὴν ἔτι μεθυσκόμενοι καὶ πίνοντες ἐξεπήδων ἐκ τῶν
10   σκηνῶν. καὶ πολλοὶ μὲν ὑφ᾽ αὑτῶν περὶ τὰς τοῦ
χάρακος ἐξόδους συνεπατήθησαν, πολλοὶ δὲ περι-
καταληφθέντες ὑπὸ τῆς φλογὸς κατεπρήσθησαν· οἱ δὲ
καὶ διαφυγόντες τὴν φλόγα, πάντες εἰς τοὺς πολεμίους ἐμπίπτοντες, οὔθ᾽ ὃ πάσχουσιν οὔθ᾽ ὃ ποιοῦσι
γινώσκοντες διεφθείροντο.

5. Κατὰ δὲ τὸν καιρὸν τοῦτον οἱ Καρχηδόνιοι,
θεωροῦντες τὸ πλῆθος τοῦ πυρὸς καὶ τὸ μέγεθος τῆς
ἐξαιρομένης φλογός, ὑπολαβόντες αὐτομάτως ἀν-
ῆφθαι τὸν τῶν Νομάδων χάρακα, τινὲς μὲν ἐβοήθουν
2   ἐξ αὐτῆς, οἱ δὲ λοιποὶ πάντες ἐκτρέχοντες ἐκ τῆς
παρεμβολῆς ἄνοπλοι συνίσταντο πρὸ τῆς ἰδίας
3   στρατοπεδείας, ἐκπλαγεῖς ὄντες ἐπὶ τοῖς γινομένοις. ὁ
δὲ Σκιπίων, τῶν πραγμάτων ὡς ἂν εἰ κατ᾽ εὐχὴν αὐτῷ

ing been, as I stated above, almost specially constructed
for the purpose of catching fire, once the front ranks of
the Romans had set the fire alight it spread at once over
the first row, and made the evil irremediable owing to the
closeness of the huts to each other and the quantity of the
fuel it fed on. Laelius remained to cover the operation, and
Massanissa, knowing the places by which those who were
trying to escape from the flames would have to pass, stationed his own men at those spots. Absolutely none of the
Numidians had any suspicion of the actual fact, not even
Syphax, but they all supposed that the camp had caught
fire by accident. So that suspecting nothing, some of them
aroused from sleep and others surprised while still drinking and carousing, they rushed out of their huts. Many
were trampled to death in the passages that led out of the
camp, and many others were caught by the flames and consumed, while all those who escaped from the fire fell into
the midst of the enemy and perished without knowing
what was happening to them or what they were doing.

5. Meanwhile the Carthaginians, when they saw the
strength of the fire and the volume of flame that rose to the
sky, thinking that the Numidian camp had caught fire by
accident, rushed some of them to give assistance, while all
the rest, flocking out of their camp unarmed, stood in front
of it in a state of terror at what was taking place. Scipio,
now that all had gone as well as he could have wished, fell

προχωρησάντων, ἐπιπεσὼν τοῖς ἐξεληλυθόσιν, οὓς
μὲν ἐφόνευεν, οὓς δὲ καταδιώκων ἅμα τὸ πῦρ ἐνέβαλλε
4 ταῖς σκηναῖς. οὗ γενομένου παραπλήσια συνέβαινε
πάσχειν τοὺς Φοίνικας ὑπὸ τοῦ πυρὸς καὶ τῆς ὅλης
5 περιστάσεως τοῖς ἄρτι ῥηθεῖσι περὶ τῶν Νομάδων. οἱ
δὲ περὶ τὸν Ἀσδρούβαν τοῦ μὲν τῷ πυρὶ βοηθεῖν
αὐτόθεν εὐθέως ἀπέστησαν, γνόντες ἐκ τοῦ συμβαίνοντος ὅτι καὶ περὶ τοὺς Νομάδας οὐκ αὐτομάτως,
καθάπερ ὑπέλαβον, ἀλλ᾽ ἐκ τῆς <τῶν> πολεμίων ἐπι-
6 βολῆς καὶ τόλμης ἐγεγόνει τὸ δεινόν· ἐγίνοντο δὲ περὶ
τὸ σῴζειν ἑαυτούς, βραχείας σφίσι καὶ περὶ τοῦτο τὸ
7 μέρος ἐλπίδος ἔτι καταλειπομένης. τό τε γὰρ πῦρ
ταχέως ἐπενέμετο καὶ περιελάμβανε πάντας τοὺς
τόπους, αἵ τε δίοδοι πλήρεις ἦσαν ἵππων, ὑποζυγίων,
ἀνδρῶν, τῶν μὲν ἡμιθνήτων καὶ διεφθαρμένων ὑπὸ
τοῦ πυρός, τῶν δ᾽ ἐξεπτοημένων καὶ παρεστώτων ταῖς
8 διανοίαις, ὥστε καὶ τοῖς ἀνδραγαθεῖν προαιρουμένοις
ἐμπόδια ταῦτα γίνεσθαι, καὶ διὰ τὴν ταραχὴν καὶ
9 σύγχυσιν ἀνέλπιστον εἶναι τὴν σωτηρίαν. παραπλήσια δὲ τούτοις ἦν καὶ τὰ περὶ τὸν Σόφακα καὶ τοὺς
ἄλλους ἡγεμόνας. πλὴν οὗτοι μὲν ἀμφότεροι μετ᾽
10 ὀλίγων ἱππέων ἐξέσωσαν αὑτούς· αἱ δὲ λοιπαὶ μυρι-
άδες ἀνδρῶν, ἵππων, ὑποζυγίων, ἀτυχῶς μὲν καὶ ἐλε-
11 εινῶς ὑπὸ τοῦ πυρὸς ἀπώλλυντο· αἰσχρῶς δὲ καὶ
ἐπονειδίστως ἔνιοι τῶν ἀνδρῶν, τὴν τοῦ πυρὸς βίαν
φεύγοντες, ὑπὸ τῶν πολεμίων διεφθείροντο, χωρὶς οὐ
μόνον τῶν ὅπλων, ἀλλὰ καὶ τῶν ἱματίων, γυμνοὶ
12 φονευόμενοι. καθόλου δὲ πᾶς ἦν ὁ τόπος οἰμωγῆς,

upon those who had come out. Killing some and pursuing others he set their huts also on fire, with the result that the scene of conflagration and general destruction I have just described in the case of the Numidian camp was reproduced in that of the Phoenicians. Hasdrubal at once entirely desisted from any attempt to extinguish the fire, as he knew now from what had befallen him that the calamity that had befallen the Numidians also was not, as they had supposed, the result of chance but was due to the initiative and daring of the enemy. He now thought but of saving himself, and there was very little hope left of even doing this. For the fire spread with great rapidity, and soon covered the whole area of the camp, the passages of which were full of horses, mules, and men, some half-dead and consumed by the flames, and some frenzied and beside themselves, so that even those ready to make a bold effort were prevented by these obstacles, and owing to the confusion and disturbance there was no hope of safety. Syphax, too, and the other officers were in the same plight. The two generals, however, managed to escape with a small body of horse, but of the rest those thousands and thousands of men, horses, and mules met with an unhappy and miserable end in the flames, while some of the men trying to escape the fury of the fire died a disgraceful and dishonorable death at the hands of the enemy, cut down as they were naked, not only without their arms but without their clothes. In a word the whole place was filled with

βοῆς ἀτάκτου, φόβου, ψόφου παρηλλαγμένου, σὺν δὲ
τούτοις πυρὸς ἐνεργοῦ καὶ φλογὸς ὑπερβαλλούσης
13 πλήρης· ὧν ἓν ἱκανὸν [ὃν] ἐκπλῆξαι τὴν ἀνθρωπίνην
φύσιν, μηδ᾽ ὅτι καὶ πάνθ᾽ ὁμοῦ συγκυρήσαντα παρα-
14 δόξως. διὸ καὶ τὸ γεγονὸς οὐδὲ καθ᾽ ὑπερβολὴν εἰ-
κάσαι δυνατὸν οὐδενὶ τῶν ὄντων ἐστίν· οὕτως ὑπερπε-
παίκει τῇ δεινότητι πάσας τὰς προειρημένας πράξεις.
15 ᾗ καὶ πολλῶν καὶ καλῶν διειργασμένων Σκιπίωνι
κάλλιστον εἶναί μοι δοκεῖ τοῦτο τοὔργον καὶ παραβο-
λώτατον τῶν ἐκείνῳ πεπραγμένων. . . .

6. Οὐ μὴν ἀλλὰ τῆς ἡμέρας ἐπιγενομένης, καὶ τῶν
πολεμίων τῶν μὲν ἀπολωλότων, τῶν δὲ προτροπάδην
πεφευγότων, παρακαλέσας τοὺς χιλιάρχους ἐκ ποδὸς
2 ἐπηκολούθει. τὰς μὲν οὖν ἀρχὰς ὁ Καρχηδόνιος ὑπ-
έμενε, καίπερ αὐτῷ προσαγγελίας γενομένης· τοῦτο δ᾽
3 ἐποίει πιστεύων τῇ τῆς πόλεως ὀχυρότητι. μετὰ δὲ
ταῦτα συνθεωρήσας τοὺς ἐγχωρίους στασιάζοντας,
καταπλαγεὶς τὴν ἔφοδον τοῦ Σκιπίωνος, ἔφευγε μετὰ
τῶν διασεσωσμένων· οὗτοι δ᾽ ἦσαν ἱππεῖς μὲν οὐκ
4 ἐλάττους πεντακοσίων, πεζοὶ δὲ περὶ δισχιλίους. οἱ δ᾽
ἐγχώριοι συμφρονήσαντες ἐπέτρεψαν περὶ σφῶν
5 αὐτῶν τοῖς Ῥωμαίοις. ὁ δὲ Πόπλιος τούτων μὲν ἐφεί-
σατο, δύο δὲ τὰς παρακειμένας πόλεις ἐφῆκε τοῖς
στρατοπέδοις διαρπάζειν, καὶ ταῦτα διαπραξάμενος
αὖθις ἐπὶ τὴν ἐξ ἀρχῆς ἐπανήει παρεμβολήν.

6 Οἱ δὲ Καρχηδόνιοι, παλιντρόπου τῆς ἐλπίδος αὐτοῖς ἀποβαινούσης πρὸς τὰς ἐξ ἀρχῆς ἐπιβολάς,

wailing and confused cries, panic fear, strange noises, and above all raging fire and flames that overbore all resistance, things any one of which would be sufficient to strike terror into a human heart, and how much more this extraordinary combination of them all. So it is impossible for any man alive to give a true picture of what happened, no matter how he might exaggerate, so much did it exceed in horror all previous events. Therefore of all the brilliant exploits performed by Scipio this seems to me the most splendid[10] and most adventurous. . . .

6. But when day dawned, and the enemy either had all perished or were in headlong flight, Scipio exhorted his officers and at once started in pursuit. The Carthaginian commander at first remained where he was, although he had received notice of the approach of the Romans; it was his confidence in the strength of the town[11] in which he was that made him act thus. But afterward, when he saw that the inhabitants of the place were disaffected, the prospect of being attacked by Scipio dismayed him and he continued his flight with all those who had escaped, and who consisted of not less than five hundred horse and about two thousand foot. Upon this the inhabitants with one accord surrendered at discretion to the Romans. Scipio spared them, but gave up two of the neighboring towns to his soldiers to pillage and after this returned to his original camp.

The Carthaginians, now that the prospect of success in their original design had been reversed, were deeply de-

[10] P. extols the deed in spite of having reported Scipio's duplicity. It is obvious that he applies standards to Scipio different from those he applies to Philip V (13.3.1–8).

[11] Not identified with certainty.

7 βαρέως ἔφερον τὸ γεγονός· ἐλπίσαντες γὰρ πολιορ-
κήσειν τοὺς Ῥωμαίους συγκλείσαντες εἰς τὴν ἄκραν
τὴν προσοῦσαν τῆς Ἰτύκης, ἐν ᾗ τὴν παραχειμασίαν
ἐποιοῦντο, κατὰ γῆν μὲν τοῖς πεζοῖς στρατεύμασι,
κατὰ θάλατταν δὲ ταῖς ναυτικαῖς δυνάμεσι, καὶ πρὸς

8 τοῦτο πάσας ἡτοιμακότες τὰς παρασκευάς, ἅμα τῷ μὴ
μόνον τῶν ὑπαίθρων οὕτως ἀλόγως καὶ παραδόξως
ἐκχωρῆσαι τοῖς ὑπεναντίοις, ἀλλὰ καὶ τὸν περὶ σφῶν
αὐτῶν καὶ τῆς πατρίδος ὅσον οὐκ ἤδη προσδοκᾶν
κίνδυνον, τελέως ἐκπλαγεῖς ἦσαν καὶ περίφοβοι ταῖς

9 ψυχαῖς. οὐ μὴν ἀλλὰ τῶν πραγμάτων ἀναγκαζόντων
ποιεῖσθαι πρόνοιαν καὶ βουλὴν ὑπὲρ τοῦ μέλλοντος,
ἣν τὸ συνέδριον ἀπορίας καὶ ποικίλων καὶ τεταραγμέ-

10 νων ἐπινοημάτων πλῆρες. οἱ μὲν γὰρ ἔφασαν δεῖν
πέμπειν ἐπὶ τὸν Ἀννίβαν καὶ καλεῖν ἐκ τῆς Ἰταλίας,
ὡς μιᾶς ἔτι καταλειπομένης ἐλπίδος τῆς ἐν ἐκείνῳ τῷ

11 στρατηγῷ καὶ ταῖς μετ' ἐκείνου δυνάμεσιν, οἱ δὲ
διαπρεσβεύεσθαι πρὸς τὸν Πόπλιον ὑπὲρ ἀνοχῶν καὶ
λαλεῖν ὑπὲρ διαλύσεων καὶ συνθηκῶν, ἕτεροι δὲ θαρρεῖν καὶ συνάγειν τὰς δυνάμεις καὶ διαπέμπεσθαι

12 πρὸς τὸν Σόφακα· καὶ γὰρ πλησίον αὐτὸν εἰς τὴν
Ἄββαν ἀποκεχωρηκέναι, συναθροίζειν δὲ τοὺς ἀπὸ
τοῦ κινδύνου διαφυγόντας. καὶ δὴ καὶ τέλος αὕτη τῶν
γνωμῶν ἐπεκράτησεν.

13 Οὗτοι μὲν οὖν τάς τε δυνάμεις ἤθροιζον, ἐκπέμ-
ψαντες τὸν Ἀσδρούβαν, καὶ διεπέμψαντο πρὸς τὸν
Σόφακα, δεόμενοι σφίσι βοηθεῖν καὶ μένειν ἐπὶ τῶν

jected. For they had hoped to shut in the Romans on the cape adjacent to Utica, which they made their winter quarters, besieging them by land with their armies and by sea with their navy and had made all preparations for this purpose; so that now when by a strange and unexpected disaster they had not only been obliged to abandon to the enemy the command of the open country but expected that at any moment they themselves and their city would be in imminent peril, they became thoroughly dismayed and fainthearted. The situation, however, demanded that they should take precautions and deliberate as to the future, and when the senate assembled it was full of perplexity and the most divergent and tumultuary suggestions abounded. Some held that they should send to Hannibal and recall him from Italy, their only remaining hope being in that general and his army, others proposed sending an embassy to Scipio to ask for a truce and speak to him about terms of peace, while others said they should pluck up courage and communicate with Syphax, who had retired to Abba[12] quite near by, and collect the troops who had escaped from the disaster. This was the counsel which finally prevailed.

The Carthaginians, then, began to assemble their forces, dispatching Hasdrubal to do so, and at the same time sent to Syphax entreating him to help them and to remain firm

12 Also unidentified.

ὑποκειμένων κατὰ τὴν ἐξ ἀρχῆς πρόθεσιν, ὡς αὐτίκα
μάλα τοῦ στρατηγοῦ μετὰ τῶν δυνάμεων πρὸς αὐτὸν
συνάψοντος·

7. ὁ δὲ τῶν Ῥωμαίων στρατηγὸς ἐγίνετο μὲν καὶ
περὶ τὴν τῆς Ἰτύκης πολιορκίαν, τὸ δὲ πλεῖον, ἀκούων
ἐπιμένειν τὸν Σόφακα καὶ τοὺς Καρχηδονίους πάλιν
ἀθροίζειν στρατιάν, ἐξῆγε τὰς δυνάμεις καὶ παρενέ-
2 βαλλε πρὸ τῆς Ἰτύκης. ἅμα δὲ καὶ νείμας τῶν λαφύρων ⟨πολλὰ μὲν τῇ στρατιᾷ, τὰ δ' ἀξιολογώτατα
πέμψας εἰς τὴν Ῥώμην⟩ τοὺς μὲν ⟨στρατιώτας οὐκ
ὠφέλησε μεγάλα, τοὺς δ'⟩¹ ἐμπόρους ἐξαπέστειλε . . .
3 λυσιτελῶς· καλῆς γὰρ τῆς ὑπὲρ τῶν ὅλων ἐλπίδος
ὑπογραφομένης ἐκ τοῦ γεγονότος εὐτυχήματος, ἑτοίμως τὴν παροῦσαν ὠφέλειαν οἱ στρατιῶται παρ' οὐδὲν ποιούμενοι διετίθεντο τοῖς ἐμπόροις.

4 Τῷ δὲ βασιλεῖ τῶν Νομάδων καὶ τοῖς φίλοις τὸ μὲν
πρῶτον ἐδόκει κατὰ τὸ συνεχὲς εἰς τὴν οἰκείαν ποι-
5 εῖσθαι τὴν ἀναχώρησιν· τῶν δὲ Κελτιβήρων αὐτοῖς
ἀπαντησάντων περὶ τὴν Ἄββαν, οἵτινες ἐτύγχανον
ὑπὸ τῶν Καρχηδονίων ἐξενολογημένοι, πλείους ὄντες
τῶν τετρακισχιλίων, πιστεύοντες ταῖς χερσὶ ταύταις
οὕτως ἐπέστησαν καὶ βραχύ τι ταῖς ψυχαῖς ἐθάρ-
6 ρησαν. σὺν δὲ τούτοις ἅμα καὶ τῆς παιδίσκης, ἥτις ἦν
θυγάτηρ μὲν Ἀσδρούβου ⟨τοῦ⟩ στρατηγοῦ, γυνὴ δὲ
τοῦ Σόφακος, καθάπερ ἐπάνω προεῖπον, δεομένης καὶ
λιπαρούσης μεῖναι καὶ μὴ καταλιπεῖν ἐν τοιούτοις
καιροῖς τοὺς Καρχηδονίους, ἐπείσθη καὶ προσέσχε
7 τοῖς παρακαλουμένοις ὁ Νομάς. οὐ μικρὰ δὲ καὶ τοὺς

to his first engagements, assuring him that Hasdrubal would at once join him with his army.

7. The Roman general both occupied himself with preparations for the siege of Utica[13] and now, on hearing that Syphax remained faithful and that the Carthaginians were again collecting an army, led out his own forces and encamped before that city. He also at the same time distributed the booty, <much to the army, but sending the best pieces to Rome. He did not enrich the soldiers greatly, but> sent away the merchants with an excellent profit;[14] for as their recent success had made them form a rosy picture of the future, the soldiers attached no value to their actual booty and were very ready to dispose of it to the merchants for a song.

The Numidian prince[15] and his friends had at first decided to continue their retreat and seek their homes, but when they were met near Abba by the Celtiberians who had been hired by the Carthaginians and who numbered over four thousand, the reliance they placed on this additional force made them halt and pluck up a little courage. And when at the same time the young girl,[16] who was, as I have said, the daughter of the general, Hasdrubal, and wife of Syphax, begged and entreated him to remain and not desert the Carthaginians at such a critical time, the Numidian prince suffered himself to be persuaded and yielded to her prayers. The Celtiberians contributed also

[13] Some thirty kilometers northwest of Carthage.
[14] For B-W's supplement see WC 2.431.
[15] Syphax.   [16] Sophoniba; see n. on 1.4.

[1] Suppl. e.g., B-W.

Καρχηδονίους ἐλπίζειν παρεσκεύασαν οἱ Κελτίβηρες·
ἀντὶ μὲν γὰρ τῶν τετρακισχιλίων μυρίους αὐτοὺς
ἀπήγγελλον εἶναι, κατὰ δὲ τοὺς κινδύνους ἀνυπο-
στάτους ὑπάρχειν καὶ ταῖς ψυχαῖς καὶ τοῖς καθοπλι-
8 σμοῖς. ἐκ δὲ ταύτης τῆς φήμης καὶ τῆς χυδαίου καὶ
πανδήμου λαλιᾶς μετεωρισθέντες οἱ Καρχηδόνιοι δι-
πλασίως ἐπερρώσθησαν πρὸς τὸ πάλιν ἀντιποιήσα-
9 σθαι τῶν ὑπαίθρων. καὶ τέλος ἐν ἡμέραις τριάκοντα
περὶ τὰ Μεγάλα πεδία καλούμενα βαλόμενοι χάρακα
συνεστρατοπέδευον ὁμοῦ τοῖς Νομάσι καὶ τοῖς Κελτί-
βηρσιν, ὄντες οὐκ ἐλάττους οἱ πάντες τρισμυρίων.

8. Ὧν διασαφηθέντων εἰς τὸ τῶν Ῥωμαίων στρατόπεδον εὐθέως ὁ Πόπλιος ἐγίνετο περὶ τὴν ἔξοδον,
καὶ συντάξας τοῖς πολιορκοῦσι τὴν Ἰτύκην ἃ δέον ἦν
πράττειν καὶ τοῖς κατὰ θάλατταν ἐξώρμησε, τὸ στρά-
2 τευμα πᾶν ἔχων εὔζωνον. ἀφικόμενος δὲ πεμπταῖος
ἐπὶ τὰ Μεγάλα πεδία καὶ συνεγγίσας τοῖς πολεμίοις,
τὴν μὲν πρώτην ἡμέραν ἐπί τινος λόφου κατεστρατοπέδευσε, περὶ τριάκοντα σταδίους ἀποσχὼν τῶν πολε-
3 μίων, τῇ δ' ἑξῆς καταβὰς εἰς τὰ πεδία καὶ προθέμενος
4 τοὺς ἱππέας ⟨ἐν⟩ ἑπτὰ σταδίοις παρενέβαλε. δύο δὲ
τὰς κατὰ πόδας ἡμέρας μείναντες καὶ βραχέα διὰ τῶν
ἀκροβολισμῶν καταπειράσαντες ἀλλήλων, τῇ τετάρτῃ κατὰ πρόθεσιν ἐξῆγον ἀμφότεροι καὶ παρενέβαλ-
5 λον τὰς δυνάμεις. ὁ μὲν οὖν Πόπλιος ἁπλῶς κατὰ τὸ
παρ' αὐτοῖς ἔθος ἔθηκε πρῶτον μὲν τὰς τῶν ἀστάτων
σημαίας, ἐπὶ δὲ τούταις τὰς τῶν πριγκίπων, τελευ-
6 ταίας δ' ἐπέστησε κατόπιν τὰς τῶν τριαρίων· τῶν δ'

not a little to inspire the Carthaginians with hope. For instead of four thousand it was announced that they were ten thousand, and that their personal courage and their armament rendered them invincible in the field. These reports and the vulgar gossip of the rabble raised so much the spirits of the Carthaginians that their confidence in being able to take the field once more against the enemy was redoubled. Finally in thirty days they encamped and entrenched themselves on the so-called Great Plain[17] together with the Numidians and Celtiberians, the whole force numbering not less than thirty thousand.[18]

8. When the news reached the Roman camp, Scipio at once prepared to advance against them, and after giving the necessary orders to the land and sea forces besieging Utica, he set out on his march, his whole force being in light marching order. On the fifth day he reached the Great Plain, and on approaching the enemy encamped for the first day on a hill at a distance of thirty stades from them, but on the next day came down from the hill, and placing his cavalry in front drew up his army at a distance of seven stades from the Carthaginians. After remaining where they were for the two subsequent days and making trial of their strength by some slight skirmishing, on the fourth day both generals deliberately advanced their forces and arrayed them for battle.[19] Scipio simply followed the usual Roman practice of placing the maniples of *hastati* in front, behind them the *principes,* and hind-

[17] Some 125 kilometers southwest of Utica; see map in WC 2.425.   [18] Another inflated number.

[19] The battle of the Great Plain is also described in Livy 30.8, who closely follows P.

ἱππέων τοὺς μὲν Ἰταλικοὺς ἐπὶ τὸ δεξιὸν ἔθηκε, τοὺς
7 δὲ Νομάδας καὶ Μασαννάσαν ἐπὶ τὸ λαιόν. οἱ δὲ περὶ
τὸν Σόφακα καὶ τὸν Ἀσδρούβαν τοὺς μὲν Κελτίβηρας
μέσους ἔταξαν ἀντίους ταῖς τῶν Ῥωμαίων σπείραις,
τοὺς δὲ Νομάδας ἐξ εὐωνύμου, τοὺς δὲ Καρχηδονίους
8 ἐκ τῶν δεξιῶν. ἅμα δὲ τῷ γενέσθαι τὴν πρώτην ἔφοδον
εὐθέως οἱ Νομάδες ἐνέκλιναν τοὺς Ἰταλικοὺς ἱππεῖς,
οἵ τε Καρχηδόνιοι τοὺς περὶ τὸν Μασαννάσαν, ἅτε
9 πλεονάκις ἤδη προηττημένοι ταῖς ψυχαῖς. οἱ δὲ Κελτίβηρες ἐμάχοντο γενναίως, συστάντες τοῖς Ῥωμαίοις.
οὔτε γὰρ φεύγοντες ἐλπίδα σωτηρίας εἶχον διὰ τὴν
ἀπειρίαν τῶν τόπων οὔτε ζωγρίᾳ κρατηθέντες διὰ τὴν
10 ἀθεσίαν τὴν εἰς τὸν Πόπλιον· οὐδὲν γὰρ πολέμιον
πεπονθότες ὑπ' αὐτοῦ κατὰ τὰς ἐν Ἰβηρίᾳ πράξεις
ἀδίκως ἐφαίνοντο καὶ παρασπόνδως ἥκειν κατὰ Ῥω-
11 μαίων συμμαχήσοντες τοῖς Καρχηδονίοις. οὐ μὴν
ἀλλ' ἅμα τῷ κλῖναι τοὺς ἀπὸ τῶν κεράτων ταχέως
κυκλωθέντες ὑπὸ τῶν πριγκίπων καὶ τριαρίων αὐτοῦ
12 κατεκόπησαν πάντες πλὴν τελέως ὀλίγων. οἱ μὲν οὖν
Κελτίβηρες τοῦτον τὸν τρόπον ἀπώλοντο, μεγάλην
[παρ' ὅλην] παρασχόμενοι χρείαν τοῖς Καρχηδονίοις
οὐ μόνον κατὰ τὴν μάχην, ἀλλὰ καὶ κατὰ τὴν φυγήν.
13 εἰ μὴ γὰρ τοῦτ' ἐμπόδιον ἐγένετο τοῖς Ῥωμαίοις, ἀλλ'
εὐθέως ἐκ ποδὸς ἠκολούθησαν τοῖς φεύγουσι, παν-
14 τελῶς ἂν ὀλίγοι ‹δι›έφυγον τῶν ὑπεναντίων. νῦν δὲ
περὶ τούτους γενομένης ἐπιστάσεως οἵ τε περὶ τὸν
Σόφακα μετὰ τῶν ἱππέων ἀσφαλῶς ἐποιήσαντο τὴν

most of all the *triarii*. He stationed his Italian cavalry on his right and the Numidians with Massanissa on the left. Syphax and Hasdrubal placed the Celtiberians in the center opposite the Roman maniples, the Numidians on the left, and the Carthaginians on the right. At the first encounter the Numidians gave way before the Italian horse and the Carthaginians before Massanissa, their courage having been broken by previous defeats, but the Celtiberians fought bravely holding out against the Romans. For they neither had any hope of safety in flight owing to their ignorance of the country, nor could they expect to be spared if made prisoners, owing to their treachery to Scipio in thus coming to fight in the service of Carthage against the Romans in spite of his never having been guilty of any acts of hostility to them during his Spanish campaigns. But when the wings gave way they were soon surrounded by the *principes* and *triarii* and cut to pieces where they stood except quite a few. Thus perished the Celtiberians after proving of the greatest service to the Carthaginians not only in the battle but in the flight. For if the Romans had not met with this obstacle, but had directly pursued the fugitives, very few of the enemy would have escaped. But as it was, owing to this stand made by the Celtiberians, Syphax with his cavalry made his way

ἀποχώρησιν εἰς τὴν οἰκείαν, οἵ τε περὶ τὸν Ἀσδρούβαν μετὰ τῶν διασῳζομένων εἰς τὴν Καρχηδόνα.

9. Ὁ δὲ στρατηγὸς τῶν Ῥωμαίων, ἐπεὶ τὰ σκῦλα
καὶ τοὺς αἰχμαλώτους εὐτρεπεῖς ἔθετο, συγκαλέσας
τὸ συνέδριον ἐβουλεύετο περὶ τῶν ἑξῆς, τί δέον ἦν
2 ποιεῖν. ἔδοξεν οὖν αὐτοῖς τὸν μὲν στρατηγὸν Πόπλιον
καὶ μέρος τι τῆς δυνάμεως μένειν ἐπιπορευόμενον τὰς
πόλεις, τὸν δὲ Λαίλιον καὶ τὸν Μασαννάσαν, λαβόντας τούς τε Νομάδας καὶ μέρος τῶν Ῥωμαϊκῶν στρατοπέδων, ἕπεσθαι τοῖς περὶ τὸν Σόφακα καὶ μὴ δοῦναι
3 χρόνον εἰς ἐπίστασιν καὶ παρασκευήν. οὗτοι μὲν
ταῦτα βουλευσάμενοι διεχωρίσθησαν, οἱ μὲν ἐπὶ τὸν
Σόφακα μετὰ τῶν προειρημένων στρατιωτῶν, ὁ δὲ
4 στρατηγὸς ἐπὶ τὰς πόλεις. ὧν αἱ μὲν ἐθελοντὴν προσ-
ετίθεντο τοῖς Ῥωμαίοις διὰ τὸν φόβον, ἃς δὲ πολιορ-
5 κῶν ἐξ ἐφόδου κατὰ κράτος ᾕρει. πάντα δ' ἦν οἰκεῖα
μεταβολῆς τὰ κατὰ τὴν χώραν, ἅτε συνεχῶς [τε]
ἐκκείμενα ταῖς κακοπαθείαις καὶ ταῖς εἰσφοραῖς διὰ
τὸ πολυχρονίους γεγονέναι τοὺς κατὰ τὴν Ἰβηρίαν
πολέμους.

6 Ἐν δὲ τῇ Καρχηδόνι μεγάλης καὶ πρότερον ὑπαρχούσης ἀκαταστασίας, ἔτι μείζω τότε συνέβαινε γίνεσθαι τὴν ταραχήν, ὡς ἂν ἐκ δευτέρου τηλικαύτη
πληγῇ ⟨περι⟩πεπτωκότων ἤδη καὶ ἀπειπόντων τὰς ἐν
7 αὑτοῖς ἐλπίδας. οὐ μὴν ἀλλ' οἱ μὲν ἀνδρωδέστατοι
δοκοῦντες εἶναι τῶν συμβούλων ταῖς μὲν ναυσὶν ἐκέλευον ἤδη πλεῖν ἐπὶ τοὺς τὴν Ἰτύκην πολιορκοῦντας,
καὶ τήν τε πολιορκίαν πειρᾶσθαι λύειν καὶ ναυμαχεῖν

safely back home and Hasdrubal also with the survivors of his force reached Carthage.

9. The Roman general, as soon as he had arranged about the disposal of the booty and prisoners, summoned the council to deliberate as to what should be done next. It was decided that Scipio with a part of his army should remain and go round to the several cities, while Laelius and Massanissa with the Numidians and a portion of the Roman legions should follow up Syphax and not give him time to stop and prepare for resistance. Having come to this decision they separated, these two going after Syphax with the troops I mentioned and the general visiting the towns, some of which surrendered voluntarily to the Romans out of fear, while he besieged and stormed others. The whole country indeed was inclined for a change, as the people had been constantly exposed to hardship and excessive taxation owing to the long duration of the war in Spain.

In Carthage itself the disorder had been serious enough previously, but now the city was still more deeply disturbed, and it seemed that after this second heavy blow they had lost all confidence in themselves. But nevertheless the advice of those who were thought to be the boldest spirits in the senate was to sail with the fleet against the besiegers of Utica and attempt to raise the siege and engage

τοῖς ὑπεναντίοις, ἀπαρασκεύοις οὖσι πρὸς τοῦτο τὸ
8 μέρος· ἐπί τε τὸν Ἀννίβαν πέμπειν ἠξίουν καὶ μηδεμίαν ὑπερβολὴν ποιησαμένους ἐξελέγχειν καὶ ταύτην
τὴν ἐλπίδα· μεγάλας γὰρ ἀμφοτέραις εἶναι ταῖς ἐπιβολαῖς ἐκ τῶν κατὰ λόγον ἀφορμὰς πρὸς σωτηρίαν.
9 τινὲς δὲ ταύτας μὲν ἔφασαν μηκέτι φέρειν τοὺς καιροὺς, τὴν δὲ πόλιν ὀχυροῦν καὶ παρασκευάζεσθαι
πρὸς πολιορκίαν· πολλὰς γὰρ δώσειν ἀφορμὰς ταὐτό-
10 ματον, ἂν ὁμονοῶσιν. ἅμα δὲ βουλεύεσθαι περὶ διαλύσεως καὶ συνθηκῶν παρῄνουν, ἐπὶ τίσι καὶ πῶς ἂν
11 λύσιν ποιήσαιντο τῶν ἐνεστώτων κακῶν. γενομένων
δὲ καὶ πλειόνων λόγων περὶ ταῦτα, πάσας ἐκύρωσαν
ἅμα τὰς γνώμας.

10. κριθέντων δὲ τούτων οἱ μὲν εἰς τὴν Ἰταλίαν
μέλλοντες πλεῖν εὐθέως ἐκ τοῦ βουλευτηρίου προῆγον
ἐπὶ θάλατταν, ὁ δὲ ναύαρχος ἐπὶ τὰς ναῦς· οἱ δὲ λοιποὶ
περί τε τῆς κατὰ τὴν πόλιν ἀσφαλείας προενοοῦντο
καὶ περὶ τῶν κατὰ μέρος ἐβουλεύοντο συνεχῶς.

2 Καὶ [ὁ] Πόπλιος, καταγέμοντος ἤδη τοῦ στρατοπέδου τῆς λείας διὰ τὸ μηδέν᾽ ἀντιπράττειν, ἀλλὰ
πάντας εἴκειν ταῖς ἐπιβολαῖς, ἔκρινε τὸ μὲν τῶν λαφύρων πλεῖον εἰς τὴν ἐξ ἀρχῆς παραπέμψαι παρεμβο-
3 λήν, αὐτὸς δὲ τὴν στρατείαν ἀναλαβὼν εὔζωνον κατα-
λαβέσθαι τὸν ἐπὶ Τύνητι χάρακα καὶ στρατοπεδεῦσαι
τοῖς Καρχηδονίοις ἐν συνόψει· μάλιστα γὰρ οὕτως
4 ἐκφοβήσειν ὑπελάμβανε καὶ καταπλήξειν αὐτούς. οἱ
μὲν οὖν Καρχηδόνιοι μετ᾽ ὀλίγας ἡμέρας τά τε πλη-
ρώματα καὶ τὰς σιταρχίας ἑτοίμας ἔχοντες ἐν ταῖς

the enemy's fleet, which was unprepared for an encounter. They also demanded that Hannibal should be summoned to return and that resource be put to the test without any delay. Both these measures, they said, offered, as far as could be reasonably judged, great chances of saving the country. But others maintained that the time for these steps was past, and that they must now strengthen the city and prepare for a siege. For if they only preserved concord, chance would afford many opportunities. They also advised them to take the question of peace into consideration, and to decide on what terms and by what means they could be delivered from the present evils. After several speeches had been made on these proposals, they adopted them all together.

10. As soon as the vote had been taken, those senators who were to sail for Italy proceeded directly from the senate house to sea, and the admiral went straight on board his ship. The remainder made it their business to see to the defenses of the city and met frequently to discuss points of detail.

Scipio's camp was now full of booty, as he met with no resistance but all gave way to him no matter what he attempted, and he decided to send off the greater part of the booty to his original camp, and taking with him his army thus lightened to seize on the entrenched position before Tunis[20] and to encamp in full view of Carthage. For this he thought would be the most effective means of striking the Carthaginians with terror and dismay. The Carthaginians had got ready in a few days the crews and stores for their

---

[20] Less than twenty kilometers southeast of Carthage.

ναυσὶν ἐγίνοντο πρὸς ἀναγωγῇ καὶ τοῖς προκειμένοις·
ὁ δὲ Πόπλιος ἧκε πρὸς τὸν Τύνητα, καὶ φυγόντων τὴν
ἔφοδον αὐτοῦ τῶν παραφυλαττόντων κατέλαβε τὸν
5 τόπον. ὁ δὲ Τύνης ἀπέχει μὲν τῆς Καρχηδόνος ὡς
ἑκατὸν εἴκοσι σταδίους, ἔστι δὲ σύνοπτος σχεδὸν ἐξ
ὅλης τῆς πόλεως, διαφέρει δ' ὀχυρότητι καὶ φυσικῇ
καὶ χειροποιήτῳ, καθάπερ καὶ πρότερον ἡμῖν εἴρηται.
6 τῶν δὲ Ῥωμαίων ἄρτι κατεστρατοπεδευκότων ἀνή-
γοντο ταῖς ναυσὶν οἱ Καρχηδόνιοι, ποιούμενοι τὸν
7 πλοῦν εἰς τὴν Ἰτύκην. ὁ δὲ Πόπλιος ὁρῶν τὸν ἀνάπλουν τῶν ὑπεναντίων, καὶ δεδιὼς μή τι περὶ ⟨τὸ⟩
σφέτερον αὐτῶν ναυτικὸν συμβῇ, διεταράττετο πάντων ἀνυπονοήτως διακειμένων καὶ ἀπαρασκεύως πρὸς
8 τὸ μέλλον. αὖθις δ' ἐκ μεταβολῆς ἀναστρατοπεδεύσας
9 ἠπείγετο βοηθήσων τοῖς ἰδίοις πράγμασι. καταλαβὼν δὲ τὰς καταφράκτους ναῦς πρὸς μὲν τὰς ἐξαιρέ-
σεις καὶ προσαγωγὰς τῶν ὀργάνων καὶ καθόλου πρὸς
πολιορκίαν εὖ καὶ δεόντως ἐξηρτυμένας, πρὸς δὲ ναυμαχίαν ἥκιστα παρεσκευασμένας, τὸν δὲ τῶν ὑπεναντίων στόλον ἐξ ὅλου τοῦ χειμῶνος πρὸς αὐτὸ τοῦτο
10 κατηρτισμένον, τὸ μὲν ἀντανάγεσθαι καὶ ναυμαχεῖν
ἀπογνούς, συνορμίσας δὲ τὰς καταφράκτους νῆας
περιέστησε ταύταις τὰς φορτηγοὺς ἐπὶ τρεῖς καὶ τέτ-
11 ταρας τὸ βάθος, κἄπειτα καθελόμενος τοὺς ἱστοὺς καὶ
τὰς κεραίας ἔζευξε τούτοις βιαίως πρὸς ἀλλήλας,
12 βραχὺ διάστημα ποιῶν, ὥσθ' ὑπηρετικοῖς ἐκπλεῖν
δύνασθαι καὶ διαπλεῖν.

510

ships and were about to put to sea to execute their purpose, when Scipio arrived at Tunis and upon its garrison taking to flight occupied the place. Tunis is situated at a distance of about 120 stades from Carthage, and is visible from nearly the whole town. As I have previously stated, both nature and art have contributed to render it a very strong place. Just as the Romans had encamped there the Carthaginian fleet was putting to sea on its way to Utica. Scipio when he saw the enemy under way was much disturbed, as he feared that something untoward might happen to his own fleet, since no one expected to be attacked or had made any preparations for such a contingency. He, therefore, at once broke up his camp and marched hastily to the help of his own people. Finding that his warships were well provided with facilities for supporting and moving forward siege machines, and in general for all siege operations, but were quite unprepared for a naval action, while the enemy's fleet had during the whole winter been equipping for this very purpose, he abandoned any idea of advancing and offering battle, but anchoring his warships in a line placed round them the transports three or four deep, and then taking down the masts and yards lashed the transports securely to each other with these, leaving a small interval for dispatch boats to pass in and out.

III. RES AEGYPTI

11. ⟨Πολύβιος⟩ ἐν τῇ τεσσαρεσκαιδεκάτῃ ⟨φησὶν⟩
Ἀγαθοκλέους τοῦ Οἰνάνθης υἱοῦ, ἑταίρου δὲ τοῦ Φιλοπάτορος βασιλέως, ⟨κόλακα γενέσθαι⟩ Φίλωνα. . . .

2 Πολύβιος δὲ ἐν τῇ τεσσαρεσκαιδεκάτῃ τῶν ἱστοριῶν Κλεινοῦς φησι τῆς οἰνοχοούσης αὐτῷ ⟨Πτολε-
μαίῳ τῷ Φιλαδέλφῳ⟩ εἰκόνας πολλὰς ἀνακεῖσθαι
κατὰ τὴν Ἀλεξάνδρειαν μονοχίτωνας καὶ ῥυτὸν ἐχού-
3 σας ἐν ταῖς χερσίν. αἱ δὲ κάλλισται τῶν οἰκιῶν,
φησίν, οὐ Μυρτίου καὶ Μνησίδος καὶ Ποθεινῆς προσ-
4 αγορεύονται; καίτοι Μνησὶς μὲν ἦν αὐλητρὶς καὶ Πο-
θεινή. Μύρτιον δὲ μία τῶν ἀποδεδειγμένων καὶ κοινῶν
5 δεικτηριάδων. τοῦ δὲ Φιλοπάτορος βασιλέως Πτολεμαίου οὐκ Ἀγαθόκλεια ἡ ἑταίρα ἐκράτει ἡ καὶ πᾶσαν
ἀνατρέψασα τὴν βασιλείαν; . . .

12. Ἴσως δέ τινες ἐπαπορήσουσι πῶς ἡμεῖς τὰς
ἄλλας πράξεις ἁπάσας κατ᾽ ἐνιαυτὸν γράφοντες τὰς
καταλλήλους περὶ μόνων τῶν κατ᾽ Αἴγυπτον ἐν καιρῷ
νῦν ἐκ πλείονος χρόνου πεποιήμεθα τὴν ἐξήγησιν.
2 ἡμεῖς δὲ τοῦτο πεποιήκαμεν διά τινας τοιαύτας αἰτίας.
3 Πτολεμαῖος ὁ βασιλεύς, περὶ οὗ νῦν ὁ λόγος, ὁ Φιλο-
πάτωρ, μετὰ τὸ συντελεσθῆναι τὸν περὶ Κοίλην
Συρίαν πόλεμον ἀποστὰς πάντων τῶν καλῶν ἐτράπη

21 From Athen. 6.251c.

22 He will reappear in 15.30.5 and 33.2. His mention here as
coming from Book 14 has given rise to a bold theory by K. Abel;
see n. on 15.24a.

III. AFFAIRS OF EGYPT
SINCE 213 B.C.[21]

11. Polybius in his fourteenth book says that Philo[22] was the flatterer of Agathocles,[23] the son of Oenanthe and the companion of Ptolemy Philopator. . . .

Polybius[24] in his fourteenth book tells us that there were many portraits in Alexandrian temples of Cleino, the cupbearer of Ptolemy Philadelphus, representing her clothed only in a chiton and holding a rhyton. "And are not some of the finest houses," he says, "called Myrtion's, Mnesis', and Potheine's? But what were Mnesis and Potheine but flute players and Myrtion one of the professional and vulgar mimae? And was not Ptolemy Philopator the slave of the courtesan Agathocleia, who overturned the whole kingdom?" . . .

12. Perhaps some of my readers will wonder why while elsewhere I dealt with the successive events of each year separately, in the case of Egypt alone I give on the present occasion a narrative of occurrences there extending over a considerable period. The reason of this I may state as follows. Ptolemy Philopator,[25] of whom I am now talking, after the termination of the war[26] for Coele-Syria abandoned

---

[23] Of Samos (*PP* 14576). In 216/5 he was eponymous priest of Alexander the Great and the deified kings and next to (and after) Sosibius the most influential member of the king's court. G. Hölbl, *Geschichte des Ptolemäerreiches* (Darmstadt 1994), 111–112 .

[24] From Athen. 13.756c.

[25] His very negative portrait in P. has been challenged by recent research, for instance by C. Préaux, *Chron. d'É.* 40 (1965), 364–375.

[26] The war that culminated in the battle at Raphia in 217.

πρὸς βίον ἄσωτον καὶ τοιοῦτον οἷον ἀρτίως διεληλύ-
4 θαμεν. ὀψὲ δέ ποτε βιασθεὶς ὑπὸ τῶν πραγμάτων
ἐνέπεσεν εἰς τὸν νῦν δεδηλωμένον πόλεμον, ὃς χωρὶς
τῆς εἰς ἀλλήλους ὠμότητος καὶ παρανομίας οὔτε
παράταξιν οὔτε ναυμαχίαν οὔτε πολιορκίαν οὔθ᾽ ἕτε-
5 ρον οὐδὲν ἔσχε μνήμης ἄξιον. διόπερ ὑπέδραμεν οὕτω
κἀμοὶ τῷ γράφοντι ῥᾳδίαν ἔσεσθαι καὶ τοῖς ἀνα-
γινώσκουσιν εὐμαθεστέραν τὴν διήγησιν, εἰ μὴ κατ᾽
ἐνιαυτὸν ἐπιψαύων μικρῶν [καὶ] οὐκ ἀξίων ἐπιστάσεως πραγμάτων ἀποδιδοίην τὸν λόγον, ἀλλ᾽ εἰσάπαξ
οἷον εἰ σωματοειδῆ ποιήσας τὴν τοῦ βασιλέως προαίρεσιν ἀπαγγείλαιμι περὶ αὐτῆς.

entirely the path of virtue and took to a life of dissipation such as I have just described.[27] Late in his reign he was forced by circumstances into the war[28] I have mentioned, a war which, apart from the mutual savagery and lawlessness of the combatants, contained nothing worthy of note, no pitched battle, no sea fight, no siege. It, therefore, struck me that my narrative would be easier both for me to write and for my readers to follow if I performed this part of my task not by merely alluding every year to small events not worth serious attention, but by giving once and for all a unified picture[29] so to speak of this king's character.

[27] In 11.1–5. So already often in Book 5.

[28] The native revolt; cf. 5.107.1–3, with W. Huss, *Ägypten in hellenistischer Zeit* (Munich 2001), 441–449. Hölbl (11.1), 135–140.

[29] This account of the entire reign of Ptolemy IV has been lost with forty-eight pages of the ms., as indicated by one of the excerptors. What is left here was obviously connected to the notice of the king's death which happened in 204 (the actual date is controversial).

FRAGMENTA LIBRI XV

I. RES ITALIAE ET AFRICAE

1. Ὅτι τῶν Καρχηδονίων λαβόντων αἰχμαλώτους τὰς φορτηγοὺς νῆας τῶν Ῥωμαίων καὶ χορηγίας πλῆθος ἐξαίσιον ὁ Πόπλιος βαρέως μὲν ἔφερεν ἐπὶ τῷ μὴ μόνον σφίσι παρηρῆσθαι τὴν χορηγίαν, ἀλλὰ καὶ τοῖς ἐχθροῖς παρεσκευάσθαι δαψίλειαν τῶν ἀναγ-
2 καίων, ἔτι δὲ βαρύτερον ἐπὶ τῷ παραβεβηκέναι τοὺς ὅρκους καὶ τὰς συνθήκας τοὺς Καρχηδονίους καὶ
3 πάλιν ἐξ ἄλλης ἀρχῆς ἐγείρεσθαι τὸν πόλεμον. διὸ καὶ παραυτίκα προχειρισάμενος πρεσβευτὰς Λεύκιον Σέργιον καὶ Λεύκιον Βαίβιον καὶ Λεύκιον Φάβιον ἐξαπέστειλε διαλεξομένους τοῖς Καρχηδονίοις ὑπὲρ τῶν γεγονότων, ἅμα δὲ καὶ δηλώσοντας ὅτι κεκύρωκε
4 τὰς συνθήκας ὁ δῆμος τῶν Ῥωμαίων· ἄρτι γὰρ ἧκε τῷ Ποπλίῳ γράμματα διασαφοῦντα περὶ τῶν προειρη-
5 μένων. οἱ δὲ παραγενηθέντες εἰς τὴν Καρχηδόνα τὸ μὲν πρῶτον εἰς τὴν σύγκλητον, μετὰ δὲ ταῦτα πάλιν ἐπὶ τοὺς πολλοὺς παραχθέντες, ἔλεγον ὑπὲρ τῶν
6 ἐνεστώτων μετὰ παρρησίας, πρῶτον μὲν ἀναμιμνή-σκοντες ὡς οἱ παρ' ἐκείνων πρεσβευταί, παραγενη-θέντες εἰς Τύνητα πρὸς σφᾶς καὶ παρελθόντες εἰς τὸ

FRAGMENTS OF BOOK XV

I. AFFAIRS OF ITALY AND AFRICA

1. The Carthaginians having captured the Roman transports[1] and a vast quantity of supplies, Scipio was much disturbed, as not only had he been deprived of his own supplies, but the enemy had thus procured for themselves abundance of provisions. What aggrieved him still more was that the Carthaginians had violated the late solemn agreement and that the war had been thus rekindled from a fresh source. He, therefore, at once appointed as legates[2] Lucius Sergius, Lucius Baebius, and Lucius Fabius, and dispatched them to confer with the Carthaginians about what had occurred and at the same time to inform them that the Roman people had ratified the treaty: for dispatches had just arrived for Scipio informing him of this fact. On arriving at Carthage they first of all addressed the senate, and afterward being brought before the popular assembly, spoke with great freedom about the situation. In the first place they reminded the assembly that when the Carthaginian envoys[3] came to Tunis to the Romans and

---

[1] They were captured early in 202, during a truce, while the parties were negotiating for peace.

[2] *MRR* 1.313 with nn. 8 and 9.

[3] Sent to Scipio after Syphax's capture (Livy 30.16.3).

THE HISTORIES OF POLYBIUS

συνέδριον, οὐ μόνον τοὺς θεοὺς ἀσπάσαιντο καὶ τὴν
γῆν προσκυνήσαιεν, καθάπερ ἐστὶν ἔθος τοῖς ἄλλοις
7 ἀνθρώποις, ἀλλὰ καὶ πεσόντες ἐπὶ τὴν γῆν ἀγεννῶς
τοὺς πόδας καταφιλοῖεν τῶν ἐν τῷ συνεδρίῳ, μετὰ δὲ
ταῦτα πάλιν ἀναστάντες [ὡς] κατηγορήσαιεν σφῶν
αὐτῶν, διότι καὶ τὰς ἐξ ἀρχῆς γενομένας συνθήκας
8 Ῥωμαίοις καὶ Καρχηδονίοις ἀθετήσαιεν αὐτοί. διόπερ
ἔφασαν οὐκ ἀγνοεῖν ὅτι πᾶν εἰκότως ἂν πάθοιεν ὑπὸ
Ῥωμαίων, ἀλλὰ τῆς τύχης ἕνεκα τῶν ἀνθρώπων ἐδέοντο μηδὲν παθεῖν ἀνήκεστον· ἔσεσθαι γὰρ τὴν σφετέραν ἀβουλίαν ἀπόδειξιν τῆς Ῥωμαίων καλοκἀγα-
9 θίας. ὧν μνημονεύοντα τὸν στρατηγὸν ἔφασαν [τὸν]
αὐτὸν οἱ πρέσβεις καὶ τοὺς ἐν τῷ συνεδρίῳ τότε
γεγονότας ἐκπλήττεσθαι, τίνι ποτὲ πιστεύοντες ἐπε-
λανθάνοντο μὲν τῶν τότε ῥηθέντων, ἀθετεῖν δὲ τολ-
10 μῶσι τοὺς ὅρκους καὶ τὰς συνθήκας. σχεδὸν δὲ τοῦτ᾽
εἶναι δῆλον ὡς Ἀννίβᾳ πεποιθότες καὶ ταῖς μετὰ
τούτου παρούσαις δυνάμεσι ταῦτα τολμῶσι ποιεῖν,
11 κακῶς φρονοῦντες· σαφῶς γὰρ εἰδέναι πάντας ὅτι
ἐκεῖνοι δεύτερον ἔτος ἤδη φεύγοντες ἐκ πάσης Ἰταλίας εἰς τοὺς περὶ Λακίνιον τόπους, κἀκεῖ συγκε-
κλεισμένοι καὶ μόνον οὐ πολιορκούμενοι, μόλις ἑαυ-
12 τοὺς ἐκσεσωκότες ἥκουσι νῦν. "οὐ μὴν ἀλλ᾽ εἰ καὶ
νενικηκότες τοὺς ἐκεῖ παρῆσαν, καὶ πρὸς ἡμᾶς ἔμελλον διακινδυνεύειν τοὺς δυσὶ μάχαις ἑξῆς ὑμᾶς ἤδη

presented themselves before the council, they not only saluted the gods and did obeisance to the Earth, as is the custom with other men, but that they debased themselves by falling prostrate on the ground and kissing the feet of the members of the council; and that afterward when they got up again they accused themselves of having been alone guilty of breaking the original treaty[4] between the Romans and the Carthaginians. Therefore, they said, they were well aware that the Romans would be justified in any punishment they inflicted on them, but in the name of the common fortune of mankind they had entreated them not to proceed to extremities, but rather let their folly afford a proof of the generosity of the Romans. The general himself, they said, and those who had been present then at the council, when they called this to mind, were amazed and asked themselves whence the Carthaginians had the assurance now to ignore what they said on that occasion and to venture on breaking this last solemn treaty. It seemed almost evident that they ventured to act thus relying on Hannibal[5] and the forces with him. In this confidence they were most ill-advised; for everyone knew quite well that for the last two years Hannibal and his troops, after abandoning every part of Italy, had fled to the Lacinian promontory,[6] and that, shut in there and almost besieged, they only just succeeded in saving themselves and leaving for Africa. "And even," they said, "if they had been coming after a victory in Italy and were about to give battle to us,

---

[4] It is not clear which of the treaties between Rome and Carthage P. has in mind.   [5] He had returned to Africa in the fall of 203 and had his camp at Hadrumetum (5.3), some 125 kilometers south-southeast of Tunis.   [6] See n. on 3.33.18.

νενικηκότας, ὅμως ἀμφιδόξους ἔχειν <ἔ>δει τὰς ἐλπίδας ὑπὲρ τοῦ μέλλοντος, καὶ μὴ μόνον τοῦ νικᾶν
13 ἔννοιαν λαμβάνειν, ἀλλὰ καὶ τοῦ σφαλῆναι πάλιν. οὗ
συμβάντος ποίους ἐπικαλέσεσθε" ἔφη "θεούς; ποίοις
δὲ χρώμενοι λόγοις τὸν ἐκ τῶν κρατούντων ἔλεον
14 ἐπισπάσεσθε πρὸς τὰς ἑαυτῶν συμφοράς; πάσης εἰκὸς ὑμᾶς ἐλπίδος ἀποκλεισθήσεσθαι καὶ παρὰ θεῶν
καὶ παρ' ἀνθρώπων διὰ τὴν ἀθεσίαν καὶ τὴν ἀβουλίαν."

2. Οἱ μὲν οὖν πρέσβεις τοιαῦτα διαλεχθέντες ἀν-
2 εχώρησαν· τῶν δὲ Καρχηδονίων ὀλίγοι μὲν ἦσαν οἱ
συναινοῦντες μὴ παραβαίνειν τὰς ὁμολογίας, οἱ δὲ
πλείους καὶ τῶν πολιτευομένων καὶ τῶν βουλευομένων
βαρέως μὲν ἔφερον τὰς ἐν ταῖς συνθήκαις ἐπιταγάς,
δυσχερῶς δ' ἀνείχοντο τὴν τῶν πρεσβευτῶν παρρη-
σίαν, πρὸς δὲ τούτοις οὐχ οἷοί τ' ἦσαν προέσθαι τὰ
3 κατηγμένα πλοῖα καὶ τὰς ἐκ τούτων χορηγίας. τὸ δὲ
συνέχον, οὐ μικρὰς ἀλλὰ μεγάλας εἶχον ἐλπίδας
4 νικήσειν διὰ τῶν περὶ τὸν Ἀννίβαν. τοῖς μὲν οὖν
πολλοῖς ἔδοξε τοὺς πρέσβεις ἀναποκρίτους ἐξαπο-
στέλλειν· τῶν δὲ πολιτευομένων οἷς ἦν προκείμενον ἐκ
παντὸς τρόπου συγχέαι πάλιν τὸν πόλεμον, οὗτοι
5 συνεδρεύσαντες μηχανῶνταί τι τοιοῦτον. ἔφασαν δεῖν
πρόνοιαν ποιήσασθαι τῶν πρεσβευτῶν, ἵνα μετ'
ἀσφαλείας ἀνακομισθῶσιν εἰς τὴν ἰδίαν παρεμβολήν.
6 καὶ παραυτίκα τούτοις μὲν ἡτοίμαζον δύο τριήρεις
παραπόμπους, πρὸς δὲ τὸν ναύαρχον Ἀσδρούβαν
διεπέμψαντο παρακαλοῦντες ἑτοιμάσαι πλοῖα μὴ

who have beaten you in two successive battles, your expectation of success should be quite uncertain and you should not only contemplate the prospect of victory but that of a further defeat. And then what gods will you have to invoke, and on what plea will you be able to supplicate the victors to take pity on your calamity? Will not your faithlessness and folly exclude you from almost all hope for the mercy of gods and men?"

2. The ambassadors after making this speech took their departure. There were but few among the Carthaginians who approved of adhering to the treaty. The majority both of their leading politicians and of those who took part in the deliberation objected to its harsh conditions, and with difficulty tolerated the bold language of the ambassadors. Besides this, they were not disposed to give up the ships they had brought into port and the supplies they contained. But above all they had no slight hopes of conquering with the assistance of Hannibal, but were on the contrary most sanguine. The popular assembly decided simply to dismiss the ambassadors without a reply, but those of the politicians who had determined by any and every means to stir up the war again held a meeting and contrived the following plan. They declared that all due care should be taken to ensure the safe arrival of the ambassadors at their own camp and at once prepared two triremes to escort them. Then they sent to the admiral, Hasdrubal,[7]

_____

[7] The son of Gisgo (Livy 30.24.11).

μακρὰν τῆς τῶν Ῥωμαίων παρεμβολῆς, ἵν᾽ ἐπειδὰν αἱ
παραπέμπουσαι νῆες ἀπολίπωσι τοὺς Ῥωμαίους, ἐπ-
αναχθέντα ταῦτα καταποντίσῃ τοὺς πρεσβευτάς.
7 ἐφώρμει γὰρ αὐτοῖς τὸ ναυτικὸν κατὰ τοὺς πρὸ τῆς
8 Ἰτύκης ἐγκειμένους τόπους. οὗτοι μὲν οὖν ταῦτα δια-
ταξάμενοι πρὸς τὸν Ἀσδρούβαν ἐξέπεμπον τοὺς Ῥωμαίους, ἐντειλάμενοι τοῖς ἐπὶ τῶν τριήρων, [ὡς] ἐὰν
παραλλάξωσι τὸν Μακάραν ποταμόν, αὖθις ἀπολι-
9 πόντας ἀποπλεῖν ἐν τῷ πόρῳ τοὺς πρεσβευτάς· καὶ
γὰρ ἦν ἐκ τούτων τῶν τόπων συνορᾶν ἤδη τὴν τῶν
10 ὑπεναντίων παρεμβολήν· οἱ δὲ παραπέμποντες, ἐπεὶ
κατὰ τὸ συνταχθὲν παρήλλαξαν τὸν ποταμόν, ἀσπα-
11 σάμενοι τοὺς Ῥωμαίους αὖθις ἐπανέπλεον. οἱ δὲ περὶ
τὸν Λεύκιον ἄλλο μὲν οὐδὲν ὑφεωρῶντο δεινόν, νομίσαντες δὲ τοὺς παραπέμποντας δι᾽ ὀλιγωρίαν αὐτοὺς
12 προαπολιπεῖν ἐπὶ ποσὸν ἐδυσχέραινον. ἅμα δὲ τῷ
μονωθέντας αὐτοὺς πλεῖν ἐπανάγονται τρισὶ τριήρε-
σιν ἐξ ὑποβολῆς οἱ Καρχηδόνιοι, καὶ παραβαλόντες
τῇ Ῥωμαϊκῇ πεντήρει τρῶσαι μὲν οὐχ οἷοί τ᾽ ἦσαν,
ὑποχωρούσης τῆς νεώς, οὐδὲ τοῦ καταστρώματος ἐπι-
13 βῆναι διὰ τὸ γενναίως ἀμύνεσθαι τοὺς ἄνδρας· ἐκ
πραβολῆς δὲ καὶ πέριξ προσμαχόμενοι κατετίτρω-
σκον τοὺς ἐπιβάτας καὶ διέφθειρον πολλοὺς αὐτῶν,
14 ἕως οὗ κατιδόντες οἱ Ῥωμαῖοι τοὺς προνομεύοντας
τὴν παραλίαν ἀπὸ τῆς ἰδίας στρατοπεδείας παραβοη-
θοῦντας ἐπὶ τὸν αἰγιαλὸν ἐξέβαλον τὴν ναῦν εἰς τὴν
15 γῆν. τῶν μὲν οὖν ἐπιβατῶν οἱ πλεῖστοι διεφθάρησαν,
οἱ δὲ πρεσβευταὶ παραδόξως ἐξεσώθησαν.

begging him to have some ships ready not far from the Roman camp, so that when the Romans were left by the ships that escorted them they might bear down upon them and sink them. For the Carthaginian fleet was now anchored off the coast close to Utica. Having given these instructions to Hasdrubal they sent off the Romans. They had ordered the commanders of the triremes, as soon as they passed the river Macar,[8] to leave the ambassadors in the strait and return, this being a spot from which the enemy's camp could already be seen. The escort acting on their orders, as soon as they had passed the river mouth saluted the Romans and sailed back. Lucius and his colleagues were unsuspicious of any danger but were somewhat put out, thinking it was due to negligence that the escort had left them too soon. But as they were continuing their voyage alone three Carthaginian triremes bore down on them as they had been directed to do. When they came up to the Roman quinquereme they could not ram her as she avoided the strokes, nor could they board her as her crew made a gallant resistance. But running alongside of her and circling round her they kept on shooting the men on board and killing a number of them, until the Romans, seeing that the men from their own camp who were foraging on the coast were running down to the beach to assist them, managed to run their ship ashore. Most of the men on board had been killed in the action, but the ambassadors, wonderful to say, escaped.

[8] The Bagradas as in 1.75.5.

3. Γενομένων δὲ τούτων αὖθις ὁ πόλεμος ἄλλην ἀρχὴν εἰλήφει βαρυτέραν τῆς πρόσθεν καὶ δυσμενι-

2 κωτέραν. οἵ τε γὰρ Ῥωμαῖοι δοκοῦντες παρεσπονδῆσθαι φιλοτίμως διέκειντο πρὸς τὸ περιγενέσθαι τῶν Καρχηδονίων, οἵ τε Καρχηδόνιοι συνειδότες σφίσι τὰ πεπραγμένα πρὸς πᾶν ἑτοίμως εἶχον πρὸς τὸ μὴ τοῖς

3 ἐχθροῖς ὑποχείριοι γενηθῆναι. τοιαύτης δὲ τῆς ἐξ ἀμφοῖν παραστάσεως ὑπαρχούσης προφανὲς ἦν ὅτι

4 δεήσει μάχῃ κρίνεσθαι περὶ τῶν ἐνεστώτων. ἐξ οὗ συνέβαινε μὴ μόνον τοὺς κατὰ τὴν Ἰταλίαν καὶ Λιβύην πάντας, ἀλλὰ καὶ τοὺς κατὰ τὴν Ἰβηρίαν καὶ Σικελίαν καὶ Σαρδόνα μετεώρους εἶναι καὶ περισπᾶσθαι ταῖς διανοίαις, καραδοκοῦντας τὸ ουμβησόμενον.

5 Κατὰ δὲ τὸν καιρὸν τοῦτον Ἀννίβας, ἐλλείπων τοῖς ἱππικοῖς, διέπεμπε πρός τινα Νομάδα Τυχαῖον, ὃς ἦν μὲν οἰκεῖος Σόφακος, ἱππεῖς δὲ μαχιμωτάτους ἔχειν

6 ἐδόκει τῶν κατὰ τὴν Λιβύην, παρακαλῶν αὐτὸν βοηθεῖν καὶ συνεπιλαμβάνεσθαι τοῦ καιροῦ, σαφῶς γινώσκοντα διότι Καρχηδονίων κρατησάντων δύναται διαφυλάττειν τὴν ἀρχήν, Ῥωμαίων δ' ἐκνικησάντων καὶ τῷ βίῳ κινδυνεύσει διὰ τὴν Μασαννάσου φιλαρ-

7 χίαν. οὗτος οὖν πεισθεὶς τοῖς παρακαλουμένοις ἧκε μετὰ δισχιλίων ἱππέων πρὸς τὸν Ἀννίβαν.

4. Πόπλιος δὲ τὰ περὶ τὴν ναυτικὴν δύναμιν ἀσφαλισάμενος καὶ καταλιπὼν Βαίβιον ἀντιστράτηγον,

2 αὐτὸς μὲν ἐπεπορεύετο τὰς πόλεις, οὐκέτι παραλαμβάνων εἰς τὴν πίστιν τοὺς ἐθελοντὴν σφᾶς αὐτοὺς

3. The consequence of this was that the war began afresh, the cause of its renewal being more serious and more productive of bitter feeling than the original one. For the Romans, thinking that they had been treacherously attacked, set their hearts on getting the better of the Carthaginians, and the latter, conscious of their guilt, were ready to suffer anything rather than fall into the power of the Romans. Both sides being animated by such fury, it was evident that the issue must be decided by a battle. Consequently not only all the inhabitants of Italy and Africa, but those of Spain, Sicily, and Sardinia likewise were held in suspense and distracted, awaiting the result.

Hannibal at this time was very poorly off for cavalry and sent to a certain Numidian called Tychaeus, who was a relative of Syphax, and was thought to have the best cavalry in Africa, begging him to help him and join in saving the situation, as he knew well that, if the Carthaginians won, he could retain his principality, but if the Romans were victors, he would risk losing his life too owing to Massanissa's greed of power. Accordingly, Tychaeus was prevailed on by this appeal and came to Hannibal with a body of two thousand horses.

4. Scipio, having taken measures for the security of his fleet, deputed the command to Baebius[9] and himself went round the towns, no longer receiving the submission of those which offered to surrender, but taking them all by as-

[9] One of the legates in 1.3.

ἐγχειρίζοντας, ἀλλὰ μετὰ βίας ἀνδραποδιζόμενος καὶ
φανερὰν ποιῶν τὴν ὀργήν, ἣν εἶχε πρὸς τοὺς πολεμίους διὰ τὴν Καρχηδονίων παρασπόνδησιν· πρὸς δὲ

3 Μασαννάσαν διεπέμπετο συνεχῶς, ἀποδηλῶν αὐτῷ
τίνα τρόπον παραβεβηκότες εἶεν οἱ Φοίνικες τὰς
σπονδάς, καὶ παρακαλῶν ἀθροίζειν δύναμιν ὡς πλεί-

4 στην καὶ συνάπτειν αὐτῷ κατὰ σπουδήν. ὁ γὰρ Μασαννάσας ἅμα τῷ γενέσθαι τὰς συνθήκας, καθάπερ
εἴρηται πρότερον, εὐθέως ἀφώρμησε μετὰ τῆς ἰδίας
δυνάμεως, προσλαβὼν δέκα σημαίας Ῥωμαϊκὰς ἱππέων καὶ πεζῶν καὶ πρεσβευτὰς παρὰ τοῦ στρατηγοῦ,
χάριν τοῦ μὴ μόνον τὴν πατρῴαν ἀρχὴν ἀπολαβεῖν,
ἀλλὰ καὶ τὴν τοῦ Σόφακος προσκατακτήσασθαι διὰ
τῆς Ῥωμαίων ἐπικουρίας· ὃ καὶ συνέβη γενέσθαι.

5 Συνέτυχε δὲ καὶ τοὺς ἐκ Ῥώμης πρεσβευτὰς περὶ
τοὺς αὐτοὺς καιροὺς εἰς τὸν ναυτικὸν χάρακα τὸν τῶν

6 Ῥωμαίων καταπλεῦσαι. τοὺς μὲν οὖν παρ' αὐτῶν ὁ
Βαίβιος παραχρῆμα πρὸς τὸν Πόπλιον ἐξέπεμψε,
τοὺς δὲ τῶν Καρχηδονίων παρακατεῖχε, τά τε λοιπὰ
δυσθύμως διακειμένους καὶ νομίζοντας ἐν τοῖς μεγί-

7 στοις εἶναι κινδύνοις· πυθόμενοι γὰρ τὴν γεγενημένην
ἐκ τῶν Καρχηδονίων ἀσέβειαν πρὸς τοὺς τῶν Ῥωμαίων πρέσβεις, πρόδηλον ἐδόκουν εἶναι σφίσι τὴν ἐκ

8 τούτων τιμωρίαν. ὁ δὲ Πόπλιος, διακούσας τῶν παρα-
γεγονότων ὅτι προθύμως ἥ τε σύγκλητος ὅ τε δῆμος
ἀποδέξαιντο τὰς γενομένας δι' αὐτοῦ συνθήκας πρὸς
τοὺς Καρχηδονίους καὶ διότι πρὸς πᾶν τὸ παρακα-
λούμενον ἑτοίμως ἔχοιεν, ἐπὶ μὲν τούτοις ἔχαιρε μεγά-

sault and selling the inhabitants as slaves, to manifest the anger he felt against the enemy owing to the treacherous behavior of the Carthaginians. He was constantly sending to Massanissa, pointing out to him how the Carthaginians had violated the treaty, and begging him to raise as strong a force as possible and to make haste to join him. For Massanissa, as I above stated,[10] immediately on the conclusion of the treaty left with his own forces, taking with him besides ten cohorts of Roman cavalry and infantry, and legates on the part of Scipio, in order not only to recover his paternal kingdom, but with the assistance of the Romans to add that of Syphax[11] to it, which he ultimately succeeded in doing.

It happened that at about the same time the envoys from Rome reached the Roman naval camp. So Baebius at once dispatched the Roman envoys to Scipio, but detained the Carthaginians, who were generally dispirited and considered themselves in great danger. For when they heard of the flagitious treatment of the Roman envoys by the Carthaginians, they thought that vengeance for it would assuredly be taken on themselves. But Scipio, on hearing from the Roman legates that both the senate and the people had readily accepted the treaty he had made with the Carthaginians and were ready to comply with all his requests, was highly gratified by this, and ordered Baebius to

[10] In a lost section.
[11] Laelius had taken him prisoner, Livy 30.12.1–2.

9 λως, τοὺς δὲ τῶν Καρχηδονίων προσέταξε τῷ Βαιβίῳ
μετὰ πάσης φιλανθρωπίας ἀποπέμπειν εἰς τὴν οἰκείαν, πάνυ καλῶς βουλευσάμενος, ὥς γ᾽ ἐμοὶ δοκεῖ, καὶ
10 φρονίμως. θεωρῶν ⟨γὰρ⟩ τὴν σφετέραν πατρίδα περὶ
πλείστου ποιουμένην τὴν περὶ τοὺς πρεσβευτὰς
πίστιν, ἐσκοπεῖτο παρ᾽ αὑτῷ συλλογιζόμενος οὐχ
οὕτως τί δέον παθεῖν Καρχηδονίους, ὡς τί δέον ἦν
11 πρᾶξαι Ῥωμαίους. διὸ παρακατασχὼν τὸν ἴδιον θυ-
μὸν καὶ τὴν ἐπὶ τοῖς γεγονόσι πικρίαν, ἐπειράθη
διαφυλάξαι, κατὰ τὴν παροιμίαν, "πατέρων εὖ κείμενα
12 ἔργα." τοιγαροῦν καὶ τοὺς ἐν τῇ Καρχηδόνι πάντας
ἥττησε ταῖς ψυχαῖς καὶ τὸν Ἀννίβαν αὐτόν, ὑπερ-
θέμενος τῇ καλοκἀγαθίᾳ τὴν ἐκείνων ἄνοιαν.

5. Οἱ δὲ Καρχηδόνιοι θεωροῦντες τὰς πόλεις ἐκπορ-
θουμένας, ἔπεμπον πρὸς τὸν Ἀννίβαν, δεόμενοι μὴ
μέλλειν, ἀλλὰ προσπελάζειν τοῖς πολεμίοις καὶ κρί-
2 νειν τὰ πράγματα διὰ μάχης. ὁ δὲ διακούσας τοῖς μὲν
παροῦσιν ἀπεκρίθη τἆλλα σκοπεῖν, περὶ δὲ τούτου
3 ῥᾳθυμεῖν· διαλήψεσθαι ⟨γὰρ⟩ τὸν καιρὸν αὐτός. μετὰ
δέ τινας ἡμέρας ἀναζεύξας ἐκ τῶν παρὰ τὸν Ἀδρύμητα τόπων προῆλθε καὶ κατεστρατοπέδευσε περὶ
Ζάμαν· αὕτη δ᾽ ἐστὶ πόλις ἀπέχουσα Καρχηδόνος ὡς
4 πρὸς τὰς δύσεις ὁδὸν ἡμερῶν πέντε. κἀκεῖθεν ἐξέπεμψε τρεῖς κατασκόπους, βουλόμενος ἐπιγνῶναι
ποῦ στρατοπεδεύουσι καὶ πῶς χειρίζει τὰ κατὰ τὰς
5 παρεμβολὰς ὁ τῶν Ῥωμαίων στρατηγός. Πόπλιος δ᾽,
ἐπαναχθέντων ὡς αὑτὸν τῶν κατασκόπων, τοσοῦτον

treat the Carthaginian envoys with all courtesy and send them home, acting, as I think, very rightly and wisely. For aware as he was of the high value attached by his own nation to keeping faith to ambassadors, he took into consideration not so much the deserts of the Carthaginians as the duty of the Romans. Therefore restraining his own anger and the bitter resentment he felt owing to the late occurrence, he did his best to preserve "the glorious record of our sires," as the saying[12] is. The consequence was that he humiliated all the people of Carthage and Hannibal himself by thus requiting in ampler measure their baseness by his generosity.

5. The Carthaginians, when they saw their towns being sacked, sent to Hannibal begging him not to delay, but to approach the enemy and decide matters by a battle. After listening to the messengers he bade them in reply pay attention to other matters and be at their ease about this; for he himself would judge when it was time. After a few days he shifted his camp from the neighborhood of Adrumetum and advancing encamped near Zama.[13] This is a town lying five days' journey to the west of Carthage. From here he sent out three spies, wishing to find out where the Romans were encamped, and what disposition their general had made in his camp. When these men were caught and brought before him Scipio was so far from punishing them,

---

[12] No exact parallel has been identified in Greek literature.

[13] See the long introductory note to the battle in WC 2.445–450, on sources, chronology, site, numbers, and tactics. The date seems to have been early autumn 202; as for the site, it has not been reliably determined. It took Hannibal after the battle forty-eight hours to reach Hadrumetum; the numbers "cannot be calculated with any certainty" (WC 2.449).

ἀπέσχε τοῦ κολάζειν τοὺς ἑαλωκότας, καθάπερ ἔθος
ἐστὶ τοῖς ἄλλοις, ὡς τοὐναντίον συστήσας αὐτοῖς
χιλίαρχον ἐπέταξε πάντα καθαρίως ὑποδεῖξαι τὰ
6 κατὰ τὴν παρεμβολήν. γενομένου δὲ τούτου προσ-
επύθετο τῶν ἀνθρώπων εἰ πάντα φιλοτίμως αὐτοῖς
7 ὑποδέδειχεν ὁ συσταθείς· τῶν δὲ φησάντων, δοὺς
ἐφόδια καὶ παραπομπὴν ἐξαπέστειλε προστάξας ἐπιμελῶς Ἀννίβᾳ διασαφεῖν περὶ τῶν ἀπηντημένων
8 αὐτοῖς. ὧν παραγενηθέντων θαυμάσας ὁ Ἀννίβας τὴν
μεγαλοψυχίαν καὶ τόλμαν τἀνδρὸς οὐκ οἶδ᾽ ὅπως εἰς
ὁρμὴν ἔπεσε τοῦ βούλεσθαι συνελθεῖν εἰς λόγους τῷ
9 Ποπλίῳ. κρίνας δὲ τοῦτο διεπέμψατο κήρυκα, φάσκων
βούλεσθαι κοινολογηθῆναι πρὸς αὐτὸν ὑπὲρ τῶν
10 ὅλων. ὁ δὲ Πόπλιος ἀκούσας ταῦτα τοῦ κήρυκος συγ-
κατετίθετο τοῖς παρακαλουμένοις, ἔφη δὲ πέμψειν
πρὸς αὐτὸν διασαφῶν, ἐπειδὰν μέλλῃ συμπορεύεσθαι,
11 τὸν τόπον καὶ τὸν καιρόν. ταῦτα μὲν οὖν ἀκούσας ὁ
κῆρυξ ἐπανῆλθε πάλιν εἰς τὴν ἰδίαν παρεμβολήν· τῇ
12 δ᾽ ἐπαύριον ἧκε Μασαννάσας, ἔχων πεζοὺς μὲν εἰς
13 ἑξακισχιλίους, ἱππεῖς δὲ περὶ τετρακισχιλίους. ὃν
ἀποδεξάμενος ὁ Πόπλιος φιλανθρώπως καὶ συγχα-
ρεὶς ἐπὶ τῷ πάντας ὑπηκόους πεποιῆσθαι τοὺς πρότε-
14 ρον Σόφακι πειθομένους, ἀνέζευξε, καὶ παραγενηθεὶς
πρὸς πόλιν Ναράγαρα κατεστρατοπέδευσε, πρός τε
τἆλλα τόπον εὐφυῆ καταλαβόμενος καὶ τὴν ὑδρείαν
ἐντὸς βέλους ποιησάμενος.

6. κἀντεῦθεν ἐξέπεμψε πρὸς τὸν τῶν Καρχηδονίων
στρατηγόν, φάσκων ἕτοιμος εἶναι συμπορεύεσθαι

as is the usual practice, that on the contrary he ordered a tribune to attend them and point out clearly to them the exact arrangement of the camp. After this had been done he asked them if the officer had explained everything to them with proper diligence. When they answered that he had done so, he furnished them with provisions and an escort, and told them to report carefully to Hannibal what had happened to them. On their return Hannibal was so much struck with admiration of Scipio's magnanimity and daring, that he conceived, curiously enough, a strong desire to meet him and converse with him. Having decided on this he sent a herald saying that he desired to discuss the whole situation with him, and Scipio, on receiving the herald's message, assented to the request and said he would send to Hannibal fixing a place and hour for the interview. Upon this the herald returned to his own camp. Next day Massanissa arrived with six thousand foot and four thousand horse. Scipio received him kindly, congratulating him on having brought under his dominion all the former subjects of Syphax. He then broke up his camp and on reaching a town called Naragara[14] encamped there, selecting a spot which was favorably situated in other respects and had water within the throw of a javelin.

6. From here he sent to the Carthaginian general saying that he was now ready for the meeting. When Hannibal

[14] This is Schweighaeuser's suggestion for the *Margaron* of the ms. It may, however, not be the known Naraggara at Sidi Youssef.

2 πρὸς αὐτὸν εἰς λόγους. ὧν ἀκούσας Ἀννίβας ἀνέζευξε,
καὶ συνεγγίσας, ὥστε μὴ πλεῖον ἀπέχειν τριάκοντα
σταδίων, κατεστρατοπέδευσε πρός τινα λόφον, ὃς τὰ
μὲν λοιπὰ πρὸς τὸν παρόντα καιρὸν ὀρθῶς ἔχειν
ἐδόκει, τὴν δ᾽ ὑδρείαν ἀπωτέρω μικρὸν εἶχε· καὶ πολλὴν ταλαιπωρίαν ὑπέμενον οἱ στρατιῶται περὶ τοῦτο
3 τὸ μέρος. κατὰ δὲ τὴν ἑξῆς ἡμέραν προῆλθον ἀπὸ τῆς
ἰδίας παρεμβολῆς ἀμφότεροι μετ᾽ ὀλίγων ἱππέων,
κἄπειτα χωρισθέντες ἀπὸ τούτων αὐτοὶ συνῆλθον εἰς
4 τὸ μέσον ἔχοντες ἑρμηνέα μεθ᾽ αὑτῶν. δεξιωσάμενος
δὲ πρῶτος Ἀννίβας ἤρξατο λέγειν ὡς ἐβούλετο μὲν ἂν
μήτε Ῥωμαίους ἐπιθυμῆσαι μηδέποτε μηδενὸς τῶν
ἐκτὸς Ἰταλίας μήτε Καρχηδονίους τῶν ἐκτὸς Λιβύης·
5 ἀμφοτέροις γὰρ εἶναι ταύτας καὶ καλλίστας δυναστείας καὶ συλλήβδην ὡς ἂν εἰ περιωρισμένας ὑπὸ
τῆς φύσεως.

6 "ἐπεὶ δὲ πρῶτον μὲν ὑπὲρ τῶν κατὰ Σικελίαν
ἀμφισβητήσαντες ἐξεπολεμώσαμεν ἀλλήλους, μετὰ
δὲ ταῦτα πάλιν ὑπὲρ τῶν κατ᾽ Ἰβηρίαν, τὸ δὲ τέλος
ὑπὸ τῆς τύχης οὔπω νουθετούμενοι μέχρι τούτου προ-
βεβήκαμεν ὥστε καὶ περὶ τοῦ τῆς πατρίδος ἐδάφους
οὓς μὲν κεκινδυνευκέναι, τοὺς δ᾽ ἀκμὴν ἔτι καὶ νῦν
7 κινδυνεύειν, λοιπόν ἐστιν, εἴ πως δυνάμεθα δι᾽ αὐτῶν
παραιτησάμενοι τοὺς θεοὺς διαλύσασθαι τὴν ἐνεστῶ-
8 σαν φιλοτιμίαν. ἐγὼ μὲν οὖν ἕτοιμός εἰμι τῷ πεῖραν
εἰληφέναι δι᾽ αὐτῶν τῶν πραγμάτων ὡς <εὐ>μετάθετός
ἐστιν ἡ τύχη καὶ παρὰ μικρὸν εἰς ἑκάτερα ποιεῖ
μεγάλας ῥοπάς, καθάπερ εἰ νηπίοις παισὶ χρωμένη·

heard this he broke up his camp and on getting within a distance of not more than thirty stades[15] of the Romans encamped on a hill which appeared to be convenient for his present design, but was rather too far away from water, and indeed his men suffered considerable hardship owing to this. On the following day both generals came out of their camps accompanied by a few horsemen, and then, leaving their escorts behind, met each other alone,[16] having an interpreter with them. Hannibal first saluted Scipio and began to speak as follows:[17]

"Would that neither the Romans had ever coveted any possessions outside Italy, nor the Carthaginians any outside Africa; for both these were very fine empires and empires of which it might be said on the whole that Nature herself had fixed their limits. But now that in the first place we went to war with each other for the possession of Sicily and next for that of Spain, now that, finally refusing to listen to the admonition of Fortune, we have gone so far that your native soil was once in imminent danger and our own still is, what remains but to consider by what means we can avert the anger of the gods and compose our present contention? I myself am ready to do so as I learnt by actual experience how fickle Fortune is, and how by a slight turn of the scale either way she brings about changes of the greatest moment, as if she were sporting with little children.

[15] A little less than six kilometers.

[16] The meeting may or may not have happened; the possibility certainly exists.

[17] For the speeches (through 8.14) P. may have had, according to WC, "a Scipionic version," but it is hard to believe that Hannibal could have proposed what P. makes him offer in 7.8–9.

7. σὲ δ' ἀγωνιῶ, Πόπλιε, λίαν" ἔφη "καὶ διὰ τὸ νέον εἶναι κομιδῇ καὶ διὰ τὸ πάντα σοι κατὰ λόγον κεχωρηκέναι καὶ τὰ κατὰ τὴν Ἰβηρίαν καὶ τὰ κατὰ τὴν Λιβύην καὶ μηδέπω μέχρι γε τοῦ νῦν εἰς τὴν τῆς τύχης ἐμπεπτωκέναι παλιρρύμην, μήποτ' οὐ πεισθῇς διὰ ταῦτα τοῖς ἐμοῖς λόγοις, καίπερ οὖσι πιστοῖς.

2 σκόπει δ' ἀφ' ἑνὸς τῶν λόγων τὰ πράγματα, μὴ τὰ τῶν

3 προγεγονότων, ἀλλὰ τὰ καθ' ἡμᾶς αὐτούς. εἰμὶ τοιγαροῦν Ἀννίβας ἐκεῖνος, ὃς μετὰ τὴν ἐν Κάνναις μάχην σχεδὸν ἁπάσης Ἰταλίας ἐγκρατὴς γενόμενος μετά τινα χρόνον ἧκον πρὸς αὐτὴν τὴν Ῥώμην, καὶ στρατοπεδεύσας ἐν τετταράκοντα σταδίοις ἐβουλευόμην ὑπὲρ ὑμῶν καὶ τοῦ τῆς ὑμετέρας πατρίδος ἐδάφους πῶς

4 ἐστί μοι χρηστέον, ὃς νῦν ἐν Λιβύῃ πάρειμι πρὸς σὲ Ῥωμαῖον ὄντα περὶ τῆς ἐμαυτοῦ καὶ τῶν Καρχη-

5 δονίων σωτηρίας κοινολογησόμενος. εἰς ἃ βλέποντα παρακαλῶ σε μὴ μέγα φρονεῖν, ἀλλ' ἀνθρωπίνως βουλεύεσθαι περὶ τῶν ἐνεστώτων· τοῦτο δ' ἐστὶ τῶν μὲν ἀγαθῶν ἀεὶ τὸ μέγιστον, τῶν κακῶν δὲ τοὐλά-

6 χιστον αἱρεῖσθαι. τίς οὖν ἂν ἕλοιτο νοῦν ἔχων πρὸς τοιοῦτον ὁρμᾶν κίνδυνον οἷος σοὶ νῦν ἐνέστηκεν; ἐν ᾧ νικήσας μὲν οὔτε τῇ σαυτοῦ δόξῃ μέγα τι προσθήσεις οὔτε τῇ τῆς πατρίδος, ἡττηθεὶς δὲ πάντα τὰ πρὸ

7 τούτου σεμνὰ καὶ καλὰ δι' αὐτὸν ἄρδην ἀναιρήσεις. τί

8 οὖν ἐστιν ὃ προτίθεμαι τέλος τῶν νυνὶ λόγων; πάντα περὶ ὧν πρότερον ἠμφισβητήσαμεν, Ῥωμαίων ὑπάρχειν—ταῦτα δ' ἦν Σικελία, Σαρδώ, τὰ κατὰ τὴν Ἰβηρίαν—καὶ μηδέποτε Καρχηδονίους Ῥωμαίοις ὑπὲρ

7. But I fear that you, Publius, both because you are very young and because success has constantly attended you both in Spain and in Africa, and you have never up to now at least fallen into the countercurrent of Fortune, will not be convinced by my words, however worthy of credit they may be. Consider things by the light of one example, an example not drawn from remote times, but from our own. I, then, am that Hannibal who after the battle of Cannae became master of almost the whole of Italy, who not long afterward advanced even up to Rome, and encamping at forty stades from the walls deliberated with myself how I should treat you and your native soil. And now here am I in Africa on the point of negotiating with you, a Roman, for the safety of myself and my country. Consider this, I beg you, and be not overproud, but take such counsel at the present juncture as a mere man can take, and that is ever to choose the most good and the least evil. What man of sense, I ask, would rush into such danger as that which confronts you now? If you conquer you will add but little to the fame of your country and your own, but if you suffer defeat you will utterly efface the memory of all that was grand and glorious in your past. What then is the end I would gain by this interview? I propose that all the countries that were formerly a subject of dispute between us, that is Sicily, Sardinia, and Spain, shall belong to Rome and that Carthage shall never make war upon Rome on ac-

τούτων ἀντᾶραι πόλεμον· ὁμοίως δὲ καὶ τὰς ἄλλας
νήσους, ὅσαι μεταξὺ κεῖνται τῆς Ἰταλίας καὶ Λιβύης,
9 Ῥωμαίων ὑπάρχειν. ταύτας γὰρ πέπεισμαι τὰς συνθήκας καὶ πρὸς τὸ μέλλον ἀσφαλεστάτας μὲν εἶναι
Καρχηδονίοις, ἐνδοξοτάτας δὲ σοὶ καὶ πᾶσι Ῥωμαίοις."

8. Ἀννίβας μὲν οὖν ταῦτ' εἶπεν. ὁ δὲ Πόπλιος
ὑπολαβὼν οὔτε τοῦ περὶ Σικελίας ἔφη πολέμου Ῥωμαίους οὔτε τοῦ περὶ τῆς Ἰβηρίας αἰτίους γεγονέναι,
2 Καρχηδονίους δὲ προφανῶς· ὑπὲρ ὧν κάλλιστα γινώσκειν αὐτὸν τὸν Ἀννίβαν. μάρτυρας δὲ καὶ τοὺς θεοὺς
γεγονέναι τούτων, περιθέντας τὸ κράτος οὐ τοῖς ἄρ-
3 χουσι χειρῶν ἀδίκων, ἀλλὰ τοῖς ἀμυνομένοις. βλέπειν
δὲ καὶ τὰ τῆς τύχης οὐδενὸς ἧττον καὶ τῶν ἀνθρω-
4 πίνων στοχάζεσθαι κατὰ δύναμιν. "ἀλλ' εἰ μὲν πρὸ
τοῦ τοὺς Ῥωμαίους διαβαίνειν εἰς Λιβύην αὐτὸς ἐξ
Ἰταλίας ἐκχωρήσας προύτεινας τὰς διαλύσεις ταύτας,
5 οὐκ ἂν οἴμαί σε διαψευσθῆναι τῆς ἐλπίδος. ἐπεὶ δὲ
σὺ μὲν ἄκων ἐκ τῆς Ἰταλίας ἀπηλλάγης, ἡμεῖς δὲ
διαβάντες εἰς τὴν Λιβύην τῶν ὑπαίθρων ἐκρατήσα-
μεν, δῆλον ὡς μεγάλην εἴληφε τὰ πράγματα παραλ-
6 λαγήν. τὸ δὲ δὴ μέγιστον ἤλθομεν ἐπὶ τί πέρας;
7 ἡττηθέντων καὶ δεηθέντων τῶν παρὰ σοῦ πολιτῶν
ἐθέμεθα συνθήκας ἐγγράπτους, ἐν αἷς ἦν πρὸς τοῖς
ὑπὸ σοῦ νῦν προτεινομένοις τοὺς αἰχμαλώτους
ἀποδοῦναι χωρὶς λύτρων Καρχηδονίους, τῶν πλοίων

count of them. Likewise that the other islands lying between Italy and Africa shall belong to Rome. Such terms of peace would, I am convinced, be most secure for the Carthaginians and most honorable to you and to all the Romans."

8. Hannibal having spoken so, Scipio replied.[18] He said that neither for the war about Sicily, nor for that about Spain, were the Romans responsible, but the Carthaginians were evidently the authors of both, as Hannibal himself was well aware. The gods, too, had testified to this by bestowing victory not on the unjust aggressors but on those who had taken up arms to defend themselves. No one, he said, was more awake than himself to the fickleness of Fortune and as far as it was in his power he took into consideration the uncertainty of human affairs. "But as for the conditions you propose," he continued, "if before the Romans had crossed to Africa you had retired from Italy and then proposed them, I think your expectations would not have been disappointed. But now that you have been forced reluctantly to leave Italy, and that we, having crossed to Africa, are in command of the open country, the situation is manifestly much changed. And—for this is the most important question—what is the position we have now reached? When your countrymen were beaten and begged for peace we framed a treaty in writing in which it was stipulated, in addition to your present proposals, that the Carthaginians should give up their prisoners with-

18 One has to be equally suspicious about Scipio's words as given here, especially 8.4–5; they anticipate how the brothers Scipio answered the envoys of Antiochus the Great in 190 (21.15.7–9).

παραχωρῆσαι τῶν καταφράκτων, πεντακισχίλια τά-
8 λαντα προσενεγκεῖν, ὅμηρα δοῦναι περὶ τούτων. ταῦτ᾽
ἦν ἃ συνεθέμεθα πρὸς ἀλλήλους· ὑπὲρ τούτων ἐπρε-
σβεύσαμεν ἀμφότεροι πρός τε τὴν σύγκλητον τὴν
ἡμετέραν καὶ πρὸς τὸν δῆμον, ἡμεῖς μὲν ὁμολογοῦντες
εὐδοκεῖν τοῖς γεγραμμένοις, Καρχηδόνιοι δὲ δεόμενοι
9 τούτων τυχεῖν. ἐπείσθη τὸ συνέδριον τούτοις, ὁ δὲ
δῆμος συγκατῄνεσε. τυχόντες ὧν ἠξίουν ἠθέτησαν
10 ταῦτα Καρχηδόνιοι, παρασπονδήσαντες ἡμᾶς. τί λείπεται ποιεῖν; σὺ τὴν ἐμὴν χώραν μεταλαβὼν εἶπον.
11 ἀφελεῖν τὰ βαρύτατα τῶν ὑποκειμένων ἐπιταγμάτων;
ἵνα δὴ λαβόντες ἆθλα τῆς παρανομίας διδαχθῶσι
12 τοὺς εὖ ποιοῦντας εἰς τὸ λοιπὸν παρασπονδεῖν· ἀλλ᾽
ἵνα τυχόντες ὧν ἀξιοῦσι χάριν ὀφείλωσιν ἡμῖν; ἀλλὰ
νυνὶ μεθ᾽ ἱκετηρίας τυχόντες ὧν παρεκάλουν, ὅτι βραχείας ἐλπίδος ἐπελάβοντο τῆς κατὰ σέ, παρὰ πόδας
13 ὡς ἐχθροῖς ἡμῖν κέχρηνται καὶ πολεμίοις. ἐν οἷς
βαρυτέρου μέν τινος προσεπιταχθέντος δυνατὸν ἀν-
ενεγκεῖν τῷ δήμῳ περὶ διαλύσεως, ὑφαίρεσιν δὲ ποιουμένοις τῶν ὑποκειμένων οὐδ᾽ ἀναφορὰν ἔχει τὸ
14 διαβούλιον. τί πέρας οὖν πάλιν τῶν ἡμετέρων λόγων;
ἢ τὴν ἐπιτροπὴν ὑμᾶς διδόναι περὶ σφῶν αὐτῶν καὶ
τῆς πατρίδος ἢ μαχομένους νικᾶν."

9. Ταῦτα μὲν οὖν διαλεχθέντες αὐτοῖς Ἀννίβας καὶ
Πόπλιος ἐχωρίσθησαν, ἀσύμβατον ποιησάμενοι τὴν
2 κοινολογίαν. εἰς δὲ τὴν ἐπαύριον ἅμα τῷ φωτὶ τὰς
δυνάμεις ἐξῆγον ἀμφότεροι καὶ συνίσταντο τὸν ἀγῶνα, Καρχηδόνιοι μὲν ὑπὲρ τῆς σφετέρας σωτηρίας καὶ

out ransom, that they should surrender their ships of war, and that they should pay us five thousand talents, and finally that they should give hostages for the performance of those conditions. These were the terms we agreed upon. We jointly sent envoys to Rome to submit them to the senate and the people, we Romans stating that we agreed to the terms offered and you Carthaginians entreating that they might be accepted. The senate agreed and the people also gave their consent. The Carthaginians, after their request had been granted, most treacherously violated the peace. What remains to be done? Put yourself in my place and tell me. Shall we withdraw the most onerous of the conditions imposed? That would be to reward your countrymen for their treachery and teach them to continue to betray their benefactors. Or shall we grant their present request in the hope of earning their gratitude? But now after obtaining their request by earnest supplication, the moment they conceived the slightest hope from your return, they at once treated us as enemies and foes. If we added some conditions even more onerous we might in that case refer the treaty to our popular assembly, but if we withdraw some of the conditions it would be useless even to make mention of this conference at Rome. Of what further use then is our interview? Either put yourselves and your country at our mercy or fight and conquer us."

9. After this conversation, which held out no hopes of reconciliation, the two generals parted from each other. On the following morning at daybreak they led out their armies and opened the battle, the Carthaginians fighting for

τῶν κατὰ τὴν Λιβύην πραγμάτων, Ῥωμαῖοι δὲ περὶ

3 τῆς τῶν ὅλων ἀρχῆς καὶ δυναστείας. ἐφ᾿ ἃ τίς οὐκ ἂν
ἐπιστήσας συμπαθὴς γένοιτο κατὰ τὴν ἐξήγησιν;

4 οὔτε γὰρ δυνάμεις πολεμικωτέρας οὔθ᾿ ἡγεμόνας ἐπι-
τυχεστέρους τούτων καὶ μᾶλλον ἀθλητὰς γεγονότας
τῶν κατὰ πόλεμον ἔργων εὕροι τις ἂν ἑτέρους, οὐδὲ
μὴν ἆθλα μείζω τὴν τύχην ἐκτεθεικυῖαν τοῖς ἀγωνιζο-

5 μένοις τῶν τότε προκειμένων· οὐ γὰρ τῆς Λιβύης
αὐτῆς οὐδὲ τῆς Εὐρώπης ἔμελλον κυριεύειν οἱ τῇ
μάχῃ κρατήσαντες, ἀλλὰ καὶ τῶν ἄλλων μερῶν τῆς

6 οἰκουμένης, ὅσα νῦν πέπτωκεν ὑπὸ τὴν ἱστορίαν. ὃ καὶ
συνέβη γενέσθαι μετ᾿ ὀλίγον. πλὴν ὁ μὲν Πόπλιος
ἔθηκε τὰς τάξεις τῶν ἰδίων δυνάμεων τὸν τρόπον

7 τοῦτον. πρῶτον μὲν τοὺς ἀστάτους καὶ τὰς τούτων
σημαίας ἐν διαστήμασιν, ἐπὶ δὲ τούτοις τοὺς πρίγκιπας, τιθεὶς τὰς σπείρας οὐ κατὰ τὸ τῶν πρώτων
σημαιῶν διάστημα, καθάπερ ἔθος ἐστὶ τοῖς Ῥωμαίοις, ἀλλὰ καταλλήλους ἐν ἀποστάσει διὰ τὸ πλῆθος
τῶν παρὰ τοῖς ἐναντίοις ἐλεφάντων· τελευταίους δ᾿

8 ἐπέστησε τοὺς τριαρίους. ἐπὶ δὲ τῶν κεράτων ἔταξε
κατὰ μὲν τὸ λαιὸν Γάιον Λαίλιον, ἔχοντα τοὺς Ἰταλικοὺς ἱππέας, κατὰ δὲ τὸ δεξιὸν μέρος Μασαννάσαν

9 μετὰ πάντων τῶν ὑφ᾿ ἑαυτὸν ταττομένων Νομάδων. τὰ
δὲ διαστήματα τῶν πρώτων σημαιῶν ἀνεπλήρωσε
ταῖς γροσφομάχων σπείραις, παραγγείλας τούτοις

10 προκινδυνεύειν, ἐὰν δ᾿ ἐκβιάζωνται κατὰ τὴν τῶν θηρίων ἔφοδον, ἀποχωρεῖν, τοὺς μὲν καταταχοῦντας διὰ
τῶν ἐπ᾿ εὐθείας διαστημάτων εἰς τοὐπίσω τῆς ὅλης

their own safety and the dominion of Africa, and the Romans for the empire of the world. Is there anyone who can remain unmoved in reading the narrative of such an encounter? For it would be impossible to find more valiant soldiers, or generals who had been more successful and were more thoroughly exercised in the art of war, nor indeed had Fortune ever offered to contending armies a more splendid prize of victory, since the conquerors would not be masters of Africa and Europe alone, but of all those parts of the world which now hold a place in history; as indeed they very shortly were. Scipio drew up his army in the following fashion. In front he placed the *hastati* with certain intervals between the maniples and behind them the *principes*, not placing their maniples, as is the usual Roman custom, opposite to the intervals separating those of the first line, but directly behind these latter at a certain distance owing to the large number of the enemy's elephants. Last of all he placed the *triarii*. On his left wing he posted Gaius Laelius with the Italian horse, and on the right wing Massanissa with the whole of his Numidians. The intervals of the first maniples he filled up with the companies of *velites*, ordering them to open the action, and if they were forced back by the charge of the elephants to retire, those who had time to do so by the straight pas-

δυνάμεως, τοὺς δὲ περικαταλαμβανομένους εἰς τὰ
πλάγια παρίστασθαι διαστήματα κατὰ τὰς σημαίας.

10. Ταῦτα δ᾿ ἑτοιμασάμενος ‹ἐπ›επορεύετο παρακαλῶν τὰς δυνάμεις βραχέως μέν, οἰκείως δὲ τῆς
2 ὑποκειμένης περιστάσεως. ἠξίου γὰρ μνημονεύοντας
τῶν πογεγονότων ἀγώνων ἄνδρας ἀγαθοὺς γίνεσθαι,
σφῶν καὶ τῆς πατρίδος ἀξίους, καὶ λαμβάνειν πρὸ
ὀφθαλμῶν ὅτι κρατήσαντες μὲν τῶν ἐχθρῶν οὐ μόνον
τῶν ἐν Λιβύῃ πραγμάτων ἔσονται κύριοι βεβαίως,
ἀλλὰ καὶ τῆς ἄλλης οἰκουμένης τὴν ἡγεμονίαν καὶ
δυναστείαν ἀδήριτον αὑτοῖς τε καὶ τῇ πατρίδι περι-
3 ποιήσουσιν· ἐὰν δ᾿ ὡς ἄλλως ἐκβῇ τὰ κατὰ τὸν κίνδυνον, οἱ μὲν ἀποθανόντες εὐγενῶς ἐν τῇ μάχῃ κάλλιστον ἐντάφιον ἕξουσι τὸν ὑπὲρ τῆς πατρίδος θάνατον,
οἱ δὲ διαφυγόντες αἴσχιστον καὶ ἐλεεινότατον τὸν
4 ἐπίλοιπον βίον. ἀσφάλειαν γὰρ τοῖς φυγοῦσιν οὐδεὶς
ἱκανὸς περιποιῆσαι τόπος τῶν ἐν τῇ Λιβύῃ· πεσοῦσι
δ᾿ ὑπὸ τὰς τῶν Καρχηδονίων χεῖρας οὐκ ἄδηλα [εἶναι]
τὰ συμβησόμενα τοῖς ὀρθῶς λογιζομένοις· "ὧν" ἔφη
5 "μηδενὶ γένοιτο πεῖραν ὑμῶν λαβεῖν. τῆς δ᾿ οὖν τύχης
ἡμῖν τὰ μέγιστα τῶν ἄθλων εἰς ἑκάτερον τὸ μέρος
ἐκτεθεικυίας, πῶς οὐκ ἂν εἴημεν ἀγεννέστατοι καὶ
συλλήβδην ἀφρονέστατοι πάντων, εἰ παρέντες τὰ
κάλλιστα τῶν ἀγαθῶν ἑλοίμεθα τὰ μέγιστα τῶν
6 κακῶν διὰ φιλοζωίαν;" διόπερ ἠξίου δύο προθεμένους,
ταῦτα δ᾿ ἐστὶν ἢ νικᾶν ἢ θνήσκειν, ὁμόσε χωρεῖν εἰς
7 τοὺς πολεμίους. τοὺς γὰρ τοιαύτας ἔχοντας διαλήψεις

sages as far as the rear of the whole army, and those who were overtaken to right or left along the intervals between the lines.

10. Having made these preparations he rode along the lines and addressed his troops in a few words suitable to the occasion. "Bear in mind," he said, "your past battles and fight like brave men worthy of yourselves and your country. Keep it before your eyes that if you overcome your enemies not only will you be unquestioned masters of Africa, but you will gain for yourselves and your country the undisputed command and sovereignty of the rest of the world. But if the result of the battle be otherwise, those of you who have fallen bravely in the fight will lie for ever shrouded in the glory of dying thus for their country, while those who save themselves by flight will spend the remainder of their lives in misery and disgrace. For no place in Africa will be able to afford you safety, and if you fall into the hands of the Carthaginians it is plain enough to anyone who gives due thought to it what fate awaits you. May none of you, I pray, live to experience that fate. Now that Fortune offers us a choice of the most glorious of prizes, how utterly craven, in short how foolish shall we be, if we reject the greatest of goods and choose the greatest of evils from mere love of life. Go, therefore, to meet the foe with two objects before you, either victory or death. For men ani-

κατ' ἀνάγκην ἀεὶ κρατεῖν τῶν ἀντιταττομένων, ἐπειδὰν ἀπελπίσαντες τοῦ ζῆν ὦσιν εἰς τὴν μάχην.

11. Ὁ μὲν οὖν Πόπλιος τοιαύτην ἐποιήσατο τὴν παραίνεσιν. ὁ δ' Ἀννίβας τὰ μὲν θηρία πρὸ πάσης τῆς δυνάμεως, ὄντα πλείω τῶν ὀγδοήκοντα, μετὰ δὲ ταῦτα τοὺς μισθοφόρους ἐπέστησε, περὶ μυρίους ὄντας καὶ δισχιλίους τὸν ἀριθμόν. οὗτοι δ' ἦσαν
2 Λιγυστῖνοι, Κελτοί, Βαλιαρεῖς, Μαυρούσιοι. τούτων δὲ κατόπιν παρενέβαλε τοὺς ἐγχωρίους Λίβυας καὶ Καρχηδονίους, ἐπὶ δὲ πᾶσι τοὺς ἐξ Ἰταλίας ἥκοντας μεθ' αὑτοῦ, πλεῖον ἢ στάδιον ἀποστήσας τῶν προ-
3 τεταγμένων. τὰ δὲ κέρατα διὰ τῶν ἱππέων ἠσφαλίσατο, θεὶς ἐπὶ μὲν τὸ λαιὸν τοὺς συμμάχους Νομάδας,
4 ἐπὶ δὲ τὸ δεξιὸν τοὺς τῶν Καρχηδονίων ἱππεῖς. παρήγγειλε δὲ τοὺς ἰδίους στρατιώτας ἕκαστον παρακαλεῖν, ἀναφέροντας τὴν ἐλπίδα τῆς νίκης ἐφ' ἑαυτὸν
5 καὶ τὰς μεθ' αὑτοῦ παραγεγενημένας δυνάμεις· τοῖς δὲ Καρχηδονίοις ἐκέλευσε τοὺς ἡγουμένους τὰ συμβησόμενα περὶ τέκνων καὶ γυναικῶν ἐξαριθμεῖσθαι καὶ τιθέναι πρὸ ὀφθαλμῶν, ἐὰν ἄλλως πως ἐκβῇ τὰ τῆς μάχης. οὗτοι μὲν οὖν οὕτως ἐποίουν τὸ παραγγελθέν.
6 Ἀννίβας δὲ τοὺς μεθ' αὑτοῦ παραγεγονότας ἐπιπορευόμενος ἠξίου καὶ παρεκάλει διὰ πλειόνων μνησθῆναι μὲν τῆς πρὸς ἀλλήλους ἑπτακαιδεκαέτους συνηθείας, μνησθῆναι δὲ τοῦ πλήθους τῶν προγεγονότων αὐτοῖς
7 πρὸς Ῥωμαίους ἀγώνων· ἐν οἷς ἀηττήτους γεγονότας οὐδ' ἐλπίδα τοῦ νικᾶν οὐδέποτ' ἔφη Ῥωμαίοις αὐτοὺς
8 ἀπολελοιπέναι. τὸ δὲ μέγιστον, ἠξίου λαμβάνειν πρὸ

544

mated by such a spirit must always overcome their adversaries, since they go into battle ready to throw their lives away."

11. Such was the substance of Scipio's harangue. Hannibal placed in front of his whole force his elephants, of which he had over eighty, and behind them the mercenaries numbering about twelve thousand. They were composed of Ligurians, Celts, Balearic Islanders, and Moors. Behind these he placed the native Libyans and Carthaginians, and last of all the troops he had brought over from Italy at a distance of more than a stade from the front lines. He secured his wings by cavalry, placing the Numidian allies on the left and the Carthaginian horse on the right He ordered each commanding officer of the mercenaries to address his own men, bidding them be sure of victory as they could rely on his own presence and that of the forces that he had brought back with him. As for the Carthaginians, he ordered their commanders to set before their eyes all the sufferings that would befall their wives and children if the result of the battle were adverse. They did as they were ordered, and Hannibal himself went the round of his own troops, begging and imploring them to remember their comradeship of seventeen years and the number of the battles they had previously fought against the Romans. "In all these battles," he said, "you proved so invincible that you have not left the Romans the smallest hope of ever being able to defeat you. Above all the rest, and apart from

ὀφθαλμῶν χωρὶς τῶν κατὰ μέρος κινδύνων καὶ τῶν
ἀναριθμήτων προτερημάτων τήν τε περὶ τὸν Τρεβίαν
ποταμὸν μάχην πρὸς τὸν πατέρα τοῦ νῦν ἡγουμένου
Ῥωμαίων, ὁμοίως τὴν ἐν Τυρρηνίᾳ πρὸς Φλαμίνιον
μάχην, ἔτι δὲ τὴν περὶ Κάννας γενομένην πρὸς Αἰμί-
9 λιον, ἃς οὔτε κατὰ πλῆθος τῶν ἀνδρῶν οὔτε κατὰ τὰς
ἀρετὰς ἀξίας εἶναι συγκρίσεως πρὸς τὸν νῦν ἐπιφερό-
10 μενον κίνδυνον. καὶ ταῦτα λέγων ἀναβλέπειν αὐτοὺς
ἐκέλευε ⟨καὶ⟩ τὴν τῶν ὑπεναντίων κατοπτεύειν τάξιν·
οὐ γὰρ οἷον ἐλάττους, ἀλλ᾽ οὐδὲ πολλοστὸν μέρος
εἶναι τῶν τότε πρὸς αὐτοὺς ἀγωνισαμένων, ταῖς γε
11 μὴν ἀρεταῖς οὐδὲ σύγκρισιν ἔχειν. ἐκείνους μὲν γὰρ
ἀηττήτους ὄντας ἐξ ἀκεραίου διηγωνίσθαι πρὸς σφᾶς,
τούτων δὲ τοὺς μὲν ἐκγόνους εἶναι, τοὺς δὲ λείψανα
τῶν ἡττημένων ἐν Ἰταλίᾳ καὶ πεφευγότων αὐτὸν πλεο-
12 νάκις. διόπερ [ᾤετο] δεῖν μὴ καταλῦσαι μήτε τὴν
σφῶν αὐτῶν μήτε τὴν τοῦ προεστῶτος δόξαν καὶ
προσηγορίαν, ἀλλ᾽ ἀγωνισαμένους εὐψύχως βεβαιῶσαι τὴν διαδεδομένην περὶ αὐτῶν φήμην, ὡς ὄντων
ἀηττήτων.
13 Ταῦτα μὲν οὖν καὶ τοιαῦτα παρεκάλεσαν ἀμφότεροι.
12. ἐπειδὴ δ᾽ ἑκατέροις ἦν εὐτρεπῆ τὰ πρὸς τὸν
κίνδυνον, πάλαι τῶν Νομαδικῶν ἱππέων πρὸς ἀλλήλους ἀκροβολιζομένων, τότε παρήγγειλε τοῖς ἐπὶ τῶν
ἐλεφάντων Ἀννίβας ποιεῖσθαι τὴν ἔφοδον ἐπὶ τοὺς
2 ὑπεναντίους. ἅμα δὲ τῷ πανταχόθεν τὰς σάλπιγγας
καὶ τὰς βυκάνας ἀναβοῆσαι τινὰ μὲν διαταραχθέντα

your success in innumerable smaller engagements, keep before your eyes the battle of the Trebia fought against the father of the present Roman general, bear in mind the battle of the Trasimene against Flaminius, and that of Cannae against Aemilius, battles with which the action in which we are about to engage is not worthy of comparison either in respect to the numbers of the forces engaged or the courage of the soldiers." He bade them, as he spoke thus, to cast their eyes on the ranks of the enemy. Not only were they fewer, but they were scarcely a small fraction of the forces that had formerly faced them, and for courage they were not to be compared with those. For then their adversaries were men whose strength was unbroken and who had never suffered defeat, but those of today were some of them the children of the former and some the wretched remnant of the legions he had so often vanquished and put to flight in Italy. Therefore he urged them not to destroy the glorious record of themselves and their general, but, fighting bravely, to confirm their reputation for invincibility.

Such was the substance of the harangues of the two generals.

12. When all was ready for battle on both sides, the Numidian horse having been skirmishing with each other for some time, Hannibal ordered the drivers of the elephants to charge the enemy. When the trumpets and bugles sounded shrilly from all sides, some of the animals

τῶν θηρίων ἐξ αὐτῆς ὥρμησε παλίσσυτα κατὰ τῶν
βεβοηθηκότων τοῖς Καρχηδονίοις Νομάδων·‹οὗ γενομένου διὰ› τῶν περὶ τὸν Μασαννάσαν ταχέως ἐψι-
3   λώθη τὸ λαιὸν κέρας τῶν Καρχηδονίων. τὰ δὲ λοιπὰ
συμπεσόντα τοῖς τῶν Ῥωμαίων γροσφομάχοις ἐν τῷ
μεταξὺ χωρίῳ τῶν παρατάξεων πολλὰ μὲν ἔπασχε
4   κακά, πολλὰ δ' ἐποίει τοὺς ὑπεναντίους, ἕως ὅτου
πεφοβημένα τὰ μὲν διὰ τῶν διαστημάτων ἐξέπεσε,
δεξαμένων αὐτὰ τῶν Ῥωμαίων ἀσφαλῶς κατὰ τὴν τοῦ
στρατηγοῦ πρόνοιαν, τὰ δ' ἐπὶ τὸ δεξιὸν μέρος παρα-
φυγόντα διὰ τῶν ἱππέων συνακοντιζόμενα τέλος εἰς
5   τὸν ἔξω τόπον τῶν στρατοπέδων ἐξέπεσεν, ὅτε δὴ καὶ
Λαίλιος ἅμα τῇ περὶ τοὺς ἐλέφαντας ταραχῇ συμβαλὼν ἠνάγκασε φυγεῖν τοὺς τῶν Καρχηδονίων ἱπ-
6   πεῖς προτροπάδην. οὗτος μὲν οὖν ἐπέκειτο τοῖς φεύγουσιν ἐκθύμως· τὸ δ' ὅμοιον ἐποίει καὶ Μασαννάσας.
7   κατὰ δὲ τὸν καιρὸν τοῦτον αἱ φάλαγγες ἀμφότεραι
βάδην ἀλλήλαις καὶ σοβαρῶς ἐπῄεσαν, πλὴν τῶν
‹ἐκ› τῆς Ἰταλίας μετ' Ἀννίβου παραγεγονότων· οὗτοι
8   δ' ἔμενον ἐπέχοντες τὸν ἐξ ἀρχῆς τόπον. ἐπειδὴ δ'
ἐγγὺς ἦσαν ἀλλήλων, οἱ μὲν Ῥωμαῖοι κατὰ τὰ πάτρια
συναλαλάξαντες καὶ συμψοφήσαντες τοῖς ξίφεσι τοὺς
9   θυρεοὺς προσέβαλλον τοῖς ὑπεναντίοις, οἱ δὲ μισθοφόροι τῶν Καρχηδονίων ἀδιάκριτον ἐποίουν τὴν φωνὴν καὶ παρηλλαγμένην· οὐ γὰρ πάντων ἦν κατὰ τὸν
ποιητὴν ὁ αὐτὸς θροῦς

548

took fright and at once turned tail and rushed back upon the Numidians who had come up to help the Carthaginians, ⟨whereupon by those with Massanissa⟩ the left wing of the Carthaginians soon became exposed. The rest of the elephants falling on the Roman *velites* in the space between the two main armies, both inflicted and suffered much loss, until finally in their terror some of them escaped through the gaps in the Roman line which Scipio's foresight had provided, so that the Romans suffered no injury, while others fled toward the right and, received by the cavalry with showers of javelins, at length escaped out of the field. It was at this moment that Laelius, availing himself of the disturbance created by the elephants, charged the Carthaginian cavalry and forced them to headlong flight. He pressed the pursuit closely, as likewise did Massanissa. In the meanwhile both phalanxes slowly and in imposing array advanced on each other, except the troops which Hannibal had brought back from Italy, who remained in their original position. When the phalanxes were close to each other, the Romans fell upon their foes, raising their war cry and clashing their shields with their swords as is their practice, while there was a strange confusion of shouts raised by the Carthaginian mercenaries, for, as Homer says, their voice was not one, but

οὐδ᾽ ἴα γῆρυς,

ἄλλη δ᾽ ἄλλων γλῶσσα, πολύκλητοι δ᾽ ἔσαν
ἄνδρες,[1]

καθάπερ ἀρτίως ἐξηριθμησάμην.

13. Πάσης δ᾽ οὔσης ἐκ χειρὸς καὶ κατ᾽ ἄνδρα τῆς μάχης [διὰ τὸ μὴ δόρασι ⟨ἀλλὰ⟩ ξίφεσι χρῆσθαι τοὺς ἀγωνιζομένους], τῇ μὲν εὐχερείᾳ καὶ τόλμῃ προεῖχον οἱ μισθοφόροι τὰς ἀρχάς, καὶ πολλοὺς κατ-
2 ετραυμάτιζον τῶν Ῥωμαίων, τῷ δὲ τῆς συντάξεως ἀκριβεῖ καὶ τῷ καθοπλισμῷ πιστεύοντες οἱ Ῥωμαῖοι
3 μᾶλλον ἐπέβαινον εἰς τὸ πρόσθεν. ἅμα δὲ τοῖς μὲν Ῥωμαίοις ἑπομένων καὶ παρακαλούντων τῶν κατόπιν, τοῖς δὲ μισθοφόροις τῶν Καρχηδονίων οὐ συνεγγιζόντων οὐδὲ παραβοηθούντων, ἀλλ᾽ ἀποδειλιώντων
4 ταῖς ψυχαῖς, πέρας ἐνέκλιναν οἱ βάρβαροι, καὶ δόξαντες ἐγκαταλείπεσθαι προφανῶς ὑπὸ τῶν ἰδίων, ἐπιπεσόντες κατὰ τὴν ἀποχώρησιν εἰς τοὺς ἐφεστῶτας
5 ἔκτεινον τούτους. ὃ καὶ πολλοὺς ἠνάγκασε τῶν Καρχηδονίων ἀνδρωδῶς ἀποθανεῖν· φονευόμενοι γὰρ ὑπὸ τῶν μισθοφόρων ἐμάχοντο παρὰ τὴν αὐτῶν προαίρεσιν ἅμα πρός τε τοὺς ἰδίους καὶ πρὸς τοὺς Ῥωμαίους.
6 ποιούμενοι δὲ τὸν κίνδυνον ἐκστατικῶς καὶ παρηλλαγμένως οὐκ ὀλίγους διέφθειραν καὶ τῶν ἰδίων καὶ τῶν
7 ὑπεναντίων. καὶ δὴ τῷ τοιούτῳ τρόπῳ συνέχεαν ἐπιπεσόντες τὰς τῶν ἀστάτων σημαίας· οἱ μέντοι τῶν πριγκίπων ἡγεμόνες συνθεασάμενοι τὸ γεγονὸς ἐπέ-
8 στησαν τὰς αὑτῶν τάξεις. τῶν δὲ μισθοφόρων καὶ τῶν

Mixed was the murmur, and confused the sound,
   Their names all various,[19]

as appears from the list of them I gave above.

13. As the whole battle was a hand-to-hand affair, the men not using spears but swords,[20] the mercenaries at first prevailed by their courage and skill, wounding many of the Romans, but the latter still continued to advance, relying on their admirable order and on the superiority of their arms. The rear ranks of the Romans followed close on their comrades, cheering them on, but the Carthaginians behaved like cowards, never coming near their mercenaries nor attempting to back them up, so that finally the barbarians gave way, and thinking that they had evidently been left in the lurch by their own side, fell upon those they encountered in their retreat and began to kill them. This actually compelled many of the Carthaginians to die like men; for as they were being butchered by their own mercenaries they were obliged against their will to fight both against these and against the Romans, and as when at bay they showed frantic and extraordinary courage, they killed a considerable number both of their mercenaries and of the enemy. In this way they even threw the maniples of the *hastati* into confusion, but the officers of the *principes*, seeing what was happening, held firm their ranks, and now the greater number of the Carthaginians and their merce-

---

[19] The quotation combines parts of Hom. *Il*. 4.437 with others of *Il*. 2.804.

[20] Translating Hultsch's emendation; but see WC 2.493.

---

[1] Homer, *Il*. iv. 437, ii. 809.

Καρχηδονίων τὸ πλεῖστον μέρος τὸ μὲν ὑφ' αὑτῶν, τὸ
9 δ' ὑπὸ τῶν ἀστάτων αὐτοῦ κατεκόπη. τοὺς δὲ διασῳζο-
μένους καὶ φεύγοντας οὐκ εἴασε καταμιγῆναι ταῖς
δυνάμεσιν Ἀννίβας, ἀλλὰ προβαλέσθαι παραγγείλας
τοῖς ἐπιστάταις ἐκώλυσε μὴ παραδέξασθαι τοὺς ἐγγί-
10 ζοντας. ὅθεν ἠναγκάσθησαν οὗτοι μὲν ποιεῖσθαι τὴν
ἀποχώρησιν ἐπὶ τὰ κέρατα καὶ τὰς ἐκ τούτων εὐρυχωρίας,

14. γενομένου δὲ τοῦ μεταξὺ τόπου τῶν καταλειπο-
μένων στρατοπέδων πλήρους αἵματος, φόνου, νεκρῶν,
πολλὴν ἀπορίαν παρεῖχε τῷ τῶν Ῥωμαίων στρατηγῷ
2 τὸ τῆς τροπῆς ἐμπόδιον· ὅ τε γὰρ τῶν νεκρῶν ὄλισθος,
ὡς ἂν αἱμοφύρτων καὶ σωρηδὸν πεπτωκότων, ἥ τε τῶν
χύδην ἐρριμμένων ὅπλων ὁμοῦ τοῖς πτώμασιν ἀλογία
δυσχερῆ τὴν δίοδον ἔμελλε ποιήσειν τοῖς ἐν τάξει
3 διαπορευομένοις. οὐ μὴν ἀλλὰ τοὺς μὲν τραυματίας
εἰς τοὐπίσω τῆς παρατάξεως κομισάμενος, τοὺς δ'
ἐπιδιώκοντας τῶν ἀστάτων ἀνακαλεσάμενος διὰ τῆς
σάλπιγγος, τοὺς μὲν αὐτοῦ πρὸ τῆς μάχης κατὰ
4 μέσους τοὺς πολεμίους ἐπέστησε, τοὺς δὲ πρίγκιπας
καὶ τριαρίους πυκνώσας ἐφ' ἑκάτερον τὸ κέρας προ-
5 άγειν παρήγγειλε διὰ τῶν νεκρῶν. ἐπειδὴ δ' ὑπερ-
βάντες ἐξ ἴσου τοῖς ἀστάτοις ἐγένοντο, συνέβαλον αἱ
φάλαγγες ἀλλήλαις μετὰ τῆς μεγίστης ὁρμῆς καὶ
6 προθυμίας. ὄντων δὲ καὶ τῷ πλήθει καὶ τοῖς φρονή-
μασι καὶ ταῖς ἀρεταῖς καὶ τοῖς καθοπλισμοῖς παρα-
πλησίων ἀμφοτέρων, ἄκριτον ἐπὶ πολὺ συνέβαινε

naries were cut to pieces where they stood, either by themselves or by the *hastati*. Hannibal did not allow the survivors in their flight to mix with his own men but, ordering the troops behind to level their spears against them, prevented them from being received into his force. They were therefore obliged to retreat toward the wings and the open ground beyond.

14. The space which separated the two armies still on the field was now covered with blood, slaughter, and dead bodies, and the rout of the enemy proved an obstacle causing considerable embarrassment to the Roman general. For he saw that it would be very difficult to pass over the ground without breaking his ranks owing to the quantity of slippery corpses which were still soaked in blood and had fallen in heaps and the number of arms thrown away haphazard. However, after conveying the wounded to the rear and recalling by bugle those of the *hastati* who were still pursuing the enemy, he stationed the latter in the fore part of the field of battle, opposite the enemy's center, and making the *principes* and *triarii* close up on both wings ordered them to advance over the dead. When these troops had surmounted the obstacles and found themselves in a line with the *hastati* the two phalanxes closed with the greatest eagerness and ardor. As they were nearly equal in numbers as well as in spirit and bravery, and were equally

γενέσθαι τὴν μάχην, ἐν αὐταῖς ταῖς χώραις ἐναποθνη-
7 σκόντων τῶν ἀνδρῶν διὰ φιλοτιμίαν, ἕως οἱ περὶ τὸν
Μασαννάσαν καὶ Λαίλιον ἀπὸ τοῦ διώγματος τῶν
ἱππέων ἀνακάμπτοντες [καὶ] δαιμονίως εἰς δέοντα
8 καιρὸν συνῆψαν. ὧν προσπεσόντων τοῖς περὶ τὸν
Ἀννίβαν κατόπιν οἱ μὲν πλεῖστοι κατεκόπησαν ἐν τῇ
τάξει, τῶν δὲ πρὸς φυγὴν ὁρμησάντων ὀλίγοι μὲν
τελέως διέφυγον, ἅτε τῶν ἱππέων ἐν χερσὶν ὄντων καὶ
9 τῶν τόπων ἐπιπέδων ὑπαρχόντων. ἔπεσον δὲ τῶν μὲν
Ῥωμαίων ὑπὲρ τοὺς χιλίους πεντακοσίους, τῶν δὲ
Καρχηδονίων ὑπὲρ δισμυρίους, αἰχμάλωτοι δ' ἑάλωσαν οὐ πολὺ τούτων ἐλάττους.

15. Ἡ μὲν οὖν ἐπὶ πᾶσι γενομένη μάχη καὶ τὰ ὅλα
κρίνασα Ῥωμαίοις διὰ τῶν προειρημένων ἡγεμόνων
2 τοιοῦτον ἔσχε τὸ τέλος· μετὰ δὲ τὴν μάχην Πόπλιος
μὲν ἐπακολουθήσας καὶ διαρπάσας τὸν χάρακα τῶν
Καρχηδονίων αὖτις ἀνεχώρησεν εἰς τὴν ἰδίαν παρεμ-
3 βολήν. Ἀννίβας δὲ μετ' ὀλίγων ἱππέων κατὰ τὸ συνεχὲς ποιούμενος τὴν ἀναχώρησιν εἰς Ἀδρύμητα δι-
εσώθη, πάντα τὰ δυνατὰ ποιήσας κατὰ τὸν κίνδυνον,
ὅσα τὸν ἀγαθὸν ἔδει στρατηγὸν καὶ πολλῶν ἤδη
4 πραγμάτων πεῖραν εἰληφότα. πρῶτον μὲν γὰρ εἰς λόγους συνελθὼν ἐπειράθη δι' αὐτοῦ λύσιν ποιήσασθαι
5 τῶν ἐνεστώτων· τοῦτο δ' ἐστὶ τοῦ προειδότος τὰ
κατορθώματα, ἀλλ' ἀπιστοῦντος τῇ τύχῃ καὶ προ-
ορωμένου τὰ περὶ τὰς μάχας ἐκβαίνοντα παράλογα.
6 μετὰ δὲ ταῦτα συγκαταστὰς εἰς τὸν κίνδυνον οὕτως

well armed, the contest was for long doubtful, the men falling where they stood out of determination, until Massanissa and Laelius, returning from the pursuit of the cavalry, arrived providentially at the proper moment. When
they fell on Hannibal's army from the rear, most of the men
were cut down in their ranks, while of those who took to
flight only quite a few escaped, as the cavalry were close on
them and the country was level. More than fifteen hundred Romans fell, the Carthaginian loss[21] amounting to
twenty thousand killed and nearly the same number of
prisoners.

15. Such was the result of the final battle between
Scipio and Hannibal, the battle which decided the war in
favor of Rome. The action over, Scipio after following up
the enemy and plundering their camp returned to his own.
Hannibal accompanied by a few horsemen never stopped
until he was in safety in Hadrumetum.[22] He had done in
the battle and before it all that could be done by a good
general of long experience. For, in the first place, he had by
his conference with Scipio attempted to terminate the dispute by himself alone; showing thus that while conscious
of his former successes he mistrusted Fortune and was
fully aware of the part that the unexpected plays in war. In
the next place, when he offered battle he so managed mat-

---

[21] The numbers are, for both sides, unreliable.
[22] See above n. on 5.3.

ἐχρήσατο τοῖς πράγμασιν ὥστε μὴ δυνατὸν εἶναι
βέλτιον πρὸς Ῥωμαίους ἀγῶνα συστήσασθαι, παρα-
πλησίῳ καθοπλισμῷ χρώμενον, οὗ τότε συνεστήσατ'
7 Ἀννίβας. οὔσης γὰρ δυσδιασπάστου τῆς Ῥωμαίων
τάξεως καὶ δυνάμεως, τὸν ἄνδρα συνέβη καὶ καθόλου
καὶ κατὰ μέρη μάχεσθαι πρὸς πάσας τὰς ἐπιφανείας
διὰ τῆς μιᾶς ἐκτάξεως, ἀεὶ <τῶν> ἔγγιστα τῷ δεινῷ
8 σημαιῶν συνεπιστρεφουσῶν πρὸς τὸ δεόμενον. ἔτι δὲ
τοῦ καθοπλισμοῦ σκέπην καὶ θράσος παρασκευάζον-
τος καὶ διὰ τὸ μέγεθος τοῦ θυρεοῦ καὶ τὴν τῆς μαχαίρας ὑπομονὴν τῶν πληγῶν, δύσμαχοι γίνονται καὶ
δυσκαταγώνιστοι διὰ τὰς προειρημένας αἰτίας.

16. ἀλλ' ὅμως πρὸς ἕκαστα τούτων οὕτως ἐνδε-
χομένως Ἀννίβας ἐκ τῶν κατὰ λόγον ἡρμόσατο παρ'
2 αὐτὸν τὸν καιρὸν ὥσθ' ὑπερβολὴν μὴ καταλιπεῖν. τὸ
μὲν γὰρ τῶν ἐλεφάντων πλῆθος ἐξ αὐτῆς παρεσκευ-
άσατο καὶ τότε προεβάλετο χάριν τοῦ συνταράξαι καὶ
3 διασπάσαι τὰς τάξεις τῶν ὑπεναντίων· τοὺς δὲ μισθοφόρους προέταξε καὶ τοὺς Καρχηδονίους ἔθηκε μετὰ
τούτους ἕνεκα τοῦ προεκλῦσαι μὲν τῷ κόπῳ τὰ σώματα τῶν πολεμίων, ἀχρειῶσαι δὲ τὰς ἀκμὰς τῶν
ὅπλων διὰ τὸ πλῆθος τῶν φονευομένων ἀναγκάσαι δὲ
τοὺς Καρχηδονίους μέσους ὄντας μένειν καὶ μάχεσθαι κατὰ τὸν ποιητὴν

ὄφρα καὶ οὐκ ἐθέλων τις ἀναγκαίῃ πολεμίζοι.

ters that it was impossible for any commander with the same arms at his disposal to make better dispositions for a contest against the Romans than Hannibal did on that occasion. The order of a Roman force in battle makes it very difficult to break through, for without any change it enables every man individually and in common with his fellows to present a front in any direction, the maniples which are nearest to the danger turning themselves by a single movement to face it. Their arms also give the men both protection and confidence owing to the size of the shield and owing to the sword being strong enough to endure repeated blows. So that for these reasons they are formidable antagonists very difficult to overcome.

16. But nevertheless to meet each of these advantages Hannibal had shown incomparable skill in adopting at the critical moment all such measures as were in his power and could reasonably be expected to succeed. For he had hastily collected that large number of elephants and had placed them in front on the day of battle in order to throw the enemy into confusion and break his ranks. He had placed the mercenaries in advance with the Carthaginians behind them in order that the Romans before the final engagement might be fatigued by their exertions and that their swords might lose their edge owing to the great slaughter, and also in order to compel the Carthaginians thus hemmed in on both sides to stand fast and fight, in the words of Homer

That e'en the unwilling might be forced to fight.[23]

[23] Hom. *Il*. 4.300.

4 τοὺς δὲ μαχιμωτάτους καὶ στασιμωτάτους τῶν ἀνδρῶν ἐν ἀποστάσει παρενέβαλε χάριν τοῦ προορω-
μένους ἐκ πολλοῦ τὸ συμβαῖνον καὶ διαμένοντας
ἀκεραίους τοῖς τε σώμασι καὶ ταῖς ψυχαῖς σὺν καιρῷ
5 χρήσασθαι ταῖς σφετέραις ἀρεταῖς. εἰ δὲ πάντα τὰ
δυνατὰ ποιήσας πρὸς τὸ νικᾶν ἐσφάλη τὸν πρὸ τού-
6 του χρόνον ἀήττητος ὤν, συγγνώμην δοτέον· ἔστι μὲν
γὰρ ὅτε καὶ ταὐτόματον ἀντέπραξε ταῖς ἐπιβολαῖς
τῶν ἀγαθῶν ἀνδρῶν, ἔστι δ' ὅτε πάλιν κατὰ τὴν
παροιμίαν

ἐσθλὸς ἐὼν ἄλλου κρείττονος ἀντέτυχεν·

ὃ δὴ καὶ τότε γεγονέναι περὶ ἐκεῖνον φήσειεν ἄν τις.

17. Τὰ γὰρ ὑπεραίροντα τὴν κοινὴν συνήθειαν τῶν
παρ' ἐνίοις ἐθισμῶν, ὅταν μὲν αὐτοπαθῶς δόξῃ γίνεσθαι διὰ τὸ μέγεθος τῶν συμπτωμάτων, ἔλεον ἐκ-
καλεῖται παρὰ τοῖς ὁρῶσι καὶ τοῖς ἀκούουσι, καὶ
2 συγκινεῖ πως ἕκαστον ἡμῶν ὁ ξενισμός· ἐπὰν δὲ
φαίνηται γοητείας χάριν καὶ καθ' ὑπόκρισιν γίνεσθαι
τὸ τοιοῦτον, οὐκ ἔλεον, ἀλλ' ὀργὴν ἐξεργάζεται καὶ
μῖσος. ὃ καὶ τότε συνέβη γενέσθαι περὶ τοὺς πρεσβευτὰς τῶν Καρχηδονίων.

3 Ὁ δὲ Πόπλιος διὰ βραχέων ἤρξατο λέγειν πρὸς
αὐτούς, ὡς ἐκείνων μὲν χάριν οὐδὲν ὀφείλουσι ποιεῖν
φιλάνθρωπον, ὁμολογούντων αὐτῶν διότι καὶ τὸν πό-

The most efficient and steadiest of his troops he had placed behind at a certain distance in order that, anticipating and witnessing from afar what took place, they might with undiminished strength and spirit make use of their qualities at the proper time. If he, who had never as yet suffered defeat, after taking every possible step to insure victory, yet failed to do so, we must pardon him. For there are times when Fortune counteracts the plans of valiant men, and again at times, as the proverb says,

"A brave man meets another braver yet,"[24]

as we may say happened in the case of Hannibal.

17. When men give expression to their feelings more violently than is the general custom of their nation, if this excess seems to spring from genuine emotion due to the magnitude of their calamities, it arouses the pity of these who see and hear it, and its very strangeness touches all our hearts; but when such extravagance seems to be a mere piece of charlatanry and acting, it gives rise not to pity but to indignation and disgust. Such was the case on the present occasion with regard to the Carthaginian ambassadors.[25]

Scipio began by stating briefly to them that the Romans were not bound to treat them with leniency for their own sakes, as they confessed that they had begun the war against

[24] The source of the quotation has been a matter of speculation.

[25] Sent from Carthage to Scipio at Tunis to ask for peace (Livy 30.35.10–36.9).

λεμον ἐξ ἀρχῆς ἐπενέγκαιεν Ῥωμαίοις, παρὰ τὰς
συνθήκας ἐξανδραποδισάμενοι τὴν Ζακανθαίων πόλιν, καὶ πρώην παρασπονδήσαιεν, ἀθετήσαντες τοὺς
4 ὅρκους καὶ τὰς ἐγγράπτους ὁμολογίας· αὐτῶν δὲ χάριν ἔφησε καὶ τῆς τύχης καὶ τῶν ἀνθρωπίνων κεκρί-
σθαι σφίσι πράως χρῆσθαι καὶ μεγαλοψύχως τοῖς
5 πράγμασι. φανήσεσθαι δὲ τοῦτο κἀκείνοις ἔφησεν,
ἐὰν ὀρθῶς διαλαμβάνωσι περὶ τῶν ἐνεστώτων· οὐ γὰρ
εἴ τι πάσχειν ἢ ποιεῖν ἢ διδόναι σφίσιν ἐπιταχθήσε-
ται, τοῦτο δεῖν νομίζειν δεινόν, ἀλλ᾽ εἴ τι συγχωρηθή-
σεται φιλάνθρωπον, τοῦτο μᾶλλον ἡγεῖσθαι παράδο-
6 ξον, ἐπείπερ ἡ τύχη παρελομένη τὸν ἔλεον αὐτῶν καὶ
τὴν συγγνώμην διὰ τὴν σφετέραν ἀδικίαν ὑποχειρί-
7 ους πεποίηκε τοῖς ἐχθροῖς. ταῦτα δ᾽ εἰπὼν ἔλεγε τὰ
φιλάνθρωπα τὰ διδόμενα, καὶ πάλιν ἃ δέον ἦν ὑπομέ-
νειν αὐτούς.

18. Ἦν δὲ τὰ κεφάλαια τῶν προτεινομένων ταῦτα.
πόλεις ἔχειν κατὰ Λιβύην ἃς καὶ πρότερον εἶχον ἢ τὸν
τελευταῖον πόλεμον ἐξενεγκεῖν Ῥωμαίοις, καὶ χώραν
ἣν καὶ τὸ παλαιὸν εἶχον, κτήνη καὶ σώματα καὶ τὴν
2 ἄλλην ὕπαρξιν, ἀπὸ δὲ τῆς ἡμέρας ἐκείνης ἀσινεῖς
Καρχηδονίους ὑπάρχειν, ἔθεσι καὶ νόμοις χρῆσθαι

---

26 In fact, probably not the *casus belli* (see nn. on 3.20.6 and
30.3). It is doubtful whether the envoys really confessed to what
Scipio says they did.

Rome by taking Saguntum[26] contrary to their treaty[27] and enslaving its inhabitants, and that they had quite recently been guilty of treachery by violating a written agreement[28] they had sworn to observe. "But for our own sake," he said, "and in consideration of the fortune of war and of the common condition of man we have decided to be clement and magnanimous. This will be evident to you also, if you estimate the situation rightly. For you should not regard it as strange if we impose sufferings and obligations on you or if we demand sacrifices from you, but rather it should surprise you if we grant you any favors, since Fortune owing to your own misconduct has deprived you of any right to pity or pardon and placed you at the mercy of your enemies." After speaking in this sense he informed them first of the indulgences granted to them and afterward of the severe conditions to which they would have to submit.

18. The principal points of the conditions proposed were as follows.[29] Carthage was to retain all the cities she formerly possessed in Africa before entering on the last war with Rome, all her former territory, all flocks, herds, slaves, and other property: from that day onward the Carthaginians were to suffer no injury, they were to be governed by their own laws and customs and to receive no

[27] Again (as in 1.7) it is not clear to which treaty P. is referring; see also n. on 3.21.7.

[28] See n. on 1.1.

[29] This chapter (18.1–9) contains Scipio's proposal for a truce. It is discussed, together with the evidence from other sources, in *StV* 548, pp. 296–302 and 304–308. *StV* 548 also includes the previous negotiations and agreements of the years 203 to 201.

3 τοῖς ἰδίοις, ἀφρουρήτους ὄντας. ταῦτα μὲν οὖν ἦν τὰ
φιλάνθρωπα, τὰ δ' ἐναντία τούτοις πάλιν τὰ κατὰ τὰς
ἀνοχὰς ἀδικήματα γενόμενα πάντα Καρχηδονίους
ἀποκαταστῆσαι Ῥωμαίοις, τοὺς αἰχμαλώτους καὶ
δραπέτας ἐκ παντὸς ἀποδοῦναι τοῦ χρόνου, τὰ μακρὰ

4 πλοῖα παραδοῦναι πάντα πλὴν δέκα τριήρων, ὁμοίως
καὶ πάντας τοὺς ἐλέφαντας. πόλεμον μηδενὶ τῶν ἔξω
τῆς Λιβύης ἐπιφέρειν καθόλου μηδὲ τῶν ἐν τῇ Λιβύῃ

5 χωρὶς τῆς Ῥωμαίων γνώμης· οἰκίας καὶ χώραν καὶ
πόλεις, καὶ εἴ τι ἕτερόν ἐστι Μασαννάσου τοῦ βασιλέως ἢ τῶν προγόνων ἐντὸς τῶν ἀποδειχθησομένων

6 ὅρων αὐτοῖς πάντα ἀποδοῦναι Μασαννάσᾳ· σιτομε-
τρῆσαί τε τὴν δύναμιν τριμήνου καὶ μισθοδοτῆσαι
μέχρι ἂν ἐκ Ῥώμης ἀντιφωνηθῇ τι κατὰ τὰς συν-

7 θήκας· ἐξενεγκεῖν ἀργυρίου τάλαντα μύρια Καρχηδονίους ἐν ἔτεσι πεντήκοντα, φέροντας καθ' ἕκαστον

8 ἐνιαυτὸν Εὐβοϊκὰ τάλαντα διακόσια· ὁμήρους δοῦναι
πίστεως χάριν ἑκατὸν οὓς ἂν προγράψῃ τῶν νέων ὁ
στρατηγὸς τῶν Ῥωμαίων, μὴ νεωτέρους τεσσαρεσκαί-
δεκα ἐτῶν μηδὲ πρεσβυτέρους τριάκοντα.

19. Ταῦτα μὲν οὖν ὁ στρατηγὸς εἶπε τῶν Ῥωμαίων τοῖς πρεσβευταῖς· οἱ δ' ἀκούσαντες ἠπείγοντο

2 καὶ διεσάφουν τοῖς ἐν τῇ πατρίδι. καθ' ὃν δὴ καιρὸν
λέγεται, μέλλοντός τινος τῶν ἐκ τῆς γερουσίας ἀντι-
λέγειν τοῖς προτεινομένοις καὶ καταρχομένου, προελθόντα τὸν Ἀννίβαν κατασπάσαι τὸν ἄνθρωπον ἀπὸ

3 τοῦ βήματος. τῶν δὲ λοιπῶν ἐξοργισθέντων διὰ τὸ

garrison. These were the lenient conditions; the others of a contrary kind were as follows: Reparation was to be made to the Romans for all acts of injustice committed by the Carthaginians during the truce: prisoners of war and deserters who had fallen into their hands at any date were to be delivered up: they were to surrender their ships of war with the exception of ten triremes, and all their elephants: they were not to make war at all on any nation outside Africa and on no nation in Africa without consulting Rome: they were to restore to King Massanissa, within the boundaries that should subsequently be assigned, all houses, lands, and cities, and other property which had belonged to him or to his ancestors: they were to furnish the Roman army with sufficient corn for three months and pay the soldiers until a reply arrived from Rome regarding the treaty: they were to contribute ten thousand talents in fifty years, paying two hundred Euboic talents each year: finally they were to give as surety a hundred hostages chosen by the Roman general from among their young men between the age of fourteen and thirty.

19. This was the communication that Scipio made to the ambassadors, and after listening to him they lost no time in conveying it to their countrymen in Carthage. On this occasion it is said that when one of the senators was about to oppose the acceptance of the terms and was beginning to speak, Hannibal came forward and pulled him down from the tribune.[30] The other members were indig-

---

[30] His intervention, described here as decisive, in the debate of the Senate at Carthage may be true.

παρὰ τὴν συνήθειαν αὐτὸν τοῦτο πρᾶξαι, πάλιν τὸν
Ἀννίβαν ἀναστάντα φασὶν ἀγνοεῖν <μὲν ὁμολογῆσαι,
δεῖν δὲ> συγγνώμην ἔχειν, εἴ τι παρὰ τοὺς ἐθισμοὺς
πράττει, γινώσκοντας ὅτι τὴν μὲν ἔξοδον ἐκ τῆς πατρίδος ἐννάετης ὢν ποιήσαιτο, πλείω δὲ τῶν πέντε καὶ
4 τετταράκοντ' ἐτῶν ἔχων εἰς αὐτὴν ἐπανήκει. διόπερ
ἠξίου μὴ τοῦτο σκοπεῖν, εἴ τι παραπέπαικε τῆς συνηθείας, πολὺ δὲ μᾶλλον, εἰ τοῖς τῆς πατρίδος πράγμασιν ἀληθινῶς, συμπάσχει· διὰ γὰρ ταῦτα καὶ νῦν εἰς
5 τὴν ἀλογίαν ἐμπεπτωκέναι ταύτην. θαυμαστὸν, γὰρ
αὐτῷ φανῆναι καὶ τελέως ἐξηλλαγμένον, εἴ τις ὑπάρχων Καρχηδόνιος καὶ συνειδὼς τὰ βεβουλευμένα καὶ
κοινῇ τῇ πατρίδι καὶ κατ' ἰδίαν ἑκάστοις ἡμῶν κατὰ
Ῥωμαίων οὐ προσκυνεῖ τὴν τύχην, εἰ γεγονὼς ὑπο-
6 χείριος τοιούτων τυγχάνει φιλανθρώπων· οὓς εἴ τις
ὀλίγαις πρότερον ἡμέραις ἤρετο πόσ' ἐλπίζουσι πεί-
σεσθαι τὴν πατρίδα κρατησάντων Ῥωμαίων, οὐδ' ἂν
εἰπεῖν οἷοί τ' ἦσαν διὰ τὸ μέγεθος καὶ τὴν ὑπερβολὴν
7 τῶν προφαινομένων αὐτοῖς κακῶν. διόπερ ἠξίου καὶ
νῦν μηδ' ἐπὶ λόγον ἄγειν, ἀλλ' ὁμοθυμαδὸν δεξαμένους τὰ προτεινόμενα θύειν τοῖς θεοῖς, καὶ πάντας
εὔχεσθαι βεβαιῶσαι ταῦτα τὸν δῆμον τῶν Ῥωμαίων.
8 φανέντος δὲ φρονίμως αὐτοῦ καὶ τοῖς καιροῖς οἰκείως
συμβουλεύειν, ἔδοξε ποιεῖσθαι τὰς συνθήκας ἐπὶ τοῖς
9 προειρημένοις. καὶ τὸ μὲν συνέδριον παραυτίκα πρεσβευτὰς ἐξέπεμπε τοὺς ἀνθομολογησομένους ὑπὲρ
τούτων.

nant with him for such a violation of the usage of the house, and Hannibal then rose again and said that he confessed he had been in error, but they must pardon him if he acted contrary to their usage, as they knew that he had left Carthage at the age of nine, and was, now that he had returned, over five and forty. He, therefore, begged them not to consider whether he had transgressed parliamentary custom, but rather to ask themselves whether or not he really felt for his country; for this was the sentiment which had now made him guilty of this offense. "It seems to me," he said, "astounding and quite incomprehensible, that any man who is a citizen of Carthage and is conscious of the designs that we all individually and as a body have entertained against Rome does not bless his stars that now that he is at the mercy of the Romans he has obtained such lenient terms. If you had been asked but a few days ago what you expected your country to suffer in the event of the victory of the Romans, you would not have been able even to give utterance to your fears, so great and excessive were the calamities then in prospect. So now I beg you not even to discuss the matter, but to agree with one accord to the proposals, to sacrifice to the gods, and to pray all of you that the Roman people may ratify the treaty." As it seemed to all that his advice was wise and opportune, they voted to make the treaty on the above conditions, and the senate at once dispatched envoys[31] with orders to agree to it.

[31] After their arrival at Rome, the Senate decided to make peace on the terms formulated by Scipio (Livy 30.42.11–43.9).

II. RES MACEDONIAE ET GRAECIAE

20. Τοῦτο δὲ τίς οὐκ ἂν θαυμάσειε, πῶς, ὅτε μὲν αὐτὸς ὁ Πτολεμαῖος ζῶν οὐ προσεδεῖτο τῆς τούτων

2 ἐπικουρίας, ἕτοιμοι βοηθεῖν ἦσαν, ὅτε δ' ἐκεῖνος μετήλλαξε καταλιπὼν παιδίον νήπιον, ᾧ κατὰ φύσιν ἀμφοῖν ἐπέβαλλε συσσῴζειν τὴν βασιλείαν, τότε παρακαλέσαντες ἀλλήλους ὥρμησαν ἐπὶ τὸ διελόμενοι τὴν τοῦ παιδὸς ἀρχὴν ἐπανελέσθαι τὸν ἀπολε-

3 λειμμένον, οὐδ' οὖν, καθάπερ οἱ τύραννοι, βραχεῖαν δή τινα προβαλλόμενοι τῆς αἰσχύνης πρόφασιν, ἀλλ' ἐξ αὐτῆς ἀνέδην καὶ θηριωδῶς οὕτως ὥστε προσοφλεῖν τὸν λεγόμενον τῶν ἰχθύων βίον, ἐν οἷς φασιν ὁμοφύλοις οὖσι τὴν τοῦ μείονος ἀπώλειαν τῷ μείζονι

4 τροφὴν γίνεσθαι καὶ βίον. ἐξ ὧν τίς οὐκ ἂν ἐμβλέψας οἷον εἰς κάτοπτρον εἰς τὴν συνθήκην ταύτην αὐτόπτης δόξειε γίνεσθαι τῆς πρὸς τοὺς θεοὺς ἀσεβείας καὶ τῆς πρὸς τοὺς ἀνθρώπους ὠμότητος, ἔτι δὲ τῆς ὑπερβαλλούσης πλεονεξίας τῶν προειρημένων βασιλέων;

5 οὐ μὴν ἀλλὰ τίς οὐκ ἂν εἰκότως τῇ τύχῃ μεμψάμενος ἐπὶ τῶν ἀνθρωπείων πραγμάτων ἐν τούτοις ἀντικαταλ-

---

32 In chapter 20 P. vents his ire on the two kings who, he says, agreed to divide the empire of the orphaned boy Ptolemy V between themselves. After much scholarly discussion it seems now fairly clear that there was, in fact, some kind of agreement between them, but it was much more modest and did not include Egypt, although P. believed so (3.3.8, confirmed by 16.10.1). It

II. AFFAIRS OF MACEDONIA AND GREECE

Conduct of Philip and Antiochus Regarding Egypt

20. It is very surprising that as long as Ptolemy in his lifetime could dispense with the help of Philip[32] and Antiochus, they were very ready to assist him, but when he died leaving an infant son whom it was their natural duty to maintain in possession of his realm, then encouraging each other they hastened to divide the child's kingdom between themselves and be the ruin of the unhappy orphan. Nor did they, as tyrants do, take pains to provide themselves with some paltry pretext for the shameful deed, but at once acted in a fashion so unscrupulous and brutal that they well deserved to have applied to them the saying about the food of fishes, that though they are all of the same tribe the destruction of the smaller ones is food and life to the larger. Who can look into this treaty as into a mirror without fancying that he sees reflected in it the image of all impiety toward the gods and all savagery toward men, as well as of the unbounded covetousness of these two kings? But at the same time who among those who reasonably find fault with Fortune for her conduct of affairs, will

---

may have extended only to Ptolemaic possessions in Asia Minor and the Aegean coast, such as Samos (conquered by Philip in 201), Amyzon in Caria (in May 203 in Antiochus' hands: J. and L. Robert, *Fouilles d'Amyzon en Carie* 1 [Paris 1983], 132–137, no. 9), and Theangela in Caria (turned over by Philip to Antiochus: *EA* 33 [2001], 7 and 12). Bibliography in *StV* 547, in addition R. M. Errington, *Ath.* 49 (1971), 376–354; WC 3 (1979), 785; Ma (11.34.14), 74–76.

THE HISTORIES OF POLYBIUS

λαγείη, διότι ἐκείνοις μὲν ἐπέθηκε μετὰ ταῦτα τὴν ἁρμόζουσαν δίκην, τοῖς δ' ἐπιγενομένοις ἐξέθηκε κάλλιστον ὑπόδειγμα πρὸς ⟨ἐπ⟩ανόρθωσιν τὸν τῶν προ-
6 ειρημένων βασιλέων παραδειγματισμόν; ἔτι γὰρ αὐτῶν παρασπονδούντων μὲν ἀλλήλους, διασπωμένων δὲ τὴν τοῦ παιδὸς ἀρχήν, ἐπιστήσασα Ῥωμαίους, ἀκεῖνοι κατὰ τῶν πέλας ἐβουλεύσαντο παρανόμως, ταῦτα κατ' ἐκείνων δικαίως ἐκύρωσε καὶ καθηκόντως.
7 παραυτίκα γὰρ ἑκάτεροι διὰ τῶν ὅπλων ἡττηθέντες οὐ μόνον ἐκωλύθησαν τῆς τῶν ἀλλοτρίων ἐπιθυμίας, ἀλλὰ καὶ συγκλεισθέντες εἰς φόρους ὑπέμειναν Ῥω-
8 μαίοις τὸ προσταττόμενον ⟨ποιεῖν⟩. τὸ τελευταῖον ἐν πάνυ βραχεῖ χρόνῳ τὴν μὲν Πτολεμαίου βασιλείαν ἡ τύχη διώρθωσε, τὰς δὲ τούτων δυναστείας καὶ τοὺς διαδόχους τοὺς μὲν ἄρδην ἀναστάτους ἐποίησε καὶ πανωλέθρους, τοὺς δὲ μικροῦ δεῖν τοῖς αὐτοῖς περιέβαλε συμπτώμασι. . . .

21. Ὅτι Μολπαγόρας τις ἦν παρὰ τοῖς Κι⟨αν⟩οῖς, ἀνὴρ καὶ λέγειν καὶ πράττειν ἱκανός, κατὰ δὲ τὴν
2 αἵρεσιν δημαγωγικὸς καὶ πλεονέκτης. ὃς πρὸς χάριν ὁμιλῶν τῷ πλήθει καὶ τοὺς εὐκαιροῦντας τοῖς βίοις ὑποβάλλων τοῖς ὄχλοις, καί τινας μὲν εἰς τέλος ἀναιρῶν, τινὰς δὲ φυγαδεύων καὶ τὰς οὐσίας τὰς τούτων δημεύων καὶ διαδιδοὺς τοῖς πολλοῖς, ταχέως τῷ τοιούτῳ τρόπῳ περιεποιήσατο μοναρχικὴν ἐξουσίαν. . . .
3 Κιανοὶ μὲν οὖν περιέπεσον τηλικαύταις συμφοραῖς οὐχ οὕτως διὰ τὴν τύχην οὐδὲ διὰ τὴν τῶν πέλας

not be reconciled to her when he learns how she afterward made them pay the due penalty, and how she exhibited to their successors as a warning for their edification the exemplary chastisement she inflicted on these princes? For even while they were still breaking their faith to each other and tearing to shreds the boy's kingdom she drew the attention of the Romans against them, and very justly and properly visited them with the very evils which they had been contrary to all law designing to bring upon others. For both of them were very soon vanquished in battle, and they were not only prevented from lusting after the property of others but were compelled to submit to pay tribute and obey the behests of Rome. And, finally, in a very short time Fortune reestablished the kingdom of Ptolemy, while as for their dynasties and successors she in one case brought utter destruction upon them and in the other calamities very nearly as grave.

Philip and the People of Cius

21. There was a certain Molpagoras at Cius,[33] a capable speaker and politician, but in character a demagogue, greedy of power. This man, by flattering the populace, by inciting the rabble against men of means, by finally killing some of the latter and banishing others whose property he confiscated and distributed among the people, soon attained by these means to supreme power. . . .

Now the people of Cius met with such disasters not so much owing to chance or to the injustice of their neigh-

---

[33] City in Bithynia, modern Gemlik. *RE* Kios 486–488 (W. Ruge).

ἀδικίαν, τὸ δὲ πλεῖον διὰ τὴν αὑτῶν ἀβουλίαν καὶ
4 κακοπολιτείαν, προάγοντες ἀεὶ τοὺς χειρίστους καὶ
5 κολάζοντες τοὺς ἐναντιουμένους τούτοις, ἵνα διαιρῶν-
ται τὰς ἀλλήλων οὐσίας, εἰς ταύτας οἷον ἐθελοντὴν
ἐνέπεσον τὰς ἀτυχίας, εἰς ἃς οὐκ οἶδ' ὅπως πάντες
ἄνθρωποι προφανῶς ἐμπίπτοντες οὐ δύνανται λῆξαι
τῆς ἀνοίας, ἀλλ' οὐδὲ βραχὺ διαπιστῆσαι [ῥᾴδιον],
6 καθάπερ ἔνια τῶν ἀλόγων ζῴων. ἐκεῖνα γὰρ οὐ μόνον
ἐὰν αὐτά που δυσχρηστήσῃ περὶ τὰ δελέατα καὶ τὰς
ἄρκυς, ἀλλὰ κἂν ἕτερον ἴδῃ κινδυνεῦον, οὐκ ἂν ἔτι
ῥᾳδίως αὐτὰ προσαγάγοις πρὸς οὐδὲν τῶν τοιούτων,
ἀλλὰ καὶ τὸν τόπον ὑποπτεύει καὶ παντὶ τῷ φαινομένῳ
7 διαπιστεῖ. οἱ δ' ἄνθρωποι τὰς μὲν ἀκούοντες ἀπολ-
λυμένας πόλεις ἄρδην τῷ προειρημένῳ τρόπῳ, τὰς
δ' ἀκμὴν ὁρῶντες, ὅμως, ὅταν τις χρησάμενος τῷ
πρὸς χάριν λόγῳ προτείνῃ τὴν ἐλπίδα τῆς ἐξ ἀλλή-
8 λων ἐπανορθώσεως, προσίασι πρὸς τὸ δέλεαρ ἀνεπιστάτως, σαφῶς εἰδότες ὅτι τῶν τὰ τοιαῦτα δελέατα
καταπιόντων οὐδεὶς οὐδέποτε σέσωσται, πᾶσι δ'
ὁμολογουμένως ὄλεθρον ἐπήνεγκαν αἱ τοιαῦται πολι-
τεῖαι. . . .

22. Ὁ δὲ Φίλιππος κύριος γενόμενος τῆς πόλεως
περιχαρὴς ἦν, ὡς καλήν τινα καὶ σεμνὴν πρᾶξιν
ἐπιτετελεσμένος καὶ βεβοηθηκὼς μὲν προθύμως τῷ
κηδεστῇ, καταπεπληγμένος δὲ πάντας τοὺς ἀλλοτρι-
άζοντας, σωμάτων δὲ καὶ χρημάτων εὐπορίαν ἐκ τοῦ

bors, but chiefly owing to their own stupidity and misgovernment. For by advancing ever the worst men to power and punishing those who opposed them in order to plunder the fortunes of their fellow citizens, they fell as of their own free will into those misfortunes of which we may say that men in general, after being caught in them with their eyes open, not only cannot cure themselves of their folly, but cannot conceive the least suspicion, as even some of the brutes do. For the latter not only when they have got into trouble themselves from snares and nets, but if they see another animal in danger will not readily approach such engines again, but are even suspicious of the place and mistrust everything they see. Men on the other hand, though they have heard that some cities have been utterly destroyed by the means I have described, and though they see ruin overtaking others, nevertheless, whenever anyone courts favor with them and holds out to them the hope of repairing their fortunes by laying hands on those of their neighbors, approach the snare without a moment's reflection, though quite aware that of those who have swallowed such baits not a single one has ever been saved, but that measures like the above are well known to have brought destruction on all governments which adopted them. . . .

22. Philip[34] having made himself master of the city was highly elated, just as if he had performed a good and noble action in coming readily to the help of his kinsman,[35] and overawing those who opposed him, and then justifiably enriching himself with the prisoners and money he laid

---

[34] During his campaign in 202.

[35] Prusias I, king of Bithynia, ca. 230–183. *RE* Prusias I 1086–1107 (C. Habicht), on this episode 1093–1095.

2 δικαίου περιπεποιημένος. τὰ δ᾽ ἐναντία τούτοις οὐ
καθεώρα, καίπερ ὄντα προφανῆ, πρῶτον μὲν ⟨ὡς⟩ οὐκ
ἀδικουμένῳ, παρασπονδοῦντι δὲ τῷ κηδεστῇ τοὺς

3 πέλας ἐβοήθει, δεύτερον ὅτι πόλιν Ἑλληνίδα περι-
βαλὼν τοῖς μεγίστοις ἀτυχήμασιν ἀδίκως ἔμελλε
κυρώσειν τὴν περὶ αὑτοῦ διαδεδομένην φήμην ὑπὲρ
τῆς εἰς τοὺς φίλους ὠμότητος, ἐξ ἀμφοῖν δὲ δικαίως
καὶ κληρονομήσειν παρὰ πᾶσι τοῖς Ἕλλησι τὴν ἐπ᾽

4 ἀσεβείᾳ δόξαν, τρίτον ὡς ἐνυβρίκει τοῖς ἀπὸ τῶν
προειρημένων πόλεων πρεσβευταῖς, οἳ παρῆσαν ἐξ-
ελούμενοι τοὺς Κιανοὺς ἐκ τῶν περιεστώτων κακῶν,
ὑπὸ δ᾽ ἐκείνου παρακαλούμενοι καὶ διαγελώμενοι καθ᾽
ἡμέραν ⟨ἠναγκάσθησαν⟩ αὐτόπται γενέσθαι τούτων,

5 ὧν ἥκιστ᾽ ἂν ἐβουλήθησαν, πρὸς δὲ τούτοις ὅτι τοὺς
Ῥοδίους οὕτως ἀπετεθηριώκει τότε πρὸς αὐτὸν ὥστε
μηδένα λόγον ἔτι προσίεσθαι περὶ Φιλίππου.

23. καὶ γὰρ ἡ τύχη πρός γε τοῦτο τὸ μέρος αὐτῷ

2 συνήργησε προφανῶς. ὅτε γὰρ ὁ πρεσβευτὴς ἐν τῷ
θεάτρῳ τὸν ἀπολογισμὸν ἐποιεῖτο πρὸς τοὺς Ῥοδίους,
ἐμφανίζων τὴν τοῦ Φιλίππου μεγαλοψυχίαν, καὶ διότι
τρόπον τινὰ κρατῶν ἤδη τῆς πόλεως δίδωσι τῷ δήμῳ
τὴν χάριν ταύτην, ποιεῖ δὲ τοῦτο βουλόμενος ἐλέγξαι
μὲν τὰς τῶν ἀντιπραττόντων αὐτῷ διαβολάς, φανερὰν

3 δὲ τῇ πόλει καταστῆσαι τὴν αὑτοῦ προαίρεσιν· καὶ
παρῆν τις ἐκ κατάπλου πρὸς τὸ πρυτανεῖον ἀναγ-
γέλλων τὸν ἐξανδραποδισμὸν τῶν Κιανῶν καὶ ⟨τὴν⟩
ὠμότητα τοῦ Φιλίππου τὴν ἐν τούτοις γεγενημένην,

4 ὥστε τοὺς Ῥοδίους, ἔτι μεταξὺ τοῦ πρεσβευτοῦ τὰ

hands on. But he did not see the reverse of the medal, however obvious it was. He did not see that in the first place the kinsman whom he came to help was not wronged, but was wronging others by his treachery, next that by thus without any justification bringing the greatest of calamities on a Hellenic city he would set the seal on the reputation he enjoyed for cruelty to his friends, and that both these crimes would justly leave him a legacy of infamy throughout the whole of Greece as a violator of all that was sacred; thirdly, that he had treated with contumely the ambassadors who came from the cities[36] I mentioned to deliver the Cianians from the perils that menaced them, but who day after day yielding to his entreaties and deluded by him were compelled to be witnesses of things they were far from wishing to see; and finally, that in addition to all he had aroused such savage hate in the Rhodians against him that they would not listen to a word in his favor.

23. Indeed, chance had very conspicuously intervened to help this matter on. For just when his envoy was speaking in defense of Philip in the theater at Rhodes and laying stress on his magnanimity, asserting that, though the city of Cius was now more or less at his mercy, he granted this favor to the people[37] and acted so with the object of confuting the slander of his adversaries and clearly revealing to the city what his true sentiments were: at this very time, I say, a man who had just landed entered the Prytaneum and announced the enslavement of the people of Cius and all Philip's cruelty on that occasion. When, therefore, while

[36] Among them was Rhodes.
[37] Of Rhodes or Chius.

προειρημένα λέγοντος, ἐπεὶ προελθὼν ὁ πρύτανις
διεσάφει τὰ προσηγγελμένα, μὴ δύνασθαι πιστεῦσαι
5 διὰ τὴν ὑπερβολὴν τῆς ἀθεσίας. Φίλιππος μὲν οὖν,
παρασπονδήσας οὐχ οὕτως Κιανοὺς ὡς ἑαυτόν, εἰς
τοιαύτην ἄγνοιαν ἢ καὶ παράπτωσιν τοῦ καθήκοντος
ἧκεν ὥστ' ἐφ' οἷς ἐχρῆν αἰσχύνεσθαι καθ' ὑπερβολήν,
ἐπὶ τούτοις ὡς καλοῖς σεμνύνεσθαι καὶ μεγαλαυχεῖν·
6 ὁ δὲ τῶν Ῥοδίων δῆμος ἀπὸ ταύτης τῆς ἡμέρας ὡς
περὶ πολεμίου διελάμβανε τοῦ Φιλίππου, καὶ πρὸς
7 τοῦτον τὸν σκοπὸν ἐποιεῖτο τὰς παρασκευάς. παραπλήσιον δὲ καὶ τοῖς Αἰτωλοῖς μῖσος ἐκ ταύτης τῆς
8 πράξεως ἐνειργάσατο πρὸς αὐτόν· ἄρτι γὰρ διαλελυ-
μένος καὶ τὰς χεῖρας ἐκτείνων πρὸς τὸ ἔθνος, οὐδεμιᾶς
προφάσεως ἐγγινομένης, φίλων ὑπαρχόντων καὶ συμ-
9 μάχων Αἰτωλῶν, Λυσιμαχέων, Καλχηδονίων, Κιανῶν,
βραχεῖ χρόνῳ πρότερον, πρῶτον μὲν προσηγάγετο
τὴν Λυσιμαχέων πόλιν, ἀποσπάσας ἀπὸ τῆς τῶν
Αἰτωλῶν συμμαχίας, δευτέραν δὲ τὴν Καλχηδονίων,
τρίτην δὲ τὴν Κιανῶν ἐξηνδραποδίσατο, στρατηγοῦ
παρ' Αἰτωλῶν ἐν αὐτῇ διατρίβοντος καὶ προεστῶτος
10 τῶν κοινῶν. Προυσίας δέ, καθὸ μὲν ἡ πρόθεσις αὐτοῦ
συντελείας ἔτυχε, περιχαρὴς ἦν, καθὸ δὲ τὰ μὲν ἆθλα

---

38 See n. on 13.5.1. 39 As they had been among the
states that tried to mediate, they were insulted by Philip's actions.

40 Philip had concluded peace with them in 206 (Livy 29.12.8–
16), and Cius was their ally.

41 Founded ca. 309 by Lysimachus in the middle of the Thracian Chersonese, not far from Gallipoli (see the discussion in

Philip's ambassador was still speaking the *prytanis*[38] came forward and communicated the news, the people could not believe it, so black was the treachery. Philip, therefore, who had rather betrayed himself than the people of Cius, had become so wrongheaded or rather so lost to all sense of decency that he gave himself credit and boasted of conduct of which he should have been most deeply ashamed, as though it were a fine deed. From this day forth the Rhodians considered him to be their enemy[39] and made their preparations accordingly, and by this action he made himself equally hated by the Aetolians.[40] For though he had but recently made his peace with that nation and was extending the hand of fellowship to them, now without the shadow of a pretext, when shortly before the people of Lysimacheia, Chalcedon, and Cius were friends and allies of the Aetolians, he first of all appropriated the city of Lysimacheia,[41] forcing them to leave the alliance with the Aetolians, then the people of Chalcedon and he now took Cius and enslaved its inhabitants, although an Aetolian strategus was present in the place and at the head of affairs. Prusias, in so far as his purpose had been accomplished, was gratified, but inasmuch as the prize of the enterprise was carried off by another and he received as his

Cohen [9.45.1], 86–87). The city served as the base for Philip's campaign in 202. After the royal garrison left in 199 or 198, the city was destroyed by Thracians but rebuilt in 196 by Antiochus III. At the site (or very close to it) were found substantial parts of a treaty between Philip and Lysimacheia (*StV* 549) and also an inscription reading "of King Philip," which must date to between 202 and 198 (L. Robert, *Hellenica* 10 [1955], 266–271 and pl. XXXV).

τῆς ἐπιβολῆς ἕτερος ἀπέφερεν, αὐτὸς δὲ πόλεως οἰκό-
πεδον ἔρημον ἐκληρονόμει, δυσχερῶς διέκειτο, ποιεῖν
δ᾽ οὐδὲν οἷός τ᾽ ἦν. . . .

24. Ὅτι Φίλιππος κατὰ τὸν ἀνάπλουν ἕτερον
ἐφ᾽ ἑτέρῳ παρασπόνδημα μεταχειριζόμενος προσέσχε
περὶ μέσον ἡμέρας πρὸς τὴν τῶν Θασίων πόλιν, καὶ
ταύτῃ φιλίαν οὖσαν ἐξηνδραποδίσατο. . . .

2   Θάσιοι εἶπον πρὸς Μητρόδωρον τὸν Φιλίππου
στρατηγὸν παραδοῦναι τὴν πόλιν εἰ διατηρήσοι αὐτοὺς ἀφρουρήτους, ἀφορολογήτους, ἀνεπισταθμεύτους, νόμοις χρῆσθαι τοῖς ἰδίοις. . . .

3   Συγχωρεῖν τὸν βασιλέα Θασίους ἀφρουρήτους,
ἀφορολογήτους, ἀνεπισταθμεύτους, νόμοις χρῆσθαι
τοῖς ἰδίοις. ἐπισημηναμένων δὲ μετὰ κραυγῆς πάντων
τὰ ῥηθέντα παρήγαγον τὸν Φίλιππον εἰς τὴν πόλιν. . . .

4   Ἴσως μὲν γὰρ πάντες οἱ βασιλεῖς κατὰ τὰς πρώ-
(24a)   τας ἀρχὰς πᾶσι προτείνουσι τὸ τῆς ἐλευθερίας ὄνομα
καὶ φίλους προσαγορεύουσι καὶ συμμάχους ⟨τοὺς⟩
κοινωνήσαντας σφίσι τῶν αὐτῶν ἐλπίδων, καθικόμε-
νοι δὲ τῶν πράξεων παρὰ πόδας οὐ συμμαχικῶς, ἀλλὰ
5 (2)   δεσποτικῶς χρῶνται τοῖς πιστεύσασι· διὸ καὶ τοῦ μὲν
καλοῦ διαψεύδονται, τοῦ δὲ παραυτὰ συμφέροντος ὡς
6   ἐπίπαν οὐκ ἀποτυγχάνουσι· τὸ δ᾽ ἐπιβαλλόμενον τοῖς
μεγίστοις καὶ περιλαμβάνοντα ταῖς ἐλπίσι τὴν οἰκουμένην καὶ πάσας ἀκμὴν ἀκεραίους ἔχοντα τὰς
ἐπιβολὰς εὐθέως ἐν τοῖς ἐλαχίστοις καὶ πρώτοις τῶν
ὑποπιπτόντων ἐπικηρύττειν ἅπασι τὴν ἀθεσίαν αὐτοῦ

share nothing but the desert site of a city, was much dissatisfied. He was, however, unable to take any action.

Conduct of Philip

24. Philip on his return voyage, committing one act of treachery after another, put in at about midday to Thasos,[42] and though that city was friendly took it and enslaved the inhabitants.

The Thasians told Metrodorus, Philip's general, that they would surrender the city if he would let them remain without a garrison, exempt from tribute, with no soldiers quartered on them and governed by their own laws. . . .

The reply was that Philip acceded to this request upon which all present applauded and admitted Philip into the city. . . .

Perhaps it may be said of all kings that at the beginnings of their reigns they talk of freedom as of a gift they offer to all and style all those who are thus loyal adherents friends and allies, but as soon as they have established their authority they at once begin to treat those who placed trust in them not as allies but as servants. Therefore they are disappointed of any credit for noble conduct, though as a rule they do not miss their immediate interest. But who would not qualify as perfectly irrational and insane the conduct of a prince, who, engaging in vast enterprises and aspiring to universal dominion,[43] with his chances of success in all his projects still unimpaired, yet in matters of no moment, in

[42] The city is situated at the northern shore of the island; it was excavated by the French.

[43] P. obviously believed that Philip had such extravagant plans.

καὶ τὴν ἀβεβαιότητα πῶς οὐκ ἂν δόξειεν ἀλόγιστον
εἶναι καὶ μανικόν;

III. RES AEGYPTI

(25a) 3   Μετὰ δ᾿ ἡμέρας τρεῖς ἢ τέτταρας ἐν τῷ μεγίστῳ
περιστύλῳ τῆς αὐλῆς οἰκοδομήσαντες βῆμα συνε-
κάλεσαν τοὺς ὑπασπιστὰς καὶ τὴν θεραπείαν, ἅμα δὲ
4 (2) τούτοις τοὺς πεζῶν καὶ τοὺς ἱππέων ἡγεμόνας. ἀθροι-
σθέντων δὲ τούτων ἀναβὰς Ἀγαθοκλῆς καὶ Σωσίβιος
ἐπὶ τὸ βῆμα πρῶτον μὲν τὸν τοῦ βασιλέως καὶ τὸν τῆς
βασιλίσσης θάνατον ἀνθωμολογήσαντο καὶ τὸ πέν-
θος ἀνέφηναν τοῖς πολλοῖς κατὰ τὸ παρ᾿ αὐτοῖς ἔθος.
5   μετὰ δὲ ταῦτα διάδημα τῷ παιδὶ περιθέντες ἀνέδειξαν
βασιλέα, καὶ διαθήκην τινὰ παρανέγνωσαν πεπλα-
σμένην, ἐν ᾗ γεγραμμένον ἦν ὅτι καταλείπει τοῦ
παιδὸς ἐπιτρόπους ὁ βασιλεὺς Ἀγαθοκλέα καὶ Σωσί-
6 (3) βιον· καὶ παρεκάλουν τοὺς ἡγεμόνας εὐνοεῖν καὶ διαφυλάττειν τῷ παιδὶ τὴν ἀρχήν· ἐπὶ δὲ τούτοις δύο
κάλπιδας ἀργυρᾶς εἰσήνεγκαν, ὡς τῆς μὲν μιᾶς ἐχούσης τὰ τοῦ βασιλέως ὀστᾶ, τῆς δ᾿ ἑτέρας τὰ τῆς
7 (4) Ἀρσινόης· εἶχε δ᾿ ἡ μὲν μία κατ᾿ ἀλήθειαν τὰ τοῦ
βασιλέως, ἡ δ᾿ ἑτέρα πλήρης ἦν ἀρωμάτων. ταῦτα δὲ
ποιήσαντες εὐθέως ἐπετέλουν τὴν ἐκφοράν. ἐν ᾧ καιρῷ
πᾶσι τὰ κατὰ τὴν Ἀρσινόην συνέβη γενέσθαι δῆλα.

---

44 Probably counting from the death of Ptolemy IV or from an
event soon thereafter. The date is 204.

the very first matters he was called upon to deal with, proclaimed to all his fickleness and faithlessness?

III. AFFAIRS OF EGYPT

Ambition and Fate of Agathocles

25.3 After four or five days,[44] erecting a tribune in the largest colonnade of the palace, they summoned a meeting of the bodyguard and household troops as well as of the officers of the infantry and cavalry. When all these had collected, Agathocles[45] and Sosibius[46] mounted the tribune, and in the first place acknowledged the death of the king and queen and enjoined the populace to go into mourning as was their usual practice. After this they crowned the boy and proclaimed him king,[47] and then read a forged will, in which it was written that the king appointed Agathocles and Sosibius guardians of his son. They begged the officers to remain well disposed and maintain the boy on his throne; and afterward brought in two silver urns, the one said to contain the bones of the king and the other those of Arsinoë.[48] As a fact, the one did contain the king's bones, but the other was full of spices. Hereupon they at once celebrated the funeral, and now the real circumstances of Arsinoë's fate became manifest to all. For on her death be-

204 B.C.

---

[45] See n. on 14.11.1.

[46] See n. on 5.35.7.

[47] It will be seen in the sequel that the solemn festival of his Proclamation (Anacleteria) was only celebrated in 196 B.C.

[48] The king's sister and wife, mother of Ptolemy V Epiphanes. She was murdered soon after Philopator's death to prevent her from becoming regent.

8 (5) τοῦ γὰρ θανάτου φωτισθέντος ὁ τρόπος ἐπεζητεῖτο
τῆς ἀπωλείας· οὐκ οὔσης δὲ προφάσεως ἄλλης οὐδεμιᾶς, τῆς ἀληθινῆς φήμης προσπεπτωκυίας, ἀκμὴν δ᾽
ἀμφισβητουμένης, τὸ κατ᾽ ἀλήθειαν γεγονὸς ἐν ταῖς
ἑκάστων γνώμαις ἐπεσφραγίσθη. διὸ καὶ συνέβη
9 (6) μεγάλην γενέσθαι τὴν σύγχυσιν τῶν ὄχλων. τοῦ μὲν
γὰρ βασιλέως οὐθεὶς οὐθένα λόγον ἐποιεῖτο, περὶ δὲ
τῆς Ἀρσινόης, ἀνανεούμενοι τινὲς μὲν τὴν ὀρφανίαν
αὐτῆς, ἔνιοι δὲ τὴν ἐξ ἀρχῆς ἐν τῷ ζῆν ὕβριν, ἣν
ὑπέμεινε, καὶ τὴν αἰκίαν, σὺν δὲ τούτοις τὸ περὶ τὴν
τελευτὴν ἀτύχημα, εἰς τοσαύτην παράστασιν ἐνέ-
πιπτον καὶ δυσθυμίαν ὥστε πλήρη γενέσθαι τὴν
πόλιν στεναγμοῦ, δακρύων, οἰμωγῆς ἀκαταπαύστου.
10 (7) ταῦτα δ᾽ ἦν τοῖς ὀρθῶς λογιζομένοις οὐχ οὕτω τῆς
πρὸς Ἀρσινόην εὐνοίας τεκμήρια, πολὺ δὲ μᾶλλον τοῦ
πρὸς τοὺς περὶ τὸν Ἀγαθοκλέα μίσους·

25. Ὅτι Σωσίβιος ὁ ψευδεπίτροπος Πτολεμαίου
ἐδόκει γεγονέναι σκεῦος ἀγχίνουν καὶ πολυχρόνιον,
2 ἔτι δὲ κακοποιὸν ἐν βασιλείᾳ, καὶ πρώτῳ μὲν ἀρτῦσαι
φόνον Λυσιμάχῳ, ὃς ἦν υἱὸς Ἀρσινόης τῆς Λυσι-
μάχου καὶ Πτολεμαίου, δευτέρῳ δὲ Μάγᾳ τῷ Πτολεμαίου καὶ Βερενίκης τῆς Μάγα, τρίτῃ δὲ Βερενίκῃ τῇ
Πτολεμαίου μητρὶ τοῦ Φιλοπάτορος, τετάρτῳ Κλεο-
μένει τῷ Σπαρτιάτῃ, πέμπτῃ θυγατρὶ Βερενίκης Ἀρ-
σινόῃ. . . .

11 (8) ὁ δὲ προειρημένος, ἐπειδὴ τὰς ὑδρίας εἰς τοὺς
βασιλικοὺς οἴκους ἔθηκε, παραγγείλας ἀποθέσθαι τὰ
φαιά, πρῶτον μὲν διμήνου τὰς δυνάμεις ὠψώνιασε,

ing made known, everyone began to inquire how she had perished. As there was no other cause assigned when the true report began to reach people's ears, though doubt still subsisted, the truth was impressed on the minds of all, and the people were much stirred in consequence. As for the king, no one cared, but concerning Arsinoë, when some recalled her orphanhood and others the insults and out-rages[49] inflicted on her during her whole life, and finally her unhappy death, the people fell into such a state of dis-traction and affliction that the town was full of groans, tears, and ceaseless lamentation, a testimony, in the opin-ion of those who judged correctly, not so much of affection for Arsinoë as of hatred of Agathocles.

25.1 Sosibius,[50] the pretended guardian of Ptolemy, ap-pears to have been a dexterous instrument of evil who re-mained long in power and did much mischief in the king-dom. He first of all compassed the death of Lysimachus, who was Ptolemy's son by Arsinoë the daughter of Lysima-chus, next that of Magas,[51] son of Ptolemy and Berenice, daughter of Magas, thirdly that of Berenice,[52] mother of Ptolemy Philopator, fourthly that of Cleomenes of Sparta,[53] and fifthly that of Arsinoë,[54] the daughter of Berenice.

25.11 The latter, after depositing the urns in the royal vaults, ordered the public mourning to cease, and as a first step granted two months' pay to the troops, feeling sure of

---

[49] Among others, Philopator's relationship with Agathoclea, the sister of Agathocles.   [50] This comes in all likelihood on the occasion of his death. See Maas (n. on 24a, below) on the in-clusion of this fragment here. Thereafter Agathocles is acting alone.   [51] See n. on 5.34.1.   [52] Magas' mother.
[53] For his end see 5.34.34–39.   [54] Above, 25.7.

πεπεισμένος τὸ παρὰ τοῖς πολλοῖς μῖσος ἀμβλύνειν
διὰ τῆς πρὸς τὸ λυσιτελὲς ὁρμῆς αὐτῶν, εἶτ᾽ ἐπεξώρ-
κισε τὸν ὅρκον ὃν ἦσαν ὀμνύειν εἰθισμένοι κατὰ τὰς
12 (9) ἀναδείξεις τῶν βασιλέων. ἐξαπέστειλε δὲ καὶ Φιλάμμωνα τὸν ἐπιστάντα τῷ τῆς Ἀρσινόης φόνῳ, ποιήσας
αὐτὸν Λιβυάρχην τῶν κατὰ Κυρήνην τόπων, τὸ δὲ
παιδίον ἐνεχείρισε ταῖς περὶ τὴν Οἰνάνθην καὶ Ἀγα-
13 (10) θόκλειαν. μετὰ δὲ ταῦτα Πέλοπα μὲν ἐξέπεμψε τὸν
Πέλοπος εἰς τὴν Ἀσίαν πρὸς Ἀντίοχον τὸν βασιλέα,
παρακαλέσοντα συντηρεῖν τὴν φιλίαν καὶ μὴ παραβαίνειν τὰς πρὸς τὸν τοῦ παιδὸς πατέρα συνθήκας,
Πτολεμαῖον δὲ τὸν Σωσιβίου πρὸς Φίλιππον τά τε
περὶ τῆς ἐπιγαμίας συνθησόμενον καὶ παρακαλέσοντα βοηθεῖν, ἐὰν ὁλοσχερέστερον αὐτοὺς Ἀντίοχος
14 ἐπιβάληται παρασπονδεῖν. προεχειρίσατο δὲ καὶ Πτολεμαῖον τὸν Ἀγησάρχου πρεσβευτὴν πρὸς Ῥωμαίους, οὐχ ὡς ἐπισπεύσοντα τὴν πρεσβείαν, ἀλλ᾽ ὡς, ἂν
ἅψηται τῆς Ἑλλάδος καὶ συμμίξῃ τοῖς ἐκεῖ φίλοις καὶ
15 (11) συγγενέσιν, αὐτοῦ καταμενοῦντα. προέκειτο γὰρ αὐτῷ
πάντας τοὺς ἐπιφανεῖς ἄνδρας ἐκποδὼν ποιῆσαι.
16 ἐξαπέστειλε δὲ καὶ Σκόπαν τὸν Αἰτωλὸν ἐπὶ ξενο-
λογίαν εἰς τὴν Ἑλλάδα, πλῆθος χρυσίου συνθεὶς εἰς
17 τὰ προδόματα. δύο γὰρ ἔσχε προθέσεις ὑπὲρ ταύτης

---

55 The mother of Agathocles and Agathoclea.
56 Son of Pelops the Macedon (*PP* 14618), commander of the
Ptolemaic garrison at Samos for Ptolemy II (*IG* XII 6, 119), eponymous priest of Alexander and the *Theoi Adelphoi* in 264/3. The
younger Pelops (*PP* 15064) had served as governor of Cyprus.

taking the edge off their hatred by appealing to the soldiers' spirit of avarice, and in the next place imposed on them the oath they were accustomed to take on the proclamation of a new king. He also sent away Philammon who had carried out the murder of Arsinoë, making him libyarch in the Cyrenaica, and he placed the child in the care of Oenanthe[55] and Agathoclea. After this he dispatched Pelops, son of Pelops,[56] to Asia, to King Antiochus to beg him to remain on friendly terms and not to transgress his treaty[57] with the young king's father, and sent Ptolemy,[58] son of Sosibius, to Philip to arrange for the proposed match[59] and to beg for his help if Antiochus attempted any serious violation of his obligations. He also appointed Ptolemy, the son of Hagesarchus,[60] ambassador to Rome, with the idea not of his hurrying to his post, but of his remaining in Greece when he reached that country and met his friends and relatives there, the object of Agathocles being to remove all men of distinction from Egypt. He also sent Scopas,[61] the Aetolian, to Greece to hire mercenaries, providing him with a large sum of money to advance to them. Two reasons underlay this plan; for in

[57] Concluded after the battle of Raphia in 217: 5.87.8.

[58] Known only from P.

[59] Most likely planned to be between Ptolemy V and a daughter of Philip V.

[60] On Hagesarchus see K. Hallof-Ch. Mileta, *Chiron* 17 (1997), 268–278. In ca. 245–44 he was governor of Caria for King Ptolemy III and is attested in this capacity in *I. Priene* 37.98 and in *IG* XII 6.156, ll. 7 and 23, from Samos. His son Ptolemy, of Megalopolis, wrote a history of Ptolemy IV in at least three books (*FGrH* 161).

[61] See n. on 4.3.5. He was last mentioned in 13.2.1.

τῆς ἐπιβολῆς, μίαν μὲν ἀποχρῆσθαι τοῖς ξενολογη-
θεῖσιν εἰς τὸν πρὸς Ἀντίοχον πόλεμον, ἄλλην δὲ τοὺς
ἀρχαίους καὶ προϋπάρχοντας ξένους ἐπὶ τὰ κατὰ τὴν
χώραν φρούρια καὶ τὰς κατοικίας ἀποστεῖλαι, τοῖς δὲ
παραγενομένοις ἀναπληρῶσαι καὶ καινοποιῆσαι τὴν
θεραπείαν καὶ τὰ περὶ τὴν αὐλὴν φυλακεῖα, παρα-
18 πλησίως δὲ καὶ κατὰ τὴν ἄλλην πόλιν, νομίζων τοὺς
δι᾽ αὑτοῦ ξενολογηθέντας καὶ μισθοδοτουμένους τῶν
μὲν προγεγονότων μηδενὶ συμπαθήσοντας διὰ τὸ
μηδὲν γινώσκειν, ἐν αὑτῷ δὲ τὰς ἐλπίδας ἔχοντας καὶ
τῆς σωτηρίας καὶ τῆς ἐπανορθώσεως, ἑτοίμους ἕξειν
συναγωνιστὰς καὶ συνεργοὺς πρὸς τὸ παραγγελλό-
19 (12) μενον. ταῦτα δ᾽ ἐγενήθη πρότερα τοῦ παρὰ Φιλίππῳ
διαβουλίου . . ., ὡς ἐδηλώσαμεν· ἀλλ᾽ ἐκείνων κατὰ
τὴν τῆς διηγήσεως τάξιν προτέρων λαμβανομένων
ἀναγκαῖον ἦν οὕτως ταῦτα χειρίζειν ὥστε πρότερον
ἐξηγεῖσθαι τὰς ἐντεύξεις καὶ τοὺς χρηματισμοὺς τῶν
πρεσβευτῶν καὶ τῆς καταστάσεως καὶ τῆς ἐξαπο-
στολῆς.

24a. Ὅτι ἐπεὶ πάσας καθ᾽ ἕκαστον ἔτος τὰς κατάλ-
(24a 4) ληλα πράξεις γενόμενα κατὰ τὴν οἰκουμένην ἐξηγού-

---

62 In a lost passage.

63 Maas (n. on 24a, below) observed that the sentence, together with 24a, is identical to 28.16.10–11 and that 24a must
therefore follow immediately.

64 These lines are identical with those in 28.16.11.

65 P. included in this book, dedicated to the year 203/2, events
that had already occurred in 204/3. He may have done so for rea-

the first place, he wished to use the troops he hired for the war against Antiochus, and next to send away the existing force of mercenaries to the country forts in Egypt and to the foreign settlements, and then with these new arrivals to fill up and remodel the household troops and the guards of the court, and of the rest of the city, thinking that the men he himself had enlisted and whom he paid, as they had no political sympathies regarding past events of which they were ignorant, and as they reposed their hopes of preservation and advancement on himself, would readily support him and join heartily in executing all his behests. All this happened before the negotiations with Philip, as I have stated,[62] but as the negotiations fell to be dealt with first owing to the order of my narrative, it was necessary for me to manage matters so as to give an account[63] of the interviews and speeches of the ambassadors before mentioning their appointment and dispatch.

24a. As I give[64] a narrative[65] of the contemporary events that happened in each part of the world in each year, it is

sons of composition (E. Bikerman) or by error (his or that of his source: Schmitt [10.28.3], 189–237). K. Abel argued that 15.25.3–37 and 15.26.1–36 came in fact from Book 14, as Athenaeus (6.251 C) attests for 15.33.2 (see 14.11.1). His thesis was attacked by Walbank, *Commentary* 3, Addenda 784–785, but defended by Abel in *Hist.* 32 (1983), 268–286. On the one hand, Abel makes some important points but has to assume substantial changes in the sequence of fragments in F and in the Constantinian excerpts. On the other hand, a new order of some fragments, proposed by P. Maas (*Mélanges. Grégoire* I, 1949, 443–448), has been widely accepted and is here followed: XV 25.3–10; 25.1–2; 25.11–19; 24a.; 26a.1–2; 25.20–37; 26.1–36.11.

μεθα, δῆλον ὡς ἀναγκαῖόν ἐστι τὸ τέλος ἐπ᾽ ἐνίων
πρότερον ἐκφέρειν τῆς ἀρχῆς, ἐπειδὰν πρότερος ὁ
τόπος ὑποπέσῃ κατὰ τὸν τῆς ὅλης ὑποθέσεως μερισμὸν καὶ κατὰ τὴν τῆς διηγήσεως ἔφοδον ὁ τὴν
συντέλειαν τῆς πράξεως ἔχων τοῦ τὴν ἀρχὴν καὶ τὴν
ἐπιβολὴν περιέχοντος. . . .

(25b) 26a. Ὅτι Δείνωνα τὸν Δείνωνος ἐπανείλετο Ἀγαθοκλῆς, καὶ τοῦτο ἔπραξε τῶν ἀδίκων ἔργων, ὡς ἡ
παροιμία φησί, δικαιότατον· καθ᾽ ὃν μὲν γὰρ καιρόν,
τῶν γραμμάτων αὐτῷ προσπεσόντων ὑπὲρ τῆς ἀναι-
ρέσεως τῆς Ἀρσινόης, ἐξουσίαν ἔσχε μηνῦσαι τὴν
πρᾶξιν καὶ σῶσαι τὰ κατὰ τὴν βασιλείαν, τότε δὴ
συνεργήσας τοῖς περὶ τὸν Φιλάμμωνα, πάντων ἐγέ-
2 νετο τῶν ἐπιγενομένων κακῶν αἴτιος, μετὰ δὲ τὸ συντελεσθῆναι τὸν φόνον ἀνανεούμενος καὶ πρὸς πολλοὺς
οἰκτιζόμενος καὶ μεταμελόμενος ἐπὶ τῷ τοιοῦτον καιρὸν παραλιπεῖν δῆλος ἐγένετο τοῖς περὶ τὸν Ἀγα-
θοκλέα· διὸ καὶ παραυτίκα τυχὼν τῆς ἁρμοζούσης
τιμωρίας μετήλλαξε τὸν βίον. . . .

20 (13) Ὁ δ᾽ Ἀγαθοκλῆς ἐπεὶ τοὺς ἐπιφανεστάτους τῶν
ἀνδρῶν ἐκποδὼν ἐποίησε, καὶ τὸ πολὺ τῆς τοῦ πλήθους ὀργῆς παρακατέσχε τῇ τῶν ὀψωνίων ἀποδόσει,
21 (14) παρὰ πόδας εἰς τὴν ἐξ ἀρχῆς συνήθειαν ἐπανῆλθε. καὶ
τὰς μὲν τῶν φίλων χώρας ἀνεπλήρωσε, παρεισαγα-
γὼν ἐκ τῆς διακονίας καὶ τῆς ἄλλης ὑπηρεσίας τοὺς
22 (15) εἰκαιοτάτους καὶ θρασυτάτους· αὐτὸς δὲ τὸ πολὺ τῆς
ἡμέρας καὶ τῆς νυκτὸς ἐν μέθῃ διέτριβε καὶ ταῖς τῇ
μέθῃ παρεπομέναις ἀκρασίαις, οὐ φειδόμενος οὔτ᾽

evident that in some cases the end must be told before the beginning, in those cases I mean where according to the general scheme of my work and the order imposed on my narrative the locality which was the scene of the final catastrophe occupies an earlier place than that which witnessed the initial stages. . . .

26a. Agathocles killed Deinon, son of Deinon,[66] and this was, as the saying is, "the justest of his many iniquities." For at the time when dispatches reached Deinon proposing the murder of Arsinoë, it was perfectly in his power to report the criminal project and save the kingdom, but he chose to take the part of Philammon and became thus the cause of all the evils which followed. However, after the murder had been committed, Agathocles found out that he was always recalling his conduct, lamenting it to many people and expressing regret for the chance he had let slip. Therefore he at once met with the punishment he merited and lost his life. . . .

25.20 Agathocles, as soon as he had removed all the most notable men and checked to a great extent by the advance of pay the disaffection among the troops, turned to his old courses. He filled up the vacant places of the royal "friends" by appointing from the body servants and other attendants those most remarkable for their effrontery and recklessness. He himself spent the greater part of the day and night in drinking and the debauchery which commonly accompanies it, sparing neither women in the

---

[66] Thought to be the Deinon who was governor of Cyprus under Ptolemy IV according to *I. Lindos* 139, 2, where however, the correct reading gives Pelops instead of Deinon (*PP* 15064).

ἀκμαζούσης γυναικὸς οὔτε νύμφης οὔτε παρθένου, καὶ
πάντα ταῦτ᾽ ἔπραττε μετὰ τῆς ἐπαχθεστάτης φαντα-
23 (16) σίας. ὅθεν πολλῆς μὲν καὶ παντοδαπῆς γινομένης
δυαρεστήσεως, οὐδεμιᾶς δὲ θεραπείας οὐδὲ βοηθείας
προσαγομένης, τὸ δ᾽ ἐναντίον ἀεὶ προσεπαγομένης
24 (17) ὕβρεως, ὑπερηφανίας, ῥᾳθυμίας, ἀνεθυμιᾶτο πάλιν ἐν
τοῖς πολλοῖς τὸ προϋπάρχον μῖσος καὶ πάντες ἀνενεοῦντο τὰ προγεγενημένα περὶ τὴν βασιλείαν ἀτυχή-
25 (18) ματα διὰ τοὺς ἀνθρώπους τούτους. τῷ δὲ μηδὲν ἔχειν
πρόσωπον ἀξιόχρεων τὸ προστησόμενον, καὶ δι᾽ οὗ
τὴν ὀργὴν εἰς τὸν Ἀγαθοκλέα καὶ τὴν Ἀγαθόκλειαν
ἀπερείσονται, τὴν ἡσυχίαν ἦγον, ἔτι μίαν ἐλπίδα
καραδοκοῦντες τὴν κατὰ τὸν Τληπόλεμον καὶ ταύτῃ
26 (19) προσανέχοντες. ὁ δὲ Τληπόλεμος, ἕως μὲν ὁ βασιλεὺς
ἔζη, τὰ καθ᾽ αὑτὸν ἔπραττεν· ἅμα δὲ τῷ μεταλλάξαι
᾽κεῖνον ταχέως ἐξομαλίσας τὰ πλήθη στρατηγὸς πά-
27 λιν ἐγενήθη τῶν κατὰ Πηλούσιον τόπων. καὶ τὰς μὲν
ἀρχὰς ἐποιεῖτο τὴν ἀναφορὰν τῶν πραττομένων ἐπὶ τὸ
τοῦ βασιλέως συμφέρον, πεπεισμένος ὑπάρξειν τι
συνέδριον ὃ τήν τε τοῦ παιδὸς ἐπιτροπείαν ἕξει καὶ
28 (20) τὴν τῶν ὅλων προστασίαν. ὡς δ᾽ ἑώρα τοὺς μὲν ἀξίους
ἐπιτροπῆς ἄνδρας ἐκποδὼν γεγονότας, τῆς δὲ τῶν
ὅλων ἀρχῆς κατατολμῶντα τὸν Ἀγαθοκλέα, ταχέως
ἐφ᾽ ἑτέρας ἐγένετο γνώμης, ὑφορώμενος τὸν προ-
εστῶτα κίνδυνον διὰ τὴν ὑποκειμένην αὐτοῖς ἔχθραν,
καὶ τάς τε δυνάμεις περὶ αὑτὸν ἤθοιζε καὶ περὶ πόρον

---

67 From hellenized Persian nobility, based at Xanthus in Lycia.

flower of their age nor brides nor virgins, and all this he did with the most odious ostentation. So that as strong dislike against him was aroused on all sides, as no attempt was made to conciliate or help those aggrieved, but on the contrary there was a constant repetition of outrage, arrogance, and neglect, the former hatred of the populace for him began to fume again, and all recalled the calamities that these men had brought on the kingdom. But since they had no leader of any weight, through whom to vent their anger on Agathocles and Agathoclea, they kept quiet, their only remaining hope, to which they eagerly clung, being in Tlepolemus.[67] While the king still lived, Tlepolemus attended to his own affairs, but on the death of Ptolemy, after quieting the populace, he then became military governor of the district round Pelusium; and at first he consulted the king's interest in all he did, believing that there would be some council charged with the guardianship of the child and the general control of affairs. But when he saw that all the men worthy of this office had been got rid of, and that Agathocles ventured to assume the reins of government, he very soon changed his attitude, as he was conscious of the danger that menaced him owing to their longstanding enmity, and collecting his forces around him took measures for providing himself with money in order that he

Tlepolemus son of Artapates won an Olympic victory in 254 and served as the eponymous priest of Alexander and the *Theoi Adelphoi* in two successive years, 247/6 and 246/5 (*PP* 5227.14618). The homonymous man attested here was honored at Delphi and served in his hometown as a priest under Ptolemy IV and, after the city had fallen to Antiochus III, in 196 (*PP* 50 and 14634). See C. Habicht, *Pausanias' Guide to Ancient Greece* (Berkeley 1985), 87.

ἐγίνετο χρημάτων, ἵνα μηδενὶ τῶν ἐχθρῶν εὐχείρωτος

29 (21) ᾖ. ἅμα δὲ καὶ τὴν τοῦ παιδὸς ἐπιτροπείαν καὶ τὴν τῶν ὅλων προστασίαν εἰς ἑαυτὸν ἥξειν οὐκ ἀπήλπιζε, νομίζων καὶ κατὰ τὴν ἰδίαν μὲν κρίσιν αὐτὸς ἀξιοχρεώτερος ὑπάρχειν Ἀγαθοκλέους πρὸς πᾶν, ἔτι μᾶλλον δὲ πυνθανόμενος καὶ τὰς ὑφ' ἑαυτὸν ταττομένας δυνάμεις καὶ τὰς κατὰ τὴν Ἀλεξάνδρειαν ἐπ' ἐκείνῳ τὰς ἐλπίδας ἔχειν τοῦ καταλύειν τὴν Ἀγαθοκλέους ὕβριν.

30 (22) οὔσης δὲ περὶ αὐτὸν οἵας εἴρηκα διαλήψεως, ταχέως τὰ τῆς διαφορᾶς αὔξησιν ἔλαβε συνεργούντων ἀμφο-

31 (23) τέρων πρὸς τὴν τοιαύτην ὑπόθεσιν. ὁ μὲν γὰρ Τληπόλεμος, ἐξιδιάζεσθαι σπεύδων τοὺς ἡγεμόνας καὶ ταξιάρχους καὶ τοὺς ἐπὶ τούτων ταττομένους, συνῆγε πότους ἐπιμελῶς, καὶ παρὰ τὰς συνουσίας τὰ μὲν ὑπὸ τῶν πρὸς χάριν λεγόντων αἰκαλλόμενος, τὰ δ' ὑπὸ τῆς ἰδίας ὁρμῆς, ἅτε νέος ὢν καὶ παρὰ τὸν οἶνον γινομένης τῆς ὁμιλίας, ἐρρίπτει λόγους κατὰ τῆς συγγενείας τῆς τῶν περὶ τὸν Ἀγαθοκλέα, τὰς μὲν ἀρχὰς αἰνιγματώδεις, εἶτ' ἀμφιβόλους, τὸ δὲ τελευταῖον ἐκ-

32 (24) φανεῖς καὶ τὴν πικροτάτην ἔχοντας λοιδορίαν. ἐπεχεῖτο γὰρ τοῦ θρανογράφου καὶ τῆς σαμβυκιστρίας καὶ τῆς κουρίδος, ἔτι δὲ τοῦ παιδαρίου τοῦ πάντα πεποιηκότος καὶ πεπονθότος παρὰ τοὺς πότους, ὅτ' ἐφ' ὠνο-

33 (25) χόει τῷ βασιλεῖ παῖς ὤν. ἐπὶ δὲ τούτοις ἀεὶ τῶν συμπαρόντων γελώντων καὶ συμβαλλομένων τι πρὸς τὸν χλευασμόν, ταχέως εἰς τοὺς περὶ τὸν Ἀγαθοκλέα

34 (26) τὸ πρᾶγμα παρεγενήθη. γενομένης δ' ἔχθρας ὁμολογουμένης εὐθέως ὁ Ἀγαθοκλῆς διαβολὴν εἰσῆγε κατὰ

might not fall an easy prey to any of his foes. At the same time he did not despair of himself obtaining the guardianship of the child and the direction of affairs, thinking that he was, if his own judgment did not deceive him, more capable in every respect than Agathocles and more especially because he heard that both the troops under his own command and those in Alexandria placed in him their hopes of overthrowing the insolent domination of Agathocles. Such being his opinion of himself, the difference between them became speedily more acute, since both of them contributed to this end. For Tlepolemus, as he was desirous of attaching to himself the commanders, taxiarchs, and inferior officers, entertained them sedulously at banquets; and on these occasions, either flattered by those who wished to make themselves agreeable to him or on his own impulse, since he was young and they were talking over their wine, he would make remarks about the family of Agathocles, at first enigmatical, then of doubtful import, but finally quite outspoken and conveying the most venomous insults. For he used to toast the wall dauber and the sackbut girl and the lady barber, and the young boy who was so complaisant at the drinking bouts when he was cupbearer to the king in his childhood's days. As his guests always laughed with him and contributed something of their own to his jests, the matter soon reached the ears of Agathocles. Their enmity was now avowed, and Agathocles

591

τοῦ Τληπολέμου, φάσκων αὐτὸν ἀλλοτριάζειν τοῦ
35 βασιλέως καὶ καλεῖν Ἀντίοχον ἐπὶ τὰ πράγματα. καὶ
πολλὰς εἰς τοῦτο τὸ μέρος εὐπόρει πιθανότητας, τὰς
μὲν ἐκ τῶν συμβαινόντων παρεκδεχόμενος καὶ δια-
στρέφων, τὰς δ' ἐκ καταβολῆς πλάττων καὶ διασκευ-
36 (27) άζων. ταῦτα δ' ἐποίει βουλόμενος τὰ πλήθη παροξύ-
νειν κατὰ τοῦ Τληπολέμου· συνέβαινε δὲ τοὐναντίον.
πάλαι γὰρ ἐπὶ τῷ προειρημένῳ τὰς ἐλπίδας ἔχοντες οἱ
πολλοὶ καὶ λίαν ἡδέως ἑώρων ἐκκαιομένην τὴν δια-
37 (28) φοράν. ἐγένετο δ' ἡ καταρχὴ τοῦ περὶ τὰ πλήθη
κινήματος διά τινας τοιαύτας αἰτίας. Νίκων ὁ συγ-
γενὴς τῶν περὶ τὸν Ἀγαθοκλέα ζῶντος ἔτι τοῦ βασιλέως καθεσταμένος ἦν ἐπὶ τοῦ ναυτικοῦ· τότε δὲ τῶν
. . .

26. Πρώτους δὲ συναθροίσας τοὺς Μακεδόνας, εἰς
τούτους εἰσῆλθε μετὰ τοῦ βασιλέως καὶ τῆς Ἀγαθο-
2 κλείας. καὶ τὰς μὲν ἀρχὰς ὑπεκρίνετο τὸν οὐ δυνάμενον εἰπεῖν ἃ βούλεται διὰ τὸ πλῆθος τῶν ἐπιφε-
3 ρομένων δακρύων· ἐπεὶ δὲ πλεονάκις ἀπομάττων τῇ
χλαμύδι κατεκράτησε τῆς ἐπιφορᾶς, βαστάσας τὸ
παιδίον "Λάβετε" ἔφη "τοῦτον, ὃν ὁ πατὴρ ἀποθνή-
σκων εἰς μὲν τὰς ἀγκάλας ἔδωκε ταύτῃ" δείξας τὴν
ἀδελφὴν "παρακατέθετο δ' εἰς τῆς ὑμετέραν, ὦ ἄνδρες
4 Μακεδόνες, πίστιν. ἡ μὲν οὖν [καὶ] ταύτης εὔνοια
βραχεῖάν τινα ῥοπὴν ἔχει πρὸς τὴν τούτου σωτηρίαν,
ἐν ὑμῖν δὲ κεῖται καὶ ταῖς ὑμετέραις χερσὶ τὰ τούτου
5 νυνὶ πράγματα. Τληπόλεμος γὰρ πάλαι μὲν ἦν δῆλος
τοῖς ὀρθῶς σκοπουμένοις μειζόνων ἐφιέμενος ἢ καθ'

lost no time in bringing an accusation against Tlepolemus, charging him with disaffection to the king and stating that he was inviting Antiochus to assume the government. He was in no lack of specious grounds for this accusation, some resting on reports of actual facts which he distorted and some being pure inventions of his own. All this he did with the object of working up the populace against Tlepolemus, but it had the contrary result. For as they had for long rested their hopes on Tlepolemus, they were exceedingly glad to see the quarrel becoming more inflamed. The popular movement originated in the following manner. Nicon,[68] who was a relative of Agathocles, had been appointed director of naval affairs during the lifetime of Ptolemy, and he now . . .

26. Agathocles in the first place summoned a meeting of the Macedonians[69] and appeared together with Agathoclea and the young king. At first he pretended that he could not say what he wished owing to the abundance of the tears that choked him, but after wiping his eyes many times with his chlamys and subduing the outburst, he took the child in his arms and exclaimed, "Take the child whom his father on his deathbed placed in the arms of this woman," pointing to his sister, "and confided to your faith, you soldiers of Macedon. Her affection indeed is of but little moment to ensure his safety, but his fate depends on you and your valor. For it has long been evident to those who judge correctly that Tlepolemus aspires to a position higher than it behooves him to covet, and now he has actually fixed the

---

[68] *PP* 13778. He reappears in 33.7–8.

[69] The guard, being the privileged part of the army. Not all were of Macedonian nationality.

ἑαυτὸν πραγμάτων, νῦν δὲ καὶ τὴν ἡμέραν καὶ τὸν
καιρὸν ὥρικεν, ἐν ᾗ μέλλει τὸ διάδημ᾽ ἀναλαμβάνειν."

6 καὶ περὶ τούτων οὐχ αὑτῷ πιστεύειν ἐκέλευεν ἀλλὰ
τοῖς εἰδόσι τὴν ἀλήθειαν καὶ παροῦσι νῦν ἐξ αὐτῶν

7 τῶν πραγμάτων. καὶ τοῦτ᾽ εἰπὼν εἰσῆγε τὸν Κρι-
τόλαον, ὃς ἔφη καὶ τοὺς βωμοὺς αὐτὸς ἑωρακέναι
κατασκευαζομένους καὶ τὰ θύματα παρὰ τοῖς πλή-
θεσιν ἑτοιμαζόμενα πρὸς τὴν τοῦ διαδήματος ἀνάδει-

8 ξιν. ὧν οἱ Μακεδόνες ἀκούοντες οὐχ οἷον ἠλέουν
αὐτόν, ἀλλ᾽ ἁπλῶς οὐδὲν προσεῖχον τῶν λεγομένων,
μυχθίζοντες <δὲ καὶ> διαψιθυρίζοντες ἐξελήρησαν οὕτως ὥστε μηδ᾽ αὐτὸν εἰδέναι [μήτε] πῶς τὸ παράπαν

9 ἐκ τῆς ἐκκλησίας ἀπελύθη. παραπλήσια δὲ τούτοις
ἐγίνετο καὶ περὶ τὰ λοιπὰ συστήματα κατὰ τοὺς

10 ἐκκλησιασμούς. ἐν δὲ τῷ μεταξὺ πολὺς ἦν ὁ καταπλέων ἐκ τῶν ἄνω στρατοπέδων, καὶ παρεκάλουν οἱ
μὲν συγγενεῖς, οἱ δὲ φίλους, βοηθεῖν τοῖς ὑποκειμένοις, καὶ μὴ περιιδεῖν σφᾶς ἀνέδην ὑφ᾽ οὕτως ἀνα-

11 ξίων ὑβριζομένους. μάλιστα δὲ παρώξυνε τοὺς πολλοὺς πρὸς τὴν κατὰ τῶν προεστώτων τιμωρίαν τὸ
γινώσκειν ὅτι τὸ μέλλειν καθ᾽ αὐτῶν ἐστι διὰ τὸ
πάντων τῶν παρακομιζομένων ἐπιτηδείων εἰς τὴν
Ἀλεξάνδρειαν κρατεῖν τοὺς περὶ τὸν Τληπόλεμον.

27. ἐγένετο δέ τι καὶ ἐξ αὐτῶν <τῶν> περὶ τὸν
Ἀγαθοκλέα συνέργημα πρὸς τὸ τὴν ὀργὴν ἐπιτεῖναι

2 τήν τε τῶν πολλῶν καὶ τὴν τοῦ Τληπολέμου· τὴν γὰρ
Δανάην, ἥτις ἦν πενθερὰ τοῦ προειρημένου, λαβόντες
ἐκ τοῦ τῆς Δήμητρος ἱεροῦ καὶ διὰ μέσου τῆς πόλεως

day and hour at which he will assume the diadem." And as
to this he told them not to rely on his own word but on that
of those who knew the truth and had just come from the
very scene of action. After speaking thus he brought forward Critolaus, who told them that he had himself seen the
altars being erected and the victims being prepared in
presence of the populace for the ceremony of proclaiming
the coronation. When the Macedonians heard this, not
only did they feel no pity for Agathocles but paid absolutely no attention to his words, and showed such levity by
hooting and murmuring to each other that he did not know
himself how he got away from the meeting. The same kind
of thing took place at the meetings of the other regiments.
Meanwhile numbers of men kept on arriving by boat from
the garrisons in upper Egypt, and all begged their relatives or friends to help them at the present crisis and not
allow them to be thus outrageously tyrannized over by
such unworthy persons. The chief incentive to the soldiery
to wreak their vengeance on those in power was their
knowledge that any delay was prejudicial to themselves,
as Tlepolemus controlled the entire supply of provisions
reaching Alexandria.

27. There was also one thing done by Agathocles and
his party which contributed to exasperate the populace
and Tlepolemus. For they took Danaë, who was the latter's
mother-in-law, from the temple of Demeter, and dragged
her unveiled through the middle of the town and commit-

ἑλκύσαντες ἀκατακάλυπτον εἰς φυλακὴν ἀπέθεντο,
βουλόμενοι φανερὰν ποιεῖν τὴν πρὸς τὸν Τληπόλεμον

3 διαφοράν. ἐφ᾽ οἷς τὸ πλῆθος ἀγανακτοῦν οὐκέτι κατ᾽
ἰδίαν οὐδὲ δι᾽ ἀπορρήτων ἐποιεῖτο τοὺς λόγους, ἀλλ᾽ οἱ
μὲν τὰς νύκτας εἰς πάντα τόπον ἐπέγραφον, οἱ δὲ τὰς
ἡμέρας συστρεφόμενοι κατὰ μέρη φανερῶς ἐξέφερον
ἤδη τὸ μῖσος εἰς τοὺς προεστῶτας.

4 Οἱ δὲ περὶ τὸν Ἀγαθοκλέα βλέποντες τὰ συμβαίνοντα, καὶ μοχθηρὰς ἐλπίδας ἔχοντες περὶ αὑτῶν,
τοτὲ μὲν ἐγίνοντο περὶ δρασμόν, οὐδενὸς δ᾽ αὐτοῖς
ἡτοιμασμένου πρὸς τοῦτο τὸ μέρος διὰ τὴν σφετέραν

5 ἀβουλίαν ἀφίσταντο τῆς ἐπιβολῆς· τοτὲ δὲ συνωμό-
τας κατέγραφον καὶ κοινωνοὺς τῆς τόλμης, ὡς αὐτίκα
μάλα τῶν ἐχθρῶν τοὺς μὲν κατασφάξοντες, τοὺς δὲ
συλληψόμενοι, μετὰ δὲ ταῦτα τυραννικὴν ἐξουσίαν

6 περιποιησόμενοι. ταῦτα δ᾽ αὐτῶν διανοουμένων προσ-
έπεσε διαβολὴ κατά τινος Μοιραγένους, ἑνὸς τῶν
σωματοφυλάκων, διότι μηνύοι πάντα τῷ Τληπολέμῳ
καὶ συνεργοίη διὰ τὴν πρὸς Ἀδαῖον οἰκειότητα τὸν ἐπὶ

7 τῆς Βουβάστου τότε καθεσταμένον. ὁ δ᾽ Ἀγαθοκλῆς
εὐθέως συνέταξε Νικοστράτῳ τῷ πρὸς τοῖς γράμμασι
τεταγμένῳ συλλαβόντι τὸν Μοιραγένη φιλοτίμως

8 ἐξετάσαι, πᾶσαν προτιθέντα βάσανον. οὗτος μὲν οὖν
παραχρῆμα συλληφθεὶς ὑπὸ τοῦ Νικοστράτου καὶ
παραχθεὶς εἴς τινα μέρη τῆς αὐλῆς ἀποκεχωρηκότα,
τὸ μὲν πρῶτον ἐξ ὀρθῆς ἀνεκρίνετο περὶ τῶν προσ-

9 πεπτωκότων, πρὸς οὐδὲν δὲ τῶν λεγομένων ἀνθομο-

ted her to prison, with the express object of exhibiting their hostility to him. This so irritated the people that they no longer spoke of the matter in private and secretly, but while some expressed their detestation of those in power by scribbling it all over the town at night, others even began to meet openly in groups in the daytime for this purpose.

Agathocles, seeing what was happening and entertaining poor hopes of his own security, began to contemplate flight; but as owing to his own imprudence he had made no preparations for this purpose he desisted from the project, and his next step was to enroll conspirators ready to join in the venture, with a view to putting to death some of his enemies at once and arresting others, after which he could possess himself of tyrannical power. While he was engaged in this project an accusation was brought against a certain Moeragenes, one of the bodyguards,[70] to the effect that he informed Tlepolemus of everything and worked for his cause owing to his relationship with Adaeus,[71] then governor of Bubastus.[72] Agathocles at once gave orders to Nicostratus, his secretary of state, to arrest Moeragenes and examine him diligently, menacing him with every kind of torture. Moeragenes was instantly arrested and conducted to a remote part of the palace, where he was at first questioned directly concerning these rumors, and on his

[70] High-ranking members of the king's personal staff.

[71] The name strongly suggests a Macedonian. A. B. Tataki, *Macedonians Abroad* (Athens 1998), 220–221, nos. 15–22, with no. 17 for the man mentioned here.

[72] B. or Boubastis, region and city in the eastern Delta. *RE* Bubastis 931–932 (K. Sethe).

λογούμενος ἐξεδύθη· καὶ τινὲς μὲν τὰ πρὸς τὰς βασά-
νους ὄργανα διεσκεύαζον, οἱ δὲ τὰς μάστιγας ἔχοντες
10 μετὰ χεῖρας ἀπεδύοντο τὰς χλαμύδας. κατὰ δὲ τὸν
καιρὸν τοῦτον προστρέχει τις τῶν ὑπηρετῶν πρὸς τὸν
Νικόστρατον, καὶ ψιθυρίσας πρὸς τὴν ἀκοὴν ἄττα
11 δήποτ' οὖν ἀπηλλάττετο μετὰ σπουδῆς. ὁ δὲ Νικόστρατος ἐκ ποδὸς ἐπηκολούθει τούτῳ, λέγων μὲν οὐδέν, τύπτων δὲ συνεχῶς τὸν μηρόν.

28. περὶ δὲ τὸν Μοιραγένην ἄφατον ἦν καὶ παρά-
2 λογον τὸ συμβαῖνον. οἱ μὲν γὰρ μόνον οὐ διατετα-
μένοι τὰς μάστιγας παρέστασαν, οἱ δὲ πρὸ ποδῶν
3 αὐτοῦ τὰ πρὸς ἀνάγκας ὄργανα διεσκεύαζον· τοῦ
δὲ Νικοστράτου παραχωρήσαντος ἔστασαν ἀχανεῖς
πάντες, ἐμβλέποντες ἀλλήλοις, προδοκῶντες ἀεί ποτε
4 τὸν προειρημένον ἀνακάμψειν. χρόνου δὲ γινομένου
κατὰ βραχὺ διέρρεον οἱ παρεστῶτες, τέλος δ' ὁ Μοιραγένης ἀπελείφθη. καὶ μετὰ ταῦτα διελθὼν τὴν αὐλὴν ἀνελπίστως παρέπεσε γυμνὸς εἴς τινα σκηνὴν
5 τῶν Μακεδόνων, σύνεγγυς κειμένην τῆς αὐλῆς. καταλαβὼν δὲ κατὰ τύχην ἀριστῶντας καὶ συνηθροισμέ-
νους, ἔλεγε τὰ περὶ αὐτὸν συμβεβηκότα καὶ τὸ παρά-
6 λογον τῆς σωτηρίας. οἱ δὲ τὰ μὲν ἠπίστουν, τὰ δὲ
πάλιν ὁρῶντες αὐτὸν γυμνὸν ἠναγκάζοντο πιστεύειν.
7 ἐκ δὲ ταύτης τῆς περιπετείας ὅ τε Μοιραγένης μετὰ
δακρύων ἐδεῖτο τῶν Μακεδόνων μὴ μόνον τῆς αὐτοῦ
συνεπιλαβέσθαι σωτηρίας, ἀλλὰ καὶ τῆς τοῦ βασι-
8 λέως, καὶ μάλιστα τῆς σφῶν αὐτῶν· πρόδηλον γὰρ
εἶναι πᾶσι τὸν ὄλεθρον, ἐὰν μὴ συνάψωνται τοῦ και-

denying every one of the charges was stripped. Some began to get the instruments of torture ready and others with
the scourges in their hands were taking off their cloaks,
when one of the servants ran up to Nicostratus and after whispering something into his ear made off in haste.
Nicostratus immediately followed him without saying a
word, but striking his thigh with his hand repeatedly.

28. It is difficult to describe the strange situation in
which Moeragenes found himself. For some of the execu-
tioners stood there with their scourges almost raised to
strike him and others were getting the instruments of torture ready before his eyes; but when Nicostratus departed
all remained in mute astonishment, looking at each other,
and each moment expecting Nicostratus to return; but after a little time had elapsed they gradually dispersed, and
Moeragenes was left by himself. After that he was able,
much to his surprise, to traverse the palace, and naked as
he was rushed into a tent belonging to the Macedonian
troops not far from the palace. Finding them by chance assembled there at breakfast he told his story and the extraordinary manner in which he had been delivered. They
were disposed to discredit it, but afterward seeing him naked they were compelled to believe him. Availing himself
of this complete change of circumstances, Moeragenes
begged the Macedonians with tears not only to help him to
save himself, but to save the king also and chiefly themselves. He urged upon them that their destruction was in-
evitable if they did not avail themselves of the present
opportunity, when the hatred of the populace was at its

ροῦ, καθ' ὃν ἀκμάζει τὸ τῶν πολλῶν μῖσος καὶ πᾶς
ἕτοιμός ἐστι πρὸς τὴν κατ' Ἀγαθοκλέους τιμωρίαν.
9 ἀκμάζειν δὲ νῦν μάλιστ' ἔφη καὶ προσδεῖσθαι τῶν
καταρξομένων.

29. οἱ δὲ Μακεδόνες ἀκούσαντες τούτων παροξύ-
νονται, καὶ πέρας ἐπείσθησαν τῷ Μοιραγένει, καὶ
πρώτας μὲν εὐθέως ἐπῄεσαν τὰς τῶν Μακεδόνων σκη-
2 νάς, μετὰ δὲ ταῦτα τὰς τῶν ἄλλων στρατιωτῶν· εἰσὶ δ'
αὗται συνεχεῖς, πρὸς ἓν μέρος ἀπονενευκυῖαι τῆς
3 πόλεως. οὔσης δὲ τῆς μὲν ὁρμῆς πάλαι προχείρου τῆς
τῶν πολλῶν, προσδεομένης δὲ τοῦ προκαλεσομένου
μόνον καὶ τολμήσοντος, ἅμα τῷ λαβεῖν ἀρχὴν τὸ
4 πρᾶγμα ταχέως οἷον εἰ πῦρ ἐξέλαμψεν. οὐ γὰρ ἐγενήθησαν ὧραι τέτταρες καὶ πάντα τὰ γένη συμπεφω-
νήκει καὶ τὰ στρατιωτικὰ καὶ τὰ πολιτικὰ πρὸς τὴν
5 ἐπίθεσιν. συνήργησε γὰρ μεγάλα καὶ ταὐτόματον ἐν
6 τῷ καιρῷ τούτῳ πρὸς τὴν συντέλειαν. ὁ μὲν γὰρ
Ἀγαθοκλῆς, ἀνενεχθείσης πρὸς αὐτὸν ἐπιστολῆς καὶ
κατασκόπων ἐπαναχθέντων, καὶ τῆς μὲν ἐπιστολῆς
γεγραμμένης πρὸς τὰς δυνάμεις παρὰ τοῦ Τληπολέμου καὶ δηλούσης ὅτι παρέσται ταχέως, τῶν δὲ κατα-
7 σκόπων διασαφούντων ὅτι πάρεστιν, οὕτως ἐξέστη
τῶν φρενῶν ὥστ' ἀφέμενος τοῦ πράττειν τι καὶ δια-
νοεῖσθαι περὶ τῶν προσπεπτωκότων ἀπῆλθε κατὰ τὸν
εἰθισμένον καιρὸν εἰς τὸν πότον, κἀκεῖ κατὰ τὴν
8 εἰθισμένην ἀγωγὴν ἐπετέλει τὴν συνουσίαν. ἡ δ'
Οἰνάνθη περικακοῦσα παρῆν εἰς τὸ Θεσμοφορεῖον,
9 ἀνεῳγμένου τοῦ νεὼ διά τινα θυσίαν ἐπέτειον. καὶ τὸ

height and everyone was ready to take vengeance on
Agathocles. This was just the time, he said, when the feeling was most thoroughly aroused and it only wanted someone to begin.

29. The Macedonians on hearing this were stimulated
to action and finally took the advice of Moeragenes, first
without delay visiting the Macedonian barracks and then
those of the other soldiers, which are all close together,
and turned toward a single part of the city. As the people
had long been disposed to revolt and required only some
man of courage to appeal to them, once the movement began it spread like wildfire. Four hours had scarcely elapsed
when men of all nationalities, both soldiers and civilians,
had agreed to attack the government. Chance too cooperated much at this time to the accomplishment of their aim.
For Agathocles, when a letter reached his hands, and some
spies were brought before him, and when the letter proved
to be one addressed by Tlepolemus to the troops announcing that he was on the point of coming, and the spies reported that he had actually arrived, so entirely lost his head
that, neglecting to take any action or to consider the news
he had received, he went to carouse at his usual hour and
conducted himself at the banquet in his usual manner.
Oenanthe, who was in great distress, betook herself to the
Thesmophoreum,[73] that temple being open for an annual
sacrifice. She first of all fell on her knees and with many

[73] The sanctuary of Demeter. For her cult in Egypt see *RE*
Demeter 2742–2743 (O. Kern).

μὲν πρῶτον ἐλιπάρει γονυπετοῦσα καὶ μαγγανεύουσα
πρὸς τὰς θεάς, μετὰ δὲ ταῦτα καθίσασα πρὸς τὸν
10 βωμὸν εἶχε τὴν ἡσυχίαν. αἱ μὲν οὖν πολλαὶ τῶν
γυναικῶν, ἡδέως ὁρῶσαι τὴν δυσθυμίαν καὶ περι-
κάκησιν αὐτῆς, ἀπεσιώπων· αἱ δὲ τοῦ Πολυκράτους
συγγενεῖς καί τινες ἕτεραι τῶν ἐνδόξων, ἀδήλου τῆς
περιστάσεως αὐταῖς ἀκμὴν ὑπαρχούσης, προσελθοῦ-
11 σαι παρεμυθοῦντο τὴν Οἰνάνθην. ἡ δ᾿ ἀναβοήσασα
μεγάλῃ τῇ φωνῇ "μή μοι πρόσιτέ" φησι "θηρία·
καλῶς γὰρ ὑμᾶς γινώσκω, διότι καὶ φρονεῖθ᾿ ἡμῖν
ἐναντία καὶ ταῖς θεαῖς εὔχεσθε τὰ δυσχερέστατα καθ᾿
12 ἡμῶν. οὐ μὴν ἀλλ᾿ ἔτι πέποιθα τῶν θεῶν βουλομένων
13 γεύσειν ὑμᾶς τῶν ἰδίων τέκνων." καὶ ταῦτ᾿ εἰποῦσα
ταῖς ῥαβδούχοις ἀνείργειν προσέταξε καὶ παίειν τὰς
14 μὴ πειθαρχούσας. αἱ δ᾿ ἐπιλαβόμεναι τῆς προφάσεως
ταύτης ἀπηλλάττοντο πᾶσαι, τοῖς θεοῖς ἀνίσχουσαι
τὰς χεῖρας καὶ καταρώμεναι λαβεῖν αὐτὴν ἐκείνην
πεῖραν τούτων, ἃ κατὰ τῶν πέλας ἐπανετείνετο πρά-
ξειν.

30. Ἤδη δὲ κεκριμένου τοῦ καινοτομεῖν τοῖς ἀνδράσιν, ἐπιγενομένης καθ᾿ ἑκάστην οἰκίαν καὶ τῆς ἐκ
τῶν γυναικῶν ὀργῆς διπλάσιον ἐξεκαύθη τὸ μῖσος.
2 ἅμα δὲ τῷ μεταλαβεῖν τὸ τῆς νυκτὸς πᾶσα πλήρης
3 ἦν ἡ πόλις θορύβου καὶ φώτων καὶ διαδρομῆς· οἱ
μὲν γὰρ εἰς τὸ στάδιον ἠθροίζοντο μετὰ κραυγῆς, οἱ
δὲ παρεκάλουν ἀλλήλους, οἱ δὲ κατεδύοντο διαδι-
4 δράσκοντες εἰς ἀνυπονοήτους οἰκίας καὶ τόπους· ἤδη
δὲ τῶν περὶ τὴν αὐλὴν εὐρυχωριῶν καὶ τοῦ σταδίου

gestures prayed fervently to the goddesses, and afterward seated herself by the altar and held her peace. Most of the women, pleased to see her so dejected and distressed, remained silent, but the relatives of Polycrates[74] and some other noble ladies,[75] who were not yet aware of the danger, came up to her to console her. "Come not near me, you beasts," she cried aloud to them, "I know well that you bear us ill will and that you pray to the goddesses that the worst may befall us, but yet I trust that, if it be the will of heaven, I shall yet make you taste the flesh of your own children." After saying this she bade her lictors drive them away from her and strike those who refused to leave. Availing themselves of this pretext all the ladies withdrew, holding up their hands to the goddesses and praying that she might be cursed with the fate that she threatened to bring on others.

30. The men had already decided on a revolution, but now that in each house the rage of the women was added to their own, the hatred of the usurper blazed up twice as violent. When day again gave place to night, the whole town was full of disturbance and torches and movement. For some collected in the stadium shouting, some were encouraging each other, others running in different directions took refuge in houses and places not likely to be suspected. The open spaces round the palace, the stadium,

[74] See n. on 5.64.4. His career with the Ptolemies spanned more than thirty years. He succeeded Aristomenes (below on 31.6–7).

[75] Prominently Zeuxo of Cyrene, the wife of Polycrates, and her three daughters, Zeuxo, Eucrateia, and Hermione. All four were victorious at the Panathenaea in the early second century as was their father (*Hesp.* 60 [1991], 229 and 231).

καὶ τῆς πλατείας πλήρους ὑπαρχούσης ὄχλου παν-
τοδαποῦ καὶ τῆς περὶ τὸ Διονυσιακὸν θέατρον προ-
5 στασίας, πυθόμενος τὸ συμβαῖνον Ἀγαθοκλῆς ἐξ-
ηγέρθη μεθύων, ἄρτι καταλελυκὼς τὸν πότον, καὶ
παραλαβὼν τοὺς συγγενεῖς πάντας πλὴν Φίλωνος ἧκε
6 πρὸς τὸν βαιλέα. καὶ βραχέα πρὸς τοῦτον οἰκτισάμε-
νος καὶ λαβόμενος αὐτοῦ τῆς χειρός, ἀνέβαινεν εἰς
τὴν σύριγγα τὴν μεταξὺ τοῦ Μαιάνδρου καὶ τῆς
παλαίστρας κειμένην καὶ φέρουσαν ἐπὶ τὴν τοῦ θε-
7 άτρου πάροδον. μετὰ δὲ ταῦτα, δύο θύρας ἀσφαλισάμενος τὰς πρώτας, εἰς τὴν τρίτην ἀνεχώρησε μετὰ
δυεῖν ἢ τριῶν σωματοφυλάκων καὶ τοῦ βασιλέως καὶ
8 τῆς αὑτοῦ συγγενείας. συνέβαινε δὲ τὰς θύρας εἶναι
δικτυωτὰς διαφανεῖς, ἀποκλειομένας δὲ διττοῖς μο-
9 χλοῖς, κατὰ δὲ τὸν καιρὸν τοῦτον ἠθροισμένου τοῦ
πλήθους ἐξ ἁπάσης τῆς πόλεως, ὥστε μὴ μόνον τοὺς
ἐπιπέδους τόπους, ἀλλὰ καὶ τὰ βάθρα καὶ τὰ τέγη
καταγέμειν ἀνθρώπων, ἐγίνετο βοὴ καὶ κραυγὴ σύμ-
μικτος, ὡς ἂν γυναικῶν ὁμοῦ καὶ παίδων ἀνδράσιν
10 ἀναμεμιγμένων· οὐ γὰρ ἐλάττω ποιεῖ τὰ παιδάρια τῶν
ἀνδρῶν περὶ τὰς τοιαύτας ταραχὰς ἔν τε τῇ Καρχηδονίων πόλει καὶ κατὰ τὴν Ἀλεξάνδρειαν.

31. Ἤδη δὲ τῆς ἡμέρας ὑποφαινούσης ἦν μὲν
ἄκριτος ἡ κραυγή, μάλιστα δ' ἐξ αὐτῆς ἐξέλαμψε τὸ
2 καλεῖν τὸν βασιλέα. τὸ μὲν οὖν πρῶτον οἱ Μακεδόνες
ἐξαναστάντες κατελάβοντο τὸν χρηματιστικὸν πυλῶ-
3 να τῶν βασιλείων· μετὰ δέ τινα χρόνον ἐπιγνόντες
ποῦ τῆς αὐλῆς ⟨ἦν⟩ ὁ βασιλεύς, περιελθόντες τὰς μὲν

and the great street were now filled by a mixed multitude, as well as the area before the theater of Dionysus, and Agathocles, when he heard what was occurring, aroused himself from his drunken slumber, having broken up the banquet a short time previously, and taking all his relatives except Philo went to the king. After lamenting his ill fortune to the boy in a few words he took him by the hand and went up to the gallery between the Maeander and the palaestra leading to the entrance to the theater. After this, having made fast the first two doors, he retired to the third with a few of the bodyguard, the king, and his own relatives. The doors were of open lattice work and one could see through them, and they were each secured by two bolts. Meanwhile the populace were assembling from every part of the city, so that not only level spaces but the roofs and steps were full of people, and there was a confused hubbub and clamor, women and children being mixed with the men. For in Carthage[76] and also in Alexandria the children play no less a part in such tumults than the men.

31. When the day began to break it was difficult to distinguish the various cries, but that of "The King" predominated. At first the Macedonians got up and seized the gate of audience of the palace, but shortly after, when they discovered in what part of the building the king was, they

[76] As the city is thought to be standing, this was written before 146.

πρώτας τῆς [πρώτης] σύριγγος ἐξέβαλον θύρας, ἐγγίσαντες δὲ τῆς δευτέρας ἠτοῦντο τὸν παῖδα μετὰ

4 κραυγῆς. οἱ δὲ περὶ τὸν Ἀγαθοκλέα, βλέποντες ἤδη
τὰ καθ᾽ αὑτούς, ἐδέοντο τῶν σωματοφυλάκων πρε-
σβεῦσαι περὶ αὑτῶν πρὸς τοὺς Μακεδόνας, δηλοῦντας
ὅτι τῆς ἐπιτροπείας ἐκχωροῦσι καὶ τῆς ἄλλης ἐξουσίας καὶ τῶν τιμῶν, ἔτι δὲ τῶν χορηγίων ὧν ἔχουσι

5 πάντων, αὐτὸ δὲ τὸ πνευμάτιον δέονται συγχωρη-
θῆναι σφίσι μετὰ τῆς ἀναγκαίας τροφῆς, ἵνα χωρή-
σαντες εἰς τὴν ἐξ ἀρχῆς διάθεσιν μηδὲ βουληθέντες ἔτι

6 δύνωνται λυπεῖν μηδένα. τῶν μὲν οὖν ἄλλων σωματοφυλάκων οὐδεὶς ὑπήκουσεν, Ἀριστομένης δὲ μόνος
ὑπέστη τὴν χρείαν ταύτην ὁ μετά τινα χρόνον ἐπὶ τῶν

7 πραγμάτων γενόμενος. ὁ δ᾽ ἀνὴρ οὗτος τὸ μὲν γένος
ἦν Ἀκαρνάν, καθ᾽ ὅσον δὲ προβαίνων κατὰ τὴν
ἡλικίαν, γενόμενος κύριος τῶν ὅλων πραγμάτων, κάλλιστα καὶ σεμνότατα δοκεῖ προστῆναι τοῦ τε βασιλέως καὶ τῆς βασιλείας, κατὰ τοσοῦτον κεκολακευ-

8 κέναι τὴν Ἀγαθοκλέους εὐκαιρίαν. πρῶτος μὲν γὰρ ὡς
ἑαυτὸν ἐπὶ δεῖπνον καλέσας τὸν Ἀγαθοκλέα χρυσοῦν
στέφανον ἀνέδωκε μόνῳ τῶν παρόντων, ὃ τοῖς βασι-

9 λεῦσιν αὐτοῖς ἔθος ἐστὶ μόνοις συγχωρεῖσθαι, πρῶτος δὲ τὴν εἰκόνα τοῦ προειρημένου φέρειν ἐτόλμησεν
ἐν τῷ δακτυλίῳ· γενομένης δὲ θυγατρὸς αὐτῷ ταύτην

10 Ἀγαθόκλειαν προσηγόρευσεν. ἀλλ᾽ ἴσως ὑπὲρ μὲν
τούτων ἐξαρκεῖ καὶ τὰ νῦν εἰρημένα· λαβὼν δὲ τὰς

---

77 He was soon to take Agathocles' place. PP 14592.

went round and after taking the first door of the gallery off its hinges approached the second and clamored loudly for the king. Agathocles was looking now to his own safety and begged the bodyguards to convey a message on his behalf to the Macedonians, stating that he abandoned the office of regent and all his powers and dignities as well as all his revenue, and begged simply for his poor life and a sufficient supply of food, so that retiring into his original obscurity he could not in future, even if he wished it, hurt anyone. None of the other bodyguards consented, but Aristomenes[77] alone, who afterward became minister, undertook this service. He was by birth an Acarnanian,[78] and the adulation he had paid to Agathocles in the season of his prosperity was no less conspicuous than his admirable and scrupulous fidelity to the interests of the king and his kingdom when later in life he was at the head of affairs. For he was the first who having invited Agathocles to dinner presented to him alone among the guests a crown of gold, an honor which is customarily paid only to the king, and he was the first who ventured to wear a ring with Agathocles' portrait engraved on it, and when a daughter was born to him he actually called her Agathoclea. Perhaps regarding his character I have said enough; but now when he had re-

---

[78] From Alyzeia, as an inscription found at Olympia and published *Hermes* 85 (1957), 86–122; cf. 501–504, has revealed (now *IG* IX 1² 583). At that time (ca. 216) he was one of eleven ambassadors who represented the League, together with the federal magistrates, in its negotiations with the member city of Anactorium. Soon thereafter he must have come to Egypt, where he served in 204/3 as the eponymous priest of Alexander the Great and the deified rulers.

προειρημένας ἐντολὰς καὶ διά τινος ῥινοπύλης ἐξελ-
11 θών, ἧκε πρὸς τοὺς Μακεδόνας. βραχέα δ' αὐτοῦ
διαλεχθέντος καὶ δηλώσαντος τὴν προαίρεσιν, ἐπεβάλοντο μὲν οἱ Μακεδόνες παραχρῆμα συγκεντῆσαι,
ταχὺ δέ τινων ὑπερεχόντων αὐτοῦ τὰς χεῖρας καὶ
παραιτησαμένων τοὺς πολλούς, ἐπανῆλθε λαβὼν ἐν-
τολὴν ἢ τὸν βασιλέα πρὸς αὐτοὺς ἄγονθ' ἥκειν ἢ μηδ'
12 αὐτὸν ἐξιέναι. τὸν μὲν οὖν Ἀριστομένην ταῦτ' εἰπόντες
οἱ Μακεδόνες ἀπέπεμψαν, αὐτοὶ δὲ ταῖς δευτέραις
13 θύραις ἐγγίσαντες ἐξέωσαν καὶ ταύτας. οἱ δὲ περὶ τὸν
Ἀγαθοκλέα θεωροῦντες τὴν τῶν Μακεδόνων βίαν διά
τε τῶν ἐνεργουμένων καὶ διὰ τῆς ἀποκρίσεως, τὸ μὲν
πρῶτον ἐπεβάλοντο διὰ τῆς θύρας προτείναντες τὰς
χεῖρας, ἡ δ' Ἀγαθόκλεια καὶ τοὺς μαστούς, οἷς ἔφη
θρέψαι τὸν βασιλέα, δεῖσθαι τῶν Μακεδόνων, πᾶσαν
προϊέμενοι φωνὴν πρὸς τὸ περιποιήσασθαι τὸ ζῆν
αὐτὸ μόνον·

32. ἐπεὶ δὲ πολλὰ κατολοφυρόμενοι τὴν αὑτῶν
τύχην οὐδὲν ἤνυον, τέλος ἐξέπεμψαν τὸν παῖδα μετὰ
2 τῶν σωματοφυλάκων. οἱ δὲ Μακεδόνες, παραλαβόντες
τὸν βασιλέα καὶ ταχέως ἐφ' ἵππον ἀναβιβάσαντες,
3 ἦγον εἰς τὸ στάδιον. ἅμα δὲ τῷ φανῆναι μεγάλης
κραυγῆς καὶ κρότου γενηθέντος, ἐπιστήσαντες τὸν
ἵππον καθεῖλον τὸν παῖδα καὶ προαγαγόντες ἐκά-
4 θισαν εἰς τὴν βασιλικὴν θέαν. περὶ δὲ τοὺς ὅλους
ἐγένετό τις ἅμα χαρὰ καὶ λύπη· τὰ μὲν γὰρ ἦσαν
περιχαρεῖς ἐπὶ τῷ κεκομίσθαι τὸν παῖδα, τὰ δὲ πάλιν
δυσηρέστουν τῷ μὴ συνειλῆφθαι τοὺς αἰτίους μηδὲ

ceived Agathocles' commission he went out by a wicket
gate to the Macedonians. After he had said a few words to
them and explained the proposal, the Macedonians at once
attempted to run him through, but when some few persons
held their hands over him and begged them to spare him.
he went back with orders either to return to them bringing
the king or not to come out at all. Aristomenes, then, was
sent back by the Macedonians with this message, and they
themselves came up to the second door and broke it in
also. Agathocles and his people, seeing the violence of the
Macedonians both by their actions and their determined
demand, at first attempted to entreat the soldiers, leaving
no word unspoken that might move them to spare their
lives at least, Agathocles putting out his hands through the
door and Agathoclea her breasts with which she said she
had suckled the king.

32. When bitterly bewailing their evil fate they found
all was useless, they sent out the boy with the bodyguard.
The Macedonians then took the king and at once setting
him on a horse conducted him to the stadium. His appearance was greeted with loud cheers and clapping of hands,
and they now stopped the horse, took him off, and leading
him forward placed him in the royal seat. The joy of the
crowd was mingled with regret, for on the one hand they
were delighted at having the boy in their hands, but on the
other they were displeased that the guilty persons had not

5 τυγχάνειν τῆς ἁρμοζούσης τιμωρίας. διὸ καὶ συνεχῶς
ἐβόων, ἄγειν κελεύοντες καὶ παραδειγματίζειν τοὺς
6 πάντων τῶν κακῶν αἰτίους. ἤδη δὲ τῆς ἡμέρας προβαινούσης, καὶ τοῦ πλήθους ἐπ᾽ οὐδένα δυναμένου
πέρας ἀπερείσασθαι τὴν ὁρμήν, Σωσίβιος, ὃς ἦν μὲν
υἱὸς Σωσιβίου, τότε δὲ σωματοφύλαξ ὑπάρχων μάλιστα τὸν νοῦν προσεῖχε τῷ τε βασιλεῖ καὶ τοῖς
7 πράγμασι, θεωρῶν τήν τε τοῦ πλήθους ὁρμὴν ἀμετά-
θετον οὖσαν καὶ τὸ παιδίον δυσχρηστούμενον διά τε
τὴν τῶν παρεστώτων ἀσυνήθειαν καὶ διὰ τὴν περὶ τὸν
ὄχλον ταραχήν, ἐπύθετο τοῦ βασιλέως εἰ παραδώσει
τοῖς πολλοῖς τοὺς εἰς αὐτὸν ἢ τὴν μητέρα τι πεπλημ-
8 μεληκότας. τοῦ δὲ κατανεύσαντος, τῶν μὲν σωματοφυλάκων τισὶν εἶπε δηλῶσαι τὴν τοῦ βασιλέως γνώμην,
τὸ δὲ παιδίον ἀναστήσας ἀπῆγε πρὸς τὴν θεραπείαν
9 εἰς τὴν ἰδίαν οἰκίαν, σύνεγγυς οὖσαν. τῶν δὲ διασαφούντων τὰ παρὰ τοῦ βασιλέως, κατερρήγνυτο πᾶς ὁ
10 τόπος ὑπὸ τοῦ κρότου καὶ τῆς κραυγῆς. οἱ δὲ περὶ τὸν
Ἀγαθοκλέα καὶ τὴν Ἀγαθόκλειαν ἐν τούτῳ τῷ καιρῷ
διεχωρίσθησαν ἀλλήλων εἰς τὰς ἰδίας καταλύσεις.
11 ταχὺ δὲ τῶν στρατιωτῶν τινες, οἱ μὲν ἐθελοντήν, οἱ δ᾽
ὑπὸ τοῦ πλήθους ἐξωθούμενοι, <παρ>ώρμησαν ἐπὶ τὸ
ζητεῖν τοὺς προειρημένους.

33. Τοῦ δὲ ποιεῖν αἷμα καὶ φόνους ἐγένετό τις ἐκ
2 ταὐτομάτου καταρχὴ τοιαύτη. τῶν γὰρ Ἀγαθοκλέους
ὑπηρετῶν καὶ κολάκων τις ὄνομα Φίλων ἐξῆλθε κραι-
3 παλῶν εἰς τὸ στάδιον. οὗτος θεωρῶν τὴν ὁρμὴν τῶν
ὄχλων εἶπε πρὸς τοὺς παρεστῶτας ὅτι πάλιν αὐτοῖς,

been arrested and punished as they deserved. So that they continued to shout, demanding that those who had caused all the evil should be taken into custody and made an example. The day had now advanced, and as the people after all could find no one on whom to vent their resentment, Sosibius,[79] who was the son of Sosibius and at the present time, being a member of the bodyguard, particularly devoted his attention to the king and to affairs of state, seeing that there was no hope of appeasing the fury of the populace and that the boy was ill at ease, finding himself among strangers and amidst all the commotion of the mob, asked the king if he would give up to the people those who were in any way guilty of offenses to himself or his mother. When the boy nodded his head in assent Sosibius bade some of the bodyguard communicate the royal decision, and making the boy get up led him away to receive attention at his own house which was quite near. When the king's consent was announced, there was a deafening outburst of cheering and applause all through the stadium. Meanwhile Agathocles and Agathoclea had separated and each retired to their own residence, and very soon a certain number of soldiers, some on their own initiative and others forced to go by the crowd, set off in search of both.

33. The bloodshed and murders which followed were due to the following incident. Philo,[80] one of Agathocles' attendants and parasites, came out into the stadium suffering from the effects of drink. When he observed the popular excitement, he said to those next him, that if

[79] The younger Sosibius, brother of Ptolemy (25.10), whom Agathocles had sent to the court of Philip V.

[80] See n. on 14.11.1.

THE HISTORIES OF POLYBIUS

καθάπερ καὶ πρῴην, ἐὰν Ἀγαθοκλῆς ἐξέλθῃ, μεταμε-
4 λήσει. τῶν δ' ἀκουσάντων οἱ μὲν ἀπελοιδόρουν αὐτόν,
οἱ δὲ προώθουν. ἐπιβαλομένου δ' ἀμύνεσθαι ταχέως οἱ
μὲν τὴν χλαμύδα περιέρρηξαν, οἱ δὲ τὰς λόγχας
5 προσερείσαντες ἐξεκέντησαν. ἅμα δὲ τῷ τοῦτον εἰς τὸ
μέσον ἑλκυσθῆναι μεθ' ὕβρεως ἔτι σπαίροντα, καὶ
γεύσασθαι τὰ πλήθη φόνου, πάντες ἐκαραδόκουν τὴν
6 τῶν ἄλλων παρουσίαν. μετ' οὐ πολὺ δὲ παρῆν ἀγόμε-
νος πρῶτος Ἀγαθοκλῆς δέσμιος· ὃν εὐθέως εἰσιόντα
προσδραμόντες τινὲς ἄφνω συνεκέντησαν, ἔργον ποιοῦντες οὐκ ἐχθρῶν, ἀλλ' εὐνοούντων· αἴτιοι γὰρ ἐγέ-
νοντο τοῦ μὴ τυχεῖν αὐτὸν τῆς ἁρμοζούσης καταστρο-
7 φῆς· μετὰ δὲ τοῦτον ἤχθη Νίκων, εἶτ' Ἀγαθόκλεια
γυμνὴ σὺν ταῖς ἀδελφαῖς, ἑξῆς δὲ τούτοις πάντες οἱ
8 συγγενεῖς. ἐπὶ δὲ πᾶσιν ἐκ τοῦ Θεσμοφορείου τὴν
Οἰνάνθην ἀποσπάσαντες ἧκον εἰς τὸ στάδιον, ἄγοντες
9 γυμνὴν ἐφ' ἵππου. παραδοθέντων δὲ πάντων ὁμοῦ τοῖς
ὄχλοις, οἱ μὲν ἔδακνον, οἱ δ' ἐκέντουν, οἱ δὲ τοὺς
ὀφθαλμοὺς ἐξέκοπτον· ἀεὶ δὲ τοῦ πεσόντος τὰ μέλη
10 διέσπων, ἕως ὅτου κατελώβησαν πάντας αὐτούς· δει-
νὴ γὰρ τις ἡ περὶ τοὺς θυμοὺς ὠμότης γίνεται τῶν
11 κατὰ τὴν Αἴγυπτον ἀνθρώπων. κατὰ δὲ τὸν καιρὸν
τοῦτον σύντροφοι τῆς Ἀρσινόης γεγενημέναι τινὲς
παιδίσκαι, πυθόμεναι παραγεγονέναι τὸν Φιλάμμωνα
τριταῖον ἀπὸ Κυρήνης τὸν ἐπιστάντα τῷ φόνῳ τῆς
12 βασιλίσσης, ὥρμησαν ἐπὶ τὴν οἰκίαν αὐτοῦ, καὶ βια-
σάμεναι τὸν μὲν Φιλάμμωνα τύπτουσαι τοῖς λίθοις
καὶ τοῖς ξύλοις ἀπέκτειναν, τὸν δ' υἱὸν ἀπέπνιξαν,

612

Agathocles came out they would have cause to repent again as they had done some days before. Upon hearing this they began some of them to revile and others to hustle him, and when he attempted to defend himself some very soon tore off his cloak and others leveling their spears at him transpierced him. Then as soon as he was ignominiously dragged still breathing into the middle of the stadium and the people had tasted blood, they all eagerly awaited the arrival of the others. It was not long before Agathocles was led in in fetters, and as soon as he entered some people ran up and at once stabbed him, an act of benevolence rather than of enmity, for they thus saved him from suffering the fate he deserved. Next Nico was brought there and after him Agathoclea stripped naked with her sisters and then all her relatives. Last of all they dragged Oenanthe from the Thesmophorium and led her to the stadium naked on horseback. All of them were delivered into the hands of the mob, and now some began to bite them with their teeth, some to stab them and others to dig out their eyes. Whenever one of them fell they tore the body limb from limb until they had thus mutilated them all. For terrible is the cruelty of the Egyptians when their anger is aroused. At the same time some young girls who had been Arsinoë's close companions, hearing that Philammon, who had directed the queen's murder, had arrived from Cyrene three days before, rushed to his house and forcing an entrance killed Philammon[81] with clubs

---

[81] 25.1.

ἀντίπαιδα τὴν ἡλικίαν ὄντα, σὺν δὲ τούτοις τὴν γυναῖκα τοῦ Φιλάμμωνος γυμνὴν εἰς τὴν πλατεῖαν ἐξέλκου-
σαι διέφθειραν.

13   Καὶ τὰ μὲν περὶ τὸν Ἀγαθοκλέα καὶ τὴν Ἀγαθόκλειαν καὶ τοὺς τούτων συγγενεῖς τοιοῦτον ἔσχε τὸ
τέλος.

34. ἐγὼ δ' οὐκ ἀγνοῶ μὲν τὰς τερατείας καὶ δια-
σκευάς, αἷς κέχρηνται πρὸς ἔκπληξιν τῶν ἀκουόντων
ἔνιοι τῶν γεγραφότων τὰς πράξεις ταύτας, πλείω τὸν
ἐπιμετροῦντα λόγον διατιθέμενοι τοῦ συνέχοντος τὰ
2 πράγματα καὶ κυρίου, τινὲς μὲν ἐπὶ τὴν τύχην ἀνα-
φέροντες τὰ γεγονότα καὶ τιθέντες ὑπὸ τὴν ὄψιν τὸ
ταύτης ἀβέβαιον καὶ δυσφύλακτον, οἱ δὲ τὸ παράδοξον τῶν συμβεβηκότων ὑπὸ λόγον ἄγοντες, πειρώ-
μενοι τοῖς γεγονόσιν αἰτίας καὶ πιθανότητας ὑποτάτ-
3 τειν. οὐ μὴν ἔγωγε προεθέμην τούτῳ χρήσασθαι τῷ
χειρισμῷ περὶ τῶν προειρημένων διὰ τὸ μήτε πολε-
μικὴν τόλμαν καὶ δύναμιν ἐπίσημον γεγονέναι περὶ
4 τὸν Ἀγαθοκλέα μήτε χειρισμὸν πραγμάτων ἐπιτυχῆ
καὶ ζηλωτὸν μήτε τὸ τελευταῖον τὴν αὐλικὴν ἀγχίνοιαν καὶ κακοπραγμοσύνην διαφέρουσαν, ἐν ᾗ
Σωσίβιος καὶ πλείους ἕτεροι κατεβίωσαν, βασιλεῖς
ἐκ βασιλέων μεταχειριζόμενοι, τὰ δ' ἐναντία τούτοις
5 συμβεβηκέναι περὶ τὸν προειρημένον ἄνδρα. προ-
αγωγῆς μὲν ἔτυχε παραδόξου διὰ τὴν τοῦ Φιλοπά-
6 τορος ἀδυναμίαν τοῦ βασιλεύειν· τυχὼν δὲ ταύτης καὶ
παραλαβὼν εὐφυέστατον καιρὸν μετὰ τὸν ἐκείνου θάνατον πρὸς τὸ συντηρῆσαι τὴν ἐξουσίαν, ἅμα τὰ

and stones; strangled his son who was hardly more than a mere boy, and dragging out his wife naked into the street slew her.

Such was the end of Agathocles, Agathoclea, and their kindred.

34. I am not unaware that some authors[82] in describing these events have introduced the sensational element and worked up their material with the object of making the whole more striking to their readers, largely transgressing the bounds of what is essential to give coherence to their narrative. Some of them attribute all to Fortune, and lay stress on her instability and on men's incapacity of evading her, while others take count of the strangeness of all that happened, attempting to assign reasons or probable causes to everything. It was, however not my own object to treat these matters in that manner, inasmuch as Agathocles displayed neither courage in war nor conspicuous ability, nor was he fortunate and exemplary in his management of affairs, nor, finally, had he that acuteness and mischievous address which serve a courtier's ends and which made Sosibius and several others so successful until the end of their lives in their management of king after king. On the contrary it was quite different with Agathocles. Owing to Philopator's incapacity as a ruler he attained an exceptionally high position; and in this position finding himself after that king's death most favorably circumstanced to maintain his power, he lost both his control and his life through his

[82] Among them probably Ptolemy of Megalopolis (n. on 25.14). It is not certain who the others were.

πράγματα καὶ τὸ ζῆν ἀπέβαλε διὰ τὴν ἰδίαν ἀνανδρίαν καὶ ῥᾳθυμίαν, ἐν πάνυ βραχεῖ χρόνῳ καταγνω-
σθείς.

35. Διόπερ οὐ χρὴ τοῖς τοιούτοις προσάπτειν τὸν
ἐπιμετροῦντα λόγον, καθάπερ εἶπα, τῷ δ᾽ Ἀγαθοκλεῖ
καὶ Διονυσίῳ τοῖς Σικελιώταις καί τισιν ἑτέροις τῶν
2 ἐν πράγμασιν ἐπ᾽ ὀνόματος γεγονότων. ἐκείνων γὰρ ὁ
μὲν ἕτερος ἐκ δημοτικῆς καὶ ταπεινῆς ὑποθέσεως
ὁρμηθείς, ὁ δ᾽ Ἀγαθοκλῆς, ὡς ὁ Τίμαιος ἐπισκώπτων
φησί, κεραμεὺς ὑπάρχων καὶ καταλιπὼν τὸν τροχὸν
⟨καὶ τὸν⟩ πηλὸν καὶ τὸν καπνόν, ἧκε νέος ὢν εἰς τὰς
3 Συρακούσας. καὶ τὸ μὲν πρῶτον ἐγενήθησαν ἀμφότεροι κατὰ τοὺς ἰδίους καιροὺς τύραννοι Συρακουσῶν,
πόλεως τῆς μέγιστον ἀξίωμα τότε καὶ μέγιστον πλοῦ-
4 τον περιποιησαμένης, μετὰ δὲ ταῦτα βασιλεῖς ἁπάσης Σικελίας νομισθέντες καί τινων καὶ τῆς Ἰταλίας
5 μερῶν κυριεύσαντες. Ἀγαθοκλῆς δ᾽ οὐ μόνον καὶ τῶν
τῆς Λιβύης ἀπεπείρασεν, ἀλλὰ καὶ τέλος ἐναπέθανε
6 ταῖς ὑπεροχαῖς ταύταις. διὸ καὶ Πόπλιον Σκιπίωνά
φασι τὸν πρῶτον καταπολεμήσαντα Καρχηδονίους
ἐρωτηθέντα τίνας ὑπολαμβάνει πραγματικωτάτους
ἄνδρας γεγονέναι καὶ σὺν νῷ τολμηροτάτους, εἰπεῖν
τοὺς περὶ Ἀγαθοκλέα καὶ Διονύσιον τοὺς Σικελιώτας.
7 καὶ περὶ μὲν τῶν τοιούτων ἀνδρῶν εἰς ἐπίτασιν ἄγειν
τοὺς ἀναγινώσκοντας, καί που καὶ τῆς τύχης ποιήσασθαι μνήμην, ἔτι δὲ τῶν ἀνθρωπείων πραγμάτων, καὶ
καθόλου προστιθέναι τὸν ἐπεκδιδάσκοντα λόγον, ἐπὶ
δὲ τῶν προειρημένων ἀνδρῶν οὐδαμῶς ἁρμόζει.

own cowardice and indolence, becoming an object of universal reprobation in quite a short time.

35. It is not therefore advisable, as I said, to deal at excessive length with the fate of such a man, but it is otherwise with the Sicilian Agathocles[83] and Dionysius[84] and certain other rulers of renown. Of these two, the latter started from an obscure and humble position, and Agathocles, as Timaeus ridiculing him tells us, was a potter and leaving his wheel and the clay and the smoke came to Syracuse as a young man. In the first place they both of them became in their time tyrants of Syracuse, a city which then ranked highest in opulence and dignity, and they were afterward recognized as kings[85] of the whole of Sicily and had made themselves masters even of some parts of Italy.[86] And Agathocles not only made an attempt to conquer Africa but retained his exalted position until his death. So that they say that Publius Scipio, who was the first to bring Carthage to her knees, when some one asked him whom he thought the greatest statesmen combining courage and wisdom, replied "Agathocles and Dionysius the Sicilians." To the careers of such men indeed it is proper for us to direct the attention of our readers, touching a little on the vicissitudes of fortune and the uncertainty of human affairs, and in general adding to our bare narrative some instructive reflections, but we are by no means called on to do so in the case of the Samian Agathocles and his associates.

[83] See n. on 1.7.2.   [84] See n. on 1.6.1.   [85] Dionysius did not take the royal title, Agathocles did in 305/4.

[86] See H. Berve, *Die Tyrannis bei den Griechen* (Munich 1967), 1.233–236 for Dionysius, 453 for Agathocles.

36. Διὰ δὴ ταύτας τὰς αἰτίας τὸν μετ᾽ αὐξήσεως
2 λόγον ἀπεδοκιμάσαμεν ὑπὲρ Ἀγααθοκλέους, οὐχ ἥκιστα δὲ καὶ διὰ τὸ πάσας τὰς ἐκπληκτικὰς περιπετείας
μίαν ἔχειν φαντασίαν τὴν πρώτην ἀξίαν ἐπιστάσεως,
τὸ δὲ λοιπὸν οὐ μόνον ἀνωφελῆ γίνεσθαι τὴν ἀκρόα-
σιν καὶ θέαν αὐτῶν, ἀλλὰ καὶ μετά τινος ὀχλήσεως
3 ἐπιτελεῖσθαι τὴν ἐνέργειαν τῶν τοιούτων. δυεῖν ⟨γὰρ⟩
ὑπαρχόντων τελῶν, ὠφελείας καὶ τέρψεως, πρὸς ἃ δεῖ
τὴν ἀναφορὰν ποιεῖσθαι τοὺς διὰ τῆς ἀκοῆς ἢ διὰ τῆς
ὁράσεως βουλομένους τι πολυπραγμονεῖν, καὶ μάλιστα τῷ τῆς ἱστορίας γένει τούτου καθήκοντος, ἀμφοτέρων τούτων ὁ πλεονασμὸς ὑπὲρ τῶν ἐκπληκτικῶν
4 συμπτωμάτων ἐκτὸς πίπτει. ζηλοῦν μὲν γὰρ τίς ἂν
βουληθείη τὰς παραλόγους περιπετείας; οὐδὲ μὴν
θεώμενος οὐδ᾽ ἀκούων ἥδεται συνεχῶς οὐδεὶς τῶν
παρὰ φύσιν γενομένων πραγμάτων καὶ παρὰ τὴν
5 κοινὴν ἔννοιαν τῶν ἀνθρώπων. ἀλλ᾽ εἰσάπαξ μὲν καὶ
πρῶτον σπουδάζομεν ἃ μὲν ἰδεῖν, ἃ δ᾽ ἀκοῦσαι, χάριν
τοῦ γνῶναι τὸ μὴ δοκοῦν δυνατὸν εἶναι διότι δυνατὸν
6 ἐστιν· ὅταν δὲ πιστεύωμεν, οὐδεὶς τοῖς παρὰ φύσιν
ἐγχρονίζων εὐδοκεῖ· τῷ δ᾽ αὐτῷ πλεονάκις ἐγκυρεῖν
7 οὐδ᾽ ὅλως ἂν βουληθείη. διόπερ ἢ ζηλωτὸν εἶναι δεῖ τὸ
λεγόμενον ἢ τερπνόν· ὁ δὲ τῆς ἐκτὸς τούτων συμφορᾶς
πλεονασμὸς οἰκειότερόν ἐστι τραγῳδίας ἤπερ ἱστο-
8 ρίας. ἀλλ᾽ ἴσως ἀναγκαῖόν ἐστι συγγνώμην ἔχειν τοῖς
μὴ συνεφιστάνουσι μήτ᾽ ἐπὶ τὰ τῆς φύσεως μήτ᾽ ἐπὶ
9 τὰ καθόλου κατὰ τῆς οἰκουμένης πράγματα· δοκεῖ
γὰρ αὐτοῖς ταῦτ᾽ εἶναι μέγιστα καὶ θαυμαστότατα

36. For these reasons I refrained from enlarging on the story of this man, and no less because all sensational occurrences are worthy of attention only when first presented to our view, but afterward it is not only unprofitable to read about them and keep our eyes on them but the vivid representation of such things produces a certain disgust. For since there are two objects, improvement and pleasure, which those who wish to study any subject either by the use of their ears or of their eyes, should keep before them, and since this is especially true of the study of history, a too generous treatment of sensational events contributes to neither. For not only do abnormal reversals of fortune arouse no emulation, but no one has any permanent pleasure in seeing or reading of things which are contrary to nature and contrary to the general sentiment of mankind. It is true we are interested in seeing or hearing of them once and for all at first, just for the sake of observing that what seemed to be impossible is possible, but once we are convinced of this no one takes any pleasure in dwelling on the unnatural, and there is none who would have the least wish to meet with frequent references to the same event of this class. Therefore what is told us should either excite emulation or cause pleasure, and the elaborate treatment of an event which does neither is suitable rather to tragedy than to history. Possibly we must excuse writers who do not draw their readers' attention to such matters as are natural or generally happen in the world. For they think that among past events the greatest and most wonderful are

τῶν προγεγονότων οἷς ἂν αὐτοὶ παρατυχόντες ἐγκυ-
ρήσωσιν ἢ πυθόμενοι παρά τινων πρὸς αὐτὰ ταῦτα
10 προσέχωσι τὸν νοῦν. διὸ καὶ λανθάνουσι πλείω τοῦ
καθήκοντος διατιθέμενοι λόγον ὑπὲρ τῶν μήτε καινῶν
ὄντων διὰ τὸ καὶ ἑτέροις πρότερον εἰρῆσθαι μήτ᾽
11 ὠφελεῖν μήτε τέρπειν δυναμένων. περὶ μὲν οὖν τούτων
ἐπὶ τοσοῦτον ἡμῖν εἰρήσθω.

IV. RES ASIAE

37. Ὅτι Ἀντίοχος ὁ βασιλεὺς ἐδόκει κατὰ μὲν τὰς
ἀρχὰς γεγονέναι μεγαλεπίβολος καὶ τολμηρὸς καὶ
2 τοῦ προτεθέντος ἐξεργαστικός, προβαίνων δὲ κατὰ
τὴν ἡλικίαν ἐφάνη πολὺ καταδεέστερος αὐτοῦ καὶ τῆς
τῶν ἐκτὸς προσδοκίας.

those which they have met in their personal experience
or which particularly arrested their attention when they
heard of them from witnesses. So that unconsciously they
devote too much space to matters which neither are novel,
others having spoken of them before, nor are able to benefit or to please us. I have now said enough on this subject.

IV. AFFAIRS OF ASIA

Character of Antiochus

37. King Antiochus[87] seems to have been at first a man
who both conceived great projects and possessed courage
and the capability of executing his designs, but as he advanced in life he showed himself much inferior to his former self and disappointed general expectation.

[87] P. observes a change for the worse in the king's reign after
the end of his expedition to the East. It is not clear what caused
him to insert these remarks here. P. made similar observations
concerning Philip V.

INDEX

INDEX

INDEX

INDEX